PENGUIN BOOKS

HUMANITY

Geoffrey Robertson QC has had a distinguished career as a trial counsel, human rights advocate and UN appellant judge. He has argued hundreds of death sentence appeals, prosecuted Hastings Banda, defended Salman Rushdie, Mike Tyson and Julian Assange and acted for Human Rights Watch in the proceedings against General Pinochet. He served as first president of the UN's Special Court in Sierra Leone, and has authored landmark decisions on the limits of amnesties, the illegality of recruiting child soldiers and the legal protections for war correspondents and human rights monitors. He serves as a 'distinguished jurist' member of the UN's Internal Justice Council and in 2011 he was awarded the New York Bar Association prize for achievement in international law and affairs.

Geoffrey Robertson is founder and head of Doughty Street Chambers, the UK's largest human rights practice, and sits as a recorder (part-time judge) in London, where he is a Master of the Middle Temple and visiting professor in human rights law at Queen Mary College and the New College of the Humanities. His books include *Freedom, the Individual and the Law; Does Dracula Have Aids?*; *Robertson & Nicol on Media Law*; and an acclaimed memoir, *The Justice Game*. In 2005 he published *The Tyrannicide Brief* – the story of how Cromwell's lawyers mounted the first trial of a head of state, and in 2010 his Penguin Special *The Case of the Pope* was published in all major languages. He has made many television and radio programmes, notably *Geoffrey Robertson's Hypotheticals*, and has won a Freedom of Information award for his writing and broadcasting.

GEOFFREY ROBERTSON QC

Crimes Against Humanity

The Struggle for Global Justice

FOURTH EDITION

PENGUIN BOOKS

For Julius and Georgina

PENGUIN BOOKS

Published by the Penguin Group
Penguin Books Ltd, 80 Strand, London WC2R ORL, England
Penguin Group (USA) Inc., 375 Hudson Street, New York, New York 10014, USA
Penguin Group (Canada), 90 Eglinton Avenue East, Suite 700, Toronto, Ontario, Canada M4P 2Y3
(a division of Pearson Penguin Canada Inc.)
Penguin Ireland, 25 St Stephen's Green, Dublin 2, Ireland
(a division of Penguin Books Ltd)
Penguin Group (Australia), 707 Collins Street, Melbourne, Victoria 3008, Australia
(a division of Pearson Australia Group Pty Ltd)
Penguin Books India Pvt Ltd, 11 Community Centre,
Panchsheel Park, New Delhi – 110 017, India
Penguin Group (NZ), 67 Apollo Drive, Rosedale, Auckland 0632, New Zealand
(a division of Pearson New Zealand Ltd)
Penguin Books (South Africa) (Pty) Ltd, Block D, Rosebank Office Park, 181 Jan Smuts Avenue,
Parktown North, Gauteng 2193, South Africa

Penguin Books Ltd, Registered Offices: 80 Strand, London WC2R ORL, England

www.penguin.com

First published by Allen Lane 1999
Published in Penguin Books with new material 2000
Second edition 2002
Third edition 2006
Fourth edition 2012

001

Copyright © Geoffrey Robertson 1999, 2000, 2002, 2006, 2012
All rights reserved

The moral right of the author has been asserted

Typeset by Palimpsest Book Production Ltd, Falkirk, Stirlingshire
Printed in Great Britain by Clays Ltd, St Ives plc

ISBN: 978-0-141-97483-5

www.greenpenguin.co.uk

MIX
Paper from
responsible sources
FSC™ C018179

Penguin Books is committed to a sustainable
future for our business, our readers and our planet.
This book is made from Forest Stewardship
Council™ certified paper.

ALWAYS LEARNING   **PEARSON**

Contents

Preface to the Fourth Edition

'I have put my death-head formations in place with the command relentlessly and without compassion to send into death many women and children of Polish origin and language. Only thus we can gain the living space that we need. Who after all is today speaking about the destruction of the Armenians?'

Adolf Hitler to chief commanders and commanding generals,
22 August 1939[1]

I happen to have been born on the day of the Nuremberg judgment – 30 September 1946 – so the length of my life provides a precise temporal measure of the extent to which the international community has delivered on the momentous promise of that day, namely that crimes against humanity would henceforth be deterred by punishment of their perpetrators. It was the judgment imposed upon the authors of the Holocaust which created international criminal law, a free-standing and universal jurisdiction to prosecute those who direct or assist a crime so heinous that it is 'against humanity' because the very fact that a fellow human being could conceive and commit it demeans every member of the human race, wherever they live and whatever their culture or creed. It is a crime confined to genocide and mass murder and systematic torture, or to atrocious acts of warfare and terror, and it imputes a special responsibility to commanders, organizers and abettors of these crimes – be they heads of state or political or military leaders, bureaucrats or theocrats, ideologues or industrialists. Since the perpetrators will generally be powerful enough to be above or beyond the law in their own state, the Nuremberg legacy depends for its fulfilment on the establishment of international institutions of justice with power to end impunity.

Sixty-five years on from that day of judgment, the nations of the world have made a start in devising institutions and procedures which work to protect the most basic of human rights: freedom from state-sponsored murder, torture and terror. This progress has been made mostly since publication of the first edition of *Crimes Against Humanity* in 1999. The book was fuelled by anger at the seemingly endless barbarities committed with impunity by governments throughout the world, some of which I had observed – officially for Amnesty International and Human Rights Watch, professionally as a barrister defending dissidents or just casually, as a television viewer. I sought to build, from the straws blowing in the *fin de siècle* wind (the arrest of Pinochet, the UN courts set up to deal with war crimes in Yugoslavia and Rwanda, the Lockerbie agreement and the Rome Statute for an international criminal court), an argument for a kind of millennial shift, from appeasement to justice, as the dominant factor in world affairs. The evolving force of international human rights law was carrying some compulsion in municipal courts and in an increasing number of international tribunals. The pioneering discovery (law being a science in its content, an art only in its practice) was how the crime against humanity, first defined in the Nuremberg Statute, might become the key to unlocking the closed door of state sovereignty, and to holding political and military leaders responsible for the evils they chose to visit upon humankind.

The preface to the first edition was completed on 24 March 1999, another red-letter day; it began with the British law lords ruling that the Torture Convention had destroyed General Pinochet's sovereign immunity, and ended with NATO bombing the sovereign state of Serbia over its 'ethnic cleansing' in Kosovo. The promise of Nuremberg, for the first time since 1946, seemed capable of realization. When, a few months later, a UN force landed on the shores of East Timor, to protect its people from massacre by Indonesian militias and to secure their right to self-determination, the era of human rights enforcement seemed to have dawned. It would, in effect, be the 'third age' of human rights: the first had been articulated in the declarations of the American and French Revolutions; the second was ushered in by the Nuremberg judgment and the triptych of treaties it directly inspired – the 1948 Universal Declaration and the Geneva and Genocide Conventions. Now, more than a half century on, human rights law was teething at last – and in this third age, its teeth would be for biting, not gnashing.

A critical response to the publication of *Crimes Against Humanity*, in the summer of 1999, nervously concentrated on practicalities rather than principles. Might Pinochet's arrest not destabilize democracy in Chile? Would Milosevic ever be surrendered to face his indictment in The Hague? These fears seem risible now. Chile's democracy has gone from strength to strength: in 2006 the nation elected a Pinochet torture victim as president and its courts lifted the old tyrant's immunity for crimes of torture and murder. The indictment of Milošević hastened his fall from power and international pressure forced Serbia to disgorge him to The Hague; the issue before his death was not whether he should be tried, but how he should be tried more effectively. The main ideological objection to the book's argument came in Europe from relics of the socialist left who cling still to nation-state sovereignty (Milošević was its embodiment) as a protection from American interference. From their perspective, 'enforcing human rights' was a euphemism for forcing American freedoms on peoples who should not be allowed to enjoy them.[2] Ironically, the vehemence of this critique was contradicted in America itself by blasts from the Republican right. Future UN ambassador John Bolton, then an obscure think-tanker, wrote that the book's advocacy of a global justice movement was a serious threat to US sovereignty and to its ability to do in the world whatever served its national interest.[3] From his perspective, international law was a set of rules that could be imposed upon other countries, but which must never be enforced against Americans.

The first edition found its way into the footnotes of many books and articles on human rights enforcement and was set on many law and international politics courses. It was tempting to leave it unamended, as a *fin de siecle* case for global justice. But international criminal justice was a work in progress, its principles developing case by case, and war by war, so I decided that this book should accompany its journey. I wrote additional material for the second (2002), third (2006) and now for the fourth (2012) editions, increasing the bulk (and perhaps the price) but also the cogency of the case for a global justice that today is rarely out of the headlines.

It must never be forgotten that international criminal law is a very recent development, dating in reality from the revival of the Nuremberg legacy by the arrest of General Pinochet in 1998. Like other branches of law it develops by the leaps and bounds of precedent, key events, and cases that are the result of happenstance as war criminals or tyrants or heads of state are arrested and sent to The Hague. Pinochet here, Charles Taylor there, then Milošević, Karadžić, Gaddafi (posthumously) and Laurent Gbagbo. Like any legal textbook, this work must be kept up to date. But unlike most other legal textbooks, its subject impacts upon international affairs by asserting the centrality of 'justice' to dealing with states that deny it to their peoples. For that reason I shall be reconsidering and recasting the material in this book every few years, doomed like Sisyphus to an uphill struggle, in my case to the improbability of ever giving a complete account of a subject under exponential expansion. Nonetheless, I hope that this edition will give a fairly clear picture of what the struggle for global justice has achieved by mid-2012.

The second edition was published in 2002, and incorporated into its thesis the fallout from the dastardly terrorist attacks on New York and Washington on 11 September 2001. This atrocity, which followed the al-Qaida bombings of USS *Cole* and American embassies in Kenya and Tanzania, precisely fits the definition of a 'crime against humanity', which covers not only genocide and torture but 'multiple acts of murder committed as part of a systematic attack against a civilian population'. Osama bin Laden was not some peripatetic gang leader but an honoured guest of Afghanistan's Taliban government during his genocidal jihad against Americans (and anyone else who happened to get in the way). I argued that the consequent war against the Taliban government by the US and its allies could not be justified as an exercise in self-defence under Article 51 of the UN

Charter: that certainly permitted an incursion on Afghan territory and sovereignty to flush al-Qaida out of its caves and to capture its adherents, but did not extend so far as to allow the overthrow of the Taliban. That action – which in reality still continues today – could be legitimate only if characterized as an operation to prevent and punish the commission of further crimes against humanity – a 'just' war if conducted by reference to the principles of human rights inter-vention for which NATO's action in Kosovo had come to stand (and which have now been generalized, not entirely satisfactorily, as the UN's 'responsibility to protect'). The ultimate principle, I suppose, is that in the twenty-first century, nations which go to war in the name of human rights must not only make good their case on the battle-field, but subsequently in a court of law. Losers must have access to justice, as well as victors.

Humanitarian intervention was not the principle invoked by the US or the UK for invading Iraq in 2003, an exercise which should not be allowed to affect the principles of humanitarian intervention other than to illustrate the risks of ignoring them. Saddam Hussein was a tyrant who mass murdered some 300,000 of his people: his regime should have been ousted when he began to use poison gas against the Kurds back in 1988. Instead, the world's advanced nations – most notably, the US and UK – vied to do business with him until he invaded Kuwait, when the coalition that counter-attacked stopped short of marching on Baghdad. Its victory in 1991 was pyrrhic, because it failed to protect Shias from Saddam's venomous reprisals and defended the Kurds only by makeshift 'no fly' zones. The US claim in 2003 of entitlement to 'pre-emptive self-defence' was no excuse for regime change in Iraq, since there was no credible evidence that Saddam was harbouring terrorists or was bent upon further unlawful foreign adventures. There was, certainly, reason to suspect him of harbouring weapons of mass destruction: he had attempted to develop them in the early 1990s and had behaved as if he *did* possess them, by obstructing UN inspectors, and there were seemingly credi-ble reports from defectors. Most members of the Security Council wanted these to be verified, but the belligerents could not wait: the US launched 'Operation Shock and Awe' before Hans Blix and his team could complete their work. It was a war commenced without UN or NATO approval, justified neither as an humanitarian intervention 'nor as a measure of self-defence. It was the latter justification, not the former, that the US invoked in support of its act of aggression.

The United Kingdom, its main coalition partner, assumed that Saddam was hiding WMD and relied upon an earlier Gulf War resolution that might, on a pettifogging reading, be 'revived' to justify enforcement action. All belligerents expressly rejected any human rights rationale: indeed, shortly before the invasion, they offered Saddam and his sons amnesty if they would leave the country. It must be said, however, that the initial support for overthrowing Saddam Hussein, certainly among Western journalists and politicians, was based on a belief that it was 'just' to use force to topple a tyrant. Belatedly, as Saddam's WMD proved a chimera and Iraq became engulfed in civil war, Western leaders have retrospectively justified the invasion by reference to Saddam's atrocious human rights record and the moral rightness of putting him on trial for it, an argument which puts the humanitarian cart before the warhorse, and has done much to discredit so-called 'liberal interventionism'. George W. Bush was no liberal, and his decision to invade Iraq was not influenced by humanitarian considerations. The subsequent trials of the Iraqi leaders were neither held in an international court nor make any contribution to international law: Saddam was convicted and executed for a local crime, after improper political interference with the independence of his judges. I participated in the training of these brave men, but cannot regard the proceedings, which ended in the squalor of the scaffold, as any precedent for international justice. Thanks to American insistence on exposing the Iraqi leaders to the death penalty, the trial of Saddam Hussein turned into an exercise in wild justice – that is, revenge.

The US, as leader of an increasingly free world, inevitably came in for further scrutiny in the third edition in respect of its denial of due process to Guantanamo Bay detainees, its responsibility for torture at Abu Ghraib and its tolerance of 'renditions' that are extraordinary because they are secret and involve the sending of suspects for brutal interrogation in foreign prisons. I noted the emergence of the 'Bush lawyer' – originally a colloquial Australian phrase for a hick counsellor ignorant of the rules, but here applied to lawyers in US government service who have misrepresented the law with opportunistic advice that the Geneva Conventions are 'obsolete', that due process is unavailable on offshore islands and that the threshold for torture should be defined as pain comparable to that suffered by the loss of a bodily organ.

It took years before the US Supreme Court could strike down the dishonourable advice of the Bush lawyers, premised on the unconstitutional notion that the President could do no wrong – indeed, in time of war (his self-proclaimed 'war on terror'), could do anything. In this fraught time, the Republican administration challenged the very idea of universal enforceable human rights – to the extent that Bush signed the Jesse Helms-inspired 'bomb The Hague' bill (the American Service-Members' Protection Act) which permitted the President to take military action to free any American 'captured' by the International Criminal Court. Nonetheless, international justice continued to have momentum: in this period I served as President of the UN's War Crimes Court in Sierra Leone, which indicted Charles Taylor, fashioned an international law against recruitment of child soldiers, and struck down amnesties for crimes against humanity. Similar progress was being made at the *ad hoc* tribunals dealing with war crimes in the Balkans (ICTY) and in Rwanda (ICTR). The third edition of *Crimes Against Humanity* took in the aborted trial of Milošević – a striking example of the power of international justice to humble demagogues, but equally a measure of the inadequacy of its procedures to cope with a truculent defendant who died mid-trial after three years of prosecution evidence.

This fourth edition comes as the ICTR is winding up efforts which have put behind bars a number of perpetrators of the 1993 genocide in Rwanda, and after the ICTY has captured its two most important fugitives, Karadžić and Mladić, now being tried on charges of genocide and crimes against humanity for Srebrenica and other massacres. The ICTY may not have worked well but at least it has worked, and its conviction of Croatian General Gotovina has reassured sensible Serbs that it has not worked one-sidedly. The demand for justice against tyrants became a catch-cry of the crowds during the so-called 'Arab Spring': in Iran (2009) Syria and Bahrain, and (more successfully) in Tunisia, Egypt and Libya. It was a cause for which many were prepared to die. The most important precedent was set in 2011 by the Security Council, which by Resolution 1970 referred the case of Libya to the ICC prosecutor (who subsequently indicted Colonel Gaddafi, his son Saif and his intelligence chief Al-Senussi). This unanimous resolution gave universal justice a great-power imprimatur it had hitherto lacked, as the US, Russia and China had always insisted on *ad hoc* courts to deal with country-specific problems. Now, by Resolution 1970, they all endorsed the International Criminal Court as the proper instrument for investigation and prosecution of the leaders of a country who were preparing to kill their own people. Back in 2005 the Security Council had referred Darfur to the ICC, but that decision was subject to a number of abstentions (including, hypocritically, that of the US, which had brought the case forward). Now, partly due to the influence at the UN of the 'Responsibility to Protect' doctrine which justified international intervention in states that could not protect their own people, the principle of universal (rather than *ad hoc*) justice was invoked, bolstered a few weeks later by Resolution 1973, which empowered NATO to use 'all necessary means' to protect Libyan civilians – the means that became necessary were aggressive armed action calculated to overthrow the Gaddafi regime.

In consequence, in 2012, the odds that nemesis will catch up with perpetrators of crimes against humanity are significantly better than they were in 1999. That means that international human rights law can be confidently said to exist in the real world, not just in the reports of non-governmental organizations or the pipe dreams of law professors. True, there is a selectivity in its enforcement at this early stage: the Security Council will not move against governments or governors allied with its 'big five' permanent members, while some pariah states and rogue statesmen may escape through its lack of interest or lack of funds. There is a 'catch as catch can' quality about international criminal justice at this point (illustrated by the failure to catch Bashir or to indict Assad) but criticism that enforcement is selective should count not as a principled objection but rather as a spur to get international justice systems up and running, creating precedents that can be universally applied. The Arab Spring, for example, produced ICC indictments on Gaddafi and his son, while Mubarak was tried domestically and Ben Ali escaped to refuge in Saudi Arabia. As for the US, even when the Bush administration adopted the 'exceptionalist' position that international law is a set of rules for the rest of the world, those rules were entrenching themselves in American legal practice. The opposition of many in the US military to undermining the Geneva Conventions was vindicated by the Supreme Court and President Obama began his term by renouncing torture and promising (albeit unsuccessfully) to close Guantanamo. The most urgent problem for international justice is no longer US exceptionalism but the failure of international courts to devise and to operate expeditious and effective (and cost-effective) procedures for delivering it.

Most cases in international courts are still excruciatingly slow and intolerably expensive. These courts have an unfortunate structural bias towards the prosecution, but have not managed to slow the flow of gravy-train motions by some defence lawyers. Judicial appointment through a UN system of state nomination does not mean selection on merit or selection of the fittest. NGOs, philosophically supportive of the international justice movement, sometimes pull punches that should be landed on international courts for costs blowouts and procedural obfuscations. The adversarial system, which works in many Anglo-American countries because defendants are prepared to co-operate with a system that offers a possibility of acquittal, can collapse in chaos when that co-operation is withdrawn. The high-profile trial of Slobodan Milošević provides a case in point: the court bent over backwards to do him justice but he mocked it by outrageous cross-examination and constant demands for adjournments. The judges can also be as slow as the lawyers: in Charles Taylor's case, for example, after a trial lasting three and a half years, there was an unexplained delay of over thirteen months in delivering judgment.

In jurisdictional terms, some of the difficulty comes from the attempted fusion of two very different doctrines: international law (which must be extrapolated from treaties, juristic writings and state practices) with criminal law, which should be a clear set of legal rules simple enough for criminals to comprehend. Although I owe my own passion for law to teachers like Julius Stone and Ronald Dworkin, I learned it in practice with John Mortimer QC down at the Old Bailey, where a rule was one of law not because it could be found in a text book or deduced from 'right reason', but because there was a prospect that someone would be sent to prison for its breach. The task of producing a workable set of rules for international criminal tribunals has been to pare away the academic excrescences of international law, with its extinct Latin phrases and its obscure theories culled from indigestible treaties and tomes and *travaux préparatoires*, and to produce a straightforward set of prohibitions and procedures, operated by confident judges skilled at applying them in adversarial proceedings. It has also been a mistake to attempt to fuse the civil law inquisitorial system with the adversarial tradition of Anglo-American trial. Many European jurists thought that this would produce the best of both legal worlds: increasingly, it can be seen to have produced the worst.

But this is not a textbook on legal procedures. It aims to tell the human rights story, with some of the spilt blood and guts, passion and philosophy that have enlivened its history and will influence its future. It is difficult entirely to avoid Latin phrases or the 'alphabet soup' acronyms which stand for the profusion and confusion of UN conventions and committees. In this book, however, I have tried to use as few acronyms as possible and have kept the Latin *de minimis*. It is, in one sense, an exciting and timely story, because it has very recently become possible – with the help of the ICC, UN war crimes courts, the European Court of Human Rights, the Privy Council and leading national courts entrusted with the interpretation of bills of rights – to synthesize a body of basic guarantees potentially enforceable throughout the world, properly described as 'international human rights law' because states publicly recognize that its rules should never be breached, however frequently or secretly they are.

The first step, it seems to me, towards having human rights respected is to enable these rules to be understood by 'ordinary people' (the condescending phrase lawyers use to describe people who are not lawyers). After all, the modern progress of human rights – from an aspiration born of the concentration camp and the gulag to a set of powerful international law propositions to which enforcement mechanisms may be attached – has been accomplished not by lawyers or diplomats but by a movement which now has millions of 'ordinary' members throughout the world: twelve million, for a start, who signed an Amnesty International petition pledging support for the Universal Declaration on its fiftieth anniversary. Some have been inspired by the courageous examples of dissidents who have suffered in freedom's cause, but many more by revulsion against the atrocities brought into their homes through a billion television sets and twice as many radios, now being superseded by electronic social connectivity through blogs, Twitter, Facebook and an Internet to which two billion people have access. This has created a vast audience which is beginning to think like global citizens and, as the Arab Spring showed, is certainly beginning to believe that democracy is a necessary, if not sufficient, condition for progress. In Václav Havel's phrase, 'the power of the powerless' is beginning to be felt. It is their reaction to human rights violations which constitutes, in Theodore Roosevelt's phrase, 'the indignant pity of the civilized world' and, when transmitted to different democratic governments, impels international and UN response. Horizons have widened: the old newspaper joke 'Small Earthquake in Chile: Not Many Dead' rings hollow when television pictures of corpses in Racak (Kosovo) can put that obscure village on the map of everyone's mind and galvanize the West to war. That crimes against humanity occur in 'a far away country between people of whom we know nothing' – Neville Chamberlain's reason for appeasing Hitler's invasion of Czechoslovakia – is no longer an excuse, as social media coverage of human rights black spots rekindles the potent mix of anger and compassion which produced the Universal Declaration and now produces a democratic demand not merely for something to be done, but for the laws, courts and prosecutors to do it.

Notwithstanding this groundswell for 'global justice', and the progress made in the years since the first edition, I have had no hesitation in keeping this book's subtitle, prefaced with the word 'struggle'. The mechanisms for delivery are imperfect and the opposition formidable.

In some of the feudal societies of the Middle East, and the war-torn areas of sub-Saharan Africa, human rights and especially women's rights are little better today than they were half a century ago. Optimism is an eye disease which inflicts many who hold court on the subject in university lecture halls or the expensive Geneva hotel suites where diplomats prefer to hold their conferences. The matter is perceived differently from the cells of political prisons and the unmarked cars of death squads. I cannot forget standing on a Belfast street shortly after 'Bloody Sunday', as an armoured car passed and it dawned upon me that there was an exact point in its passing at which, in the event of any crossfire, I would be hit by a bullet in the head. It is that point which I have tried to keep in mind while writing this book. It is a point which permits hope (since Belfast has been made safer by a peace process guaranteeing human rights) but which serves to remind how many other 'mean streets' there are in this world where you can still be caught in crossfire, and in how many of them you can now be deliberately murdered by fire from drones in the sky or snipers in the pay of war criminals.

Today 'human rights' is much in fashion, which makes it the subject of a certain amount of humbug. In a world where virtue is no longer its own reward, there are plenty of human rights prizes, many funded by corporations exposed for exploiting the poor, awarded to well-paid lawyers, well-meaning journalists, well-photographed actresses and politicians who have never had to risk their careers in a cause perceived by national authorities as subversive. Ironies abound: the Simon Wiesenthal Center, celebrated for tracking down Nazi war criminals, today gives its peace prizes to supporters of the government of Israel. Self-promoting pop stars are prepared to promote politicians if they support the right to debt relief, but not the anti-war and anti-corruption measures without which there can be no relief for the poor in countries bankrupted by armed conflict and the extravagance of their rulers. In 2005, the 'Live 8' campaign to 'make poverty history' made no mention of ending the impunity which in Africa makes poverty inevitable. In 2009 President Obama was awarded the Nobel Peace Prize, just as he was authorizing the CIA's 'drone war' to execute summarily several thousand unconvicted terrorist targets, and anyone who happened, however innocently, to be in their near vicinity. It would be churlish to decry the fashionability of human rights, but premature to think that this means the struggle to have them enforced – the crucial 'third phase' of the human rights revolution – has yet been won. Still, it is in a better position than when the first edition appeared in 1999, and a far better position than when I joined Amnesty International as a student in 1970. Then, my initial task was to write a letter to 'His Excellency Sir Idi Amin Dada, QC, MP, VC and bar' politely requesting that he hold an inquest into the deaths of three Supreme Court judges whose headless bodies had been found floating downstream after they had delivered a decision 'about which Your Excellency may well have had reservations'.

I am especially grateful to Amnesty for inviting me, years later, to conduct missions which gave me experience of the sharp end of this subject, and to Ken Roth of Human Rights Watch for preparing introductions to the American editions. I would like to record my lasting gratitude to the late Sir Robin Vincent, my Registrar in the early years of the Sierra Leone Special Court. My thanks for helping this edition to press go particularly to Lionel Nichols, whose research ability, judgement and facility with footnotes have given great comfort. The text has also benefited from discussions with Jen Robinson, Stephen Powles, Kate O'Regan, Caitlin Reiger, Nina Jorgensen, Simona Tutui-anu, Toby Collis and Luis Moreno Ocampo. My thanks to Judy Rollinson, who did sterling work on the manuscript, to Stefan McGrath, Tom Penn, Bela Cunha and Richard Duguid at Penguin and Andre Shiffrin, Marc Favreau and Azzura at The New Press. My wife, Kathy Lette, and my children, Julius and Georgina, have frequently had to remind me that the most fundamental human right begins at home.

Geoffrey Robertson QC
Doughty Street Chambers
July 2012

'And here, over an acre of ground, lay dead and dying people. You could not see which was which except perhaps by a convulsive movement, or the last quiver of a sigh from a living skeleton, too weak to move. The living lay with their heads against the corpses, and around them moved the ghastly procession of emaciated, aimless people, with nothing to do, and no hope of life, unable to move out of your way, unable to look at the terrible sights around them . . . Babies had been born here, tiny wizened things that could not live. A mother, driven mad, screamed at a British sentry to give her milk for her child, and thrust the tiny mite into his arms and ran off, crying terribly. He opened the bundle, and found the baby had been dead for days. This day at Belsen was the most horrible day of my life.'

Richard Dimbleby
BBC broadcast from Belsen, 13 May 1945

Introduction

The notion that individuals, wherever in the world they live, possess a few basic powers which no political order can remove, has had a momentous impact at various points in modern history. The first came in 1642 with the civil war in England, during which Parliament wrested power from an absolute monarch, ended torture and secured some independence for judges, with freedom of speech and (up to a point) toleration of minority religions. By putting their king on trial for tyranny (including the charge that he tortured prisoners of war), an exercise by which they aimed to end what they called (for the first time) the 'impunity' of heads of state in Europe, the English Parliamentarians began to grapple with issues that are the subject of this book. It traces the development of the 'crime against humanity' – essentially genocide and mass-murder, or torture and persecution on a widespread or systematic scale – as a basis for engaging international justice, at least as a fall-back if local justice is dysfunctional or under the control of the perpetrators. The philosophy behind the global justice principle begins with the parable of the Good Samaritan, and owes something to Shakespeare's demonstration of the quality of mercy, John Stuart Mill's defence of the dissident and, of course, Emmanuel Kant's 'categorical imperative' to treat others as you would have yourself treated by others. It took the Holocaust, however, before the free world community could agree to end the impunity of political and military leaders, and bring their depredations within the reach of international law. This book charts the efforts since to deliver on the Nuremberg legacy that crimes against humanity, committed by any human, must be punished.

The second point came in the last quarter of the eighteenth century and was in every way revolutionary: it inspired both the American battle for independence from Britain and the overthrow of the despotic monarchy in France. It endowed these upheavals with a political meaning far beyond the republics which were their immediate object, by establishing the liberty of the individual as a precondition of and restriction on the power of the state. This was not unique to America and France: in other societies limitations had been imposed by tradition or cultural convention, or (most notably in Britain) by compact and common law, but what was truly groundbreaking was the constitutional enumeration of rights which the citizen could enforce against the government by taking it to court. But the notion that 'rights' might belong to anyone, anywhere, as a human inheritance was ridiculed by nineteenth-century philosophers and when the majority of Western powers agreed to outlaw slavery, this was attributed to shared moral generosity rather than to any recognition of an inalienable individual right not to be held in bondage or servitude. It dawned on no political leader, even after the carnage of the First World War, that international institutions might tell states how to treat their nationals – the League of Nations and the Permanent Court of International Justice were untroubled by 'human rights' until Hitler rendered them irrelevant. At this point, the individual had no rights in international law, which dealt with treaties and agreements between states and was completely inaccessible to their citizens.

The Holocaust was a revelation that was to change this for ever. It crystallized the Allied war aims, and called forth an international tribunal – the court at Nuremberg – to punish individual Nazis for the barbarities they had authorized against German citizens. These charges – called, for the first time, 'crimes against humanity' – were distinct from the 'war crimes' the Axis partners had inflicted upon Allied soldiers and prisoners-of-war. The logic of the crime against humanity, first defined in Article 6(c) of the Nuremberg Charter, was that future state agents who authorized torture or genocide against their own populations were criminally responsible, in international law, and might be punished by any court capable of catching them. For the first time, it could be said that individuals had a 'right' to be treated with a minimum of civility by their own governments, which 'right' all other governments had a correlative duty to uphold by trying the torturers who fell into their hands, or else by setting up international courts to punish them. This was the legal legacy of Nuremberg, supplemented by a United Nations system which promised institutional support for a 'Universal Declaration of Human Rights' approved by the General Assembly of the United Nations.

The third great moment for human rights – the creation of a process by which it could emerge from the domestic laws and constitutions of a few countries into a universal system affording some minimum protection to everyone, everywhere – had arrived. At the Palais Chaillot in Paris, on 10 December 1948, the president of the General Assembly, Dr H. V. Evatt (the Australian foreign minister), announced the advent of a new international law of human rights, for the first time transcending the laws and customs of independent sovereign states: 'millions of men, women and children, all over the world, many miles from Paris and New York, will turn for help, guidance and inspiration to this document'.

But this moment was short-lived. The evolutionary process for international human rights law, commenced so confidently, was frozen almost to a standstill by the Cold War. The power blocs did not deny the idea of universal human rights – with shameless hypocrisy, they contentedly signed convention after convention on the subject – so long as no meaningful enforcement action could ever be taken. 'Human rights' became a phrase incorporated into insults traded between the Great Powers, as they secretly vied for the support of dictatorships which comprehensively violated them. The four decades between 1948 and the collapse of communism may be characterized – and stigmatized – as the lip-service era for human rights, when diplomats strove to ensure that they could never be meaningfully asserted against a nation state. There were times – the early days of Jimmy Carter's presidency, for example – when the idea resonated before succumbing to *realpolitik*, and undoubtedly the 'help, guidance and inspiration' of human rights was an important factor in the ultimate failure of some regimes notorious for denying them: the military juntas of Latin America, the apartheid system in South Africa, the USSR and its puppet states of eastern Europe. But all that happened to human rights *law* over those four decades was a series of academic exercises, honing and refining and putting in place international conventions – most notably the twin Covenants on Civil and Political Rights and on Economic and Social Rights – which were marvels of modern diplomacy: none of the states which signed them intended them to work.

The only progress in this regard was regional, and confined to western Europe, where a human rights court at Strasbourg gradually made guarantees of 'fundamental freedoms' more meaningful to citizens across a dozen or so harmonious continental borders. Come the communist collapse, the European Convention and its Strasbourg court were sufficiently impressive for the newly liberated nations of eastern Europe to sign up for membership, and by the time of the UN's triumphalist talk-fest at Vienna in 1993 there was a much more genuine desire to put human rights at the centre of the 'New World Order' proclaimed after the apparent defeat of Saddam Hussein following his invasion of Kuwait. It seemed possible to extrapolate the Strasbourg experiment to a global level, most optimistically by having all 193 member nations ratify the UN Covenant on Civil and Political Rights and accept the jurisdiction of the Human Rights Committee established under its Optional Protocol, so creating a forum for individuals to complain about and obtain redress, as a matter of law, against their governments. In the meantime, a start (barely noticed at first) was made to capitalize on the Nuremberg legacy – international tribunals were established, in The Hague and at Arusha, in Tanzania, to punish the perpetrators of crimes against humanity during the genocidal conflicts in former Yugoslavia and Rwanda.

But evolution of international law is not a linear progress. A backwards step came at Vienna, in 1993, in the form of belated but vehement Third World objections, not so much to the very idea of human rights as to its elucidation in the UN Declaration and the twin Covenants. These were said to embody 'Western' perceptions of freedom at odds with those in Asia and Africa, and antipathetic to states governed paternalistically by 'big men' or by religious (especially Islamic) law. This ushered in a new 'universality' debate, rekindled and rephrased from the nineteenth century when objections to the notion of 'natural' or 'inalienable' rights had successfully called into question the philosophical truth of the French and American declarations. Human rights were said to be 'culturally relative' – by such statesmen as Dr Mahathir (who found an independent judiciary inconvenient to his own aspirations in Malaysia), President Suharto (the incarnation of nepotistic corruption) and Lee Kuan Yew (whose assaults on freedom of speech in Singapore had been designed to maintain his electoral hegemony). The championship of 'Asian values' soon weakened with Asian economies, and in 1998 Dr Mahathir's behaviour over Anwar Ibrahim – gloating after he was beaten up in police custody – made many of his countrymen protest in favour of old-fashioned Western values asserted by the Indonesian protesters who had just swept Suharto from power. Following the elections of human rights activists like Kim Dae Jung in South Korea and Chen Shui-bian in Taiwan, the idea of human rights resurged in Asia.

In the Middle East, fundamentalism and liberalism as well were both kept in check by military or militarized regimes which denied citizens any democracy and forbade free speech. The occasional revolution did not result in democracy – quite the opposite in Libya, where Colonel Gaddafi ruled with unparalleled viciousness, hanging his opponents ('stray dogs') from lampposts or sending assassination squads to hunt them down abroad. (At one point he had 1,200 prisoners mass-murdered, because they had protested against prison conditions.) Iran was even worse: the torture by the Shah's brutal SAVAK was benign by comparison with the torture and execution of dissidents that followed under Ayatollah Khomeini. Thousands of political prisoners were rounded up and hanged without trial in 1988 – perhaps the worst single example of a crime against humanity committed against prisoners since the Japanese death marches at the end of the Second World War. In Iraq in the same year chemical weapons were used by Saddam Hussein to kill thousands of Kurds, and nobody much minded: Western politicians and diplomats flocked to Baghdad's next arms bazaar.

It was little wonder that when the first books hailed as dispensing millennium wisdom – Francis Fukuyama's *The End of History and the Last Man* and Paul Kennedy's *Preparing for the Twenty-First Century* – thudded on to reviewers' desks in 1993, neither made a single reference to human rights as a factor in the futures they envisaged.

Readers of these works, hailed as so prescient, could never have imagined that before the century was out a British prime minister and a US president would proclaim a duty to go to war to protect human rights – by putting the leader of a sovereign nation in the dock of an international court.

That this could happen so dramatically was a result of the return to Nuremberg, re-examining and reinstating its great legal legacy – the notion of the crime against humanity. This is a crime with a peculiar horror deriving from the fact that fellow human beings are capable of conceiving and committing it, thereby diminishing us all. Such crimes are not only unforgettable; what Nuremberg established in international law is that they are unforgivable. They cannot be the subject of amnesty or of time limits on prosecution. Punishment cannot be left to history (which depends, after all, on who writes it) or to hellfire (a sanction which would in any event be contrary to the convention against torture). There is a legal duty on all states to investigate and (if the evidence is available) to prosecute persons suspected of this class of offence, narrowly defined as the commission of widespread and systematic murder, torture, enslavement or persecution of innocent civilians pursuant to a political policy. Individuals who commit such crimes must have no hiding-place: there is a universal jurisdiction to punish them. This legal principle draws practical support from the consideration that crimes against humanity will be deterred only if would-be perpetrators – whether political and military leaders or foot soldiers and policemen – are given pause by the prospect that one day, under a different regime or in another country, they may be called to account. And irrespective of claims of state sovereignty, a government which inflicts crimes against humanity on its own people risks armed intervention, from an international community which now accepts an obligation to interfere in the internal affairs of collapsed or criminal states, under the 'responsibility to protect' (R2P) principle.

The revival and refinement of the Nuremberg legacy is best appreciated by consideration of the cumulative impact of six unprecedented events, all occurring in the last eighteen months of the twentieth century:

* *The statute to establish an international criminal court* (ICC) agreed by 120 nations in Rome in July 1998, to come into effect after 60 nations had ratified the Treaty (achieved less than four years later, on 11 April 2002). Only seven nations formally opposed it, although they included the US and China, as well as Libya, Iran and Saudi Arabia.

* *The arrest of General Pinochet* in London in October 1998, on a warrant from a Spanish magistrate alleging his systematic use of torture. The British House of Lords ruled (twice) that his sovereign immunity from prosecution as an ex-head of state did not protect him against allegations of directing systematic torture. He remained under house arrest in England for eighteen months until declared medically unfit for trial.

* *War against Yugoslavia.* NATO countries, without explicit Security Council backing, invaded Yugoslavian sovereignty by a bombing campaign designed to stop further 'ethnic cleansing' in Kosovo. A ceasefire agreement in June 1999 provided for Kosovo autonomy.

* *Freedom for East Timor.* In September 1999 a UN-backed coalition led by Australia invaded East Timor to stop massacres by militias in league with the Indonesian army, and to guarantee the island's independence after its people had voted for that status in a UN-brokered election.

* *The Hague Criminal Tribunal.* From early 1999 onwards NATO forces began to arrest major war criminals – Serb and Croat generals and their concentration camp commanders – while in Arusha, Tanzania, the former prime minister of Rwanda was convicted of genocide.

* *The Lockerbie agreement.* After a decade of economic sanctions, Libya finally agreed to surrender the two intelligence agents suspected of blowing up a Pan American jumbo jet over the Scottish town of Lockerbie. They were tried under Scots law, before Scottish judges, at an American airbase in Holland.

After a half century of ineffectual treaties and diplomatic thumb-twiddling, there came this end-of-century stampede to put global justice systems in place: an international criminal court, a 'prosecute or extradite' regime for torturers, a precedent for intervening in the internal affairs of sovereign states out of humanitarian necessity. Nations were prepared to kill for human rights in Kosovo, and more significantly were prepared for their troops to be killed for human rights in East Timor. This movement may have owed something to PMT (pre-millennium tension) – a sickness at the atrocities of the twentieth century and a wish to do better in the twenty-first. But it did seem to foreshadow a millennial shift, from appeasement to justice, as a dominant factor in diplomatic relations.

The momentum continued, most spectacularly when Slobodan Milošević appeared in the Hague dock, sold out by his country in disgust and for the price of a reconstruction loan. There were other hopeful developments in the first two years of the new century: the Hague Tribunal recorded its first genocide conviction (forty-six years in prison for a Bosnian Serb general who ordered mass murder at Srebrenica); the humanitarian crisis in Sierra Leone was finally brought under some control by a British force and the UN set up a war crimes court in Sierra Leone to try those who bore greatest responsibility for the atrocities, with the participation of international judges and prosecutors. In East Timor an international tribunal was jailing such militia leaders as it could lay its hands on, although the real culprits – officers of the Indonesian army – were playing a waiting game in Jakarta, where weak politicians and corrupt judges provide a paradigm case in favour of international criminal justice when not much is on offer locally. In other places the Pinochet precedent was beginning to bite, as old dictators realized that their prospects for longevity hinged upon the uncertain expertise of local medics, since they could not travel abroad in safety. Fear of universal jurisdiction caused Indonesian President Suharto to cancel a trip to Germany for heart surgery; Mengistu, the mass-murdering Marxist of Ethiopia, ventured from Zimbabwe to a hospital in Cape Town but scampered back to his bolt hole when his presence was mentioned in the local press. Ariel Sharon was indicted in Belgium by survivors of the Sabra and Shatila massacres, and had to hire lawyers to contest the charges in the interests of being able to undertake trouble-free European travel. A Belgian court used its universal jurisdiction over genocide to jail two Hutu nuns, Sister Gertrude and Sister Maria, who had offered their church as sanctuary for hundreds of Tutsi refugees and then bought the petrol used to incinerate them. In 2001 international judges sitting in Fiji's appeal court declared illegal the government installed by the military, which actually obeyed the court's order to hold fresh elections. Of course, there were many examples of failure and foot-dragging, of war crimes unnoticed or unpunished from Chechnya to the Congo, while NATO's inability to arrest Karadžić and Mladić remained inexplicable, but by the summer of 2001 it could confidently be said that the age of human rights enforcement had dawned.

On 11 September 2001, quite literally out of a clear blue sky, came the kamikaze attack on symbols of American hegemony, leaving almost 3,000 dead, incinerated in the remains of the World Trade Center and part of the Pentagon. This atrocity qualified as a 'crime against humanity', since it involved multiple acts of murder committed as part of a systematic attack against a civilian population (the al-Qaida organization had been responsible for previous atrocities carried out as part of the same plan, including the embassy bombings in Kenya and Tanzania which killed several hundred civilians). There was confusion, however, as to whether international law could apply to a terrorist network operating in various countries and possessing neither territory nor government. The immediate presidential declaration of a 'war on terror' was at first no more than rhetoric, although it soon decoded into the reality of a war on Afghanistan and the overthrow of the Taliban government. America claimed to be exercising its right to self-defence under Article 51 of the UN Charter, which certainly justified an initial bombing campaign to destroy al-Qaida's bases and infrastructure. But self-defence only legitimizes a military response when and so long as the necessity for it is 'instant, overwhelming, leaving no choice of means and no moment for hesitation'. As the bombing continued, the right of self-defence was expanded, and the action lacked credibility as a war to protect America. It was a war to topple the Taliban government, an objective achieved by American air power and ground forces of the Northern Alliance.

If there is any silver lining retrospectively to be found in those grotesque pictures of black clouds over Manhattan, it will be eventual US commitment to a system of global justice which alone offers a principled method of punishing terrorism on this scale. The message that much more international co-operation is needed to ensure that perpetrators of crimes against humanity have no place to hide, and no place to hide their money, was soon communicated by strengthening international extradition arrangements and (through Security Council Resolution 1373) producing a duty on all states to ban the financing of terrorist organizations. What the 9/11 atrocity highlighted – for the world in general and the US in particular – was the spectre of weapons of mass destruction, in the hands of rogue states and rogue statesmen, or obtained by terrorists.

That was the issue that poleaxed the Security Council in 2003 over Iraq, a dictatorship insufficiently punished (in the first Gulf War) for its invasion of Kuwait and not punished at all for its genocidal forays against its population of Kurds and Marsh Arabs. Saddam Hussein's minority Ba'athist regime had stayed in power by brutal repression, made easier by inconclusive US/UK attempts to bomb it into co-operation with weapons inspectors. By what mixture of arrogance and ignorance Saddam was led to act as if he did have weapons of mass destruction, and by what mix of arrogance and ignorance the Bush administration determined Iraq should be invaded without Security Council approval in order to remove these non-existent weapons, is yet to be fully unravelled: international law was much discussed in the lead-up to a war which it had neither the confidence nor the foresight to prevent. Afterwards, US 'own goals' – torture at Abu Ghraib prison, 'extraordinary rendition' of prisoners and a refusal of due process for Guantanamo detainees – made the world's most powerful nation appear the enemy of international justice. That presumption was strengthened by the Pentagon's relentless and irrational attempt to undermine the ICC – which obscured the fact that the US was the main financial supporter of '*ad hoc*' tribunals in The Hague, at Arusha (for the Rwandan genocide) and in Sierra Leone. Its rejection of international justice as the venue for Saddam Hussein's trial was another missed opportunity for progress towards a world willing to punish tyrants who mass murder their own people.

In time – a very little time – this has changed. Towards the end of the second Bush term, the realization that international justice was no bad thing began to dawn on the White House; Colin Powell went so far as to ask the Security Council to refer suspected genocide in Darfur to the ICC (although the US abstained from its vote in favour of the reference). The Obama administration has shown no such hypocrisy, and has collaborated with the ICC almost as if the US were an associate member. It has consistently renounced torture, including waterboarding; it supported Resolutions 1970 and 1973 by which the Security Council empowered the ICC to indict the Gaddafis; it invited NATO to use 'all necessary measures' to protect the vulnerable lives of Libyan citizens. But the Obama administration has been unable to summon the political resolve to close Guantanamo or to put its inmates on fair trials rather than military commissions, and the civilian death toll from its use of pilotless drones in Pakistan has become seriously unacceptable – a form of execution of terror suspects without trial or any form of due process. This reached its apotheosis in the killing of Osama bin Laden, by a mission which appears to have been directed to kill rather than capture America's public enemy number one. The opportunity lost by making him a martyr rather than defendant is discussed in chapter 11. On a more positive note, the US under Obama has shown a greater respect for international law, a greater willingness to abandon some of its 'sons of bitches' when the populace turn against them, and a new willingness to respect the 'responsibility to protect' principle as a basis for UN intervention, rather than its own exceptionalist view of what serves US interests.

It cannot be said that either Russia or China show much enthusiasm for human rights standards: China consistently opposes incursions upon state sovereignty, and defies human rights standards by passing lengthy jail sentences on dissidents and democrats, imposing firewall censorship on the Internet and inflicting more death sentences than any other country. Russia conducts a brutal war in Chechnya and manipulates the judiciary to jail Putin's political enemies, although its behaviour at the Security Council tends to be opportunistic, supporting states that it has forged friendships with through trade in arms and oil. The UK, ever since it accepted the adverse decision in the

Alabama claims case, has been the one big power prepared to take international justice on the chin and to support its development, although its record has been spotted by complicity with CIA torture and with the unlawful invasion of Iraq. France led the opposition to that venture in aggression and was the keenest advocate for humanitarian intervention in Libya, but has contrived to dodge international justice when its own misbehaviour is at stake, such as its tests of nuclear devices in the Pacific and its sinking of the *Rainbow Warrior*. It played a devious role in support of preparations for the genocide in Rwanda, and its treatment of colonies, especially in the Pacific (such as New Caledonia and Samoa) has denied the rights of indigenous peoples.

Meanwhile, the communications revolution continues its work of making human beings everywhere respond with simultaneous outrage to the images of genocide and torture through its capacity to download into every corner of the planet. CNN has in this way served as recruiting officer for the human rights movement, followed by Al Jazeera, which has played an even more important role, revealing the evils of the Arab world to the Arab street. Ignorantly demonized by Western leaders at first because of its neutral coverage of al-Qaida (President Bush privately suggested to Tony Blair that it should be made a bombing target) it has become a beacon for free-speech values, its broadcasts from Qatar being more trusted in many developing countries than those of its Western competitors. But ever since the attempted 'Green Revolution' in Iran in 2009, the role of the new electronic media in communicating information has been crucial to protest movements. Demonstrations are organized through Facebook postings and Twitter feeds, while pictures of regime brutality – for example, the death throes of Neda Agha-Soltan, the courageous young Iranian woman protestor killed in Tehran by revolutionary guards – 'go viral' on YouTube, and move people throughout the world to pity and to anger. The Syrian government in 2011 banned all foreign reporters and broadcasters, but could not stop cell-phone pictures of its army shooting at protestors being posted on YouTube. Wikileaks has added a further dimension: its founder, Julian Assange, invented an 'electronic dead letter-box' to which sources could post secret documents without ever being identified (unless, like Bradley Manning, they blabbed to untrustworthy friends). It was Wikileaks which, in 2010, revealed 'collateral murder' – the footage of a US Apache helicopter shooting at Reuters reporters and children – and a mass of information about government corruption, culled from US diplomatic cables. It also revealed the truth about casualties of the war in Iraq – much higher than hitherto admitted – and Hillary Clinton's plans to set up secret surveillance of UN diplomats, in contravention of the Vienna Convention. This revolution in information technology has in turn been a recruiting agent for human rights NGOs, many with consultative status at the UN, whose monitors in war-torn countries collect evidence, produce reports and are available to testify at international criminal courts.

Amnesty International was founded by a few English do-gooders in 1961: by 2012 it boasted over three million members, and there were more than 900 other non-government organizations sharing aspects of its work. Twelve million people from all over the world signed a petition presented to the UN's Secretary-General on the fiftieth anniversary of the Universal Declaration of Human Rights, demanding that its promises be made good after the millennium.

As this book will demonstrate, the United Nations system is not structurally or psychologically geared to deliver on these promises – other than by setting up institutions independent of its internal politics, which might make adjudicative decisions which require the enforcement powers of the Security Council (ranging from trade sanctions to armed intervention) to be deployed against states which do not accept the adjudication. Any such system would challenge both the shibboleth of the sovereignty of nation states and the obsessive neutrality ingrained in UN personnel and procedures. Such challenges have been permitted in the case of pariah states like South Africa, Iraq and Libya, and criminal justice has been imposed on those in a state of disintegration (former Yugoslavia and Rwanda) but these cases are *ad hoc* – a weasel Latin phrase used in UN resolutions as a coded diplomatic signal that the action will not be used as a precedent to threaten other members. Obeisance to member-state sovereignty is the UN's systemic defect, and it accounts for the often poor performance of the Human Rights Council and that toothless tribunal, the Human Rights Committee. If the promises of the Universal Declaration are to be realized, we must look to bodies independent of the UN, to regional treaty systems and their courts, to forge an international human rights law sufficiently understood and respected to be enforced in municipal courts throughout the world.

The UN's finest moment came in 2011 when the Security Council applied the 'responsibility to protect' principle to the situation in Libya, authorizing (by Resolution 1970) the ICC prosecutor to investigate and indict, and then (by Resolution 1973) calling upon armed intervention by NATO to protect civilians. Colonel Gaddafi, of course, was an absurd and brutal figure despised, in the end, by Arab and African statesmen as well as their Western counterparts. Satisfaction at his overthrow was diminished by the Security Council's inability to reach agreement on referring President Assad to the ICC, notwithstanding his slaughter of thousands of protestors over a period of months. He was guilty of a crime against humanity, yet his superpower protectors – Russia and China – would not agree to have the case of Syria referred to the ICC prosecutor.

But there are many reasons for caution, indeed for cynicism, about the resolve of states to enforce international human rights law, notwithstanding the fact that it is currently in fashion in diplomatic discourse and has become the United Nation's catch-cry for the twenty-first century. It is popular, certainly, in the West, where decent people do want their governments to intervene to stop the slaughter in far-off countries of which they know something from the Internet and the television news. But the project still remains in the care of diplomats and politicians, who throughout the Cold War used human rights opportunistically, as a propaganda weapon against the other side. Diplomacy is the antithesis of justice: it brokers trade-offs which allow oppressors to escape punishment. Global enforcement of human rights standards cannot confidently be entrusted to the United Nations, with its lamentable record of doing so little to staunch gross abuses by countries of any significance (or even by insignificant countries, if they are protected by powerful alignments). The very action which revived the idea of an international criminal court, namely the establishment in 1993 of the Hague Tribunal to punish crimes against humanity in former Yugoslavia, was conceived as a fig leaf to cover the UN's early reluctance to intervene in the Balkans.

However, for all the cynicism of diplomats which attended their creation, the work of the ICC, the ICTY and its counterparts in Arusha and Sierra Leone, in trying crimes against humanity, has slowly gained acceptance. Their record gives no cause for the kind of alarm that was sounded by the US delegation in Rome in 1998: there has been no prosecutorial excess, no politically motivated indictments, no judicial over-reach. There have been errors, mostly corrected on appeal, and unacceptable delays – sometimes due to painstaking regard for the defendant's rights. The evidence shows that international criminal justice is operating fairly in those limited 'ad hoc' spheres in which it is presently allowed. What is perhaps more important is the intellectual momentum of these courts, which is synthesizing and popularizing the principle of retribution for international crimes. War crimes jurisprudence has an epic quality which is beginning to be cited in national courts around the world. It is giving lawyers good ideas, not just for prosecuting and extraditing, but also for dipping into the growing body of international human rights law to find new ways of arguing cases for victims of crimes against humanity. This may smack of lawyerly hand-rubbing, but that profession exists to satisfy popular as well as individual desire for justice: what has taken politicians as well as diplomats by surprise is the public insistence that they maintain pressure on states to punish the crimes against humanity that *realpolitik* counsels them to forget. In these different ways, through *ad hoc* tribunals, international pressure for domestic prosecutions, Pinochet precedents, truth commissions and now an international criminal court, the third age of human rights – the era of enforcement – is beginning to dawn.

That era notionally began on 1 July 2002, the date after which war crimes and crimes against humanity became capable of prosecution, if overlooked by individual states, at the International Criminal Court. The Court itself came into concrete existence in 2003 when its eighteen judges were appointed, although the first indictments were not handed down until 2005 and its first conviction was in 2012. Its jurisdiction, as explained in chapter 10, is severely limited by *realpolitik*:

its prosecutor can only act after a reference from the Security Council, or else by permission of the Court in respect of crimes committed on the territory, or by nationals, of states which have ratified its convention. That 120 states have done so is a remarkable tribute to the power of the global justice idea, all the more so given the hostility of both China and the US. It is not without irony that this legacy of Nuremberg is not supported by Israel, whose government has been determined to avoid international legal scrutiny of its treatment of Palestinians. Arab nations are equally reluctant to submit to international law – of their number, only Jordan, Tajikistan and Afghanistan have ratified, although the Arab Spring brings promise that Egypt, Tunisia and Libya will follow. It will take time before the Security Council will mandate the Court to deal with civil wars other than those in failed or friendless states, but the very prospect that it may do so in some unforeseeable future will make leaders and generals in powerful places think more carefully before unleashing state violence on civilians.

In the twenty-first century, the dominant motive in world affairs is the quest – almost the thirst – for justice, replacing even the objective of regional security as the trigger for international action. It was the first demand made by the US President after the World Trade Center attack, and it won a compassionate and supportive response from almost all sectors of the international community. This quest explains, on a jurisprudential level, the refusal to accept Chile's sovereign immunity for Pinochet or Serbian sovereignty over Kosovo. It has been exemplified by the tenacity of the Lockerbie relatives (although at first their cause seemed hopeless), drawing in the UN and many world leaders who eventually negotiated a surrender of the Libyans for trial under Scottish law on a US airbase in the Netherlands, and by the international campaign to make African leaders understand why it was important that Charles Taylor should be tried, and tried fairly, at the UN war crimes court in Sierra Leone, to which he was eventually surrendered in 2006 (and sentenced in 2012). For all the attacks on the ICTY from dyspeptic Marxists and Milošević supporters, it weathered these early storms and its dogged hunts for Generals

Gotovina and Mladić, and for Bosnian Serb Prime Minister Karadžić, were eventually successful. Mladić's capture and transfer to The Hague in 2011 was greeted with satisfaction throughout Europe. Although some criticized NATO for 'exceeding its brief', the Security Council's prior decision to empower the ICC prosecutor to indict the Gaddafis met with no opposition, nor did Laurent Gbagbo's transfer to The Hague after he had blocked democracy in the Ivory Coast by allegedly ordering his troops to engage in a killing spree.

Events like these mark the end of sovereign impunity, by recognizing that political leadership (a role for which there is no shortage of candidates in any country) carries, as a concomitant of wielding state power, an accountability for abusing it. Cynics point out the present and pragmatic limitation of this principle, namely that it does not apply to high officials of states with a permanent seat on the Security Council. However, if the principle means there will be no more Rwandas or Kosovos or Darfurs, at least it will mean something. And then the challenge will be to invest the international legal system with the power to investigate the legitimacy of behaviour like Assad's in Syria or Russia's in Chechnya or America's at Guantanamo. That challenge, as superpower opposition to the Rome Statute demonstrated, will take many years before it prevails, but a start has been made. Justice, once there is a procedure for its delivery, is prone to have its own momentum.

I

The Human Rights Story

'Establish the Rights of Man; enthrone equality . . . let there
be no privileges, no distinctions of birth, no monopolies;
make safe the liberty of industry and trade, the equal distribution of family inheritances.'

Thomas Paine
Dissertation on the First Principles of Government (1795)

IN THE BEGINNING: NATURAL RIGHTS

Any system of law – including the first written Hammurabi code, several thousand years before Christ – inferentially confers 'rights' on the
citizens to whom it applies, at least in the negative and residual sense
of entitling them to behave in any manner which it does not specifically prohibit. The ancient codes of the Greek city states and of
imperial Rome conferred such 'rights', but went on to bestow positive
powers on certain classes of citizens, over and distinct from other
classes. Religions, similarly, enforced within theocratic communities
rules and taboos from which positive entitlements might be deduced.
Christianity goes further and applies its rules to all living persons,
irrespective of status or nationality: from the commandment 'Thou
shalt not steal', for example, one might infer a moral right for everybody to enjoy private property. But the closest the lawyers of the
ancient world came to the idea that some special rights were *universal*

was in the Roman concept of *jus gentium*, those rules which they discovered to be common to all civilized societies and which might therefore be catalogued specially as a kind of international law. Laws were thus categorized, not because of their intrinsic or self-evident merit or validity, but simply because they were in service in every civilized society.

This 'lowest common denominator' approach of *jus gentium* – these laws have a special quality because they are approved by rational men and regarded as binding by all civilizations – was picked up two thousand years later to justify the assertion of jurisdiction over crimes against humanity, wherever and by whomsoever committed. But in ancient times, when rules of battle were rudimentary, when the greatest of crimes were punished by the gods and extradition was unknown, the notion that *jus gentium* might reflect and even protect inalienable human rights was never coherently propounded. What did emerge, however, through the church-dominated Middle Ages, was the quasi-theological notion that there were 'laws of nature': rules ordained by God, to be observed by all His human creations on peril of divine punishment. This theory was highly attractive to the crowned heads of Europe – to princes and to popes with princely ambitions – for the first law of nature invariably imposed unquestioning obedience to the prince, as God's regent on his own little patch of the earth. The 'Divine Right of Kings' was part of the natural order of things, and from it flowed a number of legal consequences (such as the immunity from prosecution of heads of state) which international human rights law is still in the process of extirpating.

Essential to this feudal conception was *sovereignty* (the power of the divinely approved ruler over all his or her subjects), the exercise of which – however barbaric – could not be questioned either by those subjects or by or against other sovereigns. There could, of course, be treaties between two or more states, giving rise to international law, but they could only be invoked by the sovereigns who had signed them (or their heirs and successors). The only 'rights' an individual could possess in such a world was if he happened to be visiting a foreign country. Then, as a temporary 'alien', he was entitled to call on the protection of his own sovereign against infringements on his liberty threatened by the state in which he was sojourning. This had the consequence, for several centuries, of giving aliens abroad more 'rights' than the citizens of their host country.

The appearance of 'rights' as a set of popular propositions limiting the sovereign is usually traced to Magna Carta in 1215, although that document had nothing to do with the liberty of individual citizens: it was signed by a feudal king who was feuding with thuggish barons, and who was forced to accede to their demands. It had two symbols of a constitutional settlement, however: firstly, it limited the power of the state (in a very elementary way, since the King *was* the state), and secondly it contained some felicitous phrases which gradually entered the common law and have worked their rhetorical magic down the centuries. For example, in Clause 40 of Magna Carta, the King promised, 'To no man will we sell, to no man will we deny or delay justice or right.' This was the forerunner – what might be called the King John version – of Article 6(1) of the European Convention on Human Rights, 'Everyone is entitled to a fair and public hearing within a reasonable time.'

There was also the great promise of *habeas corpus* in Clause 39:

No freeman shall be seized or imprisoned or stripped of his rights and possessions, or outlawed or exiled ... except by the lawful judgement of his equals or by the law of the land ...

Magna Carta, therefore, became a weapon for opposition to absolute rule: as Tom Bingham has put it, 'King John entered the meadow [of Runnymede] as a ruler acknowledging no secular superior, whose word was law. He left the meadow as a ruler who had acknowledged, in the most solemn manner imaginable, that there were some things even he could not do ...'[1] Judges in subsequent centuries relied on Clause 39 of Magna Carta to develop *habeas corpus*: it was the one iconic precedent that even kings could not challenge.

Magna Carta was reinvented as guarantor of these basic rights by English parliamentarians as they struggled to share power with a king who insisted on absolute rule. Their Petition of Right, in 1628, was the first legislative attempt to entrench the liberty of the subject.

Charles I ignored it and suspended Parliament for eleven years, using his Star Chamber – an executive 'court' of ministers and lackey judges – to torture and imprison Puritan preachers. Some 30,000 refugees from his religious persecution settled in Massachusetts, many (including the first graduates from Harvard) returning to fight for Parliament in the English Civil Wars, begun by the King in 1642. This was a crucible period in history in which the key values of Western democracy – the sovereignty of Parliament, the independence of the judiciary and the separation of church and state – were thought out and fought for, at the cost of one in ten British lives (comparatively, a higher death toll than that suffered by Britain in the First World War). Although he was the enemy commander, defeated time and again, Charles remained the country's king, always plotting from his place of 'castle arrest' more war to restore himself to absolute power. As head of state, he enjoyed absolute immunity – a doctrine confirmed by the Treaty of Westphalia in 1648, which is regarded as the foundation of modern international law.

Westphalia was a peace treaty that brought the Thirty Years War on the Continent to an end, through recognition of the sovereignty of the nation state and the immunity of its ruler. In Philip Bobbitt's words, 'Westphalia was to the state of Europe in 1648 what Philadelphia became for the states of the American colonies in 1789: the birthplace of a new constitution for a small society of states.'[2] Its signing by or on behalf of Machiavelli's princes of Europe was truly a 'Grotian moment' that produced a new world order – in fact, a first world order, in which nations differing in religion and politics recognized that together they had power to make rules that would bind them all. It drew immediate condemnation from the Pope, appalled at the prospect that an international juridical order might threaten his pretensions to universal spiritual hegemony. Westphalia therefore spelled progress, but in structure rather than substance: as a peace treaty it legitimized war as a means of dispute settlement, and as an agreement simply of kings it embodied the philosophy of Jean Bodin, that apostle of absolutism who argued that tyranny was more congenial than rebellion and that the greatest danger to a nation came from tolerating talk of 'the people's liberty'. So the best thing about the Treaty of Westphalia was that England was not part of it.

THE TRIAL OF CHARLES I

The trial of Charles I in January 1649 was the first war crimes trial of a head of state – just three months after the Treaty of Westphalia had endorsed their immunity from prosecution. Charles had the purest form of sovereign immunity: he was sovereign, both by hereditary and (as most believed) by Divine Right. English judges, too, had always said that the King, as the source of the law, could do no wrong: '*Rex* is *Lex*' is how they had put it in the ship-money case.[3] Besides, Magna Carta promised trial by one's peers and the King's lawyers argued that since the King had no peers, he could not be put on trial at all. Undaunted, the House of Commons passed a law which established the High Court of Justice 'to the end that no chief officer or magistrate may hereafter presume traitorously or maliciously to imagine or continue the enslaving or destroying of the English nation, and expect *impunity* for so doing'. This was the origin of 'impunity' in the sense that Kofi Annan and Amnesty International now use the word, to refer to the freedom which tyrants should never have, to live happily ever after their tyranny.

What was truly astonishing about the trial of Charles I was that it took place at all. Under the laws of war as understood at the time, kings had no immunity during hostilities: 'in war the rules of honour applied universally, binding princes and men at arms equally'. The decision to put the King not before a firing squad but before a tribunal tasked to apply the common law, permitting him to justify his cause in public and requiring the prosecution to prove his guilt, was an unprecedented step. It was a daring decision, far in advance of the law as it then stood in England or, following the Treaty of Westphalia, in the known world. There was no example to suggest that the trial of a head of state was feasible: it would be necessary to find lawyers who could make it work. Parliament's brief to end impunity was sent to a barrister at Gray's Inn, one John Cooke, who prosecuted Charles

Stuart as 'the occasioner, author and continuer' of the civil wars, 'a tyrant, traitor, murderer and a public and implacable enemy to the Commonwealth of England'.⁴ 'Tyranny' was an apt description of what today would be called crimes against humanity and war crimes: Cooke used it to describe the conduct of leaders who destroy law and liberty or who bear 'command responsibility' for the starting of wars or the plunder of innocent civilians or the torture of prisoners-of-war. Cooke drew upon Magna Carta, the law of nations and the Bible to charge Charles I with a crime which only kings or other heads of state could commit by mass murdering their own people and denying them civil and religious liberties. Cooke had plenty of compelling evidence: intercepted correspondence, witnesses who had seen the King directing torture of prisoners, and so on. The King had access to the best lawyers in the land but he refused to plead, and with a courage and nobility that he had never shown previously, he attacked the lawfulness of the court and all its proceedings. He showed utter contempt for the judges, abused them and eloquently refused to recognize their jurisdiction over him. In the end, the court had to apply the contemporary rule that a refusal to plead was in law a confession of guilt: they had no alternative but to convict him and sentence him to death.

The difficulties of putting a head of state on trial had become apparent. Most judges and barristers fled town, in fear of retribution at the hands of God or of royalists if they returned to power. Eventually one judge was prevailed upon to preside (not in a wig but in a hat lined with lead) and some seventy 'judge jurors' – namely MPs, army officers and influential business and civic figures were empanelled, the closest 'peers' of the King that could be found. Westminster Hall, the largest public space in the kingdom, was chosen so that as many subjects as possible could watch – a commitment to open justice continued today in television coverage of war crimes trials. It would allow the world to witness the righteousness of their cause and 'teach all kings to know that they were accountable and punishable for the wickedness of their lives'. When Charles made his entrance on the first day, he was very much a king in command, taking his plush velvet seat beside the prosecutor. As John Cooke stood to present the charge, the King tapped the low-bred lawyer with his silver-tipped cane and commanded, 'Hold.' Had Cooke done so, the whole proceedings would have faltered, but he continued notwithstanding another royal poke. He was hit a third time, with such force that the silver tip fell off and clattered to the floor between the two men. The King motioned for Cooke to pick it up, but the prosecutor ignored his command and went on with his opening. As thousands of his subjects watched, the King stooped low to retrieve it – a portentous historical moment when Divine Majesty bowed, powerless before the majesty of the law.

The defendant quickly recovered from this symbolic set-back and his arguments in Westminster Hall are repeated (with diminishing force) today in the courtrooms of The Hague and were even heard in the Iraqi Special Tribunal – Saddam Hussein's opening words to his judges were, in translation, a paraphrase of those of Charles: 'I would know by what power am I called hither . . . by what authority, lawful I mean . . .' (see p. 721). Three centuries before the rulings against Pinochet and Milošević, this was a good question, and Charles was allowed to repeat it without entering a plea. He had refused the offer to have Matthew Hale, London's top barrister, take points of law on his behalf, since that would imply a recognition of the court and would detract from the martyr's image he wished to cultivate. After suffering him to abuse the court over four sessions, the rule that a refusal to plead had to be treated as a confession of guilt was reluctantly applied. To satisfy itself of his actual guilt, the court held a special hearing to receive the evidence of thirty-five prosecution witnesses, some eyewitnesses to his ordering the torture of prisoners-of-war and plundering and pillaging civilian homes. The King's lack of remorse – he laughed loudly in court whenever casualties were mentioned and told his guards he had not cared about what had befallen his soldiers – sealed his fate: Cromwell and the other judges believed he would remain a danger if deposed or sentenced to exile and that they had no alternative but to sentence him to execution. This was a fatal mistake – the King played the martyr's part to perfection in milking the macabre proceedings for every ounce of sympathy, and made an eloquent scaffold speech:

He nothing common did or mean
Upon that memorable scene.[5]

Come the restoration of the monarchy in 1660, the King's judges and prosecutors were condemned for treason and disembowelled ('hung, drawn and quartered') at Charing Cross in the presence of his son, now Charles II. Their courage on the scaffold won sympathy from the crowd and the government dared not bring more of these republicans to trial. Instead, they were imprisoned on offshore islands like Jersey to which the writ of *habeas corpus* would not run. This early precedent for Guantanamo Bay was regarded as devious even then: in 1679 Parliament passed the Habeas Corpus Act to give the great writ extra-territorial effect. (In 2004 the US Supreme Court would draw on this seventeenth-century precedent to permit Camp Delta inmates to challenge their offshore detention at Guantanamo Bay.)

The trial of Charles I was compulsory reading for the French revolutionaries when they put Louis XVI on trial in 1792. Louis had good lawyers who also studied accounts of the proceedings and advised him to adopt the same tactic of denying jurisdiction, since the French constitution guaranteed his inviolability, but the King doggedly insisted upon trying to establish his innocence.[6] That was a mistake. Louis was unanimously convicted by Parliament, the National Assembly that had already declared him guilty. The vote to have him executed, however, was close. Tom Paine was an honorary delegate (a tribute to his role in the American Revolution) and urged that the King should be instead exiled to Massachusetts, where he might be reformed and become a democrat. Marat jumped up to accuse Paine of being a Quaker opposed to the death penalty on principle, whilst Robespierre shouted that humanity could not pardon mass murdering despots and Saint-Just adopted John Cooke's argument that all kings were tyrants and the King must die so that monarchy would die with him. Jacobin censorship ensured that Louis did not become a martyr like Charles: they even directed army drummers to drown out his speech from the guillotine. When the British defeated Napoleon, they knew better than to put him on trial. He was exiled to St Helena, a small island in the South Atlantic.

REVOLUTIONARY RIGHTS

It took the trial and execution of Charles I to confirm the political rights won by Parliament in the civil wars, and the Restoration could not reinstate the worst features of Stuart absolutism, such as the Star Chamber. In 1688–9 constitutional monarchy was brought about by a bill of rights which followed from the so-called 'Glorious Revolution'. 'Glorious' it certainly was not at the time, for it was popularly fuelled by anti-Catholicism and resulted in the infliction of many other disabilities upon followers of that religion. It did, however, mark in England the end of the King's claims to absolute rule by Divine Right and imposed upon him a measure of accountability to Parliament. The 'rights' which it declared were for the most part those of parliamentarians, to veto royal decisions to raise new taxes and to enjoy freedom of debate without prosecution before the King's judges. But by declaring themselves 'a full and free representative of this nation' assembled 'for the vindicating and asserting of their ancient rights and liberties', the Lords and Commons purported to state rights which had been acquired by prescription – i.e. by custom and tradition – and which were capable of being upheld by the courts. Chief of these were: the right of subjects to live under the law as approved by Parliament without arbitrary royal interference; the right to due process in the selection of jurors; the right not to lose liberty through excessively high fixing of bail; and the right not to be inflicted with 'cruel or unusual punishment'. The common-law remedy of *habeas corpus* still provided the most valuable and enduring right of all: to have the lawfulness of detention tested promptly by the courts.

These 'rights' continue to have resonance today, although they are understood in ways which would have bewildered seventeenth-century parliamentarians. For example, the prohibition on 'cruel or unusual punishment' was inserted because of public outrage at the treatment of Titus Oates, the popular clergyman and perjuryman whose lies sent dozens of Catholics to the scaffold. Oates was sentenced to be defrocked, whipped and set in the pillory – indignities thought cruel and unusual for a Church of England minister by his fanatical fellow Protestants. The idea that the death penalty *per se*, or the genital mutilation, bowel-burning and drawing and quartering which often attended it, might be 'cruel' never entered seventeenth-century heads. Hence the first rule of interpreting a bill of rights: the concepts have evolved to a meaning which reflects modern humanitarian usage rather than contemporary understanding when they were first formulated.

The English Bill of Rights had its philosophical foundation in the work of Thomas Hobbes and its subsequent explication by John Locke. Hobbes, whose major work *Leviathan*, published in 1651, is often quoted in support of state tyranny, in fact broke the nexus between God and the state, because he identified the true source of political power in the consent of the people. He rolled back civil society to its most primitive and brutal and warlike manifestation, and deduced that its terrified denizens would authorize a ruler to lay down laws for their own protection, against the environment and each other. For Hobbes, an implacable opponent of individual freedom, this was a once-and-for-all surrender of individual power. For John Locke, however, the people's consent to government was continuous and capable of being withdrawn if that government broke the purpose of the compact, which was to further their majority interests. Writing in 1690, two years after the 'Glorious Revolution' and with the object of celebrating and justifying it, he developed the principle that government was by popular consent, and was contingent upon a commitment to protect liberty.

The compact, by which men gave up certain freedoms to join a body politic, meant that they were left with those freedoms which the state did not need to take away in order to maintain and protect the public good. Since the whole object and purpose of the compact was the public good, the state 'can never have a right to destroy, enslave or designedly to impoverish the subjects'. It followed that there could be circumstances when subjects were entitled to revolt, breaking the compact and renegotiating it:

The end of government is the good of mankind. And which is best for mankind: that the people should be always exposed to the boundless will of tyranny, or that the rulers should be sometimes liable to be opposed when they grow exorbitant in the use of their power and employ it for the destruction and not the preservation of the properties of their people?[7]

In the eighteenth century, Locke's argument became a threat to other absolute monarchs, like Louis ('L'État, c'est moi') XIV. They might be deposed, if their governance was so arbitrary and tyrannical that it cut down rather than protected the residual rights of their people. Locke's philosophy was embraced and developed by leading European intellectuals, who found in England a constitution which seemed to guarantee political liberty through the supremacy (although it was far from that) of Parliament. By the middle of the century they had begun to identify 'universal' rights: to person and property, and hence not to be held in slavery (Rousseau: 'Man is born free; and everywhere he is in chains'); the liberty of the press (Voltaire: 'I know many books that fatigue, but none which have done real evil'); and the right not to be subjected to torture (as Cesare Beccaria argued, the liberty which men had been forced by necessity to yield to the state was the very minimum required for the state to defend what remained: 'Punishments that exceed what is necessary for the protection of the deposit of public security are by their very nature unjust'). It was Beccaria, in his *Of Crimes and Punishments* of 1764, who first enunciated the credo of the modern human rights lawyer:

... if, by defending the rights of man and of unconquerable truth, I should help to save from the spasm and agonies of death some wretched victim of tyranny or of no less fatal ignorance, the thanks and tears of one innocent mortal in his transports of joy would console me for the contempt of all mankind.[8]

This was heady stuff to find in philosophy, but it required politicians and propagandists and indeed revolutionaries to give it any legal force. Man was born free, but at the time of Rousseau's observation was everywhere in chains. The first to break them were the American Founding Fathers in 1776, making in the potent prose of Thomas Jefferson their claim to re-acquire their inalienable human rights from the government of George III:

We hold these truths to be self-evident, that all men are created equal; that they are endowed by their Creator with certain inalienable rights; that amongst these are life, liberty, and the pursuit of happiness. That, to secure these rights, governments are instituted among men, deriving their just powers from the consent of the governed; that, whenever any form of Government becomes destructive of these ends, it is the right of the people to alter or abolish it, and to institute a new government, laying its foundations on such principles, and organizing its powers in such form, as to them shall seem most likely to effect their safety and happiness.

This was, of course, an act of defiance and not an act of law: it was the preamble to a litany of complaints against the 'tyranny' of George III. There were complaints about the unfairness of trials and lickspittle judges, although taxation without consent was the motivating grudge and the clarion cry that 'all men are created equal' hardly squared with the slaves owned (in Jefferson's case, impregnated) by many of the signatories. But it is Jefferson's preamble which resonates through subsequent centuries, identifying the denial of human rights as the *justification* for the revolution foreshadowed by John Locke. The fundamental rights to life, equality, liberty and the pursuit of happiness are not drawn from any empirical source or discovered through rational argument; they may be given by God but the proof of their existence is that we all feel and think them – they attach 'inalienably' to the human person, like a shadow. They are not the end product of philosophical inquiry but the starting point for it, imposing a duty on government to order itself in a way which will maximize opportunities for individual fulfilment.

It was the oppressive human rights record of the government, its 'history of repeated injuries and usurpations', which absolved the colonials from their duty of allegiance to the British Crown. As well as their own objectionable taxes, they also had much in mind the unlawful behaviour of George III's ministers in persecuting John Wilkes. Wilkes, a radical MP, and his printers were the targets of 'general search warrants' which allowed government spies to ransack their homes. Despite being jailed for sedition, Wilkes made constitutional history by winning damages against a government minister,

Lord Halifax, for abuse of power. Re-elected to Parliament, he tried to impeach General Burgoyne for war crimes (e.g. hiring Indians to scalp the colonists), and was the first MP to table a motion calling for universal male suffrage. His struggles against the sedition law inspired James Madison and influenced the identification of *habeas corpus* and fair trial as 'inalienable rights' in the 1789 US constitution, as well as inspiring several of the amendments which followed two years later. For example, the First Amendment provided that Congress (i.e. the state) 'shall make no law' prohibiting the free exercise of religion, or abridging the freedom of speech, or freedom of the press, or the right of peaceful assembly. The Fourth Amendment secured the people in their homes and persons 'against unreasonable searches and seizures' and the Fifth and Sixth enshrined 'due process', i.e. rights against self-incrimination and double jeopardy and expropriation of property, and the rights to speedy and public and impartial trial, with advance disclosure of prosecution evidence, the right to cross-examine hostile witnesses and to call defence witnesses, and the right to counsel. Although protection from slavery and forced servitude was not added to the US constitution until 1865 (following a civil war fought over the right of the Southern slave-owning states to secede from the Union), America had in place by the end of the eighteenth century a functioning domestic court system in which basic human rights could be enforced as such, by individual citizens. This had come about more as an act of faith than of philosophy: as the great legal architect of the American constitution, Alexander Hamilton, wrote in 1787: 'The sacred rights of mankind are not to be rummaged for amongst old parchments or musty records. They are written, as with a sunbeam, in the whole volume of human nature by the hand of divinity itself, and can never be erased or obscured.'[9]

At an intellectual level, however, this achievement owed much, and itself gave impetus, to the dissatisfactions in France which were to culminate in that 'hour of universal ferment'. Enthusiasm for the American colonists in their war against France's historic foe gave an inspirational quality to their victory and made Lafayette, who had helped to achieve it, a national hero: his popularity on his return to Paris was rivalled only by that of the American ambassador, the charismatic lightning-conductor Ben Franklin, who was succeeded in that post by Thomas Jefferson. In January 1789, Jefferson wrote to James Madison from Paris, 'Everybody here is trying their hands at forming declarations of rights.'[10] In August, during the parliament called to solve a cash-flow crisis itself partly caused by French support for the American war, it was Jefferson who helped Lafayette with the draft of 'The Declaration of the Rights of Man and the Citizen' – a detailed description of 'natural, inalienable and sacred rights' which any citizen could advance against an oppressive government. These were birthrights, which the state was constituted to protect up to the point at which their exercise might harm others, a point which had to be defined by law rather than through arbitrary exercises of government power. The Declaration was followed in 1791 by the French constitution, providing for poor relief and free public education – the first sign of what today are called 'economic and social rights'.

Up to his neck in every revolutionary movement of this incandescent era was Thomas Paine, the first writer to fuse outraged polemic and constitutional philosophy to produce a distinctive literature of human rights. This former English customs official ignited the American Revolution with his incendiary pamphlet *Common Sense*, explaining (in January 1776, when all the talk was of appeasement with the Crown) why it was ineluctable that the colonists fight for their liberty. It was Tom Paine whom President Obama quoted at his inauguration: 'Let it be told to the future world, that in the depths of winter, when nothing but hope and virtue could survive, that the city and the country, alarmed at one common danger, came forth to meet and to repulse it.' Paine helped Jefferson to draft the Declaration of Independence, fought alongside Washington and then returned to London to write (at the Angel Tavern, Islington) one of the most influential books of all time: *The Rights of Man*. This is a classic liberal text – Paine's idea was minimal government, limited to protecting individual liberty, equality and enterprise – but his fervour for free-market individualism was leavened by his novel and detailed plans for social security, family benefits and public education, not out of charity but as a right derived from membership of society. He scorned as a contradiction in terms the notion of an 'unwritten constitution', and refuted Edmund Burke's argument for monarchies as a legitimate inheritance from our forefathers: 'The vanity and presumption of governing beyond the grave, is the most ridiculous and insolent of all tyrannies.' The book came peppered with attacks on Britain's hereditary establishment sufficiently savage to have Paine prosecuted for sedition. He fled to France before being convicted *in absentia* by a rigged jury, whereupon crowds thronging the streets outside the Old Bailey set up the chant 'Paine and the Liberty of the Press'. In Paris he was elected to the National Assembly and to the committee which drafted the constitution, and spent some months in prison for failing to match the bloodthirstiness of his comrades. He wrote *The Age of Reason* – a book for which many courageous printers and booksellers would be jailed for blasphemy in nineteenth-century Britain. Tom Paine is on postage stamps in America and there is a gold statue of him in Paris (Napoleon said there should be a gold statue of Paine in every city of the universe) but the prophet has been without honour in his own country. It took two centuries before the abolition of hereditary peers finally gave acknowledgement to Paine's point that the 'idea of hereditary legislators [is] as absurd as an hereditary mathematician . . . as absurd as an hereditary poet laureate'.[11]

The American declarations were shaped by the colonial experience of indignity at the hands of British soldiers and sedition laws. Dissident Frenchmen had suffered imprisonment and confiscation of property, without trial (or any other legal process), through the system of *lettres de cachet* – warrants for arrest, search and seizure signed at the whim of the Bourbon kings. Hence the French Declaration emphasizes the presumption of innocence and the need for legal process before arrest and detention. It elevates the possession of private property to a 'sacred and inviolable right' to be expropriated only upon proof of public necessity, and then with just compensation. Freedom of speech, 'one of the most precious of the rights of man', was given special protection ('No one is to be disquieted because of his opinions') – testimony to the influence of Voltaire and reaction to the regular use of *lettres de cachet* against critics of the King and his government. This removal of censorship had a most immediate and striking effect, releasing what Simon Schama describes as a 'polemical incontinence that washed over the whole country', propelling it to a republic within two years, and thereafter inciting each increasingly bloody phase of the Terror. Unfortunately, the class-crazed and blood-thirsty Jacobins did not see human rights as universal – as one leader wrote, 'the rights of man are made, not for the counter-revolutionaries, but only for *sans-culottes*'.[12]

As the Terror became the order of the day and brought wave after wave of revolutionaries tumbrilling to the guillotine after the aristo-crats, so 'The Rights of Man and the Citizen', which had started it all, appeared a sick joke. The good old days of the King's *lettres de cachet* were contrasted with the killings ordered by the Committee for Public Safety, notwithstanding the device to reduce the length of pain invented by one assemblyman, the kindly Dr Guillotine. Victims were first put on show trial by the public prosecutor, Antoine Fouquier-Tinville. There was no 'due process' in his Revolutionary Tribunal: suspects were denied advance notice of the case against them, the right to defence counsel and the right to call witnesses; the biased jury normally convicted whenever Fouquier-Tinville asked whether they had heard enough evidence. Although blame for the barbarities of the Revolution is always fixed on its political leaders, Fouquier-Tinville emerges as the first of modern history's monster lawyers, rivalling Andrei Vyshinsky, the choreographer of Stalin's show trials. At least Fouquier-Tinville met his own fate shortly after the fall of Robespierre, appealing in vain to his judges as a 'mildmannered family man who had always obeyed the law and done his duty'.[13] What he had done, like so many state servants who only follow orders, was to deny to citizens the most fundamental of liberties guaranteed them by a law which, lacking at that time independent judicial enforcement, was just not worth the parchment on which it was written.

That was a problem for France, precisely because it left the 'rights' in the Declaration to be enforced by politicians in the National Assembly and their representatives on the Committee for Public Safety. In America, by contrast, the constitution and its bill of rights were enforceable by an independent judiciary, empowered to strike down government orders and even congressional legislation which violated the rights they guaranteed. This development in legal theory, achieved in 1803 by Chief Justice Marshall in the great case of *Marbury* v. *Madison*, provided human rights in the US with a set of teeth, by endorsing courts rather than legislatures as their enforcement machinery:

The very essence of civil liberty certainly consists in the right of every individual to claim the protection of the laws, whenever he receives an injury . . . [the] government of the United States has been emphatically termed a government of laws, and not of men. It will certainly cease to deserve this high appellation, if the laws furnish no remedy for the violation of a vested legal right.[14]

These French and American documents became models for many constitutions drafted over the next two centuries containing human rights guarantees: the struggle has always been for independent courts to enforce them, at national and now at international levels.

THE NINETEENTH CENTURY: BENTHAM, MARX AND THE HUMANITARIAN IMPULSE

The Terror that enveloped France a few years after the Declaration provided for many who had first welcomed the Revolution refutation of its claim that 'rights' were natural, let alone inalienable and sacred. 'When I hear of natural rights,' snapped Jeremy Bentham, 'I always see in the background a cluster of daggers and pikes introduced into the National Assembly . . . for the avowed purpose of exterminating the King's friends.'[15] It was Bentham who led the attack on 'natural rights' as vague and abstract nonsense – 'nonsense upon stilts' – which, by encouraging the obliteration of socially useful distinctions, tends to produce the anarchy exemplified by the Terror. Bentham's attack on the Declaration was logical – all the rights, he pointed out, including the right to liberty, were to be limited by law, thereby begging the question of what content the law should have to be compatible with liberty. He was also pragmatic. No one was in fact 'born free' – all were born helpless, and subject for years to parental authority. Men were not equal in rights: there was the master and the apprentice, the genius and the lunatic. Moreover, 'natural rights' were of uncertain provenance: if from God, their content (apart from biblical injunctions) was unknowable; if from 'nature' they were unprovable and unpredictable. The force of Bentham's arguments was partly responsible for 'natural rights' falling out of fashion in the nineteenth century and the first half of the twentieth century. When they returned, it would be as '*human* rights' rather than 'natural rights', sourced in the nature of humans rather than in the laws of God or the seasons.

The next formidable critic of 'the rights of man' was Karl Marx. In 1844 he wrote an essay, *On the Jewish Question*, which questioned whether the French Declaration could provide a way forward for Jews like himself, who were suffering from discrimination in Germany. His dismissive conclusion was that 'the so-called rights of man . . . are nothing but the rights of egotistic man, of man separated from other men and from the community'. The Declaration focused, not on man as citizen, but on man as bourgeois – an individual withdrawn from the community, motivated only by whim and self-interest. For example, the right to property was 'the right to enjoy possessions and dispose of the same arbitrarily, without regard to other men, independently from society: the right of selfishness'. The 'political emancipation' produced by the Revolution was the reduction of man to an egocentric and independent individual: true emancipation would rather enlarge him as a citizen, 'a moral person' – a theme Marx was to take up a few years later in *The Communist Manifesto*.

The force of this early critique led Marxist thinkers in the next century to characterize human rights as a device to universalize capitalist values, notably freedom of enterprise, without social responsibility. Hence socialist governments were silent or suspicious of the concept, until it proved useful to rally support for leftist causes in the later stages of the Cold War. But Marx was actually supportive of the Declaration's identification of *citizen's* rights: citing Rousseau with approval, he perceived these communal rights as new resources which could assist social transformation to a 'moral existence'.[16] This level of abstraction always infuriated Bentham, although some content would subsequently be found in the idea of 'second generation' or 'social and economic' rights of citizens to education, housing and work, and later still in the notion of a *third* generation of rights, belonging to citizens of the world, to peace and development and a clean environment. But Lenin derided the English and French revolutions as uprisings of the bourgeoisie, with freedom of speech a fraud enabling the rich to control propaganda in their interests. 'The capitalists have always used the term 'freedom' to mean freedom for the rich to get richer and the poor to starve to death.'[17] Shortly after the Bolshevik accession to power, Lenin was presented by his favourite lieutenant with a set of draft guarantees of liberty, the 'Anti-Thermidorian Catechism', as an insurance against the revolution degenerating into terror. He waved it away: 'Comrade, I see no need to circulate this . . . It is a childish idea . . . that we could stop or forestall so fatal a development with the help of this sheet of paper.' The comrade in question was Nikolai Bukharin, who in 1936 was ordered by Stalin to put his catechism into the new Soviet constitution, which did not save him two years later from being wrongly arrested, dishonestly tried and peremptorily shot.

The nineteenth century did see three humanitarian impulses which were in due course to assist the development of international law. Most notable was the legislative attack on the slave trade in England in 1807 and in America in 1865 after the Civil War. It was finally acknowledged by European nations, in the Berlin Treaty on Africa in 1885, that 'trading in slaves is forbidden in conformity with international law'. This breakthrough only applied to inter-state trading, however, and did not require states to outlaw the practice locally: the slavery convention, which did, came into force much later, in 1926, and not until 1970 did the last state – Oman – announce formal abolition of the status. None the less, this was progress – attempts made by Jefferson and Robespierre respectively to abolish slavery by the American and French declarations had signally failed. Although an international law rule did not begin to crystallize until 1885, for most of the century the British navy took upon itself a novel enforcement role, liberating victims of slavers around the African coast. Its actions in intercepting slave ships, freeing victims and even educating them in schools on the Seychelles and in Sierra Leone must rate as the first example of a humanitarian enforcement mission.

Secondly, there dawned the notion of 'a right of humanitarian intervention' in the internal affairs of a state if its rule over some of its citizens was perceived as barbaric. This right had been described by Milton as 'the right of intervention vested in humane society' when Cromwell had asserted it in 1655 to threaten the Duke of Savoy with war unless he withdrew his edict requiring all Protestants, on pain of death, to convert to Catholicism. It was invoked most vociferously by the Hellenic movement in the years 1810–30, urging Britain to intervene to free the Greeks from the Ottoman Empire. The Foreign Secretary, Lord Castlereagh, was subjected to the deathless opprobrium of the poets for standing firm to Westphalian principles and insisting there was no such right. 'I met murder on the way / He had a mask like Castlereagh,' said Shelley. On the statesman's death, it was Byron who wrote his epitaph:

> Posterity will ne'er survey
> A nobler grave than this.
> Here lie the bones of Castlereagh
> Stop, traveller, and piss.

Castlereagh's successor reversed his policy and eventually put together a 'coalition of the willing' – a British-led fleet, with French and Russian components, that annihilated the Turkish and Egyptian navies at Navarino and secured the independence of the Greek state. Later in the century came a similar intervention in Syria. Pressure was put on the Ottoman sultans in the 1880s to promulgate measures to protect Christian minorities from discrimination; when these failed, Gladstone obtained parliamentary approval to allocate ships, men and money to protect Christians from slaughter by Turks in Bulgaria.

In 1898, the US declared war on Spain because its oppressive rule in Cuba 'shocked the moral sense of the people of the United States'. It was government behaviour 'shocking to the conscience of mankind' which might justify intervention, but only as a matter of conscience and not of legal obligation. International lawyers still adamantly refused to admit that 'the so-called rights of mankind' existed. As late as 1912, a leading textbook opined that 'should a State venture to treat its own subjects or part thereof with such cruelty as would stagger humanity' public opinion might demand intervention, but this could only happen out of Christian charity and could not be defended on grounds of international law.[18] Whether these strictly count as 'humanitarian' interventions is open to question – their motivations were not entirely that of the Good Samaritan. Russia was spurred on by a desire to dismember the Ottoman Empire and some of the British actions were racist or imperialist or based on the belief that Christianity should triumph over Islam. But these instances do show that there were exceptions to the principle of Westphalian sovereignty recognized on occasion when public feeling and poetic justice demanded.

None the less, in Theodore Roosevelt's 1904 State of the Union message, the right, and indeed the duty, to intervene in the affairs of sovereign states which were committing what he almost called 'crimes against humanity' was persuasively articulated:

... there are occasional crimes committed on so vast a scale and of such peculiar horror as to make us doubt whether it is not our manifest duty to endeavour at least to show our disapproval of the deed and our sympathy with those who have suffered by it ... in extreme cases action may be justifiable and proper. What form the action shall take must depend upon the circumstances of the case; that is, upon the degree of the atrocity and upon our power to remedy it. The case in which we could interfere by force of arms as we interfered to put a stop to intolerable conditions in Cuba are necessarily very few. Yet ... it is inevitable that such a nation should desire eagerly to give expression to its horror on an occasion like that of the massacre of the Jews in Kishenef, or when it witnesses such systematic and long-extended cruelty and oppression of which the Armenians have been victims, and which have won for them the indignant pity of the civilized world ...[19]

Of course, it helped that the interests of humanity coincided with the interests of the United States – Roosevelt was retrospectively justifying US intervention against oppressive Spanish dominion over Panama and Cuba – but his inclusion of Jews in eastern Europe and Armenians in Asia Minor as within the potential protection of the world's 'indignant pity' is worthy of note. But his promise did not save the Jews from the pogroms of 1905 or the Armenians from the genocidal attacks of Turkey in 1915.

The third nineteenth-century advance was not taken for the sake of indignant pity, but rather to reduce the cost of killing soldiers in wars. The expense of new weaponry was the reason why the major powers attended a conference in St Petersburg in 1868 and later ones in The Hague in 1899 and 1907, agreeing limits on the development of poison gases and explosive and 'dum-dum' bullets. That these rules of war came to be dressed up in the language of humanity was due to the influence of the International Committee of the Red Cross, founded in 1863 by Henri Dunant, a wealthy Swiss who had been appalled at the bloody array of bodies left on mid-European battle-fields after the armies moved on. Epiphany for Dunant came in 1859 from witnessing the battle of Solferino, where 30,000 French and Austrian soldiers were killed in a single day. His object, and indeed the object of the 1907 Hague Convention (which forty-four nations signed), was not in any way to restrict the right of sovereign states to go to war, but simply to make these wars more humane for injured soldiers and prisoners. The futility of this exercise was demonstrated in the trenches of the First World War, where a million dead bodies would mock the notion that modern war could be made humane by laws which tinkered with methods of killing.

International justice made few advances before the First World War. In 1821 there had been a proposal to set up a court with American, Spanish and British judges sitting in Sierra Leone to issue warrants for the arrest and seizure of slave ships, but this faltered when the US withdrew (*plus ça change . . .*). Later, however, an international court of arbitration was established to settle a US dispute against Britain over its support, while ostensibly a neutral, for *The Alabama* and other Confederate ships which were sinking Federal merchant ships during the American Civil War. A judge from each disputant power sat in Geneva, together with judges appointed by Italy, Switzerland

and Brazil, to determine the *Alabama* claims, and it was notable that the British judge actually joined his colleagues in one unanimous finding against Britain. The award was massive, and Gladstone described it as 'harsh in its extent and punitive in its basis', yet 'as dust in the balance compared with the moral example set of two proud nations going in peace and concord before a judicial tribunal' instead of 'resorting to the arbitrament of the sword'.[20] It was an inspiring moment – indeed, it immediately inspired the first suggestions for an international criminal court[21] – although Britain's willingness (at a time when it was the world's most powerful nation) to submit to international justice was an example that other states were not prepared to follow, then or, in many cases, even now.

ARMENIAN MASSACRES, THE LEAGUE OF NATIONS AND STALIN'S SHOW TRIALS

After four years of a pointless war of unprecedented ferocity and carnage, in which 8.5 million lives were lost, it might have been thought that any new world order would aspire to some protection of human rights. But the concept was never mentioned at the Versailles Peace Conference in 1919, nor in the Covenant of the League of Nations. The closest that document came was in Article 23, whereby members promised 'just treatment' to natives in Trust territories and that they would 'endeavour to secure and maintain fair and humane conditions of labour'. This gesture, inspired more by fear that badly treated labourers would turn to Bolshevism than by any acceptance of workers' rights, at least led to the establishment of the International Labour Organization (ILO), the first rights-related global agency. Although Britain and France came to Versailles determined to set up an international court to try Kaiser Wilhelm II for commanding the brutal invasion of Belgium and authorizing unrestricted submarine warfare, their plans met with total opposition from America, which took the legalistic position that this would be retrospective punishment and breach the then sacred Westphalian principle of head-of-state immunity. The US had only become an ally towards the end of the war, and its objection to war crimes trials was opportunistic: President Wilson's real concern was that they would undermine his grand plan for permanent peace through the League of Nations. So public opinion in Britain and France was placated by a treaty proposal for an international tribunal to try the Kaiser for crimes against 'international morality', but it was never intended to take effect. The courts of Germany were made responsible for trying their own war criminals, with predictably partisan results (hardly anyone was convicted, thanks to 'loser's justice': see p. 305).

A similar fate befell the Allied effort to prosecute the Turkish leaders responsible for the Armenian genocide. That cataclysmic event – which was uppermost in the mind of Raphael Lemkin when, a year later, he coined the word 'genocide' (see p. 325) had been perpetuated by the Ottoman regime in 1915, when it killed and deported to their deaths hundreds of thousands of members of this Christian community.[22] The Young Turk government had developed race supremacy theories together with a 'Turkification' programme for language and culture, and its strident nationalism had taken it into the First World War on the side of Germany. Towns and rivers that bore Christian names were renamed, Armenian property was seized and dehumanized descriptions ('tubercular microbes') were used in government newspapers. Armenians were portrayed as fifth columnists, and the Gallipoli invasion was the trigger for lynching several hundred of their intellectuals in Istanbul and commencing the deportations through the desert, where hundreds of thousands died from starvation, disease or from marauding gangs, who killed with cries of 'God is great'. There is overwhelming evidence of how racial hatred was whipped up by the government's 'Turkey for the Turks' campaign, and whole communities of Armenians were liquidated. What Interior Minister Talaat Pasha called the 'final solution' ('a final end, in a comprehensive and absolute way') extended even to orphans whose parents had expired in the death marches: 'the government . . . considers the survival of these children as detrimental'.[23] Notwithstanding the implacable genocide-denial stance of today's Turkish government, the totality of the evidence against the Young Turk regime is overwhelming – it comes not only from missionaries and Western (especially American) diplomats, who were at that time neutral, but from German envoys, who were Turkey's allies. The German Ambassador cabled Berlin to say that the government intended 'the extirpation of the last remnants of the Armenians . . . Turkification means licence to expel, to kill, and to destroy'.[24] The German Vice-Consul reported Turkish government admissions that their purpose was 'total obliteration' of the Armenians.[25]

Retribution had been threatened by the Allies in 1915, at the time when 200,000 were massacred. A joint declaration by Britain, France and Russia was prepared, announcing that all members of the Ottoman government would be personally liable for 'crimes committed by Turkey against Christianity and civilization'. Britain was worried that reference to 'Christianity' would strike an anti-Muslim note, so the Russian foreign minister substituted 'humanity', which won unanimous approval. This declaration marked the first official use of the phrase 'crimes against humanity' in reference to charges against government officials who might be tried, irrespective of sovereign immunity, for their complicity in ethnic mass murder. Sadly, the trials did not live up to the Declaration's promise: although Britain, as occupying power, insisted on the arrest of major suspects (including religious leaders who had pronounced a jihad against Christians), it found that it had no power to prosecute some it took to Malta, whilst local proceedings became bogged down in weak local military courts which convicted very few and left no recorded judgments to persuade Turkish posterity of the evil done in its name. Turkish governments could thereafter airbrush the Armenian genocide from the nation's history: they still lodge diplomatic protests whenever any reference to the Armenians is made at official ceremonies (such as Britain's 'holocaust day') and in 2005 the distinguished Turkish novelist Orhan Parmuk was charged with the crime of 'denigrating the Turkish identity' by stating – truthfully – that, overall, one million Armenians were killed. The problem is Turkey's – it dropped the charge against him once it became clear that it could be denied entry to the European Union unless it met freedom of expression standards – but its almost pathological genocide denial would not be possible had the Young

Turk leaders been convicted by an international court of the Armenian killings, on the evidence that was amply available at the time of
Versailles.

The only lasting significance of the peace process after the First
World War was the inclusion by the Allies, in peace treaties signed
with some enemy states, of 'minorities clauses' by which they were
required to guarantee civil and political rights and religious and cultural toleration to groups (minorities) who by race or language
differed from the rest of the population. These treaties were supervised by the Council of the League of Nations (which could be
petitioned by individuals or associations) and were monitored through
the compulsory jurisdiction of the Permanent Court of International
Justice, activated by any state member. The League took this idea one
step further, and in the case of several states with bad records for
maltreating minorities (e.g. Albania, Latvia, Iraq) made their admission to the League conditional upon a similar obligation to safeguard
the rights of minorities within their borders.

These minorities clauses bound only a few countries, and after
1922 the League lacked the resolve to extend them any further. Yet
they are of some historic importance, as the first human rights limitation on sovereign states enforced by a global institution and an
international court. The Permanent Court of International Justice
showed an early awareness of the need to protect minority cultures in
its advisory opinion *Minority Schools in Albania* (1935), which condemned Albania's decision to close down private schools serving its
Greek minority, and other judgments which were supportive of German settlers in Poland and of Polish nationals in Danzig (see p. 196).
In 1933, shortly after Hitler's accession to power, the League received
an individual petition from Franz Bernheim (its first from a victim of
Nazism), whose sacking on the grounds that he was Jewish contravened a minorities treaty for Upper Silesia. Bernheim and several other
Jews were awarded compensation for discrimination by a League
commission – prompting Germany to withdraw from the League.[26] In
1939, the League's Minorities Section was disbanded.

From 1936 to 1938 there was presented in Moscow a series
of 'show trials' which was to prove, in time, second only to the

Holocaust in its impact on post-war human rights thinking. These trials were the public tip of Stalin's iceberg of terror, the means by which he sought to justify the purge of his leading opponents, and then, less publicly, of their followers. The victims of these purges are now estimated, incredibly but reliably, to outnumber the six million Jews lost in the Holocaust.[27] This is without precedent in human history at a time of peace: in Nazi Germany, only a few thousand lives were lost in concentration camps before the war, and in the French Revolution the Terror at its pre-Thermidorian height claimed no more than 17,000. But between 1936 and 1938, in Moscow alone, 30,000 defendants were tried in the Supreme Court and sentenced to death by firing squad. And these were the trials reserved for important people: in the provinces, millions were killed after summary proceedings or through beatings and starvation in the gulag.

Andrei Vyshinsky, like Fouquier-Tinville, was a hard-working lawyer devoid of any moral scruple. It was his evil genius to produce the main show trials as forensic spectacles which persuaded many in the West that they were genuine applications of criminal law. The prosecution case – that most of the old Bolsheviks were spies for foreign powers – was incredible enough, as was the theory that the moderate groups led by Bukharin had secretly joined forces with their main enemies, the Trotskyites, to sabotage the country and the communist revolution. What made these preposterous conspiracy theories seem credible in the West was simply that the conspirators confessed, in public proceedings overseen by a judge. It was not until 1956 that Khrushchev admitted what should have been obvious to observers at the time: the defendants had all been subjected to months of torture by the NKVD until they agreed to sign and speak the script prepared for them by Vyshinsky.[28] They were put on 'the conveyor' – a disorientation procedure which alternated psychological pressures of sleeplessness and starvation with interrogation to enhance suggestibility and acquiescence. This was interspersed with beatings and physical torture, such as burning the body with a molten knife. As each victim agreed to 'confess' he was confronted with others who had broken, and together they were encouraged to elaborate further hypothetical scenarios in the basic prosecution fantasy. The few who held out were shot in the secret cellars of the Lubyanka prison, while VIP defendants were required to repeat their false confessions in public, as the price exacted for saving the lives of their wives and children. (One of Stalin's first decrees in this terror period was to give the secret police special powers over the families of convicted traitors.)

The trials were held in an auditorium in front of several hundred specially invited observers from around the world – fellow travellers like the influential English QC D. N. Pritt, who could be relied upon to write dishonest propaganda pamphlets with titles like *The Moscow Trial was Fair*. The defendants were allowed counsel, but only to speak *after* their convictions, in mitigation of their confessed crimes. Vyshinsky occupied centre stage, eliciting from the dozen or so defendants their self-lacerations around which he wove his fantastical plots. The transcripts typically read like this extract, in which the old Bolsheviks Zinoviev and Kamenev play the Rosencrantz and Guildenstern of the Russian Revolution:

KAMENEV: I, together with Zinoviev and Trotsky, organized and guided this terrorist conspiracy. I had become convinced that Stalin's policy was successful and victorious . . . yet we were motivated by boundless hate and by lust for power.

VYSHINSKY: You expressed your loyalty to the Party in various articles and statements. Was all this deception on your part?

KAMENEV: No, it was worse than deception.

VYSHINSKY: Perfidy?

KAMENEV: Worse than that!

VYSHINSKY: Worse than deception? Worse than perfidy? Then find a word for it. Treason?

KAMENEV: You have found the word.

VYSHINSKY: Zinoviev, do you confirm this?

ZINOVIEV: Yes, I do. Treason, perfidy, double-dealing.

Nikolai Bukharin (who designed that *Anti-Thermidorian Catechism* precisely to prevent this turn of events) was the only one of the defendants to offer any resistance, or to show any self-control after his year on 'the conveyor'. Although he pleaded guilty to treason (to

THE HUMAN RIGHTS STORY

save his wife and baby son) he managed to blurt out that his confession had been obtained by 'medieval methods'. He tried to explain that his treason consisted in feeling his own powerlessness before the totalitarian state he had helped to construct, and the impossibility of beating it at the game it chose to play with his own life.[29] When Bukharin tried to question one of the lying prosecution witnesses, the presiding judge ruled cross-examination irrelevant. This judge was V. Ulrich, head of the military section of the Supreme Court, who reported throughout the trials to Stalin and followed his orders in respect to passing the death sentences which were imposed on most defendants. He is the archetypal scoundrel judge, but was acting in accordance with the textbook *Judicial Organization in the USSR*, written by public prosecutor Vyshinsky:

The laws of the Soviet power are a political directive and the work of the judge amounts not just to the application of the law in conformity with the needs of bourgeois judicial logic, but to the application of the law as a political expression of the Party and the Government . . . the judge must be a political worker, rapidly and precisely applying the directives of the Party and the Government.

Stalin's show trials came to haunt later generations because they proved how a system of law, with procedural forms and rituals calculated to impress, could be vulnerable to political manipulation by an all-powerful state. Vyshinsky perverted the trial process so that Stalin could rewrite history by eliminating those who made it. These 'purge' trials with their inevitable conclusion for 'enemies of the people' – a bullet in the head, followed by burial in an unmarked grave – cast a long historical shadow. The rights of defendants which later appeared in the UN Conventions and which are now written in the Statute of the International Criminal Court (the right, for example, even in the face of compelling evidence, to refuse to testify without any adverse inference being drawn) may be traced to the reaction to Vyshinsky's colossal frame-ups. No account of human rights in the twentieth century can ignore the Moscow trials: they became the model for political 'show' trials, and not only in communist countries. The truth about them that only novelists could at first tell – like George Orwell in *Animal Farm* and

Arthur Koestler in *Darkness at Noon*, followed by Khrushchev's belated acknowledgement that they were monstrous perversions of justice – did much to persuade the European left that, *pace* Marx and Lenin, human rights was not such a bad idea after all. (The fact that Vyshinsky's ashes still occupy a place of honour in the Kremlin wall may be evidence that, in Russia, the lesson has not fully been learned.)

H. G. WELLS: WHAT ARE WE FIGHTING FOR?

One of the great mysteries of the twentieth century is why, for its first forty years, there was virtual silence on the subject of universal human rights from European intellectuals, politicians and public figures. Even as Jews in Germany were forced out of jobs and professions and then into labour camps, even as kulaks, then old Bolsheviks and later millions of innocent citizens were exterminated in the Soviet gulag, still the notion of protecting human rights was not raised either at the League of Nations or in academic journals or the popular press. This may at a theoretical level owe much to the demolition of 'natural rights' by Bentham and Marx, but more pragmatically those nations which might have embraced the idea, such as Britain and France, were concerned lest it might make the natives restless in their far-flung colonial domains. For that reason, they squashed a proposal made at the League in 1934 by Haiti for a treaty to guarantee the human rights of ethnic minorities. Astonishingly, this was the League's only reference to the subject before its demise at the onset of the Second World War, and the idea does not appear to have been seriously advanced by any major thinker or statesman of the period.[30]

The revival of the human rights idea in the twentieth century really began at the instigation and inspiration of the British author H. G. Wells, in the months immediately following the outbreak of the Second World War. It can be traced to letters he wrote to *The Times* in October 1939, advocating the adoption by 'parliamentary peoples' of a Declaration of Rights – a fundamental law defining their rights in a democracy and drafted to appeal 'to every responsive spirit under the yoke of the obscurantist and totalitarian tyrannies with which all are in conflict'. The League of Nations had been too conservative, half-hearted and diplomatic throughout 'the tortuous Twenties and the frightened Thirties': now, the only sane alternative was to declare 'the fundamental law for mankind throughout the world'. It is a remarkable tribute to Wells and a few of his friends (English socialists ranging from former Labour Lord Chancellor Sankey to Barbara Wootton, J. B. Priestley and A. A. Milne, creator of Winnie the Pooh) that they were able to distil into nine short and readable principles a declaration that came to attract support throughout the world. In their modest English way, they eschewed the messianic preambles of the French and American declarations in favour of the simple observation that 'since a man comes into this world through no fault of his own' he is in justice entitled:

(1) Without distinction of race or colour to nourishment, housing, covering, medical care and attention sufficient to realize his full possibilities of physical and mental development and to keep him in a state of health from his birth to his death.

(2) Sufficient education to make him a useful and interested citizen, easy access to information upon all matters of common knowledge throughout his life, in the course of which he would enjoy the utmost freedom of discussion.

(3) That he and his personal property lawfully acquired are entitled to police and legal protection from private violence, deprivation, compulsion and intimidation . . .

And so it went on, in fine and only occasionally dated style, promising *inter alia*: 'There shall be no secret dossiers in any administrative department'; 'a man's private house or apartment or reasonably limited garden enclosure is his castle'; 'no man shall be subjected to torture, beating or any other bodily punishment, or to imprisonment with such an excess of silence, noise, light or darkness as to cause mental suffering or in infected, verminous or otherwise insanitary quarters'.

Here, for the first time since the eighteenth-century revolutions, was an attempt – by well-meaning middle-class socialists – to restate human rights in a homely way, as a talisman against the coming cataclysm. In the first months of the 'phoney war' it attracted extraordinary support in England: the *Manchester Guardian* and the *Daily Herald* took up the issue, and tens of thousands flocked to hear H. G. Wells speak under the banner 'The New World Order – The Fundamental Principles'. What gave his campaign further momentum was the swift publication of a Penguin Special, *H. G. Wells on the Rights of Man*, which sold many thousands of copies in the UK and was translated into thirty languages and syndicated in newspapers throughout the world. For the first few months of 1940, this was the idea whose time had come – in an act of utter optimism the War Ministry even had copies of Wells's booklet translated into German and dropped on SS divisions as they were overrunning France, although they did not stop to read it. It had more impact on President Franklin D. Roosevelt, a friend of Wells who was much taken by his new book: it influenced his famous appeal in 1941 for a world 'formed upon four essential freedoms' – freedom of speech and worship, and freedom from want and fear. And on 1 January 1942, a few weeks after American entry into the war, H. G. Wells secured his objective: the Allied powers declared that 'complete victory over their enemies is essential . . . *to preserve human rights* and justice in their own lands *as well as in other lands*' (my italics). Human rights was henceforth a war aim, emphasized in the rhetoric of politicians while lawyers in the back rooms of the State Department and the common rooms of Oxbridge tried their hands at drafting something that was now definitely on the post-war agenda: an international bill of rights.

They did so, inevitably, in language that lacked the passion and simplicity of H. G. Wells. His achievement was to make human rights relevant to a world from many parts of which they had vanished with the secret policeman's knock on the door, and to include in his list the social and economic rights which Western governments had refused to acknowledge during the Great Depression. His Penguin Special, which must be accounted one of the twentieth century's most influential books, was a far-sighted demand for what he was the first to call a 'New World Order', in which fundamental human rights, enforced by law, would protect individuals against governments of whatever political complexion. What made this slim volume of 128 pages so powerful was the way its author was able to mix unassuming idealism with a devastating attack on Stalin, and especially upon 'the young Germany of Hitler, wearing its thick boots (that have stamped in the faces of Jewish women), its brown shirts, that recall the victims smothered in latrines and all the cloacal side of Hitlerism; its swastika – ignorantly stolen from the Semitic Stone-age peoples; oafish and hysterically cruel, they remind us all how little mankind has risen above the level of an exceptionally spiteful ape'. Wells was the first to argue from 'those outrages upon human dignity' in the concentration camps – outrages that others only felt after seeing the pictures of the corpse-strewn Belsen, six years later.

But these examples were used to illustrate a broader thesis, namely that Western tradition required, as a response to totalitarianism, a reassertion of individual liberty, and for that liberty to be protected by an international order that relied on law rather than diplomacy. This was the prescience of Wells's vision, as astonishing, in its way, as his first novel, *The Time Machine*, half a century before. Wells's grasp of international law was negligible, and he offered no answer to the problem of how his declaration, which was to be incorporated in the domestic law of every state, might be enforced in states without independent legal systems. He was, however, positive that it would take more than diplomacy to bring them into line, and that pleas of state sovereignty must not be allowed to prevail: 'There was an extraordinary mass of foolish talk after 1918 about not interfering in the internal affairs of this, that or the other member of the League of Nations. It is time we recognized fully that the making of any lethal weapon larger than what may be required for the control of big animals, is a matter of universal concern . . .'

NATIONS UNITED

Winston Churchill, legend has it, was naked in the toilet of the White House guest wing on the morning of 29 December 1941 when Franklin Roosevelt wheeled into his bedroom bellowing 'United Nations!' Hastily donning a dressing-gown, Churchill emerged to agree to the name for the union of powers (including the Soviet Union and China) which were now waging war against the Axis countries. They rejected the US State Department's tepid suggestion ('Associated Nations') and turned instead to a line from Byron's *Childe Harold's Pilgrimage*, which had, no doubt, been recited the previous evening by Churchill:

> *Their children's lips shall echo them, and say –*
> *Here where the sword United Nations drew,*
> *Our countrymen were warring on that day!*

The existence of the United Nations was formally declared a few weeks later, in a document that built on the 'Four Freedoms' speech and the Atlantic Charter, and Roosevelt used the brand name in his rhetoric against the US isolationists (which was so successful that four years later the US Senate ratified the Charter by 89 votes to 2). There were United Nations days and rallies, a Rothko-like flag on four blue posts (long since abandoned) and even a 'United Nations march', composed by Dimitri Shostakovich, used as the finale of the 1943 Gene Kelly movie *As Thousands Cheer*.

A food and agriculture conference was organized and the Allies began to make 'declarations' in the UN's name. As early as 17 December 1942, the United Nations issued the first statement on the Holocaust ('this bestial policy of cold-blooded extermination'), by way of a declaration released simultaneously in London, Washington and Moscow. It told of a 'barbarism and inhuman treatment to which the Jews are being subjected in German-occupied Europe'. But it took a year of lobbying by governments in exile and by Jewish and Christian organizations before the UN War Crimes Commission (UNWCC) was established, with the purpose of compiling lists of war criminals and collecting evidence for their trials. (In due course the evidence came to be used in 3,470 trials throughout newly liberated Europe.) It also engaged legal experts who advised on potential charges, beginning the intellectual process of developing war crimes jurisprudence and giving shape to the demand made by Roosevelt and Churchill for retribution: as the latter put it, as early as October 1941, retribution for 'these crimes must henceforward take its place among the major purposes of the war'.[31] Its lawyers and investigators were soon confronted with a conundrum: the most 'bestial' of crimes were those committed by Germany against its own Jewish nationals, and the Westphalian principles did not permit its leaders to be prosecuted for murdering and torturing their own people on account of their race, religion or political opinions. The Commission's request to work on a new international crime was actually rejected by diplomats and lawyers in the State Department and the UK Foreign Office, so closely were they wedded to the Westphalian principle of state sovereignty. It took the public outrage at pictures from Belsen and Auschwitz, and the determination of President Truman to punish the perpetrators of the Holocaust, before the idea of a 'crime against humanity' would be permitted at Nuremberg to trump the immunity hitherto accorded to leaders of the states that exterminate their own.

In the meantime, as defeat loomed for the Axis powers, the structure of the post-war international order took shape. It was to a strengthened League of Nations model that the Allied governments turned, at the four-power conference at Dumbarton Oaks in late 1944 which led to the Charter of the United Nations, signed by forty-four nations in San Francisco on 26 June 1945. The original 'Great Power' plan was to leave the promotion of 'respect for human rights and fundamental freedoms' as merely an incidental aspiration of the new organization: that this was elevated into one of the Charter's primary purposes was due to last-minute pressure exerted on the US delegation by a group of American non-governmental organizations (notably, the American Jewish Congress and the National Association for the Advancement of Colored People). It was the US, then, which took the lead in giving human rights its prominent position in the UN Charter, both in its preamble (which evinces a determination 'to re-affirm faith in fundamental human rights, in the dignity and worth of the human person, in the equal rights of men and women') and in Article 1, which sets out as a chief purpose of the UN:

To achieve international co-operation in solving international problems of an economic, social, cultural or humanitarian character, and in promoting and encouraging respect for human rights and for fundamental freedoms for all without distinction as to race, sex, language or religion.

The Charter established an Economic and Social Council with power to set up a Human Rights Commission. Significantly, Article 55(c) says that 'universal respect for, and observance of, human rights' is essential for 'conditions of stability and well-being which are necessary for peaceful and friendly relations among nations'. To achieve this, members pledge themselves in Article 56 to take 'joint and separate action' in co-operation with the UN. But members must never forget Article 2(4), which sets up the rule that H. G. Wells identified as the road block for human rights, and at whose barrier their progress was halted for much of the remaining century:

All members shall refrain in their international relations from the threat or use of force against the territorial integrity or political independence of any state, or in any other manner inconsistent with the purposes of the United Nations.

Article 2(4) is beloved of China, and regularly cited in opposition to any form of 'humanitarian intervention'. But on a true interpretation, this is neither its meaning nor its effect, which was to outlaw interventions which are inconsistent with UN principles. Since these principles include a duty to protect innocent civilians, it could be argued that an intervention of the kind made in Libya in 2011 would not breach Article 2(4), even if made by NATO without a formal Security Council mandate. Besides, the first draft of the Article was a blanket ban on 'the threat or use of force', and an amendment (proposed by Australia) limited the prohibition to attacks against 'territorial integrity' or 'political independence': attacks to free hostages or to capture perpetrators of crimes against humanity would not be covered. So Pakistan's objection to the US helicopter raid on bin Laden's compound in 2011 on the basis that it constituted a breach of Article 2(4), was misconceived.

Article 2(7) at first blush imposes on the UN the same prohibition against force that Article 2(4) imposes on states, but then provides a way around it through the Security Council's enforcement powers in Chapter VII of the Charter:

Nothing contained in the present Charter shall authorize the United Nations to intervene in matters which are essentially within the domestic jurisdiction of any State or shall require the members to submit such matters to settlement under the present Charter; but this principle shall not prejudice the application of enforcement measures under Chapter VII.

By reference to this crippling rule, the UN and its instrumentalities declined to act against any state which objected to having its internal repression investigated or condemned. It was a restriction over which diplomats could wring their hands, whilst having no desire at all to intervene to stop barbarities perpetrated by their allies or to create precedents which might later justify intervention in the affairs of their own governments. It was not until 1993, after the Cold War was over and as the spectre of 'ethnic cleansing' returned to Europe, that there was sufficient superpower resolve to apply the proviso to Article 2(7), namely that it could be overridden by Chapter VII. This is the chapter of the Charter which permits the Security Council to order armed intervention against any state once it has determined that such a response is necessary to restore international peace and security. The appalling crimes against humanity which occurred after 1945 could have been forcibly combated by the UN under its Chapter VII power, but until the Balkan atrocities in the 1990s the Security Council never thought that military action could be a response to human rights violations.

At the conferences that turned the United Nations into an expanded (and expanding) post-war organization, voices began to be raised in favour of a more permanent international justice system. The most powerful came from Dr H. V. Evatt QC, Australia's foreign minister. He was first to propose a European Court of Human Rights, with the right of individual petition, arguing that even democratic governments could not be trusted to protect the rights of individual citizens,

as they could be ridden over roughshod by elected majorities prejudiced against them. 'State declarations, standing alone, are not
sufficient to guarantee the inalienable rights of individuals and behind
them it is essential that some sufficient sanction be established.'[32]
Evatt adopted Raphael Lemkin, the somewhat shabby Polish lawyer
who obsessively lobbied for his big idea – a convention against genocide, which came to pass under Evatt's UN presidency in 1948. Evatt's
delegates on the Human Rights Commission urged it to establish an
international human rights court, and feistily replied, to objections
that this would impinge on national sovereignty, that this Westphalian
icon was 'an outdated conception, a fetishist survival whose worship
should be anathema in the face of economic and human inter-
relationships of our one atomic world . . . Gentlemen, every international agreement is a derogation of sovereignty!' This cry roused
support from lesser powers and the British delegation even produced
a draft convention, but this time it was the French who blinked: 'the
Australian proposal (for a court) would seem to be the normal step in
the evolution of the world,' said René Cassin, 'but its realization at
this time seems unlikely.'[33] Doubtless Monsieur Cassin was looking at
the stony-faced Stalinist delegates, under orders from Soviet Foreign
Minister Andrei Vyshinsky to oppose any move towards real justice.
Vyshinsky, ringmaster of the Moscow show trials, even tried to amend
the right to 'independent and impartial' courts in the Universal Declaration to read instead a right merely to 'open' courts – Stalin's rigged
trials were always open, but its judges were never independent or
impartial.

Nevertheless, the UN Charter was the first treaty to make human
rights a matter for global concern. By identifying violations as a danger to world peace and security, it provided a mechanism for
international intervention, as a last resort, in the affairs of nation
states. What it did not do was to impose any *legal* duty on member
states to comply with human rights standards. This could have been
accomplished, as several small countries urged, by incorporating a
bill of rights into the Charter: the move was opposed by all the major
powers, conscious of the motes in their own eyes (France and the UK
had no desire at the time to grant any form of democracy to their

colonies; all the Southern states in the US had 'Jim Crow' laws discriminating against blacks; there were millions still consigned without trial to Soviet gulags). For this reason the Charter pledges on human rights were circumscribed: the duty spelled out in Article 55(c) was to *promote* respect for and observance of human rights, not to guarantee them as a matter of law for all citizens. This vagueness was quite deliberate: no Great Power was prepared in 1945 to be bound by international law in respect of the treatment of its own subjects. The only positive rule of law to which they committed themselves was to refrain from threatening or using force against the territory or independence of any other state (Article 2(4)), subject to their 'inherent right of individual or collective self-defence if an armed attack occurs against a member' (Article 51). It was the application of this formula which was mostly to exercise the Security Council in its efforts to broker peace, until the internecine bloodbaths in former Yugoslavia and Rwanda caused it to exercise a power to punish crimes against humanity that it had actually possessed from the outset.

THE UNIVERSAL DECLARATION OF HUMAN RIGHTS

In closing the San Francisco conference, President Truman had promised that under the newly minted UN Charter 'we have good reason to expect the framing of an international bill of rights (which) will be as much a part of international life as our own Bill of Rights is a part of our own Constitution'[34] The momentous task of drafting this constitution for humankind was allotted to the newly formed Commission on Human Rights, set up by the Economic and Social Council pursuant to Article 68 of the Charter. It was chaired by Eleanor Roosevelt and served by a secretariat headed by a Canadian law professor, John Humphrey, who over the next two years was instrumental in putting before the delegates drafts he culled from many sources – notably the American Law Institute, the constitutions of Latin American countries (which contained social and economic rights), drafts by Sir

Hersch Lauterpacht, H. G. Wells and the Sankey Committee, and the eighteenth-century declarations.[35]

The most profound influence on the Commission was the evidence from the trial of the Nazi leaders, which lasted from Justice Jackson's opening on 20 November 1945 to the judgment on 30 September 1946. The judgment at Nuremberg made an historic inroad into Westphalian immunity: it created an international criminal law to punish the perpetrators of crimes against humanity. The evidence upon which the judgment was based would provide the rationale for many of the clauses of the Universal Declaration.

The Commission's most severe division turned on whether the bill should be legally enforceable (either as an annex to the UN Charter or as a multilateral human rights convention) or merely take the form of a declaration – of principles without powers of implementation, other than by the slow process of acceptance as customary international law. The Soviet Union and its puppets were implacable foes of enforceability, while Britain and Australia led the demand for a binding document. Australia's delegates were the first to propose an international court of human rights, pointing out the obvious: 'a mere declaration of principles would not offer assurance against the revival of oppression'. The Americans blew hot and cold. Roosevelt initially inclined to the American Bar Association call for 'a new Bill of Rights that will be a part of law enforceable against governments which deny human rights' but she shifted towards the Soviets' position the more that US relations with them worsened: neither of those sparring superpowers wanted rules, or even a referee, when the gloves had to come off.[36] The idealistic nations gave in, and this had, with hindsight, two negative advantages: the declaration was agreed, with superpower involvement, by the end of 1948 (it might not have been agreed at all thereafter), and it came with no enforcement machinery to be discredited (as discredited it would undoubtedly have been) during the years of the Cold War.

What emerged was not a legal guarantee but a 'declaration' made by the General Assembly, putting beyond doubt the nature and meaning of the pledge to respect human rights contained in Article 55 of the Charter. The Universal Declaration of Human Rights was adopted by forty-eight members of the General Assembly on 10 December 1948. It is poignant to recall the eight member states which abstained from voting: the USSR; Czechoslovakia, Poland and two other Soviet satellites; Yugoslavia, South Africa and Saudi Arabia. (The six communist abstentions were opportunistic – these countries had played an important part in the drafting and insisted on a non-binding declaration, then abstained on the grounds that it would have little effect. South Africa could not square the non-discrimination clauses with its apartheid laws, and Saudi Arabia – unlike other Muslim countries – objected that the right to change religion prevented it from punishing apostasy.) It was to be a measure both of the triumph of human rights as an idea, and of the failure to make it a reality, that these nations came in later years consistently to endorse the Declaration, as did well over a hundred countries which emerged to independence after 1948. This is the Declaration's achievement of sorts, that no state has ever been prepared to boast of its breach.

Although it was the first modern human rights text to be drafted in the pedestrian prose of a UN committee, there is anger flashing from the Charter's preamble. After the briefest of natural law nods towards 'inherent dignity' and 'inalienable rights' (and a welcome non-sexist substitution of 'human family' for 'man'), it recites as its rationale that contempt for human rights results in 'barbarous acts which have outraged the conscience of mankind' and so human rights 'should be protected by the rule of law' in order to avoid the need to revolt against tyranny. For members of the drafting committee, and speakers in the General Assembly debate, the Holocaust had supplied human rights with the most utilitarian of justifications: the alternative to them is war.

It is possible to find, behind the adoption of most of the articles, some reference to the perversions of Nazism. Thus 'master race' ideology is refuted by Article 2, which entitles everyone to rights 'without distinction of any kind, such as race, colour, sex, language, religion, political or other opinion, national or social origin, property, birth or other status'. The Declaration was drafted by the Human Rights Commission after receiving a detailed report on the prosecution evidence at the Nuremberg trials. The killing of 'useless eaters', the

Einsatzgruppen orders to kill indiscriminately, the gas chambers, Mengele experiments, 'night and fog' decrees and the extermination projects after *Kristallnacht* were at the forefront of their minds and provided the examples to which they addressed their drafts.[37] Thus the first draft of Article 3 ('Everyone has a right to life, liberty and security of person') originally went on, 'except in cases prescribed by law' – until it was realized how many had been put to death under perfectly valid laws passed by the Nazis. (The African Charter, drafted many years later, makes this same mistake: see p. 87.) The Article 19 guarantee of freedom of expression and Article 20 guarantee of freedom of peaceful assembly were incorporated by reference to Hitler's crackdown on dissent after the Reichstag fire, and Article 21 – the right to participate in government through secretly balloted and free elections – was an attempt to address the fascist habit of rule through decree without reference to any democratic body. The clumsily drafted addendum to the right to education in Article 26, which reads like support for private and religious schooling ('Parents have a prior right to choose the kind of education that shall be given to their children'), was in fact a heartfelt reaction to Nazi brainwashing. Roosevelt explained that it was 'designed to avert situations such as prevailed in Nazi countries where education, which was entirely under state control, tended to atrophy children's intellectual facilities'.[38] The rights to an effective remedy (Article 8) and to a fair hearing by an independent tribunal (Article 10) were reactions to the puppet courts, packed with Nazi judges, established to enforce the Party's decrees.

Of course, many of these rights are to be found in similar language in H. G. Wells's draft and in the eighteenth-century declarations, but the Nazi record and the considerably more barbaric Japanese record (which was also before the Commission in digests of the Tokyo trials) gave an emphasis to those individual rights which seemed incompatible with totalitarianism. What amazes today is the contemporaneity of the document, over half a century on. Roosevelt and her drafting committee produced an imperishable statement that has inspired more than 200 international treaties, conventions and declarations, and the bills of rights found in almost every national constitution adopted since the war. There were, in retrospect, a few errors: it was not necessary to spell out as a universal right 'periodic holidays with pay' (Article 24); and the special copyright provision for the profits of scientists and authors in Article 27(2) is surely out of place (it was probably inserted because a conference on the Berne Copyright Convention coincided with the main drafting session). These are quibbles: more serious is the failure (thanks to communist objection) to make political rights depend upon multi-party democracy and a somewhat overblown definition of the freedom publicly to 'manifest' religion. The failure to provide any protection for minority rights was largely due to the prevailing fallacy that if you look after individual rights, group rights will take care of themselves (see p. 197), and by way of reaction to Hitler's exploitation of German minorities as an excuse for invading Poland and Czechoslovakia. But colonial attachments and racist assumptions played a part: for example, Australia argued that 'the principle of assimilation of all groups was in the best interests of all in the long run'[39] – a principle of white superiority for which indigenous people in that and other countries would tragically suffer. Otherwise, the Universal Declaration has stood time's test, and what resonates most loudly today is Article 28:

Everyone is entitled to a social and international order in which the rights and freedoms set forth in this declaration can be fully realized.

This was a right without precedent in the eighteenth-century declarations. It called for some international enforcement system, harking back to the provisions of the Charter which permitted Security Council intervention under Chapter VII in the event of human rights violations on a scale which threatened world peace. The French delegate, René Cassin (who played an important part in drafting the Declaration), was aware that the Charter made it possible to penetrate the sovereignty of the State: 'This was specifically put into the Charter in the hope of avoiding a repetition of what happened in 1933, when Germany began to massacre her own nationals and when other nations refused to consider this a matter of international concern.'[40]

At this point, the true significance of the Charter and the Universal Declaration for the still-distant human rights movement can with hindsight be appreciated. It lies in the nexus both these documents assert between grave human rights violations and international insecurity: atrocities within a sovereign state are a matter for international law because they upset neighbouring states in a manner likely to disturb world peace. This was the assumption of Article 55 of the Charter (promotion of respect for human rights helps create 'conditions of stability and well-being') and the preamble of the Universal Declaration ('recognition of . . . equal and inalienable rights of all members of the human family is the foundation of . . . peace in the world'). Today the rationale for humanitarian intervention might be stated differently – with more sophistication (in terms of the psychological necessity to eradicate behaviour that diminishes everyone's humanity) or less (a crime-free global village). But in 1948, US Secretary of State George Marshall explained the link that the framers had in mind:

Governments which systematically disregard the rights of their own people are not likely to respect the rights of other nations and other people and are likely to seek their objectives by coercion and force.[41]

This was true of Hitler, of course, and would be true of Saddam Hussein and Khomeini and Gaddafi, but not for countries like Zimbabwe and Burma, where domestic repression does not coincide with an aggressive foreign policy or a desire to export revolution. None the less, by making the somewhat questionable assumption that a state's respect for human rights was a precondition of international peace, the Charter and the Declaration provided the legal mechanism which could later be triggered to challenge the sovereign right of states to oppress groups of their own people.

Although a product of Allied war aims, with an intellectual provenance described above, the final draft of the Universal Declaration emerged from a geographically and culturally mixed committee on which major contributions were made by delegates from India, China and Lebanon, with further input from representatives of Chile, Iran

44

and Egypt. Many of today's African and Asian countries had not at this stage been granted independence, but fourteen members of the 56-state General Assembly were Asian, four were African and twenty came from Latin America. The communist abstainers had given assent to the individual freedom provisions: what they feared was the Declaration's bias towards democracy (to assuage them, the word itself is only mentioned once, in Article 29). So there is little historical merit in the criticism raised decades later, that the Universal Declaration embodies only liberal Western values. On the contrary, it vouchsafed economic, social and cultural rights of enormous importance to developing countries. These included the right to work and to basic standards of health, housing and education. The drafting committee, conscious of the need to avoid 'cultural imperialism', took evidence from anthropologists who warned of ethnocentrism, the assumption of the superiority of one's own cultural values. The actual drafting history reveals very few cultural divides, other than over the rights to marry and to change religion – a sticking point for the Saudis but not for other Muslim nations like Syria, Iran and Pakistan. The USSR and its henchstates championed the non-discrimination clauses and the rights to work and housing, whilst it was the bloc of Latin American states, supported by delegates from China, India and the Philippines, which successfully insisted on the inclusion of the 'new' or 'second generation' social and economic rights, despite opposition from the US and its 'liberal' Western allies. These communitarian rights are made in some cases contingent upon 'national effort' or 'the organization and resources of each state', but their inclusion was at the behest of representatives of poor and underdeveloped countries. The Australian Labour government, with its strong trade union ties, first broke Western ranks, pointing out (to the embarrassment of his widow, who chaired the session) that the third of President Roosevelt's 'four freedoms' was freedom from want.[42]

There is nothing in the Declaration that is hostile to developing countries, or to Asian and African countries, or to the culture and aspirations of ethnic groups or tribes. It sets bedrock standards, beyond which diversity is encouraged. As a matter of history, the allegation that the Declaration was intended to be an instrument of

Western hegemony fails: it was a righteous and at the time largely uncontentious response to the horrors of concentration camps in Europe and of Japanese military occupation in Asia, pithily defining the freedoms which would have to be upheld to prevent any repetition of this intolerable state behaviour. At the time, these rights were not perceived as Western or Eurocentric, but as obvious. That over the following half century the Declaration would be flouted without regard to geography, by governments of every creed and colour and often by or with the connivance of the US and its European allies, amply demonstrates that its guarantees are not 'Western' in any meaningful sense. 'Liberal' the Declaration is not, in any consistent way: philosophically it embodies a lowest common denominator of postwar decency, imbued with the dour moral conservatism of the time (adopting, for example, the family as 'the natural and fundamental group unit of society') allied to some emerging socialist ideals such as a basic wage, favourable conditions of work and the right to join trade unions. As for the individual freedom clauses, these were all made subject to the sweeping exceptions of Articles 29 and 30, which embody the communitarian philosophy that 'Everyone has duties to the community in which *alone* the free and full development of his personality is possible'. So the real failure is not to be found in a perspective skewed towards Western values, as arrogant Asian leaders and then nervous Muslim states were much later to allege, but in its lack of enforcement machinery: that could only come from progressive incorporation of its clauses into treaties and in due course into customary international law. Its original purpose was to serve as 'the measuring rod of illegitimacy and illegality of practices of power' and without it, as the leading Indian legal scholar Upendra Baxi concludes, 'there would have been no objective way of measuring and combating State-caused human deprivation and suffering'.[43]

The Declaration was proclaimed by the General Assembly as 'a common standard of achievement for all peoples and all nations', to be promoted by education and, more optimistically, by 'progressive measures, national and international, to secure their universal and effective recognition and observance'. This coy phraseology conceals the awkward fact that this proclamation lacks legal force, whilst articulating the hope that it might come to possess such force through 'progressive measures' by states and through its adoption by international law. Although its drafters had drawn heavily on the eighteenth-century declarations, they had wisely refrained from incorporating appeals to God and to nature. Instead, they invoked the 'categorical imperative' familiar from the moral philosophy of Immanuel Kant: 'Act so that you treat humanity, whether in your own person or in that of another, always as an end and never as a means only.'[44] Kant located the seat of universal laws in national respect for intrinsic human worthiness, which he termed 'dignity' – the key word in the preamble, which opens by recognizing 'the inherent dignity of all members of the human family' and goes on, by secular and rational argument, to affirm faith in 'the dignity and worth of the human person' which needs protection (a) because securing the 'four freedoms' is the highest international aspiration and (b) because of the empirical evidence that violating human rights conduces to war and barbarism.

The preamble advances, through seven powerful propositions, the logical and moral argument that human rights are universal, and proceeds to state their content: it is an exercise in persuasion rather than law. Eleanor Roosevelt prophesied that the Universal Declaration 'might well become the international Magna Carta of mankind'. But she warned the General Assembly that it would not initially have that status: 'It is not a treaty; it is not an international agreement. It is not and does not purport to be a statement of law or legal obligation.' What *was* intended to have precisely that status was the accompanying Convention on the Prevention and Punishment of Genocide, which was presented for signature the following day (it entered into force in 1951). This required states to punish, either domestically or 'by such international criminal tribunal as may have jurisdiction', acts which were intended to destroy, in whole or part, a national, ethnic or racial group, committed by anyone 'whether they are constitutionally responsible rulers, public officials or private individuals'.

These two documents – the convention placing an international law obligation on every state to act against genocide and the inspirational Universal Declaration – provide the UN with its finest historical moment. (The Geneva Conventions, presented in March 1949, completed the post-war human rights triptych.) But the starry-eyed delegates and self-congratulating diplomats present at the Palais Chaillot, in the shadow of the Eiffel Tower, at the birth of the first 'New World Order' in December 1948 failed to heed the lesson of the Berlin airlift, made necessary by Stalin's petulant decision to seal the city against road and rail transport. The USSR, for no good reason, was threatening two million West Berliners with starvation, having just abstained from voting for a declaration that every man has the 'right to a standard of living adequate for the health and well-being of himself and of his family, including food'. The Soviet ambassador to the UN gave a tight, abstemious smile as he explained the Soviet abstention to newsmen: the Declaration, he said, was 'just a collection of pious phrases'. This was Andrei Vyshinsky, the century's most polished legal liar, who had commenced his new career as communism's archdiplomat.

2

The Post-war World

'Count up the results of fifty years of human rights mechanisms, thirty years of multibillion dollar development programmes and endless high-level rhetoric and the general
impact is quite underwhelming . . . this is a failure of implementation on a scale that shames us all.'

Mary Robinson, UN Human Rights Commissioner, on the
fiftieth anniversary of the UDHR, 10 December 1998

The Universal Declaration was adopted by the UN General Assembly
on 10 December 1948: 'Human Rights Day', as it was thereafter
annually celebrated, with as much enthusiasm as the times would permit. The Declaration and the Genocide Convention had been the
high-water marks of a movement which was not so much for human
rights as against the tyranny and racist ideology of Nazism: its force
was spent in its culmination. Thereafter, it proved powerless to move
politicians or diplomats to do anything much about genocide, or any
other of the multiple and massive breaches of human rights which
took place over the next fifty years. This shameful failure occupied a
period when over a hundred international treaties and conventions
and declarations were promulgated, invariably preceded by preparatory commissions and conferences taking diplomats to the world's
most pleasant and expensive cities: Geneva (incessantly), The Hague,
Vienna, Rome and New York. (It may be no coincidence that the only
conference of much value to the cause took place, briefly, in Tehran.)

The result was to define and extend human rights on paper – endless reams of paper – but never seriously to discomfit a single torturer until Duško Tadić was put behind bars for twenty years by the Hague Tribunal in May 1997. He was, however, just a thug; the following year torturer-in-chief General Pinochet, architect of the 'disappearances' in South America which claimed thousands of lives, became a much more significant candidate for international justice after his arrest in London. The fact that Pinochet *was* arrested in 1998 – he had been a frequent visitor in previous years – was an achievement made possible by a development in a parallel universe to that occupied by politicians and diplomats and UN bureaucrats, namely the real world, where people were coming to believe in the principles to which these functionaries had for too long given lip-service.

This has been mainly achieved by the moral force of the principles themselves, promulgated by the hundreds of non-governmental organizations (NGOs) like Amnesty International and Human Rights Watch which have sprung up to promote them. Political leaders occasionally gave genuine commitment (e.g. President Carter in 1977) and inspiration came from victims whose struggles provoked anger throughout a world that by the century's end was instantaneously informed of human rights violations by satellite television. The pictures were as important as ever: just as the pitiable skeletons of Belsen haunted in flickering black and white the architects of the 1948 Declaration, so television's colour coverage of the piled-up bodies in Bosnia and Rwanda produced a public response which forced the UN to establish a court to convict those responsible for the carnage. The television pictures of refugees massed on the Kosovo borders initially swung public support behind the NATO bombing of Serbia in 1999, although had it bombed the Bosnian Serbs at Srebrenica in 1995, or demonstrated any resolve to arrest their leaders indicted by the Hague Tribunal, then the later tragedy may have been avoided. Equally, had the world worked out a way of putting Pinochet, Pol Pot and Idi Amin behind bars within a decade of their crimes against humanity, Milošević, Saddam Hussein, Bashir and Assad may have been deterred from following their example.

This chapter explains the post-war evolution of systems aiming to protect human rights, charting the progress that was made until the end of the twentieth century. Firstly, there are the institutions – courts (so called if their decisions are binding on states) – then there are the commissions and committees which receive and rule upon petitions from individuals, sometimes encouraging a government to change its mind. The treaties which set up these adjudicatory bodies, and the adjudications themselves, are 'sources' for emerging international human rights law, along with custom and state practice: if all such 'sources' point in the same direction, or a great preponderance of authority is in favour of a particular principle, it may be said to have crystallized into a 'rule' of international law. But international law, unlike municipal law, cannot be said to 'rule': it lays down a standard which independent states may in practice ignore, and often do, without suffering anything more than diplomatic embarrassment. However, sufficient sources have congealed for international human rights to be stated in terms of the elemental liberties described in chapter 3. Some of the most vexing topical issues, such as the rights of minorities and of prisoners condemned to death, receive separate treatment in chapter 4.

1946–76: THIRTY INGLORIOUS YEARS

The promise of a 'New World Order' was ushered in by the Universal Declaration and the Genocide Convention in December 1948, followed a few months later by the final part of the human rights triptych, the four Geneva Conventions requiring civilized treatment for civilians and prisoners and sick and wounded victims of war. In 1950, in the temporary absence of the Soviet Union, the Security Council took the momentous decision to commence military action under the UN Charter against North Korea. This war ebbed and flowed until 1953, costing almost a million lives. The most appalling atrocities were committed, in complete defiance of the Geneva Conventions, by the North Koreans allied with Chinese forces under the brutal and dictatorial Kim Il-sung and by the UN-supported South

Koreans led by the brutal and corrupt Syngman Rhee. The US air force carpet-bombed civilian targets with almost as much tonnage as had devastated Nazi Germany, and its soldiers (so a few confessed fifty years later) massacred hundreds at the hamlet of No Gun Ri, while North Koreans left their prisoners to die of starvation and later (when the Chinese took over the camps) introduced a technique new to the human rights lexicon: 'brainwashing'. They maintain to this day, and have a museum purporting to prove, that US planes dropped poison gas and biological bombs that spread illness and death: captured USAF pilots confessed to this before (and probably as a condition of) their release, but on return to the US they retracted their confession, widely attributed at the time to 'brainwashing'. Typically, a group of communist-supporting scientists were allowed to enter on a 'fact-finding' mission, which found the facts to be exactly as described by the North Koreans. This was how human rights issues played out in the Cold War, as propaganda claim and counter-claim: the truth of this particular allegation remains elusive, even today.

Any prospect of a 'New World Order' based on the Universal Declaration was swiftly shattered. Stalin's terror made a comeback: show trials played to capacity radio audiences throughout eastern Europe, with confessions rehearsed at gunpoint. László Rajk in Hungary and Rudolf Slánský in Czechoslovakia took the Nikolai Bukharin part, without any ambiguity in their script. Stalin remained in place until his death in 1953, as did his gulag, which devoured millions and provided slave labour to build the vast scientific complexes needed for the Soviet nuclear industry. The arms race began in 1949 when the Soviet Union first tested its bomb: the Great Powers vied to develop weapons of mass destruction in complete defiance of all Hague Conventions on this subject. Just for a moment, in February 1956, a ray of hope for human rights briefly shone, when, at the Twentieth Congress of the Soviet Communist Party, Khrushchev condemned Stalin and admitted that the show trial confessions had been obtained by torture. But the moment was lost, partly through a last gasp of colonialism by the British government, leading France and Israel into a racist war with Egypt over the Suez Canal. With UN and US attention diverted by the misbehaviour of these foolish allies, the cries for freedom sweeping Hungary (excited by Khrushchev's apparent denunciation of Stalinism) went unheeded by the West, and Soviet tanks rolled into Budapest to make mockery of the Universal Declaration promise that 'the will of the people shall be the basis of the authority of government'. Tens of thousands of Hungarians were arbitrarily detained, and hundreds were executed without any pretence at fair trial. The determination of the Soviet Union to destroy any freedom which might be asserted against the interests of communism reached its apotheosis in 1961 with the building of the Berlin Wall. Those brutal apparatchiks Walter Ulbricht and later Erich Honecker directed that anyone seeking to exercise the universal right of freedom of movement by crossing it, should be shot on sight.

Liberty took a bashing in the West as well. In the US, Senator McCarthy and his ambitious assistant, Congressman Nixon, poisoned the wells of free speech, while the electrocution in 1953 of Ethel Rosenberg – a mother of young children – was a signally cruel event. Discrimination against blacks was endemic, and in some American states there was what amounted to apartheid as petty as that which was imposed by law in South Africa. US intervention in its 'spheres of influence' was as frequent as that of the Soviet Union, although much less heavy-handed: the Americans worked their will through CIA-financed fronts rather than by sending in their own tanks. When a democratic election threw up a socialist regime in Guatemala, for example, which confiscated land owned by the United Fruit Company and redistributed it to peasants, the CIA trained and supported an insurrectionary force which in 1954 overthrew the government and installed a military junta. The junta restored the land to United Fruit and began a process of secretly kidnapping, torturing and killing its left-wing opponents (a prelude to the 'disappearances' under US-backed dictators in the 1970s). A CIA operation to overthrow Fidel Castro notoriously failed at the Bay of Pigs in 1961, prompting that agency to plot his death by poison pen and exploding cigar. He responded by inviting the Soviet Union to defend his country with nuclear-tipped ballistic missiles aimed at Washington and New York. The Cuban Missile Crisis of October 1962 came very close to triggering a third world war in which hundreds of millions would have died in a nuclear holocaust. If President Kennedy had taken the advice of the Pentagon to bomb the Cuban missile sites, provoking retaliation and counter-retaliation between the two superpowers and their European surrogates (NATO and the Warsaw Pact), mutual destruction would have been assured. Civilization would have started again, probably in Tasmania.[1]

So what had happened in the meantime to the systems for protecting human rights so confidently put in place by the UN Charter, which had created an Economic and Social Council with the duty, under Article 68, to establish a commission 'for the promotion of human rights'? The Human Rights Commission met for a few weeks each year, riven by bloc-voting and by the refusal of member states to allow themselves or other members to be criticized. It resolved at its inception in 1947 that it had 'no power to take any action in regard to any complaints concerning human rights' – a resolution which pretty much summed up its impact over the next twenty years. All that was achieved in this period was paperwork – in particular, the paper upon which the two main covenants were drafted, prior to their presentation to the General Assembly in 1966. It took a further decade for the International Covenant on Civil and Political Rights and the International Covenant on Economic, Social and Cultural Rights to attract ratification from the minimum number of states necessary for them to come into operation. The Human Rights Commission for all this time remained tight-lipped about breaches of the Universal Declaration, or the Genocide and Geneva Conventions, by any government which was a member of the UN.

At last, in the 1960s, there appeared a pariah state that the UN could do something about, especially when it withdrew its membership. That state was South Africa, with its system of apartheid, which had united the other African countries in condemnation, egged on by the Soviet Union. Drs Verwoerd and Vorster found few defenders in the West at a time when the civil rights movement was forcing the US to take minority rights seriously and when the UK was furious at the white separatists who had declared themselves the minority rulers of Rhodesia. It was in 1960 that South Africa first provoked that horrified international response which is the hallmark of crimes against humanity, when its police massacred sixty-nine peaceful protesters in the black township of Sharpeville. This state was an easy (as well as a proper) target because it had few powerful supporters besides Israel (itself a pariah in Arab eyes). In 1963 other African countries prevailed upon the Security Council to urge a trade boycott, and in 1967 the General Assembly condemned apartheid as a 'crime against humanity', calling for economic sanctions. For the first time, the prospect of *doing something* about human rights violations was on the agenda of the Human Rights Commission.[2]

There was, comparatively speaking, quite a lot of idealism swirling around the world again in early 1968, when the UN convened a conference in Tehran specifically to review the first twenty years of the Universal Declaration. In the West, much of it was a spill-over from the civil rights movement and protests against the Vietnam War, orchestrated by the 'peace and love' themes that had captured popular music. It helped that China was temporarily out of the power game, in the process of self-devastation at the hands of the Gang of Four. (The Cultural Revolution killed over a million citizens, a matter of human rights that every other country was happy to ignore.) Against this background, the Proclamation of Tehran in May 1968 won unanimous support. Its second principle was portentous:

The Universal Declaration of Human Rights states a common understanding of peoples of the world concerning the inalienable and inviolable rights of all members of the human family and constitutes an obligation for the members of the international community.

Here we go again. Only three months after the Tehran Proclamation, Soviet tanks rolled through Czechoslovakia, to nip the Prague Spring in the bud by replacing the Dubček government with hardline Stalinists. The UN Human Rights Commission did and said nothing. The General Assembly was also useless – an idle forum for diplomats, occasionally galvanized by a set-piece speech from the leader of the US or the USSR (Khrushchev's petulant behaviour in taking off a shoe and banging it on the podium was its most memorable moment). Its most damaging action, for international law, was to mis-state it when it decided to make a unanimous 'Friendly Nations Declaration' in 1970, one part of which became a tyrant's charter:

No State or group of States has the right to intervene, directly or indirectly, for any reason whatever, in the internal or external affairs of any other State. Consequently, armed intervention and all other forms of interference or attempted threats against the personality of the State or against its political, economic and cultural elements, are in violation of international law.[3]

The Human Rights Commission had nothing to say about the CIA's provocations in Chile, where the Nixon administration sponsored the military overthrow of a long-standing democracy and its elected leader, Dr Salvador Allende. The century's most vicious human rights violation – the 'disappearance' – followed en masse in the wake of General Pinochet's coup. Although Pinochet only killed about 4,000 in this way, 'Operation Condor' was a conspiracy he masterminded with leaders of five other military juntas in Latin America to secure the disappearance of left-wingers and liberal elements throughout the region.

The powerlessness – indeed pointlessness – of the Commission had been further demonstrated when it turned its back on what was, at that point, the worst human rights violation since the war: the mass-rape of up to 300,000 Bangladeshi women, and killing of even more men, in the course of the Pakistan army's invasion of a country it insisted was 'East Pakistan'. There could be no justification for the atrocities, but nobody was punished (a few Bangladeshi collaborators were finally put on trial in Dacca in 2011, forty years later) and the only assistance from the West, after India had intervened to push the Pakistani troops out, came from individual doctors (such as the celebrated Sydney abortionist Geoffrey Davis), whose consciences led them to Dacca in order to terminate pregnancies of women deliberately impregnated by soldiers whose 'ethnic policy' rapes would later be replicated by Serb troops in the Balkans.

During the 1960s, and until the final victory of the North in 1975, Vietnam proved another graveyard for the good intentions of the 1949 Geneva Conventions. It had been America's lamentable mistake to shore up the vicious Catholic dictator Ngo Dinh Diem, whose political perversity led him to offend his religious *majority* by persecuting Buddhist monks, several of whom brought their plight indelibly to world attention by setting themselves alight in front of news photographers. President Johnson began the bombing of North Vietnam in 1964 which in due course visited eighteen million gallons of 'Agent Orange' on forests and rice fields. Napalm was used against villagers – mainly women and small children – suspected of supporting the Vietcong. A few firefight atrocities were brought to account: Lieutenant Calley was convicted over My Lai, although Ernest Medina, who had greater responsibility as his commanding officer, was acquitted. Dr Henry Kissinger recommended the bombing of neutral Cambodia, which only served to rally support behind the Khmer Rouge.[4] Under Pol Pot's guidance, 1.7 million Cambodians (20 per cent of the population) were killed, in a genocidal mania which not only went unpunished for thirty-five years, but was actually rewarded by the Khmer Rouge being given a place in the anti-Vietnam coalition supported by the UN at the prompting of Reagan doctrinaires. The move to end the Vietnam War came after America wearied of television pictures of its boys being brought home in bodybags from a country where ragged children ran screaming with the pain of napalm in their eyes and where a police chief could shoot suspects in the head in full view of press photographers.

The behaviour of the superpowers in this era was motivated entirely by national and ideological interests, but some sneaking respect for the idea of international justice required aggression to be dressed in the language of legality. When the US wanted to serve its strategic or economic interests by invading a country, it took care to solicit an 'invitation' first. Makeshift principles were invented: to justify the US invasion of the Dominican Republic in 1965, for example, President Johnson declared he was merely enforcing a regional rule that communist governments were incompatible with the Inter-American system. Even more risible was the 'Brezhnev Doctrine' (hastily formulated in 1968 to excuse the Soviet invasion of Czechoslovakia) that international socialist law permitted 'fraternal military assistance' to any country whose socialist system was under threat. This bogus doctrine too could be triggered by a convenient 'request' from any apparatchik in a general's uniform or clinging to a ministerial post. The best that can be said for Cold War law was that superpowers felt obliged to resort to such fictions, covering up as best they could the atrocities committed by their own allies in order to accuse more loudly the other side. Action against South Africa excepted, it was not until the end of the Vietnam War, and the emergence in Chile of a dictator who was so confident of American support that he would openly resort to mass torture, that some states began to take human rights seriously.

It was largely in response to Pinochet's excesses (see chapter 8) that the General Assembly passed the Declaration Against Torture in 1975, the year which marked the end of the Vietnam War. About this time, also, the modern human rights movement gathered a certain strength, formally through the Helsinki Accords of 1975 in Europe and the entry into force, with thirty-five ratifying states, of the UN's twin Covenants in 1976 and the adoption of human rights as a foreign policy objective by the Carter administration in 1977. In 1976, the Security Council declared that apartheid was 'a grave threat to the peace' and urged states to support the ANC. The following year, it took the unprecedented step of imposing mandatory trade sanctions on South Africa and Rhodesia under Chapter VII of the Charter. At last, one widespread and systematic violation of human rights had been found to justify interference in a state's internal affairs, albeit that the interference amounted only to a ban on trade. The ban was not policed, however, and was easily circumvented by multinational corporations.

It was during this period that the conspicuous courage of individuals in standing up to state abuses began to matter. Andrei Sakharov, for example, gained immense moral stature. This ascetic scientist, one of the 'fathers of the Russian bomb' and hence a respected member of its privileged *nomenklatura*, put principles before preferment by publishing criticisms of Soviet policies and trenchant attacks on the abuse of psychiatry to silence dissidents. His personal clout protected him as he masterfully exploited the media to draw attention to the plight of political prisoners, through hunger strikes and letters to the US Congress urging trade sanctions. Behind the scenes, his courage was deplored by Western diplomats almost as much as by the Soviet government – Kissinger raged that he damaged *détente*. But Sakharov always and steadfastly took his stand on human rights instruments – the Universal Declaration, the Civil Covenant and the Helsinki Final Act.[5] He was the first dissident to demonstrate the counterproductive effect of censorship, through the cachet it gave to his publications in the West and their consequent popularity when they received a *samizdat* circulation back in Russia. It was noteworthy that Sakharov bypassed the UN system completely, deriding its partisan politics and its 'quiet diplomacy'.

The next valiant figure to emerge was Václav Havel, spokesman for Charter 77, a document prepared by leading Czech intellectuals which argued that their country's ratification of the Civil Covenant imported its 'rights' into municipal law, according to the promises made by parties (including hardline Czechoslovakia) to the Helsinki Agreement. This was to give Helsinki (essentially a rudimentary blueprint for political co-operation between eastern and western Europe) a legal importance it did not possess. Indeed, it was specifically made non-binding so that the Americans could sign it without the Senate's consent and the Soviet Union could agree to human rights in return for a Western promise (equally unenforceable) to respect its borders. What was significant, though, was that appeals of this kind could now gather public momentum by taking such international instruments at their face value, however little intention the diplomats who signed them had of honouring them.

The other important development was that the US, so wary of overseas entanglements, was now prepared to give the Universal Declaration its due, as a force in foreign policy. The Soviet Union responded that 'we will never tolerate interference in our internal affairs', but this formula was becoming frayed. What the entry into force of the twin Covenants had done in 1976 was to make human rights abuses a legitimate subject of international concern. There was growing acceptance of Sakharov's argument, used in his 1973 open letter to the US Congress calling for trade sanctions against

Russia until it abandoned its policy of refusing Jews the right to emigrate to Israel. Such a sanction, he contended persuasively, 'does not represent interference in the internal affairs of socialist countries, but simply a defence of international law, without which there can be no mutual trust'.

THE HUMAN RIGHTS COMMISSION AND COUNCIL

The record of the Human Rights Commission, ever since its initial resolution not to act on human rights violations, was woeful. Most of the states represented on it had no wish to create precedents for investigations or enforcement procedures which might next be used against an ally, or against themselves. (South Africa had been a different matter because the country had few allies and its racism – three million whites suppressing a seventeen-million black majority – was so egregious.) It generally avoided any criticism of states or state rulers, whether of Pol Pot's genocide or of Emperor Bokassa's primitive savagery or of mass murder by Idi Amin. Its votes came in power blocs which played games with each other on West–East, later North–South, divides. The US annually attempted to promote a resolution condemning China which was defeated by anti-US alliances even when it should unanimously have passed – in 1990, for example, after the shooting of dissidents in Tiananmen Square and in 2000, just after the jailings of the Falun Gong. The latter vote, 22–18 with 12 abstentions, demonstrates how unsatisfactory this committee had become for objective or fair adjudication. In 2001 the US was voted off for a year, as much for its attempts to 'politicize' the Committee as for the Bush administration's refusals to co-operate with other UN initiatives. The partisan behaviour of diplomat members actually damaged human rights: witness its fifty-first session in April 1995, when all Third World country members irresponsibly cast their votes to defeat a resolution critical of Nigeria, despite the military government's overthrow of democracy and its grotesquely unfair treason trials of dissidents like Ken Saro-Wiwa. A few months later, he was executed

– by a military command that knew it could get away with murder at the UN's Human Rights Commission.

It pretended to work through the 'quiet diplomacy' of its 'Resolution 1503 procedure', which encourages confidential dialogue with representatives of violating states. There is little evidence that this procedure, derided by Sakharov and human rights campaigners, has achieved any concrete results, although it has served the public relations interests of violating states which make great play of their 'co-operation' with UN emissaries who parachute in for a few days once the massacre is over. UN 'fact-finding' in such circumstances can be influenced by officials of the host state who 'look after' the emissary and determine whom he meets – usually military commanders, rehearsed prisoners and paid propagandists.

There is an open 'Resolution 1235 procedure' under which the Commission would appoint a study group for a particular country or subject, but here again it largely confined itself to studying breaches of civil rights in those countries which lacked lobbying influence at the UN. The Commission's 'fact-finding' procedures generally failed to find the facts which would discomfit powerful member states or their allies, although one rare exception was its East Timor report in January 2000 urging prosecution of Indonesian Generals. 'Special Rapporteurs' have been appointed to report on critical situations, and some have done so efficiently but as UN appraiser Philip Alston concludes, 'the selection of rapporteurs has been a quintessentially political process, the mechanics of which do little to ensure that expertise and competence will be the principal qualities sought . . . the range of people is unduly narrow . . . nominees are usually diplomats, and expertise in human rights law is often not prominent among their attributes'.[6] Alston was appointed rapporteur on extrajudicial executions, but found himself powerless to persuade the Indonesian government to drop the death penalty for drug couriers, or to protect witnesses at an enquiry he conducted into Kenyan disputes. The rapporteur for the UN on the independence of the judiciary, Brazilian lawyer Gabriela Knaul, has made little impact on this sensitive subject: in 2010 she sent only ninety-seven secret communications to states, half of which did not even bother to answer.[7]

This instrumentality of the United Nations has been crippled by that organization's instinctive deference to its own members and by its bureaucratic commitment to 'neutrality' in any fact-finding or adjudication. The crucial defect of the Commission was that its fifty-three members were representatives of *governments* rather than appointed as independent experts. They were diplomats, time-servers of states (including military juntas and feudal dictatorships) who regarded their part-time job – most representatives were fully employed in departments of their national government – as political rather than judicial. The Commission sat for only six weeks a year and, although it sometimes sent missions to human rights blackspots, it had no power to insist that they could range freely and investigate fully, or even that they should be allowed entry. It could not take on the superpower violators and equally it could not tackle the small states which ally themselves for protection to regional or political blocs. Notoriously, the Commission failed to confront Idi Amin over his years of butchery in Uganda: as president of the Organization of African Unity, he mobilized African state support in order to keep his own murders off its agenda. UN members could at any time have agreed to set up an independent appointments body to nominate members of the Commission, but this did not suit the self-interest of governments which were determined from the outset that this Commission should be kept under diplomatic control. As a result, it always had as members a number of states with appalling human rights records themselves. In 2005, for example, diplomats from Cuba, Zimbabwe, China, Algeria, Libya, Guatemala, Sudan and Saudi Arabia were purporting to sit in judgment on the human rights violations of others.

A full-time post of Commissioner of Human Rights was created after the Vienna Conference in 1993, but its first occupant was an undistinguished diplomat who refused to criticize any member state. He was succeeded by Mary Robinson, chosen (unusually) on ability rather than from diplomatic circles around the Secretary-General, but her budget was small and her influence over member states limited: Russia refused to co-operate with her visit to Chechnya and she had hurriedly to withdraw an early criticism of US bombing in Afghanistan.

She claimed to have been 'forced out' by US pressure and certainly she was replaced by a UN diplomat renowned for never criticizing anyone, but her own critics blamed the disastrous Durban 'World Conference against Racism, Racial Discrimination, Xenophobia and Related Intolerance' in August 2001, which showed the UN system at its worst. Human Rights Commission politics meant that the plight of Tibetans and the 'untouchable' low-caste Dalits would not feature on the agenda so as not to upset China and India; nor could the Taliban government be in any way embarrassed by reference to its destruction of ancient Buddhist monuments and its law requiring Hindus to wear yellow patches. What did feature was race-hatred against Jews over Israel and Americans over everything. Important issues such as the re-emergence of slavery in modern African states (Sudan, Mali, Niger and the Ivory Coast) were glossed over by a demand for compensation from the West for slavery centuries ago (the money to be paid to African states rather than to deserving descendants of victims). Israel was wildly (and wrongly) accused of 'genocide' by delegates who gave their longest ovations to Castro and Mugabe, two of the world's cruellest leaders who had turned up to bask in their applause. The Moroccan delegate, just after voting to end Third World prostitution, hired for his private pleasure several black sex workers, who robbed and then killed him: a grisly gift to the media cynics who look only at the corruption and hypocrisy on display at these UN talk-fests. The UN does not learn its lessons from such spectacles: ten years later all the usual suspects were back in Durban, to 'review progress' made by the 2001 conference. This time, sensible states like Canada, Australia and New Zealand stayed well away, but nothing could stop Iranian President Mahmoud Ahmadinejad turning up to deliver the opening speech, denouncing Israel as a state 'created on the pretext of Jewish sufferings and the ambiguous and dubious question of the Holocaust'. Thirty delegations walked out, while NGO participants who protested were formally removed: the BBC reported (once again) 'a public relations disaster for the United Nations'.[8]

The Human Rights Commission did itself disastrous and terminal damage in 2003 by electing Libya to chair its deliberations. No less than thirty-three of its fifty-three members voted for this one-time practitioner of torture, assassination and mid-flight aircraft destruction, after it was nominated by South Africa (only three countries – the US, Canada and Guatemala – voted against Libya). The Libyans claimed that the vote showed their government 'has a clean sheet with regard to human rights', but what it in fact showed was the disgusting hypocrisy and indeed stupidity of the African and Asian diplomats determined to produce, in the headline 'Libya Heads UN's Human Rights', the most indefensible of oxymorons.[9] The Commission's laughing-stock status caused an exasperated Kofi Annan to go on the attack, pointing out that 'states have sought membership of the Commission not to strengthen human rights but to protect themselves against criticism or to criticise others'. His efforts at the 2005 UN Summit to abolish the Commission and replace it with a much smaller, full-time body of states qualified by the excellence of their own human rights records was defeated – by African and Asian countries determined to stay in control.[10]

A modicum of sense prevailed in the General Assembly in 2006 when the Commission was abolished, although its replacement – the Human Rights Council – bore the hallmarks of compromise with the same African and Asian states which are determined that their violations will not be exposed or condemned. The Council now has a more positive and proactive mandate and meets for at least ten weeks a year with provision for emergency sessions, many of which were called in 2011, when the Arab Spring began to rain bullets. But the Council's composition remains unwieldy (forty-seven member states); it is made up of paltering diplomats rather than independent experts; and it will continue to meet in the expensive backwater of Geneva. Voting for candidates by General Assembly members remains secret and is divided into regional blocs. The only regional bloc consistently in support of human rights ('Western Europe and Others', i.e. the original EU countries plus Canada, Australia, New Zealand and the US) has been allotted merely seven seats. Voting states are meant to take into account 'the contribution of candidates to the protection of human rights', but this regional structure means that inevitably some of the countries whose presence disgraced the old Commission were returned to the new Council at the first election in May 2006. Some of these states have not even ratified the Civil Covenant (which ought to have been a prerequisite of membership), let alone the Optional Protocol subjecting them to the judgment of the Human Rights Committee.

In recent years, shamed by widespread criticism and dashed hopes, and with a more active Commissioner (Navi Pillay, formerly a war crimes judge), the Commission has risen to a few occasions. Its report on how in 2009 the government of Sri Lanka brutally ended the Tamil Tiger secession movement (LTTE) was independent and punctilious in criticizing both sides: the government of Sri Lanka refused all co-operation, and its friendly states at the UN blocked follow-up action (which should have been to establish a war crimes court) until March 2012, when the US took up the case and the Council called on the government to investigate properly the atrocities perpetrated by its troops. Although rightly criticized for its obsession with undermining Israel, the Council did set up a distinguished independent commission under Richard Goldstone to investigate the war in and on Gaza. Typically, Israel refused to co-operate, and viciously attacked Goldstone in various underhand ways (most disgracefully, through slanders spread among the Jewish diaspora) despite the even-handedness of his report which blamed Palestinian provocation as well as Israeli over-reaction. Its emergency report on Syria was expeditious and fair.

By 2012, after five years in operation, the Council's weaknesses had been amply demonstrated. Although states are required, when electing its members, to 'take into account the contribution of candidates to the promotion and protection of human rights,'[11] nineteen of these elected members had not ratified the Optional Protocol on the right of individual petition and three – Malaysia, Qatar and Saudi Arabia – had not even ratified the Civil Convention itself. A number of elected members had dreadful human rights records, notably *China* (which had put the 2010 Nobel Peace Prize winner, Liu Xiaobo, in prison for eleven years for advocating democracy); *Indonesia*, which viciously represses the independence movement in West Papua; *Jordan*, which stands accused by Amnesty of being 'the central hub in a global complex of secret detention centres operated by the US';[12] *Saudi Arabia*, where women are not permitted to travel abroad without written permission of a male guardian and whose male rapists can only be convicted on the testimony of four witnesses;[13] *Azerbaijan*, which jails and tortures political dissidents; *Cuba*, which represses almost all forms of political dissent and jails journalists who criticize either or both of the Castros; *The Philippines*, repeatedly condemned by the Council's own rapporteur for failing to stop 'disappearances' and summary executions by its military;[14] *Pakistan*, guilty of the worst excesses in the 'war on terror', and of permitting capital punishment for blasphemy (in 2010, Asia Bibi was sentenced to death for criticizing the Prophet Muhammed); and *Nigeria*, whose police stand accused of widespread torture and of such brutality that in April 2011 it sparked violence in which 800 were killed.[15] The election of these countries to the Council does not appear to have taken into account their 'contribution . . . to the promotion and protection of human rights'.

The main work of the Human Rights Council, by which it deserves to be judged, is its universal periodic review of every country's human rights record. This operates in three stages: 'self-assessment' by the state in a twenty-page report; public presentation of that report for thirty minutes followed by thirty minutes of questioning; then a published summary of the proceedings prepared by a working group. It is at the second stage that contributions from NGOs and independent experts may intrude, through reports and questioning, so as to give the Council's 'monitoring' exercise significant enough impact for states to take it seriously. Many do, to the extent that they send high-level delegations and take care over their reports. The problem is that Council members let them off lightly: criticisms are rare, and the reporting state can recruit its allies to 'stack' the review meeting and offer platitudinous compliments. Regional alliances protect their own members: when the corrupt and repressive Ben Ali government came up for review in 2008, for example, fifty of the sixty-five statements made on its report were of vapid praise, mainly by Tunisia's allies in African and Muslim countries.[16] These lying diplomats were confounded, three years later, by the Tunisian people, who took back their rights without the slightest help from the Human Rights Council. Even worse was the session on Iran, orchestrated by allies like Bangladesh, Lebanon and Nicaragua, which pretended that its murderous repression could be forgiven because of its history.[17] Disgustingly, the session ended with orchestrated applause. Diplomats have made a nonsense of the Council's claim to be objective and apolitical, and it is to Ban Ki-moon's credit that, in exasperation, he told its members 'you must rise above partisan posturing and regional divides.'[18]

This has proved impossible in the case of Israel, which a majority of council members cordially loathe and obsessively condemn. Since its inception, no fewer than thirty-nine (i.e. 44 per cent) of its state-specific resolutions have targeted Israel, compared with only one against Iran (passed belatedly in 2011, two years after its brutal repression of the Green Movement), one each against Belarus and Yemen, two against Syria and Libya, and none at all against Cuba, China and Saudi Arabia (which are, of course, Council members). This wildly disproportionate focus on Israel – the only state which is a standing item on the Council's agenda – seriously undermines its work, especially in regard to Israel itself. Its twenty-two-day 'war' on Gaza killed some 1,400 Palestinians – most of them civilians (including 300 children) compared with four Israeli civilians (killed by Palestinian rockets) and ten Israeli soldiers (three killed by friendly fire). This massive disparity alone demanded an enquiry into a military operation which had been provoked by years of unlawful rocket attacks on Israeli targets, launched by Hamas from the Palestine side of the border. But the Council Resolution establishing an 'independent international fact-finding mission' was tasked solely with investigating violations 'by the occupying power, Israel, against the Palestinian people', and the Resolution itself decided the issue without awaiting the found facts, by condemning Israel for 'massive violations of the human rights of the Palestinian people' and by 'recognizing' that the Israeli siege constituted 'collective punishment of Palestinian civilians'. These were the very issues that the committee should have been tasked to decide. Mary Robinson, the first human rights grandee to be asked to head the mission, sensibly declined, pointing out how one-sided the investigation would be by looking at Israel alone. She regretted the practice of the Council 'adopting Resolutions guided not by human rights, but by politics'. Richard Goldstone then accepted the poisoned chalice, but only after the President of the Council had agreed to alter his mandate to permit investigation of the Palestinian provocation.

Despite Goldstone's standing, and that of his colleagues, the inquiry was dogged by the bias against Israel so palpably displayed by the Council that commissioned it. This gave Israel an excuse not to co-operate, and a 'free kick' for its critics when it reported. The facts it found were undeniably shocking, but its inferential conclusion – that 'Operation Cast Lead' between 27 December 2008 and 18 January 2009 amounted to 'collective punishment' intentionally inflicted on the civilian population of the Gaza Strip in order to punish, humiliate and terrorize them for harbouring Hamas fighters – was predictably controversial. Israel rejected it out of hand, but many of that state's criticisms were undermined by its own failure to co-operate with Goldstone.[19] Human Rights Watch supported the report, and Amnesty pointed out that its findings were consistent with its own field observations. For all the fury on the Israeli side (and some of the critics, notably Alan Dershowitz, demonstrated that it gave Hamas the benefit of too much doubt and gave no credit to Israel for taking some steps to minimize casualties), the Report produced evidence that no honest Israeli could dispute. As Britain's UN envoy put it, 'the Goldstone report itself did not adequately recognise Israel's right to protect its citizens, nor did it pay sufficient attention to Hamas's actions. But the concerns raised in the report cannot be ignored.' They were, of course, ignored by the Security Council, even though they were replicated by other enquiries, notably by John Dugard and other distinguished human rights monitors, who conducted a parallel enquiry for the Arab League. Goldstone himself became a target for lies and smears, condemned as a 'self-hating Jew'.[20] In 2011 he wrote an article in the *Washington Post* retracting the report's most controversial claim, that Israel intentionally targeted civilians, because this was based on the 'record before us' and since when there had been fresh evidence of Israel's intentions.[21] His three colleagues however, issued a statement endorsing their report and refusing retrospectively to 'sanitize' its conclusions.[22]

For all the controversy, the Goldstone report did lead to changes in Israel Defense Forces procedures for protecting civilians in urban warfare and for using white phosphorus, and it did criticize Hamas (although not as severely as that organization deserved) for its unprovoked rocket attacks and for putting civilians at risk by deliberately having its combatants fire their rockets from densely populated areas and using mosques, hospitals and schools for military purposes. It was the political bias of the Human Rights Council which did most damage to the report's credibility, and it would be much more satisfactory if such valuable initiatives were henceforth instigated by the apolitical Human Rights Commissioner rather than by a dubious body of diplomats. Any report into state aggression is bound to attract controversy, and outrage from the state in question and its allies, but reports which turn up clear evidence of crimes against humanity should always and automatically be forwarded by the Security Council to the prosecutor of the International Criminal Court. This has not been done in respect of other reports to the Council, most notably the impressive expert report on the armed conflict in Sri Lanka, which was even-handed and found both sides guilty of war crimes. The leaders of the losing side – the Tamil Tigers – had been exterminated, and the failure of the Security Council to take steps to further investigate the actions of the government troops was deplorable. There is some hope that the Human Rights Council will serve as an early warning system to jolt the Security Council into action when it receives reports which characterize atrocities as crimes against humanity, but it is probably more realistic at this stage to see it as little more than a portent of great power reaction. In December 2011, for example, the Human Rights Council received a report on the continuing killings in Syria (4,000 at that point) and, at the insistence of the EU, condemned them as a crime against humanity – a decision that should have led to the Security Council referring the situation to the ICC. Thirty-six states of the Council voted in favour of this condemnation and only four against, but the latter included China and Russia, states which wield vetoes over any Security Council action in respect to Syria, including ICC referrals. So no referral was made, and the casualties mounted.

THE HUMAN RIGHTS COMMITTEE SYSTEM

States voting in favour of the Universal Declaration in 1948 did not anticipate for a moment that their vote meant they were assuming any obligation to enforce the rights declared. None the less, Article 28 momentously decreed that 'Everyone is entitled to a social and international order in which the rights and freedoms set forth in this Declaration can be fully realized'. So the General Assembly directed the Human Rights Commission to proceed with the drafting of a treaty which would, upon ratification, oblige states to guarantee human rights to their citizens as part of their domestic law and would set up some mechanism to monitor their progress to this end. The chill winds of the Cold War blew the Commission delegates this way and that, finally splitting along ideological lines over the relative importance of civil and political rights on one hand (favoured by western European and American states) and economic and social rights on the other (which were preferred by communist countries). With what seemed like the wisdom of Solomon, the Commission agreed to prepare a separate covenant for each set of rights, but these were not tabled in the UN until 1966. The General Assembly then expressed the pious hope that the twin Covenants would be 'signed and ratified without delay and come into force at an early date'. That date was set for the time when a mere thirty-five states would ratify them, but this did not happen for an entire decade. Even when they commenced in 1976, they had little superpower support – the US refused to put its money where Jimmy Carter's mouth was (it did not ratify the Civil Covenant until 1992) and although it now has 167 members, states which still, as of 2012, refuse to ratify include Singapore, Saudi Arabia, Malaysia, Cuba and Burma. Fewer (114) have signed the all-important 'Optional Protocol' to the Civil Covenant, which provides a means by which individual victims of human rights violations may complain to an international body, the Human Rights Committee – established by the Covenant and situated in Geneva. Of the world's ten most powerful countries, only two have signed up to the Optional Protocol. The Economic and Social Covenant provides no such complaints mechanism: member states are supposed to submit five-yearly reports on their 'progress' in guaranteeing second generation rights to a subcommittee of the Economic and Social Council, but most countries' reports are overdue and the subcommittee has no power to do anything about these defaults.

That these twin Covenants staggered into being at all, thirty years after they were envisaged as the machinery for enforcing the Universal Declaration, owed something to the atrocious brutality of events during those inglorious years: by 1976, most of the ratifying governments were sensitive enough to see that the world could not go on in this fashion, and that one way forward might be to recapture the idealism which had briefly surfaced after the war. National Socialism was aped, in a less extreme but generally vicious form, by apartheid – the one systemic violation of human rights which by this time had united almost every state in public condemnation. Its 'master race' ideology (the black majority were to be treated like children who would never grow up) was harnessed to pervasive discrimination enforced by brutal policing and controlled by a white Afrikaner minority with elders who had, during the war, supported the Nazis. But there was a good deal of hypocrisy about these attacks on South Africa: the Soviet Union was first to sponsor the International Convention on the Suppression and Punishment of the Crime of Apartheid, despite all the dissidents still in its gulags and its own suppression of majorities in satellite states. Black African countries, mired in corruption and brutal 'big man' tyranny, joined in hypocritical condemnation of court systems in South Africa and Rhodesia much fairer than their own. Notwithstanding such double standards, agreement between East and West that apartheid constituted a violation of human rights meant that a consensus could be reached on establishing some institutions to protect them. Hence, in 1969, the Convention on the Elimination of All Forms of Racial Discrimination (CERD), established the Committee on the Elimination of Racial Discrimination, which could, with the consent of a state, receive complaints by individuals. What the evils of fascism inspired in the post-war settlement, it took the evils of apartheid to put back on the global agenda.

The Human Rights Committee (HRC for short) was established

under Article 28 of the International Covenant on Civil and Political Rights. Its role is two-fold: (1) to 'study' reports submitted at five-year intervals by state parties and to relay 'observations' to those states about their performance in promoting human rights; (2) to serve as the body to which individuals or groups may complain against their state if it has signed the Optional Protocol to the Convention – a distinct treaty by which some states indicate their willingness to allow their nationals access to the HRC but not necessarily (as we shall see) to co-operate with the Committee or to implement its adjudications. Although the eighteen members of the HRC serve in theory in their personal capacities rather than as representatives of states, they are, like the members of the Human Rights Council, none the less nominated by governments which usually make sure that their nominees are 'one of us' – i.e. are fully alive to the importance of state sovereignty and the need to avoid criticism of their nominator and its allies. The HRC should operate, at least when considering individual complaints under the Optional Protocol, as a body composed of experts independent of all countries, but the UN election system does not produce a lot of HRC members in this category. Many are ambassadors, or lawyers serving in government departments, who carry their diplomatic baggage to Geneva and New York for a few weeks of HRC meetings each year, and currently the majority are academics. Few have any professional commitment to independence or impartiality – states seem reluctant to nominate real judges, or independent legal professionals.

The Human Rights Committee has a number of equivalents under separate human rights treaties. The Convention on the Elimination of Racial Discrimination has 175 state parties but only fifty-four of them have declared in favour of allowing individual complaints to its committee. The Convention on the Rights of Persons with Disabilities (2008), the first human rights treaty of the twenty-first century, already has 117 state parties: its committee is, appropriately, chaired by a blind law professor, Ron McCallum. The Convention against Torture (150 state members) has an Optional Protocol whereby its sixty-three state parties permit its subcommittee on Prevention of Cruel, Inhumane and Degrading Treatment or Punishment to access their prisons and police stations and provide confidential reports that they are encouraged to make public. This subcommittee was only established in 2007 and has the makings of a body that ought to be compulsory for all UN members: at present only states with forward-thinking penology have agreed to sign up (i.e. not China or the United States, or Russia or India). Even so, in its 2010 report it expressed some frustration at obtaining information from prisoners, who feared reprisals if they co-operated.[23] State parties should be prepared to give an undertaking to allow the Committee to meet prisoners in complete privacy and to investigate any case where they may have suffered reprisals.

The Human Rights Committee and the Committee on the Elimination of Racial Discrimination are, self-evidently, 'committees' as distinct from courts (which have adversary proceedings ending with judgments in some manner binding on parties). Their operations are circumscribed by diplomatic politesse: they do not receive 'applications' or 'petitions' or 'complaints', they merely get *written communications*. These are not 'analysed' or 'investigated', they *receive consideration*. The government concerned has the allegation *brought to its attention* and must, within a leisurely six months, submit a statement which *clarifies* the matter. The committees do not hold any hearings, in public or indeed at all: they *examine communications* in a closed meeting and in due course, instead of delivering a judgment or decision, they *forward their views* to the government and to the communicant. These excruciating euphemisms need not have prevented the HRC itself from developing into a powerful, quasi-curial body, delivering well-reasoned and intellectually respectable decisions. But throughout its history it has become submerged within the UN culture: starved of funds, with eighteen part-time members of variable quality and integrity and a handful of overworked staff, its 'views' tend to be brief, poorly argued opinions on the facts, excessively deferential to states and quick to take refuge in technicalities as a way to avoid adverse decisions. No one who has visited its offices in a nondescript UN building in Geneva could possibly think of it as an enforcer of any universal bill of rights.

Such significance as the Committee's decisions (sorry, 'views') may have is due to factors outside its control. For example, the time it takes to form 'views' on 'communications' from Caribbean death rows may save a communicant's life – but that is thanks to the Privy Council ruling in *Pratt and Morgan* v. *Jamaica* to the effect that undue appellate delay prevents imposition of the death penalty (see p. 191). Ironically, the HRC itself refused to adopt this principle, which has saved hundreds of lives in the British Commonwealth – an example of how street-ignorant HRC members can be about lives on death row and the expedients necessary to preserve them. Judges on the European Court and the Privy Council hold (and psychiatrists agree) that leaving men on death row more than five years amounts to inhumane treatment, but the HRC finds no inhumanity in keeping men there for eleven years – or even longer, should a state so choose.[24]

The HRC has served a useful purpose in cases where federal governments make use of its 'views' as a basis for taking action against their own regressive provincial legislatures, as when the HRC held that freedom of expression of English-speaking Quebecois was violated when that province passed a law forcing them to advertise in the French language.[25] Similarly, in the *Toonen Case*,[26] the federal government of Australia was able to abolish the criminalization of homosexual conduct in its least enlightened state, Tasmania, by reference to the 'view' of the HRC that this was an unreasonable measure not excused by its pretended object of curbing the spread of AIDS/ HIV. The Committee did act in this case like a court, delivering an important and well-argued decision that the Covenant right not to be discriminated against on grounds of sex included sexual orientation. This provides a rare example of how the HRC might, if cut loose from the diplomatic apron strings of the UN, function genuinely to advance the cause of human rights. But it provides that example only because the decision against Australia was actually encouraged and supported by Australia itself, embarrassed by the homophobic Tasmanians. Had Toonen been a Malaysian or a Cuban, the decision would have been different (in fact, since those states have not accepted the Optional Protocol, there would have been no decision at all).

The HRC, CERD and other obscurely acronymed UN organs have another familiar function: to 'monitor progress' by receiving reports at regular intervals – every five years or so – from state parties. This at least provides a public occasion at which state representatives – often minor diplomatic functionaries rather than government ministers – are politely questioned about their reports which claim, often falsely, that great progress is being made in protecting or extending the covenanted rights. There is endemic delay in submission of reports – most states miss the deadline, some by ten years – with no sanction for non-compliance, although CERD has recently adopted the practice of reviewing defaulting states in any event, which has increased compliance. This backlog in state submissions is matched by unconscionable delay by the Committee itself – sometimes 3–4 years – in dealing with the reports which are submitted.[27] In these circumstances the violating states are not discomfited by 'comments' the HRC chooses to make, because they can deny their relevance. The examination process itself is painless: there are no on-site inspections or demands to meet victims or oppositionists to hear their side of the story. The public presentation of the report is a polite occasion: there is no grilling, or any form of cross-examination: questions are very often parried by the delegate promising to find out the answer in order to reply later in writing. The occasion does provide non-governmental organizations like Amnesty and Human Rights Watch with the opportunity to brief sympathetic committee members and to focus public attention on a country's real failings. But the HRC strives to avoid any criticism in its reports of the states whose records it has considered: Article 40 of the Covenant permits it only to make 'such general comments as it may consider appropriate', which it generally takes to mean uncritical and unspecific comments couched in weasel words (the most appalling violations are noted with 'regret' or 'disappointment' or an 'expression of deep concern'). Thus Libya, a truly brutal state, submitted its report in 1995, just after Gaddafi had given a blood-curdling order for assassination of expatriate dissidents, and while he was thwarting justice over Lockerbie. His report was short and utterly dishonest. Three years later the HRC issued its verdict, complimenting Libya on its treatment of women and expressing polite 'concern' at the murder and torture of oppositionists and the lack of any independent legal system. Libya was unconcerned at these 'comments' – perhaps the most critical the HRC has ever issued.[28] As we have seen, in 2003 when Libya was elected to chair the Human Rights Commission, it was able to claim this was an honour bestowed because of the excellence of its human rights record.

A number of UN conventions establish a 'committee of experts' given a quasi-judicial duty to monitor compliance, consider state reports and investigate complaints. But these committees, like the Human Rights Committee itself, are relatively ineffectual. Their 'experts' are chosen by states, i.e. by diplomats, and their most common qualification seems to be a lack of resolve to rock any boat. The most notorious example is the committee of experts attached to what should be the UN's most influential Convention – that of the rights of the child, ratified by every nation in the world except the failed state of Somalia, the US (which has at least signed it) and the brand-new state of South Sudan. From 2002 onwards, it became public knowledge that the Vatican (a state party) was conniving in widespread child sexual abuse by paedophile priests, covering up their crimes and imposing 'canon law' duties on bishops to keep them hidden from police and law-enforcement authorities. As the scandal erupted in country after country (for example, judicial enquiries in Ireland published in 2010 described sexual abuse as 'endemic' in Catholic boys' institutions) it became clear that tens of thousands of children had been molested by Catholic priests.[29] Yet 'the committee of experts' did absolutely nothing about the unfolding scandal, and did not even chide the Vatican for its abject failure to deliver reports to the committee or (when it did report in 2010) for its claim that civil authorities like the police had no business intervening in matters of family privacy.[30] This argument (that families should be left in peace to decide to let the Church handle allegations of abuse, secretly and without punishing paedophile priests other than by an occasional quiet defrocking) flatly contradicted the international law duty on states, imposed by Articles 19 and 34, to require that all cases of child sexual abuse be reported to law enforcement authorities. In the case of this Church, of course, it had been established that many bishops had moved paedophile priests to unsuspecting parishes, or transferred them to other countries, placing the interests of the Church's reputation ahead of the interests of children. Amnesty International took up the issue in 2010, but not a word has been heard from the children's convention's 'committee of experts'.

The glaring weakness of the UN committee system of state reports and individual communications is that many states which violate the human rights of their citizens are not parties to the Covenant or have not ratified the Optional Protocol permitting individuals to communicate with the Committee. Among Optional Protocol refuseniks are superpowers America and China, and even Britain. Many states which are party to the Optional Protocol simply ignore the Committee: in recent cases, Libya, Peru and the Central African Republic have not bothered to reply to its letters. Equatorial Guinea told the HRC in effect to get lost when it asked why an opposition MP was abducted and tortured by security forces over a period of eighteen months: this very inquiry, apparently, constituted an 'interference into domestic affairs of Equatorial Guinea'. It is the old story: countries like Canada and Australia, which on the whole value human rights and co-operate with UN organs, can utilize the HRC, elevating its 'views' into decisions which strengthen their hand against provincial legislatures if they pass laws which discriminate against minorities. But countries which care nothing for human rights can quite brazenly ignore the HRC, or simply remain outside the voluntary covenant system. There is no 'universality' about this human rights system, even among its own signatories. The Covenant assumes that complaints will be made by one state against another, but dog does not eat dog at the UN: not a single inter-state complaint has been made since the system came into operation in 1979. By 2011, no fewer than 114 states had ratified the Optional Protocol. But its 2011 report admits that only 731 of its 2,076 communications over the past forty years had resulted in 'views' that a violation had occurred. In only 15 per cent of these cases did the defaulting state implement the HRC 'view' or provide any remedy to the complainant. This is a record of failure, and its 'grave concern over the lack of sufficient staff resources and translation services which hampers its activities' (2011 report) would perhaps be met with more sympathy were it to issue powerful and well-reasoned judgments on issues of individual liberty. Instead it too often busies itself with issues that belong to economic or social campaigns, such as its critique of government subsidies for biofuels and its solemn declaration, on World Toilet Day, that adequate access to toilets is a human right (surely it is a human necessity).

The deficiencies in the UN committee system are due to the endemic failure of that organization to allow for criticisms of its own members. If the 'views' of the HRC and its expert committees are ever to be accorded respect, the following structural problems will have to be overcome:

(1) The HRC is meant to comprise eighteen 'experts', but UN election procedures ensure that many are government mouthpieces (some being actually *in* government service) or else owe their 'expertise' to *defending* governments. Some members are reasonably independent academics or judges, but few, if any, have acted for victims. As one long-serving member writes (delicately), appointment depends on 'the lobbying effectiveness of the nominee's country's representatives at the UN, bloc voting and general diplomatic bargaining . . . as a result, a high premium is not always placed on those individual qualities which are most important, such as competence'.[31]

(2) The HRC only meets three times a year, and CERD twice, for three-week sessions. The idea that nine weeks a year is a satisfactory commitment to monitoring and problem-solving under the Covenant is risible.

(3) The HRC holds no 'hearings' and makes no provision for oral applications or adversary proceedings. Everything is done on paper, very slowly, without the benefit of live-witness testimony or cross-examination.

(4) The HRC is entirely dependent on the UN Secretariat in terms of structure, budget and status. It is not a quasi-judicial body, much less a court: most accurately, it is a UN 'organ' which goes out of its way to avoid criticizing UN members.

(5) The Civil Covenant concerns the duties of states towards individuals, not the rights of individuals against states. The HRC cannot compel or even pressure states to do these duties – most violators stay outside it, or refuse to sign the Optional

Protocol or (if they do) refuse none the less to co-operate with the HRC.

(6) The HRC and other UN committees lack any independent fact-finding capacity. Not only do they have no investigative powers, resources or personnel, but they cannot even make visits to alleged crime scenes or call for relevant documents or cross-examine witnesses and experts. This is a crippling weakness for the HRC, which makes its monitoring role ineffective (unless assisted by NGOs) and leaves it to find facts on the basis of written communications, which in many cases is not possible.

(7) The HRC work goes largely unreported and none but a handful of victims of human rights violations around the world will ever hear of it. That is partly because its proceedings are closed and its files remain confidential and its 'views', when published, are often not worth reading, in the sense that they usually lack detailed reasoning.

(8) It has no power to enforce its 'views', which states frequently ignore. Indeed, sometimes death row prisoners are targeted for execution precisely because they have written to the HRC – they, and their letters, are dead on arrival.

These problems of the HRC are endemic to CERD and all other UN bodies established to 'monitor compliance' with human rights conventions. Those oversight committees have no power to call to account states which neglect or refuse to submit reports – in its 2011 report, the HRC deprecated the large number of state parties which do not comply with their reporting obligations. The current UN Commissioner for Human Rights, Navi Pillay, has called for reforms to make the UN treaty body system more coherent and more effective, but the ideas coming out of her think-tanks on the subject are underwhelming. States that fail to report should be reviewed *in absentia* and non-compliance taken into account if they stand for election to the Human Rights Council; delegations should have more experts; elections should be more transparent, with candidates elected on merit rather than on political connections. These are all overdue reforms, but will not redress the eight defects listed above. The UN system cannot, by its very nature, offer satisfactory methods of enforcing human rights, because it cannot compel violating states to join its protocols. Should they do so, the UN's methods for 'monitoring' performance give little confidence that this would expose violations or lead to greater obedience to the rules of international human rights law.

SOME ENFORCEMENT AT LAST: THE EUROPEAN CONVENTION, AND OTHER REGIONS

Although the United Nations dropped the human rights baton soon after the Universal Declaration, it was picked up by the Council of Europe, a body which co-ordinated the dozen democracies in that region which were determined to resist the spread of communism. In 1950 it promulgated the European Convention on Human Rights, which combined the civil liberties articles in the Universal Declaration with fair trial principles drawn from English common law. Its preamble describes the Convention as one of 'the first steps for the collective enforcement of certain rights stated in the Universal Declaration', although it turned out, for many years, to be the only step. It was real progress, none the less, and a marked improvement on the Declaration in terms of a clearer definition of the rights of suspects, *habeas corpus* and the requirements for fair trial, although the rights to freedom of speech and assembly and privacy were hedged by numerous exceptions and qualifications. It established a commission which could refer cases for final decision to a court, sitting in Strasbourg: state signatories to the Convention had a duty, in the event of any adverse judgment, to change their law to bring it into conformity with the Convention. This was revolutionary enough – the first time in history that states were prepared to give an external court a treaty power to *require* changes in their domestic legislation – but there was a provision more revolutionary still. Under Article 25 of the European

Convention, 'any person, non-governmental organization or group' could petition the Commission alleging a violation of their rights, and if the Commission agreed with them it could bring their case before the European Court. States which accepted this 'right of individual petition' would in effect be giving their citizens the opportunity to bring them – or their own law and their own court decisions – before the bar of international justice.

The European Convention was something of a marvel at the time – 1953 – when it entered into force as a legal bulwark against the resurgence of fascism and as an articulation of the civil rights which were being threatened by communist regimes in eastern Europe. However, it took several decades before the European Court made its presence felt, largely because governments delayed in accepting Article 25 and refused to complain about each other (the only exceptions were cases brought by Ireland against the UK over 'in-depth interrogation', by several Scandinavian countries against Greece under the Colonels, and over torture in Turkey and UK dominion over Cyprus). After the mid-1970s, however, the court at Strasbourg grew in business and in reputation, so much so that it was besieged after 1989 by newly liberated eastern European states clamouring to be admitted as members. It now lays down quite sophisticated human rights standards for forty-seven nations, from Iceland to Turkey and from Latvia to Malta, through well-reasoned decisions which have made governments change domestic laws in all these countries. Governments can formally 'derogate' from the Convention rather than accept an adverse decision; however, compliance is normal and the quality of the human rights law emerging from the Court's Richard Rogers-designed building in Strasbourg is relatively high. Crucially, if negatively, its success may be due to the fact that it has no connection whatsoever with the United Nations.

What has made the European Court stand head and shoulders above any UN or other regional arrangement is the simple fact that adverse decisions are implemented, under supervision. State parties comply (albeit sometimes not quickly or adequately) with its rulings, even though they generally require legislation or some restructuring of the domestic legal system. It has now become a constitutional court for the whole continent. That does not, of course, mean that its decisions have always been correct or its approach beyond reproach. Under a coward's cloak called 'the margin of appreciation', this court has often dodged controversial issues by leaving them to the discretion allowed to states to protect their own values and traditions. This tendency has been particularly marked in questions of morality, where several poorly reasoned rulings have permitted censorship by rulings that bans on anti-Christian plays and films are within state 'margins of appreciation'. The Court has wrongly refused to strike down blasphemy laws in the UK and Austria, although such laws are the cause of serious human rights violations by Iran (the Salman Rushdie *fatwah*) and Bangladesh.[32] However, it has been prepared to extend a degree of tolerance to homosexuals, at least in countries where there is no 'large body of opinion hostile or intolerant towards homosexual acts committed in private between consenting adults'[33] – an unsatisfactory rationale which would allow sodomy to remain a crime in Malaysia and other Muslim states. The whole point of human rights law is to protect innocent minorities against malevolent prejudice, and the 'margin of appreciation' doctrine, appropriate for cases where there are harmless cultural differences, should not be erected into a shield for majority oppression. Outside the area of morals, however, the doctrine has been given a narrower application, and the Court has been much more rigorous in protecting the rights of suspects, even of terrorist suspects who cannot – except in times of emergency or by states (like the UK) which formally derogate from the law – be held for interrogation for longer than four days without access to a court.

The European Court of Human Rights has become the model human rights court, proof positive that international law can work to enforce fundamental freedoms across a swathe of countries despite some differences in culture and tradition. This court's decisions have seeped into the domestic jurisdictions of all its client countries, as every one of its original member governments has made changes in its laws for the benefit of groups such as immigrants, transvestites, prisoners and mental patients – reforms which would not have been sufficiently vote-winning in the absence of a decision from Strasbourg. Despite periods of unpopularity with particular governments, the

Court has won substantial respect and support, and in 1998 the Council of Europe re-established it on an expanded and improved basis. It now has a permanent and properly salaried judiciary, unlike any of the UN commissions and committees. The 'filter' device of the European Commission has been replaced by a two-tier system in which cases are heard first by a chamber of seven judges and then – if the legal point is important – it may be decided by many more judges sitting in a 'grand chamber'. The real problem for the European Court is that of becoming the victim of its own success: it is swamped with applications, especially from Turkey and Russia and former satellites of the Soviet Union. In 2010 it received 61,300 applications: over half were rejected as inadmissible, and it managed to deliver judgments in respect of 2,607 applications. But it simply cannot cope with the rising tide of complaints from Eastern Europe – many of them justified.

Unfortunately, the 1998 Council of Europe reforms retain one irritating feature of international justice which is simply not just. This is the practice, which began in the International Court of Justice, of having a judge from the 'defendant' state sit on every hearing and appeal as a full voting member of the court. This is a blatant breach of the rule against bias, since justice cannot be seen to be done by a judge who is there to look after the defendant's interests. It provides a much clearer case of bias than appeared in *Ex parte Pinochet (No. 2)*, where a judge's indirect connection with Amnesty International was held to disqualify him from sitting in a case where Amnesty was presenting argument.[34] The official reason for the practice was to reassure nervous governments that the court would have at least one sympathetic member who would know about the domestic legal system, but this is no longer a necessary political expedient. There have been some abject examples of the 'state party judge' defending his indefensible state (when the UK was held in breach for permitting the caning of juvenile delinquents, for example, the English judge dissented on the grounds that his own beatings at Eton had done him a power of good).

There are other regional arrangements outside the United Nations which offer a measure of legal protection of human rights for subscribing countries within their geographical area. There is an

Inter-American system, with a convention (1969), a commission (in Washington DC) and a court (sited in Costa Rica), which covers many Latin American and Caribbean members of the Organization of American States (OAS). There is also the African Charter on Human and Peoples' Rights (1981), with a commission to monitor and to receive complaints about its breach, which is headquartered in Banjul in the Gambia and is financed and supervised by the African Union. There have been occasional human rights initiatives on behalf of the fifty-four states comprising the British Commonwealth, which encompasses no less than one quarter of the world's population. A dozen of these countries – Mauritius, Belize, Jamaica, Trinidad and other Caribbean islands – accept the Privy Council, comprising English law lords, as their final court of appeal: its binding constitutional decisions make it in effect an external human rights court whose judgments are directly enforceable. For this reason, Singapore pulled out when it criticized Lee Kuan Yew, and some Caribbean governments have been so angered by its landmark decisions which prevent the imposition of death penalties that they are trying to replace this 'remnant of colonialism' with a court of Caribbean judges, who they think will be more likely to approve of hangings – the punishment so often meted out to black slaves by their colonial masters. Politicians in favour of hanging have greeted Privy Council decisions that have stopped executions with demands to transfer its jurisdiction to the Caribbean Court of Justice. The chances of this commercial tribunal acquiring power of final decision on human rights will depend on whether the people are prepared to vote to abolish the Privy Council in referenda or by the entrenched parliamentary majorities required by the constitutions of the various islands. The signs are that they repose more trust in judges of the Privy Council to call their politicians to account than in local judges appointed by those same politicians.[35]

Regrettably, attempts to broaden Privy Council membership and extend its jurisdiction have failed, leaving the Commonwealth with no effective mechanism for deterring oppressive conduct by its members, whether in the form of Mugabe's electoral fraud and his racist attacks on whites, or military overthrow of democratic government (in Nigeria, Pakistan and Fiji). It does little more than provide a colourful biennial, the Commonwealth Heads of Government Meeting (CHOGM), at which dictators may be pictured in national costume cosying up to the Queen (and wondering anxiously whether their absence from the presidential palace might provide – as it sometimes has – the opportunity for a coup against them). The CHOGM meeting in Perth (Australia) in 2011 ended any hope that this organization would work as a force for human rights: a recommendation to this effect by its elder statespeople was decisively and derisively rejected by politicians from the majority of its fifty-four members who did not want judges looking over their shoulders. The 'black Commonwealth', which remains in the grip of homophobia (the Ugandan parliament is seriously discussing whether to impose the death penalty) was concerned that any Commonwealth court might deliver liberal rulings on the subject, and there was much sympathy for Sri Lanka, which had so recently solved its Tamil separatist problem by the indiscriminate killing of Tamils. With a show of contempt for human rights, the organization chose Sri Lanka for its 2013 conference – thereby giving its imprimatur to mass execution without trial of people that governments designated as terrorist supporters, even though they may only be related to or living in the same geographical area as armed insurgents.

There is no external or regional system for Arab or Asian countries and the old 'regionalism versus globalism' debate now seems particularly arid: since there is no effective global system, regional arrangements are much to be encouraged if they work. The European Court and the Privy Council do work, because their judgments have power to bind governments. The Inter-American system is patchy, but better than nothing, while the African Commission is powerless. This varied performance has little to do with the core documents: the Inter-American Convention is, if anything, a slight improvement on the text of the European Convention, and both concentrate on the civil liberties protected by the overlapping UN Convention on Civil and Political Rights. The African Charter is worthy of note because it includes 'third generation' rights (e.g. to development) and counterbalances individual rights with 'peoples' duties' to African society and culture, and to its often corrupt and authoritarian governments.

The Inter-American system has had some signal successes. Its commission, operating from Washington (the US is a signatory to the treaty although it does not accept the jurisdiction of the Commission or the Court), conducted a number of expert on-site investigations into disappearances and atrocities in the military dictatorships of Latin America in the late 1970s and 1980s. To some extent its work was more political than legal, providing authoritative fact-finding reports which did something to galvanize international opinion against the worst offenders. It had a relatively small and cohesive composition of seven members, with staff well funded by the Carter administration. (There were cut-backs under Reagan, whose support for right-wing regimes in the region was undermined by the Commission's work.) It has been criticized for ignoring individual petitions, but at the time its role as a hemispheric accusatory agency, collecting and publicizing evidence against military dictators or their corrupt judges, was more valuable.[36] When Latin American countries began their transition to democracy, the Commission concentrated on finding legal ways of invalidating or sidestepping the amnesties and immunities which the Generals exacted for themselves and their henchmen as the price of giving up power. Much of its work is now directed to delaying executions of petitioners on death row in those Caribbean countries which adhere to the Inter-American Convention.

The Commission also serves as a filter for the Inter-American Court, which has (like its European equivalent in Strasbourg) treaty powers to require state parties to change their laws. Individuals have no direct right of access, but their cases may be taken up by the Commission which appears as a party on their behalf, although curiously a political rivalry between the two bodies has disinclined the Commission to make many referrals. This is regrettable, since the seven-person court has boasted some fine jurists, like the American Thomas Buergenthal and the Costa Rican Sonia Sotela, and the comparatively few judgments it has given have signally contributed to the development of human rights law. One of the first, in 1985, was a decision that requiring journalists to join a government-controlled association as a condition of practising their craft was an infringement of freedom of expression – a ruling which demolished a misguided UNESCO initiative to encourage government 'licensing' of journalists.[37] Then came the notable *Velasquez Rodriguez Case*, breaking new ground by ordering a government to pay reparations to the family of a young man 'disappeared' by the military in Honduras (see p. 362). Needless to say, the Court would gain enormously in workload and prestige were the United States to ratify the Inter-American Convention and accept its jurisdiction – an unlikely event, given the traditional refusal of Congress to bow to international judgment.

The African Charter deserves a final word, if only to explain why it fails to live up to its promise of 'third generation' rights to peace, development and a satisfactory environment. The first draft, by a Senegalese judge, Kéba Mbaye, was no doubt a worthy attempt to fuse statements of individual liberty with cultural duties believed to be distinctly African (such as the duty 'to respect parents at all times, to maintain them in case of need'). However, the Charter became the creature of the Organization of African Unity (OAU), a rabidly political organization which was dominated by some of the worst violators of human rights, such as Mengistu, Barre, Mobutu, Gaddafi and Idi Amin (whose barbaric rule in Uganda no member state except Tanzania had the decency to criticize). The OAU, ironically for all its commitment to anti-colonialism, had as its central concern the maintenance of Africa's old colonial borders, drawn haphazardly in the nineteenth century, and mindlessly opposed any form of intervention in the internal affairs of states ruled by one party, or one man. Thus, the preamble to the Charter promises the elimination of 'neo-colonialism' and 'Zionism', while the duties of the African are 'to serve his national community by placing his physical and intellectual abilities at its service . . . not to compromise the security of the state whose national or resident he is . . . to preserve and strengthen social and national solidarity . . . and the territorial integrity of his country'. These are all euphemisms for the duty to follow the leader, whose 'law' circumscribes all the individual 'rights' and 'freedoms' which are sonorously declared. Thus, under Article 10(1), 'Every individual shall have the right to free association provided that he abides by the law' – and if the law bans all but one political party, that's too bad for freedom of association. Similarly, Article 9(2) reads, 'Every individual shall have the right to express and disseminate his opinions within the law' – and if the law prohibits any criticism of the ruler, that's perfectly all right according to the African Charter on Human and Peoples' Rights, which might more accurately have been entitled the African Charter for Keeping Rulers in Power.

The African Commission, with eleven members nominated by the African Union, has the task of promoting and applying the Charter through devices familiar from the HRC: receiving and discussing state reports, and expressing opinions on individual communications. It has no enforcement power, and no court to take on its cases: its reports go in secret to the African Union, because its complaints process is confidential. Its members are not independent of their governments – several have been serving attorneys-general – although in 1999 some more impressive members were appointed, including Vera Chirwa, formerly the doughtiest (and longest-serving) prisoner of power-crazed Hastings Banda. The commission occupies an unpretentious building in Banjul, chosen because the Gambia was a small West African former British colony (known to Americans as the home of the slaves in Alex Haley's *Roots*) which seemed a very stable democracy. It suffered a military coup just after the Commission took up residence and its courts are no longer respected. The Gambia has British law, a Muslim population and a link with francophone Africa through an open border with Senegal, but it does not have adequate communications or air travel (and it does have malaria). Isolated at its base, the Commission travels for two-week sessions in other African capitals, only two or three times a year. An independent evaluation of the Commission conducted for prospective European donors identified its problems as the shortness of session time, inadequate preparation and lack of funds. Typically, some commissioners reacted by criticizing the decision to allow an independent evaluation, the Chairman said he had not read it anyway, and ordered observers out so the meeting could continue in closed session.[38] By 2010 it was complaining that its staffing situation had reached 'critical levels' and it still had no permanent headquarters. Only ten of its fifty-three state members had bothered to submit their periodic reports, and it has been deciding on average only sixteen cases a year. It insists that communications must not be 'written in disparaging or insulting language directed against the state concerned and its institutions' and has declared communications inadmissible for using such descriptions as 'regime of torturers' or 'government of barbarism'.

The Commission has been so disappointing largely because it was until recently under the thumb of a political organization even more jealous of state sovereignty than the UN. The OAU kept the Commission starved of funds and its work is largely unknown in Africa. The Commission does issue brief opinions on 'communications' received from individuals and organizations, but usually years later when condemnation of state behaviour can be safely expressed because the misbehaving government has fallen. This is a motive for its delay in some cases, but the reason for delay in almost all is that governments are not bound to respond to its inquiries within any time period, and tardiness is endemic. It repeatedly fails to find facts, resorting to the feckless formula that *if* the facts alleged by the complainants were true then they would constitute serious violations of the Charter.[39]

The OAU has transmogrified into the African Union, a body which has already strongly supported Robert Mugabe and failed to act effectively to stop the killings in Darfur: only international outrage prevented it from offering presidency in 2007 to Sudan, the most blatant human rights offender on the continent. In 2008 the African Union voted to establish the African Court of Justice and Human Rights (ACJHR). Incredibly, however, it decided to deny automatic standing to victims and NGOs unless their state permitted such actions (so much for access to international justice in Africa). The treaty has been ratified by only three states, excluding Tanzania, the proposed host country for the new court, so it is unlikely to spring into action any time soon. There is an unhappy precedent of the African Court on Human and Peoples' Rights, set up in 1998 and which celebrated its tenth anniversary in 2008 without having heard a single case. In December 2009 it held its first session, throwing out a hopeless attempt to stop Senegal putting the ex-President of Chad, Hissène Habré, on trial for crimes against humanity.[40] This court, based in Tanzania, will merge with the ACHJR when the latter comes into existence.

REALPOLITIK RULES OK

Notwithstanding the UN's failure to develop effective systems for the protection of human rights following the Universal Declaration of 1948, and the hypocrisy that attended diplomatic conferences and covenants on the subject throughout the 1970s, the cause has been advanced by victims throughout the world (in particular in Russia and eastern Europe), emboldened by such events as the Carter initiative, the Helsinki process and the coming into force of the Civil Covenant. In spotlighting their plight and rallying support, Amnesty International has been crucial. It was founded by a small group of English liberals in 1961, adopting as its first prisoners of conscience an Angolan poet who had been publicly flogged and imprisoned without trial (Dr Agostinho Neto), a priest hiding out from the communists in the US embassy in Budapest (Cardinal Mindszeny) and an elderly American writer jailed in Texas for demanding equal rights for blacks. The fledgling body had an early success when Louis Blom-Cooper's mission to Ghana in 1962 resulted in the release of 152 of Nkrumah's opponents from prison, but was mocked when one of its 1966 missions turned out to have been secretly funded by the British government.[41] The organization forswore all such government ties for the future, and began to gather members in large numbers who reach out to victims through letter-writing campaigns aimed at their oppressors. Human rights was placed on the agenda of international TV news by CNN, which in 1980 began satellite transmission across most state borders of those atrocity pictures which do so much to arouse feelings of anger or solidarity. The struggle for human rights began to succeed in the 1980s, not because its rules were enforced, but because they existed and were better known and it was widely accepted that they *should* be enforced. Charter 77 and Solidarity and the refuseniks in Russia could not appeal to a court, but they could and did appeal to the new inter-state agreements which pretended to lay down international law.

The world was still full of atrocities. In Africa, the CIA supported Holden Roberto in Angola, who armed small children with AK-47s, while the KGB backed Colonel Mengistu in Ethiopia, a tyrant even bloodier than Idi Amin (who was responsible for 75,000 deaths in Uganda). It seemed that their crimes against humanity would go unpunished, as part of the latitude allowed to sovereign states to go to hell in their own way, or at least in a way condoned by their superpower protectors. Something could be done, however, if a state was exceptionally small and its behaviour very bizarre. That was the case with Grenada in 1983, when power-crazed politicians on the tiny island (population 60,000) went berserk and killed their leader, Maurice Bishop, and his pregnant partner and fired lethally into a peaceful crowd chanting, 'We want our leader.' America invaded, arrested the killers and in due course restored democracy. It did the right thing for the wrong reason, however: in the twisted thinking of the time, the US justified its action not as humanitarian intervention but as action against a communist threat (which Grenada did not constitute) and to save a 'campus' of pampered US medical students, whose lives were not at risk. It was typical that the US was almost universally condemned – even by Mrs Thatcher, Reagan's most uncritical supporter – for daring to invade the sovereignty of a state, despite the fact that the state in question was smaller than most city suburbs and its citizens were being shot at by political maniacs. Human rights still had nothing to say to governments, even those which devoured their own members.

That this attitude started to change in the 1980s was one consequence of the communications revolution, which showed to citizens in the West, and increasingly in the East, pictures which moved them to pity, and then to anger, about the inability of politicians to stop state-sponsored killings. It helped, too, that human rights had become the rallying cry of dissidents like Sakharov and Havel, oppressed under the dying dogmas of communism. Some were put on trial, at which they exuded a dignified defiance (so different from the old show trial confessions), after which they were jailed for a few years, since even Stalinist states no longer dared provoke an international outcry by executing them. Maybe it is a mistake to characterize the revolutions in eastern Europe in 1989 as a triumph for human rights rather than a result of the demand for higher living standards through free-market reforms, but the heady rhetoric of freedom from censorship and secret policing and rigged justice certainly provided some of the inspiration for the movement that rolled up the Iron Curtain and brought down the Berlin Wall. It had been censorship, after all, which had kept even the politburos in ignorance of their financial as well as their moral bankruptcy, and it was in recognition of their economic helplessness, rather than any shame over their civil rights violations, that old communists voluntarily left the stage. Yet the bitterness of the break-up of the Soviet Union was not explained by communism's economic failure or a resurgence of ethnic pride – it was a legacy of hatred towards Moscow caused by all those decades of Stalinist repression. The revolt against Russia by the Baltic states and Central Asia illustrates one feature of crimes against humanity, namely their historical tendency to return to haunt and destroy the state that perpetrates them.

The progress towards making human rights the political slogan of our time – an apotheosis of the 'New World Order' scheduled for celebration at the UN's Vienna Conference in 1993 – was not without its ironies. For example, one early target of the human rights movement had been the Shah of Iran, a corrupt and despotic ruler whose secret police (SAVAK) was notorious for its sophisticated torture techniques. Satisfaction at the Shah's popular overthrow in 1979 turned quickly to horror at the evils committed in the name of religion by his successor, the Ayatollah Khomeini, who fanned the fanatical flames of Muslim extremism which pose the greatest contemporary threat to human rights. Muslim extremism was much assisted by the Reagan administration, not only by its arms sales through 'Irangate' but by the massive logistical and financial support it gave to the Mujahidin in Afghanistan, most of whom transmogrified in due course into the Taliban. Osama bin Laden was at this point in the 1980s a freedom fighter, backed by the CIA.

The worst crime against humanity in this period was the massacre of thousands of political prisoners in Iran in August and September 1988. Prisoners – especially in wartime – are so utterly at the mercy of their captors that international law firmly protects them from summary execution. That is exactly what captive supporters of the Mujahedin-e-Khalq suffered in Iranian prisons at the end of the Iran–Iraq War. Most of them had been in prison for years for protesting against the Islamic regime – they were Muslim, but Khomeini called them *mohareb* ('enemies of God') and decreed their deaths because they had Marxist leanings, and did not believe in his teaching that the poor must be guided by their Mullahs and not by class struggle. They were condemned by 'death committees' of Islamic judges, and hanged from cranes, four at a time, or in groups of six from ropes dropping from the ceilings in prison assembly halls. Some were taken to army barracks, directed to make their wills and then shot by firing squad. Their bodies were doused with disinfectant, packed in refrigerated trucks and buried by night in mass graves. Families were refused any information about the location of the graves and ordered never to mourn their children in public. (In 2011, families trying to lay flowers on 'places of the damned' in Tehran cemeteries, where they believed their children's mass graves could be located, were placed under arrest.) As many as 7,000 Mujahedin and Marxists were killed in this bloodbath, the former for having the wrong religion, the latter for having none. The Human Rights Commission had at the time a special rapporteur for Iran – he alerted the world (as did Amnesty) to the killings, but the weak-willed diplomat allowed himself to be fobbed off with lies by the Iranian government, most of whose high-ranking politicians had enthusiastically implemented the Ayatollah's merciless decree. They included Ayatollah Khomeini (now the supreme leader), Hashim Rafsanjani (still a force in Iranian politics) and (regrettably) Mir Hossein Mousavi, who was in 1988 the Prime Minister. He is now leader of the 'green' opposition, but at the time of these monstrous events said and did nothing to stop them. The UN rapporteur reported his belief that the Iranian government would investigate the killings (an astonishingly naïve belief, given that they had perpetrated them) and the Human Rights Commission lost interest – even after the Ayatollah launched his outrageous *fatwah* sentencing Salman

Rushdie to death. This massacre was forgotten until the publication of a number of reports into it in 2010–11, which pointed out that most of the participants are still alive and in high (or higher) office in Iran's political and legal systems.[42] The most telling objection to this regime developing a nuclear weapon is to point out that its leaders have already granted themselves immunity for mass murder, and may do so again.

Members of the vicious military juntas in Latin America took their ill-gotten gains into retirement along with their amnesties against prosecution for murder and torture, but democracy in Nicaragua, after the Sandinista movement overthrew the Somoza dictatorship, was something Washington refused to abide. Not only did it train and supply the Contra rebels, but it showed contempt for international law by having the US navy lay mines outside Nicaraguan ports and assist attacks on harbours, oil installations and naval bases. When Nicaragua brought the US before the International Court of Justice, the US argued at first that the Court had no jurisdiction. When that argument was lost, it ungraciously walked out, announcing that it would not be bound by any decision that did not suit the interests of America. Then it withdrew its agreement under the Optional Clause, so that it could not be forced before the Court again. This exceptionalist attitude did not seem to matter to Cold War allies at the time, but when it resurfaced in 1997 at Ottawa (where America refused to sign the convention banning anti-personnel land mines), and at Rome in 1998 (where the US voted against the creation of an international criminal court), they were sorely displeased. The nation with the most to offer the human rights movement in the twenty-first century was prepared to do so only on the condition that other countries were the targets.

Then there is China, which airbrushes from its school history books all mention of Mao's barbaric 'cultural revolution', and still chooses to jail for up to a decade its leading pro-democracy protesters, despite having in 1998 ratified the Civil Covenant (but not, of course, the Optional Protocol). It had joined with the US as the other superpower at Rome in that year to object to the idea of an international tribunal to bring perpetrators of crimes against humanity to justice. That, no doubt, was because the category would surely include

Premier Li Peng and his military brass who in June 1989 gave tank commanders the orders to shoot unarmed student protesters massing in Tiananmen Square. Hundreds were killed, and the media brought the wrenching horror of the massacre into homes around the world. So strong was international revulsion that smaller states and their militias began to realize that they could no longer behave in the same way. In the squares of eastern Europe a few months later, demonstrators were spared deadly attack. After, and as a result of, Tiananmen Square, the British Parliament hastily vouchsafed Hong Kong a bill of rights, before the handover to China.

There were no television cameras in the streets of Halabja in 1998 when Saddam Hussein's troops gassed the Kurdish population, killing 5,000 with an improved derivative of Zyklon-B, the gas used in Nazi concentration camps and now, by obscene irony, supplied to Iraq by German chemical companies. Genocide did not halt the rush to do business with Iraq's megalomanic dictator. Donald Rumsfeld, and trade ministers from the governments of Britain, France, Germany and Italy headed commercial delegations out to make a killing: they supplied him with arms and arms-making equipment in such abandon that he was genuinely surprised when they objected to his using them for the invasion of Kuwait. However, this was a crime against state sovereignty, and the Security Council, for the first time since Korea, decided upon armed intervention against a country which had lost all superpower support. Western public opinion, which was not much moved by the sight of corrupt Kuwaiti princes forced into five-star hotels, had to be galvanized by human rights images, especially a vivid (and completely false) story, propagated by the Hill & Knowlton advertising agency, of Iraqi troops throwing babies out of incubators in the maternity wing of a Kuwaiti hospital. 'Operation Desert Storm' carried all before it, until President Bush, out of knee-jerk respect for state sovereignty (even Iraq's), halted General Schwarzkopf's yomp towards Baghdad.

A great deal of pain and provocation would have been avoided had the allies taken the city, captured Saddam and put him on trial. There were ample precedents – the war crimes and 'crimes against humanity' defined at Nuremberg, not to mention common Article 3 of the 1949 Geneva Conventions. But there was no international court to try Saddam Hussein, even for genocide, and no sensible thought was given to setting up an *ad hoc* tribunal for this purpose. It was over the next ten years that Saddam would make his great contribution to international justice, by providing evidence through his own recalcitrant behaviour of the need for a world criminal court. Had such a tribunal been available in 1991, the UN-backed alliance may not have hesitated to capture Saddam. Instead, he remained a malevolent presence, his refusal publicly to renounce germ and ballistic warfare inviting further sanctions and bombings which caused many more deaths and an exodus of Iraqi refugees.

In America, there was euphoria at the triumph of 'Desert Storm': the television picture of the first helicopter to land on the roof of the American embassy in Kuwait was the reverse image of that shameful footage of the last helicopter scuttling from the roof of the American embassy in Saigon. Another 'New World Order' was announced by President Bush senior, in which human rights would be accorded a central place. But neither the President nor the many well-meaning proponents of this grand, if not new, idea recognized that no such 'order' could be imposed unless it had the capacity to punish those responsible for flagrant breaches. The United Nations planned a jamboree in Vienna for June 1993, at which all states would celebrate alongside representatives from the 800 non-governmental organizations by now active in the human rights cause.

But 1993 was not, as it turned out, a good year for human rights. The new belief that 'something must be done' had already persuaded the UN to intervene in Somalia, at the insistence of President Bush, once American public feeling had been aroused by shocking television pictures of the atrocities committed by its feudal warlords during a famine of biblical proportions. At first, the 25,000 UN peacekeepers of 'Operation Restore Hope' were welcomed as saviours, but soon they were perceived as the enemy when they made the mistake of taking sides in a many-sided civil war. They sided against the Mogadishu warlord General Aidid, because his followers were responsible for ambushing a UN contingent and killing two dozen Pakistani soldiers. After this, the UN forces became more concerned with capturing and punishing Aidid than with stopping the civil war or the famine.

At the UN World Conference in Vienna, the lip-service paid to human rights began to curl. From the strong men of Asia and the old men of Africa came a new and unsettling refrain: 'human rights' was an invention of Western liberalism which had little to offer countries whose values derived from tribal wisdom or other communal traditions, or which were poor and politically vulnerable. Led by China, Malaysia, Indonesia and Singapore, Asian countries caucused and then came to Vienna with their own declaration: that 'universal' human rights must evolve to accommodate 'the significance of national and regional peculiarities and various historical, cultural and religious backgrounds'. The Vienna 'Declaration of Principles' was on its surface a solemn reaffirmation of the universality of human rights, but nobody was fooled: the anodyne 'action programme' showed very clearly that state sovereignty would go into the New World Order undented. The conference itself veered between shambles and sham: for ten days, the governments of the world conducted an unrealistic and abstract discussion, in which under UN rules no state (apart from former Yugoslavia) was allowed to be mentioned by name as a place of human rights violations. Beneath the conference hall, some 9,000 representatives of the 800 NGOs which attended bickered among themselves and protested against their virtual exclusion from the conference agenda. The true tone of the event was set when China insisted that the Dalai Lama, invited by the host state (Austria) to address the conference, should be barred from entering the hall.

There was worse to come. 'Operation Restore Hope' became 'Operation Abandon Hope' when, on 3 October 1993, a mission to capture Aidid went disastrously wrong, leaving US casualties – 18 dead and 84 wounded – and abiding images of 'Black Hawk Down' as the dismembered and dishonoured body of a young American helicopter pilot was presented as though dragged by celebrating savages through dusty streets. President Clinton, who had succeeded Bush, ordered the troops home – more pictures of the last US helicopters leaving, once again, a country abandoned in an even greater mess than it was in when they touched down. This was symbolism that no

US administration could risk again: the voting public could not stand the sight of bodybags. The 'Mogadishu factor' entered American calculations at every level thereafter, and explains why the Clinton administration withheld US forces from Bosnia for the next two years and ordered that Serbia and Kosovo be bombed from a height that ensured both the safety of US pilots and the deaths of hundreds of innocents below them.

As 'ethnic cleansing' re-emerged in Europe, the Security Council reached for a dramatic and almost desperate alternative: in 1993 it used its Chapter VII powers to create a criminal court to punish crimes against humanity committed in the territory formerly known as Yugoslavia. The threat of international justice, rather than international armed intervention, deterred the Bosnian Serb commanders only for a few months. The fighting claimed up to a quarter of a million lives before the first trial – of Bosnian Serb torturer Duško Tadić – began in 1996. For the Security Council, with the US paralysed by the 'Mogadishu factor', the invocation of international criminal law was a last resort. But the gambit seemed to work, at least in convincing a sceptical world that the UN was prepared to do something about genocide. This was a false impression, as its next disaster, Rwanda, demonstrated. There, a long history of fighting between the Hutu majority (85 per cent of the population) and the Tutsi minority culminated in a ceasefire agreement in August 1993, overseen by troops (mainly Belgian) from UNAMIR (United Nations Assistance Mission for Rwanda). A particular concern, so the Commission on Human Rights was told that month by its Special Rapporteur, was the danger of genocidal attacks against Tutsis by extremist Hutu elements in the army and the presidential guard, who were being organized into a new military force (the Interhamwe – 'those who attack together'). Despite more reports implicating the French-backed Hutu government in plans for genocide, the General Assembly incomprehensibly proceeded to elect it to a seat on the Security Council. Armscour of South Africa supplied it with weapons, as did the French, who trained the murderous presidential guards and must have known of the genocide preparations. In January 1994, the UN commanders on the spot received reliable information (from mercenaries training the Interhamwe) that the object of the training was to assassinate leading Tutsis and moderate Hutu politicians and judges, and commence a systematic slaughter of Tutsis. The Canadian generals heading UNAMIR sent details to the peacekeeper-in-chief at the UN, Kofi Annan, who refused their urgent request for permission to intervene.[43]

Three months later, the cue for the genocide to begin came when the presidential plane was shot down: gangs armed with machine guns, machetes and nail-sprouting clubs roamed the capital killing Tutsis at random. The UN in New York was notified of the genocide while the numbers of dead were still in five figures: it did nothing. The Security Council went repeatedly into secret session over the next twelve weeks, cowering over the 'Mogadishu factor' which prevented action as the death toll mounted to more than 800,000. The behaviour over these three months of the US and UK – signatories to the Genocide Convention which bound them to stop the crime – was quite extraordinary. The Clinton administration, supported to the hilt by the British Foreign Office (under John Major's government), insisted that this was 'black on black' violence in which the West should not intervene. Their diplomats refused to describe the killings as genocide: they were merely 'tribal hatred' and 'a breakdown of the ceasefire agreement'. The British ambassador, as secret minutes reveal, played the most shameful part, urging the council to 'think back to Somalia' and to avoid using the term 'genocide' (later, he explained that he was not a lawyer and did not know whether what was happening was genocide: 'we knew a lot of Tutsi were being killed by a lot of Hutu').[44] In fact, right from the start there was no secret about the ethnic killings: they were done openly, in the streets, and repeatedly incited on the radio. Shortly after they began, on 19 April, Kenneth Roth wrote from Human Rights Watch to the president of the Security Council pointing out that they constituted the crime of genocide and urged the five permanent members to fulfil their duty under the Convention to stop the killings and punish the perpetrators. But for ten days the Council did not even bother to discuss the subject, and then, at the instigation of the UK and US, decided to pull out *all* its troops: had they instead been reinforced, several hundred thousand human lives would have been saved.

An independent commission headed by Bengt Carlsson later condemned UN officials for failing to act despite knowledge of the impending holocaust, and accused Britain and the US of refusing to acknowledge the killings as genocide in order to avoid their obligations under the Genocide Convention. (The only members of the Security Council who cared were New Zealand and the Czech Republic; the rest joined the pretence that the genocide was not happening.)[45] The Belgian government had a fit of cowardice after ten of its peacekeepers were killed: against the wisdom of its own commanders on the ground, it ordered the withdrawal of all its troops, despite the fact that they alone were guarding 'safe havens' for Tutsi refugees. Thousands of refugees were massacred when their UN 'protectors' fled. The French, with the finest of racist sensibilities, landed in force but only to save their white expatriates, with their dogs and other household pets: their household Tutsi servants were left behind to be slaughtered. The ensuing bloodbath in April and May 1994 left churches and rivers full of corpses:

If we consider that probably around 800,000 people were slaughtered during that short period . . . the daily killing rate was at least five times that of the Nazi death camps.[46]

After such knowledge, what forgiveness? President Clinton visited Rwanda in 1998 to apologize, but his words were spoken from the steps of his aeroplane, with its engines still running. 'We did not act quickly enough, after the killing began . . . we did not immediately call these crimes by their rightful name, genocide. Never again must we be shy in the face of the evidence.' But the case against the diplomats (the representatives of the major powers in the Security Council, the government of Belgium and the UN Secretary-General and his peacekeeping officers) was gross negligence and deliberate breach of the Genocide Convention obligation to stop the most barbaric genocide since Cambodia. By July 1994, the expatriate Tutsi army (the Rwandan Patriotic Front) had invaded and was in control of most of the country but was competing with a UN-sanctioned French expedition ('Operation Turquoise') which operated to protect French interests and save many Hutu *génocidaires* from retribution. Hutus – most of them very willing executioners of Tutsis – fled to mass camps in Zaire, to the delight of the late President Mobutu who siphoned a large proportion of the international aid into his Swiss bank accounts. These camps, supported by the UN and private charities, were run by the Interhamwe, who used them as a base for attacks on genocide survivors who might testify – an exercise they called 'killing the evidence'.[47]

Rwanda marked an all-time low for the UN, and at every level. Not only had the Security Council turned a blind eye to genocide, but its troops on the ground had been morally responsible for some of the murders – many leading Tutsis declined to flee, relying on a UNAMIR promise of protection which (in the case of the Belgian troops) had been shamefully broken. The most appalling incident involved the Rwandan chief justice, Joseph Kovaruganda, who was being guarded by a UNAMIR detachment from Ghana. These soldiers physically handed him over to a Hutu death squad from the presidential guard, then stood laughing and drinking with his killers while they assaulted his wife and two young daughters. This incident was confirmed by the Carlsson inquiry and amounted to assisting with genocide. The UN itself can hardly remain immune from legal action when it becomes complicit through this kind of misconduct, by its Belgian and Ghanaian troops, in a crime against humanity.

The UN needed a fig leaf to cover up its failures. The idea of a war crimes tribunal, which had received good publicity the year before and quietened the UN's human rights critics, had returned to the agenda. In November, six months after the killings stopped, the Security Council decided once again to invoke its Chapter VII powers to establish an international court to punish the authors of the Rwandan genocide: it would be an offshoot of the Hague Tribunal, sitting principally in Arusha (in Tanzania) but sharing the prosecutor and the appeals chamber being established in The Hague. This time China abstained, and one non-permanent member of the Security Council voted against the proposal. This state was Rwanda itself, now Tutsi-governed. Its objection was that the tribunal was not based in Kigali, Rwanda's capital, and would not exact the death penalty. But as

Richard Goldstone has pointed out, in Kigali 'no fair trials could have been held in the presence of millions of victims calling for blood'.[48] After summary conviction by biased courts, Hutu extremists captured in Rwanda were shot by firing squads, amid public rejoicing. As an alternative to this fate, most genocide commanders preferred to surrender to the more civilized justice on offer in Arusha.

THE SREBRENICA QUESTION

Once it was the bombing of Guernica, captured in all its barbarism and terror in Picasso's painting, that epitomized a crime against humanity. This has been superseded by the fall of Srebrenica, in July 1995, when 7,000 Muslim men and boys were executed by General Mladić's Bosnian Serb army and 23,000 elderly men, women and children were transported. This particular exercise in 'ethnic cleansing' needs no artist for its *frisson*: that is provided by the astonishing fact that this rankest of crimes was committed under the noses of the UN's 'Blue Helmets', and in some respects with their complicity. NATO commanders deliberately decided not to save this 'safe haven' by deploying aerial bombardment, although Security Council Resolution 819 charged them with taking 'the necessary measures, including the use of force' to protect it from attack. The fall of Srebrenica exemplifies the dangers of a fashionable human rights policy when it is decreed by states unwilling to lose a single life in its enforcement. The men of Srebrenica were caught in a human rights death trap, sacrificed to the good intentions of cowardly countries.

To state this does not detract from the prime responsibility of the Bosnian Serb commanders, who planned the massacre down to the last truck needed to transport the men – civilians and soldiers – to their mass graves. Their attack on the town was in aggressive defiance of international law. By executing prisoners-of-war, they committed a war crime in breach of the Geneva Convention. By executing civilians, the crime was against humanity as well as the Geneva Convention. As the siege intensified, General Mladić was pictured on the hill overlooking Srebrenica. He turned to his tame Serb TV crews, and emoted:

'Remember that tomorrow is the anniversary of our uprising against the Turks. The time has now come to take revenge on the Muslims.[49] His deliberate destruction of a community on ethnic and religious grounds counted palpably as genocide. It matters not how Srebrenica is characterized, because it was the worst war crime committed in Europe since the fall of Hitler – and it was committed several years *after* the United Nations had established the Hague Tribunal as a means of deterring exactly such offences.

Did Srebrenica, then, signal the futility of expecting the prospect of punishment to deter those hellbent on committing crimes against humanity?

This is an important question, but it must be remembered that by the time of the massacre – July 1995 – the Hague Tribunal was still very much a paper tiger. The intercept evidence which proves that the idea actually frightened the Bosnian Serb leaders when the tribunal was first mooted in August 1992 (and this fear seems to have contributed to a lull in the fighting) shows that insouciance quickly returned to their headquarters as the tribunal stumbled and delayed and failed to get itself off the ground. By July 1995, it had only one prisoner, a footsoldier named Duško Tadić, whom it had yet to put on trial. Its very impotence may have convinced Mladić that he could breach international criminal law so blatantly and barbarically, and avoid punishment.

In the racially jumbled geography of Bosnia, Srebrenica was a Muslim city surrounded by predominantly Serbian countryside. It might have made sense to surrender it to Serbia with guarantees (that was the Vance-Owen plan) or even – since guarantees were often dishonoured – to transport its entire population to safety, but by 1993 this would have been an unconscionable reward to the Serbs for their brutality. Instead, at the suggestion of the Red Cross, the city was one of those declared a 'safe area' by Security Council Resolution 819, passed in April 1993 – a promise to its people that international law and, 'if necessary', international forces would protect them. To fulfil this promise, the UN correctly assessed the need for 34,000 soldiers on the ground, but none of its members stepped forward to offer troops. Eventually, some 7,400 were mustered for six enclaves (sar-

ally referred to as 'safe areas lite'). Srebrenica was vouchsafed a Dutch battalion, the Netherlands being one of the few countries idealistic enough to send troops to patrol the safe areas, and naive enough not to recognize the absurdity of sending a 'peacekeeping' force to a place where there was no peace to keep.

The Dutch troops' task was doomed from the start, but it is instructive to ask why simple defeat was allowed to become a disgrace. The insufficiency of numbers, of course, meant that they simply cowered when the Serb attack came, and watched apologetically during the subsequent preparations for 'ethnic cleansing' by evacuation and massacre.[50] But their very presence prevented the UN from taking the one action which would have saved the town and honoured the promise of Resolution 819: ordering NATO air strikes to halt the Serb advance. The fear that Dutch soldiers would become hostages and that the battalion might suffer casualties caused the Dutch government (and the UN representative on the ground) to veto the essential air strikes. Unhindered, Mladić's army took the town and put into operation a carefully planned exercise in which males of arms-bearing age were separated from their families and, within sight of the Dutch 'peacekeepers', taken away ostensibly to be 'screened' for complicity in war crimes but in fact to be carted off to fields where they were killed, then buried in mass graves which have now yielded corpses with hands tied behind backs, shot from behind. The scenario is common in ethnic war: what made this massacre so horrific is that the international community stood back and allowed it to happen, as the price for protecting the peacekeepers who were there protecting the victims. The Dutch troops received heroes' welcomes on their return to the Netherlands a week after the massacre, a celebration of the fact that they were 'safe' which appeared grotesque precisely because those to whom they had promised safety had been left behind, in mass graves. The politicians who had sent these soldiers and the generals who had commanded them imposed a rule of silence which served to cover up not only their acquiescence in the genocide, but (for some months) the fact of the genocide itself. As one history of this appalling incident concluded, 'in hindsight, the Dutch failure to speak out after they left the enclave was worse than their conduct during the Serb offensive'.[51]

Srebrenica was allowed to happen because of the 'Mo[g
factor': states intervening from humanitarian motives refused t[·
the lives of their own soldiers to make that intervention effect[
The case can be put more bluntly: the Dutch government preferred
to dishonour promises and to allow Muslims to die in their thousands rather than to suffer one more Dutch casualty. This was the
conclusion of the Netherlands Institute of War Documentation,
whose seven-year investigation, published in April 2002, caused the
government to resign in shame (although only one month before its
term of office was due to end). It had sought prestige by sending
poorly prepared troops on an ill-defined mission, then panicked and
ordered them to hand the Muslims under their protection over to
the merciless Mladić. The same national funk took hold in Belgium
the previous year, when its army was 'peacekeeping' in Rwanda: it
failed to take action which might have prevented massacre (e.g. by
closing down the radio stations which were inciting the Hutus to
genocidal attacks on the Tutsis and by sending tanks against the killers on the streets). This would have been to 'take sides', stepping
down from the fence on which UN peacekeeping missions can get
impaled. Like the Dutch battalion in Srebrenica, the Belgians
watched the massacre, and then withdrew as soon as they began to
suffer casualties.

Both the Dutch and the Belgians were morally guilty for making
a fashionable gesture of sending soldiers under the impossible condition that they should not be required to fight. But the problem
was more fundamental: it stemmed from the diplomatic mindset
that assumed peace could be secured without justice. If the UN is to
protect a city or a people, it must have a clear idea of whom it is
protecting them from, and treat these aggressors as the enemy. Soldiers must be sent to fight, and politicians at home must be prepared
for soldiers to die, in the cause of protecting the innocent (or at
least the people promised protection) from attack. There is little
doubt that General Mladić, a cunning calculator of odds, would
have retreated under aerial bombardment and would not (at least
for long) have provoked the international community by holding
Blue Helmets hostage. But he knew his enemy's weaknesses: a

Dutch public desperately opposed to sacrifice and a United Nations which wanted and needed him to talk about peace. The UN diplomat responsible, along with the Dutch defence minister, for vetoing air strikes was UN Special Representative for Bosnia, Yasushi Akashi: he defended his conduct on the grounds that 'the man you bomb today is the same man whose co-operation you may require tomorrow for the passage of a humanitarian convoy'.[52] This is a very good reason for leaving humanitarian assistance to the Red Cross while the UN decides which men are in the wrong and have to be bombed. The writer Michael Ignatieff confronted the UN Secretary-General as Srebrenica was falling: 'Why,' he asked, 'insist on being neutral in the face of a clear aggressor and a clear victim, when that neutrality daily undermines the UN's moral credit?' Boutros Boutros-Ghali could only reply: 'We are not able to intervene on one side. The mandate does not allow it.'[53] Mandates to keep the peace must be interpreted as mandates to fight aggressor factions, if this is the only way the peace can be kept and genocide prevented.

The cries from the mass graves still being excavated around Srebrenica are more haunting than ever, as war crimes prosecutors unveil the evidence gathered from them to incriminate Mladić and Karadžić (both on trial at The Hague in 2012) and to shame the Dutch army and the UN. The most moving scenes were recorded on private camcorders, the grainy images of Muslim men and boys huddled in fields, surrounded by soldiers blessed by Serb Orthodox priests who wait impatiently to shoot them come nightfall. The most incriminating footage comes from Serbian television: it shows Mladić toying with the lives of his terrified hostages, and blowing lies and cigarette smoke into the face of the pathetic Dutch commander, Colonel Karremans. This soldier is seen disgracing his country and his calling by accepting drink and gifts from Mladić – a reward for following Dutch government orders and handing over thousands of Muslims who had sought refuge in their UN compound. This was the moral nadir reached by UN peacekeeping, rivalling the behaviour of the Belgian and Ghanaian 'peacekeepers' in Rwanda who handed over the Tutsis they were meant to be guarding to Interhamwe hit squads. It was this complicity in the slaughter which provoked a bleak joke about UN peacekeeping: 'If the UN had been around in 1939, we would all be speaking German.'

As the first half century of the Universal Declaration drew to a close, the failure to make its provisions stick in most countries of the world seemed both abject and irremediable. Talk of a 'New World Order' after the Cold War, the Gulf War and the Vienna Conference was just talk, by voices shrill if challenging universality or tremulous if contemplating another Mogadishu. The diplomats had drafted all the treaties necessary to define human rights, and the politicians had signed them because they would have no practical or legal effect, since violators would not be called to account other than through a polite and powerless UN committee system. What they overlooked was the gathering strength of the human rights movement and its NGO networks, galvanized by interrelated victories in the struggle for global justice at the century's close: Pinochet and Lockerbie and the ICC Treaty, Kosovo and East Timor and the work of the Hague Tribunal. These will be described in later chapters, after an analysis of the jurisprudential developments that brought them about: international human rights law, humanitarian law (i.e. the rules of war) and the legacy of Nuremberg in establishing a duty to prosecute crimes against humanity.

3

The Rights of Humankind

'You are going to have to tell me when things do become
part of international law and when they do not. It is a point
I have never understood since I was at Oxford.'

Lord Browne-Wilkinson, presiding judge in *Ex parte
Pinochet (No. 3)*, to counsel

The last quarter of the twentieth century witnessed a struggle between
the human rights movement and its enemies (especially the diplomats)
over whether the great promises made in the Universal Declaration
should be recognized as having the force of international law. The
battle was joined in 1976, when the twin Covenants became operational, one guaranteeing the 'liberty rights' the Universal Declaration
promised to individuals *vis-à-vis* the state, the other proclaiming communal or 'fraternity' rights which were generally perceived as
unenforceable aspirations, i.e. policy goals to be encouraged but not
imposed on a sovereign state by any external court of the kind which
might adjudicate infringements of liberty. This easy distinction is
untenable, as Amnesty International came to recognize in 2005 when
it announced that it would campaign for economic and social rights.
But the advantage of the narrower and more clearly defined individual rights in the Civil Covenant is that certain of these 'liberty rights'
can be said to have crystallized into rules of international law. A
human rights principle which achieves this status has a real force in
most municipal courts and before international tribunals: in the case

of the most fundamental 'physical safety' rights, their widespread and systematic breach further counts as a crime against humanity. Human rights principles which have not become part of 'customary' (i.e. binding) international law (even though they are found in treaties and are accepted by some municipal courts) remain ethically attractive, but states are under no legal obligation to honour them.

'Law', in common parlance, means a rule which (unlike a rule of ethics) is actually capable of enforcement through institutions created for that purpose. But 'law' in the phrase 'international law' does not automatically have this quality: it has no police force or bailiffs, for example, to bring malefactors before its courts. If a rule attains the status of customary international law, it will be enforced by national courts (if it is not contrary to the constitution or to local statutes). At its mundane level, international law comprises treaties between two or more sovereign states which operate more in the observance than the breach because states generally find it convenient to keep the promises they exchange with other states. Treaties which facilitate trade and commerce are usually adhered to, whether between two states or 120, and when disputes arise then the decisions of an agreed arbitrator are honoured, so international law relating to the air or the sea or the Antarctic can be stated with some confidence. But the international law of human rights is grounded on treaties like the twin Covenants, by which states solemnly undertake to treat their own nationals according to certain civilized standards. If they break the undertaking, very little can be done by other states: this would interfere with 'sovereignty', which is the most essential quality of a 'state' in international law. As we shall see, this throws up an acute paradox. A human rights rule may be crystal clear from a treaty signed by the great majority of states, but whether it counts as customary international law depends largely on whether states believe it should normally be honoured in practice. If the rule against torture, or in favour of free speech, is regularly flouted by many states, can that rule be meaningfully described as 'law'? That must depend on whether the possibility exists (however rarely it may be taken) of calling agents of the government which disobeys it to account.

The purpose of this chapter is to enumerate the 'liberty rights' of the Universal Declaration as they are reflected and extended by the

International Covenant on Civil and Political Rights (the Civil Covenant) and to identify those which have become so generally accepted as to have international legal force when asserted by or on behalf of individuals. It is first necessary to explain how an interplay of factors can turn a 'right' declared in a treaty into a 'law' which is binding internationally, and not just on states which are party to the treaty.

MAKING HUMAN RIGHTS RULE: INTERNATIONAL LAW

There are dozens of overlapping human rights treaties, signed and ratified by most countries. The Universal Declaration is now truly universal, in the sense that almost every country is a member of its declaratory body, the UN. Its offshoots, the twin Covenants, have (as of 2012) been ratified by 167 countries in the world. Treaties such as the twin Covenants do not become part of municipal law when the state *signs* them – this is an act which has no real legal significance. What matters is the subsequent act of *ratification*, the formal act by its executive government by which the state agrees to be bound. The position in some countries (including France and Spain and their former colonies in Africa and Latin America) is that ratification *automatically* incorporates the treaty as part of the national law. It is, for these so-called 'monist' nations, a very serious act with an immediate legal consequence. In Britain and Commonwealth 'dualist' countries, however, ratification is an executive decision which has no effect unless the elected parliament subsequently passes legislation to *incorporate* the treaty into its body of local law. The position in America is more complicated: the executive (i.e. the President) may sign a treaty, but ratification – his act which gives effect to it – must first be approved by a two-thirds majority in the Senate. The President may then 'proclaim' the treaty, which will thereafter override any inconsistent state or federal laws, although not the US constitution itself. This to some extent explains the poor US record on ratification of human rights treaties: the requirement of a two-thirds Senate majority means that any party-political division will kill it. (Thus President

Clinton's signature in the Rome Treaty which set up the International Criminal Court was worthless, even before George W. Bush's unnecessary and petty act of 'unsigning' it.)

The position in most countries is that, save for 'self-executing' treaties which are framed to take effect directly upon ratification (usually by granting specific rights to a class of persons, such as aliens, or those deprived of property by another state party), the rules of international law, whether derived from treaty or custom or state practice, depend for their implementation upon national law, i.e. local implementing legislation and court decisions. Once this action has been taken, the US courts, like those in Britain, will be bound (by their own case law, or particular statutes) to apply 'the law of nations', and will have to decide whether a particular human rights principle has entered customary international law.

The point at which a human right becomes part of customary international law depends upon creative interplay between a number of factors. Everyone agrees upon the identification of those factors: they are authoritatively enumerated in Article 38(1) of the Statute of the International Court of Justice, which enjoins that court to apply, in deciding inter-state disputes,

(a) international conventions, whether general or particular, establishing rules expressly recognized by the contesting States;

(b) international custom, as evidence of a general practice accepted as law;

(c) the general principles of law recognized by civilized nations;

(d) subsidiary means for determining rules of law, judicial decisions and the teachings of the most highly qualified publicists of the various nations.

The classic example of the interplay of these factors is the decision of the US Supreme Court in 1900 to award compensation to Cuban fishermen whose boat flying the Spanish flag, the *Paquete Habana*, had been destroyed by the US navy in the course of its war with Spain. The exemption of fishing vessels from capture as a prize of war was described as 'an ancient usage among civilized nations, beginning centuries ago, and *gradually ripening into* [my italics] a (settled) rule of international law'.¹ This 'ripening' process was assisted by a consistent exemption the Court detected over the centuries – in treaties between leading nations, in decisions of prize courts in other countries and in the opinions of distinguished textbook writers. But what mattered most was that the exemption appeared to have been made by most states (originally as a matter of mercy or courtesy rather than law) and was now the invariable practice of *civilized* states. The natural law origins of this 'right reason' approach are manifest: at a time when war could still be regarded as a gentlemanly affair, a rule could 'ripen' into law if it was soundly based in both decency (the Court referred to 'considerations of humanity to a poor and industrious order of men') and expedience (the next reference was to 'the mutual convenience of fishing vessels'). It is a nice case, which resulted in the poor but industrious Cubans being compensated by the US navy, but there was a vigorous dissent from a minority of judges who thought the exemption no more than a common act of mercy from which no legal right (and certainly not one against the US government) could mature. What happens if a principle recognized by *civilized* nations is not generally or customarily accepted as law by states which are, or wish to retain the option to be, uncivilized?

This is always the problem in reposing much faith in the so-called 'norms' of international law as a means of puncturing state sovereignty. No matter how persuasively 'right reason' calls for abolition or restriction of the death penalty, or prohibition of anti-personnel land mines, or an end to discrimination against women, it comes up against determined state practice: thousands of executions in countries around the world; a refusal by the United States to sign the Ottawa Agreement; the dictates of Sharia law in Islamic nations. It is not, however, a futile exercise to discover how many human rights rules have 'ripened' into rules of international law: this accords them a status which domestic courts must respect (and in some cases, apply) and it makes their breach a matter of international moment, possibly even engaging the Chapter VII enforcement powers of the Security Council. For this reason, a closer look at the four crystallizing factors is required.

INTERNATIONAL CONVENTIONS AND TREATIES

If a rule is contained in a treaty, the strength of the presumption that it is part of customary international law will vary with the number of states which are party to that treaty. There are 193 member states of the UN. Switzerland joined in 2002 (non-membership had been thought appropriate for its pretence of neutrality, which by then could no longer be sustained). Taiwan has always been vetoed by China, although there can be no doubt that it fulfils international law criteria for statehood set out in the 1933 Montevideo Convention on the Rights and Duties of States, namely: a) a permanent population; b) a defined territory; c) government; and d) capacity to enter into relations with other states. Palestine also fulfils these criteria, but its bid for membership of the UN in 2011 was resisted by the US on political grounds, namely that recognizing the obvious might give it an advantage in negotiations, or in any event remove the prospect of statehood as an incentive for its people to settle with Israel. The UN improperly accords 'non-member statehood' to the Vatican, which plainly is not a state, but rather a palace in Rome with no permanent population (no one is born to its celibate officials, other than by accident). It serves as the headquarters of a particular religious movement, which enjoys preferential treatment and diplomatic immunity from its 'statehood' status.[2] *Realpolitik* can distort the question of statehood – for many years most governments declined to recognize the Republic of East Timor (now Timor-Leste) out of a misguided support for Indonesia, which had unlawfully invaded it in 1976 and thereafter brutally oppressed its liberation movement.

The UN Charter, to which all member states subscribe, is the 'constitution' of world government. The Universal Declaration of Human Rights is not a treaty, but the Civil Covenant has 167 parties as signatories – making its rules *prima facie* candidates for the 'universal' status of international law. Treaties which are accepted by less than half the nations of the world, such as the Optional Protocol on the

Abolition of the Death Penalty (a mere seventy-four parties), cannot for that very reason be considered as serious candidates for the status. The test, incidentally, is not whether a state has signed a treaty, but whether it has agreed to be bound by it through the process known as ratification. A further complication comes from the fact that states are permitted to make reservations to their acceptance of a treaty, and subsequently to derogate from some aspect of it: these qualifications, if widely shared, will undermine the claim of the qualified rule to be part of international law. The strength of claims to customary status which can be made by the major human rights treaties, as of February 2012, may be gauged from the table of ratifications set out in appendix C (p. 864).

CUSTOM AND STATE PRACTICE

The existence of an obligation in a human rights convention is not definitive: since many states in practice ignore the duties they pledge themselves to respect, an international law rule must show a high level of compliance – as evidenced by government statements, diplomatic correspondence, support for UN resolutions and, most importantly of all, actual behaviour. Given the stark difference between what governments say and what governments do, this is a particularly slippery balance: how can there be an international law against torture when all too many governments allow armies and police forces to inflict it upon prisoners? As so often in the chimerical world of international law, this problem is overcome with the help of Latin phrases. 'Custom' in customary international law is made up of state practice (what governments have done and intend to keep on doing) on the one hand, and on the other what is termed the *opinio juris*, i.e. what governments feel they are obliged to do (even if, in practice, they do the opposite). This is the way international lawyers solve the paradox of having a rule against torture in a world where many states permit it: these states lie and hide it and pretend it doesn't exist *because they know it's wrong*, so it's contrary to the received wisdom, the *opinio juris*. And if their moral (or, more probably, psychological) sense of obligation is strong enough to amount to an imperative, then it forms part of the *jus cogens*, i.e. one of the rules defined by Article 53 of the Vienna Convention on the Law of Treaties as 'accepted and recognized by the international community of States as a whole from which no derogation is permitted'. In other words – other Latin words – it gives rise to an *erga omnes* duty, owed to the whole international community. In a much-celebrated definition offered (in passing) by the International Court of Justice (ICJ) in the *Barcelona Traction Case*,

such *erga omnes* obligations derive, for example, in contemporary international law, from the outlawing of acts of aggression, and of genocide, as also from the principles and rules concerning the basic rights of the human person, including protection from slavery and racial discrimination.[3]

An *opinio juris* that becomes accepted as part of the *jus cogens* has a dynamite quality which invalidates any conflicting treaty: it becomes in international law-speak 'a peremptory norm from which no derogation is permitted'. This is all very well but, as a leading textbook remarks, 'more authority exists for the category of '*jus cogens*' than exists for its particular content'.[4] The ICJ in the *Barcelona Traction Case* did not condescend to define 'the basic rights of the human person' that can be included, other than the right to be free from genocide, race discrimination and slavery. This is a start, but not enough of a start: the point about most human rights rules is not that governments believe them to be legally binding, it is that governments honestly believe they are not *legally* binding but that breaches are so prone to outrage world opinion that they should be hidden or, if exposed, defended on legal technicalities. But in so far as it has become common for accused states to deny human rights violations with legalistic arguments (e.g. 'psychological pressure' is not torture) without objecting to the human rights principle *per se* (that torture is always wrong), it might be said that they acquiesce in a rule of customary international law that prohibits torture. Thus the law against widespread and systematic torture belongs to this elusive body of especially powerful human rights rules, the breach of which within a state elevates its conduct from an 'internal affair' to an affront to global conscience which the world may intervene to prevent or even to punish.

PRINCIPLES OF LAW RECOGNIZED BY CIVILIZED NATIONS

Principles of law which are recognized and unanimously applied in efficient legal systems are strong candidates for international law status. The importance of providing criminal suspects with a fair trial, for example, is now universally recognized, although civilized nations may differ on whether 'fairness' requires a judge or a jury, or an adversarial or inquisitorial proceeding. There is a tendency in the ICJ to reach for this source of law only when treaties and custom are silent, or simply to confirm instinctive general principles such as the overriding importance of 'good faith', but it need not be a subsidiary source or a last resort. It was used creatively by the Permanent Court of International Justice between the wars to establish in international law the rule against expropriation of private property without compensation (see the *Chorzów Factory Case*, p. 171) and the duty of a new sovereign to honour private rights acquired under the old (the *German Settlers in Poland Case*). The very fact that most constitutions of civilized states now incorporate bills of rights which recognize many of the civil liberties in the Universal Declaration provides a powerful argument that these liberties have 'ripened' into international law. The work of identifying these principles is being done by the International Law Commission, an offshoot of the Human Rights Commission: it operates on the basis that *jus cogens* rules (i.e. those accepted by the international community as a whole) do not require universal agreement, but rather the agreement of a preponderant and sufficiently representative body of states.[5]

JUDICIAL DECISIONS AND TEXTBOOKS

These are recognized as 'subsidiary' sources, and for good reason: they are myriad, confusing and sometimes conflicting. A clear ICJ decision, although binding only on parties to the dispute, will have some force, as will decisions of the European Court of Human Rights and the Inter-American Court, and judgments by the Privy Council and respected national supreme courts. These decisions may influence international law under three conditions:

(1) if they exhibit a striking unanimity of approach to the same question, or

(2) if a particular decision has won widespread respect, either for its epic quality (e.g. the Nuremberg judgment) or for its statement of a new and subsequently accepted principle (e.g. that of compensating victims of crimes against humanity, in the *Velasquez Rodriguez Case*), or

(3) because of the power and persuasiveness of the actual opinion, even if the result is not widely accepted (e.g. the US Supreme Court ruling in *New York Times* v. *Sullivan*, which has promoted free speech 'First amendment' style, or the Privy Council decision in *Pratt* v. *AG of Jamaica*, that a lengthy stay on death row amounts to inhumane treatment, and requires commutation of the death sentence).

Textbook writers (the term used is 'publicists') come with caveats: those most venerated, from Grotius in the seventeenth century to Sir Hersch Lauterpacht immediately after the Second World War, have contributed to the theory of an international legal order at times when it barely existed or was rudimentary by comparison with the present day. Their opinions sometimes foreshadow a shift from diplomacy to law, but their optimism can do little to effect it: during the twentieth century, the writer who most accurately described state practice throughout its course remained Machiavelli.

State practice has been the most potent, and has become the most problematic, source of international law. It may be gleaned not only from national legislation and domestic court decisions, but also from such politicized examples of government conduct as diplomatic exchanges, policy statements, executive decisions, prime ministerial outbursts and press releases on foreign affairs. This 'practice' reflects the interests of the particular state – often, the interests of its ruling party or of its powerful corporate backers – rather than the interests of international justice. Drawing 'law' from the conglomeration of such usages will not necessarily produce rules which are fair and just. The problem is exacerbated by the fact that the other major source of international law – treaties – is in effect state practice writ large, since treaties require ratification by governments. So international law's development has been crucially dependent upon the consent of states, as evidenced by their practice and their treaty commitments, with little contribution from court decisions or juristic writings, or even the generally acknowledged principles of justice and equity. Indeed, Article 38(2) of the ICJ Charter specifically restricts the right of the world court to decide *ex aequo et bono* (i.e. by reference to its own determination of what is just and right) to cases in which all parties have agreed to this course. Thus does the shibboleth of state consent haunt every stage in international law-creation, except where pariah states object to a rule agreed by a great and representative majority of other states (thus apartheid violated an emerging norm of international law, notwithstanding South Africa's practice of it). The problem is that states rarely consent, genuinely and voluntarily, to external limits on their power over their own people. So the paradox of international law, from a human rights perspective, is that it remains under the thumb of the very entities it seeks to control: state conduct determines its creation, and states effectively monopolize appointments of their representatives to its adjudicative bodies. Even the International Law Commission, charged with drafting international legal rules, has most of its thirty-four members drawn from diplomats or state government legal departments, rather than appointed on merit from distinguished academic or practising lawyers. Human rights challenges international law to move in a less state-oriented direction, which means that the commissions and courts which develop and apply international human rights rules must henceforth do so by reference to what is right and good, rather than to what states have done in the past in their selfish national interests. Paradoxically, perhaps, the human rights assault on the shield of sovereignty leaves weak or 'failed' states at the mercy of powerful interveners: it is the latter's national interests, rather than international justice, which may thus become determinative.

Customary international law is an emanation of agreements between sovereign states. It has only recently been applied to individuals, and it has yet to bind transnational corporations, some of which are wealthier and more powerful than many sovereign states. One of its primary modern sources is found in the responses of millions of ordinary men and women, and of the non-governmental organizations which many of them support, to the human rights abuses they see on the television or computer screen in their living rooms. These people do not talk about *jus cogens* and *erga omnes*: they believe in the simple language of the Universal Declaration, and they are not bound by Article 2(7) of the UN Charter to avert their eyes from repression in foreign countries. The sight affects them, in a literal sense: it makes them sad and angry, it makes them shield the eyes of their children and it makes them feel diminished to be a member of a race that can act so barbarously. These citizens, of global society rather than nation state, cannot understand why human rights rules should not rule because they are just and right, irrespective of state practice.

But, for the present, international law comes courtesy of nation states if it comes at all. There is no parliament to pass it, since the General Assembly is hopelessly unrepresentative – one vote for Antigua (population 60,000) and one vote for India (population over one billion) – and the Security Council is often poleaxed by the superpower veto. The International Court of Justice, at its gothic building in The Hague, is not permitted to become the Supreme Court for Humankind: it can only decide a case between states, and then only when a defendant state agrees to accept its jurisdiction; even so, it has no power to require compliance with its judgments. All UN member states are, under the UN charter, parties to the court, but only sixty-seven have agreed to accept its compulsory jurisdiction. Superpowers often treat it with contempt: in 1974 France disdained to appear to answer a case brought by Australia over nuclear testing in the Pacific and in 1984 the United States walked out of the case brought against it by Nicaragua, announcing that it would not comply with any ICJ decision unless it suited US interests. Both France and the US, after these discomfits, revoked their automatic consent to be made a party to any case in the world court. China and Russia have never given that consent, so Britain, faithful to its *Alabama claims* position, is left as the only permanent member of the Security Council with sufficient faith in international law to accept automatically the ICJ jurisdiction. In 2004, when the ICJ was required by the UN General Assembly to give an advisory opinion on the legality of the wall that Israel was building across the land of dispossessed Palestinians, Israel did not turn up to defend its conduct. After the adverse decision, it simply relied on its superpower ally, the US, to wield its veto so as to block any Security Council resolution on the issue. Such truculence explains why the Court's impact has not been much felt in the human rights area: less powerful states have been reluctant, on the 'dog does not eat dog' principle, to accuse other governments of violations. Unless it is empowered, by an amendment to the UN Charter, to hear cases brought by NGOs or an independent Human Rights Commissioner, the ICJ will remain of marginal significance, notwithstanding its potential as the 'world court'.

In sum, international law is a system created and controlled by sovereign states, for their convenience. Some of its classic doctrines – sovereign and diplomatic immunity, non-intervention in internal affairs, non-compulsory submission to the ICJ, equality of voting in the General Assembly – continue to damage the human rights cause. Nevertheless, the incantations of *jus cogens* and *opinio juris* may turn out in time to be abracadabras which open, if only a crack, the doors of state sovereignty. For example, although resolutions of the General Assembly (which now often favour human rights) are not binding or even acknowledged as sources of customary international law, recent ICJ decisions have admitted them as evidence of *opinio juris*. By such devices, progressive claims – such as the rights of women and children – may be advanced more forcefully. The importance of customary international law is that it filters through into national law: most municipal systems have procedural and interpretative rules which permit notice to be taken in their courts of international law when it is not in direct conflict with local law. Some common law systems, including the British and American, accept customary international law as part of that common law, although treaties must be incorporated by specific legislation before they can have any direct legal effect. Even here, however, they can have an indirect effect on statutory construction: in democracies, courts must favour that interpretation of a statute which accords with an international treaty, because of the presumption that 'Parliament does not intend to act in breach of international law, including therein specific treaty obligations'.[6]

INTERNATIONAL CRIMES AND THE RULE AGAINST RETROSPECTIVITY

International law rules are binding on states, not individuals. Beginning with the Nuremberg Statute in 1945, however, states came to agree that individuals responsible for breaching certain of these rules could be punished, at least by international criminal courts. It is important to identify the process by which a norm of customary law metamorphoses into a criminal prohibition, and to identify within that process the turning point at which criminal liability arises. This is because of the rule against retrospectivity, usually expressed in the Latin phrase *nullum crimen sine lege* – conduct however awful is not unlawful unless there is a criminal law against it in force at the time it was committed. As Article 15 of the International Covenant on Civil and Political Rights puts it:

No one shall be held guilty of any criminal offence on account of any act or omission which did not constitute a criminal offence, under national or international law, at the time it was committed.

Like most absolute principles, *nullum crimen* can be highly inconvenient – especially in relation to conduct which is abhorrent or grotesque, but which parliament has not thought to legislate against. The temptation to criminalize conduct regarded as seriously anti-social or appalling but which has not yet been outlawed must be firmly resisted by national and especially international law judges who have no legislature to correct or improve upon them and are dealing with a subject – international criminal law – which came into existence as recently as Nuremberg. It is precisely when the acts are abhorrent and deeply shocking that the principle of legality must be most stringently applied, to ensure that a defendant is not convicted out of disgust rather than evidence, or of a non-existent crime. *Nullum crimen* may not be a household phrase, but it serves as some protection against the lynch-mob.

The principle of legality requires that the defendant must at the time of committing the acts alleged to amount to a crime have been in a position to know, or at least readily to establish, that those acts may entail penal consequences. Ignorance of the law is no defence, so long as that law is capable of reasonable ascertainment. The fact that the defendant's conduct would shock or even appal decent people is not enough to make it unlawful in the absence of a prohibition. It is not necessary that at the time of commission there exists an international court with the power to punish the conduct, or any foresight that such a court will necessarily be established. In every case, the question is whether the defendant, at the time of conduct which was not clearly outlawed by national law at the place of commission, could have ascertained through competent legal advice that it was contrary to international criminal law. This principle is the basis of the rule of law, because it impels governments (in the case of national law) and the international community (in the case of international criminal law) to take positive action against abhorrent behaviour, or else that behaviour will go unpunished. It thus provides the rationale for legislation and for treaties and conventions – i.e. for a system of justice rather than an administrative elimination of wrongdoers by command of those in power. It is the reason why we are ruled by law and not by police.

For an international court to recognize the creation of a new criminal offence without infringing the *nullum crimen* principle,

(1) the elements of the offence must be clear and in accordance with fundamental principles of criminal liability;

(2) that the conduct could amount to an offence in international law must have been capable of reasonable ascertainment at the time of its commission;

(3) there must be evidence or at least inference of general agreement by the international community that breach of the customary law rule would now entail international criminal liability for individual perpetrators, in addition to the normative obligation on states to prohibit the conduct in question under their domestic law.

The process described in the *Paquete Habana* decision is one of crystallization of international law rules that become binding on states. But they do not bind individuals, unless the state legislature adopts them by decree or ratification into municipal criminal law. In order to become a criminal prohibition enforceable in that sphere of international law which is served by international criminal courts, the 'norm' must satisfy a further test. It must have the requisite qualities for a serious criminal prohibition: the elements of the offence must be tolerably clear and must include the mental element of a guilty intention or *mens rea*. Its existence, as an international law crime, must be capable of reasonable ascertainment, which means that prosecution for the conduct must have been foreseeable as a realistic possibility. Most significantly, it must be clear that the overwhelming preponderance of states, courts, conventions, jurists and so forth relied upon to crystallize the international law 'norm' intended – or now intend – this rule to have penal consequences for individuals brought before international courts, whether or not such court presently exists with jurisdiction over them.

These tests are all satisfied in relation to the crimes usually prosecuted in international courts: genocide, mass murder, widespread and systematic torture, grave breaches of the Geneva Conventions and so on. But many serious crimes found in domestic criminal laws will not qualify, because there is no evidence of a general consensus in the international community that they should be treated as crimes against humanity. And when such consensus arises – as it did for many war crimes when 120 nations signed the ICC

Statute which included them in its definition of offences – there may still be ambiguities or issues relating to the time at which the crime was first created. This question arose acutely in the *Child Soldiers Case* decided by the Special Court of Sierra Leone. The country's defence minister, Chief Hinga Norman, was charged with recruiting children to fight under his command in 1996, two years before the Rome Statute made the first reference to this offence. The court majority accepted a submission by UNESCO that a consensus had emerged by 1996 to support a new international law offence of child recruitment. The better, positivist position is that the general consensus in favour of individual criminal responsibility emerged, at the earliest, with the Rome Statute in 1998 and possibly not until 2002 when that Statute came into force. All that had emerged by 1996 was a vague obligation on states (which only five had honoured) to make child recruitment for front-line fighting a domestic crime. It was ironic that Norman himself had been enlisted in the British army at the age of fourteen, but as a result of his case, there can be no doubt that charging child recruiters with an international crime today does not infringe the rule against retro-activity.[7]

The rule has been further restricted by the Sierra Leone Court decision that forced marriages are a crime against humanity, given that they amount to 'other inhumane acts of a similar character intentionally causing great suffering or serious injury to mental or physical health' under the court's statute. They are 'of a similar character' to 'rape, sexual slavery, enforced prostitution' etc., which are listed as crimes against humanity in the ICC statute, when committed as part of a widespread and systematic attack on a civilian population. The defendants, leaders of one brutal faction, had approved when their troops systematically abducted young girls from their homes, in violent circumstances, and compelled them to act as 'bush wives', accompanying their 'bush husbands' and providing them, exclusively, with sex, cleaning and cooking. They would become pregnant and bring up the children of the 'bush marriage'. They were subject to brutal discipline if they did not consent to these indignities, and evidence was called to show how deeply traumatized they were by the experience, many suffering health problems as well as from

STIs and AIDS. The Court accepted that customary 'arranged' marriages violated human rights norms, but what turned these particular unions into crimes was the violence that accompanied them, the permanence of the servitude and the outrage on human dignity they constituted.[8] The international element was provided by the systematic attacks on civilians by soldiers encouraged by commanders to abduct 'comfort women'. Although 'forced marriage' as such may not be a crime, the *nullum crimen* principle was not infringed because the defendants must have known that their actions included the recognized crimes of rape and sexual slavery, and indeed had an aggravated element because of the ongoing physical domination and lasting mental damage. This came not only from the trauma in the forced relationship but from the continuing stigma in the community because they had served as the partner of a killer. The *Child Soldiers Case* and the *Forced Marriages Case* show how international criminal law, by focusing on systematic outrages on human dignity, can produce acceptable results on a case-by-case basis. Further examples of 'other inhumane acts' are provided by convictions for desecration of dead bodies of those fallen in battle[9] and forcing women POWs to march naked in public.[10] The categories of men's inhumanity to women can never be closed.

THE STATUTE OF LIBERTY

The rights of humankind now accepted as universal have to do with individual freedoms from (a) wanton state infliction of death and torture; (b) arbitrary arrest and unfair trial; and (c) unreasonable interference with choice of religion, opinion and associates. These liberties may be classified in different ways, but on any view they are designed to keep the state at a distance, to ring-fence every adult from interference with his body or his mind, until a defined point at which social dangerousness justifies intervention. These liberties are expressed negatively, as justiciable rights against the state, i.e. the government and all its agencies. Normally it will be the state itself that is the violator, through police or army or security services, but the state may also be obliged to exercise its power to stop violations by third parties – whether they be vigilante groups, death squads or potent private organizations like media groups or multinationals or trade unions. It follows that the pivotal technical right, which must be implemented as a precondition of the enjoyment of basic liberties, is the right to an effective remedy. This is promised, in general terms, by Article 8 of the Universal Declaration:

Everyone has the right to an effective remedy by the competent national tribunals for acts violating the fundamental rights granted him by the constitution or by law.

This curiously inadequate formulation – 'law' must include 'international law', since some nations have constitutions and domestic laws which do not grant fundamental rights – is rectified by Article 2(3) of the Civil Covenant, which requires state parties to guarantee the human rights 'as recognized herein', and to ensure that when remedies for their breach are granted by national tribunals, 'the competent authorities shall enforce [them]'. In other words (and the point is surely obvious), only enforceable remedies are 'effective'. The European Court has held that to be 'effective', remedies for breaches of rights must include compensation or some other benefit to victims. It is not enough, for example, that invaders of privacy can be reprimanded or even fined by a regulatory authority – there must be realistic redress for the suffering caused – e.g. by payment of damages.[11] The principle has been most notably flouted by the Vatican (a state, even if a make-believe one) because the Catholic Church has been found in many countries to have put its own financial and reputational interests ahead of the interests of children in its care, tens of thousands of whom have been molested by paedophile priests. Its insistence that all such crimes should be dealt with under canon law, a process which imposes secrecy on all participants and involves no punishment of rapist priests (other than 'penitence' and, very rarely, defrocking), is a blatant breach of the Convention on the Rights of the Child, requiring such crimes to be reported to the police. The Vatican practice of approving the transfer of paedophile priests to unsuspecting parishes or unsuspecting countries is, of course, even more deplorable, and may amount to aiding and abetting a crime against humanity.[12]

The other pivotal principle of international human rights law is that of non-discrimination. Rights must not be vouchsafed or denied by reference to distinctions

of any kind such as race, colour, sex, language, religion, political or other opinion, national or social origin, property, birth or other status.

This organizing principle is found in Article 2 of the Universal Declaration, and it is repeated in the promise of Article 7 that

[a]ll are equal before the law and are entitled without any discrimination to equal protection of the law.

The principle is endorsed in the Covenant (Article 3 of which binds state parties 'to ensure the equal right of men and women' to the enjoyment of all its civil and political rights). But, most importantly, it is to be found entrenched in the UN Charter, the third purpose of the organization being defined to include

promoting and encouraging respect for human rights and fundamental freedoms for all without distinction as to race, sex, language, or religion.

It follows that international law is breached whenever rights of universal application are denied through racism or sexism or on religious or any other 'status' grounds. Since the UN Charter binds every state, this rule cannot be vitiated by common state practice to the contrary. But does it amount to more than a way of *testing* whether the rights are breached, or is it a freestanding right not to suffer discrimination, enforceable on behalf of individuals? If the discrimination is so widespread and severe as to amount to either apartheid or genocide, this would certainly be the case, as the conventions on these two international crimes make clear. The position would be the same if the distinct status was treated by national law as criminal or as entailing quasi-criminal consequences: hence municipal laws penalizing Jews or gypsies or homosexuals must be in breach of this international rule notwithstanding the number of countries which still make homosexuality, for example, a crime. The rule against discrimination may also come into play to determine whether other, entrenched rights have been breached – as it did to characterize as 'degrading' the racially discriminatory treatment of Asians holding British passports who were denied entry to Britain when they exodused from Kenya and Uganda in 1973.[13] Race discrimination is more clearly condemned than that on grounds of gender – the United Nations itself and most of its principal organs are dominated by men, notwithstanding Article 8 of the Charter which requires appointments to be made 'on conditions of equality'. Recently the UN has taken steps to redress this imbalance by advertising senior positions for which applications from women are 'particularly encouraged'.

The Convention on the Elimination of All Forms of Discrimination against Women entered into force in 1981 and has been ratified by most states, but with reservations which preserve for Muslim countries the indelibly sexist legal regime of Sharia law, and for the United States the power to deny any woman either an abortion or paid maternity leave. This must be compared to the equivalent Convention on the Elimination of All Forms of Racial Discrimination, which has been almost universally and unreservedly ratified, thereby establishing an international law against systemic racism. So it is idle to pretend that at this point in time equal treatment for women is a rule of international law. It should be, of course, but so long as discrimination remains a basic tenet of many national legal systems, the *opinio juris* necessary to make international law is lacking, other than where violations of womanhood are so systematic and gross that the state fails in its internationally recognized duty to protect victims, if it does not possess or does not enforce laws against their violators.

Even at this elemental level, international law has been slow to recognize rape for the war crime it invariably constitutes when inflicted with impunity by victorious armies. Although prohibited in terms by Geneva Convention IV and as a form of torture by all human rights conventions, 'spoils of war' rapes (such as those in Bangladesh in 1971) were not taken seriously until they featured in war crimes indictments handed down by the International Criminal Tribunal for the Former Yugoslavia (ICTY) at The Hague. States are in consequence under the clearest international law duty to ensure that military commanders take all reasonable steps to prevent and punish sexual abuse of civilians, and the commanders themselves as well as their soldiers will be criminally liable for any failure. It is not sufficient for a state to point to a domestic legal prohibition, if in practice its police force does little to implement the law – a commonplace throughout the world in cases of wife-beating and domestic violence. This duty is difficult to enforce, unless police or prosecution inaction is caused by procedures which the state can alter. (Examples include the Sharia evidence rule in Pakistan that rape convictions require four witnesses who must all be male and Muslim, and the macho 'honour' defence in parts of Latin America which in practice produces acquittals for husbands who kill adulterous wives.)

There are special international law duties imposed on a state in respect to persons under eighteen. Children are a very recent subject of human rights law, omitted from the eighteenth-century declarations because they were then regarded as the property of their parents. The League of Nations, moved by the numbers orphaned in war, issued a declaration in 1924 about the duty of governments to provide food, shelter and medical attention for poor children, but although the Universal Declaration stands up for bastards (by insisting that illegitimates should not suffer discrimination), it says no more than 'Motherhood and childhood are entitled to special care and assistance' (Article 25). The Civil Covenant, too, is vague, giving protection to children only as part of a family and affording them just one right – to acquire a nationality. Eventually, in 1989, came the Convention on the Rights of the Child: its importance is demonstrated by the fact that it has been ratified by every nation. Article 3 imposes a pivotal duty:

In all actions concerning children, whether undertaken by public or private social welfare institutions, courts of law, administrative authorities or legislative bodies, the best interests of the child shall be a primary consideration.

This principle is now part of international law and is reflected in the custody laws of most states, although in tandem with Article 9 (which imposes a duty to avoid separating a child from its parents) it often comes into conflict with penal decisions – e.g. to jail a child or to deport a parent. It was in the latter situation that the High Court of Australia in the *Teoh Case* invoked the Convention as a means of reviewing a decision made without considering the interests of the deportee's children. (This was a groundbreaking decision for international law generally, because a local court found a way of holding the state to the principles of a treaty it had signed but not incorporated.)

States must take effective steps to protect children from economic or sexual exploitation and abolish 'traditional practices prejudicial to the health of children' – a firm rejection of the 'cultural relativism' arguments which attempt to justify tribal maiming. Significantly, Article 23 endows mentally or physically disabled children with a special right to claim such assistance from the state as may be necessary to develop into full and useful members of society. Children must not be executed or jailed for life; they must not suffer imprisonment with adult offenders and states must establish a minimum age for criminal liability (many do, but since the range is between seven and sixteen, this rule is of scant assistance). These provisions may draw additional *opinio juris* support from general human rights provisions: thus under the 'inhumane treatment' prohibition in the European Convention, the European Court has held that the birching of juvenile offenders, even those convicted of acts of violence, was degrading treatment, a form of 'institutionalized violence' constituting an assault on the individual's dignity and physical integrity. School canings too were unlawful, the court later ruled, if suffered by children contrary to their parents' wishes and beliefs about how they should be educated.[14] In its controversial but correct *Bulger Case* decision in 1999, this court ruled that children charged with heinous crimes must be tried with a fairness which reflects their tender age.[15] Two ten-year-olds who had murdered a small boy were put on trial in the dock of an adult court packed with prying journalists and old men in pantomime wigs and gowns, quoting Latin. The youths were traumatized by proceedings they had not understood. The decision requires states to provide special treatment for children appearing in court as witnesses or as defendants.

SAFETY OF THE PERSON

The most basic right of all is that to life – guaranteed by Article 8 of the Universal Declaration. At its highest, namely when the State takes life pursuant to a policy of genocide, this right is so forcefully protected by international law (it carries every Latin tag from *jus gentium* and *jus cogens* to *opinio juris* and *erga omnes*) that it justifies armed intervention by other states, whether pursuant to Chapter VII or by way of a unilateral humanitarian mission, and the ICJ may order 'provisional measures' against a government under the Genocide Convention. The right to life stands as fundamental and non-derogable in all human rights conventions, the barrier against all forms of summary execution without a fair trial, whether of soldiers shot as they surrender or dissidents assassinated by death squads. This right is the basis for imposing duties on the state to investigate and prosecute any of its agents reasonably suspected of unlawful killings. (See chapter 7.)

Article 5 is also fundamental:

No one shall be subjected to torture or to cruel, inhuman or degrading treatment or punishment.

There can be no doubt that the rule against torture has evolved into a *jus cogens* prohibition which every state has a duty owed to the international community to outlaw and to punish. This follows from a multitude of sources, most notably the 1984 Convention on Torture, ratified by 150 states, which requires torture suspects to be put on trial or else extradited to a country which *will* put them on trial. The force of the prohibition was described by the Hague Tribunal in *Prosecutor* v. *Anton Furundžija* as 'designed to produce a deterrent effect, in that it signals to all members of the international community and the individuals over whom they wield authority that the prohibition of torture is an absolute value from which nobody must deviate'.[16] The *Furundžija Case* was specifically approved by the House of Lords in *Ex parte Pinochet (No. 3)*.[17] Torture is defined by the Convention as the international infliction of *severe* pain or suffering, whether physical or mental, by or with the consent of a public official, although it specifically excludes suffering attendant upon the imposition of lawful punishments (see pp. 330–36). Whether there is a binding international law against 'degrading treatment' must be open to doubt, given its breach in prisons and interrogation centres in many countries. The distinction most commonly quoted comes from a case brought in the European Court by the Republic of Ireland against the UK over the 'in-depth interrogation' to which internees in Belfast in 1970 were subjected by the British army: they were hooded and ordered to stand for several hours spreadeagled against a wall, while questioning was interspersed with disorienting effects like sleep deprivation and high-pitched noises. This was held to be degrading treatment but not torture, which the Court defined as 'deliberate inhuman treatment causing very severe suffering'.[18] In cases brought against the fascist military junta in Greece, the Court had no hesitation in finding that electric shocks, *bastinado* (beating of feet so as to produce pain and swelling), genital assault, burning with cigarettes and sticking pins under nails would all cause pain of sufficient cruelty and intensity to satisfy this definition of torture.[19] The Civil Covenant, with a nod to victims of the Auschwitz doctors, spells out that, when in the hands of the state, subjection to medical or scientific experimentation without consent is also a form of torture.

It is instructive to note how countries which have not signed the Covenant or the Convention against Torture are none the less anxious to deny that their harsh treatment of prisoners satisfies the definition. In 1988, Singapore made this claim in respect of its policy of applying 'psychological pressure' to political detainees (young Catholic lawyers and playwrights who had dared to criticize Lee Kuan Yew). They were denied sleep for up to seventy hours at a time, and kept standing directly under the blast of a freezing air-conditioner. During the interrogation period they were repeatedly slapped on the face and doused with cold water, warned that their friends and relatives would be arrested and that they would be detained indefinitely, unless they confessed. This 'psychological pressure' was cunningly devised to leave no permanent physical mark: it was that very cunning, and the fact that its object was to elicit a false confession (which they were required to repeat on state television), that justified its characterization as torture.

The right to life and to be spared torture are connected with the rights under Article 4:

No one shall be held in slavery or servitude; slavery and the slave trade shall be prohibited in all their forms.

Freedom from slavery was the first human right to crystallize as international law: the Covenant expressly prohibiting it dates from 1956 and has been ratified by 123 nations. Like the right to life and to humane treatment, it is made non-derogable by the Civil Covenant, which means that it cannot be curtailed or derogated from, even in a public emergency. (This let-out is provided by Article 4 of the Civil Covenant, although 'derogable' civil liberties, such as freedom of speech, may be suspended only while the emergency lasts.) The right to avoid 'forced or compulsory labour' is not made non-derogable, so this lesser freedom cannot be regarded as entrenched in international law: it is subject to numerous exceptions, such as 'hard labour' during imprisonment, conscription and 'any work or service which forms part of normal civil obligations'.

An associated non-derogable provision, Article 6 of the Universal Declaration, occurs in identical terms in the Civil Covenant:

Everyone has the right to recognition everywhere as a person before the law.

This overlaps with the prohibition on slavery, a crime which denies legal status to its victims in the sense that it treats them as property rather than as persons. It may also be relevant in attacking the most fundamental form of discrimination, which denies civic rights to persons defined in human categories, such as women or homosexuals or Jews. Religious laws in many countries breach Article 6 by treating such groups not as 'non-persons' but as 'lesser persons', e.g. women and non-Muslims in Sharia law. India is in breach of Article 6 by maintaining laws and caste systems which in practice discriminate against millions of 'untouchables' like the Dalits. Such blatant breaches do not attract international action unless the state becomes a pariah for other reasons: in overthrowing the Afghanistan government for its involvement in 9/11, the US and its allies claimed added justification from the Taliban's obnoxious laws against women being seen, heard or educated beyond the age of twelve.

A crucial physical safety right for individuals is to leave a state where their lives are in danger, and to be permitted entry to the first country they come to where they need have no fear of persecution. Sadly, the millions of refugees in the world and the reluctance of safe countries to admit them has made this a right honoured much more in the breach than in the observance. It is of historical interest to note that it appears in fairly expansive terms in the Universal Declaration, to shame all the states which turned away Jewish refugees from Nazism:

Everyone has the right to seek and to enjoy in other countries asylum from persecution.

This was a precious but increasingly inconvenient right, jettisoned by the Civil Covenant. Fortunately, the world was still idealistic enough in 1951 to agree to the International Convention on Refugees, albeit in a much narrower formulation. That covenant, which has now been ratified by 145 countries (but few from Asia), provides international law protection in the negative sense that no country can deport a refugee to a state

to which he is unwilling to go owing to a well-founded fear of being persecuted for reasons of race, religion, nationality, membership of a particular social group or political opinion.

This Convention establishes the 'Good Samaritan' principle that no state can expel from its territory any persons likely to be murdered or maltreated at their destination for reasons of race or religion or politics. It is supplemented by the Torture Convention, which prohibits deportation to countries where torture probably awaits. The Convention does not protect criminals or terrorists, who are excluded, and does not allow oppressed persons to travel abroad: it applies only to provide a sanctuary for those who have managed to escape, if they can prove that they are not 'economic immigrants' and that prosecution back home is both a near certainty and likely to lead to loss of liberty, if not of life. The UN's High Commission for Refugees (UNHCR) is tasked with supervising millions of asylum seekers each year, manning refugee camps and (if governments are unable to do so) interviewing claimants to decide whether their fears of persecution are well-founded. This agency performs a herculean task, but has been criticized for making it more difficult for members of groups formerly involved in armed struggle – the Tamil Tigers, for example, or the Iranian dissidents, the Mujahedin-e-Khalq – to have their claims accepted. Whilst those facing terrorist charges should be returned to countries where courts are independent and impartial, there is no basis in the Convention for denying or delaying refugee status to those who would, in their native land, be persecuted for present or previous political allegiance to an opposition group. It was wrong for the UNHCR to discriminate in this way in 2011 against several thousand Mujahedin refugees in Camp Ashraf in Iraq, who were in danger of death had they been returned ('refouled') to Iran.[20]

Europe has been particularly concerned to turn itself into a 'fortress' against the 'onslaught' of refugees, and France and Germany restrict the Convention's protection – wrongly, as a matter of law – to those at risk only from government forces, and not from local militias, warlords and terrorists. Many Asian countries refuse to sign the Convention and have become notorious for pushing 'boat people' back to sea as prey for pirates (Malaysia) or for turning a blind eye to the bribery which makes them a transit point for people-smugglers (Indonesia). A dishonourable precedent was set in 2001 by Australia, which refused landing rights to a Norwegian merchant vessel, the *Tampa*, which had rescued several hundred refugees after their boat had sunk. Captains have a maritime law duty to rescue those in peril on the sea, and Australia bore a correlative humanitarian duty, on which it reneged, to land them and then consider their claims to asylum. (It later bribed the tiny Pacific state of Nauru to take most of the *Tampa* refugees.) This episode may be explained by the fact that the government was in the throes of an election, and took the opportunity to boost its popularity at the expense of refugees and respect for international law – an ironical example of how the emerging right to democracy (see p. 239) is no guarantee that less popular rights, like asylum, will be protected. Australia, for all its size, takes only 23,000 refugees: states bearing the heaviest burdens are Pakistan (almost two million), Iran (1.1 million) and Germany (0.6 million).

The only long-term solution to the refugee problem is for the international community to put an end to the persecution which causes the exodus in the first place. The 1951 Convention was a Cold War device to give sanctuary to those fleeing from the onset of Stalinism in eastern Europe. In today's world, the people most in need of succour are those the refugees leave behind, who lack the money, health or connections to seek a better and less brutal life abroad. It is illogical to make successful escape a precondition for protection: in a sense, those who get away are less deserving, precisely because they have managed to leave. The overthrow of the Taliban gained added justification from the fact that, like Milošević in Kosovo, they persecuted civilians so severely as to cause a refugee crisis. There is certainly an emerging rule of international criminal law that the forcible displacement of a settled population amounts to a crime against humanity if conducted as an act of state policy and may, if undertaken ferociously and on a large scale, justify armed intervention by other states on the grounds of humanitarian necessity. On this basis NATO countries justified the bombing of Serbia in 1999.

The Universal Declaration aimed to make everyone a citizen of the world. Article 13 provides

(1) Everyone has the right to freedom of movement and residence within the borders of each state.

(2) Everyone has the right to leave any country, including his own, and to return to his country.

This is one of many articles stated in absolute terms, subject to the all-purpose caveat of Article 29(2) that they may be made the subject of legal restriction to secure the rights of others or to meet 'the just requirements of morality, public order and the general welfare in a democratic society'. States have given an expanded meaning to these exceptions on the basis they are fighting a 'war on terror': immigration officials have lengthy watch lists of suspected terrorist sympathizers who are turned away at borders. Interpol, an international policing operation based in Lyon, France, issues notices to all countries about persons who are 'wanted', although not always for serious or substantiated crimes. Its 'red notice' procedure can be exploited for political purposes – an outrageous example being the 'red notice' it issued in 2011 against Benny Wenda, head of the West Papuan freedom movement, at the behest of the Indonesian government, after he had already been given political asylum in the UK because of that government's persecution of him.[21] Interpol cravenly complies with Iranian government requests to issue 'red notices' against its escaped dissidents. It is difficult to believe that politics did not play a part in the issue of a 'red notice' against Wikileaks founder Julian Assange, accused in Sweden of having consensual sex but without a condom required by his partners, when the country that really wanted him to be treated like a terrorist was the United States (where popular talkshow host Rush Limbaugh demanded that 'Assange die of lead poisoning, from a bullet in the brain'). What this clause of the Universal Declaration does give rise to is an international 'due process' rule requiring some prospect of opening that door through legal action. East German border guards who shot on sight anyone attempting to exercise an Article 13(2) right to leave their country have been convicted of crimes against humanity. It should be possible to test the necessity of the restriction through action under municipal law, as in the notable case of *Kent* v. *Dulles*, where the US Supreme Court refused to allow the State Department to withhold passports from citizens merely because they were communists.[22]

The passport is not a legal document, although it provides *prima facie* evidence of nationality and identification and its convenience makes it indispensable for the modern traveller. It serves as the symbol of nationality, the possession of which is a separate right under Article 15 of the Universal Declaration, together with the right to change nationality. This supports an international law rule against statelessness, under which nationals are absolutely entitled to return to their own country. Many states jealously retain petty regulations which discriminate in favour of those born within their borders, or against them when they take up another nationality, and laws like these unnecessarily hinder the working and family lives of many peripatetics. If the right to change nationality were to include a right to *dual* nationality (which some states accept), many of these problems would disappear.

Magna Carta was first to proclaim the right of every free man to leave the realm at his pleasure in time of peace. The Universal Declaration reasserts this, although subject of course to the Article 29(2) public order exceptions (used to justify travel restrictions on British football hooligans) but also to Article 29(3):

These rights and freedoms may in no case be exercised contrary to the purposes and principles of the United Nations.

Governments could by reference to Article 29(3) justify keeping both sanctions-busting sportsmen and would-be suicide bombers at home. A state is entitled – indeed, obliged – to stop anyone within its borders from leaving to fight for forces which are committing war crimes. As a last resort – and only if measures such as confiscation of passports and 'house arrest' will not work – a state may be justified in interning those within its borders determined to leave to fight for such a cause.

INDIVIDUAL FREEDOMS

A cluster of rights in the Universal Declaration serves communal ends as well as personal development. The right to marry, and to give full and free consent to that marriage, and to found a family protected by the state *as a family*, all derive from Article 16. These principles are often asserted in municipal law to challenge immigration decisions which have the effect of breaking up families, e.g. by deporting one member or refusing entry to another. Article 16 does not strike in terms at 'arranged' or proxy marriages, such as are common on the Indian subcontinent, but it does require that each partner approve of the arrangement (if not of each other). It specifically entitles them to equal rights 'during marriage and at its dissolution', thus conflicting with patriarchal systems where the father is designated head of the household, and with divorce laws which expressly favour custody for the wife or automatically penalize a 'guilty' party.

Further protection to the individual as part of a family is provided by Article 12, which prohibits 'arbitrary interference with . . . privacy, family, home or correspondence'. A few sophisticated legal systems provide their citizens with a right to privacy (generally by permitting the recovery of damages for deliberate violation) but it cannot be said that international law requires states to go that far: the right can only be universalized as one to challenge by legal process any form of bugging or burglary of the home by a state agency. In other words, as the European Court has repeatedly held, each state must put in place a system of prior authorization (normally, by way of warrants obtained on application to a judge after production of evidence of 'reasonable suspicion') before its police may enter and search a home, or intercept private mail or telephone conversations. This rule has proved useful for curbing the 'Big Brother' tendency of the state, especially in Europe, where the right to privacy in the European Convention has been held to oblige member states to introduce laws that punish flagrant media intrusions. In the UK, the mighty Murdoch media was brought low when its stories about celebrity sex turned out to have been obtained by illegal telephone hacking.

Privacy is a value which calls for protection because of the individual's psychological need to preserve an intrusion-free zone of personality and family. For that reason, it appears in all the main human rights treaties, although they speak in the same breath of the 'right' to freedom of expression. These two rights are often perceived to conflict and, influenced by the media's self-interest, the West has become much more concerned about free speech violations than privacy violations. The former attract the undivided attention of human rights organizations (some formed solely for this purpose) while the latter are rarely condemned. For the media, lack of privacy is perceived merely as a *quid pro quo* for being rich and famous, forgetting (as Orwell never did) that communism deprived *all* citizens of any right to privacy from the state. What matters is that municipal law should enforce respect for a few fundamental decencies, so that privacy and freedom of expression are recognized as values which are universal and complementary. Public figures, whether crowned or elected or created by happenstance, might then enjoy reputations based on truthful appreciation of all significant aspects of their lives *except* that part they live behind a door marked 'Do Not Disturb'. This cannot be dictated by international law: it needs to be located culturally, according to local conceptions of dignity and decency, and may legitimately deny the media (and other intruders) access to private places like the bedroom, the bathroom, the hospital and the grave.

That said, freedom of expression should be regarded, like the right to a remedy, as a pivotal right in international law. That is because, quite simply, international attention and action against human rights abuses cannot be aroused without it. Richard Dimbleby's broadcast from Belsen, the sound of gunfire in Tiananmen Square, the television pictures of 9/11 and 7/7, and the children dead at Beslan and starving in Darfur, Neda, the young protester deliberately murdered on a street in Iran – reports of atrocities incite people throughout the world to put pressure on governments to do something about them. There was certainly a time – during the Second World War and for many years afterwards – when the extent of human rights abuses in far-flung countries was known only to the intelligence services of major powers. Gradually, NGOs like Amnesty were able to build their own intelligence networks, drawing on low-key missions and on sources promised confidentiality, and they filtered the information into the public domain through annual and special reports. Although many countries have some degree of news and opinion censorship, most information of importance to human rights can be placed on the

Internet, where it cannot be jammed or blanked out, although some states, notably China and Zimbabwe, prohibit access to critical sites, and even Turkey closed down Internet traffic so its people could not access a site which suggested Atatürk was gay. What is needed, therefore, is a rule framed in terms which enable the media to *extract* information from governments, as well as provide freedom to disseminate it when extracted.

Article 19 provides:

Everyone has the right to freedom of opinion and expression; this right includes freedom to hold opinions without interference and to seek, receive and impart information and ideas through any media and regardless of frontiers.

Article 19 of the Universal Declaration is reproduced as Article 19 of the Civil Covenant. The latter spells out the standard qualifications, which allow the right to be overridden by considerations of reputation, national security, public order or morals. But it makes clear, like the European and American Conventions, that these exceptions are to be narrowly construed and applied only when truly necessary to protect the excepted values. They are, moreover, exceptions that can never apply to thought, which remains the one natural right – or at least capacity – that can never be shackled. Attempts to scramble or punish thought, by 'brainwashing' or psychiatric treatment or laws which permit detention of persons suspected of harbouring disloyal imaginations, are in fundamental breach of the most elemental guarantee of freedom. Article 20 of the Covenant goes on to make two controversial provisos:

(1) Any propaganda for war shall be prohibited by law.
(2) Any advocacy of national, racial or religious hatred that constitutes incitement to discrimination, hostility or violence shall be prohibited by law.

These prohibitions on hate speech were formulated in memory of Hitler's ranting rallies and the obscene racism of *Der Stürmer* magazine (whose editor, Julius Streicher, was convicted and hanged at Nuremberg). Article 20(1) has been universally ignored, especially by the superpowers and other states involved in Korea, Vietnam and Iraq, wars which were trumpeted among their own people and to the world as 'just'. It can, however, justify bans on advocacy of war crimes, or 'holy war' crimes like suicide-bombing. Many countries have implemented Article 20(2) by enacting race-hate legislation, which the European Court has consistently held to correspond to that 'pressing social need' which overrides free speech in a democracy. America, however, regards its constitutional right to free speech as virtually absolute (other than to stop people shouting 'Fire!' in crowded theatres) and has entered a reservation to Article 20. The position was famously epitomized in the 1977 action of the American Civil Liberties Union (ACLU), supporting the right of a group of fascists to march through the predominantly Jewish town of Skokie, Illinois. The organization's stand on principle – that the free-speech guarantee of the First Amendment was absolute – cost it thousands of members and brought it close to bankruptcy, although its stand in support of hate speech was upheld by the court and confirmed by the Supreme Court in 1992 when it struck down as unconstitutional a ban on racist symbols like swastikas and Ku Klux Klan crosses.[23] But the ACLU gesture was on behalf of a handful of racist malcontents of no political importance, attempting to provoke safe, prosperous and peaceful citizens. This was a world away from the teeming hamlets of Rwanda and Burundi, where in 1994 terrified Tutsis huddled to hear their own slaughter being urged from Hutu-controlled radio station Libre des Mille Collines: 'The grave is only half full. Who will help us fill it?' A barbaric genocide followed which cost 800,000 human lives: its scale can partly be attributed to these ferocious broadcasts, and there has been no criticism of the jailing by the International Criminal Tribunal for Rwanda of the 'journalists' responsible for them.

The most significant feature of common Article 19 for international law is that it is designed to protect the free flow of information and ideas 'through any media and regardless of frontiers'. Throughout the 1990s, states went to extraordinary lengths to impose political censorship, especially on outside criticism of their leaders: the Sey-chelles banned all fax machines and Burma refused to permit satellite television, while in Malawi Dr Banda made it a crime to own a televi-sion set or to tune a radio to any but his own one-party station. Singapore even contrived a ridiculous law to ban foreign publications while pretending not to ban them: papers like the *Asian Wall Street Journal* and the *Far Eastern Economic Review* were adjudged to have 'interfered in local politics' (i.e. they accurately reported opposition to Lee Kuan Yew), whereupon their circulation was cut by ministerial order from 10,000 copies to a few hundred, distributed to govern-ment departments and tourist hotels. Lee Kuan Yew made the risible claim that by this means the international press was not banned, but merely 'restricted' for its temerity in reporting what his opponents were saying. In reality, of course, he was using the device to stop his own people from reading in the 'foreign' press the kind of news which the government-controlled Singapore press refused to print. Many states are at present trying to restrict access to the Internet, either by criminal laws which prohibit it entirely (in Iraq, North Korea, Burma and Syria) or by controlling a sole service provider (in Saudi Arabia, all traffic goes through a ministry which disallows access to sites offering 'information contrary to Islamic values'). A similar 'fire wall' has been erected by China, not only to stop information coming in other than through the official gateway, but to stop 'official secrets' (i.e. criticisms of the regime) being e-mailed abroad. China's surf wars are fascinating to watch, given popular expertise with the technology: the Falun Gong cult was banned more for its ability to organize dem-onstrations by e-mail than for its meditation techniques.[24] In Harare, a secret-police division is devoted to scouring the web for libels on Robert Mugabe. A local correspondent for the *Guardian*, which is not distributed in Zimbabwe, was prosecuted in 2003 for 'spreading false news' in an article that appeared on the newspaper's London website. He was acquitted at trial when the prosecution was unable to access the article (because it had been taken off the site) but Mr Mugabe, a bad loser, had the journalist deported.

International law provides a presumption in favour of free speech, but this protection is not (as in the First Amendment) absolute in the absence of malice. Depending on the degree of public interest in the information which it is desired to communicate, the value may be overborne by other considerations. That most commonly invoked by governments is 'national security' – often a bogus reason, especially after the end of the Cold War. The European Court has made clear, in its *Spycatcher* judgment, that suppression orders and injunctions which impose 'prior restraint' are to be avoided if possible.[25] An exception which is more formidable, both because it protects the citizen rather than the government and because Article 12 of the Universal Declaration promises protection against 'attacks upon honour and reputation', is that newspapers which publish defamations or damaging falsehoods about individuals and organizations should be obliged to correct them. On the assumption that there is a reasonable system available for adjudicating where the truth lies this is unobjectionable: in some states, however, plaintiff-friendly legal systems can cause media defendants to suffer heavy financial penalties. This is particularly so in Commonwealth countries like Malaysia and Singapore, where government ministers and their business cronies obtain massive libel awards to bankrupt political opponents and disrespectful journalists. Such awards constitute an improper restraint (a 'chilling effect') on freedom to communicate, so held the European Court in *Tolstoy* v. *UK* (in which the author of a book imputing war crimes to a former British general had been ordered to pay £1.5 million in damages).[26] An unattractive consequence of wide variations in press laws across the globe is that wealthy and powerful 'public figures' seek out the forum which has the most plaintiff-friendly law for their actions against newspapers, books and magazines which are distributed for worldwide sale, as well as against satellite television and the Internet. (The favourite forum at present is the UK, which places a heavy burden on the media to prove the truth of the stories and permits libel actions if only a few copies of the offending publication are circulated within the country.) This ability to forum-shop for the jurisdiction which is least tolerant to free speech should be curtailed: in a global village it makes no sense for the new breed of 'international' public figures to enjoy different reputations in different parts of town.

Common Article 19 bestows a right to 'seek' information as well as to receive and impart it. This must imply more than a right to ask questions, and may be used to support three implications of the Article 19 right: (1) to impose duties on governments to divulge information; (2) to protect whistleblowers who breach secrecy laws and employment contracts in order to speak out, in conscience, from within a government agency; and (3) to permit journalists to refuse to divulge their confidential sources for stories, no matter how much the identity may be of interest to police or security services, or to government or big business. In this last respect, in 1996 the European Court held in *Goodwin* v. *UK* that the right to freedom of information carries the implication that journalists must be permitted to protect their sources, otherwise there would be no information to be free with – sources of news would 'dry up'.[27] Although the finest 'free speech' rhetoric comes from the US, especially from its Supreme Court when it allowed publication of the 'Pentagon Papers', the behaviour of the Pentagon itself, and of the US politicians and commentators, was deplorably hypocritical when Wikileaks published secret US diplomatic cables revealing (amongst much useful information) serious political corruption in some countries and many human rights abuses. Julian Assange was subjected to a grand jury investigation and his alleged source, the young soldier Bradley Manning, was the victim of degrading treatment in his first eight months of incarceration. Although US diplomats suffered embarrassment, nobody's life was put at risk (the cables were not *top* secret) and the public was better informed about what their rulers were up to. Governments are responsible for keeping their own secrets: unless those are extracted by bribery or duress, journalists should not be prosecuted for passing them on to the public.

Linked to freedom of speech is the freedom of belief guaranteed by Article 18:

Everyone has the right to freedom of thought, conscience and religion; this right includes freedom to change his religion or belief, and freedom, either alone or in community with others and in public or private, to manifest his religion or belief in teaching, practice, worship and observance.

This right is made non-derogable by common Article 18 of the Covenant, more perhaps as a measure of its symbolism for a world with a history scarred by religious wars than for its contemporary relevance to conflicts produced by ethnic and political hatreds, although religious differences still fuel these fires in places as far removed as Bosnia, Iraq, Afghanistan and Northern Ireland. International courts can try to reduce the dangers of religious fanaticism – by, for example, ensuring that no religion gets preferential treatment, that secularists and atheists are not discriminated against, and that educational institutions do not engage in 'brainwashing'. The European Court has promised to intervene if state schools engage in religious proselytizing, although this was said in *Lautsi* v. *Italy*, a case where it decided that the display of a Catholic cross in every state school classroom did not cross this legal line.[28] Its decision was reached on the ground that it had no expert evidence to assume – and the judges were not prepared to use their common sense to recognize – that forcing children to stare at a Catholic symbol every minute of their schooldays might incline them to adhere to that religion.

The right vouchsafed by Article 18 appears somewhat overstated at a time when Islamist extremists claim that suicide-bombings of civilians are a public manifestation of religious belief, and it must be read down, by reference to Article 29, to protect only those public manifestations that cause no public offence. A tougher, more secular approach to religious freedom was apparent in 2005 in the European Court of Human Rights case of *Sahin* v. *Turkey* which approved a ban on the wearing of headscarves at Istanbul University.[29] Freedom of conscience and religion was 'a precious asset for atheists, agnostics, sceptics and the unconcerned' as well as for believers, but it did not protect every religiously motivated action. Regulation was necessary to achieve toleration, especially in respect of wearing religious symbols in educational institutions. The Court observed, with an unusual acidity, that wearing the headscarf 'might have some kind of proselytizing effect, seeing that it appeared to be imposed on women by a religious precept that was hard to reconcile with a principle of gender equality'. It could not easily be reconciled with the 'message of tolerance, respect for others and, above all, equality and non-discrimination, that all teachers in a democratic society should convey to their pupils'. Religions and cults are riddled with sexist and superstitious practices: the overdue message of *Sahin* is that they will receive scant protection if there is a rational justification for denying them public display in places or at times when they are calculated to cause offence or disharmony.

International law condemns discrimination on all grounds, and the right to one's religion is in effect a right not to suffer unfairly for practising it. Its non-derogable status does not give a dominant religion any special claim to override minority rights or to have its doctrines – themselves often cruel and prejudicial to women and adherents of other religions – specially exempted from the ground rules set out in Articles 29 and 30 for respecting the rights and freedoms of others. Thus, the inequities of Sharia law are not excused by its claim to be based on Islam (its penalties for apostasy are grotesquely incompatible with the right to change religion) any more than the right to practise Catholicism gives a state comprised mainly of Catholics the right to prevent women from choosing birth control or from going abroad for abortions. The *fatwah* on Salman Rushdie and his translators and publishers imposed by Iran for his 'crime' of apostasy was not only a breach of Article 18, but an act of international terrorism.

This article, like the others, is principally concerned to protect individuals against state tyranny, including attempts to impose religious orthodoxy, and so it must be read as a right to choose atheism, or Rastafarianism, as well as any 'recognized' religion. This follows, in any event, from the promise of freedom of thought and conscience. Religion has been objectively defined as having two criteria, 'first, belief in a supernatural Being, Thing or Principal and second, acceptance of canons of conduct in order to give effect to that belief'.[30] This means that it includes nonsense like scientology and Satanism, and that in theory 'cults' enjoy the same international law protection as the great faiths, subject always to the state's duty to curtail such of their activities as may damage the general welfare. The state is not prohibited from making one creed its own 'national' religion, although it may not place severe restraints on free speech in protecting adherents from insult. Blasphemy laws which cover a number of faiths can probably be upheld if they protect adherents from obscenity or offensive abuse, but not from criticism or contempt. The right to practise religion is a right to go to heaven in your own way, while tolerating others who choose different paths or none at all.

Another overlapping right is that of association. Article 20 provides:

(1) Everyone has the right to freedom of peaceful assembly and association.

(2) No one may be compelled to belong to an association.

International law thus recognizes the right of peaceful protest, which, notwithstanding its tendency to clog the traffic, remains a potent method for demanding and obtaining change. It was the crowds who stayed for weeks in the streets which brought about the 'Velvet Revolution' in Prague in 1989, the fall of the Suharto regime in Indonesia in 1998 and the fall of Ben Ali (Tunisia) and Mubarak (Egypt) in 2011. The crowds in Tiananmen Square and in Uzbekistan might have had a similar impact, had they not been dispersed by real, rather than rubber, bullets. The right of peaceful assembly is constrained by the need for public order; however, there is a correlative duty upon the state to disperse peaceful assemblies by peaceful means. That these may include tear gas, rubber bullets and water cannon is regrettable, but most demonstrators would rather be gassed and splashed than shot. International law accepts a proportionality test, condemning the use of excessive force in crowd dispersal. Breaches of this rule can have international criminal consequences: commanders who order their soldiers to fire upon peaceful demonstrators will be liable to trial under the Rome Statute for a crime against humanity. (This may be one reason why China voted against the creation of the International Criminal Court.)

Article 20(2) moves on to a different dimension, where it protects associations as well as assemblers. This has been of great importance to oppositionists battling against one-party states in eastern Europe and Africa, since the article is incompatible with bans on membership of non-violent political parties. Thus Paul Muite, a courageous president of the Kenyan Law Society, argued that a constitutional right in identical terms permitted his countrymen to form and belong to parties opposed to that of Daniel Arap Moi, even though local law prohibited them from contesting elections. The members of the Czech Jazz Society – the cultural front for Charter 77 in its battle against the state – kept making music and mischief together by invoking their constitutional entitlement to this right through the society's membership of UNESCO. It did not prevent their prosecution, but it forced the communist regime to frame them on fraud charges because it could find no legitimate basis for jailing them for belonging to a peaceful organization. The right does not admit 'semi-peaceful' organizations to its protection: only if an organization is demonstrably non-violent need the state tolerate it on an equal footing with others.

Article 20(2) is commonly taken to prohibit the 'closed shop', i.e. the use of trade union muscle to force members to join the union or else be sacked. It cannot be argued that a choice to be unemployed is any choice at all, and the European Court in *Young James and Webster* v. *UK* said as much in upholding the rights of railway workers to remain in employment notwithstanding their refusal to join a union with political commitments they did not share. This is a good example of a state being required to introduce laws to prevent the violation of individual rights by powerful private organizations, in this case the trade union which had effectively blackmailed the employer into sacking the complainants. Trade unions are beneficiaries of the freedom of association principle, through the individual worker's right to join them which is vouchsafed by Article 23(4).

THE RIGHT TO FAIRNESS

International law acknowledges, through its Conventions and case law, the right to fair treatment of women and children, and of racial, religious and even sexual minorities. But the rights of the mentally disabled to participate fully in human society are the last to have been recognized. It took until the 2006 Convention on Rights of Persons with Disability before there was a guarantee that such persons should have equal access to community services and facilities. It has been a long process, from the welfare model embodied in the Poor Law (which formally removed social rejects from the community and diminished the quality of their life by unnecessary institutionalization) to a rights-based approach which entitles those wrongfully detained or discriminated against on grounds of mental handicap to use the law as a weapon for redress. In 1948, the destruction in part of a race or ethnic group was outlawed by the Genocide Convention, but it made no reference to groups that had been exterminated as 'useless eaters' by the Nazis, or discarded as 'feeble-minded' by the eugenics movement in the US and the UK or had been the potential victims of sterilization programmes with the slogan 'three generations of imbeciles are enough', or actual victims of 'breeding out' programmes, like the 'stolen generation' of Australian Aborigines. The public intellectuals who made eugenic euthanasia fashionable in the 1920s were, of course, still in the grip of the nineteenth-century rationalist fallacy that rights should belong only to those capable of logical thought – a principle that in the Victorian age excluded 'women, dogs and lunatics' from the professions, the universities and the franchise.

The Universal Declaration made no mention of those with mental disabilities, and the position changed only as the European Convention on Human Rights took hold, through decisions of its Court in Strasbourg. In Britain, for example, the problem for mentally disordered offenders was that any kind of liberty – release, recall, discharge – depended not on a review tribunal (its decisions were no more than recommendations) but on the politician – easily deterred by fear of adverse publicity – who happened to occupy the office of Home Secretary. Human rights law requires decisions about restoration of liberty to be a matter of independent judgment rather than political discretion, and Article 5(4) of the Convention gives all detainees the right to have the lawfulness of their confinement decided by a court. The Strasbourg judges ruled that the Review Tribunal was not a 'court', because it had no power to do other than make recommendations to the minister. The law in the UK had to be changed so that it was henceforth for the minister to make recommendations to the Review Tribunal.[31] This was an example of a significant contribution by human rights law to ensuring fairness for mentally disordered offenders, by insisting that decisions about their liberty are made independently and impartially.

There is, of course, much more to be done. At present, the international reporting system which covers all state parties to human rights conventions still fails to include 'mental health' as a matter on which these states must report. This must change, and urgently. The true test of a nation is how it treats its most vulnerable citizens, and mentally disabled people still have their lives made miserable – sometimes too miserable to bear – by being bullied and scapegoated and taunted. Persecuting people on account of or by reference to their mental capacity should be made a specific criminal offence. Laws and practices that have the effect of excluding the mentally disabled from community experiences and duties – jury service, for example – must be reconsidered. Slowly, in a few countries, human rights rules are promoting the happiness of those who, through no fault of their own, have minds less adjusted to a world which should value them none the less, and especially.

Legality is essentially a promise of fairness: that in the criminal and (where appropriate) civil systems there will be no arbitrary arrests, biased judges and oppressive procedures. Derogation from these rights may be permitted at times of 'emergency' – when there is a war or a continuing terrorist threat or a natural disaster – but not disproportionately to the exigencies of the situation and never for the purpose of racial, religious or sexual discrimination. The one principle which permits of no derogation is the rule against retroactivity: no person may be convicted for an act which was not a crime at the time it was committed (Universal Declaration, Article 11(2)). Importantly for prosecutions of war criminals and perpetrators of crimes against humanity, this rule means that the act must have been punishable under either national or international law. The Nuremberg defendants could not argue (although they tried) that it was a breach of the rule to try them for offences which had no equivalent in the law of Nazi Germany, when the offence existed in *international* law. The Covenant (Article 15(2)) makes plain that nothing in the rule against *ex post facto* laws shall prejudice trial or punishment for any act which was, at the time of its commission, 'criminal according to the general principles of law recognized by the community of nations'. The Pitcairn islanders who had sex with their children were on this basis guilty of rape, despite the absence of any law or law book on the island for 200 years.

The Universal Declaration does not detail the rights which must be afforded a defendant at the time of arrest and detention, and then at time of trial. The major powers had commonly interned 'fifth columnists' on the flimsiest suspicion, and they routinely detained colonial leaders under internal security laws. So the only detention right which can be spelled out, and with some difficulty (by coupling Article 9, below, with the right to an effective remedy), is that of *habeas corpus*:

9. No one shall be subjected to arbitrary arrest, detention or exile.

The Civil Covenant elucidates this right: detention must be in accordance with a settled procedure, and the detainee has to be (1) informed of the grounds for his arrest, (2) brought promptly before a judge, (3) given the opportunity to test the lawfulness of the detention and (4) entitled to ask for bail. An important new right was added that had no resonance in state practice at the time, but which is now gaining acceptance: the wrongly detained victim 'shall have an enforceable right to compensation'. The Covenant also adds some basic humanitarian rules about jails – for example, requiring remand prisoners to be segregated from convicts and juveniles from adults. Its drafters had read Charles Dickens on the evils of the debtors' prison: they made it a non-derogable duty to ensure that 'No one shall be imprisoned merely on the ground of inability to pay a debt'.

Articles 10 and 11 of the Universal Declaration identify, in the briefest terms, the rights to fair trial:

10. Everyone is entitled in full equality to a fair and public hearing by an independent and impartial tribunal, in the determination of his rights and obligations and of any criminal charge against him.

11(1). Everyone charged with a penal offence has the right to be presumed innocent until proved guilty according to law in a public trial at which he has had all the guarantees necessary for his defence.

To identify the necessary guarantees, turn again to the Covenant. In Article 14 they include the defendant's right to:

(1) be informed promptly of the nature of the charges;

(2) adequate time and facilities to prepare the defence;

(3) trial without undue delay;

(4) be present at the trial, and to be defended by counsel of his own choosing, or (if indigent) to have legal aid for counsel where the interests of justice require it;

(5) cross-examine hostile witnesses and to require the attendance of witnesses who can give evidence for the defence;

(6) have an interpreter where there are language difficulties;

(7) not to be compelled to testify against himself or to confess guilt;

(8) if convicted, to have the right of appeal;

(9) have a remedy in the event a miscarriage of justice can be demonstrated, and to receive compensation for wrongful conviction;

(10) never be placed in double jeopardy, i.e. not to be retried after a final acquittal or conviction.

These fair trial rights have been recently entrenched in the international tribunals set up in The Hague and Arusha to conduct trials relating respectively to former Yugoslavia and Rwanda, and in the UN war crimes court for Sierra Leone, and they are reflected (or, in some cases, such as the right to silence, extended) in the Rome Statute of the International Criminal Court. They show some bias towards the Anglo-American system of adversarial trial, although they are not inconsistent with inquisitorial systems – the latter placing more emphasis upon the judge as investigator and determiner of truth than on the creative play of a defence team. Most of the guarantees can never be cast iron: the trial may need to go into closed session to protect child witnesses or rape victims; a defendant may be excluded from his own trial if he tries to disrupt it; 'counsel of choice' may be unavailable and trials cannot be scheduled for the convenience of lawyers. Defendants in receipt of legal aid have no such right: they are entitled to express preferences, but the authorities have an overriding duty to provide them with counsel of competence and of sufficient independence to defend with vigour, especially in 'political' cases.[32] The double jeopardy rule, when applied inflexibly, can produce shocking results – as when persons acquitted of serious crimes through lack of evidence subsequently confess to guilt or have it conclusively established by advances in forensic science like DNA tests, but cannot be reprosecuted. For this reason the UK has provided that the double jeopardy rule may be set aside by an appeal court if fresh and compelling evidence of guilt emerges after an acquittal. It is difficult to accept that every specific guarantee has ripened into international law, although this certainly is the case with the more general requirement that these rules be sufficiently respected to produce a trial which is fair.

Four guarantees do seem to possess that 'normative' quality which makes them part of customary international law. First and foremost is the presumption of innocence, described as the 'golden thread' of common law.[33] It appears in every human rights treaty and in Rule 21 of the Hague Tribunal and as Article 66 of the Rome Statute of the International Criminal Court. This presumption has two effects: the prosecution must always bear the burden of proof, and must shoulder this responsibility in criminal cases to a high standard, proving the case beyond reasonable doubt. Although some latitude is allowed in requiring defendants to prove matters of which they should have a special knowledge (such as the possession of a licence to do an otherwise unlawful act), the general burden at the end of the day must fall on the prosecution. International case law is remarkably unanimous on this point.[34]

Secondly, serious criminal trials must be open to the public. Publicity, as Jeremy Bentham put it, 'is the very soul of justice. It keeps the judge, while trying, under trial.' The 'secret court' has been associated over many centuries with gross abuses of power. The public nature of the trial remains the greatest safeguard against the unfair use of criminal proceedings, although Sweden, in an excess of zeal to encourage women to testify, holds all its rape trials in secret.

The third great safeguard is the 'independence and impartiality' of the judges, as individuals with sufficient confidence and backbone to stand up to governments and other power-wielders in the society (not excluding the power of terror and intimidation wielded by criminal gangs). This principle is so important – and so endangered – that it receives special treatment at the end of this chapter. It was breached by the Zimbabwe government in 2001, which permitted its 'war veterans' and other supporters to intimidate the Chief Justice and force his early retirement; he was replaced by Mugabe's former attorney-general. It was breached by the 'Special Military Commission' ordered for Guantanamo Bay detainees, who are being tried by career army officers and not judges. Impartiality is provided for by a rule disqualifying judges for bias, on the principle that 'justice must be seen to be done'. It has been rigidly applied by the European Court, ordering the disqualification of judges if they have come from offices connected with the prosecution or, as in *Hauschildt* v. *Denmark*, have made any prior decision in the case as a result of which bias as to its outcome might reasonably be inferred.[35] The rule was most notably applied by the House of Lords in 1998 when it bent over backwards to do justice to General Pinochet by annulling its initial 3–2 decision against him because one of the majority judges had served (unpaid) on a charity connected with Amnesty International, which had intervened to argue that the ex-head of state was not immune from prosecution. This tenuous non-financial link was sufficient to disqualify the judge: although justice had undoubtedly been done, it had not been seen to be done.[36]

The most serious problem with many Third World judiciaries is corruption, because judges are paid so little that they become prey to temptation from richer litigants. In Indonesia until recently, for example, corruption was institutionalized as a means of paying the judiciary. Judges indicated their needs – a car, a refrigerator or whatever – and on receiving a gift from each party tried to mediate a mutually acceptable solution to their dispute. In many countries, corruption comes through political connections: since judges are appointed and promoted by governments, lickspittles are common. Some judges actually take orders from government (this was common in the Soviet Union and eastern Europe until the fall of communism) while others (in Singapore, for example) reflect a culture where the government is always right. But, for all the examples of judicial corruption, there are heartening (indeed, heart-rending) cases from Italy and Colombia of judges prepared to do their duty according to law, notwithstanding the danger to their lives.[37]

The fourth guarantee which may have achieved international law status, although it is not to be found in the Universal Declaration, is the defendant's right 'not to be compelled to testify against himself or to confess guilt'. Article 14 of the Covenant begs the question of what amounts to compulsion: a gun to the head, clearly, and brutal inter-rogation and threats to family of the kind made to elicit the public confessions at Stalin's show trials. But the somewhat mundane prom-ises and inducements ('You can have bail if you spill the beans') which can serve to exclude confessions in Anglo-American law are not com-pelling. The right against self-incrimination has been taken so far as to require in the Rome Statute of the International Criminal Court a rule against the drawing of inferences of guilt from a defendant's refusal to testify. This is illogical and Britain, which pioneered this 'right to silence', abandoned it in 1994. Such an extensive defence right seems incompatible with the rights of victims of crimes against humanity to have the truth about them told – the most important reparation of all. Where evidence establishes a *prima facie* case of genocide or torture, the defendant surely has a moral duty to respond: common sense would infer guilt from a defendant's refusal to explain the blood that the evidence plainly shows to be on his hands.

Both the Universal Declaration and the Covenant are silent on one important consequence of the right to liberty: the principle that the state should neither spy on law-abiding citizens nor incite them to commit crimes. But there is a general rule in the Hague and Rome statutes entitling these international criminal tribunals to exclude unfairly obtained evidence, and it is through this back door – an aspect of the duty of fair trial – that the use of state *agents provoca-teurs* may be attacked. The principle is of importance, given the history of states fomenting crimes as an excuse for aggression, the blackmailing of diplomats and the use of stool pigeons to frame dis-sidents. There is also concern at the clandestine operations of intelligence and security agencies, especially when they are directed to entrapment.[38] State agencies which routinely or randomly test the vir-tues of citizens they have no reason to believe are engaging in crime put liberty at risk in a manner which was classically condemned by Justice Felix Frankfurter in *Sherman* v. *US*:

The power of Government is abused and directed to an end for which it was not constituted when employed to promote rather than to detect crime and to bring about the downfall of those who, left to themselves, might well have obeyed the law. Human nature is weak enough and sufficiently beset by temptations without Government adding to them and generating crime.[39]

Most legal systems strive to avoid the spectacle of trial and punishment of those who would never have broken the law without the urgings of state agents.[40] An international law rule against state instigation of criminal offences is in the process of crystallizing: what does emerge consistently in human rights jurisprudence is a duty on the state to draw up strict protocols governing undercover investigations and to monitor their observance effectively. International criminal courts should decline to lend authority and approval to improper and unlawful conduct by investigators and prosecutors. This is the approach taken by the US Supreme Court,[41] the High Court of Australia,[42] the House of Lords[43] and the Supreme Court of Canada.[44]

The European Court of Human Rights has developed a stringent rule against entrapment, which breaches the fair trial guarantee of Article 6(1) of the Convention, and further against the unsupervised deployment of secret surveillance, which offends the privacy guarantee in Article 8, because:

the public interest cannot justify the use of evidence obtained as a result of police incitement, as to do so would expose the accused to the risk of being definitively deprived of a fair trial from the outset.[45]

This was said in *Bannikova* v. *Russia*, which set out a number of tests for determining entrapment, the most important of which is the question of whether the offence would have been committed in any event without the intervention of state agents.

Police incitement occurs where the officers involved – whether members of the security forces or persons acting on their instructions – do not confine themselves to investigating criminal activity in an essentially passive manner, but exert such an influence on the subject as to incite the commission of an offence that would otherwise not have been committed, in order to make it possible to establish the offence, i.e. to provide evidence and institute a prosecution . . .[46]

This test requires consideration of whether the suspect was predisposed to commit the crime; whether the government had ulterior motives for mounting the 'sting' operation (the 'good faith' issue); whether any form of financial or other pressure was applied, and whether undercover agents merely joined a conspiracy already afoot or whether they initiated or induced the criminal act by their words or deeds. As the court put it in *Bannikova*:

When drawing the line between legitimate infiltration by an undercover agent and instigation of a crime, the court will examine the question whether the applicant was subjected to pressure to commit the offence. It has found the abandonment of a passive attitude by the investigating authorities to be associated with such conduct as taking the initiative in contacting the applicant, renewing the offer despite his initial refusal, insistent prompting, raising the price beyond average . . . or appealing to the applicant's compassion . . .[47]

Importantly, when applying this test for entrapment the court insists that the burden of proof must be placed on the state, unless the defendant's allegations are 'wholly improbable'.[48] The state will be unable to discharge the burden if its agents have embarked on an undercover operation – especially one involving secret surveillance – without formal (usually judicial) authorization and supervision.[49] In *Khudobin* v. *Russia* the Court ruled that there must be a 'clear and foreseeable procedure for authorizing investigative operations, as well as for their proper supervision'.[50] The burden cannot be discharged by the state unless it puts all relevant information openly before the trial court to enable it to be tested in an adversarial manner.[51] Although Article 8(2) of the Convention permits secret surveillance operations in combating crime, a long line of European cases[52] insists that this is conditional upon there being a law in place which provides sufficient guarantees for authorization and judicial oversight.

In several recent cases the court has condemned abuses of state power in the form of a trick played or a trap set by a state agency acting in bad faith. In *Conka* v. *Belgium*,[53] for example, officials issued false and misleading statements to lure Roma asylum seekers into a police station on the pretext that they would be helped to file their applications: when they arrived they were arrested and held for deportation. They had been deprived of their liberty in a manner incompatible with the purpose of Article 5, which is to protect individuals from arbitrary arrest. Instead, the state agents had issued official communications dishonestly to gain the trust of individuals and to lure them into a situation where they were deprived of their liberty. This form of entrapment violated Article 5, notwithstanding that they were illegal immigrants. In *Gusinsky* v. *Russia*,[54] an oligarch detained on fraud charges was offered a deal whereby these would be dropped if he ended a commercial dispute by transferring his media company to a government corporation. The Court found a violation of Article 18 (which requires that Convention exceptions – e.g. which justify actions taken in order to combat crime – should be strictly applied to their stated purpose) together with a violation of Article 5. Although Gusinsky had been detained on reasonable suspicion of fraud, the state's ulterior motive was to put pressure on him to transfer his media business. Criminal charges and detention without bail, the court said, cannot be 'used as part of commercial bargaining strategies'.[55]

The most that international human rights law can require, given the prevalence of international terrorism, drug trafficking and money-laundering crimes which require undercover methods to detect, is that states provide sufficient safeguards within their domestic justice systems for defendants to challenge the misconduct by secret police to which they have been subjected – an aspect of the guarantee of fair trial. The freedom to assemble and to speak openly will be infringed by secret-police infiltration of political parties or pressure groups if done with the objective of turning organizations committed to lawful change into seditious and treasonable conspiracies. All secret surveillance undertaken by the state should be conducted according to clear rules and procedures, with the additional safeguard that the risk of unreliability should be guarded against by monitoring the behaviour of those agents with a motive – be it money or political spite or a wish to win immunity – to incriminate those they are sent to spy on. States which cannot produce legal rules for limiting undercover operations cannot claim that their citizens enjoy the right to liberty.

JUDICIAL INDEPENDENCE

Independence means putting judges in a position to act according to their conscience and the justice of the case, free from pressures from governments, funding bodies, armies or any other source of state power and influence that may possibly bear upon them. That an independent judiciary is a prerequisite for any society based on the rule of law cannot be doubted. Conditions for independence are set out in the International Bar Association (IBA) rules, the *Minimum Standards of Judicial Independence*, agreed in 1982, and in the *Basic Principles of the Independence of the Judiciary*, adopted by the General Assembly of the United Nations in 1985.[56] These instruments lay down guidelines for appointment and removal, for tenure, conduct and discipline, which are generally designed to ensure that 'judges are not subject to executive control' (personal independence) and that in the discharge of judicial functions 'a judge is subject to nothing but the law and the commands of his conscience' (substantive independence). The latter formulation is high-sounding but inadequate: a judge is subject additionally to certain public expectations arising from the constitutional importance of the office. These should be spelled out in a Code of judicial conduct, requiring justice to be done efficiently and decently, without fear or favour, discrimination or discourtesy.[57] Any complaints about breaches of the Code should be decided by a tribunal which includes senior judges, and is itself free from executive influence.

The preamble to the UN's 'Basic Principles' notes: 'whereas frequently there still exists a gap between the vision underlying these principles and the actual situation'. In 2011, this was an understatement, as some random examples show:

* In Uganda, President Museveni mounted a direct attack on the Constitutional Court for doing its constitutional duty by striking down an inconsistent Act of Parliament. He made a televised address accusing the judges of 'usurping the power of the people' and claimed that 'the major work for the judges is to settle chicken and goat theft cases but not to determine the country's destiny'. The government orchestrated a large demonstration against the Court.[58]

* In Belarus, Judge Siarhei Bandarenka jailed a human rights activist, Ales Belyatsky, for four and a half years and ordered the seizure of his property. Although it masqueraded as a tax offence, the crime was brought under retrospective legislation banning NGOs from receiving donations from abroad. The defendant's real crime in the eyes of the regime was leading an organization that defended protesters arrested for demonstrating against dictatorial Belarus President Lukashenko.[59]

* In 2008, three judges were summarily dismissed by order of the President of The Gambia, in reprisal for decisions they had taken in politically sensitive cases.[60]

* In Ukraine, Judge Rodion Kireyev was condemned by the European Union for sentencing opposition leader Yulia Tymoshenko to seven years in prison (with an order to pay £120 million to the state and a three-year ban on political participation). As she said to the court, 'You know very well that the sentence is not being pronounced by Judge Kireyev, but by President Yanukovych.'[61]

* In Russia, old habits die hard: two constitutional court judges were forced to resign after making critical comments about how judicial decisions were really taken by an 'authoritarian' government.[62] There has been worldwide criticism of the Mikhail Khodorkovsky decision, with credible allegations that the judge was directed to convict.

These are all public examples of cases where the high principles of judicial independence have been breached or at the very least put in jeopardy. In some cases the issue is well publicized, by courageous judges or by the resignation of the judge under pressure, but in others it depends on the happenstance of a human rights report on the country in question or whether an alert journalist has identified and publicized a behind-the-scenes government manoeuvre.

Subtle political influences on the judiciary are difficult to detect and can be inferred only from evidence of pattern or system. Take Georgia, for example, where the government, after its 'Rose Revolution', purported to crack down on corruption and to allow democratic freedom to flourish. Yet the conviction rate remains, today, a staggering 99.6 per cent. Is it possible to believe that Georgian policemen arrest only those whose guilt can be proved beyond reasonable doubt? That Georgian judges are not independent can be inferred from this statistic, which is provided by the courts themselves, as if proud of their performance. Suspiciously high conviction rates demand an explanation. When Georgia came up before the Human Rights Commission in 2011, only one country asked about judicial independence, and was of course told that it was improving. If the Commission is to function effectively on this issue, it must assume that any country with more than a 90 per cent conviction rate does not have an independent judiciary.

The real problem is that there is no way to detect whether a judge, or a court of judges, has made a perverse decision in order to curry favour with a government other than by close and expert analysis of the decision itself. This is easier when the intellectual dishonesty involves bending rules of law, but is more difficult to uncover if it has involved twisting the facts that the judge had to 'find' by believing or disbelieving witnesses. In other words, the bias of a good bad judge is very difficult to detect.

What can be done to detect the judicial lickspittle, when the pro-government pressure under which he or she has buckled is secret, or psychological, or generated by ambition or hope for post-retirement reward? The first step, namely analysing for perverse judgments in favour of the executive, must obviously depend upon their accessibility, and many even at appeal level are not officially reported. Publicity, as Jeremy Bentham pointed out, is a precondition of justice: 'it keeps the judge, whilst trying, under trial'. The IBA, in conjunction with the UN and interested foundations, could help by fostering the electronic availability of judgments.[63] It should be a duty on states to ensure that all final judgments are publicly reported, or at least available to the public if requested – a matter essential to checking judicial independence but overlooked both by the IBA minimum standards and by the UN principles. Secret or 'in chamber' judgments can be a vehicle for criminality: these were used by the corrupt Malaysian judges recently exposed as having conspired with lawyers to favour their clients. A right of public access to unreported judgments is the first step in identifying judges who are actually or intellectually corrupt.

Then, expert analysis of the suspect judgment is essential if perversity is to be exposed. The UN Rapporteur on Judicial Independence should undertake research into the quality of the jurisprudence of courts suspected of truckling to governments. A great deal of aid money is spent on judicial training, and indeed on judicial networking, but very little on assessing judicial performance and identifying cases where facts have been ignored or twisted, or rules of law misstated or bent, to reach politically convenient conclusions.

There is another danger to judicial independence on the horizon, as a consequence of financial constraints. The justice system – especially criminal justice and justice for unpopular people like immigrants and asylum-seekers – is a favourite target for politicians in times of financial stringency. Indeed, Greece has cut its immigration tribunals so close to the bone that the ECHR held in 2011 that it is denying access to justice. The IBA 'minimum standards' assert 'the duty of the state to provide adequate financial resources to allow for the due administration of justice'.

More worrying are cuts in court funding which may reduce the capacity to do justice. At what point should the judges of an underfunded court have a duty to resign? This question was addressed by the Special Court for Sierra Leone in *Prosecutor* v. *Hinga Norman*. Defendants argued that the independence of their judges had been imperilled by a 'voluntary donations' system in which some thirty UN countries paid for the Court's upkeep, by way of voluntary infusions of funds which they had no obligation to give or repeat. Significantly, the Court acknowledged that if funding did fall below a certain level, its judges would pack up their tent and depart:

It would be an act of moral irresponsibility for the international community to establish a criminal court system, necessarily involving loss of liberty by arrest and detention as well as by custodial sentence, which lacked the financial guarantees necessary to complete its task. Paying judicial salaries – conventionally set at a high level to remove the temptation to bribery – is but one essential requirement. There must be sufficient funding to keep prisoners in humane conditions and to provide indigent defendants with adequate legal representation. Were a budgetary cut made which removed the right to legal assistance, for example, then the Court could not afford fair trial and should not attempt to do so.[64]

It is not unknown for judges appointed under one government to fall foul of the next, whose attorney-general may be invidiously tasked with bringing criminal charges against them or alternatively moving for their dismissal. In such circumstances, judicial independence requires that they be accorded fairness at every stage: when the allegations analogize to a criminal offence, the tribunal must not recommend dismissal unless satisfied to the criminal standard, i.e. beyond reasonable doubt. This was the conclusion of the Mustill enquiry, which exonerated Chief Justice Sharma of Trinidad, whom the government accused of interfering in a trial in order to favour the defendant (who was leader of the opposition). In cases which involve both personal and political animosities, fairness to a chief justice may require a determination of his conduct to be made by outside jurists (in the *Sharma* case, Lord Mustill sat with judges from Caribbean islands other than Trinidad).

Dissidents on trial in Eastern Europe prior to the velvet revolutions were familiar with the phenomenon of 'telephone justice', where the case would be decided not by the evidence but by a telephone call to the judge by the party boss, who had calculated the sentence according to its effects on 'the public good', which was usually a euphemism for the party's interests.[65] Honest and open criticism by politicians or members of the public is not, however, objectionable. In America, judges may be 'the least dangerous branch' of government, but none the less have a power vouchsafed to few other Supreme Courts, namely to directly strike down acts of the legislature. They cannot complain when legislators make them the target of political attack, or when they become the butt of popular displeasure, even in the form of bumper-stickers (e.g. 'Impeach Earl Warren'). What stands out in US politico-legal history, for all the virulent calls for 'court curbing', is the fact that Roosevelt's notorious attempt to pack the court failed, and that no Supreme Court judge has ever been successfully impeached (it was only tried once, on the elderly William O. Douglas, who had emphasized his belief in free speech by giving an interview to *Playboy* magazine).

The right to trial of civil and criminal cases before an independent tribunal is so fundamental that it should now be part of *jus cogens* – an international law obligation binding on all governments. Article 14(1) of the ICCPR encapsulates this rule, and the Human Rights Committee describes it in General Comment 32 (2007) as 'an absolute right that is not subject to any exception'.

Where a state party to the ICCPR fails to guarantee the rights contained in Article 14(1), an individual may initiate a complaint to the Human Rights Committee, provided that their state has ratified the First Optional Protocol to the ICCPR. (To date, 114 states have ratified.) Unfortunately, however, even those that have signed are prone to ignore an adverse decision by the Committee. An example is the case of *Oló* v *Equatorial Guinea*.[66] The complainant claimed that the judges in Equatorial Guinea could not act independently or impartially, since all judges and magistrates were directly nominated by the President. The Committee found that 'a situation where the functions and competencies of the judiciary and the executive are not clearly distinguishable or where the latter is able to control or direct the former is incompatible with the notion of an independent tribunal'. But the government has yet to issue a formal response to this decision. In its Concluding Observations, published on 13 August 2004, the Human Rights Committee merely 'expresses its concern at the absence of an independent judiciary in the state party'.

A few successful outcomes do occur. For example, in *Busyo, Wongodi, Matubuka* v. *Democratic Republic of the Congo*, the complainant judges were dismissed from office by Presidential Decree after allegations of corruption.[67] They did not receive a hearing before the

Supreme Council of the Judiciary, and the President of the Supreme Court had publicly called for the dismissals. The Committee found that 'the dismissal of the authors was ordered on grounds that cannot be accepted by the Committee as a justification of the failure to respect the established procedures and guarantees that all citizens must be able to enjoy on general terms of equality'. Following this decision, the judges were admitted to practice and received compensation for their arbitrary suspension from office. This case was satisfactorily concluded because there was ample and public evidence of the breach and the government was prepared to submit to the adjudication – conditions which are not often satisfied.

Another possible remedy is offered by complaining to the office of Special Rapporteur on the Independence of Judges and Lawyers, established by the Commission on Human Rights (Resolution 1994/41, extended through subsequent resolutions of the Human Rights Council). The Special Rapporteur responds to individual complaints, sends letters to concerned governments and summarizes these communications in an annual report, in which she comments on various country situations. Her effectiveness, however, is limited by the willingness of states to cooperate, or even to correspond with her. The Special Rapporteur's 2011 report reveals that she sent a total of ninety-seven communications but received only forty-one replies (a 42 per cent response rate). The current rapporteur, Ms Gabriela Knaul, usually postpones any comment or recommendation until a reply is received, but the low response rate suggests she should take the initiative if there has been no reply after a reasonable time. It also casts doubt on the clout of the Special Rapporteur, operating a system which relies on responses to confidential communications and is not equipped with resources to monitor courts in countries where the conditions for judicial independence are not fulfilled.

The method of appointing judges to international courts and tribunals raises important independence issues. Until recently, UN judges were nominated by states, with all the familiar UN problems of nepotism and horse-trading. There have been cases where friends or relatives of prime ministers, possessing no judicial experience, have been nominated; where judges who have attracted domestic scandal have been 'kicked upstairs' (out of sight and out of mind in a UN tribunal in Africa) and where diplomats with, and even without, law degrees have been transmogrified into judges by their fellow diplomats. Fumiko Saiga, a career diplomat from Japan, was elected as an ICC judge and oversaw its DRC proceedings despite the fact that he did not have a law degree.[68] His death avoided an appeal on the basis that he was unqualified, but Japan then nominated Kuniko Ozaki who had not yet finished her law degree, although it was said she had relevant experience – in Japan's Ministry of Justice.[69] Such appointments are bound to bring international justice into disrepute – and worryingly the ICC in September 2011 was forced to extend its deadline for new appointments because good judges had been reluctant to apply.[70] States take pride in having their nationals elected as UN judges (so long as they are loyal government supporters), and they lobby excessively for them – Nigeria even had T-shirts printed to support a recent candidate. The first academic study of UN judicial appointments concluded that the election of judges was indistinguishable from elections for political offices, and that 'vote-trading, campaigning, and regional politicking invariably play a greater part in candidates' chances of being elected than considerations of individual merit'.[71] The authors conclude that good judges are overlooked and bad judges are sometimes elevated to important and lucrative places (the ICC pays US$250,000 tax-free and a half-salary pension).

A better approach would be to take the nomination process out of the hands of states and entrust it to an expert and independent panel. This was achieved in 2008 in relation to the UN's internal judicial appointments by pressure from its staff unions, which insisted upon having the employment, disciplinary, sexual harassment, etc. cases brought by their members decided by judges who were independent of the organization. So the Internal Justice Council – a five-person body, constituted by a distinguished jurist and a union representative selected by staff, and a distinguished jurist and a UN executive nominated by management, chaired by a distinguished jurist selected by them (the first was South African Justice Kate O'Regan). The Council selects two or three of the best applicants and recommends them to the General Assembly for each judicial position. The appeal for candidates of ten or fifteen years judicial experience is made through papers like *The Economist* and *Le Monde*, and elicited in 2011 about 500 applications. The Council then meets to identify the top thirty to forty candidates, who are brought to The Hague to be invigilated by way of a two-hour competitive examination paper and a one-hour interview. Although all candidates will have had long judicial careers, an exam paper can detect those who have lazily allowed their judgments to be written by their associates or law clerks.

There are many judges of conspicuous (and inconspicuous) courage, who in some countries manage to do their duty in the face of quite awesome pressures. Gabriel García Márquez reminds us of how in Colombia, 'Judges and magistrates, whose miserable salaries were barely enough to provide for the education of their children, were faced with an impossible choice: either to sell out to the traffickers or to be killed by them. The most admirable and heartrending thing is that over forty of them chose to die.' Courage of that order is astounding, but it is necessary, in order to salute the brave and steadfast judges, to condemn the judicial cowards and the fellow-travellers, the time-wasters and the incompetents. The difficulty, of course, is to uncover threats to judicial independence and identify the lickspittle judges who bow to them. Naming and shaming judges is dangerous in many countries, thanks to Napoleonic insult laws bequeathed by the French and the arcane British contempt law against 'scandalizing the court' (in Scotland, it is called 'murmuring judges'). In America this crime has been abolished[72] and in Canada it is a dead letter,[73] but in many countries journalists find themselves threatened, arrested and even jailed for making imputations against the judiciary. These strict liability offences – of 'insulting' and 'scandalizing' – cast a chill over investigative reporting, especially investigations into judges who are controlled by or in awe of the government. In Singapore, the proprietor and two journalists from the Asian *Wall Street Journal* were held in contempt and fined merely for reporting the publication of an IBA report questioning the independence of the Singapore judiciary.[74] These offences have no place in a democratic society, where judges should be confident enough either to ignore criticism or to sue for libel if it seriously impugns their integrity. But they should welcome

– and even assist – journalists who seek information about hidden political pressures.

PEACEFUL ENJOYMENT OF PROPERTY

International law classically protected aliens from seizure of their land or goods on arbitrary or discriminatory grounds and additionally required expropriating states to pay appropriate compensation to foreigners deprived of their possessions. The right of nationals, too, to enjoy property was a central preoccupation of the American and French revolutions and their declarations. But subsequently, Marxist philosophy and practice favoured nationalization of industry and confiscation and redistribution of land, while independence movements, on attaining government, wished to extirpate foreign corporations regarded as agents of imperialism: they had stolen natural resources from the people, so they did not deserve compensation. Since this was the outlook of many states by the 1960s, little progress was made in putting further flesh on Article 17 of the Universal Declaration, which, at the insistence of President Truman, provided:

(1) Everyone has the right to own property alone as well as in association with others.

(2) No one shall be arbitrarily deprived of his property.

By the time the International Covenant on Political and Civil Rights had come to be drafted in 1966, there was serious disagreement over whether private property was a human right or any sort of right at all. Article 17 of the Declaration was but palely reflected in a rule against arbitrary deprivation of *privacy*, which would cover intimate personal possessions and, at most, the family home. One regrettable result was that this omission in the Covenant would, over the next quarter century, be cited by Jesse Helms and other isolationists in the US Senate as grounds for refusing its ratification. But as the Cold War ideological debates over property rights have receded, so Article 17 has crystallized into a rule of international law: there would at present be a broad consensus in its favour. The principle is embodied in Article 1 of the First Protocol to the European Convention on Human Rights, namely:

Every natural or legal person is entitled to the peaceful enjoyment of his possessions. No one shall be deprived of his possessions except in the public interest and subject to conditions provided for by law and by the general principles of international law.

In this formulation, state acquisition of private property is viewed as arbitrary where it is not in the public interest, although Article 1 goes on to allow governments a considerable margin of appreciation to control property in 'the general interest' by pursuing radical measures of economic reform or redistributive social justice. The European Court has held that governments do not breach Article 1 by acquiring ancestral estates or nationalizing private industry, so long as they provide appropriate compensation.[75] 'Arbitrary deprivation' in contravention of international law would have to be evidenced by personal malice or favouritism, such as the confiscation of the property of a dissident in order that it can be given to a party official, or depriving one ethnic or racial group more readily or severely than others – a feature of the government's confiscation of farms owned by whites in Zimbabwe. In the absence of discrimination, however, any form of 'public interest' will suffice, however economically or politically controversial: governments may acquire private land to return it to indigenous inhabitants or 'lock it up' to protect environmental values. They may redistribute land to peasants, or take land away from peasants to build dams or railways. The state's sovereign power to act in the general interest trumps the individual's right to enjoy private property, subject always to such duty as it has under international or national law to provide an appropriate measure of compensation.

The nature and extent of the obligation to compensate is a subject of a debate which is still tinged with ideological differences. In customary international law there is a duty to compensate aliens whenever their property is lawfully expropriated: this was settled by the Permanent Court of Justice in 1928 in the *Chorzów Factory*

Case.[76] Historically, aliens were owed special protection by their host state, and were more vulnerable to confiscations motivated by racism or jingoism. But it would be anomalous if the rule did not apply to nationals,[77] because it stems from a general principle of justice and equity ('Thou shalt not steal') and in modern times it is nationals who are most vulnerable to having their property confiscated arbitrarily. The 'right to own property' which Article 17 enunciates must carry as a corollary a right to compensation in the event of arbitrary deprivation: as the European Court has pointed out in respect of the First Protocol, 'the protection of the right to property . . . would be largely illusory and ineffective in the absence of a duty to provide compensation'.[78]

When a foreigner's property is expropriated, what measure of compensation must the state pay to its former owner? The words of US Secretary of State Cordell Hull, deployed by way of demand to the Mexican government when it confiscated the holdings of American landowners, provides the formula preferred by Western governments: compensation must be 'prompt, adequate, and effective', reflecting the full market value of the property which has been lost. It was described in the *Chorzów Factory Case* as 'the value of the undertaking at the moment of dispossession, plus interest to the day of payment'.[79]

These 'full compensation' principles are all very well when applied by claims tribunals assessing compensation due to foreign oil companies whose operations have been taken over as a going concern by oil-rich governments. But where inherited estates or areas of national heritage or precious ecology are taken into public ownership, a lesser standard – that of 'appropriate compensation' – may be deployed to give the former owner a reasonable sum, albeit one which falls considerably below market value. This standard was adopted by the UN in 1962 in its Declaration on Permanent Sovereignty over National Resources,[80] and again in 1974 in its Charter of Economic Rights and Duties of States.[81] These declarations were devised as justifications for developing nations who wished to 'buy back the farm' from colonial corporations at less than the market value, but in such cases a discount is fair only if the object of the acquisition is to right historical wrongs or to deprive former owners of windfall profits as the result of artificial inflation of property values prior to state acquisition. The European Court has consistently held that 'legitimate objectives of public interest, such as pursued in measures of economic reform or measures designed to achieve greater social justice, may call for less than reimbursement of the full market value'.[82]

So far as individuals are concerned, it may be said that international law recognizes in principle everyone's right to own private property, as declared in Article 17. It requires that right to be protected by states in the case of non-nationals, who must not have their property confiscated unless for a purpose which serves the general interest, and for compensation, if offered, to be given on just terms. There is an emerging international law rule requiring nationals to be compensated on the same basis. They certainly have international law rights if state action invades their privacy, which it would do by taking an individual's 'living space' – a family home, personal possessions and private goods with some element of sentimental value, and what are quaintly termed in bankruptcy law 'tools of trade'. Should the state trespass on this protected area, it can only do so in the public interest and by offering just compensation. The annexation of farms owned by white Zimbabweans was an outrageous breach of this principle: not only was it discriminatory and achieved by government-supported thuggery, but no compensation was offered.

The difficulty, as ever, is in finding a forum with the power to order compensation. Investors in countries where court systems are impotent or corrupt are well advised to ensure that any contract with the government or its enterprises contains an ICSID (International Centre for Settlement of International Disputes) clause which entitles them to appoint an independent arbitral panel to decide any dispute. The government becomes liable, under the ICSID Treaty, to pay the award, which in cases of expropriation may be in many millions, or even billions, of dollars, and can be enforced by sequestration of the government's commercial assets. Each side will choose an arbitrator from an approved list, and the two arbitrators select a chairperson, thus ensuring the tribunal's independence. The ICSID system has worked well, although a misguided decision by one panel, in the *World Duty Free* v. *Kenya* case, has limited its use as a means of exposing corruption.[83] It decided that the claimant should lose because although its business had been expropriated, its chairman had admitted that he had been forced to pay a bribe by President Arap Moi in order to obtain the contract. The Tribunal naively thought that its ruling would discourage bribery, although in the real world all it would discourage was telling the truth about bribery.

There is another right which is in the process of ripening rather quickly, as a result of international law's especial abhorrence of crimes against humanity. Any victim who has lost property in the course of such a heinous crime – the Jews who had their assets, their houses and their works of art confiscated in the course of the Nazi genocide, for example – have a right to its return, *in specie*, which trumps all local laws capable of creating difficulties (such as time bars). This is not just a right against the immediate Nazi beneficiaries, or those who acquired the property from them with knowledge of its origin. Such is the tenderness shown by international law towards victims of these crimes that their right can be asserted against third parties who purchased the property in ignorance of its origins. This right received grudging recognition from Swiss banks which allowed Nazi withdrawals from the bank accounts of genocide victims. What began as a class action in US courts brought by Holocaust survivors ended in a US$1.25 billion pay-out by a Swiss banking and political establishment terrified that exposure of their complicity with the Nazis would provoke US boycotts and a withdrawal from Geneva of the international organizations headquartered there.

The fact that the case was arguable in law meant that the morally guilty Swiss banks could not bear it to be argued: nor could Germany and its best-known companies when similarly sued by victims and relatives of victims of their wartime slave labour programmes. In frenzied pre-millennium negotiations, half a million claimants were bought off with a massive US$6 billion – half contributed by the German government. Had this case been fought, the courts might well have decided that inter-state arrangements (e.g. made between Germany and the Allies in 1951 to draw a line under the Holocaust) cannot bind individuals by stopping them from suing private companies which had once tried to work them to death. Establishing that this international right of the individual cannot be overridden by the sovereignty of states, and exposing the appalling history of the manufacturers of celebrated cars and cameras and clothing (Hugo Boss, for example, was tailor to the SS), might have been more valuable to the plaintiffs (and to everyone else) than obtaining an estimated US$5,000 per head in a settlement which made hundreds of millions of dollars for their contingency-fee'd lawyers. None the less, lawyers have been necessary to achieve a belated justice for victims whose governments ignored their rights when doing peace deals with Axis powers. In 2004, the US Supreme Court allowed an action against the Austrian government, over some Gustav Klimt paintings hanging in its National Gallery: they had been looted by Nazis from a Jewish family which now wanted compensation and the Court held that Austria could not hide behind state immunity in order to take the benefit of a crime against humanity. Apartheid victims are trying to sue the banks which propped up the South African state, in breach of trade sanctions ordered by the Security Council. They have had difficulties showing that apartheid was at the time an international crime (see p. 341), but the action at least sends a warning signal to corporations that disregard for human rights can have serious financial consequences.

4

Twenty-first Century Blues

'From this day forward, I no longer shall tinker with the machinery of death. For more than twenty years I have endeavoured . . . along with the majority of this court, to develop procedural and substantive rules that would lend more than the mere appearance of fairness to the death penalty endeavour. Rather than continue to coddle the court's delusion that the desired level of fairness has been achieved . . . I feel mentally and intellectually obligated simply to concede that the death penalty experiment has failed.'

US Justice Harry Blackmun, from his judgment
in *Callins* v. *Collins* (1994)

Human rights standards are becoming rules of international law because a campaigning mass movement is putting pressure on democratic governments to practise what they preach when they ratify treaties which embody these standards. Some national courts, too, are finding ways to hold governments to the 'liberty' rights of the Universal Declaration and the Civil Covenant. But what has happened to the 'lost rights' to social and economic development which were thought non-justiciable and sloughed off into a separate covenant? In 2005, Amnesty International announced that it would work to promote them – a policy shift that disturbed many members, who pointed out that the struggle for liberty rights, especially to abolish the death penalty, was far from over. This chapter will first examine that unresolved problem, and then consider another burning issue: the law's potential for advancing the political and social rights of minorities. The importance of making legal provision for ethnic minorities and indigenous peoples is underlined by the ethnic cleansing in the Balkans and Rwanda, and the potential of other melting-pot states to boil over. Can international human rights law do anything to ameliorate or mediate the blood feuds, or will nothing succeed like secession – the most fundamental of all attacks on the sovereignty of the state? And another vital issue: can it do anything to curb abuses by multinational corporations – entities wealthier and more powerful than many states, but traditionally beyond the jurisdiction of international law? Finally, it will be suggested that the direction in which the nations of the world are moving indicates that democracy – a political system which actually had a minority of adherents in the United Nations in 1948, and for decades afterwards, will eventually become a generally accepted form of government, and that Article 21 of the Universal Declaration will be freshly interpreted to make free electoral choice (between parties as well as candidates) an international law right in the course of the twenty-first century.

FREEDOM FROM EXECUTION

Executioners no longer burn the bowels of their victims before their very eyes or pluck out their hearts and hold their severed heads aloft, although the practice of stoning to death, still followed in some Islamic states, is of equivalent barbarity when inflicted for the 'crimes' of adultery or sodomy. Most retentionist states adopt more discreet modes of killing criminals, but no method is free from 'execution glitches'. Electrocutioners often miscalculate voltage or use faulty electrodes – the third-degree burns on the head and leg usually suppurate before the dead prisoner is unstrapped from the electric chair and his cooked flesh falls from the bone. In gas chambers in America, as in Auschwitz, prisoners fight in panic against the cyanide, 'eyes popping, tongue hanging thick and swollen from a drooling mouth'.[1] Hanging requires macabre preparation, weighing the prisoner and greasing the trap, and the strangulation (occasionally, decapitation) is traumatic: disposal of the stinking body with its elongated neck and diarrhoea-filled underwear is also a problem. The axe and the guillotine, much favoured historically for English and French aristocrats, are swift but too bloody and mutilating for Western liking, although several Middle Eastern countries still behead felons with a sword. Lethal injection is the preferred American mode of dispatch, although it leads to unseemly last-minute struggles to find a workable vein in some prisoners' drug-abused bodies and places attendant doctors in breach of their Hippocratic oaths. Missouri allows executees to invite friends to join the audience for their lethal injection: the first of such victims was seen to mouth 'I love you' to his wife before choking over his last breath. This is a more romantic ending than the offer of poison (now unfashionable, since few prisoners are prepared to drink it like Socrates), although it does not quite reach the operatic pitch of death by firing squad, where the ritual demands that the victim has a target pinned to his chest before being offered a last cigarette, and that one of the firing squad must, for the sake of its collective conscience, shoot a blank.

All these methods of execution cause intense physical pain, of varying duration, after the mental agonies during the preparation period of maybe several days. It was Stalin, ironically, who devised the demise least painful physically and mentally for political prisoners – a bullet fired at point-blank range into the back of the head when the victim was least expecting it, usually while being escorted down a dark corridor. This method is reliable, painful for the splittest of nanoseconds, and avoids the mental anguish of brooding over the appointed time and place of death. However, it offends both the legal requirement of due process and the religious rule that life must not be taken unless and until the prisoner has had an opportunity to prepare himself for its loss. It is a method used today mainly in China.

The cold-blooded killing of a healthy human being, other than in war or in order to save other lives, is an act universally condemned as evil. It does not entirely lose that quality when committed by the state, no matter what incantations of law or religion are used to absolve the officials obliged (albeit by their own choice) to carry out executions in one of the ways described above. The law against murder, which purposes to promote reverence for human life, cannot achieve that aim when the state itself takes life in the name of its people. There is no system which can be devised for inflicting the death penalty without cruelty or degradation, or for selecting condemned persons other than arbitrarily or without lurking doubts as to their guilt. Luck can play a preposterous part: Eduardo Agbayani, condemned to die when capital punishment was restored in the Philippines, was being led to his place of execution when President Estrada granted him a last-minute reprieve. Unfortunately, the prison telephone was engaged and news of the presidential pardon arrived seconds after his death. No research has confirmed the retentionist credo that the death penalty deters crime, other than in disappearing a criminal who would be neutered as effectively by an alternative sentence of life imprisonment. The US, for all its executions, still has the highest murder rate in the industrialized world, and is especially high in those states (Texas and Florida) which conduct the most executions. Significantly, the states which have not reintroduced the death penalty have comparatively fewer homicides than those which execute.[2]

The fallibility of human justice is underlined by the fact that DNA tests have scientifically proved the innocence of 130 men consigned to death row in America, and an authoritative study of all 5,760 capital cases between 1973 and 1995 showed that about two-thirds were vitiated by legal error, with 7 per cent of defendants demonstrably innocent and serious doubts about guilt in 60 per cent of these flawed cases.[3] However, in 2011 there were 3,251 inmates on death rows in the thirty-four US states that retain capital punishment, and Texas (with Supreme Court approval) executed Troy Davis despite substantial doubts about his guilt. The five main reasons for 'miscarriages' are: incompetent defence lawyers; prosecution suppression of evidence; black defendants convicted by all-white juries; and the prejudicial impact of two classes of unreliable evidence – eyewitness identification and the 'jailhouse snitch'. Capital punishment is reckoned to be four times more expensive to the state than life imprisonment. This is because of the extra appeals, security arrangements and so forth that must attend death penalty processes: Florida has costed each execution at $24 million, and Americans are asking, increasingly, whether the death penalty – abolished by all its main allies except Japan – is really worth it.[4]

In 1995 such arguments had persuaded South Africa's Constitutional Court to strike down, unanimously, the punishment which had so often served the apartheid regime. 'Death is different,' declared Ismail Mahomed, the nation's first black Chief Justice. 'The dignity of all of us, in a caring civilization, must be compromised by the act of repeating, systematically and deliberately, albeit for a wholly different objective, what we find to be so repugnant in the conduct of the offender in the first place.'[5] The Court concluded that the death penalty was an infringement both of the right to life and of the right to avoid 'cruel, inhuman or degrading treatment', because these rights were unqualified in the new post-apartheid constitution. Although it acknowledged that capital punishment was not yet contrary to international law, the force of its decision helps to inch international law slowly in that direction. Just how slowly is demonstrated by the Tanzanian Supreme Court, which decided in the same month that the mandatory death penalty, while cruel and degrading, was none the less constitutional because it was a 'reasonable and necessary measure to protect the 'right to life' of law abiding citizens'.[6]

There is no issue more politically polarized, or more heavily litigated, in human rights law than the sentence of death and its modes and rituals of execution. Most national constitutions reflect international human rights instruments in avowing respect for the 'right to life' and in prohibiting 'cruel or unusual' or 'inhumane or degrading' punishments and treatments – descriptions which were not thought, at the time of their adoption, to apply to the sentences of death regularly passed on persons convicted of serious crimes like murder or treason. No nation of any significance had abolished the death penalty by the time it was imposed on Nazi war criminals at Nuremberg in 1946, but the half century which elapsed before the next trial of an ethnic cleanser saw abolition – by law or in practice – in most of the 193 countries of the world, leaving fifty-three retentionist states, only twenty-three of which carried out executions in 2010. In

Amnesty reported a sharp rise in executions in the Middle East, Iran leading the way (ostensibly killing mainly drug traffickers, although there were suspicions that some dissidents were numbered amongst their ranks), followed by Saudi Arabia, Iraq and Yemen. It may be that the rise had more to do with deterring uprisings during the Arab Spring than with a serious outbreak of criminality. The good news was that executions in the US had reduced in the previous year to forty-three, with Connecticut following Illinois to become the seventeenth state to abolish the death penalty. However, China was believed to have dispatched several thousand victims – no reliable figures were available because many executions are in secret. Eighty-two prisoners in Saudi Arabia had been executed by beheading, and in Iran at least three children had been hanged in blatant violation of international law. Another violation was to use the death penalty for crimes that were not of the greatest seriousness – in Iran, for sodomy and drug offences, and in Saudi Arabia for sorcery. The International Criminal Court and the courts established by the UN to deal with war crimes in former Yugoslavia, Rwanda and Sierra Leone are prohibited by their statutes from imposing death sentences. It follows that, despite the clear modern trend in state practice towards abolition, there is still not a sufficient consensus for executions to be prohibited as a matter of customary international law.

The most signal failure of human rights law, at this stage of its development, is that it does not condemn the formal extinction of the lives of those human beings convicted of crime. Although Article 6 of the Civil Covenant is worded in a way which has led the Human Rights Committee to believe that it 'strongly suggests' the desirability of abolition, which represents 'progress in the enjoyment of the right to life',[7] the second Optional Protocol to the Civil Covenant – the treaty by which states can solemnly pledge themselves to abolish capital punishment as a step towards human progress – has only attracted seventy-three signatories.[8] In Europe, however, there is a consensus for abolition, reflected in the fact that all the Council of Europe members which have ratified the Sixth Protocol of the European Convention on Human Rights have forsworn the imposition of the death penalty as a punishment in peacetime. Many executions go unrecorded:

liquidations of state enemies in places like North Korea and Burma are presented as accidents or the result of private feuds. The US has over 3,500 men and women on death row, engaged in see-sawing legal battles to avoid the lethal injection that has largely replaced the gallows and the electric chair.

'Everyone,' says Article 3 of the Universal Declaration, 'has the right to life.' Article 6(1) of the Civil Covenant insists that 'No one shall be arbitrarily deprived of his life'; however, 'arbitrarily' may mean no more than 'without trial', in which case it merely requires a finding of guilt duly rendered by a court competent under national law. There was no consensus as to the meaning of 'arbitrarily' at the time the Covenant was drafted and it is apt to cover not only secret police or death squad killings and other executions which take place in defiance of the due process of law, but those that are inflicted within legal systems which do not measure up to international human rights standards.[9] Yet even with due process, those selected for capital punishment will generally be poor and will have been poorly defended. The question of commutation may depend upon the subjective view of jurors or of judges, or of the governor or committee of worthies endowed with the power of mercy. As Justice Stewart remarked in *Furman* v. *Georgia* (the 1972 Supreme Court case that *almost* abolished capital punishment), 'Death sentences are cruel and unusual in the same way that being struck by lightning is cruel and unusual.' It is in this sense that every prisoner who is actually executed may be said to have been 'arbitrarily' deprived of his life, simply because others who may be equally, or more, 'deserving' of death have avoided the same fate. Racism is inherent in capital punishment in the US: blacks convicted of killing whites were sentenced to death fifteen times more often than whites convicted of killing blacks. In the case of executed felons, since 1973 only seventeen whites have been executed for killing black victims, as against 254 blacks executed for killing whites.

A constitution which avows respect for life should not permit the state cold-bloodedly and purposefully to take it.[10] But many constitutions expressly preserve the death penalty, so international human rights instruments need to be realistic. The Civil Covenant, in Article 6(2), seeks to limit rather than abolish capital punishment:

In countries which have not abolished the death penalty, sentence of death may be imposed only for the most severe crimes in accordance with the law in force at the time of commission of the crime and not contrary to the provisions of the present Covenant . . . This penalty can only be carried out pursuant to a final judgment rendered by a competent court.

Although Article 6(6) pleads that 'nothing in this article [i.e. subparagraph (2), above] should be invoked to delay or to prevent the abolition of capital punishment by any State Party', Article 6(2) is in fact routinely invoked by retentionist states to prove that executions after due process do comply with international law. But the very next article of the Covenant, Article 7, provides that 'no one shall be subjected to torture or to cruel, inhuman or degrading treatment or punishment', and since executions undoubtedly fit that description it is logically impossible to execute anyone in a manner 'not contrary to the provisions of the present Covenant'. This is a circle which cannot be squared, and the intellectually disreputable attempts of the Human Rights Committee to do so (for example, in holding that execution in a gas chamber is cruel but killing by lethal injection is not) should be abandoned.

DEATH PENALTY SAFEGUARDS

Judges in most countries fight shy of striking down the death penalty *per se*, but what national and international courts are increasingly prepared to do is to make executions as difficult as possible, by applying human rights principles so as to limit the classes of offenders who may undergo it, or the ways in which it may be carried out. The role of international law, at this stage of its development, is to play Portia: the state may have its pound of flesh, on the condition that it sheds no drop of blood. A set of safeguards has developed which limit the applicability of the death penalty in retentionist countries.

The international law status of these safeguards follows from a reference to them in common Article 3 of the 1949 Geneva Conventions, which prohibits executions 'without previous judgment pronounced by a regularly constituted court, affording all the judicial guarantees which are recognized as indispensable by civilized people'. Common Article 3 has been recognized by the International Court of Justice (in *Nicaragua* v. *US*) as expressing customary international law applicable in times of war and insurgency, so it follows that the rule must apply with all the more force in peacetime. The 'indispensable judicial guarantees' are laid down in Articles 6 and 14 of the Covenant, and most are collected in Safeguards Guaranteeing Protection of the Rights of Those Facing the Death Penalty, adopted by the Economic and Social Council and endorsed by the UN General Assembly in 1984 (the ECOSOC safeguards). They draw support from treaties on other subjects (such as the rights of children and the mentally handicapped) which make passing reference to the death penalty or are applications of other general international law rules, such as the guarantee of fair trial and the prohibition on torture and cruel and inhumane treatment. The following eight limitations on the application of the death penalty are required at this juncture by international human rights law:

MANDATORY DEATH SENTENCES

Death, the most severe punishment, 'may be imposed only for the most serious crimes' (Covenant, Article 6(2)). This rule, states the Human Rights Committee, 'must be read restrictively to mean that the death penalty should be a quite exceptional measure'.[11] Murder is the crime for which it is most commonly and most appropriately (in the retributive sense) inflicted, although murders vary so much in heinousness (from euthanasia and domestic crimes of passion to contract killings and hostage executions) that any *automatic* infliction of the death sentence on all murderers, or on all murderers within a defined category, is contrary to international law prohibitions on arbitrary and inhumane treatment. As Justice Stewart put it, for the plurality in *Woodson* v. *North Carolina* which struck down a mandatory death penalty for certain murder categories:

A process that accords no significance to relevant facets of the character and record of the individual offender or the circumstances of the particular offence excludes from consideration in fixing the ultimate punishment of death the possibility of compassionate or mitigating factors stemming from the diverse frailties of humankind. It treats all persons convicted of a designated offence not as uniquely individual human beings, but as members of a faceless, undifferentiated mass to be subjected to the blind infliction of the penalty of death.[12]

This passage was approved by the Privy Council in 2002, when it struck down mandatory death penalties in the Commonwealth Caribbean on the grounds that it is inhumane and degrading to impose the most severe punishment without considering factors which might mitigate culpability.[13] Put simply, international law (in this respect, with US backing) endorses the proposition that not everyone convicted of murder deserves to die.

The only other serious crimes for which the death penalty can be justified are those assumed to involve indirect taking of life, such as by peddling heroin or by serving an enemy. However, the latter offence, generally termed espionage or treason, cannot today be regarded as requiring the ultimate punishment.[14] Article 6(2) of the Covenant requires that a capital crime must not be 'contrary to the provisions of the present Covenant', which protect the freedoms of conscience and speech and association which are often involved in treason or sedition. The frequent condemnation by the UN General Assembly of 'politically motivated executions' adds weight to the view that imposition of the death sentence for political offences short of murder is contrary to international human rights law, certainly if the offence has been motivated by ideology rather than greed or revenge.

UNFAIR TRIALS

It follows from the irrevocability of the sentence that it should not be carried out unless trial procedures have been scrupulously fair. This is the main objection to US plans to try alleged al-Qaida members before a biased military commission which could sit in secret and apply a lower standard of proof. The 'equality of arms' principle, whereby defendants are entitled to sufficient legal resources to assert their innocence realistically against the state, has a particular force in this context. Those sentenced to death are predominantly poor and illiterate, and the spectacle of them being tried and sentenced without legal representation, or else defended by newly admitted advocates of questionable competence acting without fee, is one which no nation, however impoverished, should permit. The cost of inflicting the death penalty in conformity with international law includes the cost of providing potential victims with access to advice and assistance at every stage in the proceedings. In *Robinson* v. *Jamaica*,[15] the HRC considered it 'axiomatic' that legal assistance should be provided in capital cases. In *Mbenge* v. *Zaire*, it ruled that violation of any due process rights in Article 14 of the Covenant in a capital case is a breach of Article 6(2), because this would mean the sentence would be imposed 'contrary to the provisions of the Covenant'. The state was then under a duty to vacate a death sentence passed *in absentia* and to compensate Mbenge – probably for shock, since he first heard of his trial and conviction when he read about it in a newspaper.[16]

Another aspect of fundamental fairness is that the death penalty must not be applied retrospectively, i.e. as punishment for a crime which did not carry that penalty at the time it was committed.[17] This is emphasized by the Geneva Conventions, which protect prisoners-of-war and civilians under enemy occupation.[18] It is sometimes argued that states which have abolished the death penalty cannot lawfully reintroduce it, but such a rule is found only in the American Convention on Human Rights. What is emerging, however, is a rule that executions should not take place in any period during which there is a real political prospect that the death penalty will be abolished. Thus death sentences were commuted in Britain in 1948 during a period when Parliament was divided over abolition, and executions were suspended in Jamaica between 1977 and 1981 while a Royal Commission studied the issue.

RIGHTS OF APPEAL

One of the abiding arguments against the death penalty is the fallibility of human justice, and the consequent prospect that it will sometimes be imposed on the innocent. The UN safeguards for capital convictions require 'clear and convincing evidence leaving no room for an alternative explanation of the facts' and there must be a right to appeal to a higher court. These rules require that each capital case is carefully scrutinized by domestic courts for the possibility of error. If, in the course of the appellate process, there is a judgment which dissents from the majority decision to uphold the conviction, the death sentence should in principle be commuted because any judicial disagreement will leave a question mark over guilt, or at least over the propriety of the procedures used in establishing guilt.

MERCY PETITIONS

The condemned prisoner must always be accorded the right, under Article 6(4) of the Covenant, to seek a pardon or commutation of sentence after appeals to the courts have been exhausted.[19] It is essential to provide an extra-legal forum in which the issue of whether the prisoner really deserves to die may be resolved as a matter of common humanity. There may be a residual uncertainty about guilt (despite the rejection of all appeals); there may be evidence that the prisoner is of unsound mind; there may be mitigating features which make execution a punishment disproportionate to his moral culpability. The ultimate question of whether the public interest demands death is usually left to the judgment of the head of state or a senior government minister, often advised by a specially appointed 'mercy' committee. International law requires that the condemned person be given facilities to petition the appropriate body. Little attention has been paid, however, to the procedure for clemency petitions: the executive, charged with making what is literally a life or death decision, should on principle be bound to act fairly and consistently, and the Privy Council has been prepared to quash execution warrants when it does not. In *Lewis* v. *Attorney-General of Jamaica* the court reasoned from the right to due process and the specific right, in Article 4 of the 1969 American Convention, of condemned persons to apply for pardon or commutation, that the officials empowered to grant mercy must give condemned men reasonable opportunity to make representations (after disclosing to them any adverse representations) and must take into account any recommendations made by an international or regional human rights body to whom they have appealed.[20]

STAYS OF EXECUTION

The rule that executions must not be carried out while appeals or clemency petitions are pending is of increasing importance to legal struggles against the death penalty. Derived from the principle of legality and the prohibition on 'arbitrary' deprivation of life, it has the backing of General Assembly resolutions and the American Convention (Article 4(6)), and is spelled out in Article 8 of the Economic and Social Covenant safeguards. Unhappily, governments capable of inflicting death penalties often resort to devious ways of carrying them out. Trinidad, for example, hanged Black Power leader Michael X a few hours after serving the execution warrant late at night, when the court registry was closed and his lawyers were asleep. In 1994 it deliberately executed a prisoner named Glen Ashby while the court was considering his application for a stay, and after its attorney-general had given an undertaking to the Privy Council the previous day that the execution would not proceed. Ashby had been on death row for almost five years, and the government feared that, unless he were killed quickly and secretly, he would not be killed at all.[21] One death penalty phenomenon is that it drives otherwise civilized states to resort to this degree of dishonesty.

Many lives have been saved by the rule that no execution should take place while an appeal is still under consideration, even if it is to an external body like the HRC or the Inter-American Court. The International Court of Justice has held, unanimously, that a stay of execution should be granted pending determination of a point of international law. In *Paraguay* v. *US* (1998) it issued an order for 'interim measures' against the US to stop the state of Virginia from lethally injecting a Paraguayan national who in breach of the Vienna Convention had not been told, on his arrest, of his right to consular advice. The US, required by this Convention to appear at the Court, apologized to Paraguay for the police oversight but still went ahead and executed its national, in breach of the ICJ order. The Clinton administration did ask the governor of Virginia and the Supreme Court to stay the execution in compliance with the ICJ request. Both refused (the court by 6 votes to 3) and the senator who was then the major human stumbling block to human rights, Jesse Helms, condemned the President's request as 'surrendering US sovereignty'. It did no such thing, of course, because the US (like every other state) made a sovereign decision to ratify the Vienna Convention in order to protect its own diplomats and its nationals when abroad: Helms would have been the first to bellow if an American were sentenced to death in Paraguay after a legal process he could not understand, having been denied US consular assistance.[22] In 2001 the ICJ ruled in the *LaGrand Case* that the USA had not only violated the Vienna Convention by failing to inform a German national of his right on arrest to communicate with his consulate, but had committed a contempt of the Court's own processes by defying its provisional order that Walter LaGrand should not be executed pending its decision.[23] This is a landmark judgment in two respects: it recognizes that a treaty between states can confer rights on individuals (in this case, the right of an alien to consular access on arrest) and it insists that interim orders made under the ICJ's power to grant 'provisional measures' prior to judgment must be obeyed. Henceforth, aliens may have imminent execution stayed if their state of nationality is prepared to send its lawyers hotfoot to The Hague to obtain a provisional order.

EXEMPTED PERSONS

International law firmly forbids the execution of pregnant women – a rule found in all conventions and in domestic laws of most retentionist states, only one of which, Iran, is reported still to engage in this practice. Anglo-American tradition required a special jury to decide whether a woman prisoner was 'quick with child', in which case execution was stayed until after the baby's delivery. The rationale of allowing an innocent child to be born should extend to its interests in being suckled and mothered, yet only the additional Geneva Protocols forbid execution of women with dependent infants: state practice variously allows execution after delivery (United Arab Emirates, Turkey, South Korea), forty days after birth (Indonesia), two months after birth (Egypt and Libya), or later – Yemen allows a full two years for lactation to finish before orphaning the child.[24] A pregnancy planned to delay execution is a ploy familiar to female felons in such countries, although there are a few sexist governments, such as Jamaica, which always commute death sentences on women no matter how heinous their murders.

There is also a clear rule of international law which forbids the execution of children who are under eighteen at the time of the commission of the offence (rather than at the date of passing the sentence).[25] Such executions amount to cruel and unusual punishment, as the US Supreme Court finally recognized in 2005, after a decade in which it had been inflicted on fifteen youth offenders. The majority accepted that international human rights law now reflected 'a world that has turned its face against the juvenile death penalty'.[26] Only Iran and the Congo still execute teenage offenders. In 1986, the Inter-American Commission ruled that this violated an 'emerging norm' prohibiting the execution of persons who committed capital crimes before the age of eighteen.[27] This norm may be considered as having 'emerged' in 1989, when it was embodied in Article 37 of the Convention on the Rights of the Child, which all countries have ratified except for the US, Somalia (which intends to ratify) and South Sudan, which has not had time to consider the question. The Inter-American Convention also prohibits the execution of persons over seventy, although this respect for old age has not found much support: is the taking of a life which has almost run its course logically any less distasteful than cutting one off in its prime?

Most domestic legal systems jib at carrying out death sentences on mentally handicapped offenders. Even in an age of the most savage punishments, English judges who had no compunction in burning witches drew the line at hanging village idiots. As Chief Justice Coke explained, four centuries ago:

The execution of an offender is for example, but it is not when a madman is executed; that should be a miserable spectacle, both against law, and of extreme inhumanity and cruelty, and can be no example to others.

This blunt reasoning applies to render the execution of insane persons a form of cruel and inhuman treatment which is plainly contrary to international law. The US Supreme Court has ruled that execution of the mentally incompetent is unconstitutional, and that procedures must be available for testing the prisoner's sanity prior to carrying out the sentence.[28] There is evidence that this decision is ignored. The lobotomized Ricky Roy Rector had his sentence approved by Arkansas governor Bill Clinton in order to win votes in the 1992 presidential election: Rector ordered a pie for his last meal, ate half and then requested that the remaining portion be saved for later. It should make no difference whether mental incapacity was present at the time of the crime or supervened subsequently, except that in the latter case a state could theoretically be entitled (subject to the rule against delay) to execute a prisoner who in due course recovered.

DELAYED EXECUTIONS

Two important international courts – the Privy Council and the European Court of Human Rights – have accepted that it is unlawful to execute a prisoner who has been held for a substantial period of time under death row conditions, because there has to come a point at which he is deemed to have suffered cruel, inhuman and degrading treatment. Subjection to such treatment is outlawed by the Universal Declaration (Article 5) and by all human rights conventions, in terms which derive from the prohibition on 'cruel and unusual punishments' in the 1689 English Bill of Rights. This phrase originally referred to unreasonably severe or disproportionate penalties: in human rights law (where the adjectives 'inhuman and degrading' are often used instead), it refers to premeditated ill-treatment of such severity that it produces mental or physical anguish beyond that which is inevitable in the infliction of a legitimate form of punishment.[29] The brooding horror of contemplating one's own death, alternating between hope and despair over a period of years, in a specially sterile environment and in the company of other men who are also liable to be taken out and executed, creates what the European Court describes as a 'death row phenomenon' – a trauma which exceeds the severity threshold imposed by human rights law. The Privy Council put it more simply:

There is an instinctive revulsion against the prospect of hanging a man after he has been held under sentence of death for many years. What gives rise to this instinctive revulsion? The answer can only be our humanity; we regard it as an inhuman act to keep a man facing the agony of execution over a long extended period of time.[30]

In that case – *Pratt and Morgan* v. *Jamaica* – the senior court of the Commonwealth decided that no executions can take place within its jurisdiction (which embraces sixteen independent nations and all British colonies) of prisoners still alive more than five years after sentence was passed. This ruling in 1993 led to the immediate commutation of sentences of death on 160 prisoners in Trinidad and Jamaica and has required many more commutations since in retentionist countries of the Commonwealth. It was preceded, in 1989, by a European Court ruling that the United Kingdom could not extradite a man named Soering to the US to face trial for murder in Virginia, where conviction for a capital offence entails an average wait of between five and seven years before execution.[31] It is frequently much longer: in 1999, Justice Breyer noted that 125 prisoners on US death rows had been there before 1980, twenty-four of them having been sentenced more than twenty years ago. He was in favour of *Pratt and Morgan* ('willingness to consider foreign judicial views in comparable cases is not surprising in a nation that from its birth has given a "decent respect to the opinion of mankind"') but his was a dissenting judgment, in a case where Justice Clarence Thomas made clear his ignorance of and lack of interest in such 'obscure' courts as the Privy Council and the European Court of Human Rights.[32]

The focus in *Pratt and Morgan* is on the peculiar nature of an institution – death row – which is common to prisons in most retentionist states. Its special regime seems to have originated in England in 1752, when 'an Act for better preventing the horrid crime of murder' attempted to do so by providing that executions should take place two days after sentence, and that until that time the condemned person should be kept in a special place within the jail, isolated from all other prisoners. In due course rituals developed in this place of dread, where no productive work or education was permitted: the execution warrant was formally read; the prisoner was weighed for the trap-door and measured for the noose; a 'last supper' was permitted, and so on. The institution and its special regime was exported to many other countries through British conquest and colonialism, and some of its features have remained post-independence, despite the fact that men may spend years there before the government decides to hang them. Common to all such institutions is the alternating hope and despair provoked by legal actions and mercy petitions; the traumatic awareness of the execution of fellow prisoners; the inability to engage in productive work; the reading of warrants and the preparations for death. All these become part of the mounting anguish of awaiting execution. If permitted to continue for years, this will exceed the 'severity threshold' set by the prohibition on cruel and inhuman behaviour. To the objection that condemned prisoners welcome delay and most of them try to cause it by filing appeals and petitions, the Privy Council points out that 'it is no answer to say that the man will struggle to stay alive. In truth, it is this ineradicable human desire which makes prolongation inhuman and degrading.'

The practical issues which arise from this determination are: firstly, how long a prisoner must wait on death row before the severity threshold is exceeded; and secondly, whether any adjustment should be made for delays induced by the prisoner's own actions in taking legal proceedings which stave off the evil day. There is a general consensus in the cases that five years' delay gives rise to an irrefutable presumption that the threshold has been exceeded, no matter how relaxed the physical conditions on the particular death row may be. The period to be measured is that between the passing of the death sentence and the date of the proposed execution, although account may be taken of any inordinate delay in bringing the prisoner to trial after his arrest. Obviously, any period of time during which the prisoner is at liberty as a result of escape must be discounted, as should periods attributable to legal proceedings which are unarguable and vexatious. But delay caused by exercise of rights of appeal, motions based on tenable (albeit not upheld) arguments, petitions for mercy and complaints to international human rights bodies cannot be overlooked merely because they are self-induced by the prisoner. As the Privy Council ruled in *Pratt and Morgan*, 'It is part of the human condition that a condemned man will take every opportunity to save his life through use of the appellate procedure.' Where the severity threshold has been exceeded, the proper remedy is to commute the sentence to life imprisonment.

MODES OF EXECUTION

The rule against cruel and inhuman treatment prohibits modes of execution which inflict torture and degradation, such as burning at the stake, or drawing (i.e. disembowelling) and quartering, or the Chinese procedures which have reportedly been designed to keep the prisoner alive while organs (mainly kidneys and corneas) are removed for subsequent transplant to worthier citizens. Public executions are regarded as degrading in some countries and as essential for deterrent purposes in others, and there is a serious legal issue being litigated in America as to the right of television to transmit death scenes live to what would probably be massive audiences. Public execution cannot, therefore, be considered cruel and inhuman, at least by the standards of countries which permit executions at all, although the Taliban government's fixation for stringing up its opponents in a crowded football stadium (donated by the European Union) was often listed among the reasons justifying its overthrow. It may well be that televised hangings, gassings and injectings (and the reaction to them) would provide the proof necessary to establish their inhumanity *per se* as punishments: the film taken in Spandau prison in 1944 of Adolf Hitler gloating while the bodies of his would-be assassins danced on piano wire (an example of the conduct Montaigne envisaged as the ultimate in cruelty) helped to convince many European statesmen to abolish the death penalty. Stays of execution have been ordered in American courts where there is reason to suspect that the lethal apparatus will malfunction, and either botch the job or kill slowly and with unnecessary pain; the rule might also be invoked where conditions on death row are particularly gruesome (e.g. where inmates watch their fellows being put to death) or in the case of prisoners who have had a number of death-defying last-minute reprieves. In 2005, the *Lancet* published evidence that death by lethal injection could be accompanied by excruciating pain, and several executions were stayed when anaesthetists decided that facilitating deadly anaesthesia would breach the Hippocratic oath.

Human rights law has had a dramatic effect on the death penalty by enabling appellate judges throughout the world to find good legal reasons for staying executions – the decision in *Pratt and Morgan* has already saved over 1,000 lives in the Commonwealth Caribbean, and is now being followed in a number of African countries. Prisoners facing execution in circumstances which infringe the international law rules described above may be able to seek relief in their national courts, failing which they can complain to the United Nations Human Rights Committee (if their country has signed the Optional Protocol) or to a regional human rights court, if there is one available. The *LaGrand Case* is ICJ authority for postponing the prisoner's execution while the claim is investigated and, if held admissible, while it is being adjudicated. Failing such recourse, there is the possibility of attracting the attention of the UN Special Rapporteur on 'summary and arbitrary' executions, at least if there has been a demonstrable failure by the State to comply with the safeguards referred to in the Covenant. The Rapporteur is then entitled to send a formal 'urgent message' to the defaulting government, followed by intervention from the Secretary-General pursuant to his 'best endeavours' mandate. As an absolute last resort, the Pope may intercede. None of these expedients worked on George W. Bush, who sent 152 prisoners to their deaths during his term as Governor of Texas – a record for a US state governor.

In 1958, Chief Justice Warren briefly fashioned the US constitution into an instrument for striking down the death penalty by reference to 'the evolving standards of decency that mark the progress of a maturing society'.[33] But thirty years later, Justice Scalia could joke that 'the risk of assessing evolving standards is that it is all too easy to believe that evolution has culminated in one's own view'.[34] There are signs, however, that Americans are growing weary of 'tinkering with the machinery of death', the one thousandth victim since *Furman* v. *Georgia* was lethally injected in December 2005, but fewer death sentences were being passed and fewer felons brought to execution. There was widespread revulsion when Californian governor Schwarzenegger refused clemency for 'Tooky' Williams, a reformed gangster, because he had not admitted his crime – unsurprisingly, since he denied committing it (and over 120 death row inmates have subsequently been able to disprove their guilt). China is believed to kill several thousand felons each year, while Singapore operates a merciless mandatory death sentence for drug couriers, but there has been a gradual increase in the number of abolitionist nations or nations where courts have made executions all but impossible to carry out.

MINORITY, CULTURAL AND INDIGENOUS RIGHTS

From the sixteenth century onwards, treaties were haphazardly entered into by European rulers which guaranteed to minorities within their domain the enjoyment of their 'traditional religious liberties'. The most influential – the Treaty of Westphalia of 1648, the first pact to recognize sovereignty in nation states – granted religious freedom to German Protestants on the same terms as Roman Catholics. Centuries later, the League of Nations at its inception took this idea a step further by promoting 'minorities treaties' by which Allied powers required states with minorities problems to guarantee civil and political rights and religious and cultural toleration. These treaties were enforceable at the instance of a state signatory, through the compulsory jurisdiction of the Permanent Court of International Justice, and were also supervised by the League Council, which could be addressed by a petition from an individual or association. In the case of other states with poor records in minorities treatment – Albania, Latvia and Iraq, for example – admission to the League was made conditional upon their acceptance of an equivalent obligation to safeguard the rights of minorities within their borders.

So between the wars the international community was alive to the significance of minority rights and the attention given to the subject recognized its importance as a precondition for peace in Europe. The Permanent Court of International Justice began to develop a jurisprudence which addressed the problem of reconciling, on the one hand, demands for equality and non-discrimination with, on the other, the special need to preserve the characteristics and culture of minority groups. Thus its advisory opinion *Minority Schools in Albania* (1935) condemned that government's decision to close private schools serving the Greek minority, on the grounds that 'there would be no true equality between a majority and a minority if the latter were deprived of its own institutions'. The Court held that peaceful coexistence required two legally enforceable objectives:

The first is to ensure that nationals belonging to racial, religious or linguistic minorities shall be placed in every respect on a footing of perfect equality with the other nationals of the State. The second is to ensure for the minority element suitable means for the preservation of their racial peculiarities, their traditions and their national characteristics.[35]

The Court adopted these principles to support German settlers in Poland and Polish nationals in Danzig, but these promising beginnings came to a sudden end in 1939, when the League's Minorities Section was disbanded and its subjects thrown to the werewolves of the Second World War. What emerged from that darkness – in which minorities suffered horrifically – was a new way of thinking about human rights which ironically denied them any special protection. It was the notion, which seemed blindingly obvious to Eleanor Roosevelt and the brahmins of war-free Washington as they planned a 'New World Order', that all relevant human rights belonged to individuals: take care of the rights of persons, and the rights of peoples would as a matter of logic take care of themselves. As Sumner Wells, US Secretary of State, concluded in 1943, 'in the kind of world for which we fight, there must cease to exist any need for that accursed term "racial or religious minority"'. So it came to pass that neither the Charter of the United Nations in 1945 nor the Universal Declaration of Human Rights in 1948 made any mention of minority rights. The UN adopted the position that everyone would be protected by guarantees of rights for individuals and adherence to the principles of equality and non-discrimination.

The unreality of this position should have been evident from the beginning: the Nuremberg trials, after all, concerned the rights of Jews and gypsies to survive not merely as individuals, but as ethnic groups. The 1948 Convention on the Prevention and Punishment of Genocide outlawed serious crime committed 'with an intention to destroy in whole or in part a national, ethnic, racial or religious group'. In 1951, the International Court of Justice declared genocide a crime under customary international law, confirming that such groups had at least a right to exist, maintainable against states which sought to splinter or extinguish them by physical force. The definition of the crime did not, however, cover state actions designed to subvert or eliminate minorities indirectly, such as the destruction of an environment which sustains them or abolishing their schools, and so prevent them from thriving. Remarkably, it was not until the advent of Article 27 of the Civil Covenant that even this modicum of protection was extended by international treaty. As early as 1946, the UN had set up a subcommittee on the Prevention of Discrimination and the Protection of Minorities, which must be ranked as one of its laziest and least effective organs, since it did nothing for minorities in fifty years except to define them. Even this was the work not of the subcommittee but of Francesco Caportorti, the UN's Special Rapporteur, whose report in 1977 provided a definition of a minority as a 'group numerically inferior to the rest of the population of the State, in a non-dominant position, whose members – being nationals of the State – possess ethnic, religious or linguistic characteristics differing from those of the rest of the population and show, if only implicitly, a sense of solidarity, directed towards preserving their culture, traditions, religion or language'.[36]

THE RIGHT TO EXIST

For all the talk at the UN about 'minority rights', it is only possible to say that minorities have two rights: to exist, and to be different in their existence from the majority of people in their state. The right to exist derives from the Genocide Convention, and is enforceable according to the post-Nuremberg theory of a universal jurisdiction to try 'crimes against humanity'. This right has been boosted by the establishment of tribunals to punish genocide in Rwanda and former Yugoslavia and Cambodia, although it remains a protection only against *deliberate* steps taken by the state to 'destroy in whole or in part' a national, ethnic, racial or religious group. It does not protect such peoples against wanton destruction of the environment or culture which sustains them, or against acts intended to prevent them from thriving or developing; nor does it provide redress against a state which 'accidentally' extinguishes a group by neglect or by creating conditions which conduce to the dissolution of the group by death or departure from it. The 'right to exist' is a basic but bare right, which protects against ethnic cleansing by threatening prosecution of perpetrators – if they can be captured – and by inviting the intervention of other states, on the 'humanitarian necessity' principle of Kosovo, if breached on a large scale. Such breaches should – at a point yet to be defined by international law – give rise to a right of secession (see p. 738).

THE RIGHT TO BE DIFFERENT

The right to be different has now crystallized into a rule of international law, to the extent that it is expressed in Article 27 of the International Covenant on Civil and Political Rights:

In those states in which ethnic, religious or linguistic minorities exist, persons belonging to such minorities shall not be denied the right, in community with other members of their group, to enjoy their own culture, to profess and practise their own religion, or to use their own language.

'Persons', be it noted, rather than the minorities to which they belong, are the subject of Article 27. Its language hovers uneasily between treating minority rights merely as individual rights writ large, the sum total of the rights to religious or cultural tolerance enjoyed by individual 'persons' or individual 'members' of the group, and a genuinely collective right exercisable on behalf of all members either by the group leader, or by any one member as representative of the others. It is a negative right which has supported very few complaints to the Human Rights Committee, and those which have succeeded might have done so because individual rights were also breached. The classic case is that of Sandra Lovelace, a Canadian Indian who left her tribal reserve to marry a non-Indian, thereby losing her status under the Canadian Indian Act and hence being refused permission to return to the reserve after her divorce. The regulations under which she was excluded plainly discriminated against her as an individual woman, and additionally infringed her right to freedom of association, although the HRC made great play of condemning the regulations as contrary to Article 27.[37] It would be interesting to know whether the result would have differed had the legislation (which Canada changed in consequence of the HRC decision) reflected an inflexible tribal rule, or indeed had her expulsion been ordered by the tribal council.

The HRC has so far dodged this sensitive question of what happens when minority rights under Article 27 conflict with individual rights. The answer must be that the minority right gives way: cultural traditions which infringe basic human rights cannot be supported. Decisions will doubtless depend on findings of fact and degree: some level of sex discrimination may be acceptable in harmless tribal or religious rituals, but if it amounts to inhuman or degrading treatment (e.g. clitoridectomies on young girls) or threatens the right to life (the practice of *sati*, which requires newly widowed women to commit suicide) or the right to education (the Taliban prohibition on teaching girls over twelve), it is nonsensical to accord such barbarism the description of a minority 'right'. Minorities are as capable of breaching human rights as majorities, and it is absurd to elevate Article 27 into a general licence for them to maintain cruel or discriminatory practices. On the other hand, Article 27 should mean more than just a general right to be tolerated, although that has often been its interpretation. Unhappily, it does not grant *locus standi* for domestic public law purposes to minorities, or even give them the standing to petition international bodies like the HRC. It does not carry the crucial right to representation in government, nor to manage their own communal affairs within the structure of the state. It does not include any right to communicate with minorities or majorities of the same ethnic origin in other states, or even to enjoy affirmative action programmes. Beyond existing guarantees to individuals (and hence to groups of individuals) of equality, non-discrimination, freedom of worship and freedom to assemble, Article 27 has added little in practice except the right to use the minority language in courtrooms and in schoolrooms. Even this is qualified by reference to the reasonable needs of the state to 'strike a fair balance' in its allocation of resources: affirmative action is not a duty, even if it is the only effective way to maintain minority culture.[38]

Politicians find it difficult to admit to the existence of minorities, for fear that any such concession will encourage separatist claims. The states of Latin America have been particularly critical of 'collective rights', while Turkey could not until recently bring itself officially to acknowledge the existence of the millions of Kurds within its borders: they were always described by its diplomats at international gatherings as 'mountain Turks'. No state has, however, gone quite so far as France to deny any meaning to Article 27: that nation refuses to be bound by it, on the grounds that 'Article 27 is not applicable so far as the Republic is concerned' because there *are* no minorities in Greater France. The peoples of Papeete, who rioted in 1995 in protest against the pollution of their culture and environment by the French nuclear tests at Mururoa Atoll, are not entitled to complain to the HRC under Article 27 because France has entered this reservation. The Tahitians are deemed to be French, so far as France is concerned, as are the peoples of New Caledonia, Guadeloupe, Martinique and any minorities inhabiting the suburbs of Paris. The French state claims the right to annihilate their culture, language and religion if it chooses, on the grounds that 'minorities' can be constitutionally defined out of existence. This claim to immunity is such a sleight of hand that the HRC should have rejected it outright. Regrettably, in a series of cases brought against France by its Breton minority seeking protection against the defilement of their language, the HRC upheld the French reservation to Article 27.[39] To add insult to injury, it obliged the complainants to use the French language to challenge the domestic laws which required them to use French at the expense of their mother tongue!

THE RIGHT TO RETURN OF
CULTURAL PROPERTY

The right of minorities – and indeed of majorities and of nation states – to retain and enjoy the treasures of their culture is acknowledged by a widely supported 1970 UNESCO Convention, which requires states to ensure the return of 'cultural property' stolen from public museums or monuments in the country of its origin. This is a very limited right, however, directed against illicit trafficking in antiquities, and imposes no obligation on US or European museums to return the donated or displayed treasures that were plundered from other nations by nineteenth-century explorers and archaeologists. These looted treasures acquired long ago are lodged in national museums pursuant to local laws preventing their 'de-accession' – in some countries even if the museum trustees wish to de-access them (the British Museum was debarred by such a law from returning artworks stolen by the Gestapo from a murdered Jewish collector).[40] There is considerable support for the emergence of an international law norm that would trump such national laws, so long as it is confined to cultural treasures of great national significance. Such a norm would not result in the emptying of Western museums: it would only require the return of items of unique cultural significance, so the British Museum could keep its Egyptian mummies, but not its Greek marbles. It is a right that would derive in law from the Article 27 right of nations 'to enjoy their own culture' together with the right to cultural identity derivable from human dignity and privacy rights and from the 1970 UNESCO Convention. The US Court of Appeals for the Seventh Circuit used the Convention to restore some historical mosaics to Cyprus, on the basis that the mosaics before us are of great intrinsic beauty. They are the virtually unique remnants of an earlier artistic period and should be returned to their homeland and their rightful owner . . . not only because the mosaics belong there, but as a reminder that greed and callous disregard for the property, history and culture of others cannot be countenanced by the world community . . . This is particularly true where this sort of property is important to the cultural heritage of a people because of its distinctive characteristics, comparative rarity, or its contribution to the knowledge of origins, development, or history of that people.[41]

There has been no international court case to develop from Article 27 a norm to require the return of unique cultural treasures. The ICJ ruled in 1962 that religious relics taken by Thai authorities had to be returned to Cambodia, but that decision turned on locating in Cambodia the temple from which they had been taken, rather than on their cultural significance.[42] There have been some deeply unattractive decisions by British courts – e.g. refusing to stop Sotheby's from selling Maori relics unlawfully exported from New Zealand, on the technical ground that the New Zealand government which brought the case could not prove title.[43] Until a cultural property rule develops, peoples whose heritage has been exploited will have to rely on public protest: the Maori had more success in 2001 when they stopped Lego from merchandising a trivia game which made use of sacred words from their legends. The company withdrew the game and apologized for its cultural insensitivity.

The true test of a right of cultural return is – or should be – *the case of the Elgin Marbles*:

The Parthenon is a symbol of the glory that was Greece, and the new Acropolis Museum stands ready to receive the fifty-six panels of this world-heritage-listed, fifth-century-BC frieze carried off 200 years ago by Lord Elgin and subsequently sold to the British Museum. Elgin managed this act of despoliation by abusing his diplomatic status to obtain a licence from the Ottoman occupiers, the terms of which he massively exceeded, bribing the local commander to turn a blind eye while his workmen chiselled the marble from the building. British denials notwithstanding, the evidence clearly points to the illegality of his taking so significant a part of Greece's cultural treasure, a taking which the country's Ottoman Empire had in any event no right in international law to permit. Greece has asserted its claim to return of the Parthenon sculptures under the UNESCO Convention (which has no enforcement mechanism), but the UK adamantly refuses to consider any form of arbitration or mediation which might conceivably result in their extraction from the British Museum. What the Greek government has failed to do is to bring any international legal action to recover them based on the argument that nations have a sovereign right to repossess and enjoy the keys to their ancient history and cultural heritage. The case could (and should) have been brought either in the ICJ, on the basis that customary international law requires the return of cultural property of great significance to the peoples of a nation if it has been lost or misappropriated by an occupying power, or else under the European Convention.[44] There is a 1993 EU directive on the return of cultural property, and Article 8 of the Convention has been held to cover 'cultural identity' (thus the Roma people were entitled to maintain their 'travelling lifestyle'). The Parthenon marbles go to the core of Greek identity as a living symbol of their history and culture and of what it means to be the successor to a political community which originated democracy. In 2011, after so many years of complaining, the Greek government finally approached international lawyers, but its projected case against the UK was dropped because of the debt crisis: trying to recapture the symbol of the glory that once was Greece would be too embarrassing at a time when that country was sliding so ingloriously into bankruptcy.

INDIGENOUS MINORITIES

Article 27 has more resonance when applied to indigenous peoples, when in the minority, than to other minorities. This may be appreciated from the HRC decision in the case of the Lubicon Lake Band, a Canadian Indian tribe whose traditional land had in the distant past been seized by the province of Alberta, and whose very existence was precarious as a result of industrial development of that land's oil and gas deposits. The tribal chief claimed that the state was engaged in a process of non-deliberate genocide by permitting the degradation of the environment to such an extent that it was now impossible for the tribe to survive as a people. The Committee ruled that 'historical inequities (conceded by Canada) and certain more recent developments threaten the way of life and culture of the Lubicon Lake Band, and constitute a violation of Article 27 as long as they continue'.⁴⁵ The Canadian government was obliged to pay $45 million compensation, to set aside a reserve for the tribe and to sustain its separate existence with special community services.

Indigenous peoples have been regarded as an emerging object of international law, although it may be more logical to regard them as one class of minority group which has a particularly strong claim for fair treatment from a nation state with a majority of settler descendants. The strength of indigenous peoples' claims derives not only from sentiment: their forebears will usually have been massacred or enslaved by settlers, or at very least cheated out of their land, to which they will often retain a quasi-spiritual attachment. Reckoned to comprise 300 million people from 5,000 groups, and defined as 'descendants of the original inhabitants of conquered territories preserving a minority culture and recognizing themselves as such',⁴⁶ indigenous peoples have a powerful claim under Article 27 to maintaining their cultural traditions. Much is fashionably made of their 'right to development', although more often their claim is to a right *not* to develop in ways which their state of residence wishes. Their claim is 'promoted' at UN level by its Working Group on Indigenous Populations, which is driven by the statist strategy of avoiding demands for secession by offering indigenous leaders lesser alternatives, described in buzzwords like 'self-management' and 'cultural integrity' or 'cultural independence'. Its work was boosted in 2007 when the General Assembly adopted the Declaration on the Rights of Indigenous Peoples, which on the one hand recognized their 'distinct political, legal, economic, social and cultural institutions' and on the other 'their right to participate fully, if they so choose, in the political, economic, social and cultural life of the State'. If they do not so choose, the Declaration does not promise them autonomy, independence or any other form of self-determination, or any claim to tribal land or the minerals beneath it. The Declaration is exactly that – a non-binding statement of good intent – but its widespread support does edge customary international law towards recognition of native title and their right to share in mining royalties.[47]

A grisly form of cultural property is the remains of humans – the skulls and bones of tribespeople killed by colonists and despatched to European museums for anthropological comparisons or public amusement. The British Natural History Museum alone has 20,000 remains of long-dead warriors, whose descendants can powerfully claim to have them returned for proper burial after an important case in 2010 concerning the skulls of Tasmanian Aborigines, a tribe largely exterminated by English settlers in the early nineteenth century. The museum decided to conduct some DNA experiments – shaving off pieces of bone for dissolution in acid in an effort to glean information, e.g. about their eating habits. Their descendants objected – it would be sacrilegious, and contrary to Aboriginal custom and law, to interfere with remains which required decent burial before their wandering spirits could rest. The Tasmanian Aboriginal Centre, backed by the Australian government, sought an injunction to stop experiments on the skulls of victims of genocide. The museum was forced to accept mediation, before the former Chief Justices of England and of New South Wales. In the result, the museum agreed to cease its experiments and to return the remains for traditional burial. It handed over the DNA preparations as well, to be kept under lock and key in Tasmania unless and until the Aboriginal community consented to further access. Respect for religious beliefs requires that a community be permitted to bury its ancestors according to its own rituals, rather than to leave their skeletons immured or on display in some foreign museum. If there is anthropological value to be extracted from experimentation, the museum must first convince the descendant community, rather than take the decision without its consent.

In the case of indigenous peoples, Article 27 has been used to overrule the traditional doctrine that conquest extinguishes native land claims. The pernicious common law theory of *terra nullius* – which in countries 'discovered' by European explorers meant that native inhabitants were treated as if they were part of the flora and fauna – was condemned by the Australian High Court in 1992, in the course of allowing Aborigines to claim historic title to land still in state (although not private) ownership.[48] In other countries, treaties signed centuries before with tribal chiefs terrified by guns or bribed by trinkets have been renegotiated to provide descendants with some compensation in cash or kind or status. These developments have been essentially domestic, although they have in common the recognition that indigenous minorities have a special relationship with the land and a claim to benefit from its wealth, of which their forebears had been wrongfully dispossessed. It is a matter for individual states as to how they should right their historic wrongs and give meaning to the cultural and spiritual traditions of their particular indigenes: Article 27 is easily satisfied by avoidance of discriminatory laws and practices. What states have never countenanced is any right of an ethnic minority to a share in sovereignty, even when history and anthropology establish that an indigenous people, now a minority among the descendants of its invaders, governed themselves and their territory, prior to the invasion, through tribal or other communal structures. None the less, progress is slowly being made. In 2007 the General Assembly adopted the Declaration on the Rights of Indigenous Peoples, recognizing both their rights to distinct political, social and cultural institutions and to full participation in the political, social and cultural life of the state. There are ambiguities in the Declaration, especially over the scope of self-determination, but it does serve to strengthen arguments for preserving indigenous culture and language and for earmarking seats in parliament for indigenous candidates.

It should be stressed that the indigenous rights that are slowly being recognized are only apt for assertion by ethnic minorities, and cannot be proclaimed as an instrument of race superiority by indigenous *majorities*. This was the perverted principle of 'ethnic paramountcy' promulgated in 2001 by an indigenous regime in Fiji, installed by the army after it ousted the Prime Minister, an Indian, and his democratically elected, racially mixed government. The country comprises a narrow majority of ethnic Fijians, whose chiefs insisted that they should occupy as of right positions of political power (including the presidency and prime ministership) and that indigenous status should prevail over descendants of Indians who had arrived as plantation workers in the nineteenth century, and who now comprised over 40 per cent of the population. The Court of Appeal (made up of five international judges) emphatically rejected the notion that 'ethnic paramountcy' could justify the overthrow of a democratically elected government.[49]

SELF-DETERMINATION

At first blush, independence for ethnic minorities – whether indigenous or not – appears to be promised by Article 1 of the Civil Covenant, which announces that 'All peoples have the right of self-determination'. But this blunt language is deceptive, because minorities are not peoples. 'Peoples' refers to *all* inhabitants of *each* existing state, and the guarantee denotes little more than the right of the population of every sovereign state to determine their own form of government without interference from other states. This is made clear by Article 1(2) of the UN Charter, which declares the UN's purpose, *inter alia*, 'to develop friendly relations among nations based on respect for the principle of equal rights and *self-determination of peoples* . . .' – the collective noun again defining the sovereign nation which is to be protected from unfriendly interference by other nations. 'Self-determination' does not entail the right to be independent, or even to vote for independence: as Rosalyn Higgins succinctly puts it, 'International law provides no right of secession in the name of self-determination.[50] At best, the people's right to self-determination connotes the right of all citizens to participate in the political process, but this gives power to majorities and not minorities.

However much a minority may be oppressed by a majority, and however geographically obvious and politically convenient secession may be (for a province with a majority for secession either to become a self-governing state or to join another state with which it has ethnic congruence), the UN Charter sets its face against any change to the territorial integrity or political independence of its member states, other than by peaceful agreement. When the Grand Captain of the Mikmaq tribe complained that the Canadian government was denying his members their Article 1 right to self-determination (they wanted to form an independent state), rather than reject his argument the HRC refused to hear it, on the ground that this right belongs not to individuals as a group, but to 'peoples'.[51] But even when 'peoples' properly so called are truly claiming a right to self-determination against an aggressor state, international law speaks with a forked tongue. Throughout the decolonization period, the right of peoples to reject imperial rule, by free vote for independence at a UN-monitored plebiscite, was such an article of faith that the ICJ described it as having an 'erga omnes' character. But now that decolonization has been deemed complete, the application of the self-determination principle comes up against the brick wall of state sovereignty. In 1995, the ICJ pusillanimously refused to adjudicate the clearest possible case of a breach of the right – Indonesia's invasion of East Timor – and there has been a marked nervousness in applying the doctrine to other cases, for example to the five million Palestinian Arabs or even to those (about half this number) who live in the territories annexed by Israel through military conquest in 1967, only one of which – Gaza – has been returned, as belatedly as 2005.

A textbook example of the emptiness of the right to self-determination in the face of global *realpolitik* is provided by the case of West Papua – occupied from time immemorial by a proud Melanesian people who have little in common with their Muslim rulers, the Indonesians. They had been colonized by the Dutch, cruelly enough, and 'liberated' even more cruelly by the Japanese, so they helped American and Australian allies drive them out during the Second World War. The country reverted to the Netherlands, which belatedly acknowledged a 'sacred trust' (imposed by Article 73(e) of the UN Charter) to bring it to self-government: educational and technical progress was made in the 1950s, and in 1961 elections were held for a national parliament. That was when Indonesia invaded, supported behind the scenes by the US which sought Indonesia as a Cold War ally against communism. An agreement brokered in New York by the UN required the Netherlands to cede the country to Indonesia in 1963 on condition that it then held a referendum in which Papuans could freely vote on whether they wanted independence or integration with Indonesia. The latter 'prepared' the people for their free choice by arresting and in some cases killing independence movement leaders.[52] Its 'act of free choice' was an act of no choice at all: 1,025 hand-picked local men were invited to indicate in public their support for integration, in what was an atmosphere of violence and intimidation after President Suharto had warned that opponents of integration were guilty of treason.[53] This so-called 'act of free choice' was an absurdity, but the UN (under US pressure) betrayed its principles and gave its approval. General Assembly Resolution 1541 had insisted that no self-governing territory could be integrated into another state except as the result of 'the freely expressed wishes of the territory's people . . . expressed through informed and democratic processes, impartially conducted and based on universal adult suffrage'. The 'act of free choice' violated West Papua's right to self-determination, violated the 'sacred trust' under the UN Charter and the obligations under the New York Treaty.[54] Ever since, Indonesia has brutally repressed the civilian population – presuming (probably correctly) that they mostly support the independence movement – by forced disappearances, summary executions, and killings by Kopassus, its feared paramilitary police. Victims have been estimated at over 100,000. So much for the UN's 1960 Declaration on Granting Independence to Colonial Countries and Peoples, which states:

the subjection of peoples to alien subjugation, domination and exploitation constitutes a denial of fundamental human rights, is contrary to the Charter of the UN and is an impediment to world peace and co-operation.

Since the UN Charter, the right of self-determination has implied the right of 'peoples' of a territory to decide the status of their homeland, by voting for independent statehood, integration with another state, or some form of political association with another state (such as autonomy within it).[55] However, an irrational but apparently insurmountable qualification to self-determination has been the '*uti possidetis*' rule that its exercise must not involve changes to existing frontiers, other than by agreement between the states concerned. Since states rarely concede territory, *uti possidetis* has prevented the early and sensible resolution of disputes which later flare into ethnic violence. The rule was applied by the Arbitration Commission set up by the EC conference on Yugoslavia in the early 1990s to decide, according to the principles of self-determination, the fate of that dissolving state. Instead of attempting to carve a Bosnian Serb republic out of the Serb-dominated areas of Bosnia-Hercegovina and Croatia, and recommending independence for Kosovo, the Commission decided that the wishes of the minorities must be denied because they would require border changes opposed by Croatia and Serbia. Fatuously, it emphasized instead the international law duties of a state towards its minorities.[56] As the Serbs in the Krajina soon discovered, followed by the Muslims in Kosovo, this was akin to leaving the fox in charge of the hen house with a reminder of its duties towards the chickens. As with so many international law rules fashioned to perpetuate the territorial status quo, *uti possidetis* can be a potent recipe for that which it claimed to prevent, namely fratricide and oppression. And, as Diane Orentlicher points out, coupling the right of self-determination with the restraint of *uti possidetis* drains the right of its point for minorities who are in a majority in a province or part of a state: 'Through this legal alchemy, international law could claim to preserve a principle that had acquired a potent symbolic power while simultaneously depriving that principle of its power to threaten established states' "territorial boundaries".'[57]

An example of how great powers will ignore the *uti possidetis* principle when it suits them is provided by the treatment of the sixty-four coral islands of the Chagos Archipelago, whose Chagossian people were deceitfully expelled by Britain when it traded their birthright for a discounted price on the Polaris missile – the price America was prepared to pay in the 1960s for their naval base at the main island, Diego Garcia. Had the principle been applied, Chagos would have been part of Mauritius, to which it had always belonged. But Britain severed the islands from the territory to which it granted inde-

pendence in 1968, and leased them instead to the United States. It lied
– barefacedly – to the UN about the Chagossians, pretending they
were merely casual labourers from Mauritius rather than permanent
residents whose ancestors – slaves brought to the islands by French
planters in the late eighteenth century – had their graves on the
islands.[58] They were rounded up, their homes demolished and their
pet dogs shot in front of them, and transported like criminals to Mauritius, where they remain without adequate compensation. They have
been allowed only once to return, very briefly, to tend the cemeteries,
at what is now an American Archipelago. Diego Garcia has become a
massive naval base and the other Chagos islands – the nearest over
one hundred miles away – have been kept empty at the absurd American insistence that this is necessary for 'security concerns'. The UK's
indifference to indigenous rights, and subservience to US interests,
was on display in 2010 when it purported to establish a 'marine protected area' around the Chagos Archipelago. Although several
environmental organizations, through naivety (or, in the most notable
case, with financial interest) hailed this as 'the world's largest marine
park', the real purpose of the zoning was revealed by a cable published by Wikileaks, from the UK Foreign Office to the US State
Department: 'establishing a marine park would, in effect, put paid to
the resettlement claims of the Archipelago's former residents'. 'We do
not regret the removal of the population,' the British said – 'there
would be no human footprints' and no 'Man Fridays' on the islands if
the marine protection zone went ahead, because 'the environmental
lobby is far more powerful than the Chagossians' advocates'.[59]

International law advances not so much by justice as by state
practice: since 'territorial integrity' is in the self-interest of every
state, boundaries have become shibboleths. In Africa, where many
boundaries were drawn arbitrarily and artificially by colonial powers
in the nineteenth century (at places, for example, where the English
explorer met the German missionary) and today make no ethnic or
economic sense, the first principle of the Organization of African
Unity was to maintain and protect the colonial carve-up of the continent at the Berlin Conference on Africa in 1885. The African
Charter on Human and Peoples' Rights actually imposes duties on

individuals to preserve and strengthen 'national solidarity' and 'territorial integrity' – in other words, to forget about minority rights or discrimination against particular tribes and follow the national leader, who has the all-purpose excuse for infringement of civil liberties, namely that he is 'building the nation'. African political leaders claim that any alternative would lead to chaos: a more cynical view is that any alternative would in fact reduce bloodshed, but would also reduce the power of African political leaders. This subversive thought is not permitted to intrude at the UN General Assembly, or even in the ICJ – where judges might be expected to give 'self-determination' some meaning. When the opportunity arose, in 1986, in the case of *Burkina Faso* v. *Republic of Mali*, they sacrificed it to the principle of territorial integrity, with a gratuitous compliment to some violent and corrupt African leaders:

[A]t first sight this principle [of territorial integrity] conflicts outright with another one, the right of peoples to self-determination. In fact, however, the maintenance of the territorial status quo in Africa is often seen as the wisest course . . . The essential requirement of stability in order to survive, to develop and gradually to consolidate their independence in all fields, has induced African States judiciously to consent to the respecting of colonial frontiers, and to take account of it in the interpretation of the principle of self-determination of peoples.[60]

The right of self-determination is rendered meaningless by the Machiavellian fiction that 'peoples' and their government ('the state') are conceptually interchangeable. Although the right has been deployed, historically, to justify the overthrow of colonialism and the attainment of independence, it has thereafter been disallowed to ethnic minorities living within the independent state, however reasonable their claims to autonomy. It has also been withheld from peoples (such as the inhabitants of islands in the Pacific and Caribbean colonized by the French) when their colonizers have adopted the device of making them citizens of the 'mother country'. The UN General Assembly, in its Declaration on Granting of Independence to Colonial Countries and Peoples in 1960, made clear that self-determination did not mean secession: 'Any attempt aimed at the partial or total disruption of the national unity and the territorial integrity of a country is incompatible with the UN Charter.'

The International Labour Organization, in its 1957 Convention on Indigenous and Tribal Populations, rejected self-determination for indigenous peoples in favour of 'their progressive integration into the life of their respective countries'. This 'assimilation' doctrine, so popular in the 1950s, led to the degradation and destruction of peoples perceived as 'primitive' in an effort to have them accept 'superior' white values, laced with alcohol. It should not be forgotten that the UN's insistence on reconciling minorities to their fate within a larger polity (throwing to them the scant consolation of Article 27) reflects the interests of the old USSR (struggling to suppress the nationalities which became sovereign states on its collapse in 1991), France (justifying its colonial retentions), India (afraid of its own fragmentation) and the bully boy leaders of some African and South American nations, who insist that the penalty for promoting irredentism must be death. These are the bad reasons why there is no support in UN instruments for construing 'self-determination of peoples' in a manner helpful to minorities or indigenous populations within a state, or to transfrontier minorities like the Kurds, whose homelands cross national borders and who were vouchsafed 'safe havens' by the UN only when they were threatened with extinction by Saddam Hussein.

It is open to future international courts to give the right of peoples to self-determination some meaning beyond the historic process of decolonization (a process now artificially deemed to have ended). Pressure from African countries has allowed the right to include 'liberation from racist domination' (revolution was always acceptable against minority white governments in South Africa and Rhodesia) and Arab countries have wanted it to include liberation from some forms of foreign domination (i.e. from Israel occupying Palestinian territories). In due course the Charter principle of self-determination of peoples came quite illogically to denote the right of governments to avoid interference from other states.[61] But now that the main progenitor of this doctrine, the USSR, has collapsed under the weight of its own ethnic minorities, while South Africa and Zimbabwe have conceded majority rule, there must be some hope that the right of peoples to self-determination can revert to something akin to its true meaning, namely a right conferred on peoples against their own governments.[62] That right is assuredly engaged when the peoples in question are victims of crimes against humanity – as was implicitly acknowledged in 1972 by the instant recognition of Bangladesh, formerly the eastern part of Pakistan, after the Pakistani army had run amok, and by the international community which supported East Timor's independence. The right of unilateral secession as a last resort when there is subjugation or a 'complete blockage' of aspirations was cautiously acknowledged by the Supreme Court of Canada in 1998.[63]

The reason why international law has made so little contribution to the reduction of ethnic strife is because it constructs its rules as a synthesis of what states in fact do, rather than by reference to what they *should* do according to principles of fairness and justice. This approach has denied to minorities all but the bare rights to exist, to maintain innocuous cultural differences and to avoid overt discrimination. In 1966, the ICJ had an opportunity to give self-determination some meaning in terms of justice when it adjudicated upon Namibia's right to independence, but the timorous majority of its judges insisted that secession – however morally, politically or socially necessary – was beyond the cognizance of international law.[64] By erroneously ruling the very subject non-justiciable, they withheld from the world the one tried and tested means of resolving grievances short of conflict and strife, namely the submission of the question to impartial arbitration.

The ICJ and a host of *ad hoc* arbitral tribunals have developed principles and precedents for dealing with land ownership disputes between states: it is not an impossible step to adjudicate claims by ethnic minorities to statehood or to increased political recognition. Teams of lawyers are less expensive than armies, and do not slaughter each other, and a reasoned adjudication would provide some guide as to whether and on what side other states or the Security Council should intervene. Imbroglios in places like former Yugoslavia and

Somalia, where politicians and diplomats could not agree on which ethnic claims were justified, might well have been better handled had UN action been preceded and guided by an international court decision as to the sovereign rights of competing groups. It may be over-idealistic to imagine that blood feuds can be diverted to courtrooms, or staunched by the redrawing of boundaries, but the massive loss of life occasioned by secessionist movements surely warrants an attempt. However, as international law now stands, it offers no means of relieving ethnic strife: only states are entitled to be parties to cases before the ICJ. 'As a result, indigenous peoples cannot under any likely set of circumstances have their claims of abuse resolved under international law as assessed by the International Court, or even by some special tribunal with any authority to assess claims put forward on behalf of indigenous people.'[65]

Preservation of minority culture is not achievable merely by recognizing the group's right to exist alongside the majority and to receive equality of treatment: those who are members of ethnic minorities are also entitled to special protection by law to secure that same enjoyment of their language, religion and lifestyle which the majority (at least in democracies) may take for granted. Thus, Article 27, and the domestic law which reflects it, should not only work to allow members of minorities a level playing field when competing with other citizens for jobs and services, but must also give them a communal right to enjoy a culture about which those other citizens are uninterested. It is necessary to recognize these 'communal rights' (the portmanteau phrase 'minority rights' is misleading) as genuinely belonging to groups, rather than to individuals who happen to be members of groups, and to allow them to be asserted by group representatives in domestic or international tribunals seized of their grievances. In an ideal world, such tribunals would have power to decide at what point minorities deserve representation in government or some measure of self-management or territorial autonomy within the framework of the wider state, or even when they should be permitted to secede. The simple procedural way forward is to give minorities the standing to bring cases before the ICJ: exclusion from the Court of all potential litigants except states has prevented it from picking up the pioneering pieces of PCIJ jurisprudence on the minorities treaties. This solution, however, would have to be accompanied by an extension of the ICJ's jurisdiction beyond the consent-based optional covenant which only sixty-five states at present accept.

The value of this approach over the individual rights focus would be to give minorities as such the opportunity to submit their disputes with states – in effect, with the majority in their state – to arbitration rather than to the sword, by seeking a peaceful resolution instead of embarking upon guerrilla action. While some blood feuds are much too bitter to be amenable to law, the prospect of adjudicative settlement must be worth exploring by an international community whose diplomacy and politicking has failed for too many years in too many places. For example, the Vale of Kashmir must be amenable to an arbitrated solution; misgoverned by India and then torn by terrorism sponsored by Pakistan, over 30,000 people have died there in the past decade, but the rival states irresponsibly refuse to negotiate, and mutter nuclear threats instead. Neither government will give up its claim to a province which should enjoy some form of independent statehood – a solution only feasible if imposed by the Security Council with the full and forceful support of the US and China.

THE QUESTION OF PALESTINE

There is no more important, yet no more intractable, international question than how to secure a relatively peaceful coexistence between Jew and Arab in a 'holy land' divided between the focused power of the state of Israel and the ramshackle 'authority' of Palestine. Peace proposals seemingly agreed at Oslo (1993), Camp David (2000) and Geneva (2002) have faded; the 'road map' has thus far led to a brick wall. These political and diplomatic efforts have failed, often through the truculence of Palestinian leaders and their Arab state backers, although international law has been marginalized by Israel's all-purpose justification of 'self-defence', even for the expansion of settlements. That defence has in recent years been made more credible by a crime against humanity – the campaign of suicide-bombing – perpetrated by Hamas, regarded by the US as a terrorist organization, which in 2006 became the democratically elected government of Palestine.

The phenomenon of large-scale, well-organized suicide bombing has been openly espoused by Hamas, Islamic Jihad and the al-Aqsa Martyrs' Brigade. These human bombers are not martyrs but war criminals (deceased), and leaders of the organizations that recruit and plan attacks on a widespread and systematic basis are guilty of crimes against humanity. Death has put Yasser Arafat, who must bear some 'command responsibility' for failing to arrest and punish organized terrorism, beyond the jurisdiction of the International Criminal Court, although neither he nor the proponents of these atrocities could be brought before that court in any event, because of Israel's refusal to ratify the Rome Treaty.

The question of Zion in many ways began as a question of justice. It was the appalling injustice done to Alfred Dreyfus, the Jewish officer wrongfully convicted by French court martial and sent to 'Devil's Island', which convinced Theodor Herzl that Jews would never be permitted to be 'assimilated' in Europe. His inspirational pamphlet *The Jewish State* launched political Zionism, a claim that the British equivocally accepted in 1917. 'His Majesty's government views with favour the establishment in Palestine of a national home for Jewish people,' said the Balfour Declaration. But how could 'a national home' mean 'a national state', in a land of 400,000 Arabs and 30,000 Jewish settlers? 'Nothing shall be done which may prejudice the civil and religious rights of existing non-Jewish communities in Palestine,' the Declaration added ambiguously: in 1917, these 'rights' did not include self-determination. For the next thirty years, Britain ruled Palestine in a kind of colonial fugue, permitting some Jewish settlement but incapable of appreciating the impossible demographic tensions its policy would produce. In the end, for these unwise administrators, partition seemed the Solomonic solution.

It still seems reasonable enough, amongst the 'rights of peoples' guaranteed by the Universal Declaration, to acknowledge a 'people's' right to a homeland from which they can draw cultural identity and, in the case of a wickedly persecuted race, to recognize their right to a safe haven carved out of the lands of their persecutors. In retrospect, this would have meant a retributive right to a Jewish homeland asserted against Hitler's willing executioners – a large slice of Prussia, perhaps. But that was not the Zionist dream (although in 1903 many of its early supporters, reluctant to risk their destiny in the desert, had been prepared to accept Britain's offer of a slab of Uganda). The creation of Israel involved a different kind of claim, which had a different consequence – the domination of indigenous Arab people who also called Palestine 'home', and were already in residence. This difficulty was fudged by the slogan 'A Land Without People for a People Without Land'. But Palestine was not *terra nullius*; by 1947 it contained 1.3 million Arabs and a small minority of Jewish settlers. Yet in that year, to compensate for the Holocaust, Security Council Resolution 181 ceded over half the land to Israel. That state came into being as a result, but against the wishes of neighbouring Arab states, who declared war and, by losing it, doomed Palestinians to the refugee camps. In 1967, after the Israeli annexation of the West Bank and the Gaza Strip following renewed Arab aggression and the Six-day war, the UN Security Council produced the first 'road map': its Resolution 242 correctly emphasized 'the inadmissibility of the acquisition of territory by war' and called both for withdrawal of Israeli armed forces from the occupied territories and for cessation of violence by or against Israel. This resolution recognizes the sovereign existence of the state of Israel: to deny it, as does the constitution of Hamas, is insupportable.

Other countries where an indigenous population has been dispossessed or humiliated or deprived of political power have turned to the law – national or, failing that, international – to protect that people from discrimination, in a way that respects their dignity and gives them fair shares in the fruits of the land they have lost. In this respect Israel is in breach of international law. For all its achievements in 'making the desert bloom', its curfews and checkpoints have had what the UK government describes as a 'catastrophic' effect on the Palestinian economy: over half the people live in poverty on less than $2 a day. The Red Cross despairs, because humanitarian aid cannot help until Israel allows Palestinians 'to live as normal a life as possible'. It is impossible to approve the Knesset's discrimination against Arab Israelis (20 per cent of the population) or the 'targeted killings' (execution without trial) of suspected terrorist leaders or the loss of innocent lives – over 500 children killed by army incursions into the occupied territories since the last intifada – many of them in 'Operation Cast Lead', Israel's twenty-two-day war of bombing and shelling the people of Gaza by air, sea and land at the end of 2009. It was, of course, provoked by Hamas rocket attacks, to which it was so dispropor-tionate a response (1,000 civilians killed, 3,000 homes destroyed along with factories, hospitals and mosques) that it could not be accounted a legitimate exercise in self-defence. War crimes were committed on all sides: the Palestinian Authority made an effort to investigate, but Hamas (doubtless because it was guilty as charged) did nothing. Israel lifted no finger against those responsible for conceiving, organizing or commanding this exercise in urban mili-tary aggression. It did commence over 400 investigations of allegations against individual soldiers, but only two were brought to trial and the only prison sentence – of seven months – was imposed on a soldier for stealing a credit card. It has made great play of Richard Goldstone's subsequent doubt over one allegation – that Israel had a policy of targeting civilians – and pretends that his retraction invalidates his report. It does no such thing. Unre-tracted, and unpunished, are facts about civilian families wiped out, civilians shot whilst waving white flags, intentional attacks on a hospital, on chicken farms, sewage works and water wells, and the use of white phosphorus and heavy artillery in built-up civilian areas. Whilst the Goldstone report was a fact-finding exercise and not a Court judgment, there has been no proper investigation of these *prima facie* war crimes in Israel. Nor, of course in Palestine, where Hamas continues to commit war crimes by firing rockets over the border, no doubt in the hope of provoking another unlaw-ful Israeli response.

In fairness, there is another side to this story and it is a consequence of the continuing unrealistic and unlawful refusal in some Arab quarters, backed by states like Iran, to accept Israel's right to exist and indeed to flourish in a security enforced not only by its own army but by the policing powers of the Palestinian authority. Sadly, Hamas continues to make rocket attacks on Israel, and the Palestinian authority has taken insufficient action to punish those responsible for inciting suicide-bombing. That such criminals are posthumously hailed as martyrs is a reason to despair, and defiance by both sides of the Geneva Conventions during the 2009–10 Gaza war makes Auden's weary point:

> *I and the public know*
> *What all schoolchildren learn,*
> *Those to whom evil is done*
> *Do evil in return.*[66]

None the less, the international law position is tolerably clear. In Justice Rosalyn Higgin's pithy summary: 'Israel is entitled to exist, to be recognised and to security, and the Palestinian people are entitled to their territory, to exercise self-determination and to their own state.'[67] Both sides are under a duty to negotiate to achieve this position, but neither has been prepared, at least simultaneously, to give peace this chance. At a time when, in Barbara Tuchman's phrase, 'history is still smoking', it would be over-optimistic to predict an international law solution, or any solution at all.

ECONOMIC AND SOCIAL RIGHTS

Civil and political rights may be fundamental, but they cannot be enjoyed on an empty stomach. Talk to Holocaust survivors, and they will tell you that racial discrimination, slavery and loss of liberty were not their immediate concern in the concentration camps, but rather an aching and all-enveloping hunger. Of course, starvation was inflicted as a consequence of an inhumane racist policy, but it endangered their 'right to life' more directly than depriving them of civil liberties. The Universal Declaration recognizes that the duty of states to protect the 'inherent dignity' of humankind goes much further than clothing individuals with legal powers: they must be clothed with clothing. They must be fed and housed and educated; given access to medical and social services when needed; able to find work paid sufficiently to make leisure time – spent with family and in the cultural life of the community – a fulfilling experience. States' duties to afford a basic standard of living for their peoples are expressed in Articles 22–27 of the Universal Declaration as 'rights' which are 'indispensable for dignity and the free development of personality'. But the highly politicized Human Rights Commission of the UN decided that these 'socialist' ideals were qualitatively different from liberty rights, both in theory (they must depend on government policies, not court decisions) and in practice (they need a great deal more money to implement). So when they were consigned to a separate treaty, the International Covenant on Economic, Social and Cultural Rights, it was decided that this covenant should have no adjudicatory body like the Human Rights Committee. It would instead be overseen by an Economic and Social Committee, which would receive and study reports provided by states on their progress towards realizing the treaty goals. It was noised abroad that these 'second generation' rights were not *real* rights but merely aspirations, ideals for states to achieve under their own steam or with charitable assistance from the international community, and they would never reverberate in international law because living standards were within the sovereign domain of the nation state for which it could never be called to account.

This approach has had a baleful influence, withdrawing from the scope and hope of international enforcement the set of Economic Covenant rights which are not only justiciable, but essential to human dignity. While it is true that no one can insist on the right to work (let alone in chosen employment with paid holidays) in a country where there are no jobs on offer, that does not preclude a legal right to such modicum of care and subsistence as is necessary to sustain life. The French Conseil d'État has declared that the more specific provisions of the ECOSOC Treaty (such as parental liberty to choose children's schools) are judicially enforceable,[68] and the South African courts are having no difficulty enforcing the socio-economic rights (such as the right to housing) adopted by that country's constitution.[69] And if that provision is beyond the resources of the particular state, then there should arise an international law duty upon other states to assist, on terms which may properly entail some breach of sovereignty. A government which abjectly fails in its duty to feed and clothe its citizens should be liable to international intervention, all the more so because in practice its failures will often be caused by the corruption of the ruling élite or a preference for spending the national wealth on armaments.

State sovereignty has been a crumbling stumbling block in the advance of *civil* rights, but it has proved a complete impasse to securing economic and social rights for citizens of many countries in the world. The state sovereignty principle affords protection to rulers who loot or otherwise misappropriate vast sums of public money, generally transmitted to Swiss bank accounts or tin-pot tax havens like Belize, the Cook Islands and Monaco. The careers of Marcos and Suharto, and especially Abacha, who looted a breathtaking US$3 billion from Nigeria (only $1 million of which could be recovered, mainly from Swiss banks) testify to the brazenness with which some rulers enrich themselves and their families, and most 'developing' countries have high-level institutionalized corruption which hinders their development. (For example, it has been estimated that up to 30 per cent of World Bank loans to Indonesia went into the pockets of Suharto and his cronies.) Studies by the International Monetary Fund have shown that endemic official bribery, usually laundered through the device of 'commission' payments to intermediaries, operates as a tax on foreign investment, and works to reduce growth and to divert resource allocation from essential services like education and health (where bribery potential is low) to grandiose projects and expenditure in areas riddled with massive bribes (such as armaments and acquisitions for national airlines).[70] The chief villains are rapacious rulers and politicians, but equally responsible are the multinational corporations which queue up to pay the 'commissions'. To combat this, the US has taken the lead, firstly with its Foreign Corrupt Practices Act (which prohibits American companies from bribing foreign officials) and then (because the Act put American business at a competitive disadvantage) by promoting an OECD convention, which became effective in 1999, under which the major trading states pledge to pass similar laws. Further daylight will come from initiatives against money laundering through Security Council Resolution 1373, taken in the wake of 9/11: corrupt rulers may henceforth have to stash their loot under their beds rather than in Swiss or offshore banks.

The United Nations system of 'state reporting', which avoids hurtful criticism, has been inadequate other than in helping to pinpoint priorities for the UN's aid agencies, which cannot be seen to take issue with the political policies of member states which are assisted. More has been achieved through the muscle of the main donor countries, which in the last decade have sometimes imposed conditions on aid grants – such as transition to democracy. The World Bank and the International Monetary Fund also have the power to make client states change their policies, although the price they exact will often be to the detriment of economic and social rights (usually, it will involve an insistence on free market reforms, and often a dismantling of social security arrangements). The international community has failed to establish any system by which collective claims to economic and social rights can be heard and determined, and which directs the aid necessary to satisfy them to states on conditions that address their failings, such as requiring them to reduce their military budgets or to take steps to combat political corruption.

Contemporary statistics show that hundreds of millions of people live in utter poverty, without access to basic health care. Two million children die annually from preventable diseases, while eight million lose one or both parents from HIV/AIDS and half a million women lose their lives in childbirth. Over a hundred million children receive no schooling and adult illiteracy is massive. These statistics arise primarily from Africa, but the problem is not confined to that disastrous continent: one-fifth of the world's population is affected. The failure of governments, either regionally or in political blocs or through the UN, to establish any framework for allocating resources to cope with a fight against immunizable disease and illiteracy is tragic: Western aid is subject to the 'compassion fatigue' which affects both foreign policy and NGO funding. Equally striking is the failure of governments to provide legal mechanisms for people (or 'peoples') whose economic or social rights have been violated. This is evidenced by their slow progress towards an optional protocol to the Economic Covenant, permitting individual complaints to a committee equivalent to the HRC: it did not become open for membership until 2009, and by mid-2012 had only eight parties. The United States, which has been particularly opposed to this step, is inclined to forget that President Roosevelt nominated 'freedom from want' as one of his four basic freedoms in the speech in 1941 which launched the modern human rights movement. Without any sensible direction from a respected and objective agency, private charity is often badly directed, whether or not through NGOs – e.g. food aid to camps controlled by guerrillas fighting a genocidal war. The best-known private initiative – Bob Geldof's Live Aid – is now criticized by Médecins Sans Frontières for dispatching one billion dollars' worth of food mostly for the benefit of the mass-murdering troops of Colonel Mengistu. The well-intentioned rock extravaganza, it alleged, was responsible for 'saving 1,000 lives to condemn 100,000'.[71]

For all the conscience-waving and consciousness raising, there is one culture in Africa that self-promoting pop stars rarely mention. It is the culture of impunity, the miserable acceptance that nobody is ever going to be held to account for the wars and the malfeasance which will continue to make poverty a reality rather than history. 'Justice' is a word that NGOs misapply to demands for debt relief and fairer terms of trade: the focus on these issues obscures the more pressing need for justice according to law. This must be the first step to addressing poverty, because it is the only cure for the armed conflicts and corruption that keep people poor. The demonstrable fact is that the 'big men' of Africa always get away with it, as do their henchpersons and hangers-on. Smaller men – policemen, judges, government inspectors and licensors – observe their unpunished venality and grasp at whatever money or position they can to benefit extended families. Foreign companies characterize bribery as the price of doing business in Africa and they do it, by 'consultancy payments' or through local partners. Wealth is extracted and exported with little local benefit: the best-resourced countries in Africa are amongst the poorest and most war-ravaged.

The culture of impunity has allowed leaders like Amin and Abacha, Mobutu and Mengistu to flourish. Daniel Arap Moi, responsible for massive corruption in Kenya, enjoys his ill-gotten gains in immune retirement, while his cronies returned to wallow at the same trough. Colonel Gaddafi, who hosted the 2005 assembly of the African Union, and was then its most influential member, bore an historic responsibility for sponsoring war throughout the continent and terrorism throughout the world. He was too powerful to be called to account (other than by his own people in 2011) and the African Union is obsessively protective of heads of state, so long as they remain heads. In 2006 Charles Taylor, former president of Liberia, was at last surrendered for prosecution at the UN war crimes court in Sierra Leone. He had been indicted in March 2003 but had been allowed to live unmolested for three years in Nigeria until the newly elected Sirleaf government in Liberia requested his transfer. The African Union was disposed to consent only once his 'state immunity' had effectively been withdrawn by his own state: it will otherwise insist on impunity for rulers, and for ex-rulers, too, if they can still pull strings in their former governments.

Measures to combat impunity are complicated and definitely 'non-sexy'. They include increased pay for law enforcers and judges; boosting the African Commission for Human Rights and rewriting some of the nationalist nonsense in the African Charter; abolishing criminal libel and francophone 'insult' laws used around the continent to lock up, journalists who expose corruption; banning sales of small-arms; setting up a rapid-reaction force with the firepower to arrest the Darfur suspects and the Congo killers and the child-kidnappers of the Lord's Resistance Army; establishing 'hybrid courts' (international judges and prosecutors working, in a majority, with local law enforcers) to deal with corruption cases and war crimes.

It is a good thing that the 2005 G8 summit wiped off a lot of African debts, mostly run up by crooked or bloodthirsty leaders with whom lending institutions should never have dealt and which would not have been repaid in any event. Unless impunity is comprehensively confronted, however, there is every likelihood that the same overdrafts will be run up again.

Impunity in Africa aside, what is certain is that many of the economic and social rights listed in the Universal Declaration are appropriate for enforcement by individuals, or better still by groups, in national courts. Examples are the right to receive equal pay for equal work, to access a social security system, to join trade unions, for children to have free education at primary level, and to have the overarching right of non-discrimination which can be asserted in respect of every welfare service. States with advanced legal systems have experienced no difficulty in having their courts and administrative tribunals deliver 'distributive justice' in respect of both individual and group entitlements to housing and social services. There is no reason in principle why decisions as to whether states are in breach of their obligations under the Universal Declaration and the Economic Covenant could not be made by an international body of experts sitting as the equivalent of the Human Rights Committee, or even by the Human Rights Committee itself (suitably enlarged and resourced).

What the world community must be entitled to do, in minimum recognition of Articles 22–27, is to create a quasi-legal system for (a) ensuring that a reasonable amount of resources actually available to the state are spent on providing for basic rights of health and education and social security (as distinct from being spent on armaments and monuments and the servicing of debts rather than people), and (b) identifying those states where available resources, although reasonably allocated, are simply insufficient to satisfy basic rights. This situation attracts the duty which falls on other states to provide aid and assistance.

Poor states never jib at (b) because they will always accept (and often demand) hand-outs from the West (to be geographically more accurate, the global North). But they cannot accept the logical consequence that such hand-outs should be predicated upon the exercise described at (a) which would entail not only independent and external evaluation of domestic policy but the ultimate insult to a state's sovereignty – by subjecting it to an international body with power to force policy change by making aid conditional upon it. Although some direction is suffered, usually with ill grace, when loans and debtreschedulings are held out as carrots by the IMF, these preconditions usually relate to management of the economy, free market reforms and greater financial stringency: the IMF and the World Bank are not in the business of setting human rights targets as priorities. Ultimately, some international adjudicatory body must be empowered to do so, if the great pledge of Article 28 of the Universal Declaration is to be honoured, namely:

Everyone is entitled to a social and international order in which the rights and freedoms set forth in this Declaration can be fully realized.

Under Article 2 of the Economic Covenant, each state party (and by 2012 there were 160 of them)

undertakes to take steps, individually and through international assistance and co-operation, especially economic and technical, to the maximum of its available resources, with a view to achieving progressively the full realization [of the Covenanted rights].

This can be construed as imposing on wealthier states a 'Good Samaritan' duty to help neighbours in distress, at least when they are in the grip of famine or poverty or natural disaster. First World countries agreed in 1990 to donate 0.7 per cent of their GNP for overseas development aid, although very few came even close to meeting this target. The collective right of victims to press the international community for a relief allocation cannot be formally asserted at the bar of any adjudicative body, not because it would be incapable of adjudication but because no such body exists. Should one be established, it would need the power to make the state of which its supplicants are nationals a party to the action, in order that its government could be given directions on how to change its present policies so as better to satisfy the basic needs of its citizens. Whether this would be hailed as a sensible step in global governance or as human rights imperialism is beside the point, since it would empower those most affected by poverty, transforming them from passive recipients of aid into plaintiffs who had obtained their due by asserting before the international community their human right to a remedy for the hopelessness of their collective life.

The same procedure, if established to enforce the 'lost rights' of Articles 22–27 of the Declaration, could be used as a means of securing other collective rights which have come to be recognized in recent years as fundamental. The most important of these relate to the environment: they range from the right to enjoy the natural wonders of the world (which requires states to preserve natural heritage areas falling within their territorial domains) to the right to breathe clean air, now and in the future. These 'prospective rights' could be exerted on behalf of future generations, much as parents and guardians may litigate on behalf of children in most domestic legal systems, to achieve a degree of inter-generational equity. International conferences on such subjects as greenhouse gases and CFCs occur regularly, of course, and occasionally sovereign governments manage to agree upon coordinated action. Their failures are more notable than their successes, and if real progress is to be made in respect of any treaty or agreement, it will turn on states' willingness to accept the decision of an international arbiter as to whether and when they are in breach and the nature of any penalty.

The 'right to development' has been solemnly identified by the General Assembly as a new 'inalienable human right'. Governments which had bridled at the very mention of human rights suddenly rallied to a concept which seemed to offer something to *them*, in the name of the human beings within their borders who – thanks largely to governmental incompetence and corruption – were not 'developing'. Fraternal obligations on rich states to help the poor are much to be encouraged, but not by a process which devalues *human* rights by trusting governments with them. The agenda behind this 'right' is recognizable in its advocacy: 'the most important and comprehensive aspect of [the right to development] is the right of each people freely to choose its economic and social system without outside interference or constraint of any kind, and to determine, with equal freedom, its own model of development'.[72] In other words, more power to one-party or oligarchic government, so long as it claims that its system has been chosen by the people, however long ago. Beware a 'right to development' which asserts the right of underdeveloped states to receive money without strings attached because its promoters fear strings which will require government ministers to reduce their military budgets or their Swiss bank accounts or the monuments they build to perpetuate their memory.

LABOUR RIGHTS AS HUMAN RIGHTS

The Universal Declaration promises workers of the world certain rights in their workplaces: Article 23 endorses fair conditions, equal pay for equal work, a just remuneration 'ensuring for himself and his family an existence worthy of human dignity' and 'the right to form and join trade unions for the protection of his interests'. This last guarantee is repeated in the same words in the Civil Covenant (Article 22) and the European Convention (Article 11), in both places presented as a derivative of the right of association. Protection of these workplace rights has been left to the International Labour Organization (ILO) founded as long ago as 1919, which has developed its own conventions and committees for advising on labour laws, mediating between employer organizations and trade unions, and serving as 'guardian' of the labour principles in the Global Compact, a UN initiative to encourage multinational corporations to respect human rights (see p. 237). But there is a conceptual difficulty in universalizing, as a 'human right' necessary for individual development and dignity, workplace practices mainly valued because of their role in achieving fair wages and conditions for workers collectively. Scholars have noted how labour rights and collective bargaining have been overlooked in the post-war struggle for human rights, despite these references to them in international human rights treaties.[73] The collective nature of labour rights did not always sit easily with the individualist interpretations dominant in the human rights field and the ILO system, which is based on traditional respect for trade unions, is being challenged by governments obsessed with shrinking their public sectors and influenced by multinationals with greater power and resources.[74]

However, the entitlement to join trade unions and to have those unions bargain collectively are both clearly enshrined in the human rights pantheon, drawn expressly from the right of association. That clearly means a right to join trade unions, whose main purpose is to bargain collectively for their members. Collective bargaining is not only a practice which has overcome inequalities that result from market forces by counterbalancing the bargaining strength of employers; it may also be perceived as an individual right to combine with other individual workers in an association to achieve wage justice, decent workplace conditions, fair disciplinary treatment, comradeship and so forth, objectives which are all associated with human dignity. Dignity is equally the object when the right to combine is deployed as a means of standing up to abuses of power by employers backed by the state. (Trade unions backed by the state may, of course, also be involved in breaches of individual human rights, e.g. through supporting 'closed shop' legislation.)[75] Although the early history of collective bargaining is associated with campaigns to protect domestic workers from foreign competition, its emergence as a human right has been hailed as necessary to enable the international legal order to protect individual human dignity in an age of economic globalization and transnational production.[76]

The HRC decisions on Article 22 have been, typically, poorly argued and often wrong. An early case held that the Covenant does not implicitly protect a right to strike, although there was a powerful and persuasive dissent joined by the more distinguished members of the Committee, on the basis (which must be correct) that the existence of the right to belong to a trade union would be valueless unless some concerted activities were also permitted.[77] There has been a more satisfactory approach by a more satisfactory tribunal (the European Court of Human Rights) interpreting the Article 11 right of the worker 'to join trade unions for the protection of his interests'. This means more than simply a right to join trade unions: the state must protect the union as it strives to advance the occupational interests of its members, at least to the extent that 'the trade union should be heard'.[78] In the case of *Wilson* v. *UK*, the Court made clear that the union's 'right to be heard' did not imply that a state must *oblige* employers to recognize unions, much less compel them to enter into collective bargaining. What it must protect is the right of an individual employee to instruct his union to seek to persuade his employer to listen to what it has to say on his behalf. 'If workers are prevented from so doing, their freedom to belong to a trade union, for the protection of their interests, becomes illusory.'[79] *Wilson* stands for the proposition that to effectuate the individual's right to have a trade union represent his or her interests, the law must permit him or her to join the workplace union and that union must be free to try to persuade the employer to enter into collective bargaining, and free to organize strike action if the employer remains unpersuaded. State laws cannot permit employers to make it an inflexible condition of employment that either union membership or collective bargaining be abjured. The state's obligation under Articles 20 and 23(4) of the Universal Declaration, as explicated by Article 22 of the Civil Covenant and Article 11 of the European Convention, is to insist that new employees in any industry have a choice, i.e. they should be free to choose to work for whatever wage collective bargaining can bring, or else to make personal contracts which may offer additional payments for more flexible work but must not come with any incentive, in cash or in kind, to abandon their right to association. For an employer to say that job applicants may remain trade union members on condition that they renounce the defining attribute of union membership such as the right to strike or collective bargaining is akin to offering women a job on the condition that they do not become pregnant (although they are not obliged to undergo a sex change) or to consider Catholics for job vacancies only if they undertake not to go to mass (although they can remain church members).

These rights are further supported by two ILO conventions, the Freedom of Association and Protection of the Right to Organize (Number 87 of 1948) and the 1949 Right to Organize and Collective Bargaining (Number 98). In 1998, the ILO issued a declaration of the four 'core labour rights' which it regards as protected by human rights treaties and as obligatory for its states 'to respect, to promote and to realise in good faith'. These rights are:

(1) freedom of association and the effective right of collective bargaining;
(2) the prohibition of forced or compulsory labour;
(3) the effective abolition of child labour; and
(4) the elimination of discrimination in respect of employment or occupation.

There can be no doubt that abolition of slave and child labour and the elimination of discrimination are fundamental human rights: not only do states have an international law duty to guarantee them, but corporations (or the individuals who direct them) have equivalent duties under the OECD guidelines and the Global Compact. Slave labour, in fact, can constitute a crime against humanity and those who arrange it are liable to prosection in international courts, even if it is lawful in the place where the slaves are forced to work.

THE DUTIES OF MULTINATIONAL CORPORATIONS

The most glaring illogicality of Westphalian international law is that it applies only to states and not to the transnational corporations whose global activities generate more product and greater influence than many UN member states will ever possess. Over half of the 100 wealthiest entities in the world today are corporations, not countries (Texaco, to take a random example, has four times the assets of Ecuador). So long as they obey local laws and the laws of their state of incorporation, transnational behemoths are safe; yet in today's world some of them are directly responsible for, and take vast profits from, human rights violations. Working (usually through subsidiaries) in partnership with military juntas or corrupt politicians, they have been known to exploit slave labour and child workers, to hire paramilitaries to destroy inconvenient villages, pillage homes and transfer populations. On their behalf, protesters have been jailed and murdered and even (in the case of Ken Saro-Wiwa in Nigeria) tried and executed. They have inflamed wars by selling arms or dealing with 'conflict commodities' like diamonds. The bribery and corruption which is endemic in Africa and in many parts of Latin America and Asia has often been instigated by multinational companies. Given their actual and potential complicity in human rights violations and their capacity – so much greater than individuals – for paying reparations, how long can multinationals keep their heads below the parapet of international law?

The systemic failure to impose corporate criminal liability began at Nuremberg, with the decision to select individuals as 'representatives' of corporations which had profited from aggression, but not to charge the corporations themselves. Gustav Krupp, scion of the armament family, was chosen as the representative of private business in the main trial but escaped due to the onset of senile dementia. His son, Alfred, subsequently received a twelve-year sentence in one of the minor trials. The entire board of IG Farben were tried for employing slave labour and prisoners-of-war and most were convicted on the theory that they had aided and abetted Nazi administrators. So too were executives of companies which manufactured poison gas used for killing rats: their complicity derived from proof that they knew their supply of vast amounts of Zyklon-B to concentration camps would be used for killing humans. In such cases, the knowledge of executives fixed their company with guilt under the Anglo-American common law of corporate criminal liability, but the prosecution did not bother to add corporate entities to the indictment because the focus was on punishing individual Nazis, not artificial entities. Besides, corporate assets had already been seized by the Allies and the notion of compensating victims was not in those days on the agenda. The need for corporate liability did not seem pressing when the UN set up its war crimes courts for Yugoslavia and Rwanda and so there was no precedent when it came to negotiating the jurisdiction of the ICC at the Rome Conference in 1998, where some states objected that their own criminal codes made no provision for corporate punishment. Some NGOs irrationally thought that the step would mean 'collective punishment' – although a punishment which deprives shareholders of unlawfully derived profits, redirected by court order to the families whose slavery had earned them, is hardly an injustice. But for these inadequate reasons, transnational corporations remain untouched by international criminal law.

In the meantime, victims of multinationals or (more often) of their local agents have been able to make aggressive use of the Alien Tort Claims Act (ATCA) to sue for damages any company that has offices in the United States. This remarkable statute dates back to 1789 and permits victims to sue for a civil wrong 'committed in violation of the law of nations'. Since the landmark *Filártiga* judgment in 1980 (see pp. 333–4), it has been used to sue resident torturers or passing dictators, who generally do not stay in the US to fight the allegation. Corporations, however, cannot so easily flee the jurisdiction, especially if they are multinational oil giants. A spate of ATCA claims caused the corporations of the world to unite with the Bush administration in 2004 in an attempt to have the US Supreme Court eviscerate ATCA. The test case, *Sosa* v. *Alvarez Machain*, involved a Mexican plaintiff (Dr Machain) who had been suspected by the US's Drug Enforcement Administration (DEA) of involvement in the murder of one of its Mexican agents. Sosa was the Mexican policeman who detained the doctor and brought him to California to stand trial. The trial collapsed when the DEA could not begin to justify its suspicions and the doctor was awarded $25,000 for emotional distress. Sosa's appeal to the US Supreme Court was the opportunity for the US Department of Justice to file a brief inviting the Court to eliminate the use of the statute by human rights victims. It was joined by foreign governments, notably the UK and Australia, which argued that the Act should be restricted to activities by US nationals because it interfered with their sovereignty and exposed their own multinational companies to punitive damages for violating human rights in the Third World. But the Supreme Court unanimously upheld the right of aliens to sue for violations of international rules which 'rest on a norm of an international character accepted by the civilized world and defined with specificity'. Norms recognized as *jus cogens*, such as those against genocide, forced labour, torture, crimes against humanity and breaches of common Article 3 of the Geneva Conventions, will still meet the *Sosa* standard.

Two post-*Sosa* cases provide examples. UNOCAL was sued by Burmese villagers for the torts of negligence and emotional distress during construction of a gas pipeline. A local joint venture subsidiary had engaged the Burmese army to assist with security: its soldiers tortured and raped natives and forced them to act as slave labour. The ninth circuit court sent the case to trial to decide whether the corporation had aided and abetted these crimes by giving practical assistance, encouragement and even moral support, so long as that support made a substantial contribution to the crime. Evidence of payments to the military, despite knowledge of its repressive tendencies, to act as corporate agents was particularly important. 'The evidence suggests UNOCAL knew that forced labour was being utilized and benefited from it: forced labour is a modern variant of slavery to which the law of nations attributes individual liabilities.' This case must be contrasted with the *South African Apartheid Litigation* against City Bank and other transnationals which supplied technology, money and oil to the South African government during the apartheid years after the UN Convention labelled apartheid a crime. Here, the court applied *Sosa* and decided that ATCA only relates to laws 'accepted by the civilized world and defined with a specificity comparable to eighteenth century paradigms' such as piracy. The Apartheid Convention had not been ratified by major world powers such as the US, Great Britain, France and Japan. 'Without the backing of so many major world powers, the Apartheid Convention is not binding in international law.' However, in 2007 the New York 2nd Circuit Court of Appeals permitted an ATCA case against Barclays Bank (once nicknamed 'Boerclays Bank' because of its closeness to the apartheid regime) to go ahead on the basis of aiding and abetting the crime of apartheid.[80] US Federal courts have delivered inconsistent rulings on liability of multinationals: an action against Shell over human rights abuses in Nigeria was struck out in 2010, but the following year a similar action against Exxon Mobil over abuses in Indonesia was given a green light. The issue is expected to return to the Supreme Court in the near future.

There is an even more serious, and indeed fundamental, ATCA issue that arises from a split 2010 decision of the 2nd Circuit Court of Appeals, namely whether corporations can be sued at all under ATCA for 'violations of the law of nations', because 'the concept of corporate liability for violations of customary international law has not achieved universal recognition or acceptance as a norm in relations of states with each other'.[81] This controversial conclusion, if upheld by the Supreme Court, would mean that the claimants would have to sue CEOs and individual directors and prove they had actual knowledge of the corporate wrongdoing – and would need to develop a theory of vicarious liability before they could recover the kind of damages that only corporations can afford to pay. This gap in international law is an unforeseen consequence of the Nuremberg judgment's insistence that crimes against international law 'are committed by men, not by abstract entities' – the phrase 'abstract entities' was intended to refer to states, and overlooked the fact that crimes are also committed by corporate entities, with their amoral commitment to shareholder profit and their vast wealth, and that such crimes require both punishment and compensation. At Nuremberg many of the lesser trials were of directors of I.G. Farben, Krupp, Siemens and the like, whom the prosecution was able to prove guilty of war crimes of pillage and plunder for receiving and keeping property that had been wrongfully confiscated from Jewish businesses. The main Tribunal convicted Walter Funk of pillage: his company exploited oil-wells seized by Nazi forces in occupied territories. At a time when transnational corporations are being accused of profiteering from human rights abuses and in some places exploiting resources in connivance with occupying foreign forces, an inability to sue corporations would considerably reduce the protection ATCA offers. It is a measure of the mistake made at the Rome Conference in refusing to clothe the ICC with jurisdiction over corporations – a mistake that no state was interested in rectifying at the 2010 Kampala Review Conference, which was indicative of the reluctance of governments to upset multinationals.

Although *Sosa* eliminates ATCA claims based on 'new and debatable violations on the law of nations', it encourages claims against corporations which can plausibly be said to have aided and abetted genocide, breaches of the Geneva Conventions, widespread and systematic torture, forced labour and war crimes. The test should not deter the filing of claims accusing economic actors of engaging in working relationships with brutal host governments whose police or military go on to commit, in the interests of the company, systematic violations of human rights such as torture or murder.

Any ATCA claim is a damaging prospect for a multinational, bringing with it not only the cost of defending conduct against contingency fee'd lawyers for the victims, but the potential for very damaging publicity. In an attempt to avoid this and as a means of promoting their own efforts at human rights compliance, many companies have been prepared to subscribe to a UN initiative, the Global Compact. This is an entirely voluntary, somewhat 'feel-good' exercise: in order to join, the chief executive simply writes a letter to the UN's Secretary-General declaring support for the Compact's ten principles and undertakes to promote them inside and outside the company and to publish a declaration of support for them in the company's annual report. Membership of the Global Compact has no legal consequences and corporate conduct is in no way regulated or even monitored, other than by expelling companies (3,000 so far) who join but then fail to communicate with the Secretariat. The UN makes no judgments on corporate performance and has not devised any means of 'delisting' companies that breach the 'motherhood' principles which their CEO has formally embraced in the following model declaration:

I am pleased to confirm that (name of company) supports the ten principles of the Global Compact in respect to human rights, labour rights, the protection of the environment and anti-corruption . . .

The Compact's advisory council has had various discussions about how to deal with companies engaged in 'egregious violations' but no serious steps have been taken to set up an investigatory or disciplinary mechanism. There is some talk of 'problem-solving dialogue' with recalcitrants. Many NGOs consider that the Global Compact, far from enhancing humanitarian standards, is being exploited by corporations for public relations purposes: e.g. the 3,000 companies which boast of joining but do not (or cannot) report any progress. None the less, the public commitment to the ten principles and the requirement to express support for that commitment in annual reports does permit some measure of corporate accountability if these statements are demonstrably false and the company can be made liable under local laws which punish false and misleading statements in annual reports.

There are unenforceable OECD 'guidelines' for multinational corporations directed particularly to reminding them to observe the four 1998 ILO core principles (see p. 232) when they conduct operations outside their headquarter states. The guidelines disavow any purpose of overriding local law: they are intended to supplement inadequate domestic legislation by encouraging respect for human rights and fair employment practices. Once again, observance of the guidelines by enterprises is voluntary and not legally enforceable. The most that governments do is to hold the occasional forum for discussion of possible breaches, but since those breaches will not normally infringe the government's own laws, this is usually an unprofitable occasion. The OECD guidelines and the Global Compact have serious limitations: weak implementation mechanisms; highly generalized and vague responsibilities; absence of clear practical precedents for companies seeking to comply. The Global Compact, for example, says that corporations 'should make sure they are not complicit in human rights abuses' but does not specify the rights that businesses should not abuse.

It was, ironically, the war on terror which made it essential to bring corporations within the grasp of international law and the very first Security Council resolution following 9/11 – Resolution 1373 – placed onerous duties on states to monitor closely the flow of money from their banks and financial institutions. 'Know your customer' guidelines required legal underpinning, to stop the funnelling of funds to terrorists through bogus charity clients, especially in Saudi Arabia.

Inspired by this precedent, the Subcommission on the Promotion and Protection of Human Rights, a branch of the Human Rights Council, published in 2003 its *Norms on the Responsibilities of Transnational Corporations and other Business Enterprises with Regard to Human Rights*. These seek to bind transnationals not only to international criminal law but to rules against discrimination, child labour, indecent pay and even consumer protection. They seek to set up an international agency to monitor compliance and adjudicate complaints and even to grant compensation and restitution. The draft has been tabled for comment and the comments of the US government have been predictably apoplectic: 'attempts to craft norms of this nature dangerously shift the focus of accountability for human rights violations away from states and towards private actors, thus creating the perception that states have less of a responsibility to end human rights abuses for which they are responsible'. The US says that voluntary self-regulation is the way forward, rather than legal rules. But Amnesty International and Human Rights Watch point out that the application of law is the only way to minimize the negative effect of corporate activities on human rights.

A RIGHT TO DEMOCRACY?

Customary international law has been profoundly apolitical, in the sense that its rules have been carefully tailored to suit sovereign states irrespective of whether that sovereignty inheres in a monarch or a military dictator or a popularly elected president. Treaties are ratified by whomsoever holds executive power, and the rule of non-intervention applies no matter how unpopular the head of state may be. 'Sovereign immunity' is often claimed by, and always accorded to, rulers and their diplomats whose own people, if given the vote, would emphatically cast them from power. But the most remarkable feature of the last two decades of the twentieth century was the triumph of democracy as the central organizing principle for the nation state: many of those in Latin America had made the transition from military dictatorship; one-party rule was diminishing in Africa and in Asia; the USSR had splintered into a dozen crypto-democratic pieces. More countries within the Muslim tradition were turning to democratic elections – most notably, Indonesia. In 2011, the Economist Intelligence Unit listed half of the world's significant countries as democratic, although only twenty-five of them qualified as 'full democracies' while a further fifty-three were rated as 'flawed democracies' and thirty-seven as 'hybrid regimes' lacking fundamental democratic attributes such as unrigged elections and independent judges. Fifty-two countries were considered to be authoritarian regimes. It would be wishful to think that dictators are a dying breed, but they are certainly in a defensive minority. So is a rule of international law, requiring democratic elections, in the process of developing?

The problem is 'state practice', because states have always condemned – loudly, and in the UN – any other state which has acted unilaterally by armed invasion to restore democracy. This is invariably described as a 'blatant breach' of international law and Article 2(7) of the Charter. This was the fate of Tanzania, when it courageously sent its troops to overthrow Idi Amin, the bloody tyrant of Uganda, and of the US for ridding Grenada of the fratricidal maniacs who murdered their elected prime minister. Among sensible observers, these 'unlawful' interventions are followed by universal sighs of relief. Of course, they antagonize diplomats, but were morally justified by the Security Council's failure to act in cases which demand humanitarian intervention.

The right to participate in democratic government *is* ripening, in favour of what Winston Churchill described as 'the worst system of government except for all the others'. Its seed is Article 21(1) and (3) of the Universal Declaration:

(1) Everyone has the right to take part in the government of his country, directly or through freely chosen representatives.

(3) The will of the people shall be the basis of the authority of government; this will shall be expressed in periodic and genuine elections which shall be by universal and equal suffrage and shall be held by secret vote or by equivalent free voting procedures.

This is the language of democracy, but it is broad enough to include systems which grant the right to vote only if it is a vote for candidates approved by a single political party. Rousseau's 'general will' is identified as the source of state power, and its mode of expression must be through the ballot box, although beyond this the Article (and its counterpart in Article 25 of the Covenant) does not go. But the argument for a right to democracy is given additional force by the Charter and Covenant principle of 'self-determination of peoples'. Although this originally meant no more than the right of the whole populace to select its form of government – democratic, communist or whatever

– it is now being hailed, post the Cold War, as a right to participate in democratic government, or at very least a right to a referendum on any alternative system.[82]

On any sensible reading, Article 21 of the Universal Declaration and the Charter principle of 'the self-determination of peoples' invalidate all remaining military regimes run by savage soldiers in places like Burma, where the patient courage of Aung San Suu Kyi, an elected leader detained by military despots for most of the time since her election in 1988 until her release in November 2011, elicited much sympathy. The United Nations is by definition undemocratic: the superpowers rule the Security Council, and in the General Assembly the vote of a country with 10,000 inhabitants is worth exactly the same as the vote of a country with a population of 900 million. Although history shows that democracies are less inclined to go to war against each other, rarely suffer famine and have better track records on human rights than alternative systems, they score just as badly on corruption levels (especially in the small islands and African nations which make up many UN votes) and 'the will of the people' – which brought Hitler to power in Germany in 1933 – often urges capital punishment and discrimination against minorities, and may inconveniently be attracted to parties of fundamentalist extremes, as in Algeria and Pakistan. It was noticeable how the latter's General Musharraf, internationally reviled when he overthrew the country's democratic government, became internationally acceptable as soon as he helped the US and its allies during the war on the Taliban.

None the less, international law is nudging domestic and international courts towards decisions which favour the democratic process,[83] and it is likely that the Article 21 guarantee of 'genuine' elections will eventually be interpreted to mean 'democratic' elections. The monitoring of elections by observers from the UN or the Council of Europe, to decide whether they are truly democratic, has become a feature of 'transitional' states, which increasingly need a clean bill of health as a condition both for recognition by the world community and for loans from the World Bank. The problem in achieving customary international law status for a right to democracy is not the number of surviving military regimes or absolute monarchies, but China – the superpower and Security Council member which signed the Civil Covenant in 1998 but thereafter continued to impose long prison sentences on pro-democracy campaigners. It may therefore be said that although the loss of democracy through a military coup or suchlike is a matter which concerns the law of nations, and restoration of democracy may therefore be a Chapter VII objective, there is as yet no right to democracy in countries which have not enjoyed that system of government in the past.

In particular, there is no right to invade a sovereign state in order to impose democracy. This may be a welcome consequence of procedurally lawful armed action – by unanimous Security Council resolution under Chapter VII, as with Libya in 2011, or by a justified exercise of the right to self-defence or of humanitarian intervention. But unless these preconditions are satisfied, 'regime change' is not a lawful option if based on the totalitarian structure of the regime itself. Although the siren slogans of 'democracy' and 'freedom' were much touted by the US to justify its 'liberation' of Iraq in 2003, much as they had similarly featured in its benighted war against North Vietnam forty years previously, this was rhetoric, ungrounded in international law. Although totalitarian and feudal regimes are more given to aggression abroad and oppression at home, this is by no means a general rule and it was the people's will, after all, that swept Hitler to power. Iraq's Ba'athist constitution was fascist in inspiration and effect, and was the convenient organizational structure for Saddam's aggression and secret killing of political opponents. But it was not intrinsically programmed to that end, and some of the chaos of post-war Iraq can be attributed to mindless and precipitate 'de-Ba'athification' of the country's law enforcement and civil society personnel, as a secular structure that had served to restrain outbursts of religious intolerance. When the international community eventually comes to define the kind of tyranny that will justify intervention by force of arms, the absence of 'periodic and genuine elections' through which the will of the people can be expressed will certainly be a factor, but what the rulers do to their people, rather than the system under which they do it, will be decisive.

In the important *Prasad* decision in 2001, the Fiji Court of Appeal (in effect, an international court with judges drawn from Australia, New Guinea, New Zealand and Tonga) declared the nation's post-coup government unlawful because it could not demonstrate any right to rule by virtue of a constitutional election (the constitution having been suspended) or by proof that it enjoyed popular support.[84] Previous cases from the Commonwealth had always held post-coup governments to be lawful if they were firmly established and administratively effective, however tyrannical: *Prasad* places the burden on the usurping regime to provide evidence that its rule is positively accepted and not just passively suffered as a result of fear or oppression. The peaceful but widespread opposition to the junta installed by the army was attested, to the Court's satisfaction, by churches, women's groups, trade unions, business groups and human rights NGOs, and the judgment (which led to the government's resignation and a fresh election) testifies to the ability of an impartial court to decide a 'political' issue upon the evidence.

An ironic indicator of the emergence of an international law rule requiring a democratic process before a political party can legitimately claim to exercise state power is the extreme to which leaders of such parties will go to ensure ballot-box victory. Lee Kuan Yew's favourite device was to disqualify opposition MPs through bankruptcies brought on by his libel actions. Robert Mugabe rigged Zimbabwe's election in March 2002: massive fraud by election officials, violent and sometimes murderous intimidation by his 'war veterans', treason charges against his opponent, voters terrified (or turned away) at polling stations – the only surprise in the 2002 elections was that his rival took 40 per cent of the vote. These tactics – especially the misuse of the army to shore up support for the government – are all too common: what the Zimbabwe elections brought to the surface was the tension between election observers from Africa, who refused to denounce the result, and those from Europe, who declared the whole process unfree and unfair. The advent of the 'election monitor' – often part-time worthies with little or no local knowledge, parachuted in by the UN or the OSCE or the Commonwealth shortly before polling day – has become an amateurish feature of human rights scrutineering. If international oversight of controversial elections is to be made meaningful, it must take a more hands-on, professional approach than hitherto. 'Monitors' need more than the evidence of their eyes on polling day: some must be permitted to serve as registrars and officials in the months before polling day, whilst others should be measuring the fairness of the political playing field in the months rather than the days before the ballot, at which they should serve as scrutineers. The Zimbabwe turbulence demonstrates that when democracy does become an international law right, it will be necessary to develop more objective methods for measuring whether the people of a country actually enjoy it by voting at an election.

Democracy cannot be regarded as an international 'right' so long as countries can get away with jailing those who advocate it. The most blatant offender in this respect is China, which condemns them to ten to fifteen years in prison. Very often, in undemocratic countries where dissidents are jailed for sedition or treason, their real offence has been to urge political reform. In the United Arab Emirates, for example, republicans who urged free elections were jailed in 2011 for three years for 'insulting the Royal Family' although they were released by the Sheikhs after an outcry in the West. In such cases, pro-democracy advocates will be better protected by protest movements than by the Human Rights Council. Opposition to democracy can provide a motive for crimes against humanity: Ivory Coast President Laurent Gbagbo was indicted by the ICC when he refused to stand down after losing a UN-sponsored democratic election (his troops had been ordered to protect his illegitimate presidency by attacking a UN compound and killing civilians it was trying to protect). That there is a certain inevitability about the onset of democracy is shown by the steady increase in states which are adopting this method of government, although its advocacy in China brings severe repression – lengthy prison sentences and menacing threats against partners and friends. As in the dying days of communist rule in Eastern Europe, charging them with 'financial crimes' is a favourite tactic in the persecution of dissidents: in 2011 the artist Ai Weiwei was detained for three

months by secret police and then prosecuted over a tax bill of
£845,000. (It was paid by foreign supporters, initially to China's
fury, but when greed got the better of moral outrage the government sent its tax inspectors back for more.)[85]

5

War Law

The twentieth century ended much as it began, in a world of small wars and occasional genocides combated by great powers if it suited their national interest. Yet there was no diplomatic exercise so persistent, throughout that century, as the search for a law to preserve the peace of the world. A century of arms control efforts, commencing in 1899 with a peace conference in The Hague at which twenty-six nations debated whether to use dum-dum bullets, ended with 50 million Kalashnikov rifles in circulation and without an international rule preventing the use – let alone the development – of nuclear weapons. Innumerable treaties, conventions and conferences, and the charters of the League of Nations and the United Nations, have made all the provision for world peace that language can describe, but the failure to establish authoritative bodies to interpret and to enforce that language has turned the laws against war into a graveyard of good words.

International law has sought to regulate wars in two ways: initially, by restricting the justifications for waging them, and (when that failed) by prescribing rules for conducting them humanely. But the notion of a 'humane war' is a contradiction in terms, while wars always seem 'just' to those prepared, on whichever side, to die fighting them. Today, states which are civilized enough to abide by the letter of the Geneva Conventions on the Treatment of Prisoners-of-War and of

Non-Combatants in Occupied Territories do not, on the whole, start wars or occupy territories, and the states which do are unlikely to treat prisoners and civilians with any degree of decency. None the less, the detailed conventions on these subjects serve to set standards, any obvious breach of which will result in a propaganda windfall for the enemy. The importance of the Hague and Geneva Conventions is that a party ignores them at its peril precisely because its behaviour is now caught on images taken by a hand-held camera or cell-phone and transmitted by satellite television to an international public whose outrage pressures politicians to 'do something' by way of armed intervention. The laws of war may not be directly enforceable, but they do function to help viewers know a war crime when they see it on CNN, Al Jazeera or BBC World. It is the collective anger produced by that knowledge and its application to the conduct of one side in a foreign war which serves both to tilt international opinion towards intervention on behalf of the opposing side and (more importantly) to overcome the 'Mogadishu factor' – that low tolerance of military casualties which can militate against any intervention at all.[2] In this way, rules of war are important, as providing a basis for UN intervention, or even for humanitarian intervention without specific UN approval, if they are regularly or dramatically flouted by one side in the course of a conflict.

Most of the rules discussed in this chapter were formulated or consolidated after the Second World War, and hence were designed for a drawn-out conflict between Great Power opponents which would ebb and flow across land borders and open sea. What they did not cater for was the low-intensity civil war or internecine struggle in which one state seeks to suppress rebel militias or armed dissidents, much less for a war against America waged by a shadowy terrorist network with allies in fifty countries. The idealists who drafted the UN Charter and the 1949 Geneva Conventions could not have foreseen the eruptions of nationalist and racist blood feuds in the Middle East, on the Indian-Pakistani border, in an eastern Europe ultimately liberated from communism, or between African tribes corralled in artificial colonial borders. The rules for POWs drafted so painstakingly to perpetuate memories of the RAF officers' mess at Colditz would hardly serve for wars in which combatants took no prisoners or, if they did, where the diet prescribed for them at Geneva was beyond the wildest dreams of their ill-fed captors. The traditional etiquette of European war, with its prohibition of poisons and dirty tricks, makes no sense to liberation front guerrillas fighting for their lives and their lands against states which deploy tanks and ballistic missiles, and it is rejected, like every Western ideal, by barbaric Islamists who decapitate their hostages with videotaped delight. It does not chime, moreover, with the dilemmas of 'virtual war', of the kind waged by NATO against Serbia. What entitles a combatant to value the lives of its pilots so highly that all bombs are dropped from a height at which the pilots are safe and civilians are certain to die? The availability of 'smart' weaponry capable of distinguishing between a barracks and the hospital next door carries a moral obligation to use these weapons to make such distinctions. As advances in military technology lift the 'fog of war' and facilitate surgical strikes and drone attacks, the law of war may come to include features of the law of tort, with combatants liable to be sued if deliberately or through gross negligence they miss their approved military target and kill or maim civilians.

The other fundamental flaw in customary law is that it accepts war as a legitimate and inevitable instrument of national policy, which can be made more bearable for both soldiers and non-combatants if armies follow rules. The task of law for the future is to change that assumption: war is unnecessary and starting war without Security Council approval or international law justification may in future count as the crime of aggression, so that those who foment war, as well as those who conduct war with exceptional viciousness, will be punished. There has to be a defined point, a trigger test, for the international community to intervene forcibly to restore the peace and round up those who can be held criminally responsible for its breach. Planning or waging a war of aggression is a crime against humanity, which the statute of the International Criminal Court recognizes in its terms, but it left implementation until a definition could be agreed at the 2010 Kampala Conference, which in turn decided that the agreed definition should not come into effect until 2017.

There have, however, been modest advances as a result of the Second World War. The right of self-defence (which America invoked to bomb terrorist bases in Afghanistan and illegitimately gave as the reason to invade Iraq) is preserved by Article 51 of the UN Charter, but made expressly subject to a duty to report to the Security Council and to desist if the UN decides to intervene. Under Chapter VII of the Charter, the Security Council is the body empowered, if the 'Big Five' permanent members agree, to marshal international forces and to wage a war the justice of which is widely recognized. Although its first such excursion, to Korea in 1950, was owed to happenstance (the USSR was absent from the Council when the vote was taken), forty years on there was sufficient unanimity among its permanent members to invade Iraq because of its annexation of Kuwait. That too owed much to expediency: Iraq in 1991 had no powerful allies, and the punishment of Saddam Hussein's breach of international law coincided with the economic interests of most states prepared to hazard their armed forces in the venture. This national interest was not a motive for the subsequent military action to create 'safe havens' for Iraq's Kurdish people, which was taken by the US, UK and France for reasons of urgent humanitarian necessity, and which retrospectively received the unanimous blessing of the UN Security Council. Since the approval of that politicized body cannot be counted upon in cases where a grave emergency is caused by a state with one friend among the 'Big Five', can the right to breach sovereignty as a matter of humanitarian necessity be claimed in the absence of Security Council approval?

This was the legal issue raised by NATO's aerial bombardment of Serbia in 1999. It was plainly a breach of Article 2(7) of the Charter (non-intervention against a sovereign state) because it was not taken pursuant to a Security Council resolution under Chapter VII. Although the Council had adopted various resolutions to the effect that the situation in Kosovo constituted a threat to international peace, these did not authorize military action, which Russia and China would certainly have vetoed. But in the three months before the air strikes, evidence emerged of massacres of ethnic Albanians by Serb troops, directed from Belgrade, going far beyond what could ever be justified as reprisals for some terrorist killings committed by an insurgent Albanian group, the Kosovo Liberation Army. Evidence mounted that Serbia was engaged in a plan to terrorize the ethnic majority in the province, to 'ethnically cleanse' it by persecuting the Albanian majority so severely that most would flee, creating a refugee crisis for neighbouring states. This would amount to a crime against humanity under Article 7 of the Rome Statute, which set up the International Criminal Court. The legal justification for NATO's attack, without Security Council approval, was that (a) the Serbian state was engaged in an ongoing conspiracy to commit a crime against humanity; (b) this conspiracy was producing a humanitarian emergency which threatened international peace; and (c) military intervention in the form of air strikes was a proportionate deterrent offering a reasonable prospect of avoiding the tragedy, or at least of punishing its perpetrators. The satisfaction of conditions such as these could provide a legal basis for humanitarian intervention, certainly by a united and regional bloc like NATO, when the Chapter VII mechanism is blocked by superpower politics under a rule by which any one of five governments may outvote the rest of the world.

In 2003, the Security Council was bypassed by the US and the UK over the invasion of Iraq, but they recognized the desirability of obtaining its approval and their failure to do so convinced most international lawyers that the invasion was unlawful – although in the absence of any defined crime in the Rome Statute of waging aggressive war, the calls for the ICC to indict Bush and Blair were fatuous. The war was swiftly won on the ground and progressively lost during the occupation in the hearts and minds of many onlookers as civil war engulfed the country, whilst 'sadists on the nightshift' at Abu Ghraib and soldiers on the day shift at Falluja made a mockery of the Geneva Conventions. The invasion brought democracy to Iraq and Saddam Hussein to trial. Neither consequence could justify the invasion as international law now stands, and whether they morally made up for the deaths of (at last count) over 4,000 coalition soldiers and at least 100,000 Iraqi civilians, will be a judgment-call for history.

IN SEARCH OF THE JUST WAR

DR LIEBER'S CODE

All civilizations have fought wars according to rules designed to make them marginally less bloody. Humanitarian concerns may sometimes be detected in the customs of Greek and Roman armies, through the chivalrous Christian tradition of St Augustine which forbade attacks on women and the wounded, and the heraldic influences on medieval city states. But the main purpose of war law was to cut the losses and distribute the gains of the potentates and princes who joined battle in the first place. Scholars like Grotius and Vattel who rationalized war law in the seventeenth and eighteenth centuries were at pains to identify 'just' wars and to protect non-combatants, but always subject to military exigency and to the policy requirements of rulers for whom wars, like marriages, were necessary diplomatic activities. None the less, Christian soldiers in this era were well aware of the professional duties to give 'quarter' to opponents who surrendered to them on the battlefield, to respect the lives and property of civilians and to treat their prisoners humanely: as early as 1419, Henry V promulgated ordinances of war that forbade rape of women and desecration of churches. Shakespeare's pedantic Welsh captain, Fluellen, could point out that killing the boys in the baggage train was 'expressly against the law of arms'.[3] The three armies that fought the English Civil War – for the King, Parliament and Scotland – all had codes of conduct which included the common rule that 'none shall kill an enemy who yields and throws down his arms, upon pain of death'. At his trial in 1649, Charles I was accused of ordering the pillage and plunder of civilian homes and commanding the torture of prisoners-of-war.[4] This was literally a civil war, fought between English gentlemen, in the sense that it was a good deal more civilized than the religious wars that had raged for thirty years on the continent of Europe. The Irish have never forgiven Cromwell for switching to Continental rules of battle and killing all men-at-arms after besieged Drogheda had refused his offer to surrender.

The first modern set of war rules was compiled by Dr Franz Lieber in 1863 at the direction of Abraham Lincoln, anxious that fellow Americans who followed the Confederate flag should not be permanently disaffected by brutalities committed by his government army. While it was no doubt true that 'what could be got away with in wars against Red Indians and Mexicans would not wash in a contest with Southern gentlemen',[5] the Lieber code – *Instructions for the Government of Armies of the United States in the Field* – remains the first source of modern military law. It was the model for military codes in many other countries (ironically, for the Serbian army in 1879) and its principles are even now being applied by tribunals in the Hague to help ascertain customary international law.

The military manual has been supplemented by innumerable treaties and conventions and by the principles distilled from the Nuremberg and Tokyo Tribunals. The modern rules governing the conduct of hostilities are now collected in the four Geneva Conventions of 1949, which all states have ratified. The earlier treaties remain of some importance, however, in tracing the extent to which various rules have entered customary international law – a body of principles which draws upon treaty law as a source, but exists independently of it. This is recognized in the treaties themselves, through a sweeping-up provision (called the 'Martens Clause') which acknowledges the duty of all belligerents, quite apart from the treaty, to obey the rules of customary international law 'as they result from the usages established between civilized nations, from the laws of humanity and the requirements of the public conscience'.[6]

THE HAGUE CONVENTIONS

The origin of the modern 'humanitarian' law of war lies less in concern for humankind than for the coffers of the warring states. This was the motive for holding the first international conferences, at St Petersburg (1868) and The Hague (1899), to limit the development of expensive armaments, notably poison gases and the newly invented explosive bullet. The 1868 conference dressed up this desire to save money in the language of humanity: projectiles weighing less than 400 grams which were explosive or inflammable were denounced because they 'uselessly aggravate the sufferings of disabled men'. So the conference fixed 'the technical limits at which the necessities of war ought to yield to the requirements of humanity', and promised to maintain this balance 'in view of future improvements which science may effect in the armament of troops'. The 1899 conference ended with a convention which followed Dr Lieber in codifying the rules of land warfare. It issued special declarations against the use of dum-dum bullets and 'projectiles the sole object of which is the diffusion of asphyxiating or deleterious gases'. The first Hague Convention, notwithstanding its financial motivation, may be seen as an application of a traditional principle (reflected in the ancient codes prohibiting poison and in the Lateran Council's 1139 edict against the 'unchristian' crossbow):

That the right of belligerents to injure the enemy is limited by their duty to avoid doing so by methods which cause unnecessary suffering, and which are either novel or generally perceived as dishonourable.

At the second Hague Peace Conference in 1907, forty-four states reached general accord on the basic rules of war, but signally failed to put in place any mechanism for limiting armaments. They repeated the fundamental principle that 'the right of belligerents to adopt means of injuring the enemy is not unlimited' – a principle objectionable today not so much for the questions it begs as for the notion that states have any right to be belligerent in the first place. It forbade the use of poison and poisonous weapons, attacks on surrendered soldiers, the killing or wounding of the enemy 'treacherously' or by weapons 'calculated to cause unnecessary suffering'. Attacks on undefended towns were prohibited, and belligerents were required to spare hospitals, churches, universities and historic buildings 'provided they are not being used at the time for military purposes'. There was a duty placed on all belligerents to treat prisoners-of-war humanely, to allow them to keep their personal belongings and to practise their religion, and to exempt officers from work and spare their men from tasks connected with the war. A further convention dealt with duties owed to peaceful shipping by belligerents who laid mines; it prohibited bombardment by naval forces of undefended ports and asserted the immunity of hospital ships, fishing boats (see the *Paquete Habana Case*, p. 111) and neutral shipping.

THE WORLD WARS

All of these rules were broken, sometimes systematically, by all the belligerents in the First World War. War criminals – even among the defeated Germans – escaped punishment (see p. 23), although in 1921 one German court set an important precedent in the case of *The Llandovery Castle* by convicting machine-gunners who massacred defenceless sailors as they took to the lifeboats after their ship was sunk. The defence of superior orders was rejected because the order in question was 'universally known to be against the law'.[7]

After the war, and as a result of its horrors, the futile movement to humanize conflict was superseded by the idealistic goal of preventing it altogether. The Covenant of the League of Nations pledged renunciation of 'resort to war', and provided a resort instead to settlements brokered by the League Council or adjudicated by the Permanent Court of International Justice. To this end in 1928 was directed the Paris General Treaty for the Renunciation of War (the Kellogg-Briand Pact) by which the signatories (including the US, which never joined the League) renounced war as an instrument of national policy and agreed to settle disputes by 'pacific means'. With these fine, unreal words the nations of the world hastened towards the Second World War, pausing only to clarify the rules relating to their new weaponry.

Aerial warfare had been on the agenda at The Hague in 1923: bombing was only legitimate 'when directed at a military objective', and not when used 'for the purpose of terrorizing the civilian population', although causing civilian terror is, as both the Luftwaffe and the RAF were to prove twenty years later, a modern military objective *par excellence*. In NATO's 'espresso machine war' on Belgrade, too, the enemy appeared to weaken only when bombing of power plants and water supplies deprived its middle classes of their morning coffee. The problem – encountered acutely in the war over Kosovo – is that many installations have dual civilian/military uses.

A television station, for example, may provide news and entertainment to the public while also being used to send military signals: it will usually have a propaganda function and may be used (like radio in Rwanda) to incite crimes against humanity. At what point does targeting such a station become legitimate because it is a 'military objective'?

In 1925 came a Geneva protocol prohibiting the use of poisonous gases, immediately ratified by Italy (which then gassed the Ethiopians) and Japan (which used gas in its war on China). This protocol had some relevance when both Britain and Germany seriously considered using chemical weapons at various stages of the Second World War. Their decisions against doing so, however, were taken not to comply with the protocol but out of fear that the other side's chemical weaponry, unleashed in reprisal, might do more damage. Finally, as late as 1936, there was an agreement in London on the rules of submarine warfare, unrealistically (given the possible presence of destroyers with depth charges) requiring submarines to surface and to save the crew of any merchant vessel it had just torpedoed. Unrestricted submarine warfare was soon conducted in breach of these rules by all major belligerents in the Second World War: Admiral Dönitz had to be acquitted at Nuremberg for ordering his U-boats to attack merchant convoys crossing the Atlantic, after US Admiral Chester Nimitz confessed to issuing similar orders to his submarines in the Pacific.

It was in the Nuremberg Charter and judgment, and in the war crimes trials which followed in Germany and Japan, that the rules of war first took on the true meaning of law, namely a rule for the breach of which there is some prospect of punishment. The Charter empowered the Tribunal to punish not only war crimes, as they could readily be described from the earlier conventions, but crimes against peace (i.e. waging a war of aggression, in violation of international treaties) and a new category of 'crimes against humanity'. This was to prove highly significant in the development of international justice, even though this category was initially limited to heinous large-scale persecution of civilians in pursuance of a war.

THE GENEVA CONVENTIONS

THE 1949 CONVENTIONS

There was one final achievement of humanitarian law before the Cold War set in. The four Geneva Conventions of 1949 state the principles of international law as they had by then emerged in relation to the treatment of: sick and wounded combatants on land (I) and at sea (II), prisoners-of-war (III) and civilians (IV).

The 1949 Geneva Conventions provide:

I *Rules for humane care of sick and wounded combatants on land*, irrespective of their race, religion or politics; immunity for hospitals and medical personnel and army chaplains; special recognition of the role of the Red Cross and Red Crescent organizations.

II Similar provisions apply to those *wounded, sick or shipwrecked at sea*, with detailed rules for the immunity of hospital ships.

III *Rules for securing the humane treatment of prisoners-of-war*, protecting them from being used for military labour or in medical experiments or as objects of public insult or curiosity. Use of POWs as hostages in combat zones (i.e. to deter enemy fire) is absolutely forbidden, as is torture or any form of coercion designed to extract information. The prisoner must give his name, rank, regimental number and date of birth: on thus achieving POW status he is entitled to 'be quartered under conditions as favourable as those for the forces of the detaining power' and to have nutritious food, warm clothing and bedding, and permission to pray and to smoke. POWs are to receive monthly pay (75 Swiss francs for generals, 8 Swiss francs for privates) and must be allowed to receive food parcels and send and receive mail. They must be given one musical instrument of their choice (a requirement in memory of the music at Terezin and other ghettos). They must be permitted to organize discipline in their own camps, and to make formal complaints about their treatment.

IV *Rules for the Protection of Civilian Persons in Time of War*. This Convention secures humane treatment for persons in occupied territories and those who have been interned on suspicion of involvement in resistance movements. The former class of 'protected persons' are entitled to respect for their family, customs and religion, and women are guaranteed protection from rape and forced prostitution. Civilians must not be used for reprisals or as hostages, or as forced labourers or subjects of mass deportations. The occupying power cannot punish civilians for activities prior to the occupation, and is entitled to execute them only for acts of spying, sabotage or murder.

These Conventions begin, most importantly, with three articles which are common to each of them. The first (common Article 1) pledges respect for the Convention 'in all circumstances', thereby excluding any excuse of national necessity or self-defence. Common Article 2 applies the Convention rules not only to declared wars but to 'any other armed conflict' arising among the parties, and requires signatories to abide by the rules even if other states do not (thus excluding a familiar reservation to previous treaties entered into by states only prepared to stick to the rules as long as their enemies did). The point at which 'armed conflict' begins, thereby attracting the Geneva regime, is not defined. It would require hostile acts by an army rather than a police force, and would seem to exclude occasional border skirmishes and destabilizing tactics which did not involve the use of force. However, the extent to which a government is entitled to use force to put down an insurgency has not been the subject of specific case law: it would have been an issue had Colonel Gaddafi survived and been put on trial at the ICC.

It is important to note that the Geneva Convention scheme which state parties promise to enforce by tracking down individuals suspected of 'grave breaches' and putting them on trial applies only to crimes committed in the course of *international* armed conflict. Although common Article 3 promises a minimum of humane treatment in 'armed conflict not of an international character' to all civilians and non-combatants, this promise comes without an enforcement mechanism for breaches, however grave. This is because in 1949 no state was prepared to allow international law to intrude upon its sovereignty when it came to putting down insurgencies and armed revolt. Genocide apart, states were not ready to concede to the international community a jurisdiction by treaty to punish their officials for torture or other brutalities inflicted upon citizens within their own borders. It was the achievement of international human rights law, by the time of the *Tadić Case* in 1996, to render largely academic this difference between 'international' and 'internal' atrocities although the distinction still has some significance. For example, the Geneva Conventions with their 'grave breaches' regime did not apply to the civil war in Afghanistan between the Taliban and the Northern Alliance until October 2001 when the United States intervened with B-52s and turned the fight into an international armed conflict. Even then, the US denied that Convention III was applicable to Taliban and al-Qaida fighters captured on the battlefield, since the former were not in a military uniform and the latter were, in addition, under no clear chain of command (see chapter 12). Common Article 3 extends the promise of a minimum standard of humanity to wars that are not declared, and to violent insurgencies, internecine struggles and armed resistance to state power (although not to riots, criminal disorder or sporadic outbreaks of civil disturbance). There has been some dispute over the level of internal violence covered by common Article 3: there would have to be fighting between two armed forces with the rebels having a sufficiently organized command structure to impose discipline.

Common Article 3 is apt to protect all non-combatants who are caught in the crossfire of a civil war. It specifically prohibits murder, torture, hostage-taking, 'outrages upon personal dignity' and extrajudicial executions, and covers any military, police or guerrilla action which has the deliberate result of killing or maiming civilians or prisoners. It applies to the 'High Contracting Parties to the Conventions', which today means every state, and must also as a matter of customary law apply by analogy to the leaders of organized guerrilla forces, since those who seek forcibly to control the state take on the basic humanitarian duties of the government they wish to supplant.

Common Article 3 helps to integrate human rights with the law of war. It was no mean achievement to persuade colonial powers that their right to put down rebellions should be limited by some basic humanitarian duties to citizens and to injured rebels. Nuremberg idealism played some part (as, more craftily, did the Soviet Union's desire for a propaganda stick with which to beat Western states opposed to the rebellions it was fomenting in their colonies). Asian countries, led by Burma, opposed the article on the ground that it was bound to 'incite and encourage insurgency', apparently by encouraging rebels to believe they would be protected from summary execution and by giving their causes some form of legitimacy by making *them* subject to international legal obligations. At a sensible level, common Article 3 does no more than record the obligation undertaken by all state parties to observe basic human rights in times of conflict, thereby imparting to conflicts within a state an obligation recognized in wars between states.[8] The position has been confused, however, by a 1977 protocol relating to the Protection of Victims of Non-International Armed Conflicts (Protocol II), which covers similar ground to common Article 3. The diplomats who did the drafting were much more careful, and clearly wished to take a step backwards. Their definition of armed conflict is much narrower (the rebel force must possess troops and control territory).

Each state has a duty, under articles common to the four Conventions which deal with 'repression of abuses and infractions', to search out suspects alleged to have committed 'grave breaches' of the Conventions and to put them on trial, regardless of their nationality. 'Grave breaches' are crimes so serious that in 1949 states were prepared, by ratifying the Conventions, to undertake to put the suspect on trial themselves or to extradite him to a country prepared to do so. They do *not* encompass crimes against common Article 3 committed in civil war, but include the following crimes if committed in *international* conflict:

wilful killing, torture or inhuman treatment, including biological experiments, wilfully causing great suffering or serious injury to body or health, and extensive destruction of property, not justified by military necessity and carried out unlawfully and wantonly.[9]

This is, inevitably, a 'catch as catch can' approach, in which few in practice are caught. Occasionally, ratifying states have acted to bring their own officers to justice – most notoriously, Lieutenant Calley for the My Lai massacre in Vietnam. Calley was properly convicted of complicity in the deaths of seventy innocent Vietnamese villagers by ordering his troops to 'waste them': he personally shot a two-year-old child. He was sentenced to life imprisonment, but President Nixon ordered this be reduced to three years. Calley served only three days in prison, spending his sentence at his home on a military base, complete with live-in lover. Thirty years on, there was no presidential clemency on offer for Lynndie England and her lover, Charles Graner, the 'sadists on the nightshift' who photographed themselves as they sexually humiliated Iraqi suspects at Abu Ghraib. Their crimes were less serious than Calley's, but nobody gave them any support: Americans had at last come to appreciate that cruelty in the course of a war hands a propaganda victory to the enemy.

Convention III (treatment of prisoners-of-war) and Convention IV (treatment of civilians) adopt an enforcement mechanism through the agency of 'protecting powers' – one nominated by each combatant – tasked with visiting prisons and war zones and generally monitoring the treatment of persons caught up in the conflict. This was always an unworkable idea (adopted from the role played by 'seconds' at a duel) and has generally been ignored: in only four conflicts have 'protecting powers' been appointed, and their role has been limited to exchanges of diplomatic niceties. More helpful work on the ground has been done by the International Committee of the Red Cross (ICRC), whose role is written into the Conventions (common Article 3 gives it a right to enter into battlefields and war zones). However, the Red Cross, to justify this privilege, makes a fetish of its commitment to confidentiality, both in observations within war zones and in its dealings with governments and militias. Its present ethics of humanitarian intervention (which are not shared by other aid agencies) require its workers to turn a blind eye to human rights violations, in the belief that their silence is the price of being invited back, or into the next war zone. It has declined for this reason to allow its employees, and even former employees, to give evidence to the Hague and Arusha Tribunals, which have upheld this absolute privilege against testifying although it deprives them of valuable first-hand accounts of atrocities and reliable evidence against those responsible.

The problem is important, since Red Cross officials always acquaint commanders with evidence of atrocities being committed by their troops, and if they take no action then these commanders will be guilty of 'command responsibility' for any war crimes those troops subsequently commit. Their conviction, however, may depend on evidence from the Red Cross officials – who will refuse to breach confidence. In consequence, ICRC inspection is a very limited safeguard. The abuse of prisoners by US guards at Abu Ghraib and other Iraqi prisons was the subject of five specific (but secret) Red Cross complaints in the latter months of 2003. Its full report, in February 2004, was sent to Paul Bremer, head of the interim administration. The US Defense Department completely ignored the report for two months, until it was leaked to the *Wall Street Journal* in April.[10] In how many other prisons has the Red Cross found evidence of torture, and found its reports consistently ignored, yet it still refuses to speak out, knowing that the torture is continuing? The ICRC alone has been permitted to inspect the prison at Guantanamo Bay, but its reports to the US authorities have not been made public, despite Donald Rumsfeld's boast in April 2006 that ICRC presence meant that mistreatment did not occur. If there *is* torture in Guantanamo, despite President Obama's promise to outlaw it, the Red Cross will never expose it.

This fetish for confidentiality seems unconscionable. The ICRC made a deal with the Nazis – it was aware of Auschwitz and other death camps, but kept quiet in order to help prisoners-of-war. This was a Faustian pact. If torture is a crime against humanity (and it is) then covering it up must also be ethically questionable. The Red Cross justifies secrecy on the basis that if its reports were published, many governments would not allow it access to their prisons. This argument seems overstated: the Geneva Conventions give it access by right, and countries that refuse would suffer aid and trade sanctions and turn the human rights spotlight on themselves, since the refusal would signify that they had something – namely torture – to hide. But the Red Cross is adamant, with the result that its monitoring can never be a satisfactory safeguard. There are, no doubt, a few governments that would deny it access if its reports were to be made public: the government of Sri Lanka, for example, gave it exclusive access to the war zone where it was later alleged to be killing and raping Tamils, safe in the knowledge that such war crimes would never be exposed. Surely it is time for those countries – like the US, UK and Australia – which both condemn torture and maintain they have nothing to hide to take the lead by *waiving* their right to confidentiality in Red Cross reports within, say, a year from their receipt. This would ensure that the right to Red Cross visits would become a meaningful safeguard against torture in prisons run by states prepared for this degree of transparency.

THE 1977 PROTOCOLS

The Geneva Convention system comprises a fine set of rules for the protection of the victims of war, but relies on states for their enforcement. Protocols I and II update the language of the 1949 Conventions and elaborate, in particular, the duties owed to civilian populations by military commanders. Protocol I summarizes, in Article 35, the three basic rules of war:

(1) In any armed conflict, the right of the parties to the conflict to choose methods or means of warfare is not unlimited.

(2) It is prohibited to employ weapons, projectiles and material and methods of warfare of a nature to cause superfluous injury or unnecessary suffering.

(3) It is prohibited to employ methods or means of warfare which are intended, or may be expected, to cause widespread, long-term and severe damage to the natural environment.

Rule 3 is elaborated in some detail, confining bombardment to military targets in the hope of minimizing civilian casualties and avoiding damage to churches, historic monuments or other cultural property. Special provision is made for the treatment of spies and mercenaries (the latter making their first appearance in these treaties) and henceforth warring parties must take care not to cause serious damage to the natural environment. Specially defined protection is given to refugees, women and children, and even to journalists, who on the production of an identity card from their government are to be accorded civilian status so long as they take no action inconsistent with that status (a reference, presumably, to shooting for one side, not to the practice of propagating one side's disinformation).

Swelling the ranks of 'diplomats' in Geneva to produce these protocols were, for the first time, representatives of national liberation fronts, and care was taken to apply Protocol I to 'armed conflicts in which peoples are fighting against colonial domination and alien occupation and against racist regimes in the exercise of their right to self-determination' (Article 4). This definition extends a full-blooded humanitarian regime (rather than just the 'elemental decency' guarantee of common Article 3) to many civil wars. An international element must be proved, however, to attract the full Protocol I regime, and will generally be found in countries where the belligerent parties are supported by foreign powers.

Protocol II applies extensive humane treatment principles (taken from the Civil Covenant) to victims of government or anti-government forces in *non*-international armed conflicts, so long, at least, as the dissident forces are armed, under responsible command and 'exercise such control over a part of its territory as to enable them to carry out sustained and concerted military operations and to implement the Protocol'.[11] This formulation gives rise to definitional difficulties. It is not even clear that it would apply to organizations like the ANC in South Africa or the 2011 Benghazi insurgency in Libya in the period when they had no 'territories' of their own but operated from bases provided or suffered by other countries, and it would not seem to apply to an armed underground resistance, however disciplined and justified in its cause. It would apply to forces like those of al-Qaida (made up of Arabs, Pakistanis, Chechens and even a few Chinese Muslims) which fought alongside the Taliban in the civil war against the Northern Alliance, unless they could be described as mercenaries – which they cannot, since Protocol I defines this unprotected species as 'motivated essentially by the desire for private gain', by which it means wealth rather than promise of paradise. Since neither the US nor Afghanistan had ratified the 1977 Protocols, the status of Taliban fighters captured during the international armed conflict in 2001 fell to be determined under the 1949 Convention, much to the disgruntlement of President Bush, who bridled at the notion that US taxpayers should supply the prisoners with musical instruments. (He forgot that the Taliban ban all music: a Guantanamo Bay prison orchestra was always an unlikely prospect.)

But definitions do not much matter, because neither protocol has teeth. Protocol II, indeed, lacks gums: its Article 3 ('non-intervention') provides:

(1) Nothing in this Protocol shall be invoked for the purpose of affecting the sovereignty of a State or the responsibility of government, by all legitimate means, to maintain or re-establish law and order in the State or to defend the national unity and territorial integrity of the State.

(2) Nothing in this Protocol shall be invoked as a justification for intervening, directly or indirectly, for any reason whatever, in the armed conflict or in the internal or external affairs of the High Contracting Party in the territory of which that conflict occurs.

So what is the point of Protocol II? A state party might openly order genocide, rape, pillage and torture of POWs, and bomb all Red Cross hospitals: however barbarically its own rules are broken, Protocol II refuses to contemplate even indirect intervention by other states. It has provided a possible argument against the legality of NATO's attack on Serbia in 1999: Milošević claimed that his army was 'maintaining law and order' in Kosovo against an insurrectionary terrorist force, the Kosovo Liberation Army. No doubt Colonel Gaddafi, had he lived to go on trial at the ICC, would have justified his attacks on the people of Benghazi as necessary to 'defend the national unity'.

The enforcement provisions of Protocol I (applying in situations of international armed conflict) appear at first blush to be an improvement on the 1949 Conventions which merely called on states to investigate and punish 'grave breaches' (presumably identified by the 'protecting powers' which would hover like referees over the contest). There are provisions introduced in 1977 to emphasize 'command responsibility', requiring military commanders to ensure their troops were aware of their obligations and making them 'responsible' (but to whom?) for violations. There are pious duties imposed on states to assist other states in respect of criminal proceedings and extradition involving war crimes (subject always to the terms of extradition treaties) and there is an impressive provision that states whose armies violate the Geneva Conventions or the Protocol shall 'if the case demands, be liable to pay compensation'. But there is no court or tribunal nominated or given the power to assess any such payment, let alone order it to be made.

Most fantastical of all is Article 90, which provides that serious violations of the 1949 Conventions or of Protocol I should trigger the establishment, in conjunction with the United Nations, of an international fact-finding commission, comprising fifteen members 'of high moral standing and acknowledged impartiality' who shall inquire into 'grave breach' allegations by seeking out evidence and visiting the *locus in quo*. The commission must send its report to all parties, but '*shall not report its finding publicly* [my italics], unless all the parties to the conflict have requested the Commission to do so'.[12] No international fact-finding commission has ever been set up, notwithstanding repeated violations of the Conventions and the Protocol since 1977, although the UN's Human Rights Council does occasionally set up an investigative commission which – in the cases of Gaza and Sri Lanka – was not allowed entry in order to investigate. The 1949 Geneva exercise was informed by a genuine optimism that it would work, and (having been ratified now by all nation states) is properly regarded as the modern bedrock of international humanitarian law. The 1977 Protocols, however, are struggling to achieve normative status, because a number of powerful nations have refused to ratify them, including the US, Israel, Pakistan, Turkey and Iran (although, remarkably, both China and Russia have endorsed them).

GOOD CONVENTIONS

The result of these exercises is a set of overlapping war laws that are, on paper, exquisitely humane. It is difficult indeed for many Third World readers of Geneva Convention III not to yearn for the pleasures of POW status, given the two-star treatment they mandate, at least for the officer class. Convention IV accords rights to civilians in occupied territories which many impoverished peoples in unoccupied territories do not possess. As one delegate put it, 'The cure for all China's problems would be to persuade some other power to occupy the entire country.' It is ironic to have to condemn humanitarian law for being *too* humane, but that fact has undoubtedly contributed to the flouting of some of its important provisions.

Vietnam refused to recognize the 'bourgeois' POW convention: the experience of US soldiers in their 'tiger cages' is a reminder that the prisoners they took could have done without an officers' mess or regular wages in Swiss francs or musical instruments, if only they had been accorded a 'bread and water' prison existence monitored by the Red Cross, which in some cases (notably Israel and Palestine) has been able to negotiate entry to prisons. In others, it has signally failed to obtain access to government torture chambers or to the makeshift jails of guerrilla groups.

The test of international law is not, however, whether it is regularly flouted but whether it is occasionally enforced – a prospect which is apt to diminish the number of future floutings. The enforcement machinery does not need to involve criminal responsibility: in the case of obnoxious weaponry, for example, what matters most is a proper verification system. And as a last resort there must be a rule requiring the international community to take preventive action to demolish weapons of mass destruction before they destroy masses. On this most anxious score, how does international humanitarian law rate? Regrettably, even when conventions, conferences, treaties and the pronouncements of the UN's General Assembly all lead logically to one result under customary international law, it is more customary to ignore that result if it interferes with military thinking.

Take, for example, the practice of carpet-bombing an area of both military significance and high population density. This is directly contrary to the Hague Rules of Aerial Warfare, which require all bombing to have a military objective. Aerial bombardment which 'terrorizes the civilian population' is prohibited. Nothing could be plainer than this rule against indiscriminate bombing; yet Allied embarrassment over the RAF's use of 'area bombardment' against Dresden and other German cities means that this war crime does not feature in the 1949 Geneva Conventions (a point unpersuasively made in defence of Nixon and Kissinger when they ordered the bombing of Cambodia). Saturation bombing of a city is a crime, and the failure of the plenipotentiaries in Geneva to acknowledge it either in 1949 or 1977 meant that Picasso painted *Guernica* in vain. It is still not specifically listed among the war crimes in Article 8 of the ICC Statute.

CHEMICAL AND BIOLOGICAL WEAPONS

There has been rather more agreement over atrocious weaponry which the military is either prepared to give up or regards as incapable of further development. History is full of examples of warped warmongering, from 600 BC when Solon of Athens poisoned the wells of his enemies, to the Tartar armies which threw plague victims over the walls of medieval cities to infect the populace. Even the British used lethal gas against the Boers.[13] The use, or at any event the first use, of chemical weapons has been contrary to international law since 1925, when a surprisingly large number of states ratified the Protocol for the Prohibition of the Use in War of Asphyxiating, Poisonous and Other Gases and of Bacteriological Methods of Warfare. These signatories did not raise so much as an eyebrow to stop Italy using poison gas a few years later in its Abyssinian campaign. Although chemical weapons have been routinely condemned at the UN Conference on Disarmament held in Geneva every year since 1972, most states looked the other way when Iraq and Iran mustard-gassed each other's troops during the Iran–Iraq War. In March 1988 Iraq used gas to kill 5,000 Kurds at Halabja, thanks to German and Dutch companies shipping stocks of Zyklon-B gas, of the kind once used to exterminate Jews in the concentration camps. It was not until 1997 that the UN conference caravanserai finalized the Convention on the Prohibition of the Development, Production, Stockpiling and Use of Chemical Weapons and on Their Destruction.

In due course, 188 states pledged to forswear the manufacture or use of chemical weaponry, and were this time prepared in principle to permit their good intentions to be checked by an organization head-quartered in The Hague, the Organization for the Prohibition of Chemical Weapons (OPCW), which has made over 1,000 inspections since 1997, and banned fourteen substances (including Sarin gas, used by terrorists in the Tokyo subway). But it has no power to order the destruction of stocks, and inspections are not compulsory: states cruel enough to contemplate manufacture and/or use of chemical weapons (e.g. North Korea, Iraq, Syria and Somalia) have all refused OPCW inspections. The real need is to establish a system for policing the manufacturers and merchandisers of biological and chemical weapons, so that they become liable to individual prosecution for knowingly assisting the production, distribution or use of such weapons in breach of the Convention.

There is some overlap with the earlier Convention on the Prohibition of the Development, Production and Stockpiling of Bacterial (Biological) and Toxic Weapons and Their Destruction (1972), which has 165 state parties. This treaty has yawning gaps – there is no prohibition, for example, on research into biological warfare or on the sale of toxins to individuals or organizations rather than to states. Attempts have recently been made to strengthen it by setting up an international body to conduct mandatory inspections, but the Bush administration (under pressure from pharmaceutical companies fearing discovery of their commercial secrets) announced its opposition in July 2001 – a few months before America was reeling from anthrax in the mail. On this, as in so many other respects when it comes to international law, America is its own worst enemy: after 9/11 it called for an effective UN procedure to investigate suspicious outbreaks, to produce an ethical code for scientists and to permit the speedy extradition of those who breach it, but remains adamantly opposed to compulsory inspections which might embarrass its big pharmaceutical companies.

NUCLEAR WEAPONRY

Chemical weapons pale by comparison with nuclear arms, and it is in respect of this terrifying force that international humanitarian law has failed. The letter of the law is not to blame. If the Geneva principles have any meaning, then:

(1) if the right to choose methods of warfare is not unlimited, the very first limit must be upon use of nuclear weapons;

(2) if it is prohibited to employ weapons which cause superfluous injury, then *a fortiori* nuclear weapons are prohibited;

(3) if it is prohibited to use means of warfare which will cause severe damage to the natural environment, then it follows that nuclear weapons are prohibited.

So it is as clear as the noiseless flash which blinded Hiroshima's citizens on 5 August 1945 and killed 100,000 of them, that 'the threat or use of nuclear weapons would generally be contrary to the rules of international law applicable in armed conflicts, and in particular the principles and rules of humanitarian law'. This was the conclusion in 1996 of the International Court of Justice, although it was carefully limited to times of war (and hence has no impact on acquisition or testing of nuclear weaponry in peacetime) and was undermined by this astonishing proviso:

The Court cannot conclude definitively whether the threat or use of nuclear weapons would be lawful or unlawful in the extreme circumstance of self-defence, in which the very survival of a state would be at stake.[14]

The nuclear bomb has been unlawful ever since its drop in 1945 proved massively, indiscriminately and environmentally damaging. That first use on Hiroshima was justifiable on the grounds of military necessity, since nothing less than a demonstration of its annihilatory power would move Emperor Hirohito to even contemplate surrender. It incinerated thousands, but it saved the lives of hundreds of thousands of Allied forces, as well as Japanese soldiers and civilians who would otherwise have been killed in the invasion of Japan. The second bomb on Nagasaki three days later may not strictly have been necessary and should have been dropped elsewhere than on a city – and on an army base rather than on a civilian population – but it does seem to have been the crunch for Japanese capitulation, which came five days afterwards. Many authors and commentators glibly assert that Hiroshima was a war crime – they fail to understand the principle of necessity when applied to a barbadous, racist and kamikazi regime which refused to honour the Geneva Conventions and which, so the more reliable historians aver, would not have surrendered in the face of superior conventional firepower from the US and from Russia. The fundamental principle of criminal law is that it is not retroactive: you judge people by the circumstances and mindset at the time they take the action, and not with hindsight, so Truman's reputation can in this respect rest in peace. The war crimes of Hirohito and Tojo, enthusiastically endorsed by their people, provoked the worst spectacle ever seen – the mushroom cloud – to which the response can only be to develop an international law that prevents it ever being seen again.

At first, the bomb remained in Allied (in effect, US) possession, and there was a remarkable moment in 1946 when President Truman, encouraged by Clement Attlee and advised by Henry Stimson and Dean Acheson, actually offered to put all atomic weapons (at the time there were only three) under UN control.[15] That would have required a renunciation of nuclear development by every other nation and careful control of uranium through an environmental agency, but the plan could have worked. It did not: the Soviet Union exploded its own bomb three years later and the nuclear race began, joined enthusiastically by France, Britain and (in 1964) by China.

These 'Big Five', having established their own nuclear arsenals, were mainly concerned to prevent other states from joining them, and brokered a series of non-proliferation treaties under the aegis of the UN which created the International Atomic Energy Agency (IAEA) in order to inspect signatory countries and verify compliance. There are testban treaties and regional nuclear-free-zone treaties and treaties by which even the Big Five powers promise to keep their nuclear bombs away from the Antarctic, the sea bed, the moon and other celestial bodies and outer space. These faintly absurd pacts, solemnly ratified by governments prepared to use nuclear weapons in places where human life *does* exist, were undermined when the 'Star Wars' programme was approved for development in 1983, heedless of the Outer Space Treaty of 1967 which obliges states 'not to place in orbit around the Earth any objects carrying nuclear weapons'. Fortified by American and French contempt for international treaties, some middle-rank nations developed a secret nuclear agenda of their own. Israel has stockpiled nuclear bombs since the 1970s and, in 1998, first India then Pakistan broke cover with nuclear tests. By that time, there were more than 40,000 nuclear warheads in existence with a total destructive capacity about a million times greater than the bomb dropped on Hiroshima. The prospect raised by Bertrand Russell and Albert Einstein in their 1955 manifesto, that 'a war with H-bombs might possibly put an end to the human race', was given new relevance by the discovery, in 'safe houses' in Kabul, that al-Qaida members had been working out how to make a nuclear bomb. They might have succeeded had they obtained the necessary fissile material (highly enriched uranium or plutonium), some thousand tons of which is to be found in former (and none too stable) states of the Soviet Union and fifty tons in Pakistan, where the sinister Dr Khan was prepared to sell nuclear science secrets to any Islamist bidder. The prospect of a small bomb detonated in Manhattan or London (100,000 dead immediately, with another 100,000 to die in drawn-out Hiroshima-like agony) or of a hijacked plane flying into a nuclear reactor, should concentrate the mind.

Such comfort on this score as presently exists hinges on the Non-Proliferation Treaty (NPT) regime, under which in 1995 the Big Five powers renewed their solemn promises (originally made in 1970) not to use nuclear weapons against those states which had promised to abjure nuclear ambitions by becoming parties to the NPT. This is all very well, but it does not affect pariah states such as Iran and North Korea, which (along with Libya, before Gaddafi reformed and exposed the plot) were clients of the AQ Khan network, which secretly sold enrichment technology. Nor does it frighten states like India, Pakistan and Israel, which deliberately shun the NPT regime in order to cling to their nuclear bombs. One paradox in the treaty itself is that it encourages the use of nuclear energy for peaceful purposes, which entails the 'inalienable right' of a state to enrich uranium and develop a fuel cycle – the 'right' that Iran claimed in 2006, but in circumstances where it was reasonably suspected of wanting to develop nuclear weaponry. Even full accession to the NPT has not stopped wealthy states equipping themselves with the technology and material to produce nuclear weapons within a few months (or, in the case of Japan, within a few weeks) of any decision so to do – about twenty such countries possess or are on the point of possessing the technology to make nuclear missiles. Even Sweden was at one point making a Scandinavian nuclear bomb.[16] A general scepticism about the NPT is demonstrated by the fact that although 189 states have felt obliged to sign it, few are prepared to observe it. The refuseniks – India, Israel, North Korea and Pakistan – do not sign because the NPT confines the bomb to the Big Five permanent members of the Security Council. But at the last five-year review conference, in May 2010, IAEA Director General Yukiya Amano estimated that up to twenty-five nations would have the bomb within twenty years. President Ahmadinejad (the only head of state to attend) criticized the US efforts to deny Iran access to peaceful nuclear power, although by November 2011 the IAEA could report with some certainty that Iran was in the early stages of developing a nuclear explosive device. This has been followed by the assassination of several Iranian scientists (presumably by Israel) and by the ravages of the 'Stuxnet worm' (a computer virus induced, so President Obama has admitted, by the US), but the weapons programme remains on course – a course that may see its facilities attacked by Israel.

The Comprehensive Test Ban Treaty (CTBT) was negotiated by the Clinton administration in 1996, only to be defeated by Republican senators who refused to contemplate a world in which America would not be free to experiment with bigger and better bombs. This position was maintained throughout the Bush years, Condoleezza Rice predicting that 'we may find at some future time that we cannot diagnose or remedy a problem in a warhead critical to the US nuclear deterrent without conducting a nuclear test'.[17] But Obama was committed to 'a world without nuclear weapons' and shortly after his election, Hillary Clinton announced that the CTBT was 'an integral part of our non-proliferation and arms control agenda[18] and in 2011 began a campaign to educate the public and the Senate on the importance of ratification. At present the Treaty has 157 state parties, but cannot enter into force until each of the forty-four states regarded as 'nuclear capable' in 1996 (when the treaty was negotiated) have ratified it. There are still eight refuseniks: China, the US, Egypt, India, Iran, Israel, North Korea and Pakistan. India has asserted its sovereign right to test – which is not a 'right' at all if testing damages the health of other peoples or provokes a breach of international peace. North Korea has actually conducted underground tests in 2006 and 2009 and its position after the death of Kim Jong Il is unpredictable.

The NPT has served as a useful brake on nuclear development, but what steps may lawfully be taken to destroy the nuclear arsenal of a state which has a potential for aggression? In 1981, the Israelis bombed Iraq's nuclear facility at Osiraq, to general condemnation – and general relief. The weakness of the NPT as an international safeguard against nuclear war is that it contains no provision for preventative action against a non-party which has obtained nuclear weapons, and no provision for preventative action against *any* state which tests or even uses them. This was the quandary that in April 2006 divided the Security Council over what to do about Iran's nuclear ambitions: a truculent non-NPT member that insisted on its right to develop nuclear energy for civil use but refused a Security Council request to allow inspections by Mohamed ElBaradei, head of the NPT watchdog, the IAEA. The treaty has no provision for dealing with non-members or members which obstruct inspectors. That is left to the Security Council, which in the case of Iran has been split – between the US and the UK (which want severe sanctions) and Russia and China (which want Iranian oil and trade). In 2010 Wikileaks revealed that the rulers of Saudi Arabia and Jordan had begged the US to bomb Iran before its development of a nuclear weapon destabilized the region. A compromise, by which Iran would only be allowed to develop a civil nuclear programme under the most rigorous and intrusive IAEA inspection regime, may offer the best long-term solution: if Iran is really willing to forgo the bomb, it should be prepared to prove it to the IAEA beyond reasonable doubt. The alternative may be Israeli or US air strikes on its nuclear facilities in a purported exercise of 'preventative self-defence'.

On these matters, so crucial to the survival of humankind, international human rights law should speak very clearly. After all, it has rules prohibiting the use of dum-dum bullets and setting the size of blankets in POW cells; it must have rules for a weapon which, if exploded over a city, could kill a million people and maim and poison millions more for generations to come. This, perhaps the ultimate test for international law, has been collectively failed by the International Court of Justice, which has, in two important cases, found nuclear bombs too hot to be handled by the law of nations.

The ICJ exists to declare international law based 'on certain general and well-recognized principles, namely: elemental considerations of humanity, even more exacting in peace than in war, and every state's obligation not to allow knowingly its territory to be used for acts contrary to the rights of other states'.[19] This simple approach was first adopted in the *Corfu Channel Case* of 1949, where Albania was ordered to pay compensation for failing in its elemental humanitarian duty to notify foreign shipping of a minefield it had secretly laid in international waters. This finding of state responsibility for creating a hazard to human life was relied upon by Australia in its attempt to stop France from conducting atmospheric tests in the Pacific. The question was eminently justiciable, but nine of the ICJ's fifteen judges in the *Nuclear Tests Case* found an excuse not to decide it: since France announced that its 1974 series of atmospheric tests was the last it would hold, 'the claim of Australia no longer has any object' and thus did not need to be adjudicated.[20] This reasoning was disingenuous: the case was of crucial and continuing importance, since atmospheric testing by other countries continued, and France was soon to dishonour the spirit of its undertaking by further testing in the Pacific, albeit underground rather than in the atmosphere.

The ICJ displayed the same jurisprudential funk in the face of nuclear *realpolitik* two decades later when called upon by the World Health Organization to decide the case of the *Legality of the*

Use by a State of Nuclear Weapons in Armed Conflict. As a UN body, the World Health Organization (WHO) has the standing to request an advisory opinion on any question which arises 'within the scope of its activities'. In a piece of breathtakingly specious reasoning, the ICJ decided that since 'whether nuclear weapons are used legally or illegally their effects on health would be the same',[21] the issue was *outside* the scope of the WHO's activities! As one of three dissenting judges observed, noting the evidence of the health and environmental devastation wrought by the bombing of Hiroshima and Nagasaki, 'to hold as the court has done that these matters do not lie within the competence or scope of activities of the WHO borders on the unreal and smacks of cynicism, and the law is not cynical'.[22]

However, an advisory opinion, *Legality of the Threat or Use of Nuclear Weapons*, had been requested by the UN's General Assembly under Article 96(1) of the Charter. The ICJ could not refuse, although the Western superpowers curiously claimed that any decision that nuclear weapons were illegal would be bad for disarmament.[23] They may have succeeded in rattling the judges by intimating that they would ignore any decision which did not suit their military plans. The majority opinion (adopted only by the casting vote of the president) notes: 'The destructive power of nuclear weapons cannot be contained in either space or time. They have the potential to destroy all civilization and the entire ecosystem of the planet.'[24] The principles of humanitarian law, from St Petersburg in 1868 onwards, certainly apply to nuclear weapons: 'States must never make civilians the object of attack and must consequently never use weapons that are incapable of distinguishing between civilian and military targets . . .'[25] However, nuclear weapons are not unlawful *per se*, and all states individually and collectively have a right to self-defence under Article 51 of the UN Charter, although as the Court ruled in *Nicaragua v. US*, 'self-defence would warrant only measures which are proportional to the armed attack and necessary to respond to it'.[26] It follows that any threat to use nuclear weapons which is disproportionate or unnecessary would be unlawful under the Charter, but there is no specific prohibition against recourse to nuclear attack in any of the treaties concerned with weapons of mass destruction. The NPT and other 'nuclear-free' conventions can be seen as 'foreshadowing a future general prohibition on the use of such weapons, but they do not constitute such a prohibition by themselves'.

In other words, the bomb is not banned by law. States can make it, and even use it according to the rules of self-defence, the occasion for which they alone are judge. The US treated the right of self-defence (preserved in Article 51 of the UN Charter) like a piece of elastic after 9/11. ('Anticipatory self-defence' was talked up as a reason for invading Iraq, because it had refused inspections and might be stockpiling chemical weapons which it might use in the future.) The UK specifically envisaged 'the use of a low-yield nuclear weapon against warships on the high seas or troops in sparsely populated areas', a prospect which, however likely to lead to escalation into a full-scale nuclear imbroglio, gave the ICJ the key to switch itself off: 'The Court considers it does not have sufficient elements of fact to enable it to *conclude with certainty* that the use of nuclear weapons would *necessarily* be at variance with the principles and rules of law in armed conflict *in any circumstance*.' These are weasel words, although the judges nervously venture the thought that, given the characteristics of nuclear weapons and the requirements of international humanitarian law, 'the use of such weapons in fact seems scarcely reconcilable with respect for such requirements'. Such use is not reconcilable at all, as a matter of the meaning of language, or of common sense, but this passing comment is the furthest they are prepared to go, because 'the Court cannot lose sight of the fundamental right of every state to survival and thus its right to resort to self-defence, in accordance with Article 51 of the Charter, where its survival is at stake'. For this reason, 'in view of the present state of international law viewed as a whole, as examined above by the Court, and of the elements of fact at its disposal, the Court is led to observe that it cannot reach a definitive conclusion as to the legality or illegality of the use of nuclear weapons by a state in an extreme circumstance of self-defence in which its very survival would be at stake'.[27]

What the ICJ opinion means is that states are not acting unlawfully by stockpiling nuclear weaponry or by acquiring the technology to build the bomb or by testing that technology. It means that states do not act unlawfully by threatening to use the bomb, or indeed by using it, so long as their leaders genuinely believe that their survival is at stake – an excuse for states outside the NPT, like India and Pakistan, to have a nuclear weapons programme. The notion of a state securing its survival by actions which threaten to exterminate all human life is risible, as is the British 'low-yield' scenario in which combatants politely nuke each other's ships on the high seas or aim their nuclear missiles only at military targets located in deserts. What the Court is saying (by reference to 'inadequate elements of fact at its disposal') is that international law contains no general prohibition against nuclear weapons, but must judge each use according to the actual 'elements of fact' surrounding it. By the time those 'elements' can be presented, as evidence of what caused nuclear war, we may all be dead. Some future form of life may stumble upon these 300 pages, carefully paragraphed both in English and French, and wonder how international law in 1996 could circumlocute itself to death.

There is an equal number of dissenting judgments, but they do not speak with the same voice. There are judges who confidently declare nuclear weapons illegal, and judges – like the American Steven Schwebel – who declare their own country's possession of them to be the best guarantee of world peace. The majority is accused (reasonably enough) of evasiveness and indecisiveness, to which accusation some of its number respond by pointing out that international law is a 'defective legal system' – which it will remain, if the ICJ continues to render judgments like this one. The decision entirely fails to elucidate the question of whether and *when* the Security Council can forcibly override state sovereignty to remove nuclear weaponry from nations which are not party to the NPT, and it fails to explain whether the Israeli bombing of Osiraq was a crime or a legitimate prophylactic. The case of the *Legality of the Threat or Use of Nuclear Weapons in Armed Conflict* stands for not much more than the rule that a state must not stockpile nuclear weapons in numbers far beyond the reasonable needs of deterrence or self-defence.

CONVENTIONAL WEAPONS

The urgency of controlling the weapons of mass destruction – nuclear, ballistic and chemical – has obscured the problems of policing the traffic in the ordinary guns and bombs which cause 90 per cent of casualties in modern wars. This has been left, unsatisfactorily, to domestic laws and to the policies of individual states, except in relation to conflicts condemned by UN imposition of arms sanctions. There is unanimity in favour of maintaining effective controls over the sales of conventional weapons and supervision over their trans-shipment to ensure that they do not fall into the hands of terrorists and criminals, but the frequency with which they do is indicative of the failure to police such controls at an international level. There are an estimated 875 million small arms in the world today, most in private hands. Eight million new weapons are produced every year, along with sixteen billion bullets. The AK-74, the most recent Kalashnikov, fires 650 rounds per minute. The small-arms scourge in Africa ranks alongside HIV/AIDS, malaria and impunity as the prime factors hindering the continent's development. The Red Cross estimates that almost one million people are killed each year by small-arms fire and that 85 per cent of them are civilians. Though Mr Kalashnikov was quoted in 2002 as expressing the wish that he had invented a lawn-mower instead of a rifle, other arms manufacturers will never be prepared to beat their swords into ploughshares.[28]

Article 26 of the UN Charter called on the Security Council, way back in 1946, to make plans for 'the establishment of a system for the regulation of armaments' but sixty-five years later, still no system has been produced – doubtless because the Big Five in the Council are also the world's largest armaments suppliers, together with Israel, the Netherlands and Germany. These countries earn most of the $55 billion that derives from global arms sales, their profits from sales to developing countries being more than they give back in aid. In 2006 the General Assembly initiated a move towards an Arms Trade Treaty, which has proceeded through its preparatory stages with Security Council support, and was being finally negotiated in 2012. It will require member states to undertake a risk assessment before selling lethal goods, against criteria (set out in the Treaty), which have yet to be agreed. The Obama administration is supportive so long as the Treaty body 'operates under the rules of consensus decision-making' – Hillary Clinton's euphemism for the US having a veto. The fervent opposition to any arms control by the National Rifle Association calls future US support into question, and Canada is anxious that weapons used for sport and hunting should be exempted.

The beginning of what should be an international law rule was first stated in the 1937 Draft Convention for the Prosecution and Punishment of Terrorism, which required states to avoid assisting wilful acts causing death to public officials or endangering the lives of members of the public. States were obliged to prohibit within their borders the manufacture, possession or supply of arms, ammunition, explosives or harmful substances with a view to assisting unlawful terrorist organizations in other countries. Although this convention never entered into force, these provisions were embodied in the Friendly Relations Resolution passed by the General Assembly in 1970 and are echoed in a number of international and regional conventions agreed since then, all endorsing an international duty on states to prohibit the supply of lethal weapons to unlawful organizations in other countries.

Where there is probably a consensus in state practice as well as in principle is in forbidding military assistance to criminal organizations which have no political agenda. Thus, Israel and Antigua were condemned in 1990 when it emerged that negligence in the former's defence department, and corruption in the latter's government and army, had combined to permit a large order of machine guns, rifles and ammunition to reach the forces of the Medellin drugs cartel, who used them in the assassinations of judges and political leaders.[29] This was one of the rare occasions on which illegal arms traffic was exposed: usually it thrives under the system of 'end-user certification', by which arms-dealing nations purport to comply with their international law obligations. In fact, the end-user system is farcical: compliance is achieved merely by asking the purchaser to make a statement to the effect that the weapons will be kept and used in a particular country for a legitimate purpose. This is not worth the paper it is written on: it is not legally binding in the country of import, and is required only to protect the exporting state from criticism when its weapons are found in the wrong hands or in the wrong place. The commission which exposed the scandalous way in which Israel and Antigua armed the Colombian drug cartels recommended that an international register of end-user certificates should be established under the auspices of the United Nations, so that at least arms exports by member governments would be identified and monitored.[30] This necessary step is resisted by many arms-exporting states fearing for the 'commercial confidentiality' of their arms merchants and, in some cases, for exposure of their own links with unsavoury regimes or guerrilla forces.

In the aftermath of international action against Iraq over its invasion of Kuwait, more attention was focused on the need to regulate the traffic in conventional weapons. Most arms-exporting nations were complicit in Saddam Hussein's massive military build-up in the years before the invasion, notwithstanding his record of brutal internal repression, his use of chemical weapons and the appalling casualty figures of the drawn-out war between Iraq and Iran. Assistance was not merely afforded by export of lethal weapons, but by providing pilot training and fighter planes for his air force (France); by building him a navy (Italy); and by supplying chemicals for poison gas (Germany). Companies from Britian (notably Matrix-Churchill, helped by the government to evade its own sanctions) made machine tools programmed to provide Iraq with the indigenous capacity to produce bombs and rockets. Sanctions were circumvented by accepting false end-user certificates from Jordan for arms obviously intended for Iraq. Considerations such as maintaining employment at home and enhancing military or diplomatic leverage abroad disincline arms-exporting states to reduce their trade with governments prone to use those arms for repression or for unnecessary enhancement of their military strength.

If international law is to have an impact on the trade in arms, it must impose incremental duties requiring states to prohibit exports to:

(1) criminal gangs and cartels;
(2) political or religious groups which engage in terrorism;

(3) governments or armies which are subject to UN arms embargoes;

(4) states which are engaging in, or are likely to initiate, hostilities with other states in breach of the UN Charter;

(5) states which intend to use the arms for domestic repression in breach of human rights law; and

(6) governments of developing countries whose arms budget is disproportionately high compared with their spending on public welfare.

At present, (1) reflects an established rule of international law, while (6) remains wishful thinking from a few NGOs. There is some movement towards (2) as a result of 9/11, subject to the inevitable dispute over whether militant resistance movements are 'terrorists' or 'freedom fighters', and towards (3): state practice is to talk as if UN arms sanctions are binding, although non-compliance by nationals is infrequently the subject of prosecution. There will be little progress without a compulsory UN register of end-user certificates and the establishment of an international monitoring body with powers to investigate and prosecute unlawful arms deals and to apply to an international court for injunctions against states which permit the export of arms to prohibited destinations. The situation at (4) and (5) above will sometimes call forth UN sanctions, or embargoes imposed by individual states with particular foreign policies: what needs to be acknowledged, however, is an international law obligation to prevent export to forces which are committing war crimes or crimes against humanity. This was the crucial issue as delegates from 150 countries hunkered down at the UN for the month of July 2012 to attempt to agree a global arms treaty prohibiting conventional weapons sales to countries where there is a 'substantial risk of a serious violation' of human rights. Such a treaty would have prevented Russia selling arms to Syria – which is why Russia may not support the treaty, along with the US, which insists that ammunition should not be subject to any ban (so existing guns could be readily supplied with bullets, and bombs) and which wants to water down the obligation on states, so they would only have to 'consider' the human rights record of the country ordering the weapons – an approach that would make the treaty of little worth.

There is a further definitional problem which must be addressed, namely the nature of the goods that are to be embargoed. States which are prepared to impose sanctions on warring parties do so by imposing export restrictions on lethal weaponry and various descriptions of arms-related equipment. The Iraqgate scandal exposed how easily these regulations could be circumvented by the export of 'dual use' machinery such as machine tools, not specifically designed to make arms but when *in situ* in Iraq easily programmed to produce bombs and rockets. Another area of unprohibited export was the provisioning of the Iraqi army with 'non-lethal' material, such as communications equipment, radar and mine-detection devices – all helping to locate and kill the enemy in greater numbers. The problem is acute for aid programmes: since armies march on their stomachs, it can clearly be contemplated that a proportion of the food charitably distributed to refugee camps will be passed over the wire to feed the soldiers fighting in genocidal conflicts. In Africa, it is estimated that up to 20 per cent of food aid provided by tender-hearted donors in the West is diverted to 'the boys in the bush' to fuel the genocide which has produced the refugee problem in the first place. Governments frequently make absurd 'humanitarian' distinctions: Britain refused to supply Iraq with guns and fuselages for 'lethal' fighter planes, but happily trained fighter pilots and provided them with ejector seats so that they could live to fight (and kill) another day.

LANDMINES

The one conventional weapon which the international community has made recent progress towards outlawing is the anti-personnel landmine. These objects, each sold for about £2.00, are designed to blast off the foot which steps on them and to project metal upwards into the stomach and chest. There are about 70 million of them lurking beneath the surface of former and present conflict zones, and as many in stockpiles in countries like Singapore, Chile, India, Israel, the USA and even Sweden. In 1997, some 26,000 people – many of them children – were killed or maimed by the weapons (that's seventy victims a day, or one every fifteen minutes). These statistics (and a glamorous campaign featuring Princess Diana) brought forth in that year the Convention on the Prohibition of the Use, Stockpiling, Production and Transfer of Anti-Personnel Mines and on Their Destruction. It was ratified in double-quick time by over seventy states, and came into force in March 1999. The Convention itself shows the limits of what states – i.e. politicians and diplomats – are prepared to do, even for such a cause, because, for all the hideousness of the anti-personnel mine:

(1) Nobody was prepared to ban the real killer, i.e. the anti-tank mine. This blows up trucks and passenger cars as well as tanks, and has caused far more casualties among UN peacekeepers and aid workers.

(2) The most significant mine-producing nations have refused to sign the Convention: China, India, Pakistan, Iran, Cuba, North Korea and Israel (to name but a few of the 'usual suspects') and Russia and the United States.

(3) The Convention's compliance provisions, in Article 8, are excruciatingly weak. As usual, in deference to state sovereignty only a 'state party' may complain that another state party is in breach – there is no provision for NGO complaints, or for an independent enforcement agency. A complaint is euphemistically called 'a request for clarification' and is submitted through the Secretary-General to the suspected violator. If the answer is unsatisfactory, a majority of state parties 'may' (not 'must') order a 'fact-finding mission'. If its report concludes that there has been a violation, then the government might be 'requested', ever so politely, to comply with the Convention in the future, if (and only if) such a 'request' is first approved by more than two-thirds of the state parties.

The Convention on landmines is instructive, because it demonstrates the difficulty for even the most fashionable and acceptable human rights cause to intrude on state sovereignty so as in any way to curtail the military might of the major powers. At the very time the

Convention was receiving its ratifications, anti-personnel mines were being laid with abandon by Serbian forces along the borders between Kosovo and Albania, by India and Pakistan, Ethiopia and Eritrea, and by Savimbi's troops in Angola – if the US, Russia and China can do it, they said, why can't we? UNICEF has estimated that there are up to 20,000 casualties from landmines each year, 80 per cent of them civilians and about 30 per cent of these being children.

CLUSTER BOMBS

These are containers dropped from aeroplanes or launched by ground rockets which open in the air and scatter lots of explosive 'submunitions' or 'bomblets' over a wide area. Many – up to 40 per cent – fail to detonate, although the bomblets sometimes ignite after the war, killing civilians and hindering the rebuilding of infrastructure. Cluster munitions were widely used in Vietnam and Laos, by the Russians in Chechnya and by American-led forces in Kuwait and Afghanistan – all countries where civilians have been injured long after the war has ended. In 2008, 107 countries signed up to the Convention on Cluster Munitions, which came into force in 2010 and has seventy-three ratifications. They undertake 'never in any circumstance' to use, produce or stockpile cluster munitions. However, non-ratifying states do all these things, and they include China, the US and Russia, each of which is estimated to have more than a billion cluster munitions. The Bush administration described them as 'legitimate weapons with clear military use in combat'[31] and Russia is alleged to have used them during its South Ossetia war. Since the Convention came into force, however, they have been used only by Colonel Gadaffi's troops during the battle for Misrata.

PILLAGE

Pillage, or Plunder, has been a war crime for many centuries. At one level, it has served the interests of discipline: Cromwell, on the way to slaughter his enemies at Drogheda, stopped to execute a soldier who stole a chicken from a local farmer; Napoleon ordered that thieving soldiers should be shot (whilst his armies ransacked Europe to bring its treasures to Paris). But the crime of pillage has a wider potential: it was a basis for the prosecution of Charles I, who had ordered his troops to burn houses and ransack towns. At the lesser Nuremberg trials it was used to convict company directors and bankers who had been permitted by Nazi officialdom to exploit property they knew had been seized from Jews and from the conquered peoples of Eastern Europe. There was a specific prohibition of pillage in the Lieber code, and the prohibition is now a norm of customary international law, applicable in civil wars as well as international conflicts. The crime essentially involves the appropriation of private property without the consent of its owner, in the context of an armed conflict. The perpetrator does not need to be involved directly in the conflict – most who exploit or deal with stolen property will be businessmen – and the war may have ended, in cases where the property is transferred with knowledge that it originated as spoils of war. The 1949 Geneva Conventions apply 'to all cases of partial or total occupation of a territory . . . even if the said occupation meets with no armed resistance'[32], so the theft of resources or of property does not have to have taken place during a shooting war. The crime is (or should be) of particular relevance where corporations are permitted to extract mineral resources from land traditionally owned by people who are under an oppressive occupation. Companies that collaborate with armed occupiers – e.g. in extracting or buying 'conflict diamonds' or in exploiting resources confiscated from the civilian population – would be guilty of pillage, subject to the vexed question of whether corporations, rather than individuals, can be liable at customary law for committing an international crime.

As we have seen, it was a serious mistake to exclude corporate liability from the ICC Treaty, thus perpetuating the error made at Nuremberg. The war crimes trials of the individual company directors do, however, provide a wealth of jurisprudence on the crime of pillage when committed by individuals through the agency of corporate entities. Rulings establish that the guilty link can be found through co-operation with an occupying army, or obtaining licences from an occupying authority to exploit seized property, or by subsequently acquiring property with knowledge that it has been wrongly requisitioned from lawful owners.[33] Executives of Krupp and IG Farben were convicted of pillage for purchasing offices and machinery seized from Jews, even though it came to them by purchase from a Nazi administrator.

Natural resources are generally regarded in international law as the permanent property of the state itself, although there seems no reason why they cannot be 'pillaged' if wrongfully appropriated and used for the advantage of a multinational corporation rather than for the benefit of the people of the state. Native title, which has accorded property rights to traditional owners of land, might also be the subject of pillage if without fair compensation the land was made available, e.g. to a mining corporation, by an occupying power. That power is entitled to sell the country's resources in order to fund the needs of the local populace during the occupation, but it would commit pillage were it to permit its own nationals to take over and profit from confiscated oil and mineral resources. IG Farben were further convicted of pillaging French chemical industries by using their clout with the German army of occupation so that it would pressure the French companies into a disadvantageous merger with IG Farben which gave the latter the majority shareholding – a form of economic blackmail.[34] This case shows that the ancient crime of pillage, certainly if charged against company directors at the ICC or in ATCA proceedings, may have some life left in it, as a means of punishing multinationals which make their money on the back of the suffering of the people caught up in civil conflict.

THE CRIME OF AGGRESSION

The Nazi leaders were prosecuted at Nuremberg for the crime of waging aggressive war, but the major state parties at the Rome Conference were nervous about incriminating their political and military leaders if they went to war without Security Council cover – as indeed happened, five years later, when Bush and Blair took their countries to war against Iraq. A compromise was reached: the crime of aggression was placed within the jurisdiction of the ICC by Article 5, but it was left undefined and would be operational only after a definition had been approved at the first review conference. This was held in Kampala in 2010 and it came up with the following definition:

'Crime of aggression' means the planning, preparation, initiation or execution, by a person in a position effectively to exercise control over or to direct the political or military action of a State, of an act of aggression which, by its character, gravity and scale, constitutes a manifest violation of the Charter of the United Nations.

It will be for the ICC judges to decide what is meant by a 'manifest' violation of the Charter, i.e. whether this refers to a violation that is clearly illegal, or which has serious consequences, or both. It is uncertain as to when the amendment will become operational: there needs to be ratification by at least thirty state parties and two thirds of all state parties must agree on a time for the amendment to come into force. In any event, there can be no prosecution for the crime at least until after 1 January 2017. Prosecutions may be initiated by the Security Council, by referral from a state party (whether or not a victim of the aggression), or – controversially – on the initiative of the prosecutor. There are other complications, although cases where it would be appropriate to prosecute the crime are fairly clear cut. An Iraqi-style invasion of Kuwait would attract liability and the hand of those who objected to the Bush/Blair invasion of Iraq would have been greatly strengthened had they been able to point to the clear-cut existence of such a crime in 2003. For all the popular books, movies and TV shows that have postulated their guilt and imagined a potential prosecution at an international court, the absence of any war crime of aggression made it merely abusive to describe them as war criminals.

But there has been a remarkable lack of interest in endorsing the new crime – three years after the Kampala Conference, only Liechtenstein had bothered to ratify the amendment. It is therefore unlikely that the ICC will be equipped to prosecute crime aggression until well after 2017.

THE DOGS OF WAR

The international community has been slow to act against ex-soldiers, often dishonourably discharged from élite national forces, who make themselves available for hire to fight in internecine wars raging in countries which are not their own. Although most nations have domestic laws prohibiting preparations made within their borders for levying war against friendly foreign governments, few deign to stop their 'soldiers of fortune', in that over-romantic phrase, from travelling abroad to kill and maim the innocent victims of conflicts with which they have no patriotic connection. In Britain, memories of the 'soldiers of conscience' who fought against Franco stay sentimentally alive in the literary works of Orwell and Hemingway, updated by the disgusting record of British mercenaries in Angola in 1976 who killed civilians indiscriminately and then turned their guns on each other.[35] During the Reagan administration, the CIA aided the recruitment of mercenaries to fight with the Contra forces against the government of Nicaragua, while 'dogs of war' from Belgium and France served national interests brutally but unaccountably in the Congo and in other parts of Africa and Asia. Bin Laden and his Arab fighters were encouraged to join the Mujahidin resistance to Russia by the very Western nations that have successfully stopped the development of international law rules against the recruitment and deployment of mercenaries.

In 1989, the General Assembly condemned states which permit the recruitment or training of mercenary soldiers,[36] although its denunciation was based on their use for aggression against established governments and (note the contradiction) 'for fighting against national liberation movements of peoples struggling for the exercise of their right to self-determination' (in which case they were fighting for established governments). The armed forces of most states voting for the motion were in receipt of weapons and training and logistical support from Russia or America, but since they had themselves emerged as a result of armed struggle against colonialism, they took care to note that the legitimate struggles of peoples for independence 'can in no way be considered as or equated to mercenary activity', even when assisted by foreign powers, or, presumably, mercenaries! Notwithstanding these confusions, the UN went on to establish the International Convention against the Recruitment, Use, Financing and Training of Mercenaries (1989), which finally came into force in October 2001 but has only thirty-two (mainly insignificant) state ratifications, so has virtually no authority.

The states from which mercenaries are normally recruited remain adamantly opposed to any general prohibition, citing the rights of their citizens to risk their lives in a cause in which they believe, and the practical difficulties of deciding which wars are so unjust that joining the wrong side should be condemned by prosecution and the withdrawal of passports. If, however, a particular conflict has been made a subject of UN sanctions, it seems entirely reasonable for international law to place a duty upon states to prohibit mercenaries from departing to fight in it, certainly if that would mean fighting against UN forces or in a war of aggression which the Security Council has condemned.

In one significant respect, the Convention against mercenary activity is acquiring the status of an international law rule, namely in its concern 'at the new unlawful international activities linking drug traffickers and mercenaries in the perpetration of violent actions which undermine the constitutional order of States'. There is a fundamental difference between allowing mercenaries to travel abroad to fight for one side – even a despised side – in a civil war, and allowing them to travel to help a gang of criminals. The Convention was established in the year in which it was revealed that Israeli and British mercenaries had run camps in Colombia teaching commando techniques to the forces of the Medellin drug cartel, turning untrained killers into trained killers who used those techniques to commit crimes against humanity, namely systematic assassinations of judges, journalists and elected politicians. Cartel money was behind an audacious plot to bribe the Antiguan government to permit the establishment of a permanent training school for narco-terrorists and to order lethal weapons from Israel for trans-shipment to cartel forces in Colombia.[37] In Jerusalem the leader of the mercenaries, Colonel Yair Klein, was mildly fined for 'exporting warlike equipment and military knowledge' from Israel, and in Antigua one minister identified with the corruption was relieved of his office, but because he was the Prime Minister's son he remained an MP. This was meagre retribution for an international conspiracy to aid a criminal organization to murder the defenders of Colombian democracy.[38]

The 1989 Convention should be redrafted and limited to prohibiting the recruitment of mercenaries to commit crimes against humanity, whether for criminal gangs or sovereign governments. At present, most states will only contemplate a ban if required by UN sanctions: few have laws which prevent enlistment, outside the jurisdiction, in foreign forces of states which are not current enemies.[39] In America, the First Amendment prohibits the suppression of *Soldier of Fortune* magazine, which remains the house journal of the modern mercenary.

There is, however, one contrary development which is turning some dogs of war into angels of mercy. Western commitment to privatization coupled with the reluctance of governments to risk the lives of their own soldiers – the 'Mogadishu factor' – has tempted them to risk instead the lives of employees of private corporations like Sandline, directed and staffed by recruits from senior or seasoned positions in the British and South African armies. They are prepared, for increased payment, to do exactly what they would have done in government service, namely to wage and win small wars. The prospect of democratic governments hiring 'legitimate' mercenaries to do dirty work that might decimate or divide their own troops began controversially when in 1997 New Guinea hired Sandline to put down a secessionist movement on Bougainville island. New Guinea's own army revolted. Then Sandline was hired to help restore a democratically elected prime minister to Sierra Leone and British diplomats argued that the end (of restoring democracy) justified the means (of hiring mercenaries to do so). There has been serious talk of hiring 'corporate security services' to conduct dangerous peacekeeping operations for which countries like the US would be prepared to pay – in money, if not in the lives of their own soldiers. South Africa has been the first government to make a virtue of necessity and to 'license' its private security firms to conduct particular overseas operations, and the British Foreign Office encourages the use of what it euphemistically renamed 'private military companies' (PMCs).

So the mercenary may make a comeback – not as a soldier of fortune but as a well-insured employee of a multinational corporation, directed by decorated officers who have taken early retirement from a national army in order to do some real fighting. There is no doubt that Sandline and Executive Outcomes were better disciplined and equipped and more effective in Sierra Leone than the ragtag soldiers mustered by the UN: corporate mercenaries are not only cheaper, but more likely to stick to peacekeeping mandates and to obey orders and the law of war. But the prospect of their deployment requires an urgent change to Protocol I of the Geneva Conventions, Article 47 of which unconscionably exempts them (and spies) from the protection of humanitarian law. That any class of combatants should be liable to torture and summary execution in a modern war cannot be countenanced, and the old rule that any enemy out of uniform can be regarded as a spy and similarly shot must be abolished (it put Western journalists, disguised in robes and burkhas, at considerable risk during the Afghan war).

WAR REPORTING

International criminal justice is heavily dependent for its evidence upon reportage from conflict zones, which is why governments, like those of Sri Lanka and Iran in 2009 and Syria in 2011, ban the media. Whether truth becomes a casualty of war depends on the presence and freedom of action of information purveyors – journalists and cameramen (whether employed by media organizations or freelance); human rights monitors (sent by NGOs), who develop an expertise and understanding of the particular society; and citizens on the ground whose ability to transmit text and pictures from computers and mobile telephones has, certainly during the Arab Spring, confounded state censorship. The combatant forces supply facts and briefings, of course, but these are usually propagandistic: Wikileaks, by publishing confidential US army records and diplomatic cables, showed that the casualties in the Iraq and Afghanistan wars were much higher than officially admitted, as was the tolerance of mistreatment of civilians. The 'collateral murder' video, which showed two Reuters employees and several children gunned down from an American helicopter, revealed a war crime. Television pictures of Mladić blowing cigar smoke into the face of the commander of the Dutch battalion and strutting around Srebrenica shortly before the massacre was shown as part of the prosecution case at his trial. Because photographic and eye-witness testimony from impartial observers is a staple of war crimes trials, international law has an important part to play in protecting reporters and human rights monitors, and in particular in protecting their neutrality and their sources.

Regrettably, the law as it has developed thus far anachronistically assumes a war fought between armies of reasonably civilized states. The Hague Convention of 1907 and the Geneva Conventions of 1949 require captured correspondents to be treated as prisoners-of-war, so long as they possess accreditation from the armed force they are following – which of course they do not have if they are freelancing or covering rebel forces. The only specific protection for journalists is contained in Article 79 of Geneva Protocol I:

Journalists engaged in dangerous professional missions in areas of armed conflict shall be considered as civilians . . . provided they take no action adversely affecting their status as civilians.

This gives journalists, like all civilians, immunity from military discipline and they must not be made specific targets for attack or become the victims of reprisals by any party to the conflict, although their entitlement to civilian status will be jeopardized if they take any action which indicates support for a belligerent – for example, carrying a gun or rendering special assistance to one side or the other. This 'civilian status' is vague and unsatisfactory: is it lost by a reporter who agrees to be 'embedded' in an army? There should be a specific war crime of killing journalists or human rights monitors or fact-finders, for the simple reason that in conflict zones they are not perceived as innocent civilians, but as enemies, real or potential, of those whose criminal acts they may expose to the world. A war crime of wilfully killing a journalist during an armed conflict, whether international or internal, should be added to the war crimes listed in

Article 8 of the Rome Statute. Such a specific crime would emphasize the essential role played by war correspondents, including cameramen and human rights monitors. Merely to include them as 'civilians' does not highlight the vital public interest role they serve and does not comport with the reality that they are targeted precisely because they are reporters. Soldiers would then be taught about the crime as part of their war-law training, and it might deter killings like that of ITN reporter Terry Lloyd, who was recklessly shot by US troops during the 2003 invasion of Iraq, and of Marie Colvin, targeted by Syrian attack troops in Homs in 2012.[40]

COMPULSION TO TESTIFY

Many human rights reporters and journalists are only too pleased to give evidence to international courts. But others, especially those still in the field, are horrified at the prospect of losing their perceived neutrality by appearing to endorse the prosecution (if the prosecution asks them to give evidence) or else by appearing in the witness box called by (and therefore appearing to support) the defence. Neutrality is vital to war correspondents and to human rights reporters working in war zones, and their own and their colleagues' safety may be put at risk if they are perceived to be 'spies' for the prosecutor of an international criminal court.

This was the dilemma that faced Jonathan Randall, a *Washington Post* correspondent who had interviewed a local Serb official named Brdanin, subsequently charged in the ICTY with complicity in war crimes. Randall was still actively engaged in reporting on terrorism, and did not want to be perceived by potential sources as a journalist who co-operated with prosecutors. He and his newspaper believed that his neutrality would be compromised. The ICTY Trial Chamber insisted that he had no testamentary privilege and had to give evidence against Brdanin, but the Appeals Chamber decided that war correspondents could not be compelled to testify unless the party which subpoenaed them could establish that their evidence would be 'really significant'; that is, of direct and important value in determining a core issue in the case. Moreover, the party seeking to call the reporter had to establish that his evidence could not reasonably be obtained elsewhere. The Court said:

In war zones, accurate information is often difficult to obtain and may be difficult to distribute or disseminate as well. The transmission of that information is essential to keeping the international public informed about matters of life and death . . . there is public interest in the work of war correspondents, which requires that the news gathering function be performed without unnecessary constraints so that the international community can receive adequate information on issues of public concern.[41]

The Court concluded that compelling war correspondents to testify on a routine basis 'may have a significant impact upon their ability to obtain information and thus their ability to inform the public on issues of general concern'. In this context there can be no meaningful distinction between the war correspondent and the human rights reporter or investigator, in terms of the importance of the information they gather or the public interest that its publication will serve. In both cases there is the danger that information will dry up if courts routinely order them to identify their sources.

SOURCE PROTECTION

In the important case of *Goodwin* v. *UK*, the European Court decided that a qualified privilege to protect journalistic sources followed from the right to freedom of expression. The public right to newsworthy information entails that those who supply information to journalists, frequently in breach of the confidence of their employers or colleagues, should none the less be protected because otherwise these sources would 'dry up' – i.e. stay silent, and much newsworthy material would not be imparted and would not in consequence be published. The European Court of Human Rights stated:

Protection of journalistic sources is one of the basic conditions for press freedom. Without such protection, sources may be deterred from assisting the press and informing the public on matters of public interest. As a result the vital public watchdog role of the press may be undermined and the ability of the press to provide accurate and reliable information may be adversely affected. Having regard to the importance of the protection of journalistic sources for press freedom in a democratic society and the potentially chilling effect an order of source disclosure has on the exercise of that freedom, such a measure cannot be compatible with Article 10 of the Convention (the freedom of expression guarantee) unless it is justified by an overriding requirement in the public interest.[42]

This reasoning can be applied to protect the sources of human rights reporters and fact-finders, who are tasked with collecting information for public purposes – to inform the reports of the UN Secretary-General or to research reports issued to the public by NGOs such as Amnesty and Human Rights Watch. The issue arose in the UN Special Court for Sierra Leone, when the prosecution called a staff member of the United Nations, who was a human rights monitor, as a witness. The UN waived its immunity so that he might testify freely, on condition that he be permitted to do so in closed court and that, when giving his evidence, the witness should not be compelled under cross-examination to name any human source from which he had received information. None the less, one trial chamber decided that the witness should be compelled to name his sources. The Appeal Chamber majority decided in favour of the witness (primarily on the wording of the Special Court Rules of Procedure) and it was the view of this author in his concurring judgment that the principle set out in *Goodwin* was equally applicable to human rights monitors giving evidence in war crimes courts:

There is, in my judgment, little meaningful difference in this respect between an investigative journalist tracking a story in a war-torn country, a war correspondent reporting on the ebb and flow of the conflict, and a researcher for a human rights organisation filing information for an 'in-depth' report or for filtered use in an annual report, or for a UN monitor gathering information for the Secretary-General to report to the Security Council. All are exercising a right to freedom of expression (and, more importantly, assisting their source's right of free speech) by extracting information for publication from people who would not give it without an assurance that their names will remain anonymous. The reprisal they often face in such circumstances, unlike the risk run by Mr Goodwin's source of being sacked or sued for breach of confidence, is of being killed as an 'informer' – a traitor to the organisation or community on whom they are silently squealing. To identify them in court would betray a promise and open them to such reprisals: more importantly, if courts routinely ordered witnesses to name their sources, then information about human rights abuses would diminish because reporters could not in good conscience elicit it by promises to protect their sources. For these reasons, I consider that 'human rights monitors', like journalists, have a privilege to refuse to name those sources to whom they have promised anonymity and who are in danger of reprisal if that promise is broken. In practical terms, that means that they must not be compelled to do so by threats to invoke the court's power to hold them in contempt and to fine or imprison them. It does not mean, of course, that the evidence that they give, based on information from sources they decline to name, will be accorded normal weight. Their entitlement to protect their source has this downside for the party that calls them: it may lose some and perhaps all of the weight that might otherwise have been placed on the evidence that is given based on the anonymous source material.[43]

There is an overriding international public interest in UN human rights reporters being able to give an assurance of confidentiality to those who put their necks on the line to inform on the murderous activities of powerful supporters or figures within their community; for example, two witnesses who gave evidence to UN Rapporteur Phillip Alston in Kenya suffered lethal reprisals. The public interest in protecting UN sources applies with the same force to fact-finders engaged by Amnesty and Human Rights Watch who collect and expertly analyse information about human rights abuses, later published in annual or special reports which serve to inform governments and international institutions, as well as the interested public, about such abuses and are used as a basis for campaigns to end them. The public interest in the free flow of information to such publications is at least as great as to other news media. Moreover, the consequences of exposure of sources of this kind can be calamitous.

In repressive countries, sources for fact-finding missions who tell of torture, death squads and arbitrary imprisonment may, if exposed, face these very consequences. Not only may they be brutally treated as punishment for embarrassing the government or other power-brokers, but their family and friends may also face reprisals. This fact underlines the need for the protective rule, usually identified as a 'privilege' belonging to the witness, although that 'privilege' is a reflection of the rather more weighty 'right' of the source. The privilege is qualified, not absolute, because it must yield in cases where the identification of the source is necessary either to prove guilt or to establish a reasonable doubt about guilt.

Courts must always guard against allowing prosecutors to present evidence which amounts to no more than hearsay demonization of defendants by human rights groups or by the media. The right of sources to protection is not a charter for lazy prosecutors to make a case based on second-hand reports or investigations. Unchecked hearsay has an inevitable place in the factual matrix upon which expert opinion is based: for example, in *Prosecutor* v. *Bizimungu*, the late Dr Alison Des Forges was called as an expert: she based her opinion upon two accounts of a meeting with Rwanda's ex-president, given by her confidential sources. Her right to withhold their names was upheld, although the court pointed out that this would be an important factor to consider in evaluating her evidence. Defendants must never be convicted solely on evidence from anonymous accusers: the court effectuates that principle by excluding or else devaluing hearsay accusations, rather than by compelling a witness who reports them to divulge the identity of the confidential source who made them.

Journalists, NGO monitors and members of fact-finding missions to repressive, war-torn or post-conflict societies must respect the undertakings they give to sources and must refuse to answer questions that might expose their informants when they are summoned to testify in a war crimes court. Courts should respect that refusal, and decline to make any finding of contempt against a fact-finder, unless the source is crucial to establishing the defendant's guilt or innocence. This approach should be applied pragmatically, by judges who recognize the danger that sources embroiled in armed conflict may be partisan and in some cases malicious, even to the extent of inventing or fabricating the information they give to fact-finders. Fabrication may, without identification or cross-examination of its source, fool even the most experienced human rights monitor. It was, after all, an experienced ex-Amnesty researcher who passed on the notoriously false story about the Kuwaiti babies being thrown out of hospital incubators by Iraqi troops during the first Gulf War. On the other hand, there must be an equal recognition that score-settling will continue for long after the conflict and that sources may be assaulted, killed or driven out of their communities as the result of exposure. But testimony based on information from anonymous sources should never be the sole or dominant basis for findings of guilt.

CHILD SOLDIERS

There are some 300,000 serving soldiers aged under eighteen presently fighting in armed conflicts in Africa. It was the CIA-backed Holden Roberto who was first to recognize how much it demoralizes an enemy village to have its chief executed by a child, and his behaviour in Angola has been emulated by both rebel groups and government militias throughout the continent. Posed photographs of small boys toting AK-47s have become the stuff of NGO fundraising, but the real problem is how to take the war out of the boy, not the boy out of the war. Attempts by UNICEF to amend the Convention on the Rights of the Child to ban recruitment of combatants under eighteen was vigorously opposed by both the UK and the US because their armies wished to continue recruiting sixteen- and seventeen-year-olds. For all the obloquy and hand-wringing that recruitment of children as frontline fighters receives, it was not until 2004 that the Special Court for Sierra Leone produced its landmark *Child Soldiers Case* judgment that recruitment of children under fifteen, at least for frontline service, was contrary to international criminal law.[44]

Attention to the problem of child soldiers has been relatively recent. The use of children in war (e.g. to load naval cannons) was ended – like their use to sweep chimneys and to go down mines – as much by the advent of new technology as by humanitarian sentiment.

Children are a very recent subject of human rights law in any event: they were omitted from the eighteenth-century Declarations on the Rights of Man because they were then regarded as the property of their parents. The Universal Declaration says no more than that 'motherhood and childhood are entitled to special care and assistance'. Article 24 of Geneva Convention IV set out a protective principle, treating children as victims of war:

Parties to the conflict shall take the necessary measures to ensure that children under 15, who are orphaned or are separated from their families as a result of the war, are not left to their own resources and that their maintenance, the exercise of their religion, and their education, are facilitated in all circumstances.

This Article identified 'children under 15' as a class which required special protection in war, along with other vulnerable categories like the sick and wounded and expectant mothers. They were to be accommodated, if possible, in 'safety zones'. But it was not until the 1977 Geneva Protocol I that parties to the conflict were directed 'to take all feasible measures in order that children who have not attained the age of 15 years do not take a direct part in hostilities and in particular, they shall refrain from recruiting them into the armed forces'. Even then, Article 77(3) accepts that there will be exceptional cases where children will take a direct part in the fighting, and requires them to be treated as protected civilians and not as prisoners-of-war. Geneva Protocol II, which applies to internal conflict, says in terms that children who have not attained the age of fifteen years shall not be recruited into the armed forces or allowed to take part in hostilities. But it was not until 1996, when Graça Machel reported on the subject for the UN, that the campaign against child recruitment took wing, and the Rome Statute defined war crimes to include 'conscripting or enlisting children under the age of 15 years into the national armed forces or using them to participate actively in hostilities'. There are different levels of seriousness: what the international crime should target is the use of children 'to participate actively' in hostilities – putting at risk the lives of those who have scarcely begun to lead them. 'Conscription' connotes the use of some compulsion, and although 'enlistment' may not need the hype of the recruiting officer, it must nevertheless involve knowledge that those enlisted are in fact under fifteen and that they may be trained for or thrown into front-line combat.

The appalling impact of war on children in Africa is well established, especially in Sierra Leone. Many were killed or wounded in that ten-year conflict, while others were forced to kill and maim – their victims including members of their own community and even their own families. The consequences for these children have been traumatic – they continue to suffer reprisals from communities they were ordered to attack and they exhibit behavioural problems and psychological difficulties related to the horrors in which they have been involved by adults in positions of 'command responsibility'. Children may be induced to risk their lives in war in a variety of ways. 'Some are conscripted, others press-ganged or kidnapped, still others joined armed groups because they are convinced it is a way to protect their families . . .'[45] Even 'voluntary enlistment' is not as benign as it sounds. Children who 'volunteer' may do so from poverty (so as to obtain army pay) or out of fear – to obtain some protection in a raging conflict. They may do so as the result of ideological inducement or psychological indoctrination to fight for a particular cult or cause, or to achieve posthumous glory as a 'martyr'. It follows that although forcible recruitment of children for actual fighting remains among the worst of war crimes, the lesser 'enlistment' offence may do the same damage. There may be a distinction in this respect: forcible recruitment is always wrong but the enlistment of child volunteers might be excused if they are accepted into the force only for non-combatant tasks, behind the front lines. Indeed, at the preparatory conference before the Rome Treaty it was agreed that the crime of using children in hostilities would 'not cover activities clearly unrelated to the hostilities such as food deliveries to an airbase or being used as domestic staff'.[46] This distinction is somewhat dubious – the baggage train, as Shakespeare's *Henry* V reminds us, is not always a place of safety for children.[47] Besides which, kids enlisted for duties 'unrelated to hostilities' may be all too willing to help on the front line, dying on the barricades like the powder monkey Gavroche in Victor Hugo's *Les Misérables*.

6

An End to Impunity?

'That four great nations, flushed with victory and stung with injury, stay the hand of vengeance and voluntarily submit their captive enemies to the judgment of the law is one of the most significant tributes that Power has ever paid to Reason.'

Justice Robert Jackson,
opening the prosecution case at Nuremberg

It is trite, and therefore true, to say that there are no 'rights' without remedies: equally, there are no human rights without remedies for human wrongs, in the sense of arrangements for punishing those guilty of crimes against humanity. These were defined, broadly but clearly, by the Nuremberg Charter provision (Article 6(c)) under which a number of Nazi leaders were convicted on 30 September 1946:

murder, extermination, enslavement, deportation, and other inhumane acts committed against any civilian population, before or during the war, or persecutions on political, racial or religious grounds in execution of or in connection with any crime, within the jurisdiction of the tribunal, whether or not in violation of the domestic law of the country where perpetrated.

Leaders, organizers, instigators and accomplices participating in the formulation or execution of a common plan or conspiracy to commit any of the foregoing crimes are responsible for all acts performed by any person in the execution of such plan.

International law is binding on states, not on persons. To this classic doctrine the Nuremberg Charter made an exception in the case· of individuals who commit crimes which – whether at a time of war between sovereign states or not – are of such ideologically motivated heinousness as to permit their classification as crimes against humanity. Crimes of that class are distinguished from acts which may have the same result – murder, torture and the like – by virtue of the fact that they are perpetrated by state officials or agents, systematically and in furtherance of an unlawful policy of denying to political or racial groups the right to life or physical integrity. They are also distinguished, in practical terms, by the perpetrator's impunity from domestic law-enforcement measures: he is punished, if at all, only after a change of government or in a foreign or international court. As one Nazi war crimes tribunal explained, 'crimes against humanity . . . can only come within the purview of this basic code of humanity because the State involved, owing to indifference, impotency or complicity, has been unable or has refused to halt the crimes and punish the criminals'.[1]

INTERNATIONAL CRIMINALS: PIRATES, SLAVERS AND KAISERS

The first individuals to be brought within the reach of international criminal law were pirates or 'sea brigands'. They were fair game for any state to capture and punish, irrespective of their nationality or whether their depredations on the high seas involved the murder or robbery of its subjects. Piracy may be regarded as the very first 'crime against humanity', its peculiarly barbaric quality deriving from the taking of lives which were especially vulnerable while outside the protective realm of any nation. It took much longer for states happy to hang pirates as if they were highwaymen to conceive a similar fate for slave traders, whose contribution to their economies was generally welcomed until the nineteenth century brought in its course a series of international treaties prohibiting the practice as 'contrary to justice and humanity'. These mark the gradual recognition of a crime against humanity so repulsive that all states are assumed to have a legal interest in its suppression: they become bound by what the International Court of Justice later termed 'an obligation *erga omnes*'[2] once treaties on the subject and the decisions of important courts are virtually unanimous. Principles of morality or dictates of humanity are a necessary but not sufficient condition for the emergence of an international law rule: as explained in chapter 3, there must be evidence of widespread 'state practice'. Thus, as late as 1825, the US Chief Justice was able to demonstrate in the *Antelope Case* that slave-trading was lawful, notwithstanding international condemnation of its immorality, because it was then 'sanctioned by the laws of all nations who possess distant colonies'.[3]

The precise point at which slavery became prohibited by international law is impossible to fix: there was no defining moment like the Nuremberg judgment, but rather an accumulation of treaties throughout the nineteenth century and a gradual abandonment by the Great Powers of their toleration of the practice, marked in turn by military offensives against traders (such as British naval action to liberate victims of Arab slavers along the east coast of Africa) and by domestic court declarations that freed any slave brought within the jurisdiction. The point came somewhere between 1885 (the Treaty of Berlin forbidding slave-trading) and 1926, when the Slavery Convention confirmed that states had jurisdiction to punish slavers wherever they were apprehended. That Convention defined the crime as reducing an individual to the status of a person over whom powers of ownership are exercised, but gave no reason why this was wrong: a supplementary Convention in 1956 explained that the basis for the prohibition was the freedom, dignity and worth of the human person. To this end it added 'practices similar to slavery', such as serdom and debt bondage, and the purchase from their families of women as wives or children as labourers. Arranged marriages can fall into this category, although NGOs have been reluctant to say so despite the ruling by the UN's Sierra Leone Court that ordering forced marriages is an international crime. A shotgun marriage, when soldiers wield the gun, overrides freedom to enter into a family relationship, but so too when parents, backed by a culture and a community, force young people into nuptials that neither party wants. Parties are not permitted to make reservations to this Convention because *erga omnes* obligations admit, by definition, of no qualifications.

The other class of individuals to be brought within the purview of international law at its pre-Nuremberg stage were soldiers, as explained in chapter 5. There was the customary right of belligerents to punish captured enemy soldiers who could be proved individually to have violated the laws of war, but heads of state and senior military commanders were traditionally immune from any trial, on the theory that as the embodiment of the state they were entitled to sovereign immunity. This metaphysical proposition was perceived as a diplomatic necessity: leaders would be less willing to settle or surrender if there was any likelihood that they would lose their necks. It was a doctrine congenial to all leaders, who could never be sure that in future conflicts they would be always on the winning side.

The first major challenge to this principle of head-of-state immunity came at the Versailles peace conference after the First World War. A commission appointed by the Allies to examine the responsibility of the 'authors of the war' rejected the sovereign immunity of high officials, including chiefs of state, who had been guilty of offences against the laws and customs of war or the laws of humanity. This was logically justified in order to refute trial claims by lesser ranks that in, for example, sinking passenger ships, they were merely following the orders of immune superiors. But it also reflected Lloyd George's campaign to prosecute the Kaiser, based on the simple principle that 'there is no right you can establish, national or international, unless you establish the fact that the man who breaks the law will meet inevitable punishment'. His attorney-general, F. E. Smith, rejected sovereign immunity for war crimes by quoting from Burke's speech indicting the Indian Viceroy, Warren Hastings – 'if you strike at him with the firm and decided arm of justice, you will not have need of a great many more examples. You strike at the whole corps if you strike at the head'. This is, of course, the deterrence argument for the 'command responsibility' theory, but as Smith also recognized, the argument does not work 'if the fairness of the tribunal can be plausibly impeached' or the head of state is summarily executed without even the trappings of a trial. He agonized over whether to recommend an impartial tribunal, with judges from neutral countries or even from Germany itself, but eventually suggested that 'grave judges' from the main Allied combatants should form a tribunal to try the Kaiser for criminal responsibility for the invasion of Belgium and for authorizing unrestricted submarine warfare. But this UK recommendation was vehemently opposed by America, since President Wilson believed that a trial would jeopardize his dream to restore such good relations with Germany that the country could be included in a 'League of Nations' which would guarantee peace.[4]

Although Article 227 of the Versailles Treaty formally proposed the establishment of a special tribunal, 'international' in the sense that its five judges would come, one each, from Britain, the US, Japan, France and Italy, this was designed as an empty gesture to Allied public opinion – Lloyd George's slogan 'Hang the Kaiser' required token acknowledgement. The Kaiser remained in Holland, as a guest of the Dutch government, until his death in 1941, leaving one of history's great hypotheticals: would Hitler have been given pause if the Kaiser had faced an international criminal court? (A prosecution might well have unearthed the evidence that has only recently come to light about the Kaiser's aggressive intentions to acquire 'lebensraum', which were not dissimilar to those of the Führer.) Articles 228 and 229 of the Treaty provided that Germany should try its own war criminals: evidence against 901 of its nationals was handed over, and they were duly arraigned in Leipzig. There, 'loser's justice' proved farcical: 888 were acquitted, and of the thirteen convicted several were allowed to escape by prison officers who were publicly congratulated for assisting them. The Leipzig trials of 1922 were a complete flop: they produced no sense of shame for inhumane actions in wartime, since the verdicts emphasized with shoulder-shrugging resignation that the 'fog of war' remained an effective defence. The trials in Constantinople of the 'Young Turk' leaders accused of the Armenian genocide were mishandled by Ottoman military authorities and abandoned after initial executions inflamed rather than shamed Turkish nationalists. The lack of any definitive verdict at a time when the evidence was fresh permits the Turkish government today to deny that the genocide ever took place, although it was fully reported (with photographs) by the British and American press in 1915 and remains well documented.[5] So it seemed that the only way to stop war crimes was to stop war – a solution embraced in 1928 with the Kellogg–Briand Pact, by which state signatories disingenuously promised to renounce war as an instrument of national policy. The League of Nations, concerned by random assassinations of politicians and diplomats, managed by 1937 to draft a convention for the creation of an international criminal court with jurisdiction to try terrorist offences, but it failed to attract many signatories before most of its members slid into another world war.[6]

THE NAZI LEADERS: SUMMARY EXECUTION?

That the course of international law was changed so dramatically by the Nuremberg Charter, trial and judgment, is attributable to a curious mixture of American idealism and Stalinist opportunism, overcoming British insistence on summary execution for the Nazi leaders. As early as 1941, punishment for war crimes was declared by Churchill to be a principal war aim and by 1943 the Allies were sufficiently confident of victory to set up a commission to gather evidence. But Nazi crimes against humanity did not figure expressly in this thinking (the Allies themselves did not, for instance, bomb the railway lines to Auschwitz) and the idea of any trial process was the last thing that British leaders had in mind. Churchill, who was an admirer of Cromwell but thought that he had made a mistake in putting Charles I on trial because it had made him a martyr and given him a platform, simply wanted a political decision made as to whom to kill – a list of fifty prominent Nazis was proffered, to be executed without trial as and when they were captured. 'All sorts of complications ensue as soon as you admit a fair trial,' he warned. Hitler was not a head of state like the Kaiser, he told the War Cabinet: he should die like a gangster 'in the electric chair, no doubt available on lend lease' (a sarcastic reference to the deal under which

the US financed the British war effort – at great profit to itself).[7]
Eden, his foreign secretary, observed that 'the guilt of such individuals as Himmler is so black that they fall outside and go beyond the
scope of any judicial process'.[8] Lord Chancellor Simon decided that
they should revive the medieval concept of 'outlawry', a status
imposed by a grand jury on suspects believed guilty of serious crimes
who did not turn up for trial: they could be killed by anyone who
captured them. Cabinet would declare the Hitler gang 'world outlaws', who must be executed six hours after their arrest – a period
thought sufficient for their final prayers.[9] On no account should
there be a trial: 'It would not rest with judges, however eminent or
learned, to decide finally a matter like this, which is of the widest
and most vital public policy.' The Foreign Office pointed to the lack
of precedent for a trial, and the danger that any charges formulated
might breach the *nulla poena sine lege* rule against retroactivity.
More persuasively, it warned of delays and procedural problems and
(even more persuasively) of the risk of defendants propagating their
policies from the dock and pointing an accusing finger at Allied war
crimes. The UK maintained its position 'that execution without trial
is the preferable course' until mid-1945, citing these 'dangers and
difficulties' of attempting to do justice to international arch-crimi-
nals.[10] At first, its view won American support: when the question
was first discussed – at the Moscow conference of foreign ministers
in November 1943 – US Secretary of State Cordell Hull declared, 'If
I had my way I would take Hitler and Mussolini and Tojo and their
accomplices and bring them before a drumhead court martial, and
at sunrise the following morning there would occur an historic incident.'[11]

That Hull did not have his way was due to the fact that it repelled
Henry Stimson, the secretary for war. He wrote to Roosevelt the following year: 'The very punishment of these men in a dignified
manner consistent with the advance of civilization will have the
greater effect on posterity . . . I am disposed to believe that, at least
as to the chief Nazi officials, we should participate in an international tribunal constituted to try them.' Hull was eventually
persuaded, and joined with Stimson to urge that 'a condemnation

after such a proceeding will meet the judgment of history so that the Germans will not be able to claim, as they have been claiming with regard to the Versailles Treaty, that an admission of war guilt was exacted under duress'. Roosevelt wavered, but his successor, Harry S. Truman, had utter contempt for the British solution of summary execution, which was anathema to his idealistic belief in the 'beneficent power of law and the wisdom of judges'.[12] He appointed Supreme Court Justice Robert Jackson to report on the feasibility of a trial, and approved his conclusion:

To free them without a trial would mock the dead and make cynics of the living. On the other hand, we could execute or otherwise punish them without a hearing. But undiscriminating executions or punishments without definite findings of guilt, fairly arrived at, would violate pledges repeatedly given, and would not sit easily on the American conscience or be remembered by our children with pride. The only other course is to determine the innocence or guilt of the accused after a hearing as dispassionate as the times and horrors we deal with will permit and upon a record that will leave our reasons and motives clear.[13]

Truman wanted an international tribunal to try the Nazi leaders, but Churchill insisted on summary execution. It was a deadlock, broken by the casting vote of Joseph Stalin, who loved show trials as long as everyone was shot in the end. His UN ambassador, the vicious ex-prosecutor Andrei Vyshinsky, had rigged such trials for him in the 1930s: proceedings in which guilt was predetermined, confessions unravelled according to a rehearsed script and, most important of all, each defendant would be convicted and executed. So for this unprepossessing reason, the Russians voted for American idealism. De Gaulle cast the French vote the same way, and the British reluctantly fell into line, consoling themselves that the suicides of Hitler, Himmler and Goebbels had diminished the danger that the trial would become a soapbox for Nazi self-justification. Supreme Court Justice Robert Jackson was nominated by Truman as chief prosecutor, and the tribunal at Nuremberg took shape with eight judges (two from each of the four Allied powers) presided over by

English Lord Justice Geoffrey Lawrence. International law would never be the same again.

THE TRIAL

The dispute between the Allies over whether Nuremberg should have happened at all is important in any analysis of its achievement. The bleak alternative – summary execution of the German political and military leaders – would have left their crimes against humanity to be revealed by posthumous propaganda rather than in an open forum where only those facts which were incontestable were not subjected to examination. Nuremberg was a show trial, but one in which the victors' sense of fairness was as much on show as the vicissitudes of the vanquished. The odds were stacked, of course: all prosecutors and judges were nationals of the Allied powers, and all defendants and, more regrettably, all their lawyers were German. (It was a measure of the contemporary collapse of adversarial ethics that the General Council of the English Bar refused to allow an English barrister to defend the Krupp family, while several provincial Bar associations in Germany later took reprisals against members who had defended Nazis 'too vigorously' at Nuremberg.) The German defence lawyers, floundering in the alien Anglo-American environment of the adversary trial, were given limited facilities to prepare their cases and little notice of prosecution evidence.

The counts in the indictment prosecuted by the Americans (conspiracy to wage aggressive war) and the British (crimes against peace) were overblown and hypocritical: as E. L. Woodward, the Foreign Office historical adviser, noted on the eve of the trial, 'up to September 1st 1939, His Majesty's Government was prepared to condone everything Germany had done to secure her position in Europe'.[14] The Russian prosecution team had the easiest task of proving war crimes, but did so with the most repellent dishonesty, insisting on laying Soviet guilt for the Katyn Forest massacre of Polish officers on the Wehrmacht (the court, wisely, made no finding on this allegation). And if anyone was guilty of being an accessory to the crime of aggression it was Stalin, who approved the Molotov-Ribbentrop Pact of August 1939 with its secret promise of a slice of *Lebensraum* for Russia as a reward for acquiescing in Nazi conquest. (Jackson, in a rare example of prosecutorial misconduct, did not disclose this secret protocol to the defence: at Soviet insistence, it remained locked in his files.)[15] Convictions for the war crime of 'wanton destruction' came ironically from judges whose nations had bombed Dresden and Hiroshima, and that strand of the Nazi conspiracy alleged to consist in 'subverting the League of Nations' was positively comic, given that the US had never joined it and the USSR had been expelled from it for attacking Finland.

These elements of humbug in the first three counts were not exposed in the court; the defence of '*tu quoque*' ('I did it, but you did it too', or 'You did it first') was ruled irrelevant with such a predetermined speed and emphasis that it was obvious that the judges were bent on silencing any allegations about Allied war crimes. As a matter both of law and of morality, they were plainly wrong: *tu quoque* evidence is highly relevant to any assessment of whether a particular mode of warfare is justified by military necessity, or is sufficiently beyond the common pale to count as a war crime. (It remains relevant in modern war crimes trials: Laurent Gbagbo, for example, sent to the ICC in 2011, will argue that his troops were entitled to respond in kind to the brutality of the opposing army.) So far as the counts alleging the conspiracy to wage aggressive war and the commission of crimes against the peace were concerned, the *tu quoque* argument was most pertinent: the Germans were charged *inter alia* with violating the rearmament provisions of the Versailles Treaty which the French had ignored and the British had joined the Germans in circumventing. As Jackson confessed to Truman, the Allies had 'done or are doing some of the very things we are prosecuting Germans for. The French are violating the Geneva Convention in their treatment of prisoners of war . . . we are prosecuting the Germans for plunder and our allies are practising it . . . we say aggressive war is a crime and one of our allies asserts sovereignty over the Baltic States based on no title except conquest.'[16] This double standard pervaded the trial, until counsel for Admiral Dönitz persuaded the Americans and the French that evidence from Admiral Chester Nimitz, commander of the Pacific fleet, should be admitted to show that American submarine practices had been the same as those his client was standing accused for ordering.[17] Dönitz was in consequence acquitted of this charge. Otherwise, the *tu quoque* objection continued to be taken and upheld throughout the trial, depriving the court of the opportunity to make any meaningful comment on the irregular commando practices of both sides, the criminality of carpet-bombing, or on the distinction, if any, between the deportations and the forced labour which the Germans were accused of ordering and the deportations and forced labour to which the Soviets were enthusiastically subjecting the people they now had at their mercy.

For all these failings, Nuremberg stands as a colossus in the development of international human rights law, precisely because its charter defined crimes against humanity and its procedures proved by acceptable and credible evidence that such crimes had been instigated by most of the defendants. The spontaneous drama of the courtroom provided the defining moment of de-Nazification on the afternoon when the prosecutor showed newsreels of Auschwitz and Belsen, and the defendants, spotlit for security in the dock, averted their eyes in horror from the ghastly screen images of the emaciated inmates of their concentration camps. Some sobbed, others sweated, or put their heads in their hands; they sat in stunned silence until the court rose, their individual and collective guilt and shame brought home to them for ever and beyond reasonable doubt.[18] This was the moment – or at least, the afternoon – of truth, but it came after painstaking months of meticulously translated documentary evidence, showing the defendants' signatures on 'night and fog' decrees, on orders for the extermination of 'useless eaters' and 'lives unworthy of living', a record the judgment accurately described as one of 'consistent and systematic inhumanity on the greatest scale'. It was that record, emerging in a largely truthful evidential shape, which can be credited with effectively destroying any future for Nazism. It prevented – as summary executions of the Nazi leaders could not – myths and fantasies about the Second World War developing in Germany in the way they did about the First in the 1920s. For that reason alone, international justice worked.

In retrospect, the most astonishing feature of Nuremberg was how the adversarial dynamics of the Anglo-American trial sucked in the defendants, who played an earnest and polite, at times desperate, part in making it work. Their leader, Göring, had initially advised them to adopt the strategy of Charles I – the King's opening gambit. They must confine their evidence to three words, 'Lick my arse' – the defiant catchcry of one of Goethe's warrior heroes.[19] But as months passed they became flattered by the fairness (at least, fairishness) of the procedures and rose to the bait of making their excuses to posterity. So they played the justice game – none more effectively than Göring himself. His defence (that the resurgence of Germany after the failure of both democracy and communism was only achievable by total support of Nazi ideology) drove Jackson, his American cross-examiner, to petulant rage. At this level, Göring was able to rebut the absurd conspiracy charge, which sought to try Germany alone for its pre-war political manoeuvrings. To his French accuser, who unemotionally put the case for his involvement in crimes against humanity, he had no answer.

What mattered above all else was that justice was seen to be done: the accused were accorded the right to defence counsel (but only from Germany), to a trial translated into their own language, to a detailed indictment and copies of all documents relied on by the prosecution, to the right both to give evidence on oath and to make unchallenged final summations. The only serious departures from Anglo-American trial procedures were standard features of Continental systems, namely the absence of any jury and the admissibility of hearsay evidence. Neither were disadvantages. Jurors drawn from the post-war populace of Nuremberg would have been biased *against* the defendant: they had lost all love for the Nazi politicians who had led them to ruin, to such an extent that they demonstrated in their thousands against the acquittals of three defendants. The hearsay rule is a shibboleth which can handicap the defence as much as the prosecution, by excluding important evidence of what was said and done by persons who cannot be called to testify. In both these respects, Nuremberg set a precedent followed by the Hague Tribunals and by the International Criminal Court statute. Guilt on charges of crimes against humanity should be based on logical reasoning by experienced judges and not on the inscrutable verdict of a jury potentially prejudiced by media attacks on the defendant. And all relevant evidence should be available to a court where the discovery of truth is more important than in the ordinary adversarial process: the weight of hearsay evidence (because it cannot be cross-examined) may be less than direct testimony, but it should not be discarded whenever it raises doubts or confirms suspicions, or accurately depicts the historical background.

JUDGMENT DAY

Nuremberg changed and clarified international law in many ways. The Charter itself was the outcome of the four-power agreement signed in London on 8 August 1945, which provided for 'an international military tribunal for the trial of war criminals whose offences have no particular geographical location'. This was, in form, no more than the exercise by belligerents of an established customary right to try captured enemies who had infringed the laws of war as defined by the early Hague Conventions. The definition of crimes against humanity in Article 6(c) of the Charter, however, was not found in these earlier conventions, and was applicable to tyrannous behaviour within a state as much as to wartime conflict between states. Article 7 expressly rejected the 'sovereign immunity' principle which the Americans had at Versailles insisted must protect military and political leaders:

The official position of defendants, whether as Heads of State or responsible officials in Government Departments, shall not be considered as freeing them from responsibility or mitigating punishment.

It was on this basis that Jackson blew away the dust of sovereignty in his prosecution opening, rejecting the notion that individual leaders could escape responsibility by arguing that they were merely agents of an immune state:

The idea that a state, any more than a corporation, commits crimes, is a fiction. Crimes always are committed only by persons . . . It is quite intolerable to let such a legalism become the basis of personal immunity.

The charter recognizes that one who has committed criminal acts may not take refuge in superior orders nor in the doctrine that his crimes were acts of state. These twin principles working together have hitherto resulted in immunity for practically everyone concerned in the really great crimes against peace and mankind. Those in lower ranks were protected because their orders were called acts of state. Modern civilization puts unlimited weapons of destruction in the hands of men. It cannot tolerate so vast an area of legal irresponsibility.

These defendants were men of a station and rank which does not soil its own hands with blood. They were men who knew how to use lesser folk as tools. We want to reach the planners and designers, the inciters and leaders . . .

The Tribunal, in its judgment, anchored its Charter in 'an exercise of sovereign legislative power by the countries to which the German Reich had unconditionally surrendered'. It was 'an expression of international law existing at the time of its creation; and to that extent is itself a contribution to international law'. It rejected the argument that international law is concerned only with the actions of states, and therefore cannot punish individuals, or (alternatively) cannot punish them for carrying out the orders of a sovereign state: 'the very essence of the Charter is that individuals have international duties which transcend the national obligations of obedience imposed by the individual state . . . if the state in authorizing action moves outside its competence in international law'.

The significance of this ruling is that it provides an authoritative basis for holding individuals at all levels, whether footsoldiers or leaders, liable for crimes against humanity. The torturers cannot rely on the defence of superior orders, any more than the commanders can rely on the privileges and immunities of the state they serve. Article 8 of the Charter provides:

The fact that the defendant acted pursuant to the order of his Government or of a superior shall not free him from responsibility, but may be considered in mitigation of punishment . . .

The true test, the Nuremberg judgment decided, was 'whether moral choice is in fact possible' for a soldier or official ordered to kill or torture in defiance of international law.[20] This leaves the proven perpetrator of a crime against humanity only two avenues of exculpation if the action was taken under orders: either that he did not appreciate its unlawfulness, or that he acted under a duress so threatening to himself or his family that it left him no reasonable option but to comply. The Nazi leaders tried at Nuremberg were superiors who gave the orders. In the follow-up trials, duress usually failed as a defence for bankers and doctors, industrialists and bureaucrats, who were personally or politically disposed in any event to carry out Nazi orders,[21] or for officers and soldiers who feared disciplinary sanctions or minor punishment in no way comparable to the gravity of the harm they inflicted by choosing to obey the order.[22] But it was crucial to the perceived fairness of these trials that 'duress' was available and availed of as a defence, however rarely it succeeded.

Nuremberg was not the model of an unbiased international tribunal (that would have required judges from countries which had remained neutral); counts one and two (conspiracy to wage aggressive war and crimes against peace) were novel and infringed the rule against retrospectivity; the fairness of the trial on count three (war crimes) was affected by the ruling against *tu quoque* evidence. But the great achievement of Nuremberg was count four: the crime against humanity – in effect, an ordinary crime committed on a scale of barbarism unimaginable until the Holocaust. This was the crime recognizable even to its architects when they saw the concentration camp films: the words of the Charter – 'extermination, enslavement, deportation and other inhumane acts . . . persecution on political, racial or religious grounds in connection with any crime' – hardly convey the unspeakable horror. These were not war crimes against enemy soldiers, but against German civilians – Jews, gypsies, homosexuals, the handicapped – who were regarded as pseudo-humans. They were not committed because of the exigencies of war, but because of the vicious racism of Nazi leaders. Unlike the crimes of pirates and slave traders, the traditional targets of individual responsibility in international law, they did not need any international or transborder element to attract jurisdiction: these were crimes that the world could not suffer to take place anywhere, at any time, because they shamed everyone. They were not, for that crucial reason, crimes against Germans (which therefore only Germans should punish); they were crimes against humanity, because the very fact that a fellow human could conceive and commit them diminishes every member of the human race. For this precedent alone, with its potential to destroy sovereign immunity, the Nuremberg judgment was one large legal step forward for humankind.

NUREMBERG AND TOKYO: VICTOR'S JUSTICE?

That humankind did not progress much beyond the Nuremberg verdicts for the next fifty years was due to many factors, only one of which can be laid at the door of the Tribunal. In its end lay the negation of its beginning: it created crimes against humanity and then punished them inhumanely. Twelve defendants were sentenced to death by hanging, after which – by some grisly irony appealing to the Allied high command – the bodies were cremated in the ovens at Dachau. The ashes were consigned to an unidentified fast-flowing river so no grave would ever serve as a place of neo-Nazi pilgrimage. Göring eluded this act of vengeance by taking a capsule of poison on the night before the executions, choosing to die privately in brief convulsive agony rather than in a macabre ritual laid on for the Allied press. The worst feature of the executions was that they had been preordained, at least by the Russians. As early as the Tehran Conference, Stalin had proposed that the trial dispense 'the justice of the firing squad'. Very early in the trial he had it visited by Andrei Vyshinsky, choreographer of his own show trials. It was an excruciating occasion, as the Allied judges and prosecutors hosted a dinner in honour of a man who had been complicit in more crimes against humanity than those they were trying. True to form, Vyshinsky raised his glass and proposed a toast 'to the speedy conviction and execution of the defendants'. The judges drank it, to their subsequent mortification. The British attorney-general Hartley Shawcross clamoured for death sentences, in breach of an ethical rule of the English Bar that prosecutors must not urge a particular punishment. He argued, perversely, that upon executing these defendants depended 'the ways of truth and righteousness between the nations of the world'.[23] Since he also accepted that they were broken and discredited men, 'the ways of truth and righteousness' were hardly paved by killing them.

But victor's justice required executions, as it still does in post-war societies where revenge is the dominant emotion, and where death sentences are imposed without fair (or any) trial – the only sure way for an ex-tyrant to save his life may be to surrender to the ICC. The Russian judges followed their orders from Stalin and insisted on the death penalty for everyone, while only one of the French judges, De Vares, was in principle opposed to hanging. That three of the twenty-two defendants were acquitted, and seven spared the death penalty, gave the Tribunal's decision that element of weighing and balancing which is necessary to any 'judgment', but its punishments subsequently provided a precedent used to excuse the politically motivated execution of other fallen leaders from Eastern Europe, and those like Pakistan's Zulfikar Ali Bhutto whose guilt was much less clearly proven. Something of this stain was removed in the 1990s, when the death penalty was abjured as an option for the international tribunals for former Yugoslavia and Rwanda, and then as a penalty available to the International Criminal Court. It remains historically the most regrettable aspect of the Allied war crimes trials that a process which commenced with Henry Stimson's call to punish 'in a dignified manner consistent with the advance of civilization' should end at Hamelin prison with the English hangman Albert Pierrepoint slavering over Irma Griese ('as bonny a blonde as one could ever hope to meet') as he measured her for the drop.[24]

Once the Nazi leaders had been tried, interest in prosecuting underlings and accomplices waned. A few industrialists – notably Alfred Krupp – received jail sentences, but the corporations which had profited by deliberately working Jews to death, such as Siemens, Volkswagen and IG Farben, were not prosecuted or forced to compensate their surviving relatives until fifty years later, when there were far fewer survivors. By the end of 1947 the Allies ran out of both money and motivation for war crimes trials, and the onset of the Cold War brought a new and powerful reason to disband them: Nazi scientists and businessmen who might be of use in the forthcoming battle between communism and capitalism had to be given immunity, by East and West alike. Justice became a mockery of power politics: while the palpably insane Rudolf Hess remained incarcerated at Soviet insistence for the rest of his life, the US helped Klaus Barbie to escape and released Krupp in 1951, before half his sentence had expired. This caused Jackson (who had returned to the US Supreme Court) to write despairingly to Shawcross: 'This country is so heated up about communism at the present moment that the public temper identifies as a friend of the United States any person who is a foe of Stalin.'[25]

It had been fear of 'communism and chaos' which determined the fateful decision of General MacArthur's administration in occupied Japan to exempt from trial – indeed, from all retribution – the worst surviving war criminal of all, the Emperor Hirohito, who had personally approved all his country's barbaric military ventures and had held out against surrender until the radioactive dust cleared from Hiroshima. It was this crucial decision which made the Tokyo trials a mockery of justice, with their death sentences on politicians and generals who had served as the Emperor's accomplices. The French judge, Henri Bernard, said that the failure to prosecute the Emperor vitiated the entire proceedings, while the presiding Australian judge, Sir William Webb, argued that because 'the leader of the crime, though available for trial, had been granted immunity', his accomplices should have their death sentences commuted to life imprisonment. This was the tragic flaw in a trial which should have been as significant as Nuremberg and was in some ways an improvement on it – for example, the defendants were provided with American lawyers, who were permitted to challenge the jurisdictional basis of the Tribunal on the grounds that it was 'victor's justice' imposing '*ex post facto* criminality'. The proceedings dragged on, from May 1946 to November 1948, because most of this time was occupied with the defence case

(George Kennan commented caustically that 'at no time in history have conquerors conferred upon the vanquished such elaborate opportunities for public defence and for vindication of their military acts').[26] The Tokyo prosecution served the historical purpose of collecting hard documentary evidence of systematic atrocities which in their elemental bestiality were beyond even Nazi contemplation: this imperial army impaled women on stakes, after raping them and cutting their children in half. It dropped bubonic plague germs on Chinese citizens, and boasted of its contempt for the laws of war by executing Allied airmen alongside their parachutes and by sending surviving prisoners, at war's end, on death marches. The sadism that flourished with official approval in the prisoner-of-war camps cost 27 per cent of the Anglo-American prisoners their lives (compared with 4 per cent who died in German or Italian captivity). While Nuremberg had confined the concept of the crime against humanity to the wartime genocide of civilian Jews in concentration camps, the Tokyo trial extended the description to peculiarly barbaric acts of murder, generally of prisoners-of-war, in circumstances which amounted in isolation to war crimes, but which were given the extra dimension of guilt because they were proved to be widespread and systematic emanations of a policy approved (or at least tolerated) by Japan's military and political leadership.[27] The Tokyo trial's contribution to humanitarian jurisprudence was the concept of criminal liability for permitting, as distinct from intending, atrocities: this was the 'command responsibility' theory, approved by the US Supreme Court in rejecting General Yamashita's appeal, which half a century afterwards would become the basis for the ICTY indictments of Karadžić and Mladić and later for the ICC indictments of the Gaddafis and Laurent Gbagbo.

The absence of Hirohito, the supreme commander, undermined the trial both as a precedent and as a method of guilt acknowledgement. The Emperor, who had previously been psychologically incapable of contemplating surrender, did so on 14 August 1945, only because the atom bomb had been dropped on Hiroshima eight days before. His 'surrender' broadcast to his people was a monument of evasion ('the war situation has developed not necessarily to Japan's advantage, while the general trends of the world have all turned against her interests') and he should have occupied Göring's place in the Tokyo dock. But MacArthur and his right-wing advisers decided that the imperative of avoiding 'communism and chaos' required the Emperor to remain in place, as an American puppet, even though this meant rigging the Tokyo trial to pretend that he was innocent. The proceedings were very much an American affair: the International Military Tribunal of the Far East was established by MacArthur's declaration, rather than by any international agreement, and he appointed the judges (eleven which proved too many). His chief counsel, Joseph Heenan, edited Hirohito out of the prosecution evidence and encouraged the twenty-five defendants to make no mention of him (they happily colluded, 'for the future of the Japanese race'). When Tojo accidentally testified that it was inconceivable for a high Japanese official to take any action against the wishes of the Emperor, Heenan stage-managed a bogus retraction. Other indefensible decisions were taken by the American prosecutors: they exempted Japan's warmongering industrialists and its violent (but violently anti-communist) nationalist leaders; they overlooked the enslavement of Koreans and Formosans and hundreds of thousands of 'comfort women' forced to slake the lust of the imperial army. They made a Faustian bargain with the wicked scientists of Unit 731 in Manchuria (where thousands of human guinea pigs were killed in the course of Mengele-type experiments), giving them immunity in return for disclosing the results of their 'research' to the US rather than the USSR.[28]

Although there can be little quarrel with the actual verdicts of the Far East military tribunals, which tried some 6,000 war criminals (imposing 900 death sentences but acquitting about one-fifth of all defendants), these inadequacies diminish the main Tokyo trial as a historical example of international justice. Bizarrely, the Americans decided not to publish an official transcript of the judgments: in consequence, the best known is a querulous dissent by Justice Pal, privately published by the author in 1952 and distributed in Japan under the title *On Japan Being Not Guilty*. Pal (who did not bother to attend many trial sessions) declared everyone innocent. He made the correct criticism that criminal liability for 'crimes against the peace' could not be derived retrospectively from the Kellogg-Briand Pact, but irresponsibly he chose to turn a blind eye to the amply proved charges of war crimes, and unforgivably tried to justify the summary murder of captured Allied airmen ('the conscience of mankind revolts not so much against the punishment meted out to the ruthless bomber as against his ruthless form of bombing').[29]

Pal's dissent provides an example of how a judge's nationality and politics (he was a bitter Indian anti-colonialist) can override his duty to do justice, but it proved influential – especially through its denunciation of the US bombing of Hiroshima. The absence of the Emperor from the dock meant that the US lost for all time the opportunity of proving in court that Truman's first use of the A-bomb did indeed, as he predicted, save hundreds of thousands of Allied and Japanese lives, since it was the only way to force this implacable man to surrender. More significantly, of course, the Emperor's immunity sent the indelible message that the nation itself was guiltless: subsequent generations felt no shame in having an executed war criminal in the family, and the Japanese government even today refuses to contemplate compensation for the victims of its atrocities (such as the death marches in Ambon), unlike the German government, which in 1999 stumped up over £1 billion in the settlement with wartime slave labourers.

The received wisdom in the US supreme command was that Japanese crimes against humanity were more readily forgivable than German, because the latter race were so much more civilized and hence deserved more punishment because they 'knew better'. This thinking, articulated by MacArthur in evidence to a US Senate inquiry, was ignorant as well as paternalistic. Imperial Japan was in fact more thoroughgoingly racist than Nazi Germany, its innate superiority lauded over other Asian races as well as over 'decadent' Europeans. Japanese generals, diplomats and government lawyers knew all about the pre-war Hague and Geneva Conventions, and boasted of flouting them. The arrogant amorality with which Japanese soldier and general alike would hack or march to death inconvenient prisoners was arguably as wicked as the perverted ideology which could justify the destruction (by working them to death) of Jews, gypsies and homosexuals. The Nuremberg trial saw off the racist perversion of Nazism, but the Tokyo trial did nothing to deter the bestial military blood-vengeance that has been the hallmark of modern crimes against humanity, from Rwanda and Bosnia to East Timor. Emperor Hirohito stayed on his throne until his death in 1989, masquerading as a meek marine biologist, touring in 1971 to meet Queen Elizabeth II and in 1975 to meet Mickey Mouse and Dr Kissinger: in that era when crimes against humanity were so regularly overlooked, few bothered to demonstrate against him. For all the promise of Nuremberg, the equivalent trial in Tokyo served more to underline a traditional Japanese song:

> *There is a law of nations, it is true,*
> *But when the moment comes, remember,*
> *The strong eat up the weak.*

Meanwhile, in Cold War Europe, the Nuremberg precedent was being ignored (although in West Germany, once the country had recovered, it was commendably applied in over 6,000 cases of Nazi war crimes). Once the Allies lost interest, nobody bothered to investigate thousands of crimes against humanity whose perpetrators quietly shipped themselves off to begin new lives in Allied countries which accepted them as refugees and did not wake up to their past until the 1990s, by which time most were too old to be satisfactorily tried. Some Nazi criminals found refuge in nations which needed them or sympathized with their crimes. In Perón's Argentina, they organized the army and much of industry; in East Germany, they occupied political positions as administrators and propagandists.[30] President Stroessner of Paraguay personally protected the Auschwitz doctor Josef Mengele, while successive Syrian rulers not only extended hospitality to Alois Brunner, Eichmann's exterminator-general, but employed him in anti-Israeli work and rejected every request for his extradition.[31]

More positively, however, the United Nations General Assembly in December 1946 unanimously confirmed that the Nuremberg Charter and reasoning of the Tribunal reflected the principles of international law.[32] As the House of Lords was to recognize in the *Pinochet Case*, this set the seal on Article 6 of the Charter, which proclaims that there shall be 'individual responsibility' (notwithstanding that individual's exercise of state power or obedience to superior orders) for

(a) Crimes against peace (waging or initiating a war of aggression or a war in violation of international treaties);
(b) War crimes (violations of the law or customs of war); and
(c) Crimes against humanity.

Questions remained, however, about the latter category, which the Nuremberg judgment itself had treated as if they were particularly heinous examples of war crimes rather than as a separate category of crime which could be committed irrespective of the existence of any inter-state conflict. On this approach, one significant distinction between a war crime and a crime against humanity would be that the latter could be committed by a government against its own nationals (e.g. the Nazis against German Jews), while war crimes could be perpetrated only upon enemies or foreigners. Article 6(c) of the Charter defines crimes against humanity as 'murder, extermination, enslavement, deportation and other inhumane acts committed against any civilian population *before or during* [my italics] the war', and is therefore apt to cover barbarities committed within a state against its own nationals, irrespective of the onset of war. Although the Charter may not have been intended to render individuals responsible in international law for the crimes against humanity they committed in time of peace, the question is now academic since 6(c) designated a class of crime which later treaties and precedents – culminating in the appeal judgment in the *Tadić Case* (see p. 453) – have recognized as capable of punishment, whenever and wherever committed.

It should be noticed, however, that an ingredient of the crimes defined as 'against humanity' in Article 6(c) was that they are committed 'in execution of or in connection with any crime within the jurisdiction of the Tribunal'. This suggested (ambiguously, since the absence of a prefatory comma could indicate that this was a requirement only for charges of 'persecution on political, racial or religious grounds') that any prosecution would have to prove a nexus with other crimes over which the Tribunal had jurisdiction, namely war crimes or the crime of aggression. The Tribunal itself adopted this approach, declining to convict any defendant for persecution of German Jews before the outbreak of war, and the Allies in the Tokyo and post-Nuremberg trials confined their crimes against humanity charges to conduct clearly linked with armed conflict. A requirement to prove such linkage can therefore be said to have been an ingredient of the offence at the time it was established by the Nuremberg Charter and judgment. However, it was to disappear as a customary international law requirement over the following decades as treaties (beginning with the Genocide Convention) and the draft criminal codes promulgated by the International Law Commission contained no such limitation. The statutes for the Rwanda Tribunal and the International Criminal Court exclude this artificial linkage requirement, and after the *Tadić* decision it can be confidently stated to have withered away as an element of the offence.[33] Crimes against humanity may therefore be committed in peacetime, and irrespective of any internal conflict (although the requirement for widespread and systematic oppression will normally mean that such crimes will be committed at times of civil unrest). An element that does remain is the linkage of the conduct charged as a crime against humanity with an exercise of the power of the state, or state-like power asserted by a political organization. The Nuremberg Charter provided authority to punish persons 'acting in the interests of the European Axis countries', but decisions of the Hague and Rwanda tribunals establish that the act need not be carried out on behalf of a recognized state. However, there must be some connection with an 'official' body which governs *de facto* or which aspires to govern through organized terror.

TOWARDS UNIVERSAL JURISDICTION

THE GENOCIDE CONVENTION

The first liberation of crimes against humanity from any temporal connection with a declared war came while the Nuremberg judgment still reverberated, in the form of the 1948 Convention on the Prevention and Punishment of Genocide. This word – a hybrid of the Greek *geno* meaning 'race' and the latin *cide* (from *caedare*, i.e. 'killing') was coined by Raphael Lemkin, a Polish law professor, as he pondered the 1923 trial of Soghomon Tehlirian. This young Armenian had seen his family wiped out in the 1915 massacres, and in reprisal had come to Berlin and assassinated Talaat Pasha, the former Ottoman minister primarily responsible for them. The evidence called for the defendant, after which he was acquitted, proved Talaat's intention to destroy his race, but Lemkin demurred at a verdict in favour of a vigilante acting as the 'self-appointed legal officer for the conscience of mankind'.[34] As Hitler rose to power, Lemkin argued that the world needed a new definition for an offence committed by state leaders who chose to exterminate racial or religious minorities comprising their own nationals. Later he adopted Churchill's description of the Holocaust ('We are in the presence of a crime without a name') as his premise for urging the United Nations to adopt a Convention against genocide. Drawing upon historical examples – the Huguenots in France, the Protestants in Bohemia, the Hottentots and then (and always) the Armenians, he added the Jewish, gypsy and Slavic victims of the Nazis.[35] A one-man lobby at the post-war conferences, Lemkin saw his cause eventually taken up by Dr H. V. Evatt, the third President of the General Assembly, who introduced the Convention with its preamble recognizing 'that at all periods of history genocide has inflicted great loss on humanity'. Article I simply states that 'genocide, whether committed in time of peace or time of war, is a crime under international law'. This treaty has been ratified by one hundred and forty-two states and the crime has been often recognized by international courts, so it can now be considered a rule of modern customary international law, binding on all states (whether they have ratified the Convention or not) and *requiring* them to prosecute acts of genocide. As the ICJ explained in its decision in the *Reservations to the Convention on Genocide Case*, 'The origins of the Convention show that it was the intention of the UN to condemn and punish genocide as 'a crime under international law' . . . involving a denial of the right of existence of entire human groups, a denial which shocks the conscience of mankind and results in great losses to humanity, and which is contrary to moral law and to the spirit and aims of the UN.'[36]

The Convention defines genocide as the committing, with the intention to destroy in whole or in part a national, ethnic, racial or religious group 'as such', of any one of the following five acts:

(a) killing members of the group;
(b) causing serious bodily harm or mental harm to members of the group;
(c) deliberately inflicting on the group conditions of life calculated to bring about its physical destruction in whole or in part;
(d) imposing measures intended to prevent births within that group;
(e) forcibly transferring children of the group to another group.

This definition reflects contemporary preoccupation with genocidal Nazi policy towards the Jews as revealed at Nuremberg: it is wide enough to cover ethnic cleansing and religious pogroms, but it does not address Stalin's extermination of a particular economic class (the kulaks) or the millions he liquidated for suspected dissidence or disloyalty. It would cover gypsies and Rastafarians, but not homosexuals or members of a political or social organization unless membership was confined to a particular tribe, race or nationality. On this basis the British government declined to credit the Spanish prosecutor's allegation of genocide against General Pinochet: it could not by definition cover his attempts to exterminate left-wingers. Attempts to liquidate a political group could, however, be prosecuted as a crime against humanity consisting of 'persecution on political grounds': on this basis the French Court de Cassation held that Klaus Barbie could be prosecuted for eliminating members of the French Resistance.[37] Although it is common to refer to the dislocation and massacre of 1.7 million Cambodians by Pol Pot's regime as genocide, and its surviving leaders have been indicted for this crime in the UN's Special Court in Cambodia, there is some doubt over whether the killings, in the case of most of the victims, were actually motivated by racial, religious or ethnic hatred. They were political, inspired by an extreme ideology theory of 'survival of the fittest', namely the survival of loyal cadres of the Khmer Rouge. To avoid such arid legal debates, it is easier to charge a crime against humanity, and the Cambodian Court has decided to proceed first against its main indictees on non-genocide charges. There is difficulty in proving a special 'genocidal intent' in many cases where an intention to mass-murder is all too evident, and therefore sufficient to enable a conviction for a crime against humanity.

There is a nice, if unresolved, point as to whether atheists count as a political or a religious group. It is not academic: in Iran in 1988 thousands of prisoners were killed because they were Marxists, and hence '*mohareb*' – enemies of God. The proposition that 'religious groups encompass both theistic, non-theistic and atheistic communities which are united by a single spiritual ideal' was upheld by Judge Baltasar Garzón. He ruled, in relation to an application alleging genocide in Argentina, that

to destroy a group because of its atheism or its common non-acceptance of the Christian religious ideology is . . . the destruction of a religious group, in as much as, in addition, the group to be destroyed also technically behaves as the object of identification of the motivation or subjective element of the genocidal conduct. It seems, in effect, that the genocidal conduct can be defined both in a positive manner, vis-à-vis the identity of the group to be destroyed (Muslims, for example) as in a negative manner, and indeed, of greater genocidal pretensions (all non-Christians, or all atheists, for example).[38]

The motivation of the exterminators may have been political, namely to extinguish opposition to their theocratic state, but their intention was also genocidal in that they sought to eliminate those 'religious groups' most likely to challenge their theology – the Mujahidin who promoted a different version of Islam, and the atheists of militant Marxist disbelief. The religious underpinning of the offence for which they were convicted is clear, for the crime of 'waging war against God on Earth' is an offence which must be punished by execution according to the Koran (Koran 5: 33–4). Its genocidal aspect arises out of political realities rather than sacred texts, however: the Iranian government considered itself to be 'God on Earth', a theocracy which could not suffer impenitent apostates to remain in its prisons, awaiting release into the community that might be influenced by their disbelief. Religion was uniquely suffused by politics in Iran, but there was a clear genocidal purpose underlying its policy of killing all prisoners who did not accept the God of its theocratic state.[39]

Genocide is limited to *material* destruction of a group, either by physical or biological means, rather than the destruction of the national, linguistic, religious, cultural or other identity of that group.[40] The concept of 'cultural genocide' – by prohibiting the use of a group's language, rewriting or obliterating its history or destroying its icons – did not appeal to members of the UN in 1948, many of whom were engaged in doing just that to troublesome minorities within their own borders. In *Prosecutor* v. *Akeyesu*,[41] the Rwanda Tribunal stressed that genocide required a specific intent to destroy a group as such, and on this basis Australian courts have held that degradation of Aboriginal people through confiscation of traditional lands cannot justify a charge of genocide against the government ministers responsible.[42] What would, however, now be classed as genocide was the policy of 'breeding out' what was once regarded as the degenerate trait of Aboriginality. In the 1930s, Aboriginal girls were placed in institutions which stripped them of cultural memories and prepared them for work as domestics, where they were expected to mate with white men. In due course, several generations of miscegenation would 'breed out' the gene, in the interests of a homogenous white society. This was an application of fashionable eugenics theories which inspired sterilization of the 'feeble-minded' in Nazi Germany and eugenics laws in a number of US states which were notoriously upheld by the Supreme Court on the basis of Oliver Wendell Holmes's vicious comment: 'Three generations of imbeciles are enough.'[43]

The procedural provisions of the Convention are of some significance. Parties must: legislate to punish the crime effectively; make it extraditable irrespective of any political motivation; and have it tried 'by such international penal tribunal as may have jurisdiction' – an indication in 1948 that recurrence of this crime against humanity should in the future call forth an international criminal court. Article

VIII permits any signatory to call upon the UN Security Council to act under the UN Charter to suppress genocide or incitements to commit it. There have been compensation demands by victims of Rwandan genocide against the US and UK, for breach of their Article I undertaking to prevent genocide by dishonestly pretending that it was not happening. But this undertaking does not require states to act unilaterally, rather (so Article VIII suggests) collectively through the Security Council. Although the Genocide Convention places a primary duty to prosecute on the state where the genocide occurs, it expressly contemplates that other courts – including international tribunals – will have jurisdiction. That there is universal jurisdiction to punish this offence has been confirmed by courts in Israel (the *Eichmann Case*) and America (the *Demjanjuk Case*)[44] and by the House of Lords in the *Pinochet Case*. The first conviction for genocide recorded at The Hague was of Bosnian Serb General Krstić, who was sentenced to forty-six years in prison for his part in directing the mass murder of men and boys at Srebrenica. He was himself under the command of General Mladić, who will presumably receive life imprisonment if convicted.

The importance of the Genocide Convention is that it obligates states to take action to stop any outbreak of the crime and envisages an international court to try the criminals. It was overlooked in 1988, when Saddam Hussein began his genocidal Anfal campaign against the Kurds, but it was the reason why at the Security Council in 1994 the US and Britain pretended that genocide was not happening in Rwanda, so that they could avoid their obligations under the Convention. A more honourable approach was taken by the US in 2005, when it took the lead in pointing to evidence of genocide in Darfur, and accepted, reluctantly, that the International Criminal Court was best placed to prosecute. The Genocide Convention is important because it has US backing – it was ratified by President Reagan in 1986 to appease Jewish fury over his visit to Bitburg cemetery. The outrage was provoked by a hitherto unknown young man, fat and bearded, who staged a demonstration at the cemetery, pointing out that it contained SS graves. This was Michael Moore's most significant protest.

THE TORTURE CONVENTION

Torture is the other crime to be recognized post-Nuremberg as involving individual responsibility under international law. For many centuries, torture was regarded as a legitimate, and indeed necessary, method of obtaining information and confession: its use by the Star Chamber and the Spanish Inquisition was ordered and regulated by judicial authorities. Evidence of torture's unreliability as a means of eliciting truth has been as much a reason for its official abandonment as revulsion at its inhumanity, but it is still widely practised by police and military forces around the world. Reaction to Stalin's deployment of 'medieval methods' led to the proscription of torture in Article 5 of the Universal Declaration of Human Rights, which has been followed by the rule against torture or other inhuman and degrading punishment found in every comprehensive human rights treaty and in many national constitutions and bills of rights. It was not until the brutal overthrow of Dr Allende's democratic government in Chile, however, accompanied by widespread torture of his supporters by the Pinochet military junta, that the General Assembly was moved to do anything to make these guarantees effective. The first step was to have them crystallize as a rule of international law.

This process began in 1975, drawing upon the obligation of states under the UN Charter to take 'effective measures' to prevent torture and to provide redress for its victims. This Declaration Against Torture asserted that no exceptional circumstances – war, instability or public emergency – could justify torture, defined as

any act by which severe pain or suffering, whether physical or mental, is intentionally inflicted by or at the instigation of a public official on a person for such purposes as obtaining from him or a third person information or confession, punishing him for an act he has committed or is suspected of having committed, or intimidating him or other persons.

Declarations of this kind assist the emergence of international law rules, but do nothing to enforce them. It took the death after police torture of Steve Biko to provoke the General Assembly into drafting and accepting the 1984 Convention against Torture and Other Cruel, Inhuman and Degrading Treatment or Punishment, which requires state parties (including the US, which is one of the 150 nations which have ratified it) to take jurisdiction to punish torture committed within their territory either by or against their nationals. The definition of torture was taken from the Declaration, which requires the pain to be inflicted by or with the consent of a 'public official', but excludes suffering 'arising only from, inherent in, or incidental to, lawful sanctions'. Significantly, the Convention requires states to arrest and bring proceedings 'where the alleged offender is present in any territory under its jurisdiction' and has not been subject to a request for extradition.

The 1984 Convention establishes a Committee Against Torture, which can receive complaints (including complaints from individuals) and conduct investigations with the co-operation of signatory states. (This has not proved very effective, since offending states are either amongst the fifty-three that refuse to ratify the Convention or else do not co-operate with the committee.) A more worthwhile deterrent within its region is the European Convention for the Prevention of Torture or Inhuman and Degrading Treatment or Punishment, which has established a committee empowered to visit prisons and police cells in signatory countries and to publish reports and recommendations following its visits. This non-judicial exercise has served to monitor and improve prison conditions in a number of European countries, but the committee is unable to sheet home responsibility for torture to particular individuals by commencing prosecutorial action against them.

For all this array of international condemnation, torture remains a malignant reality throughout the world, routinely exposed by human rights organizations but rarely punished by the states – seventy-three at Amnesty's last count – which connive in its use by their functionaries. The UN has appointed a Special Rapporteur on the subject (who counts the states who torture) and the Human Rights Committee has found some complaints proved, but the most concrete form of assistance, the Voluntary Fund for Victims of Torture, set up by the

General Assembly to finance medical and psychological support schemes for victims, is a *de facto* recognition that preventative measures have failed. The most that can be said is that the treaties evidence a state practice that torture is contrary to international law, with the corollary that individuals accused of inciting or directing it must be detained wherever they are found and either brought before a court in that country or extradited to a state prepared to exercise what is now generally regarded as a universal jurisdiction over them.

The most significant recognition of criminal liability in international law for torture was in the *Pinochet Case*, where the House of Lords confirmed that torture was a *jus cogens* offence over which universal jurisdiction exists:

The Torture Convention was agreed not in order to create an international crime which had not previously existed but to provide an international system under which the international criminal – the torturer – would find no safe haven.[45]

The torturer who found safe – indeed luxurious – haven for twenty years in Senegal was Hissène Habré, the mass-murdering dictator of Chad, whose techniques ranged from compressing the heads of victims, to forcing their mouths onto the exhausts of running cars, to leaving them for weeks in small cells in the company of rotting corpses. He bribed officials in Senegal so they would always make excuses for not prosecuting him, so Belgium (where he had been charged under its universal jurisdiction law) brought a case in the ICJ. Senegal argued that it really wanted to prosecute Habré but lacked the money to do so. The ICJ was unimpressed with its equivocation and its prevarication: in July 2012 its *Belgium* v. *Senegal* decision found that the state had violated its obligations under Article 7(i) of the Torture Convention and must 'take without further delay the necessary measures to submit the case to its competent authorities for the purpose of prosecution, if it does not extradite Mr Habré'.

The most remarkable feature of the Torture Convention is that it applies the universal jurisdiction principle – either you extradite or you punish – to any person suspected of committing a single act of official torture. In this respect it is wider than the crime against humanity constituted by the official use of torture, which must be part of a widespread or systematic attack directed against civilians as a measure of state policy. The *Pinochet Case* galvanized compliance with the Torture Convention: in 1999 a seventeen-judge Grand Chamber of the European Court of Human Rights unanimously condemned France for sustained truncheon assaults by its gendarmes on an arrested drugs suspect. This decision established that repeated beatings during interrogation, causing severe pain over a period of time, amount to 'torture' rather than inhuman treatment. In the same year, the Israeli Supreme Court, notoriously reluctant to rein in the nation's security service (the Shin Bet), at last decided that the extraction of information from terrorist suspects did not justify the continual 'violent shaking' which had become a trademark torture technique of Israeli secret agents.

Although the European Court of Human Rights has confirmed the *Pinochet (No. 3)* finding that the international prohibition against torture has a *jus cogens* character which overrides sovereign immunities in criminal cases, in 2002 in *Al-Adsani v. UK* it narrowly declined to apply this principle to require member states to permit civil claims for damages against foreign states accused of permitting torture within their borders.[46] The majority were concerned to protect diplomatic property against distraint (although embassies are made invulnerable by the Vienna Convention) and were worried that refugees would congest the courts with torture claims against the state from which they had fled (claims that could be winnowed by curial insistence on corroboration before they were allowed to proceed). The decision is over-cautious, and does not of course preclude individual states from permitting civil claims over torture abroad, as the US does pursuant to its Alien Tort Statute. It was indeed an action under that statute which produced in 1981 the precedent for the Pinochet ruling, which was issued by the New York Court of Appeals. It was brought by the Filártiga family, whose young son had been kidnapped and tortured to death by a Paraguayan police chief subsequently resident in the United States. The statutory claim for damages hinged upon whether the action, committed abroad, had been 'in violation of the law of nations', and the

court had little hesitation in ruling that 'deliberate torture perpetrated under colour of official authority violates universally accepted
norms of the international law of human rights, regardless of the
nationality of the parties ... among the rights universally proclaimed
by all nations is the right to be free of physical torture. Indeed, for
the purposes of civil liability, the torturer has become – like the
pirate and slave trader before him – *hostis humanis generis*, an
enemy of all mankind.'[47]

While torture is defined by the Convention as the intentional
infliction of severe pain or suffering, whether physical or mental, by
or with the consent of a public official, the Convention on Torture
also outlaws 'inhuman and degrading treatment', and there have been
several unsatisfactory attempts to draw a distinction. As previously
noted, the treatment by the British Army of internees in Belfast in
1970 was held by the European Court of Human Rights to be degrading rather than amounting to torture, while the interrogation
techniques of the fascist military junta in Greece were deemed by the
Court to have caused sufficient pain to be categorized as torture. Likewise in the case of the French drugs suspect, beatings over a period of
time were termed 'torture' rather than 'inhuman treatment'. There is
an ongoing debate over whether the punishment of beating the soles
of the feet with whips or canes (in Iran, with electric cables) can be a
'lawful sanction', especially in Koranic countries where it is justified
as a religious punishment (*tazir*). The answer was given as long ago as
1969, in the landmark *Greek Case* brought against that government
by other European states. The European Commission on Human
Rights found that the use of *falange* (involving beating on the soles of
the feet which is excruciating and causes swelling but leaves no other
physical trace) amounted to torture and ill-treatment.[48] In a series of
cases from Turkey, where this technique is known as *falaka*, the European Court of Human Rights had no hesitation in treating it as
torture.[49]

In 1978 the European Court in *Ireland* v. *UK* ruled that torture, as
distinct from ill-treatment, required a severity threshold so as to
'attach a special stigma to deliberate inhuman treatment causing very
serious and cruel suffering'.[50] The current definition takes account of

whether the acts were 'such as to arouse feelings of fear, anguish and inferiority capable of humiliating and debasing (the victim) and possibly breaking his physical and moral resistance'.[51] This was exactly the purpose of the waterboarding and humiliation techniques at Guantanamo and the *bastinado* used at Evin prison in Tehran. The ICTY Appeal Chamber in *Prosecutor* v. *Brdanin* reiterated that 'the purpose and seriousness of the attack upon the victim sets torture apart from other forms of mistreatment'.[52]

For the purposes of the European Convention, the distinction between 'torture' and 'inhuman treatment' does not matter other than to calculation of damages. Both techniques are prohibited. But post-9/11, 'Bush lawyers' seized upon the distinction, claiming that the war on terror justifies 'inhuman or degrading treatment' which does not amount to 'torture'. They argued that certain intentional forms of suffering, euphemistically called 'augmented techniques of coercive interrogation', may be inflicted upon terrorist suspects. This is wrong, as President Obama accepted, because the Geneva Conventions, which protect prisoners-of-war, specifically prohibit 'outrages upon personal dignity', and the Torture Convention prohibits 'cruel, inhuman and degrading treatment'. But the US military used euphemisms: *forced standing* for hours on end; taking advantage of *individual phobias*; *environmental manipulation* (this may involve *adjusting temperature* – presumably to freezing point to obtain a confession, a tactic used by the ISD in Singapore); *dietary manipulation* (i.e. temporary starvation); *deprivation of light and deprivation of auditory stimuli* (blindfolding, or solitary confinement in a darkened cell); *stress positions* (painful shackling and contortions); *forced nudity* (especially in the presence of dogs); *isolation* (solitary confinement for thirty days); *working dogs* (one way of taking advantage of *individual phobias*, i.e. the Arab fear of dogs).

All these degrading techniques were at one time or another approved by Donald Rumsfeld or his senior commanders to 'soften up' detainees in Guantanamo and Iraq (see chapter 13). All of them breach the Geneva Conventions, whether or not they amount to torture, and their approval sent a supportive signal to Lynndie England and other 'sadists on the night shift' whose behaviour at Abu Ghraib provoked hatred of America throughout the Arab world. 'Bush lawyers' have in this respect proved bush lawyers: Jay Bybee (promoted to a federal judgeship), assisted by John Yoo (now a professor of law at Berkeley), defined torture so tightly ('extreme acts . . . of an intensity akin to that which accompanies serious physical injury such as death or organ failure') that pulling fingernails would not qualify. Alberto Gonzales, who became US Attorney-General in 2005, thought that Islamic terrorism 'renders obsolete Geneva's strict limitations on questioning of enemy prisoners and renders quaint some of its provisions'. But the Geneva Conventions have saved (and made bearable) many American servicemen's lives, in Korea and Vietnam, and the US diminishes the Conventions at its own peril. 'Obsolete' they may be in part (the right of prisoners to smoke cigarettes is certainly outdated, and privileges for the officers mess reflects an antiquated British class system). 'Quaint' they may seem, but only to those ignorant of how they arose from the Holocaust. 'The American people are never going to pay for Taliban prisoners to have a musical instrument!' fumed a White House spokesman, failing to appreciate (a) that this rule came about because of the importance of orchestras in Jewish ghettoes like Terezin and (b) that the Taliban hate music.

PIRACY AND SLAVERY

These were the first crimes against humanity. So far as piracy is concerned, the old definitions[53] have been updated by Article 15 of the Convention on the High Seas, which provides that piracy shall consist of any illegal act of violence, detention or depredation, committed for private ends by the crew or passengers of a private ship or aircraft, and directed (on the high seas or in space) against persons or property aboard another ship or aircraft. This definition represents modern international law, and justifies any state in assuming jurisdiction to try attackers of ships or aircraft who are acting for private gain and not on behalf of governments. One of the least attractive human rights failures has been the refusal of states to deploy these traditional powers so as to protect refugees in Southeast Asian waters: here, the pirates come from fishing communities on the coasts of countries hostile to the boat people, while the states best equipped to provide naval protection (Indonesia, America and Australia) fear that by doing so they will incur responsibility for guaranteeing refugee status. Pirates and slave traders no longer serve the interests of sovereign states, and their international outlawry is uncontroversial: their atrocities are no longer formally regarded as crimes against humanity since they have no linkage with governments. However, there is some overlap with crimes against humanity in the 1979 Convention against the Taking of Hostages, which can apply to hijacking by terrorist groups or hostage-taking by death squads linked to military juntas. It provides an example of what is termed compulsory universal jurisdiction, in that states are required either to prosecute suspects or to extradite them to a country which will prosecute.

That is not, however, what is happening to the Somali pirates who have been marauding in the Gulf of Aden and the Indian Ocean, off the coast of Somalia, down to Mombasa (Kenya) and as far as the Seychelles. This massive criminal enterprise, which has held several thousand people and dozens of vessels hostage and was estimated in 2011 to have cost the international community over $8 billion, began after the 2005 tsunami destroyed fishing villages on the Somali coast, where irresponsible dumping of toxic waste by foreign ships over the years had also damaged the local industry.[54] Piracy was briefly held in check in 2006 when Somalia last had a government – the Union of Islamic Courts, which stopped the bloody feuding between rapacious warlords but was itself toppled by an Ethiopian invasion foolishly backed by the US.[55] In consequence, this failed state has descended into tribal conflicts and a spluttering war between African Union forces and the Jihadist Al-Shabaab, now affiliated to al-Qaida. There is no authority from the centre, and pirate lairs dot the coast of Punt-land, Somalia's northern province. NATO patrols have deterred attacks in the Gulf of Aden, but pirates infest an area of the Indian Ocean that is the size of Western Europe.

The returns on piracy are high, as insurers find ways of paying millions to secure the release of hostages and ships, and the chance of capture is low – NATO warships are usually hundreds of miles away from vessels when they come under attack.[56] Even when apprehended,

90 per cent of the pirates have been released without being prosecuted. The UN's special adviser on piracy says that the trade is 'perceived as a virtually foolproof way of getting rich'.[57] Although international law regards pirates as the 'enemies of all mankind' and bestows jurisdiction on any country's courts, the reluctance to accept the expense of prosecuting and imprisoning Somali criminals has made this a rule that rarely deters. Somalia is a failed state which cannot police its booming pirate towns, and the only way of exterminating the menace is by land attack – an invasion of the kind for which the international community has had no stomach since 'Black Hawk Down' over Mogadishu. However, when pirates took hostages from Kenyan resorts in 2011, effectively destroying the local tourist trade, the Kenyan army did invade in hot pursuit, with some success. The danger of piratical impunity, of course, is that an international crime becomes a routine trading expense, as shadowy business figures in Europe and Asia act as go-betweens with the shipowners and the insurance companies, private security firms flourish by providing on-board guards, while the hostages arouse a sympathy in their homelands which puts pressure on governments to pay up, despite the disadvantages of rewarding criminals. The reality is that although the Somali pirates are apolitical there is evidence that they are paying terrorist groups like Al-Shabaab a percentage of every ransom they get, in order to buy protection.[58] The danger of indulging piracy is that it may well provide a means for funding terrorism.

Thus far, the international community has handled the problem with restraint. NATO's 'Operation Ocean Shield' has intercepted some skiffs and 'motherships' (captured vessels used to launch raiders from offshore), but has either released the suspects, or has deposited those caught red-handed in the jails of Kenya or the Seychelles. But the present UN strategy of trying Somali pirates in local courts has not been a success, and Kenya – which has processed most pirates – in 2011 withdrew from its agreement to undertake further trials because it was not being reimbursed for the cost and the congestion in its court system.[59] The UN's special adviser on piracy has come up with a plan to build a new specialized court in Somalia (with a designated 'piracy prison' capable of holding 500) which could be operational by 2015.[60]

This court would, however, be a Somali rather than an international court, and would have to apply Somali law. A better alternative has come from Tanzania, which offered to host an international court using the facilities in Arusha of the ICTR, which is finishing its work. Both solutions are expensive, and neither offers much hope of ending piracy: whilst NATO ships play cat and mouse with suspect boats, the Indian navy has sunk a pirate ship, killing the pirates but drowning their hostages – a 'solution' that solves nothing. The first steps should be to arrest and prosecute the intermediaries and financiers of piracy, who are based in Asia and Europe, and then to proffer – through the offices of the UN – a deal which would persuade fishing communities (if backed by a credible threat of a land and sea invasion) to surrender their hostages and abjure the piracy business. Without some central government, however, and a workable international court and prison (perhaps in Arusha, or else in India), the world community appears powerless to eradicate this crime.

Action there will have to be: attacks are increasing – there are now several hundred each year – with 3,500 hostages and sixty-two hostage deaths (mostly accidental) between 2007 and 2010, with ransom payments rising to totals estimated at up to $238 million per year. (It now takes $5–$10 million to free a ship, and the return for an investor in a pirate syndicate can be 10,000 per cent). In 2012 a UK Parliamentary Committee derided the British navy for releasing 90 per cent of the pirates it apprehends because of difficulty keeping evidence: 'it beggars belief that they cannot be prosecuted.'[61] Subsequently, the navy commenced some raids on pirate lairs on the mainland, destroying skiffs but releasing no hostages. Many seagoing countries are now allowing armed guards on merchant ships but there is doubt about their right to 'shoot to kill' should they see a skiff approaching at high speed. This is a problem that international criminal law cannot solve, however many pirates are machine-gunned in hot pursuit and however many special courts and prisons await those who are captured. The only long-term solution is for the international community to establish a central government in Somalia, even if this means bringing back the Islamic courts movement and supporting its efforts to transform the pirate towns into more law-abiding coastal communities permitted to apprehend only vessels intercepted in the act of dumping toxic waste.

The only discomfiture which modern governments may feel from the prohibition on slavery derives from treaties which condemn compulsory labour practices akin to it. The first Forced Labour Convention was agreed by the General Conference of the International Labour Organization (ILO) in 1930: it justified the conviction at Nuremberg of Albert Speer and other architects of Nazi deportation and forced labour schemes, which were devised quite literally to work Jews to death. In 1957 it was valuably supplemented by the Abolition of Forced Labour Convention extending the prohibition to the punitive 'political re-education camps' which were becoming such a common feature of post-revolutionary communist states. Prohibition of child labour and work in conditions akin to slavery are two of the ILO's four 'core principles', enunciated in 1998 – labour rights that are also human rights, and more resonant as a result. If the labour in question serves multinational corporations, pressure to improve conditions may come from the threat of damaging publicity over breach of OECD guidelines or the Global Compact. In serious cases, where workers are subjected to physical assault or starvation by militias hired by multinationals, as has happened in Burma and Indonesia, actions may be brought on behalf of victims under the Alien Tort Claims Act in the US (see p. 237). In other cases, the 'good offices' of the Director-General of the ILO may have some effect, at least if labour policies antagonize international trade union bodies, although the victims most in need of assistance do not belong to trade unions. All these conventions are silent on one objectionable form of compulsory forced labour, namely conscription for military service. Indeed, they exempt 'any work or service which forms part of the normal civic obligations of the citizens of a fully self-governing country'. They do not prohibit governments from forcing nationals to fight against their will or compelling citizens to do 'civic duty' in labour camps or on national service.

APARTHEID

As a doctrine which asserts the genetic inferiority of non-white races, apartheid constitutes a breach of the anti-discrimination clause of every human rights convention, and it was the determination of a growing number of states to attack the architects of apartheid which contributed most to the development of enforcement measures such as economic sanctions. By 1973, when the Soviet Union (busily engaged in jailing its own dissidents) sponsored the International Convention on the Suppression and Punishment of the Crime of Apartheid, South Africa had become a pariah state and its policy of separate development could be condemned as a violation of international law. In so far as apartheid involved genocide, torture or slavery, it already amounted to a crime against humanity, albeit one which was not native to South Africa. There was a propagandist flavour to this loosely drafted convention, and its main significance lies in further recognition of the fact that crimes against humanity could be committed in peace as well as in war, and by a single sovereign state within its own territory.

The consequence that individuals should be held responsible for committing apartheid was spelled out in Article 3:

International criminal responsibility shall apply, irrespective of the motive involved, to individuals, members of organizations and institutions and representatives of the State, whether residing in the territory of the State in which the acts are perpetrated or in some other State, whenever they commit, participate in, directly incite or conspire . . . (or) . . . directly abet, encourage or co-operate in the commission of the crime of apartheid.

This broad definition would incriminate most of the white population of South Africa for 'co-operating' with their own government by obeying its laws – as if they were the equivalent of SS officers obeying orders to execute innocent Jews. Although 108 nations have signalled their good intentions by signing this Convention, South Africa has, ironically, declined to join. It must clearly be understood that in order to fix individual responsibility for a crime against humanity in international law, the act committed must be politically motivated commands or conduct which result in a pattern of serious crimes (torture or murder, for example). The millions who obeyed the apartheid laws without personal responsibility for its acts of violence may be condemned for apathy and acquiescence, but it is absurd to require, as does the Convention on Apartheid, that they be tried and punished wherever they are found. Needless to say, none were, and not a single prosecution anywhere in the world for the 'crime' of apartheid was recorded before the policy was progressively dismantled by South Africa under the impetus of economic sanctions. Apartheid reappears in the 1998 Rome Statute of the International Criminal Court, but the lesson has been learned: the crime against humanity constituted by apartheid is confined to systematic murder, enslavement and torture committed with the intention of maintaining the hegemony of the dominant racial group. The best that can be said about the Convention is that it can deter states from excluding racial groups from political power: in the *Prased Case* it helped to reject the Fijian government's claim that 'ethnic paramountcy', the exclusion of Indian Fijians from high political offices, was legitimate. It amounted to 'ethnic apartheid'.

THE NUREMBERG LEGACY

The Nuremberg legacy, distilled from the work and words of Justice Robert Jackson, may be simply stated: crimes against humanity will only be deterred when their would-be perpetrators – be they political leaders, field commanders or soldiers and policemen – are given pause by the prospect that they will henceforth have no hiding-place; that legal nemesis may some day, somewhere, overtake them. That prospect is only realistic if there exists an international criminal court cognizant of their offence, or, in its absence, a rule permitting their punishment by courts of countries into whose jurisdiction they may come or perchance be brought. It is this practical consideration which makes universal jurisdiction the most important attribute of a crime against humanity: it is an offence so serious that any court anywhere is empowered by international law to try it and to punish it, irrespective of its place of commission or the nationality of the offender or the victims. Jurisdiction arises, in other words, wherever an offender is found, and it arises because he is alleged to have offended in a particularly outrageous way.

There is no doubt that universal jurisdiction is recognized in customary international law as the basis for proceedings in domestic courts against pirates and slave traders, torturers and *génocidaires*. Equally, universal jurisdiction over aircraft hijackers, hostage-takers and other types of international terrorists has been partially achieved through the modern machinery of an international treaty requiring signatories to punish offenders found within their borders or else to extradite them to countries which will put them on trial. But these are all crimes which occur across borders, or on the open seas, or in air space of questionable ownership: universal jurisdiction arises not because they are crimes against humanity, but because they are crimes *simpliciter* under any domestic law, which might otherwise go unpunished. As the Permanent Court of International Justice explained in the *Lotus Case*:

It is an offence against the law of nations; and as the scene of the pirate's operations is the high seas, which it is not the right or duty of any nation to police, he is denied the protection of the flag which he may carry and is treated as an outlaw – as the enemy of mankind – *hostis humanis generis* – whom any nation may in the interest of all capture and punish.[62]

In fact, pirates – and modern criminal equivalents such as hostage-takers and international drug traffickers, against whom universal jurisdiction is developing through treaties – are not usually implicated in crimes against humanity. It follows that those courts and writers who have argued that universal jurisdiction for crimes against humanity arises on the same basis as universal jurisdiction over piracy are advancing a fundamentally flawed argument. Piracy occurs in a place, the high seas, which requires universal jurisdiction, as the alternative to there being no jurisdiction at all. The crime against humanity normally occurs in a country where there is jurisdiction, albeit one which (because of the power of the state-backed perpetrator) will not be exercised, and the issue arises years, perhaps decades, later, when the perpetrator is found (or brought) within the jurisdiction of a nation with the exceptional resolve to bring a prosecution.

One case which stands as an authority for the right of universal punishment of crimes against humanity is in some respects an unhappy precedent. Adolf Eichmann was without doubt guilty of directing much of the Holocaust: he would inevitably have been convicted at Nuremberg had he not escaped to Argentina, a country which would not have put him on trial. He was kidnapped by Israeli agents and subsequently brought to trial in Jerusalem under a local law condemning to death anyone who had participated in Nazi atrocities. Eichmann's challenge to the law was rejected on the principle that jurisdiction to try crimes against humanity was universal. Both the Israeli District Court and Appeal Court relied on precedents from piracy and slavery, which do not go far enough to establish the principle in relation to state persecution of its own people within its own territory.[63] A much better – because it was more honest – explanation was given by the French Court of Appeal in brushing aside a challenge to Klaus Barbie's arrest by French officials in Guyana: the crimes against humanity of this SS officer, who sent thousands of Jews to their deaths from Lyon, 'do not simply fall within the scope of French municipal law but are subject to an international criminal order to which the notions of frontiers and extradition rules arising therefrom are completely foreign'.[64]

This is the best, because it is the simplest, statement of the Nuremberg legacy. Article 6(c) of the Charter defined a class of crime which is so peculiarly horrific that the very fact that educated, rational and otherwise respected rulers of men were capable of conceiving and committing it must diminish whatever value there is in being human. The judgment at Nuremberg and the Conventions which followed gave this particular crime a special status in international law, as imposing an *erga omnes* obligation on every state to assist in its trial and punishment. This power to bring alleged perpetrators to justice is described by the phrase 'universal jurisdiction': states have the power, individually or collectively, to conduct a trial even if they have no link with the place where the crime was committed, or with its perpetrator or its victims. Jurisdiction over ordinary crime depends on a link, usually territorial, between the state of trial and the crime itself, but in the case of crimes against humanity that link may be found in the simple fact that we are all human beings. So an international tribunal, a court without a country, may be empowered to punish, as may (if no such tribunal exists) the courts of any other country which gets its hands on an accused. Of course, universal jurisdiction in any state will normally proceed under a local statute empowering a court to exercise it, and any international tribunal will require a charter or statute subscribed to by the states which bring it into existence, either collectively through the UN (as a subsidiary organ of the Security Council) or individually through a treaty like the Nuremberg Charter or the Rome Statute of the International Criminal Court. The concept of universal jurisdiction for crimes against humanity is the solution that international law offers to the spectacle of impunity for tyrants and torturers who cover themselves with domestic immunities and amnesties and pardons. They can still hide, but in a world where jurisdiction over their crimes is universal, they cannot run.

In 2012 it can be asserted with some confidence that an international law principle has evolved which permits states to punish foreign nationals arrested on their territory, as well as their own citizens, for certain crimes against humanity, notably genocide and torture, wherever committed. Some have incorporated aspects of this principle into domestic legislation, giving jurisdiction to their courts to try Nazi war criminals, and many have incorporated provisions to implement the 'prosecute or extradite to a state which will prosecute' principle of the Genocide and Torture Conventions. These offenders against the law of nations may now, like pirates, be punished if they are captured and may be the subject of extradition requests and international arrest warrants by states prepared to put them on trial. The only state at present which has been prepared to clothe its courts with full-blooded universal jurisdiction (i.e. to try anyone for any crime against humanity) is Belgium, by way perhaps of a belated atonement for King Leopold's atrocities in the Congo. Such universal jurisdiction must of course be exercised in conformity with international law, by respecting diplomatic immunity under the Vienna Convention and immunities that customary law grants to incumbent heads of state and foreign ministers so that they may travel abroad on inter-state business. Over-zealous Belgian prosecutors who issued, via INTERPOL, an international warrant for the arrest of the Congo's foreign minister were forced by the ICJ to withdraw it, on the grounds that it breached customary international law protection for foreign ministers so long as they were in office: it could be reissued as soon as the person relinquished the office, in respect to crimes against humanity committed while he occupied the position. Immunity does not confer impunity – it operates only to bar prosecution for a certain period or for certain offences.[65] The significant feature of the 2002 ruling was that the Court did not dispute Belgium's right to put the Congolese national on trial for heinous crimes committed in the Congo, and three of its most respected judges (Higgins, Kooijmans and Buergenthal) in a joint concurring opinion authoritatively endorsed the universal jurisdiction principle as a means of combating impunity. A state which contemplates its exercise must, however,

i)   first offer the state of which the suspect is a national the opportunity to try him

ii)   ensure that the prosecution is brought by a law enforcement office which is independent of the government

iii)   act only where there are special circumstances justifying the exercise of international jurisdiction (e.g. the availability of witnesses in the state, or requests from the victims that it should act)

iv)   limit the charges to the most heinous international crimes – i.e. war crimes and crimes against humanity

v)   respect temporal immunities bestowed by treaty or customary law.

Court rulings upholding the principle of universal jurisdiction before the *Pinochet Case* were confined to cases involving old Nazis extradited to jurisdictions anxious to try them. This in itself poses a problem which cannot be brushed under the carpet: the danger of a show trial. There has never been any doubt about the indelible guilt of Eichmann and Barbie, or of the fairness of most of the recent trials of old Nazis, like Sawonick in Britain, Priebke in Italy and Maurice Papon in France. But the case of John Demjanjuk, extradited from the

US and sentenced to death in Israel on the false finding that he was Treblinka concentration camp guard Ivan the Terrible, demonstrates the potential for injustice in a country bent on revenge. The Demjanjuk proceedings were a disgrace. The televised trial was held in a theatre, as an avowed exercise in 'Holocaust education'; the audience was permitted to display its emotions as elderly survivors came on stage to misidentify the defendant as their tormentor half a century before. The judges permitted the most hysterical and prejudicial media publicity, ignored the clearest evidence that the crucial documents were forgeries, and even ended the reasons for their decision by emotionally dedicating their judgment 'to the souls that have been lost'.[66] Demjanjuk stayed on death row for some years until an appeal court grudgingly accepted that fresh evidence, forthcoming from Poland, proved that he had been wrongly identified. The trial stands not only as another warning of the unreliability of eyewitness evidence and of the risk of justice miscarrying when it is too long delayed, but more importantly of the danger that some states will exploit universal jurisdiction for political ends. Israel wanted so badly to convict Demjanjuk that three experienced judges ignored exculpatory evidence and presided over an unfair show trial. (He was subsequently convicted in Germany for a different war crime in another camp.)

The episode is not an argument against universal jurisdiction, but rather in favour of it being exercised in many cases by an international criminal court, free from municipal pressures, whether political or psychological. These pressures were increasingly evident in the trial of Saddam Hussein, which began in 2005 before Iraqi judges in a special tribunal established and funded by the US, in a country rent by civil war. Even before any evidence on the first charge was called, one judge and two defence counsel had been assassinated and the defendant assaulted by court clerks. The moral claim of the Iraqi people to exact retribution sounds fine in theory – as President Bush argued, 'They were the people who were brutalized by this man.' But if justice can neither be done nor be seen to be done in Baghdad, in the midst of what had become a civil war, then Iraq's claim should have given way to the moral and legal right of the international community to try international crimes. The genocide charges which were included in

Saddam's indictment accused him of gassing the Kurds and mass murdering the Marsh Arabs: these are crimes against humanity and the world was entitled to an authoritative judgment on his responsibility. This judgment was never rendered: he was executed after conviction for a non-international crime. The Genocide Convention requires trial and punishment for this most heinous of all crimes, if not by a 'competent national court' then by an international penal tribunal which could have been established by the parties or by the Security Council at US request, sitting somewhere in safety and with both international and Iraqi judges (see chapter 13).

The issue arose again in 2011, after the capture of Saif Gaddafi following the brutal murder of his father – beaten, sodomised with an iron bar and shot by a detachment of rebel troops after his convoy had been hit by a NATO air strike. Given the thirst for revenge after the savage war against a loathed family regime, the prospects of Saif receiving a fair trial before an independent court were remote, and trial under local law would probably lead to a death sentence. The EU, together with most human rights NGOs, called for his transfer to The Hague, where his trial would be fair and could be relayed by television to Libya. Libya, as a member of the UN, was bound by Resolution 1970 to 'co-operate fully' with the court. But its acting junta wanted Saif to suffer in Tripoli, not The Hague. The Security Council had referred the situation in Libya to the ICC, which under its own statute (Article 17) had to consider whether Libya could give fair trial in an independent court system before relinquishing its jurisdiction.

One factor that should be taken into account in such decisions is whether the death penalty is likely to be imposed: the ICC statute is silent on this all-important issue, but international law shuns the death penalty and no international court should be complicit in surrendering, or relinquishing jurisdiction over, an indictee if he is to face execution under his national law. This may, ironically, result in an international justice system that saves the lives of the tyrants and mass-murderers that it keeps secure in its comfortable prison near the beach at Scheveningen, well away from the abused victims who want to string them up from local lamp-posts. But this is its contribution to the hope of future peace amongst factions and tribes which would otherwise remain divided by the memory of what Milton called 'unjust tribunals, under change of times' which leave the carcasses of defendants 'to dogs and fowls a prey'. It was for this reason fortunate for the Ivory Coast, as well as for Laurent Gbagbo, that he was air-lifted to The Hague to face charges of command responsibility for killing civilians: if he is followed by commanders from the other side, credibly accused of the same crime, justice will be seen to be done, or at least to be done better than by executions after a biased trial.

For all its mythic quality, Nuremberg had defects that should not be replicated (the death sentence, for example, and poor-quality defenders). It had achievements that cannot be replicated in places like Baghdad and Freetown. It succeeded for three very practical reasons:

(1) As Jackson admitted, Nuremberg worked 'because of the Teutonic habit of writing everything down'. Göring's signature was on the 'night and fog' decrees. There are no such contemporaneous documents in places like Sierra Leone: inferences have to be drawn from mass graves and from informers who may be self-serving and who must be protected against reprisals.

(2) The population of Nuremberg was on the side of the Allies. The three defendants who were acquitted could not be released for several weeks for fear that the people of Nuremberg, starving and angry and betrayed by the Nazis, would lynch them. A war crimes trial in a country still at war, where defendants have substantial and armed support amongst sections of the population, is a very different matter.

(3) The defendants played the justice game, not the King Charles gambit (see pp. 5–8). They recognized the court, respected the judges and politely faced cross-examination. In consequence, the judgment was perceived as fair and authoritative, after both sides had been fully heard.

When the security situation in the former war zone remains unsettled, the trial may have to be at The Hague rather than at the scene of the crimes. For that reason, the Special Court for Sierra

Leone in 2006 requested the Security Council to transfer Charles Taylor's trial to the Netherlands, although many thought that for symbolic reasons it should be held in a safe African country. Even when security is not a problem, witnesses will need protecting and lesser co-conspirators may have to be given immunity in return for their testimony; lawyers may have to be imposed on uncooperative defendants and trials may have to proceed in their self-induced absence. These problems may mean that the Nuremberg legacy will be delivered differently, but not that it will be diminished.

The reason why crimes against humanity, unlike ordinary crimes, in the absence of treaties attract universal jurisdiction is not found in the seriousness of the actual offence – the psychopathic serial killer may do more harm than the casual police torturer. Nor is it found by any literal analogy with the pirate or slave trader – unattractive criminals certainly, but ones who are rarely acting on government service. What sets a crime against humanity apart, both in wickedness and in the need for special measures of deterrence, is the simple fact that it is a crime of unforgivable brutality ordained by a government – or at least by an organization exercising political power. It is not the mind of the individual torturer, but the fact that this individual is part of the apparatus of a state, which makes the crime so horrific and locates it in a different dimension from ordinary criminality. This factor also explains why individual responsibility and universal jurisdiction are necessary responses if any deterrence is to be achieved. There is a reasonable chance that torture and murder will not be committed by secret police, or ordered by generals or ministers, if they believe they may one day, under a different regime, or in another country, be called to account for their participation in criminal acts of state. Crimes against humanity are committed confidently, by officials who believe that their regime will continue in power – that, after all, is often the purpose of committing the crime. In the unlikely event of its collapse, a negotiated withdrawal is possible: at best, you keep the Swiss bank account; at worst you appear before a truth commission. The doctrine of universal jurisdiction over crimes against humanity is justified because it may make some torturer pause at the prospect that sometime, somewhere, some prosecutor may feel strongly enough about his crime to put him on trial.

7

Slouching Towards Nemesis

'The idea of insecurity became increasingly entrenched in society: the dark fear that anybody, no matter how innocent, could fall victim to that infinite witch hunt. Some were absorbed by overwhelming fear, while others were controlled by the conscious or unconscious proclivity to justify horror: "There is something she must have done" was the whisper, looking at the children or parents of the disappeared as if they were pest ridden. These sentiments were vacillating, because it was known that so many had been swallowed up by that abyss without bottom without being guilty of anything: because the struggle against the "subversive", with the drift that characterizes the hunting of witches and the possessed, had turned into a demented generalized repression. Because the epithet "subversive" had such a vast and unpredictable reach.'

Ernesto Sábato
Prologue to *Nunca Más*[1]

In the half century which followed the Nuremberg judgment, leaders were rarely made responsible, precisely because their political power gave them the ability to negotiate their exit from the bloodstained stage, secret Swiss bank accounts intact, to discreet retirement in places like Panama and the south of France. The legion of crimes against humanity committed since the masters of war stood in the

Nuremberg dock were brought home to very few of those responsible for committing them. '*Impunity*' – leaving retribution for such crimes to history or to God – began immediately, with the American decision not merely to exempt Emperor Hirohito from trial but to keep him on the throne of Japan, relieving him from the prosecution he deserved for approving a war of aggression and smoothing away any sense of national shame or guilt over the atrocities committed by Japanese forces: the generals executed by military tribunals were regarded as patriotic heroes and in due course their ashes were placed in the holiest of Shinto shrines at Yasukuni (the imperial equivalent of the Kremlin wall). Blame for the war was erased from the national consciousness, as school textbooks (including 2012 editions) omit all mention of Japanese atrocities and explain their nation's aggression as a justifiable response to economic encirclement. Reparations to enslaved and tortured prisoners-of-war were fixed at a risible amount in 1951, and the country has steadfastly refused to increase them.

Barbaric leaders of more recent times, even when overthrown, have lived happily ever after, protected by amoral governments like that of Panama, a retirement home for the mass-murdering military of Latin America. African states are all too happy to forgive and forget: Hissène Habré, who killed 40,000 and tortured 200,000 during his rule in Chad, fled with $12 million looted from his country's treasury to Senegal in 1990 and has lived there in luxury for two decades despite repeated attempts to have him tried for these crimes under Belgium's universal jurisdiction law or else prosecuted in Senegal. All the perfumes of Arabia may not wash away the crimes of Idi Amin, but those of Saudi Arabia sweetened his retirement in Jeddah, where he lived happily for twenty-five years after his tyranny in Uganda had ended. He killed 73,000 people – fewer than the mass-murdering Marxist of Ethiopia, Colonel Mengistu, who now lives under the personal protection of Robert Mugabe in Zimbabwe. The late Pol Pot went into hospital in Thailand periodically for haemorrhoid treatment, protected by the UN's need to keep the Khmer Rouge from upsetting its peace plans in Cambodia, while its former Secretary-General, Boutros Boutros-Ghali, warmly embraced the bloodiest Khmer leaders when they emerged from hiding in 1998. In

1994, the Haitian generals provided a copybook example of how to ransom their crimes against humanity: they were prepared to stop committing them in the future in return for being allowed to keep the profits from those they had committed in the past.

This was all the doing of international diplomacy, which until the Bosnian crisis simply pretended that Nuremberg had never happened. The diplomats who represented national leaders were instructed not to countenance the prosecution of other national leaders: tyranny was a matter for negotiated climbdowns, never for justice. This approach has been reflected at a national level by the choice of amnesties and 'truth commissions' over trials for the crimes committed by former regimes. Thus, the middle-ranking military officers of the Argentinian junta who waged the 'dirty war' against dissidents by torturing and then causing them to disappear – often by having them pushed out of aeroplanes over the Atlantic – received a blanket amnesty in 1987. Leaders of the death squads in El Salvador received an amnesty in 1994, which embraced those responsible for killing over a hundred children in the El Mozote massacre. Go to South Africa today, and for the price of a few drinks you can listen to loquacious ex-majors tell how they tortured and killed the opponents of apartheid: the Truth and Reconciliation Commission forced them to talk, but did not reconcile them with many relatives of their victims. Those who order atrocities believe at the time that their power will always enable them to bargain with any new government to let bygones be bygones, and history has tended to prove them correct – for example in Sierra Leone, when by the Lomé agreement in July 1999 the UN not only amnestied Foday Sankoh, but rewarded his pathological greed and brutality by making him deputy leader of the government and giving him control of the diamond mines. Until the turn of the century, the main resolve to punish crimes against humanity had been to prosecute in national courts a handful of very old Nazis suspected of war crimes. Some of these trials (hinging on identification evidence, hopelessly unreliable after fifty years) have collapsed: with war crimes, as with other crimes, justice long delayed can be justice denied.

It has been the great achievement of international law, twelve years into the twenty-first century, to lift the veil of sovereign statehood far enough to make individuals responsible for the crimes against humanity committed by the states they formerly commanded, while at the same time developing a rule that those states have a continuing duty to prosecute and punish them, failing which another state or the international community may bring them to justice. This chapter places that achievement in historical perspective by examining the duty to prosecute and the rival temptations of amnesties and truth commissions.

OUT OF THIS BLACKNESS

Notable improvements in human rights came from the toppling of tyrannous regimes: the military juntas in South America in the early 1980s, followed at the end of that decade by the party machines of eastern Europe and eventually of the Soviet Union, and then the disintegration of apartheid and the onset of democracy in South Africa. These governments were all characterized by systemic violations of the rights of their citizens through the brutal secret policing which kept them in power: at worst, by torture and murder committed by death squads, and at best by harassment and detention of dissidents through the apparatus of state spies and informers. The political changes had in common both a suddenness and a comparative lack of violence: old and discredited regimes gave up the struggle against civilian rule, or took little by way of pushing. Although the Ceauşescus had to be executed in Romania to prevent counter-attack by their secret police (the Securitate), other communist dictators slunk from the stage after token resistance, while the generals and juntas in South America negotiated well-pensioned retirement. Dr Hastings Banda even presided over his own electoral demise in Malawi, in the misapprehension that the fear he had instilled in his people over thirty years would follow them into the polling booths. In all these countries, transition to democratic rule begged one crucial question: whether the new government had a duty to investigate and to punish the unforgivable crimes of its predecessors.

That the answer differed from country to country should not

obscure the importance of the question. Usually, an investigation was initially ordered, before the pressure for pardons, amnesties and 'national reconciliation' set in. Ironically, this pressure proved most successful in respect of the perpetrators of atrocious human rights abuses, generally because these had been sanctioned by senior police-men or military officers who still commanded some power – or at least, loyalty – within their old organizations. In some countries, impunity was the price exacted by the military for giving up its pre-tensions to govern; in others, it was a realistic way of avoiding a counter-coup. The organizers of these atrocities were therefore safe for the transitional period, but there are increasing doubts about whether their amnesties are valid. A few nations have exhumed old Nazis for trial fifty years after they thought that nemesis had been indefinitely postponed, while in 1998 no less than 120 nations sup-ported the Rome Statute for an international criminal court. That statute, to appease present leaders, denied the logic of universal juris-diction by excluding all crimes committed before it came into force on 1 July 2002, so the torturers of South America are safe from its clutches. They might, however, be brought to trial in civil or criminal suits at some point, should courts in their country of residence accept the view that there can be no amnesty for crimes against humanity.

There has recently been a sea change in attitudes towards impu-nity, a growing recognition that human rights cannot be secure unless political and military leaders tempted to breach them can be deterred by the real prospect of trial and punishment. A more critical attitude towards amnesties came in the 1970s as a result of terrorism and torture: governments had to respond to pardon demands from hijack-ers, whilst human rights courts in Latin America had to work their way around 'acts of oblivion' before they could require the state to investigate death-squad killings or compensate victims of state tor-ture. For all the favourable connotations of amnesty in the context of clemency by a state towards enemies whose cause may well have been politically or morally justified, immunity for perpetrators of serious crime is a betrayal both of the rule of law and of innocent victims of the crime. It is usually the product either of convenience (e.g. where a state does not have the resources to prosecute and imprison) or of duress, where a government has to offer amnesty as the price of ending a rebellion or of saving the lives of hostages. When international terrorism recrudesced in the 1970s, some governments refused to do deals with terrorists. Those which did felt obliged to keep the bargain, if only because the practical consequence of reneging would be that they could never deal with terrorists again. The common-law approach has been to read amnesty grants restrictively, while international law refuses to recognize them at all in respect of crimes against humanity.

Of all such crimes, the most evil and most poignant of modern examples is causing a 'disappearance' – a process by which a citizen suspected of harbouring subversive sentiments is kidnapped, detained and tortured for some time before being finally killed, all within a secret police or military operation which is utterly unlawful but none the less agreed in outline by the government. As a method of disposing of suspected dissidents without the inconvenience of proving guilt at delayed trials, and as a means of terrorizing others, the device is useful to a lawless government, which can pretend it has no responsibility because it knows nothing about any specific crime. For the victims, and for their society, disappearance at the hands of police or military forces amounts to the most complete abnegation of human rights imaginable: arbitrary arrest, detention without trial, inhumane and degrading treatment and torture, followed by murder and secret disposal of the body. For friends and relations, the continuing horror of not knowing any details of the victim's fate adds a special layer of cruelty, driving them either to despair or to the courage displayed by the Mothers of the Plaza de Mayo, whose weekly demonstrations on behalf of their lost children did more than anything else to expose the wickedness of the Argentinian junta.

The rise of the death squad is a late-twentieth-century phenomenon, and ironically an offshoot of international concern about human rights violations. In the past, tyrannies publicly detained and executed opponents, as a lesson to other would-be dissidents. In the 1970s, many did it clandestinely and deniably, in an attempt to avoid international condemnation. As a means of destroying dissent without answerability, the disappearance seems to have begun on a widespread scale in Guatemala in the 1960s (when the word *desaparecidos* was first used for victims);[2] it was adopted by Pinochet in Chile in 1973 and then at his urging in Operation Condor by other military governments in South America – Uruguay, El Salvador and, most barbarously, by Argentina. The technique has also featured in Uganda and South Africa, Sri Lanka and the Philippines. Typically, disappearances are planned by a central agency within the military (such as the notorious DINA – Directorate of Intelligence – in Chile) and distance from government is often sought by using retired or off-duty soldiers or policemen, albeit under overall military command.

The science of physical terror was taught by Pinochet's torturers to the military junta which ruled Argentina between 1976 and 1983. The grill (*parrilla*) was inflicted upon more than 10,000 'suspects', the great majority of whom the military took care to 'disappear' (by dropping them from planes or burying them in mass graves) so they would not live to tell the tale, unlike many of Pinochet's victims who had been released in order that they should spread fear. *Nunca Más* records the testimony of one Argentinian survivor:

I was taken straight to the *parrilla*. That is, I was tied to the metal frame of a bed, electrodes were attached to my hands and feet, and they ran an electric prod all over me, with particular savagery and intensity on the genitals . . . When on the 'grill' one jumps, twists, moves about, and tries to avoid contact with the burning, cutting iron bars. The electric prod was handled like a scalpel and the 'specialist' would be guided by a doctor who would tell him if I could take any more . . . The worst was having electrodes on your teeth – it felt as if a thunderbolt was blowing your head to pieces.[3]

The complicity of the medical profession – hooded doctors were normally present, to advise on the voltage that would maximize suffering without causing unconsciousness or premature death – gives the grill a peculiar clinical horror. To this was frequently added the excruciatingly inhuman dimension of the presence of a partner or family member, to suffer vicariously the agonies of a loved one prior to their own. Jacobo Timerman, another rare Argentinian survivor, notes that 'of all the dramatic situations I witnessed in prison, none can compare with those family groups who were tortured, often together, sometimes separately but in view of one another . . . the entire world of affection, constructed over the years with the utmost difficulty, collapses with a kick in the father's genitals . . . or the sexual violation of a daughter'.[4]

Some retribution came in 1985, when five of the junta leaders were sent to prison after a five-month trial which featured the testimony of the torture survivors and the striking debut of a new breed of prosecution expert – part forensic scientist, part archaeologist – whose skill was to put names to skulls, matching dental, medical and DNA records of the 'disappeared' with skeletal remains excavated from mass graves. Liliana Pereyra was a 21-year-old pregnant law student at the time she was abducted by the military in 1977 and taken to a special section of the Navy Mechanics School in Buenos Aires, where she was permitted to give birth (so the child would be adopted by a loyal naval family) before she was murdered. It was her picture, and photographs of remains from a mass grave, which produced the most dramatic moment at the trial. There were X-ray pictures of her skull, with a single gunshot hole to the head; of a ribcage, identified as hers with the help of a chest X-ray from her childhood; then the close-up of the telltale shallow trench in front of the sacroiliac joint which meant she had just given birth.[5] The defence of Generals Videla and Galtieri – that the battle against terrorism necessitated 'unconventional methods' – could never begin to excuse the inhuman treatment of Liliana Pereyra.

Can crimes of this blackness be forgiven, or at least allowed to go unprosecuted? In El Salvador, death squads sometimes massacred dozens of people at a time, including children, while in Argentina the treatment of women like Liliana Pereyra became a speciality: pregnant women were deliberately kidnapped and, when they had given birth, their children were fostered to military families loyal to the junta. If the phrase 'human rights' has any meaning, the perpetrators of such crimes must be punished, even more surely than the old Nazis who are occasionally dragged to trial a half century or so after their offences. (Ivan Demjanjuk, convicted in 2011 of helping Treblinka's 'Ivan the of Terrible' to kill 27,000 Jews, is likely to be the last.) Indeed, it is precisely because the death squad organizers are part of a modern militia, fully aware of the requirements of law and morality in a way that many brainwashed Nazi stormtroopers were not, that their crimes are more serious. Prosecution is the only real means of retribution, and certainly the only process which offers any hope of deterring such crimes in the future.

THE DUTY TO PROSECUTE

If crimes like this engage the world's conscience sufficiently to attract universal jurisdiction, it must follow that the state where they have been committed has the primary duty to investigate and prosecute them unless prejudicial conditions (e.g. after a civil war) make a fair trial impossible. A local court will usually be the most convenient and most fitting forum, in terms of witness availability, local knowledge and language, and the desirability of confronting and understanding the past. Although it cannot be said that the Nuremberg judgment established an *obligation* to punish crimes against humanity, it served to delineate those offences which, by virtue of their level of atrocity, attract universal jurisdiction. The work of the lesser Nuremberg tribunals was useful in making this distinction: expropriation of Jewish property and other acts of callous but not life-threatening discrimination did not produce sufficiently harsh consequences to amount to crimes against humanity.[6] This latter class of offence attracted international jurisdiction, so some military tribunals reasoned, precisely because 'the State involved, owing to indifference, impotency or complicity, has been unable or has refused to halt the crimes and punish the criminals'.[7] The corollary is that such involved states do have a duty to act, at least when conditions become propitious. Thus, when West Germany recovered its confidence and independence, it accepted responsibility for prosecuting Nazi war criminals: its courts convicted 6,000 of them between 1959 and 1981.

The duty to bring perpetrators to justice may also be deduced from international human rights treaties. By Article 2(3) of the Civil Covenant, state parties undertake to ensure that victims of rights violations 'shall have an effective remedy, notwithstanding that the violation has been committed by persons acting in an official capacity'. This imposes on states the obligation to permit civil actions for damages, although in cases of violations as grave as crimes against humanity, no remedy short of prosecution and imprisonment could be considered 'effective'. The HRC has repeatedly held that Article 2(3) does not provide a right in individuals to force a state to prosecute, but does impose a duty on the state to investigate, and thereafter to prosecute any suspects who have been convincingly identified. Thus, in 1995, it ordered Colombia to compensate the family of Nydia Bautista, a suspected M19 sympathizer abducted and killed by Brigadier-General Velandia Hurtando.[8] Since the government had promoted and honoured this officer after the evidence of his guilt had emerged, it also directed the government to pay for protection of Nydia's family against military reprisals.

The Torture Convention is explicit in requiring each state party to 'establish its jurisdiction' over offences committed in its territory either by or against its nationals (Article 5) and to 'submit the case to its competent authorities for the purpose of prosecution' (Article 7). Each state must ensure that its appropriate authorities promptly and impartially investigate torture allegations (Article 12) and 'ensure in its legal system that the victim of an act of torture obtains redress and has an enforceable right to fair and adequate compensation' (Article 14). Governments which refuse to prosecute persons reasonably suspected of causing 'disappearances', or which grant them amnesties, are plainly in breach of these 'no safe haven' provisions. Similarly, the Genocide Convention imposes an obligation to punish, irrespective of whether perpetrators are 'constitutionally responsible rulers, public officials or private individuals' (Article 4), after trial either by 'a competent tribunal' of the state where the act occurred or by an international penal tribunal (Article 6). The 1949 Geneva Convention provides that states have an obligation to search for war criminals, and to bring them (irrespective of their nationality) before their own courts or else extradite them for trial in another jurisdiction. Although the main human rights treaties – the Civil Covenant and the European and Inter-American Conventions – have no comparable provisions, they all affirmatively require that rights (notably the right to life) be respected and protected by law and that victims shall have an effective remedy: objectives which presuppose deployment of the legal process against perpetrators.

The UN's most recent Convention, for the Protection of All Persons from Enforced Disappearance, which entered into force in 2010, requires state parties to investigate and prosecute those responsible for enforced disappearances and to compensate the families of the disappeared. It defines such disappearances as deprivation of liberty by persons 'acting with the authorization, support or acquiescence of the state' followed by a concealment of the whereabouts of the detainee, who is thereby placed outside the protection of the law. Article 6 of the Convention defines such enforced disappearances as crimes against humanity, and provides that 'no exceptional circumstances whatsoever' – war, act of God or national emergency – can justify an enforced disappearance. This explains why the US refuses to sign the Convention – its CIA renditions clearly fall within the definition.[9]

The duty is supported by implication from other international instruments. In 1967, the UN adopted a resolution urging states not to grant asylum to anyone seriously suspected of committing crimes against humanity, because such suspects should be returned to face trial in their own countries.[10] The following year it opened for signature the Convention on the Non-Applicability of Statutory Limitations to War Crimes and Crimes against Humanity, a self-explanatory Convention which assumes both that there is a duty to punish such offences and that this duty cannot be attenuated by the passage of time. (It is a measure of the political reluctance to accept the principle that only forty-five states have ratified this Convention.) In 1973, the General Assembly adopted a set of Principles of International Co-operation in the Detection, Arrest, Extradition, and Punishment of Persons Guilty of War Crimes and Crimes against Humanity, Principle 1 of which is that 'crimes against humanity, wherever they are committed, shall be subject to investigation and the persons against whom there is evidence that they have committed such crimes shall be subject to tracing, arrest, trial and, if found guilty, to punishment'.

There are other declarations and statements of principle, and a section of the 1993 Vienna Declaration, to the same effect.[11] All this goes to show that there is in international law a duty on states to punish crimes against humanity, even if there is in international practice a failure to do any such thing.

In classical international law, a state has always had a duty to investigate and punish serious crimes committed against innocent foreigners ('aliens') resident within its borders. The clearest precedents were set by the US-Mexican General Claims Commission, a tribunal established in 1926 to decide, according to rules of international law, on claims by US citizens for damages arising from the Mexican Revolution. In the *Janes Case*, the court awarded damages to relations of an American killed by a Mexican who had been allowed to escape by the local authorities: Mexico was 'liable for not having measured up to its duty of diligently prosecuting and properly punishing the offender'.[12] Damages were not merely compensatory: in this context, they were increased because of both the insult to the family and the fear and instability caused by the Mexican government's behaviour. This principle was applied to the same government's decision to grant an amnesty to rebels who killed an American oil company employee: the legal formality of the grant was not allowed to disguise the fact that it amounted to a state refusal to bring the killers to justice, as much as if prison officials had deliberately permitted them to escape.[13] This precedent (the *West Case*) is important for the proposition that the granting of a lawful amnesty in order to save lives or bring a civil war to an end does not affect a state's international obligations, or the right of any state which has not granted an amnesty to prosecute and punish the beneficiaries of amnesties granted elsewhere.

That this international law duty imposed on states in their treatment of foreign residents is now being extended to their treatment of their own citizens is clear from the important 1988 decision of the Inter-American Court in the *Velasquez Rodriguez Case*. Velasquez was a student activist who disappeared after being abducted by the Honduran military, which subsequently carried out an investigation and declared itself innocent of his kidnap and murder. The Court had no difficulty in deciding, from the evidence of a pattern of disappearances of radicals in Honduras at the hands of the military, that the snatching of Velasquez was part of the pattern. It condemned the Honduran government for its failure to 'ensure' the civil rights of its citizens, holding that this language in the Inter-American Convention (IAC) implied an affirmative obligation:

The state has a legal duty to take reasonable steps to prevent human rights violations and to use the means at its disposal to carry out a serious investigation of violations committed within its jurisdiction, to identify those responsible, impose the appropriate punishment and ensure the victims adequate compensation.[14]

This decision is a logical consequence of the language of the IAC and other conventions. What else can be meant by a state undertaking to 'respect the rights and freedoms recognized herein and to ensure to all persons subject to their jurisdiction the free and full exercise of those rights and freedoms' (IAC, Article 1)? Similar language is found in Article 2 of the Civil Covenant, and the HRC has repeatedly asserted a duty upon states to investigate, to prosecute suspects (and punish them in the event of their conviction) and to provide compensation for victims and relatives.[15] These conventions promise an 'effective remedy' for violations – but what remedy can be effective in the case of persons who have disappeared? *Habeas corpus* – a demand to produce the body, dead or alive – will be met with an official pretence of ignorance and, too often, with judicial handwashing. (Velasquez's relatives brought three *habeas corpus* petitions against Honduran officials, who ignored them because intimidated judges refused to convene hearings.) Compensation may be a sufficient remedy if state authorities are in no way complicit in the disappearance – if it really is a result of factionalism in which military and police have not taken sides. But where the state is implicated, either directly or through failing to establish a system to prevent disappearances, then the remedy must include some public examination (preferably through the trial process) and accountability of those officials whose negligence or malfeasance has permitted the violation.[16] There must be a truthful accounting, a naming of the names of all those involved in the kidnap, torture and death. Preferably, they should be prosecuted or at very least stripped of rank – in appropriate cases the state should be required to disband that section of its security forces which has organized the disappearances.

Velasquez was followed in 1993 by *Aloeboetoe* v. *Suriname*,[17] a case which arose from an incident where Suriname government soldiers had arrested and tortured a group of innocent Indian fishermen, ordering them to dig their own graves before shooting them. The Inter-American Commission gathered sufficient evidence to prove Suriname's responsibility for the crime: the court ordered that it pay some half million US dollars for the benefit of the victims' children and relatives. These reparations were made up of *actual damage* (compensation for the trauma of having a close relative viciously assassinated) and *moral damage* (compensation for the terror suffered by the victims in the hours before their deaths, the right to which becomes enforceable by their heirs). This latter head of damages is particularly appropriate in the familiar case where the right to life is extinguished after torture and terror. The court sensibly ordered the government to establish a trust fund and arrange for the award to be distributed through a foundation, and further (and imaginatively) directed it to establish a school and a clinic in the village where the massacre had taken place.

If perpetrators of crimes against humanity cannot be prosecuted or even sued for damages in their home state – because they remain in power or have been granted amnesties – then a secondary duty may devolve upon another state to bring or permit proceedings should they come within its jurisdiction, on the principle that crimes against international law 'may be punished by any state which obtains custody of persons suspected of responsibility'.[18] It follows that civil actions can be brought as well, certainly where the damage flowed from an act of genocide or torture or other breach of a *jus cogens* rule (i.e. a rule defined by Article 53 of the Vienna Convention on the Law of Treaties as one 'accepted and recognized by the international community of States as a whole from which no derogation is permitted'). Since the infringement of such a compelling law – even by a state itself – involves the breach of an *erga omnes* obligation to the international community of all states, there is no reason why one of those states should not make its courts available for a victim to sue any torturer who wanders within its jurisdiction. This is the express result of the 'try or extradite' duty on all 150 state parties to the Torture Convention, and the implicit result of Article 2(3) of the Civil Covenant, which calls upon state parties to provide an effective remedy for victims of human rights abuses – a duty which must devolve on these parties if, because of an amnesty or a lack of prosecutorial will, no effective remedy is available in the country where the abuse took place. This duty is fulfilled in the US by statutory provision: the 1789 Alien Tort Claims Act permits suit for any tort 'committed in violation of the law of nations' and the 1992 Torture Victim Protection Act extends the right to US victims or relatives in respect of acts of torture and summary execution committed by officials in foreign countries where there is no remedy. In Britain, a 1988 provision gives criminal courts extraterritorial jurisdiction to try any suspected torturer whatever his or her victim's nationality and irrespective of where the torture took place. There is, however, no equivalent to the US statutes which permit civil actions.

The efficacy of civil remedies is limited by the doctrine of state immunity, which will preclude the state itself from being made a defendant, even in respect of acts of torture and extrajudicial killing which it has authorized. This means that a human defendant will have to be found, in the form of an individual who ordered or carried out the atrocity. It will not be often that such persons will reside beyond the protection of their own state, and if served with a writ it is even less likely that they will stick around to contest the case. Civil actions, therefore, are only feasible in respect of torturers who are exiled or 'on the run' from their own country, and have assets within the foreign jurisdiction which can be frozen or otherwise used to satisfy damages awards. That was the case with Ferdinand Marcos: despairing of the cowardice of the Filipino government and the corruption of its courts, victims of torture and relatives of those who 'disappeared' under the Marcos regime brought a class action against him in Hawaii, where he was living in exile. Their evidence established that he had taken personal charge of the state security apparatus and must have personally approved the atrocities which were the subject of the suit – such as the kidnap, torture and murder of student Archimedes Trajano, whose only crime had been to ask embarrassing questions of Marcos's daughter when she was head of the national youth organization. Marcos pleaded that, as president at the time, he was immune under the 'Act of State' doctrine, but in *Trajano* v. *Marcos* the Federal Appeals Court held that this doctrine did not apply to acts of torture, kidnap and murder. For the same reason, he could not invoke the claim of sovereign immunity.[19] Marcos died while the litigation was in progress, and damages of US$150 million were awarded against his estate. Eventually, in 1999, this sum was split between 10,000 plaintiffs in the class action, the money having been recovered from the dictator's Swiss bank accounts. This happy happenstance, however, is uncommon: most foreign defendants to Alien Tort Statute claims do not stay for the verdict. In the leading case, *Filártiga* v. *Peña-Irala* (1980), the relatives of a Paraguayan victim were awarded $1,000,000 damages against his torturer who evaded payment by fleeing the US.[20] In 2000 a New York jury awarded $745 million to victims of Radovan Karadžić. (He had been served with the writ while visiting the US in 1993 at the invitation of the UN.)[21] In the same year Premier Li Peng was sued over Tiananmen Square; so too was Robert Mugabe for directing mass murder in Matabeleland: the writs were served on the doormen of their New York hotels. Their presence in the US (Mugabe was attending the UN's millennium meeting) was sufficient to found jurisdiction, although none of these defendants has plans to return for the trial.

At best, such civil actions *in absentia* give victims and relatives an opportunity to present their case in a legal forum and to have it assessed by a judge: witnesses against Karadžić said that it helped them to grieve and to put their evidence against him on public record. But it may be doubted whether civil proceedings bring much satisfaction other than to the individual plaintiff. A criminal conviction, for relatives of the deceased in domestic murder cases, has a cathartic effect: it enables them to end their grieving and get on with their lives. An award of damages for the loss of a loved one through abuse of state power can be demeaning unless it comes with an acknowledgement of guilt. The Lockerbie relatives objected to compensation offered by Libya in 2002, because that state refused to acknowledge its responsibility, despite the fact that one of its security agents had been convicted and was serving his sentence in Scotland. Two years later, when Libya upped the compensation to $2.7 billion and accepted a measure of liability, the offer was accepted because the better alternative – the trial of Colonel Gaddafi, the prime suspect – was not on offer. This oil-rich ex-terrorist had at this point become an ally of America in the war on al-Qaida, their common enemy.

Civil actions are therefore second best, although if the defendant does contest them, they may have advantages in circumventing obstacles inherent in a criminal prosecution such as a higher burden of proof, time bars, stricter exclusion of hearsay evidence and the right of criminal defendants to remain silent. Civil proceedings may also be a means of circumventing the reluctance of Western governments to prosecute dictators and generals who have come within the jurisdiction to retire or to benefit from advanced medical treatment: old allegiances die hard (as right-wing British politicians showed by supporting General Pinochet) and where politicians control the prosecution process there will be a natural reluctance to cause diplomatic uproar. In such cases, civil proceedings will be better than no proceedings at all. Under the ruling in *Pinochet (No. 3)*, however, it will be much easier to prosecute under the Torture Convention, which extinguishes sovereign immunity, than to sue for damages and face an immunity defence (see chapter 8).

THE LIMITS OF AMNESTY

Every state has power – normally but not necessarily defined by its constitution – to pardon those who offend against its laws. A pardon offered or proclaimed to a whole class of offender is described as an amnesty, a word bearing favourable connotations in the human rights lexicon through its association with Amnesty International. Pardons and amnesties have been used from time immemorial, benevolently (as a measure of forgiveness to those who have already suffered some punishment for their crimes), politically (to bring to an end civil wars and insurrections), legally (to absolve convicts who later appear innocent), and even festively (to celebrate a ruler's birthday). In England the early common law developed a set of rules for pardons at a time when they were a regular feature of law enforcement by the King and his officials, and then adapted these rules to cover pardons that were offered to informers and criminals who turned 'Queen's evidence'. They would operate 'to clear the person from all infamy . . . it makes him, as it were, a new man' although it did not create the legal fiction that the beneficiary never committed the crime in the first place.²² Following the Civil War, Parliament passed various 'Acts of Oblivion' to immunize its own forces and to rehabilitate royalists, but the most significant legislation came in 1660 when Parliament, by tacit agreement with Charles II, amnestied its own supporters in the run-up to the Restoration. Significantly, this amnesty excluded those who bore greatest responsibility for the key revolutionary act of executing Charles I: not only his judges, but prosecuting counsel and several 'intellectual authors' of the regicide, including Cromwell's chaplain Hugh Peters (a founder of Harvard) and Sir Henry Vane, the former governor of Massachusetts, were excluded from this statute, and subsequently tried and executed.

None the less, amnesties get favourable treatment in American law, as a result of the litigation from the amnesty proclamations by President Abraham Lincoln to encourage defection in Confederate ranks during the American Civil War. Lincoln had insisted, against heavy congressional criticism, that former enemies should be forgiven and former enmity forgotten once the oath of allegiance (the condition of obtaining an amnesty) had been taken. In his State of the Nation message to Congress in 1863, he declared that any reneging on an amnesty would be 'a cruel and astounding breach of faith'. The Supreme Court agreed, ordering the return of property seized from 'amnestied' ex-Confederates and striking down all congressional laws discriminating against them.²³

Pardon is unexceptionable when it is used like this, as a military option that can save many lives by ending a war or revolution. Indeed, the wide presidential pardoning power in the US constitution was put there precisely because, as founding father Alexander Hamilton explained, 'In seasons of insurrection or rebellion, there are often critical moments, when a well-timed offer of pardon to the insurgents or rebels may restore the tranquillity of the Commonwealth; and which, if suffered to pass unimproved, it may never be possible afterwards to recall.'[24] Hamilton could hardly have had in mind the occasion almost 200 years later on which his words were used to justify the pardon granted by President Gerald Ford to his crooked predecessor, Richard Nixon, saving him from the impeachment proceedings commenced by Congress. Ford acted, so he claimed, in the public interest 'to end the divisions caused by Watergate', an unravelling scandal which had already seen criminal convictions imposed on sixty-six senior officials of the Nixon government (including his vice-president and three cabinet ministers) for 'high crimes and misdemeanours'. Ford's pardon was upheld on the ground that the pardoning power was, under the constitution, unlimited and thus could extend to offenders prior to their conviction: the court found that Nixon, in Hamilton's terms, was 'conducting a covert assault on American liberty and an insurrection and rebellion against Constitutional government itself and so his successor was entitled to restore the tranquillity of the Commonwealth'.[25]

The Nixon pardon, widely condemned as a political interference with the legal process, had great appeal to corrupt politicians throughout the world, conscious of their own vulnerability once they left or were excluded from office. The government in Trinidad, for example, immediately pushed through a constitutional change enabling the island's president to grant pardons for any offence prior to conviction. Ironically, the first beneficiaries were a group of Muslim terrorists who broke into Parliament House and held hostage the country's prime minister and cabinet. Eventually these MPs were released after an amnesty was granted to the terrorists by the President, but the government then proceeded to dishonour it by detaining and prosecuting them on capital charges of treason and murder. The ensuing legal proceedings, in the Privy Council, illuminate the moral difficulties in the modern concept of amnesty, a device which can be used by the state to save lives in the short term, at the expense of injustice to the victims of those pardoned. In this case the Muslims had killed eight policemen, injured dozens of citizens and caused millions of dollars of damage, yet after obtaining *habeas corpus* on the strength of their amnesty, they turned around and sued the state for damages for wrongfully detaining them. The decision of the Privy Council in *Attorney-General of Trinidad and Tobago* v. *Lennox Phillip* establishes that while an amnesty may expunge past offences, it cannot be used to immunize future lawbreaking: 'The State cannot be allowed to use a power to pardon to enable the law to be set aside by permitting it to be contravened with impunity.'[26] The significance of this ruling for invalidating amnesty laws purporting to pardon death squads is that kidnapping is a continuing offence until the body is found – and no statute can forgive a crime which is still afoot.

The Trinidad case demonstrates how 'amnesty' – that word associated with peace and compassion and forgiveness – can be exploited by the perpetrators of appalling crimes. So an increasingly important issue in human rights law is whether states can be bound by amnesties extracted under duress – for example, by a threat on the part of the army to revolt unless its officers are given amnesties for crimes against humanity. Clearly, no pardon signed under threat of direct physical violence – a gun at the head of the president – can be valid: it is not the deliberate act of a head of state.[27] But pressure, even to the point of threatening calamitous loss of life, cannot invalidate through duress the presidential act of granting an amnesty if the president is physically free and makes a deliberate decision that amnesty is in the public interest as the lesser of two evils. Thus, in the Trinidad case, the Privy Council declined to invalidate the amnesty on the ground that it was extracted from the president by threats to kill the prime minister and cabinet ministers who were all being held as hostages. The court invalidated it, instead, because the Muslims did not immediately accept its condition – that they surrender their hostages unharmed – but continued to hold them for several days while negotiating an eventual surrender. With Solomonic wisdom, the court thus denied murderous fanatics any damages for wrongful arrest, but at the same time stopped the state from proceeding to hang them by ruling that it would be an abuse of process to continue prosecution because they had surrendered in the belief (induced by the government) that they were entitled to a pardon once they did eventually comply with the condition. The repugnant prospect that terrorists who killed and caused vast damage to the country might actually be awarded millions of dollars of compensation for false imprisonment (they had been detained for two years while the validity of the amnesty was considered by the courts) was a Gilbertian conclusion to be avoided at all costs, and the Privy Council avoided it by ruling that the insurgents had not surrendered quickly enough. This useful precedent was applied by the Fiji courts in 2001 to invalidate the amnesty given by the army to George Speight, leader of a gang of ethnic supremacists who had held the prime minister and cabinet hostage for some weeks while they bargained for a place in a new government.

In both cases, the prosecutions were permitted to go ahead because the rebels had not been misled as to the condition of the amnesty, but their eventual surrender without harming the hostages was accepted as a mitigating factor in their sentences. The modern common-law approach to amnesties, exemplified by the Trinidad case, thus embodies a compromise in which the rule of law is limited by the demands of necessity, i.e. the moral imperative of saving innocent lives. The courts will uphold the right of the state to grant pardons, even for the most heinous offences (in the Trinidad case itself, for the murder of eight policemen and an attempt to overthrow democratic government). If such pardons were automatically invalid, then governments could never induce terrorists or rebels to surrender in reliance upon them and governments should at least have power to decide whether to proffer them. All such amnesties are really procured through a form of duress, i.e. by criminal elements putting unbearable pressure upon the authorities to grant the amnesty as the lesser of two or more evils. The common law does not adopt duress as a basis for invalidating them, but does require strict interpretation of the grant of amnesty and it does imply surrender conditions whenever they can be shown to be the *quid pro quo* of the grant. No amnesty can validly permit future law breaking, even in the course of negotiations over a surrender, so the surrender conditions implied in the pardon must be complied with 'either promptly or as soon as practicable'. So insurgents, terrorists and common criminals who want to obtain the protection of a pardon must comply with its conditions forthwith or else it becomes valueless, not worth the paper on which it is written or agreed or proclaimed.

There is, of course, no reason why a government which does grant a conditional amnesty may not vary the conditions in order to permit surrender and disarmament within a reasonable time, so long as no fresh offences are committed in the meantime. The approach of the Privy Council in the context of an amnesty designed to defuse an attempted coup and hostage crisis may be extrapolated to cover an amnesty which is part of an agreement to end a civil war. In other words, the protection afforded to rebel and government militias by an amnesty which is part of or conditional upon a peace settlement is irredeemably lost if they resume fighting.

It may seem a harsh rule that deprives combatants of the benefit of an amnesty because their leaders have resumed hostilities. But that is the inevitable result of an amnesty which is part of a peace agreement between leaders who subsequently breach it. An amnesty is, after all, an enormous indulgence to persons who have murdered and tortured prisoners-of-war, or directed genocidal attacks. There may be scope in domestic law for abuse of process applications to avoid serious injustice, for example to a former combatant who deserted or disassociated himself from the renewed fighting, or a militia commander who had strictly observed the ceasefire conditions until subjected to an unprovoked attack by the former enemy. But it follows from the rule in the Trinidad case that amnesties bestowed for the purpose of securing the peace have no force once war breaks out again.

AMNESTIES IN INTERNATIONAL LAW

Domestic law can limit and restrict grounds for amnesty but international criminal law, which operates in a different dimension, has the power to invalidate those which purport to pardon persons who bear prime responsibility for initiating crimes against humanity. That was the conclusion of the Appeals Chamber of the Special Court for Sierra

Leone (SCSL) in *Kondewa* and other cases which have invalidated the amnesty provisions of the Lomé Accord.[28] This was a ceasefire agreement concluded in 1999 between the Sierra Leone government and the main rebel faction led by Foday Sankoh. It was brokered by 'moral guarantors' such as Jesse Jackson (President Clinton's peace envoy), Charles Taylor (who would later be convicted of aiding Sankoh's crimes against humanity) and a very anxious representative of the UN Secretary-General. The intention of the parties was that this amnesty would cover all crimes committed by the combatants on either side of the conflict. There was to be an 'absolute and free pardon' for all 'combatants and collaborators' who were to suffer 'no official or judicial action' for *anything* done in the pursuit of their objectives, which included mass mutilation, mass murder and some of the worst butchery seen on the continent of Africa. The special representative of the UN signed the agreement, but after a call from Kofi Annan he hastily scribbled a note to the effect that 'the United Nations interprets that the amnesty shall not apply to international crimes of genocide, crimes against humanity, war crimes and other serious violations of international law'. This interpretation did not accord with the intentions of the parties in signing the agreement, but the Court held that it accurately stated the effect of the international law rule that strikes down amnesties which purport to bestow impunity on those who bear the greatest responsibility for crimes against humanity.

That decision was taken in the context of a 'peace settlement' amnesty, which has traditionally been treated as if supported by valuable consideration on both sides, namely to stop all fighting. This kind of blanket amnesty provides an almost totemic absolution of rank and file combatants at the end of a civil war. One example is found in the peace agreement reached in Liberia in August 2003, with UN support, which requires the transitional government to consider a 'general amnesty'.[29] Those who claim that international law invalidates all amnesties for all combatants for all international crimes face not only the reality of state practice, where amnesties in peace agreements are common, but also Article 6(5) in the 1977 Protocol II to the Geneva Conventions:

At the end of hostilities, the authorities in power shall endeavour to grant the broadest possible amnesty to persons who have participated in the armed conflict, or those deprived of their liberty for reasons related to the armed conflict, whether they are interned or detained.[30]

Protocol II has not been ratified by some important states (such as the US and Turkey) and Article 6(5) should be understood as a 'best endeavours' provision. Although 'broadest possible amnesty' would seem to apply to all crimes, and all criminals of whatever rank, it is plain from the context (Section 6 of Protocol II provides minimum standards for war crimes prosecutions) that it is not intended to encourage amnesties which would infringe international law, such as unilateral pardons for crimes (e.g. genocide) which the state is under a compelling duty to prosecute. The drafting history of the subsection shows that it contemplates a Lincoln-style amnesty ('to restore the tranquillity of the Commonwealth') for rank and file combatants who have fought on opposite sides according to the laws of war, especially for soldiers on the losing side who have been detained at the end of the conflict. This is the basis on which some commentators have reinterpreted 'broadest possible amnesty' to exclude violations of international law, for which an amnesty is unavailable.[31] This point was not specifically considered by the South African Constitutional Court in the AZAPO case,[32] which approved an amnesty that was not 'blanket' because each person had to be considered in the circumstances of individual cases by a truth and reconciliation commission. The Court drew support from Article 6(5), but did not consider whether 'broadest possible amnesty' would exclude prosecutions for international crimes. But it obviously encourages *domestic* amnesties, to restore tranquillity to states that have been at war with themselves, by pardoning 'persons who have participated in the armed conflict'. Sensibly, it would apply to rank and file participants, but not to the authors of such conflicts. Thus, tranquillity might well be assisted by pardoning the mass of soldiers in rival armies – the purpose of Article 6(5) – but whether it is assisted by pardoning leaders who gave orders for mass murder of civilians is quite another matter. In South Africa, the Commission of Truth and

Reconciliation itself used pardon as a plea-bargaining device, requiring those who wished to obtain an amnesty to tell, in public, the whole truth and to give evidence against accomplices in the event that any were put on trial (see p. 390).

One of the difficulties about invalidating peace settlement amnesties which apply to armies numbering tens of thousands is the practical impossibility of holding effective trials for all accused of war crimes. Another is in distinguishing between the 'ordinary' crimes, for which the defendant is immune to prosecution, and the international crimes for which he is not, although both kinds of charges will be based upon the same events. One feature that gives an international crime its special gravity is the fact that it is commonly conceived and directed by state or group leaders, as part of a widespread and systematic persecution. But even within these horrific categories of mass murder and mass torture, there are obvious distinctions in moral culpability between foot soldiers, accomplices, military authorities and national leaders. The 'authors' of international crimes are those with the imagination or the authority – the power to conceive or to implement, or the power to stop. The sea change in the international community's approach to amnesty, from regarding it as the blessing of forgiveness to reproaching it as the curse of impunity, has turned on the dawning realization of the unacceptability of amnesties for the 'authors' of crimes against humanity, i.e. those who bear the greatest responsibility. International criminal law has developed at least so far as to make this same distinction, namely that amnesties cannot absolve the political and military leaders who bear greatest responsibility for genocide, torture, crimes against humanity and grave breaches of international and humanitarian law. This development has come, somewhat ironically, by way of reaction to the very power that political and military leaders have exploited, especially in Latin America, to pardon themselves or to manipulate or pressure new governments to bestow pardons upon them.

It is well established that new governments inherit the legal responsibilities of their predecessors. The principle of the continuity of the state in international law means that state responsibility exists independently of change of government and continuously from the time of the act for which the state is responsible to the time when the act is declared illegal. The state cannot therefore obliterate its own crimes, or those of its agents, committed against its subjects. This is the case whether the government granting the amnesty is the government at fault or the successor to that government. Just as genocide and torture are repugnant to international law to such an extent that no circumstances can justify them (hence these Convention obligations are non-derogable), so amnesties given to perpetrators of such deeds by frightened or blackmailed governments cannot be upheld by international law, even when agreed by international diplomats.

In other words, states which pardon torturers before trials have taken place are in breach of their international obligations to bring perpetrators of crimes against humanity to justice. The amnesty may be valid under domestic law, and the action justified in international law either under Article 4 of the Civil Covenant (a derogation taken 'in time of public emergency which threatens the life of the nation') or under the accepted customary law notion of necessity: obligations may be ignored to save a state from grave and imminent peril. Governments which fail in their duty to prosecute the military sometimes do have reason to believe that to do so would amount to 'political suicide' by provoking another takeover. But such amnesties are not binding on other states, which may take universal jurisdiction to try a torturer who comes within their borders, or on the International Criminal Court, as established under the Rome Statute. And since a grant of amnesty can under most constitutional arrangements be revoked by whichever body has plenary power in the state, a duty to do so may retrospectively arise under international law once the danger of reprisals has passed. This is the position taken by the HRC in respect of the covenant obligation to provide an effective remedy against official violation of guaranteed rights. Amnesties granted for acts of torture, it has ruled, 'are generally incompatible with the duty of states to investigate such acts; to guarantee prosecution of such acts within their jurisdiction; and to ensure that they do not occur in the future. States may not deprive individuals of the right to an effective remedy, including compensation and such full rehabilitation as may be possible.'[33]

This is the position favoured by the Inter-American Commission, which has had to cope with the rash of amnesty laws in Argentina, Brazil, Chile, Uruguay, Guatemala, El Salvador, Nicaragua and Suriname. Most of them have been passed under pressure from the military, although in Uruguay's case the measure was approved at a referendum. This cut no ice, however: the excuse that it showed 'the express will of the Uruguayan people to close a painful chapter in their history' was condemned by the Commission as contrary to the obligation to investigate and punish human rights violations and hence a violation of the rights of relatives of the disappeared.[34] All too typical of the cases it has had to adjudicate was that of the 1983 Los Hojas massacre, in which seventy-four civilians, most with no known subversive connections, were shot in the head by members of the Salvadorian security forces and their bodies dumped along the banks of a river. The prosecution brought charges against thirteen soldiers, including the captain and major who led the death squad and Colonel Araujo, who directed its operations. After several frightened low-level judges had refused to hear the case, the Appeal Court directed that the trial go ahead, whereupon the Legislative Assembly passed an amnesty decree specifically providing impunity for all who participated in politically motivated massacres (or, lest the large number of non-subversives left dead at Los Hojas put political motivation in question, 'common crimes in which the number of persons involved is no less than twenty'). The Inter-American Commission ruled that 'the present amnesty law, as applied in these cases, by foreclosing the possibility of judicial relief in cases of murder, inhumane treatment and absence of judicial guarantees, denies the fundamental nature of most basic human rights. It eliminates perhaps the single most effective means of enforcing such rights, the trial and punishment of offenders.[35] The government responsible for the massacre was, by whitewashing it, breaching the victims' rights to life (Article 4), personal security and integrity (Article 5), due process (Article 8), and judicial protection (Article 25), and had failed to comply with its Article 1 obligation to guarantee human rights to all its citizens. El Salvador was ordered not only to pay compensation to the massacre victims, but to prosecute the perpetrators irrespective of the amnesty. Instead, its government passed an even broader amnesty law, which its constitutional court ruled to be valid.

Although the Los Hojas decision was treated disrespectfully, it marked the beginning of a refusal by international courts and commissions to countenance the spectacle of a state forgiving itself its own wrongs or the increasing phenomenon of new governments giving amnesties at the insistence of continuing branches of the old – the military, security and police.

An important example is the Inter-American Court judgment in the *Barrios Altos Case*, which confirmed the responsibility of senior government officials (including ex-President Fujimori) for authorizing a mass killing of fifteen students at their university. The Court held in terms that blanket amnesties were incompatible with the duties of state parties to the Inter-American Convention (IAC):

This Court considers that all amnesty provisions, provisions on prescription and the establishment of measures designed to eliminate responsibility are impermissible, because they are intended to prevent the investigation and punishment of those responsible for serious human rights violations such as torture, extra-judicial summary or arbitrary execution and forced disappearance, all of them prohibited because they violate non-derogable rights recognised by international human rights law.[36]

A Hague Tribunal Trial Chamber has ruled that a domestic amnesty covering crimes the prohibition of which has the status of a *jus cogens* norm 'would not be accorded international legal recognition'. In *Prosecutor v. Anton Furundžija* the court noted:

It would be senseless to argue, on the one hand, that on account of the *jus cogens* value of the prohibition against torture, treaties or customary rules providing for torture would be null and void *ab initio*, and then be unmindful of a state say, taking national measures authorising or condoning torture or resolving its perpetrators through an amnesty law. If such a situation were to arise, the national measures, violating the general principle and any relevant treaty provision, would produce the legal effects discussed above and would not be accorded international legal recognition . . . What is even more important is that perpetrators of torture acting upon or benefiting from these national measures may nevertheless be held criminally responsible for torture, whether in a foreign state, or in their own state under a subsequent regime.[37]

There is a substantial body of cases, comments, rulings and remarks which denies the permissibility of amnesties in international law for crimes against humanity and war crimes (although the HRC adds 'in general'): they produce impunity and violate state duties to investigate and punish perpetrators as well as the victims' rights to justice. But to survey all these statements is necessarily to observe the depressing number of occasions on which they have been provoked by state practice to the contrary. The fact that international legal bodies universally condemn states which grant amnesties for crimes against humanity has not stopped states, including the most powerful (as with the US/UK amnesty offer to Saddam Hussein in 2003) from resorting to them in cases of perceived necessity. How can the practice of states to grant amnesties be explained away? To some extent, perhaps, by the fact that state practice looks not only to what states do, but whether they have any qualms about doing it. There is a handwringing quality about the excuses for amnesty by states which grant them: these can range from Peru's confession (in the *Barrios Altos Case*) that international law was thereby violated, to the reaction of the UK foreign minister when taxed with his offer of impunity to Saddam: 'the world is imperfect'.[38] States condemned for granting amnesties are beginning to show some embarrassment when called to account by the human rights NGOs for breaching legal obligations. This official response of 'confession and avoidance' is taken into account in identifying the crystallization of a rule of customary international law, in the way described by the ICJ in *Nicaragua* v. *US*:

If a state acts in a way *prima facie* incompatible with a recognised rule, but defends its conduct by appealing to exceptions or justifications contained within the rule itself, then whether or not the state's conduct is in fact justifiable on that basis, the significance of that attitude is to confirm rather than to weaken the rule.[39]

It may therefore be said that state practice is changing to conform with the consistent view that blanket amnesties are, at least 'in general', impermissible in international law for international crimes. What can also be detected, in what may be the development of an interim position, is a focus on major malefactors, the intellectual or commanding 'authors' of torture and genocide, who will not be permitted to escape through a pardon that exonerates their underlings. The mesh of the dragnet may be excessively loose at this rudimentary stage of international law development, but it none the less serves to entangle the biggest fish – those who can credibly be accused of bearing the greatest responsibility for international crimes.

This is not so much a limitation on the rule as an application of it to those whose level of responsibility demands retribution, irrespective of cost or convenience or other apparently countervailing public interests. The obligation to prosecute must be more powerful – indeed, overwhelming – when applied to those political and military leaders without whose authorization or encouragement the crimes against humanity would not have been committed by 'small fry' soldiers. Such leaders are the real 'perpetrators of serious crimes under international law' who cannot benefit from a peace agreement under the simple principle of the Vienna Declaration that 'states should abrogate legislation leading to impunity for those responsible for grave violations of human rights such as torture and prosecute such violations, thereby providing a firm basis for the rule of law'.[40] There is no doubt that the sea change in international opinion is a reflection of public concern at the spectacle of truculent leaders, credibly accused of the worst human rights violations, living happily ever after, thanks to an amnesty. Removing them from the stage is no longer enough: the clear implication from all human rights treaties is that they must face justice, although their followers may be spared as a reconciliation measure. The rule against impunity that has crystallized in international law is a norm which denies the legal possibility of pardon to those who bear the greatest responsibility for crimes against humanity.

The real purpose of an amnesty statute in times of transition is not to promote 'national reconciliation' or to diminish in a new democratic society the debilitating desire for revenge, it is to enable government officials, and military and police officers, to escape responsibility for the crimes against humanity which they ordered or committed. The new government may be acting under direct threat: General Pinochet warned Chile's elected president, as he handed over power in 1990, 'No one is going to touch my people. The day they do, the state of law will come to an end.'[41] It took five years before a democratic government dared to put Pinochet's vilest henchman, Manuel Contreras, the head of DINA, on trial – and only because the US insisted on his prosecution for organizing the Letelier bombing in Washington. Contreras was sentenced only to seven years' imprisonment. Argentina's elected President Alfonsín, who subsequently abrogated the amnesty law passed by the military junta in order to put that junta's leaders on trial, was then forced to abandon consequent proceedings against more junior officers as a result of army rebellions. His achievement, however, was to have military leaders fairly tried and five of them convicted for overseeing crimes against humanity, after persuading his congress to declare null and void the amnesty which they had granted themselves, on the grounds that it was imposed by an authoritarian government and did not emanate from the democratic process.[42] Alfonsín's Perónist successor, Carlos Menem, undid his work by pardoning the convicted generals.

This highlights the failure of other transitional governments in Latin America and elsewhere to bring torturers to justice. In the Philippines, Cory Aquino's refusal at the outset of her term of office to call the military to account cannot be put down to necessity or public emergency: to nervousness, certainly, and her desire to be supported by the military to the same extent as it had supported her predecessor Ferdinand Marcos. Her most notable failure, however, lay in her inability to reform the notoriously corrupt Filipino judiciary, from whom little 'justice' of any kind could be expected. In consequence, of the thousands of cases brought by human rights bodies, only six resulted in convictions, allowing the subsequent Ramos government to introduce a total amnesty for crimes against humanity committed under Marcos, as part of a package deal promising immunity to leftist guerrillas.[43] More sinister uses of amnesty powers have occurred in Zimbabwe, for the benefit of members of the security forces accused of participating in massacres in Matabeleland in the 1980s, years after the Lancaster House Agreement which gave amnesties to all participants in the civil war. This had been reasonable enough, on the precedent set by Lincoln, but it hardly behoves the state to deploy the same power long after the war had ended to exempt its soldiers from liability for violating the human rights of the citizens they are meant to protect.[44] These failures, however, are to be set against the comparative success of the Karamanlis government, which re-established civilian rule in Greece while permitting prosecutions of senior officers for torture and murder. This produced dissension in the armed forces, but they were weakened and dishonoured by their failure to stop the Turkish invasion of Cyprus, and thus unable to destabilize the democratic government which insisted upon prosecution.

In summary, international law now imposes an *erga omnes* obligation on states to investigate and prosecute crimes against humanity, even if this means rejecting or annulling amnesty laws and taking some risk of counter-revolution. If the risk is significant, the state may rely on necessity or emergency to postpone its obligation, which can be reasserted years later, when the danger has passed. In the meantime, the rules of universal jurisdiction mean that political torturers and murderers later found in other states may be tried there, depending upon the willingness to punish offences committed in other times and other countries. A number of European countries provide for a measure of universal jurisdiction: Spanish magistrate Baltasar Garzón has deployed it against former Latin American torturers, while Belgium ignored appeals from the Vatican and convicted two Hutu nuns who had bought the petrol used to incinerate hundreds of Tutsis they had lured into the 'sanctuary' of their church. International law does not allow states to prosecute incumbent heads of state and foreign ministers, at least until after their retirement from office: the ICJ in 2002 had to curb Belgium's zeal in issuing an arrest warrant for the Congo's foreign minister – customary international law, reflecting the need to encourage such personages to travel to peace conferences and UN assemblies, gives them a temporary immunity. But the cost of such prosecutions is high, since evidence must be brought from abroad, and this factor will generally make the proceedings hinge on some co-operation from the state which has original jurisdiction, i.e. the country where the crimes were committed. Outside the traditional concern about Nazi war criminals, this co-operation has been achieved in relation to drug trafficking (notably Panama's support of the prosecution in the US of its former ruler General Noriega) and fraud – the Aquino government supported the prosecution commenced against Marcos in the US for corruption and refused to protect him by claiming sovereign immunity for his actions when they became the subject of claims by torture victims. Neither state had the confidence in itself to pursue the charges of crimes against humanity which should have been levelled at their former leaders. This is the clinching argument for the need of an international criminal court with power to prosecute those former rulers whom transitional governments lack the resolve or the political power to indict.

TRUTH COMMISSIONS AND TRANSITIONAL JUSTICE

A 'truth and reconciliation committee' (TRC) is a portentous name for the inquiries set up by reforming – generally democratic – governments which have just taken over from brutal military rulers or dictators or have emerged from brutal civil wars. Established in the first flush of popular freedom, their reports should be a prelude to the trial of the old regime's murderers and torturers, although they have often been used as alternatives to justice. That is because truth commissions have reported enough of the truth to discomfort the perpetrators of crimes against humanity who still hold rank in the military and the police: their continued influence frightens politicians, who in consequence invoke the 'interests of national reconciliation' as an excuse for granting them amnesties and pardons, despite emerging evidence of their guilt.

Most governments establish commissions of inquiry to ascertain the truth about matters of public concern. However, the only 'truth commission' that is relevant to international human rights law may be defined as an inquiry established by a government pursuant to its international law duty to investigate and to establish the truth about war crimes or crimes against humanity committed by state agents (and others) in the past, such inquiry having duties (*inter alia*) to take evidence from victims, to uncover perpetrators and to deliver a public report. The 'right to life' includes the right to know the truth about every life lost by the action of the state or its agents: as the UN Commission on Human Rights puts it, 'victims and their families have the imprescriptible right to know the truth about the circumstances in which violations took place and, in the event of deaths and disappearance, the victim's fate'. This is the main role of a truth commission, and in circumstances where there has been a pattern or system of killings or disappearances by police or military, the government has a duty to set one up. It is not an alternative to prosecutions and trials (as some governments hope it will be) but rather an adjunct, usually preliminary to the criminal process. There have been truth commissions documenting human rights abuses in more than thirty countries in the last thirty years, although their performance and impact has varied considerably, and they provide a low level of accountability – bad publicity, rather than prison. Although they are untrammelled by rules of evidence, and able to absorb history and discover global information to an extent that courts cannot, care must be taken before accepting everything in their reports as truth. Indeed the very lack of evidential awareness among amateur and somewhat naive commissioners (who are often bishops or academics) conduces to generalizations and to recommendations based on hope rather than experience. There is, of course, a perennial danger that commissioners will be chosen because they support the new and usually avenging government – which is why the most successful commissions have been hybrid, with international members in the chair and in the majority.

TRC reports can assist war-ravaged societies to move forward and beyond the hatreds that fuelled the conflict. Truth commissions offer two distinct prospects for victims: of truth – learning how and why they or their loved ones were murdered or maimed; and of reconciliation – through understanding and forgiveness of the perpetrators, or at least of those who genuinely confess and regret. The TRC methodology, which generally permits victims to give their accounts in public, can assist grieving and provide some measure of closure, certainly when perpetrators are prepared to apologize. This is rare, however, and the main satisfaction comes from official acknowledgement of suffering. Although truth commission procedures sometimes adopt forensic styles, by sitting in public and leading victims through their testimony and permitting examination and confrontation, any impression that justice is being done would be misleading. TRCs have a chequered history: the most valuable are those that are independent of the new government and concentrate their reports on the pressing needs of victims, which tend to be for medical and financial support rather than the more elusive value of 'reconciliation'. The 2005 TRC report for East Timor was a well-documented 2,500 pages, based on interviews with 8,000 witnesses and victims and a searing condemnation of the Indonesian military's use of starvation and torture to suppress popular resistance to unlawful occupation. Those responsible for it have earned promotion rather than prosecution, the report pointed out, and it embarrassed the Gusmão government by urging further trials for these Indonesian generals and by recommending civil legal claims against 'friendly' governments like the US and Australia, which had supported or acquiesced in the unlawful Indonesian invasion of the island in 1975. The Sierra Leone truth commission similarly provided an excellent analysis of the causes of that conflict, although some of its legal conclusions were shaky and its recommendations for lavish compensation to victims were far beyond the capacity of the government. Some TRC recommendations will invariably be over-idealistic or too expensive or otherwise impractical: it is important that they be seriously considered, but not necessarily implemented.

There has been a good deal of speculation over whether truth commissions can 'coexist' with war crimes courts. Ideally, TRC reports should come first, in order to verify the need for a court, or else after the court's work has been done so that its evidence and judgments can be used for an overall assessment of the causes of the conflict. However, the parallel processes are by no means incompatible: a war crimes court and a truth commission coexisted in Sierra Leone without treading on each other's toes. The prosecutor defused the initial concern by announcing that he would not compel TRC witnesses to give evidence at trials, and the only problem arose when the truth commission refused to reciprocate. It sought to summon defendants who were in detention and about to stand trial, to give public testimony in front of a bishop and other commissioners, over several days where they would be subjected to cross-examination and their speeches would be broadcast live to the nation on radio and television. The court was not prepared to permit this usurpation of its function: it was concerned that live-to-air testimony in an uncontrolled environment by alleged war criminals could stir trouble in an insecure country, frighten witnesses, lead to unfair self-incrimination or cause intense anxiety to defendants from rival factions who had not been asked to testify. (Would Hermann Göring have been allowed to broadcast to the German nation a few weeks before his trial?) In the interests of free speech and to provide as much help as possible to the TRC, the court was prepared to allow detainees to make written statements to the commissioners, who could visit them in prison for further elucidation. Defendants who had hoped to address their supporters on television declined this compromise.[45]

In transitional periods, truth commissions may be the only option for weak governments. In this context, they were common in South America in the 1980s and 1990s. They were usually preceded by blanket amnesties and were not permitted to 'name names' of perpetrators – not to avoid prejudice to trials (which were not in prospect) but to avoid political embarrassment. The reports none the less shed some light on human rights abuses – in the case of *Nunca Más* in Argentina (see below), very great light. They achieved a degree of truth, but without justice and in many cases without reconciliation – hence the later public demands in such countries to vacate the amnesties and prosecute the perpetrators. In Bolivia, for example, a National Commission of Inquiry into Disappearances was set up within days of the restoration of democracy in 1982. It produced no report and inspired no prosecutions, to the palpable relief of a government which had starved it of funds.[46]

After the restoration of democracy in Chile in 1990, a Commission for Truth and Reconciliation was established under Senator Rettig. It was not permitted to name individuals responsible for the crimes or to recommend sanctions. Its report analysed several thousand disappearances, but the new government dared not lift a finger against assassins who remained in high positions in (or in honourable retirement from) the armed forces. Pinochet personally described the TRC report as 'unpardonable' and announced that the 'army certainly sees no reason to ask pardon for having fulfilled its patriotic duty'.

A Commission on the Truth for El Salvador was established in 1991, headed by three respected international jurists, and was staffed and financed by the United Nations. It managed to identify forty individuals connected to the armed forces who had been involved in committing crimes against humanity, and its forensic scientists confounded a cover-up by the Reagan administration by proving that a massacre of almost a thousand villagers, including hundreds of children, had taken place at El Mozote.[47] The Commission found so much corruption, complacency and bias in the judges of the Supreme Court that it called on them all to retire (an invitation to which the Court responded by declaring the Commission 'subversive of the Constitution').[48] It named René Ponce as the general who ordered an élite military unit to kill six Jesuit priests (one the rector of the Central American University, another the head of its Human Rights Institute). But Ponce had played a vital part in negotiating a peace settlement between the military and the FMLN: his retirement (there was never any prospect of his prosecution) was only achieved by the new Clinton administration threatening to withhold $11 million in aid after he had been exposed. The TRC report was rejected by the Salvadorean president because it 'did not respond to the wishes of the majority of Salvadoreans who seek to forgive and forget everything having to do with that very sorrowful past'. The government immediately granted a comprehensive amnesty for all political crimes, including El Mozote and the Jesuit murders. In 1995, the corrupt Supreme Court judges declared this blanket amnesty to be valid, although it could never now prevail in any international court.

When the Argentinian military skulked in shame from government after defeat in the Falklands War in 1983, new civilian president Raúl Alfonsín had no hesitation in annulling the amnesty they had bestowed on themselves. He set up a Commission on the Disappeared, and its report, *Nunca Más (Never Again)*, became a national bestseller. This commission – the most successful of its kind in Latin America – amassed evidence which led to prosecutions and prison sentences against the five most senior members of the military junta. But when the prosecutors indicted some middle-ranking soldiers and police who had manned the 'Dirty War' detention centres and participated in the killing of at least 9,000 of the disappeared, this triggered an army revolt. In 1987, its junior officers staged a series of rebellions against the government, which Alfonsín could only dissipate by agreeing to end the trials. He refused to give any permanent pardons – that was the craven act of his Perónist successor, Carlos Menem, who pardoned ex-President Videla and the other convicted leaders on the familiar ground of 'national reconciliation'. Argentina is now making some efforts to confront its past by prosecuting men like Jorge Acosta, head of the Navy Mechanics School in Buenos Aires where some 300 mothers were murdered after the births of their children, subsequently stolen for adoption by loyal army families, and in 2012 Videla was at last sentenced to prison for ordering these disappearances after the court found a way around this amnesty.

What emerges from recent South American legal and political history is that the process of transition from military dictatorship to popular rule is not a good time for local courts to punish crimes against humanity: 'transitional justice' is a contradiction in terms. Democracy may be a necessary, but certainly not a sufficient, condition for retribution. In Argentina, for example, the colonel who led the rebellion against the Alfonsín government because it was threatening to put military torturers on trial formed a political party which had striking electoral success, and one general responsible for the murder of many prisoners enjoyed widespread support as a political candidate (he was narrowly beaten by a Perónist pop singer).[49] There is always some popular support for human rights violations: they are measures taken against persons suspected of subversion, and as Sábato reminds us in his prologue to *Nunca Más*, even innocent suspects 'must have been up to something' in the eyes of the public. Hitler's willing executioners, although not so many as Goldhagen would have us believe, were legion. In Latin America the military remained powerful, if not in power: many of the worst offenders were, precisely for that reason, crucial to peace agreements and democratic transition. They were unrepentant, and still capable of staging a coup if provoked.

But what the history of 'transitional justice' – or the lack of it – in Latin America demonstrates in the longer term is that the emergence of any measure of truth is not a basis for reconciliation. Quite the contrary, since revelation of the details of official depravity only makes the demands for retribution by victims and their sympathizers more compelling. Time wounds all heels: democratic governments become more confident, prosecutors more daring, the public more inclined to do something about old men whose behaviour in uniform has brought their country international contempt. Thus it has proved in Argentina, after a retired navy officer, Adolfo Scilingo, confessed in 1995 to his junta days of throwing political prisoners out of aeroplanes over the Atlantic. General Martin Balza, the new army chief, refuting all the 'national reconciliation' rhetoric of frightened presidents, announced that he was in favour of 'initiating a painful dialogue about the past that was never sustained and that acts like a ghost within the collective consciousness of the country, always returning from the shadows where it occasionally hides'.[50] It was then discovered that the amnesty did not cover the crime of child-stealing, so prosecutors began preparing cases against the generals involved in 'disappearing' pregnant women like Liliana Pereyra, whose babies were handed over to military families. The former dictator, Jorge Videla, pardoned by Menem in 1990, was re-arrested for this crime (which had not been included in the previous amnesty) in 1998.

Guatemala has exposed the weakness of TRCs in a country where rulers do not wish to hear whatever truth it can stumble across. Its commission had no power to search or subpoena or even 'name names' or sit in public. Although its report was devastating (the government was accused of directing the army to engage in genocidal violence against the Mayan people – deaths were estimated at 200,000) no action has been taken against perpetrators (they are covered by amnesty laws) and none of the recommendations have been adopted. The establishment of a truth commission served only to relieve the government of Alfonso Portillo from international pressure to punish human rights abusers, the worst of whom was his father-in-law, General Rios Montt, the country's former dictator who was not charged with any of his notorious crimes until 2012.[51] The lesson has gone unlearnt in Latin America: as recently as November 2011 Brazil finally created a commission to investigate all the killings and the torture inflicted during military rule (1964–85). The government of Dilma Rousseff refused, however, to repeal the amnesty law, which means that the guilty generals will not be held to account.

In principle, of course, forgiveness is the prerogative of the victims, not of the majority of members of the society in which they happen to live, let alone of any government. As crimes against humanity leave few victims living, it may be said that forgiveness is the prerogative of humanity, which generally extends it only by way of lighter sentence after a confession, the sincerity of which is supported by a willingness to give evidence in court against accomplices.

This is to some extent consonant with the approach of the Commission of Truth and Reconciliation established in 1995 in South Africa with powers (not vouchsafed to the less successful commissions) of search and seizure and Court-backed subpoenas. It offered immunity from prosecution only to political criminals prepared to earn it by testifying fully and frankly, and if necessary testifying as prosecution witnesses at subsequent trials. This is not so much an amnesty as a form of plea-bargaining, familiar for centuries in most common-law countries: conspirators may turn informers, acknowledge their guilt and earn their pardon by convicting their associates. It is not a perfect system, because it provides informers with an incentive to make false allegations. None the less, it has proved an essential weapon in ordinary law enforcement and the South African Supreme Court defended truth commission immunities for witnesses on the pragmatic basis that survivors would prefer to grieve over the truth than over prosecutions which failed for lack of evidence. In the *Azanian People's Organization Case* it upheld its constitutionality on the basis that it was not a Pinochet-style immunity given by the state to cover up its own crimes, but was more a Lincoln-style pardon to restore the tranquillity of a state which had been at war with itself.[52] Bishop Tutu, while waxing over-lyrically about the virtues of forgiveness, has portrayed his South African exercise as a negotiated part of a peace settlement and has been anxious to distinguish it from the kind of amnesties insisted upon by juntas in Latin America as a condition of giving up power, or granted by dictators to themselves.[53] The poor record of truth commissions in South America emphasizes the distinction, and the danger of promoting them as alternatives to trials. The real success of South Africa's commission was achieved through its plea-bargaining powers, which made it possible to emulate one of the values of criminal proceedings, namely the presentation of evidence that proves to doubters and to later generations that what happened did happen. TRCs can be useful additions, but not alternatives, to the trial process.[54]

In the case of crimes against humanity, however, it sticks in the craw to allow torturers and assassins to walk entirely free as a reward for talking to a truth commission. Bishop Tutu's pleas for forgiveness sounded hollow to Steve Biko's widow, and ridiculous to Marius Schoon, an anti-apartheid activist whose wife and six-year-old daughter were blown apart by a letter bomb sent on the direction of notorious double agent Craig Williamson. As Schoon put it:

There can be no indemnity, no forgiveness, without remorse. We see no signs of Craig being sorry. I mean, are we going to have a situation where people can qualify for indemnity just by saying, as if they were reeling off a grocery list, 'I killed this one and poisoned that one and beat the shit out of the third one'. It seems untenable to me, morally and philosophically.[55]

It is unacceptable that state torturers and assassins should go scot free: confessions, followed by pleas of guilty and evidence against colleagues and superiors, may earn pardons or light sentences but it is absurd to believe that such crimes will be forgiven or that reconciliation with the families of victims is possible. Amnesty is always excused as an exercise in *realpolitik*, a crude accommodation which avowedly subordinates justice to political expediency. What cannot be countenanced is any attempt to dress up expediency *as* justice, which is one mistake Bishop Tutu's truth commission made, by adopting 'principles' drawn up by Professor Nørgaard to determine whether an act of violence is 'political' (and hence indemnifiable). These so-called 'principles' were largely derived from the criteria once used in extradition law, and so are not directly relevant to the question of whether a particular criminal deserves amnesty. What makes the Nørgaard–Tutu criteria particularly unattractive is that they pardon crimes against humanity on grounds that should never amount to a defence, e.g. because they were committed under superior orders or for a political master. It angered the white and Afrikaans communities when judges on the Commission's amnesty committee granted blanket pardons to thirty-seven ANC leaders (including Thabo Mbeki) without requiring disclosure and then amnestied necklace killers and the bombers who had massacred a church congregation at prayer. The black community was similarly outraged by amnesties granted to Dirk Coetzee, commander of the Vlakplaas secret killing unit, and other senior police torturers, for no better 'political' reason than that they had carried out orders to murder Griffiths Mxenge, a defence lawyer who had 'become a thorn in their flesh by enabling persons charged with political offences to obtain the protection of the courts. . . they relied on their superiors to have accurately and fairly considered the question as to whether assassination was necessary'.[56] Gillian Slovo, daughter of the ANC's Joe Slovo, probably spoke for most victims' relatives after hearing Craig Williamson testify that 'it made absolutely no difference to me' that the letter bomb he sent to her father killed instead her mother, the academic Ruth First. 'I thought that coming here would give me some sense of closure. But I have been shaken in that belief . . . I cannot believe that my mother, not even in their terms, was a legitimate target.' Bishop Tutu had no warrant for imputing his own brand of forgiveness to those entitled not to forgive.

None the less, the South African commission succeeded where the

South American commissions failed, in identifying criminals and either shaming them (if they testified) or recommending their prosecution (if they did not apply for amnesty or did not receive it or failed to tell the truth). Its report, published in October 1998, did expose the most shocking crimes against humanity (including the unrepentant Dr Basson's scientific experiments to create bacteria that would kill only blacks and a vaccine to make black women sterile) and demonstrated the complicity of P. W. Botha and some ministers in approving the bombings of cinemas and the headquarters of the Council of Churches. It also obtained evidence of Winnie Mandela's vicious penchant for murder and torture. That it produced a lot of truth but not much reconciliation is shown by the numerous legal actions it attracted, including writs from the ANC (which tried to injunct the report), Chief Buthelezi, F. W. de Klerk and Steve Biko's widow. It did, however, contribute to today's climate where few hanker after the good old apartheid days.

Bishop Tutu's truth commission sat in public, 'named names' and had its conclusions fully reported. The 1985 commission of inquiry into the Matabeleland atrocities in Zimbabwe has still not been published, because the government claims it will 'open old wounds'. The point, of course, is that wounds of this kind – army killings of several thousand people – do not close without the application of some balm of retribution, or at least compensation. At Prime Minister Mugabe's hands, the families have received nothing, the main army murderers have been promoted, and the report which fastens guilt upon them remains suppressed. A more satisfactory approach was taken by the democratic government of Malawi which in 1991 succeeded the tyrant Hastings Banda. It established a commission of inquiry into the deaths of four cabinet ministers, which he had attributed to a road accident. The commission reported that they had been murdered at Banda's instigation, and at subsequent trials some of the Special Branch killers confessed their crimes and offered testimonies against their accomplices in return for short prison sentences. Banda was then accorded the fair trial that he had denied so many of his own citizens – so fair, in fact, that the case was heard by a jury of his own tribespeople, who acquitted him on evidence that pointed compellingly to his guilt. But overall justice was done, in that historical truth was told and Banda was, at the age of ninety-six, finally disgraced and prosecuted.

The continual problem for truth commissions is to find impartial commissioners. Just as local judges are inevitably affected with hostility to dictators under whose rule they and their families have suffered, so local lawyers, prelates, historians and other worthies will be – and will, if appointed by a new government, be seen to be – biased against the *ancien régime*. In 2010 the Supreme Court of the Philippines actually struck down a law establishing a truth commission, ruling that it violated the constitution by targeting only one side of politics. In Kenya the 2009 Truth Justice and Reconciliation Commission spent its first year in stasis because of a public outcry against its chairman, who had himself been accused of culpability for an atrocity.

The truth commission set up by the Sri Lankan government had no distinguished international figures among its members and was overconcerned in its report to find that all the human rights abuses against the Tamils – which it could hardly deny – were committed by rogue elements of the army, and not by any senior officer or government figure. The Liberian Truth and Reconciliation Commission's report in 2009 was an horrific document recounting murder, torture, rape by rebel commanders and their responsibility for the vilest abuse of children – including cooking and then serving their body parts. The Commission was inaugurated with great fanfare by Liberia's President, Ellen Johnson Sirleaf, despite which it found her to be complicit in the abuses by Charles Taylor, in whose government she had served. It recommended that she be barred from public office, together with other politicians active in the war. Sirleaf responded by announcing that she would run for re-election. She was successful and the Supreme court duly found the recommendation unconstitutional (an otiose finding, since it was merely a recommendation).

An Independent Commission of Inquiry was set up by the King of Bahrain in July 2011 to investigate human rights abuses which took place in February/March of that year, when some protesters were killed and many were tortured and unlawfully detained by the police and by an army bolstered by Saudi tanks. The five commissioners, chaired by

Professor Cherif Bassiouni, were all respected foreign experts and were provided with the funds to hire a large investigative staff. They were given access to government departments and servants, and to the sites where abuses had taken place. Their 500-page report, produced in five months, is a model of its kind, pulling no punches in its account of torture and illegal detention, and recommending sensible ways to end the culture of impunity which had come about through failures in both the prosecution department and the judiciary. As a result of the report, several thousand detainees were released and a number of retrials ordered in civil courts of cases which had been unfairly tried in military courts.

Bahrain's international image was burnished by the King's apparent conversion to human rights (Formula One, which cancelled its Grand Prix there in 2011, was brought back on track in 2012). However, he has quite cleverly used the Truth Commission as a means of promoting his openness to the world, and of ensuring the protesters are better treated, without giving them what they want, which is democracy. The Commission can be criticized on this score: its recommendations for improvements in criminal procedure are first rate, but it made none in respect of the autocratic government, and made no mention of democracy as a human right. Nor did it expose the reason for the judiciary's lack of independence, namely the regime's appointment to it of members and retainers of the royal family. To this extent it failed the Arab Spring. The people will only be reconciled to the royal family if it takes the further steps to share power: current predictions are that, despite the legal quality of the Commission's report, the country faces prolonged low-intensity unrest.[57]

The experience of Latin American and African countries in the hard-won transition from dictatorship to democracy is very different from that of eastern Europe, where repressive communist regimes collapsed rapidly at the end of the 1980s. Communism subjected its citizens to the scrutiny of secret policemen and their networks of informants, to political trials and oppressive prison sentences: dissidents were denied many of the freedoms guaranteed by human rights conventions. There was a massive institutional invasion of privacy: in

East Germany, the Stasi kept files on six million – one in three – citizens. It even monitored the angle of television antennae, arresting citizens who had turned their aerials to the West.[58] In general, however, these systematic human rights violations were committed under cover of law and did not often extend to genocide, torture, disappearances or other measures extreme enough to warrant the description of crimes against humanity. So 'settling accounts with communism' cannot be compared with settling accounts with torturers in uniform: the former must, in Václav Havel's phrase, be settled in the pages of history books (and in movies like *The Lives of Others*); the latter, eventually, in the criminal courts. In eastern Europe, commissions have had a different and difficult truth to tell: not of massacre, but of friends and relations who turned informants; of dissidents who betrayed their colleagues and apparatchik judges and prosecutors who decided cases according to political commands. The purging process (inappropriately known in Czechoslovakia as 'lustration') has undoubtedly removed dishonest timeservers from political and public life, at the expense of some unfair accusations based on unreliable records made by secret policemen prone to exaggerate or even fictionalize their dealings with 'informants' in order to claim credit or expenses. Most Eastern-bloc countries were reluctant to allow unrestricted access to secret-police files, fearing for the consequences when citizens discovered how their neighbours and even their children had spied on them. Only East Germany has had the courage to face the whole truth about its time as Stasiland.

There are, however, several significant post-communist precedents. In 1993, the Hungarian Constitutional Court paved the way to prosecuting the persons responsible for mass shootings of innocent civilians during the 1956 uprising, on the basis that this was a crime against humanity under international law (pursuant to the Nuremberg Charter and common Article 3 of the Geneva Conventions) and so statutes of limitation could apply no time bars. Domestic law, the court ruled, must secure the enforcement of 'universally accepted rules of international law'.[59] In 1999, trials were held in Budapest of elderly ex-army officers accused of firing into unarmed crowds protesting against the Soviet invasion. In former East Germany, appellate courts have used international human rights law to justify the conviction and sentencing of soldiers and senior politicians responsible for the slaying of unarmed civilians as they endeavoured to flee across the Berlin Wall. These homicides (there were over 200 killings at the border between 1961 and 1989) inexcusably breached the right to life and the right to leave a country (Articles 6(1) and 12(2) of the Civil Covenant). It followed that orders to shoot to kill unarmed fugitives were unlawful, as even indoctrinated and 'intellectually simpleminded' border guards must have realized: their convictions have been approved by the European Court of Human Rights. The last GDR leader, Egon Krenz, was jailed in 1999 for six and a half years.[60] His defiant claim of 'victor's justice' (his Leipzig appeal judges were from West Germany) fell on deaf ears. This is an important contribution to the *Yamashita* line of precedents for prosecuting commanders and political decision-makers: their liability as accessories to manslaughter was fixed by their knowledge that the orders violated internationally protected rights and by proof that they intended that those unlawful orders should be routinely carried out. The proceedings against Erich Honecker, the former East German leader, were abandoned, however, because of his terminal illness.

No such mercy was extended in Romania to President Ceauşescu and his wife Elena, who were executed during the revolution after a short and farcical trial in which their appointed defence lawyer declared them guilty of genocide. Their summary execution could have been justified on grounds of necessity, since some units of the Securitate (their secret police) would otherwise have rallied against the people, causing extensive loss of life. The mistake was to hold a mock trial, which breached every principle of fairness and demeaned all who participated (the judge, who could not live with his conscience, committed suicide soon afterwards). Some of Ceauşescu's henchmen were rushed into televised show trials, appearing with heads shaven and in striped prison pyjamas to confess to complicity in genocide – the whole proceedings smacked of an update of the Moscow trials. Meanwhile, in Moscow the victims of those trials were all 'rehabilitated' in the course of *Glasnost*, and Russia's transition to democracy was marked more by desecration of statues of old

Bolsheviks than by trials of Stalin's willing executioners. Stalin, in his embalmed self the perpetrator of more crimes against humanity than anyone else in this or any other century, has been removed from public display beside the body of Lenin. But he is not dishonoured in death: his remains were cremated and sealed respectfully in the Kremlin Wall, close by the ashes of Andrei Vyshinsky, the producer of his show trials who had called upon the Nuremberg judges to drink a toast to the death of the defendants they were trying. Stalin's victims, shot without warning in the back of the head and buried in unmarked or mass graves, may have been posthumously rehabilitated and remembered, but they have not been avenged.

THE CASE FOR RETRIBUTION

There is now little dispute in Europe about the need to bring Nazi war criminals and their collaborators to justice: their crimes, ironically, seem to gain in magnitude as they recede in time. Not a single voice was raised to protest against the conviction of 83-year-old Anthony Sowaniuk, who had shot Jews as if they were wild geese in the swamps of Latvia, before working happily for a half century as a guard on British Rail. Unlike the Demjanjuk trial in Israel, his Old Bailey proceedings were demonstrably fair and the evidence, despite the passage of time, was overwhelming. The European Court of Human Rights firmly rejected his complaint that fifty years on he could not receive a fair trial. It applied both the 1968 UN Convention and the 1974 European Convention on non-applicability of statutory limitations to war crimes and crimes against humanity. Only death, or senile dementia, can extinguish liability.[61] The same court in 2001 deployed the non-derogable 'right to life' as the basis for a duty on states to investigate and (where appropriate) to prosecute killings suspected to have been carried out by state agents.[62] This line of authority supports the existence of an international law duty to prosecute crimes against humanity, however long ago they were committed.

More difficult, but much more significant, have been the war crimes trials which have forced countries to confront their Nazi past.

Croatia bowed to pressure from the European Union over the commandant of its worst concentration camp. In 1999, at the age of seventy-eight, Dinko Šakić was sentenced to twenty years for killing 2,000 Jews and Serbs, some of whom he personally bludgeoned to death with sledgehammers.[63] In France Maurice Papon, at eighty-nine, received a ten-year sentence for complicity in crimes against humanity – he had arranged the arrest and transportation to death camps of many Jews while he was an official of the Vichy regime. The reckoning had been stalled for many years by his friends in high places, but although France has a time limit of twenty years for the prosecution of murder, it makes an exception for crimes against humanity. The documentary evidence against Papon was devastating, although the gravity and fairness of the trial was jeopardized by the loud posturing of lawyers for victims' families who were permitted to appear as 'civil parties'. None the less, the proceedings served as a long-overdue reminder that pushers of pens can be as guilty of crimes against humanity as pushers of people into gas ovens. Papon was a functionary who signed deportation orders: his guilt was fixed by the fact that he knew that he was implementing a state policy of racial persecution, even though he had no ideological commitment to that policy. Papon was jailed for what the prosecution described as an 'office crime', because 'genocide could be abetted by the routine obedience of functionaries'.[64] His claim to have been a scapegoat was true enough, but irrelevant: he was guilty, along with many other Vichy officials who happened to evade justice.

Crimes against humanity are, by definition, unforgivable, even if the worst in Latin America were committed by devoted members of a Roman Catholic faith which offers forgiveness in return for a secret confession. Any church which can in this way become complicit in the crimes of René Ponce, who ordered the gunning-down of the Jesuit priests, or of Jorge Videla, who directed the theft of the babies of 300 murdered women, cannot expect others to believe its promise of damnation for sinners in some afterlife. Nor can nervous politicians be credited in their claim that amnesties will 'secure the stability of democracy' or 'promote national reconciliation'. This is just an excuse for cowardice or inaction: as Hannah Arendt has noted, 'men are unable to forgive what they cannot punish'. International law is entitled to ignore the special pleading of the prelates and the politicians, who speculatively invite us to leave these crimes respectively to God or to history, and insist that they be left to prosecutors, as soon as it is safe to arrest the suspects. That is the position taken by the 1968 Convention on the Non-Applicability of Statutory Limitations to War Crimes and Crimes against Humanity, which has been said (by the French courts in the *Barbie Case*) to reflect customary international law in requiring some retribution for these classes of crime, no matter how long it may take. The duty, it is suggested, is not actually to punish, but only to prosecute: the outcome of a fair trial, no matter how compelling the evidence, can never be pre-ordained. A serious prosecution discharges the duty to victims, forces the perpetrator to explain or expiate, and allows some truth to be told in public proceedings. Prosecution is not revenge, because it does not necessarily entail punishment: fair trials sometimes acquit the guilty. It is justice by the very due process that torturers and death squads deny to their victims.

The duty to prosecute the perpetrators of crimes against humanity will also serve the right in their victims' families to truth and to compensation. As the Inter-American Commission put it, surveying the closed ranks of army death squads throughout Latin America, 'every society has the inalienable right to know the truth about past events, as well as the motives and circumstances in which aberrant crimes came to be committed, in order to prevent repetition of such acts in the future';[65] more simply, families have the right to know the fate of their members. Torture victims or, in the event of their death under torture, their dependants deserve some recompense for pain and suffering, and anyone who has been the victim of unlawful arrest and detention must be accorded an enforceable right to compensation, under Civil Covenant Article 9(5). TRC reports cannot order compensation, although they can recommend payments and even psychiatric assistance to victims of torture. (The Rettig Committee in Chile went so far as to propose psychological care for the torturers themselves.) Where prosecution is a political impossibility, commissions of inquiry can bring benefits if they recommend for violators the alternatives of disqualification from public office or dishonourable discharge from police or army.

Does the duty to prosecute extend to trying *in absentia* defendants who are in hiding or beyond the jurisdiction? If their escape is made prior to the commencement of proceedings, there is nothing (short of extradition requests) which can properly be done – such as in the 1979 trial *in absentia* of Pol Pot and Ieng Sary, which presented overwhelming evidence of their guilt, but so lacked due process (the defendants were safely across the border in Thailand) that it had little impact. The absurd sentence of death *in absentia* (why not execution *in absentia*, as well?) made the proceedings a mockery. An independent international inquiry, establishing facts rather than purporting to punish, would have had much more credibility. The position is different if defendants absent themselves in the course of proceedings, or formally request to be excused. The Bolivian Supreme Court was right to uphold the conviction of General García Meza, who went into hiding only after his initial testimony to the court and who had his case presented by lawyers appointed by the government to do their best for him. Similarly, the trial of Malawi's Dr Hastings Banda cannot be criticized on this score, since his absence was at his own request: he informed the court that he 'would rather die than face cross-examination' and was permitted to remain at home, a few miles away, while his imported QC challenged the evidence against him. There can be no objection to such a trial if the defendant deliberately waives his right to be present.

Undoubtedly the greatest obstacle to fair trial, whether in a society transiting from dictatorship to democracy or one in which the old repressive order has suddenly collapsed, is corruption in the judiciary and weakness of the local legal profession. One depressingly familiar feature of states in which crimes against humanity are committed is how judges connive at them by declining to investigate or hear *habeas corpus* petitions. It is difficult enough for transitional governments to reform the police and the army: invariably, they inherit judges with a vested interest in protecting the regime by which they were appointed. The failure of civil rights prosecutions in the Philippines after the fall of Marcos was largely the responsibility of that country's corrupt and incompetent judiciary. In El

Salvador, the UN-appointed truth commission explained that the reason it hesitated to recommend prosecutions was because the country's judiciary lacked integrity and had perverted justice in order to protect the death squads. The commission particularly condemned the president of the Supreme Court, Gutierrez Castro, for his attempts to stop cases arising from the El Mozote massacre: the government responded by appointing him to sit on important international judicial committees.

Diplomats, political leaders and UN officials have become notorious for cosying up to perpetrators. One of the most bizarre sights of recent times was Boutros Boutros-Ghali, recently retired as UN Secretary-General, embracing as 'an old friend' the genocidal Cambodian killer Khieu Samphan, when the latter emerged from hiding. Diplomats have been notorious for covering up crimes against humanity, both of their own and of other countries, and even when perpetrated against their own people by other countries. For example, in 2005 it came to light that the UK ambassador to Indonesia had claimed that British and Australian journalists massacred by the Indonesian army had been accidentally caught in crossfire, because he did not want to tell a truth that would embarrass the invaders and their supporters, the US government.[66] Politicians and diplomats, lawyers and judges have all been complicit in covering the trails of governments who kill: it will be necessary to develop a crime of *perverting the course of international justice* to punish those who aid and abet individuals they know to be responsible for mass murder.

If the crimes of such individuals are the most heinous of all, because they touch not only the families of victims but decent people throughout the world, then some retribution at international level is required. It is difficult to understand why states should ignore the question of punishing identifiable persons for massacres in Latin America, Africa and Asia. For them awaits no avenging Israel, no assiduous Simon Wiesenthal to track them down: they remain, many still in positions of continuing power, sheltered by unlawful pardons given under duress or by the collective guilt of societies which silently condoned crimes too monstrous for the world to forgive. Death has robbed us of the satisfaction of seeing Milošević, Foday Sankoh, Pol Pot, Hirohito, Pinochet, Honecker, Gaddafi, Amin and Tudjman behind bars, but by 2012, after the ICTY had captured all its indictees, most verdicts in Arusha and Sierra Leone had been delivered and Laurent Gbagbo, Saif Gaddafi, Ieng Sary, Nuon Chea, Karadžić and Mladić and others were awaiting or undergoing trial, nemesis was on the cards for future atrocitarians.

8

The Case of General Pinochet

Compatriots, I take leave of you. The air force is bombing the radio towers, but I will not resign. Placed in this historical timewarp, I will pay with my life for my people's loyalty, telling you that conscience will not be blindfolded for ever. They have the power, and they will dominate us, but social progress cannot be halted by criminal force. History is ours, determined by you the people. Defend but do not sacrifice yourselves. Do not let yourselves be humiliated, do not for my sake let yourselves be crushed or murdered. I have faith in the destiny of Chile, to rise above this grey and bitter moment when treason prevails. Sooner rather than later free men and women will walk our avenues full of trees to construct a better society. These are my last words. I die knowing that there will come a moral law to punish the felony and the cowardice and the treason.

Thus did Dr Salvador Allende, the elected head of the state of Chile, bid a broadcast farewell to his people on 11 September 1973 as war planes circled to bomb the presidential palace. That day's putsch was joined by General Pinochet in his role as commander-in-chief of the armed forces: he unlawfully commanded his forces to overthrow the democratic government and to murder its most prominent supporters, whether they resisted or not. The conspiracy, soon led by Pinochet, envisaged not only these extrajudicial executions but the capture of thousands of potential opponents and their vicious suffering at centres which were already designated and equipped with electrodes and iron beds (for 'the grill') and other torture paraphernalia. About 4,000 people were 'disappeared' over the next few years, and tens of thousands were processed through the torture centres as part of a preconceived plan to break the spirit of opposition to military rule and to spread terror among potential dissidents. The torture always involved infliction of physical pain by electric shocks, and in many cases it included degradation of the human personality through rape and bestiality, and ritual humiliation in front of family and friends. Pinochet appointed himself president of a military junta, and in due course styled himself 'Supreme Chief of the Nation' and then 'President of the Republic'. He ruled in this capacity, as self-appointed head of state, until 1990.

What sets Pinochet's behaviour so high on any scale of wickedness was his systematic and institutionalized use of torture as a device to keep himself in power by terrifying and demoralizing potential opposition from unarmed and unorganized civilians. The rituals of the torture centres were intended to send horrific whispers throughout the populace: this was the punishment for thinking and speaking ill of the regime. For this reason, many were eventually released, broken in body and spirit, to tell of the disappearance of those who had been killed and secretly buried. What fixes Pinochet with personal responsibility is that he set up an organization – DINA – within the military to supervise the operations of the torture centres under the directorship of Colonel Manuel Contreras, who reported daily and directly to him.[1] Pinochet extended the torture conspiracy to Chilean subversives abroad, targeting potential victims in Spain and Italy.

After a meeting in 1976 with Henry Kissinger, who sympathized with his complaints about the activities of Orlando Letelier, Allende's popular ambassador to the US, Pinochet arranged Letelier's assassination: the car bomb, detonated in Washington, also took the life of his driver, a US citizen. Pinochet exported his revolution through Operation Condor – a grandiose plan to rid Latin America of left-wingers, which involved co-operation with other military juntas, most enthusiastically that of Argentina. But since Pinochet's strategy necessarily involved the release of some victims to spread alarm, the evidence quickly mounted and in 1975 became the subject of debates and resolutions in the UN General Assembly. There, Chile's diplomats dishonestly denied that torture had taken place, but significantly they voted for one resolution (No. 3452) which recognized the practice as an international crime.

In 1978, Pinochet granted an amnesty to 'all persons who as authors, accomplices, or accessories committed . . . criminal offences during the period of the State of Siege between 11 September 1973 and 10 March 1978', excluding only (at the insistence of the Carter administration) the Letelier car bombing. This ludicrous self-amnesty was upheld in every case by the country's pro-Pinochet judiciary (two days after the coup, its Supreme Court expressed its 'most intimate pleasure' at the new military regime) despite two rulings by the Inter-American Commission that it violated the American Convention's guarantee of an effective remedy for human rights violations.[2] After seventeen years, Pinochet made Hastings Banda's mistake of holding a referendum in the belief the people loved him or else feared him too much to vote against him: they voted instead for democracy, which he had to grant, although on terms which allowed him to appoint some senators and remain as commander-in-chief of the armed forces. On retirement from that position in 1998 Pinochet was made senator-for-life, which carried under Chilean law yet further immunity from prosecution. Although cases were brought against him that year in Santiago, the judge recognized that the immunity left him powerless to arrest the senator-for-life.[3] It was from this impregnable position in 'the Fatherland' that he sallied forth in October 1998, to have his bad back attended to by doctors in Harley Street, London W1.

AN ARREST IN HARLEY STREET

That Augusto Pinochet felt free to travel the world in 1998 was a measure of the impunity which had to this point been enjoyed in practice by tyrants, notwithstanding the accumulation of treaties under which their crimes were declared contrary to international law. Never before had a former head of state, visiting another friendly country, been held legally amenable to its criminal process. Little attention was paid when the 'Association of Progressive Prosecutors of Spain' began a private action in 1996 against Pinochet and members of the Argentinean junta, or when their action was taken over by Madrid investigating magistrate Baltasar Garzón (whose previous investigation into the Spanish state involvement in 'death squads' in the Basque country had helped to bring down the Gonzalez government). Garzón's case against Pinochet over 'Operation Condor' and DINA torture and killings of Spanish nationals began to gel when Manuel Contreras testified that DINA had followed the dictator's personal orders.[4] But Garzón was in Spain, the evidence was in Chile, and Pinochet was careful to travel only to Britain, where he was a frequent and frequently honoured visitor. He had always received red-carpet treatment: as commander-in-chief of the Chilean army he was fêted by the Ministry of Defence in the hope he would purchase British arms. These previous visits had been open and uneventful, even when he dined at the gastronomic hub of London's liberal intelligentsia, the River Café: its proprietress, Ms Ruthie Rogers (wife of the architect who designed the European Court of Human Rights), was so stomach-churned at the sight of his name on the gold card print-out that she donated the cost of his meal to Amnesty International. In October 1998 he did not even bother to take the elementary precaution of obtaining a diplomatic visa: he was, so he thought, clad in the impregnable armour of state sovereignty, which had for centuries shielded every tyrant against legal attack. On arrival at Heathrow Airport, Senator and Mrs Pinochet were duly met by representatives of the UK's Foreign Office, who ushered them to the Hounslow Suite, a VIP room hired for their comfort while FO lackeys went to collect their bags and have their passports stamped. The ageing mass murderer later took tea (I am reliably informed it was whisky) with his good friend Lady Thatcher and then went into the private clinic.

It was then that the *Guardian* reported Pinochet's presence in London. Under the headline 'A Murderer Among Us', the paper's Latin American veteran Hugh O'Shaughnessy tongue-in-cheekily reported, 'there is a foreign terrorist in our midst who is hiding somewhere in London . . . If you are a patient in the London Clinic, be particularly alert. Some people say General Augusto Pinochet Ugarte is holed up there for treatment.'⁵ This tipped off magistrate Garzón, who through the Spanish embassy made a request for Pinochet's arrest under the European Convention on Extradition by which Continental countries agree to surrender persons wanted for serious criminal offences. The post-operative Pinochet became nervous and prepared to flee on the next plane, scheduled to depart for Chile at 7 a.m. on Saturday 17 October. On 16 October, Garzón obtained a warrant in Spain for Pinochet's arrest: it was rushed to London where late that evening Scotland Yard anti-terrorist officers moved in to surround the clinic and its recumbent torturer, just a few hours before his flight. This arrest, one of Scotland Yard's finest operations, was greeted at first with astonishment and even outrage: Lady Thatcher condemned the inhumanity of the police, disturbing the rest of a 'sick and frail old man'. The Chief Justice refused the Spanish government (represented by the Crown Prosecution Service) an adjournment to prepare its case, and after a two-day hearing pronounced it plain that an ex-head of state had sovereign immunity for every crime he committed in exercising the functions of office, no matter how heinous. The argument that this immunity did not cover torture and other crimes which are contrary to international law had 'some attraction', said the Chief Justice, but 'where is one to draw the line?' Crimes against humanity were committed by heads of state pursuant to their official functions, said another judge, because 'history shows that it has indeed on occasions been state policy to exterminate or oppress particular groups'.⁶ General Pinochet was granted *habeas corpus*, but was ordered to stay in the clinic to recuperate from his operation and his law suit pending a prosecution appeal.

The *Pinochet Case* proceeded directly to Britain's highest court, the House of Lords. Amnesty International and Humans Rights Watch, concerned that developments in international law had not been appreciated in the lower court, were given leave to intervene in the action in support of the prosecution. After hearing argument for six days and deliberating for two weeks, the judges announced their decision, standing at the dispatch box at the House of Lords and delivering a pithy summary of their opinion. It was an event televised throughout the world and it had the impact of a penalty shoot-out, as the first two judges held for Pinochet but the next two levelled the score at 2–2. An authentic 'Grotian moment' came when the last judge, Lord Hoffman, indicated his agreement with the reasoning of Lord Nicholls, who favoured Pinochet's extradition. In the square outside Parliament, a mass of demonstrators – many of them torture victims – exploded into cheers and tears. International law would never be the same again: the basis of the majority decision was that sovereign immunity applied only to sovereigns who were exercising *legitimate* state functions and by no stretch of the imagination could widespread torture be regarded as legitimate conduct by anyone, let alone a head of state.

It followed that the doctrine of sovereign immunity did not bar Pinochet's extradition to stand trial in Spain, if the Home Secretary decided in the exercise of his discretion that to do so would be nei- ther unjust nor oppressive. The spotlight swung from the legal to the political arena as Home Secretary Jack Straw was showered with demands that he should show 'compassion' for an old man and respect for the state sovereignty of Chile by sending its former ruler back where he belonged, where his impunity was said to be part of the deal for 'national reconciliation'. The Chilean government made loud diplomatic noises that refusal to return the Senator would be to insult its sovereign dignity. In the end, Mr Straw played a scrupu- lously straight bat, finding no reason not to let the law take its course. So it came to pass that on 11 December 1998, fifty years almost to the day after the Universal Declaration, a man who had done much to destroy its promises finally stood in the dock of a top-security court in London.

A few days later, however, another panel of law lords was per- suaded that Lord Hoffmann should not have sat because he had helped to fundraise for Amnesty International. On the grounds, therefore, that justice had not been seen to be done, Pinochet was entitled to a fresh hearing before a court comprising seven judges who had never manifested support for human rights by connections with Amnesty.[7] Their 6–1 judgment on 24 March 1999 proved his- toric: they held that an international law prohibition which had achieved *jus cogens* status, such as the rule against torture committed systematically for policy reasons (i.e. a crime against humanity) dissolved the sovereign immunity which customery law granted to former officials and heads of state. However, a quirk of statutory extradition law – the 'double criminality' principle that Britain could not extradite for a crime it could not itself punish at the time it was committed – meant that Pinochet could be sent to Spain only for crimes committed since 1988, when Britain introduced extra-territorial torture as an offence in its own law. Since his conspiracy to use torture to maintain power lasted until 1990, Pinochet could not hide behind the shield of Chile's immunity in respect of his last two years as dictator. In due course, the indefatigable Garzón uncovered thirty more cases of torture in 1988–9 for which Pinochet could be held responsible, and on 8 October 1999 the Bow Street magistrate ordered his extradition to Spain.

Terrified of facing trial, Pinochet launched an appeal, but shortly before it was due to be heard, medical experts pronounced him unfit for trial due to brain damage caused by a stroke, whereupon the Home Secretary extended to Pinochet a compassion notably denied to victims of his own secret police, and he fled back to Chile. There, he underwent what seemed the most miraculous recovery since Lazarus, but when Chilean courts (shamed by the House of Lords) found ways around his various immunities, he lapsed back into a certified state of dementia for several years, until lured by US television to give a coherent interview describing himself as an 'angel of democracy'. A judge thereupon declared him fit to stand trial for authorizing Operation Condor, and in August 2004 the Supreme Court stripped him of immunity. By the time he turned ninety, his twilight years were disturbed not only by fleeting ghosts of his victims, but by new evidence of tax fraud and money laundering, which lost him much of his earlier support. In 2005 the whirligig of time brought to the presidency of Chile Michelle Bachelet, once a medical student tortured at Villa Grimaldi after her father, a loyal air force general, had died from torture ordered by Pinochet after his coup.

Meanwhile, the *Pinochet Case* had come to crystallize the legal and political problems of accountability for crimes against humanity. It was the potency, in international law, of that concept which finally found the Achilles heel in the armour of state sovereignty, that organizing principle of international affairs which is based on the fiction of the state as an entity that can do no wrong. Governments may come and go, with more or less barbarity, led by kings or by generals or by demagogues, but the shell of statehood remains impregnable: there must be no intervention in the internal affairs of 'the state', so the theory goes, even if it is run by Idi Amin or Adolf Hitler. Its ambassadors and diplomats must carry with them the shield of immunity from prosecution, whether for non-payment of parking fines or for mass murder. The *Pinochet Case* was momentous because – for the first time – sovereign immunity was not allowed to become sovereign impunity. The great play of sovereignty, with all its pomp and panoply, can now be seen for what it hides: a posturing troupe of human actors, who when off-stage are sometimes prone to rape the chorus.

The line that the Chief Justice could not at first locate turned out on closer examination to be plainly drawn by the concept of a crime against humanity: a crime so heinous it does not admit of human forgiveness. Pinochet's crimes in this class were no more Chile's business than they were Britain's business or Spain's business: they were committed against humanity in general because the very fact that a person can order them diminishes the human race. That such crimes override sovereignty was a doctrine first propounded by Robert Jackson at the Nuremberg trial, and remained for decades a talking point in university common rooms and post-graduate theses; however, until the Serb and Croat blood feuding it had no practical application other than as a legal lasso for old Nazis like Eichmann and Barbie. Convicting war criminals in Yugoslavia and Rwanda was no great jump: these were states in the process of dissolution, their armour of sovereignty cracked in the course of their disintegration. Apparently helpful precedents forged in the United States in respect to General Noriega and the ex-Philippines president, Ferdinand Marcos, were not true exceptions to the sovereignty rule, because the Philippines government waived its immunity over Marcos, while Noriega, never formally Panama's head of state, was prosecuted not for abusing state power but for his private criminal enterprise in running drugs. So the *Pinochet*

Case became the first and paradigm test of international human rights law, because Pinochet travelled to Britain with the sovereignty of Chile wrapped as tightly around him as the felt-collared military cloak which featured in most of his posed photographs. For that collar to be felt by Scotland Yard required twelve law lords to leap over the fiction upon which modern nation states have always based their conduct towards one another.

THE STATE IN INTERNATIONAL LAW

A state, for the purposes of international law, is an entity which possesses a defined territory, occupied by a permanent and governed population, and has a recognized capacity to enter into relations with other states.[8] Frontiers may be uncertain or disputed, but there must at least be a community occupying some territory which is subject to a nominally independent political authority, however organized. Size does not matter, hence statehood is accorded to tiny islands like Nauru (population 12,000, on ten square miles of bird-droppings) and Tuvalu, which sold its internet domain name (.tv) for US$50 million as it started to sink beneath the Pacific waves. It will be the first UN member extinguished by climate change within the next half century, and its 11,000 population will be evacuated to New Zealand (under the 'Toodle-oo Tuvalu' programme). Statehood undeservedly belongs to the sleazy casino land of Monaco (0.4 square miles and 32,000 people) and the tax havens of San Marino and Liechtenstein (twenty-four and sixty-two square miles respectively) with some 30,000 occupants, mainly accountants. These are states with equal sovereign rights and the same voting powers in the UN General Assembly as China (1.3 billion people) and India (1.2 billion). For political reasons Palestine (which fulfils the legal criteria of statehood) has been denied UN membership, as has Taiwan. Statehood is, quite wrongly, accorded to the Holy See, although the Vatican City is 0.2 square miles and is occupied only by 800 celibate Catholic bureaucrats, with no potential to propagate a population. It is really a religion which has, through historical anomalies and lack of principle, been accorded the status of a 'party' to many international treaties.[9] The behaviour of its diplomats ('papal nuncios') has often damaged the cause of human rights – as with their obsessions about abortion (they even attempted to stop NATO supplying 'morning-after' pills to victims of Serb rapes), the catastrophic consequence for the spread of HIV/AIDS in Africa of their disapproval of condoms, and their attempts to evade arrest warrants issued by the Rwanda Tribunal for Catholic priests wanted for genocide. The Pope personally urged the British government, through the high diplomatic channels which statehood accords the Vatican, to release Pinochet, as did Cardinal Ratzinger, then Pope-in-waiting, who was responsible at the time for the Vatican's cover-up of the sexual molestation of tens of thousands of children by paedophile priests.[10]

'Recognition' of statehood has been a matter of *realpolitik* rather than law, and 'puppet' or 'client' states of major powers have usually passed muster. However, an important principle was established by the world's refusal to recognize the bantustans granted nominal independence by South Africa: they were no more dependent than some Soviet puppets, but the difference was that they were emanations of apartheid, an illegal policy amounting (when imposed by violence) to a crime against humanity.[11] Although this was not the reason advanced for denying recognition to Transkei, Ciskei, Venda and 'Bop', it may be seen in retrospect as the rationale. It was certainly the UN's rationale for depriving South Africa of its long-standing mandate over Namibia (South-West Africa) and the ICJ eventually confirmed that introducing apartheid was a breach of its trust obligations.[12] There was a principle here, beginning to chip away at sovereignty, but it was not yet identified as having that effect.

One important attribute of sovereignty is jurisdiction – in other words, power – to try criminal offences and to adjudicate civil disputes. The state, through its legal system, exercises power over acts which take place on its territory or disputes which are brought there by agreement. A state's power to try an offence which has taken place abroad must be exercised with respect to international law – and, apart from treaties which make up that law, it may not exercise jurisdiction over actions by non-nationals taken outside its boundaries unless these impact adversely on its own people. When an alleged offender is found in a foreign country, it must make a formal, state-to-state request for his extradition. What will halt any of these legal processes in their tracks is a claim to 'state' (or 'sovereign') immunity asserted on behalf of a defendant, whether that defendant is the state itself (sought to be made liable in a civil action for damages) or a present or past official or diplomat on whose behalf the immunity attaching to the state itself may be asserted to stop any proceedings, be they civil or criminal. Immunities are of two kinds, and are (naturally) expressed in Latin. Absolute immunity (*ratione personae*) is bestowed upon those who embody or represent the state (i.e. on heads of state and heads of diplomatic missions) but it lasts only during their tenure of office. Ex-heads, along with agents such as generals and police chiefs and ministers, enjoy only restrictive immunity (*ratione materiae*), which covers all acts performed officially but does not include actions taken for private gratification. Whether such people can be sued or prosecuted in a foreign court depends first on the nature of their immunity, if any, and then on whether the case is barred by the 'Act of State' doctrine – a self-denying ordinance by which municipal courts refuse to sit in judgment on politically fraught questions about how foreign sovereigns have behaved within their own territory. These issues are said to be 'non-justiciable' because the court finds them too hot to handle. These doctrines are different – sovereign immunity is a limit on the court's power imposed by international law and 'Act of State' derives from the court's own nervousness about its competence to decide a foreign political issue – but both tend to be raised whenever and wherever litigation seeks to make a foreign state and its officials responsible for human rights violations.

SOVEREIGN IMMUNITY

Sovereign immunity followed in the first place from the Divine Right of kings: you could not put an infallible ruler on trial since, if you did, the verdict must always go in his favour. Machiavelli's princes were attracted by its convenience in the city states of Renaissance Europe: it reduced the need for poison and gave them some protection while travelling. It was viewed as a logical development from old heraldic principles which allowed emissaries to pass unmolested through the battlelines. The Puritans, and their men from Massachusetts, had worked out how to put Charles I on trial, but later, American courts followed the English 'Divine Right' authorities on the immunity of a head of state. Quite why a country which had fought to free itself from this very tyranny should adopt its organizing principle that the King could do no wrong is 'one of the mysteries of legal evolution'.[13] The answer is probably found in the nineteenth-century preference for positivism, reflected in the acceptance of the doctrine that international law could bind states only when they consented to be bound, and not (as the natural lawyers asserted) whenever an objective morality required some limit on their power. This latter position had been commonly accepted in the sixteenth century by natural lawyers as a necessary precondition for peaceful coexistence:[14] they never doubted a head of state's liability for war crimes.[15] Positivism denied such liability, as inconsistent with political convenience and reality. It followed that only states could be subject (and only if they agreed) to international law, which could afford no rights of any kind to individuals. These nineteenth-century positivist doctrines fashioned the wide state immunity rule, which prevailed until Nuremberg gave back to international law a principle of external moral restraints on sovereign action and a precedent for incriminating individuals.

A country's deference to 'sovereigns' – its own, and those who visit – fluctuated between according them complete exemption from the law and a 'restricted immunity', which covered them only in their public capacity and not for 'private' acts which had nothing to do with their leadership of the state. The choice between the two theories – immunity 'absolute' or 'restrictive' – became of increasing commercial importance as the twentieth century progressed, because sovereign immunity was state immunity, and states (especially those run by communist and socialist governments) began to engage in commerce through nationalized industries and wholly owned trading corporations which were legal emanations of the state. If these state traders were to enter the market on a fair and rational basis, it was obvious that 'absolute' immunity would have to be abandoned, because it did not permit them to be sued for debt or breach of contract or anything else. But for many years the English judiciary resisted any change to the absolute immunity principle suggested in 1880 by the case of the *Parlement Belge*, namely that the courts of every state must decline to exercise jurisdiction over 'the person of any sovereign or ambassador of any other State, or over the public property of any state . . . though such sovereign, ambassador or property be within its jurisdiction'.[16] Consequently, later courts refused to impound a ship owned by the Portuguese government which failed to pay up on contracts in Liverpool, even though it was engaged in non-government trading operations; and they refused to allow the Tass news agency to be sued for libel because it was a propaganda organ of the USSR.[17] In 1977, in the *Trendtex Trading Case*, the Court of Appeal at last looked at the reality: a Nigerian government bank trading in Britain was not entitled to immunity. Executive government has no need to set up a bank to trade abroad; if it decides to do so, the bank must pay its debts or else be sued on them, like any other company.[18]

This was the position which had been reached by the courts of a number of other European countries, on the basis that state commercial activity had made the absolute immunity theory an anachronism. The US State Department had been wont formally to restrict state (or sovereign) immunity, but in practice restricted it to those states and sovereigns which supported the US. The government claimed the right to 'suggest' to courts by formal letter whether immunity requests by foreign states were valid, and its determinations were made not upon objective criteria but upon current considerations of diplomacy and US interests.[19] Immunity was for friends, not foes. In 1976, Congress enacted the Foreign Sovereign Immunities Act (FSIA), which set out clear tests, hinging on the commercial nature of the activity, for deciding whether sovereign immunity was lost, and a State Immunity Act to similar effect was adopted in Britain in 1978. These two statutes were passed in the interests of certainty and of trade, but they gave sovereign immunity an inflexible, once-and-for-all meaning which drained the law of its dynamism and capacity to evolve. At that stage of its development, the doctrine was moving from an absolute jurisdictional bar to a position where interference would be permitted in respect of a state's trading activities or its ex-head's private transactions. The distinction which emerged in this period, expressed as usual in Latin, was between governmental actions (*jure imperii*), which remained immune, and acts of a private or commercial nature (*jure gestionis*), which were amenable to justice in foreign courts. The distinction was never very satisfactory in practice, and local courts attempting to apply it came to different decisions on similar subjects, such as the purchase of military equipment and the promotional activities of government tourist agencies.[20] The House of Lords split 3–2 over whether an action for breach of contract could proceed when a ship operated by an agency of the Cuban state was prohibited by that government from delivering its contracted cargo to Chile, as a political protest against the Pinochet coup.[21] It is hardly surprising that a doctrine productive of such confusion in commercial cases should prove even less satisfactory when invoked to stop torture victims from attempting to sue their tormentors.

It is only necessary to revisit the rationale of state immunity to recognize its irrelevant and ceremonial basis where crimes against humanity are concerned. The classic statement is that of Chief Justice Marshall in the 1812 US Supreme Court case of *The Schooner Exchange* v. *McFaddon*:

One sovereign being in no respect amenable to another, and being bound by obligations of the highest character not to degrade the dignity of his nation, by placing himself or its sovereign rights within the jurisdiction of another, can be supposed to enter a foreign territory only under an express licence, or in the confidence that the immunities belonging to his independent sovereign station, though not expressly stipulated, are reserved by implication, and will be extended to him.[22]

But this imputes dignity to a state which has none, whenever the shell of statehood covers a government which engages in torture and murder. It was based as well on the classic fiction that all states are equal, although in the real world some states are more equal than others, especially in their level of respect for international human rights law.

Whether or not one state has immunity from civil suit in another state will therefore depend on whether the action which causes the damage is characterized as 'sovereign' or 'non-sovereign', but this distinction is entirely unhelpful for victims of human rights abuses who seek to sue the states where they have been falsely imprisoned or tortured. First they have to squeeze their case within statutory exceptions to the immunity rule (which usually relate to a commercial context), and then they must confront the characterization problem that police or military action will be classified as 'governmental' rather than 'private'. Scott Nelson, a US citizen recruited through an American company to do engineering work in Saudi Arabia, fell at both hurdles when he tried to sue that state for the wrongful imprisonment and torture he suffered as a reprisal for publicizing the safety hazards at his workplace. Although he entered Saudi Arabia pursuant to a contract for his services, the Supreme Court ruled that he was not within the FSIA's 'commercial activities' exception (hurdle one) because his action arose from the tortious conduct of the Saudi police. He fell at hurdle two (characterization) because the conduct alleged 'boils down to abuse of the power of its police by the Saudi Government, and however monstrous such abuse undoubtedly may be, a foreign State's exercise of the power of its police has long been understood for purposes of the restrictive theory as peculiarly sovereign in nature'.[23] The solution to this problem was duly provided by another American case, namely that 'international law does not recognize an act that violates *jus cogens* as a sovereign act. A State's violation of the *jus cogens* norm prohibiting official torture therefore would not be entitled to the immunity afforded by international law.'[24] However, victims like Nelson would still fall at hurdle one: the impossibility of bringing torture within the commercial exception to the FSIA would deny them the right to sue the foreign state.

A similar result was reached in Britain under the 1978 State Immunity Act, which expressly permits actions against foreign states in relation to loans, contracts and other commercial transactions, but which is silent about human rights violations. The Court of Appeal in *Al-Adsani* v. *Government of Kuwait* said the scheme of the 1978 Act was to give full force to sovereign immunity subject to limited statutory exceptions, and since torture and human rights abuses were not listed as exceptions, Parliament must have intended to leave them out.[25] This case, decided in 1996, illustrates the damage that was done by freezing the law of sovereign immunity in 1978 legislation. These period immunity statutes permit civil actions against governments where agents are responsible for negligent loss of cargo or failure to pay debts, but not if they engage in kidnap or torture or murder. *Nelson* and *Al-Adsani* were relied upon to give Pinochet total immunity, until the House of Lords pointed out that they turn on distinctions made by statutes which apply only to civil actions, and not to crime or to extradition (which is a criminal process).

The one exception is where agents of a foreign state engage in torture or murder or other tortious acts within the territory of the forum (i.e. the state in whose courts the action is brought). It is this territorial connection which permits jurisdiction over another 'sovereign'. In 1976 General Pinochet and his henchman Manuel Contreras ordered the assassination in Washington of Chile's former ambassador Orlando Letelier: agents killed him with a car bomb which also took the life of his driver. Their relatives sued the Chilean government in the American courts, and its claim to sovereign immunity was rejected on the ground that the lawless act which caused the deaths took place in the US.[26] The relatives were awarded $5 million in damages. Anomalously, sovereign immunity reasserts itself with absolute force in respect of execution of judgment orders against diplomatic property, so the relatives could not levy execution against the Chilean government's property in the US.[27]

While the 'territorial tort' exception to sovereign immunity is welcome, it remains a logical curiosity: why should the liability of a state for an international crime depend on the happenstance of where the outrage eventually took place? The assassination of Letelier was plotted in Santiago and might have been perpetrated outside the US, in which case his relatives would have had no access to the American courts. And when the territorial connection suspended the immunity and they obtained a judgment in their favour, it sprang back to life to deny them any right to recover their damages from property and bank accounts owned in the US by the sovereign but murderous state.

The change made to sovereign immunity by statute for civil actions was necessitated by the needs of global commerce, but the settlement with global human rights had to begin with criminal offences contrary to *jus cogens* – the peremptory rules of international law, which no state or state official can ever claim a licence to breach. State practice forswears genocide and torture and extrajudicial execution, and consequently gives such international crimes the status of *jus cogens*, which in turn means that each state has an *erga omnes* obligation to the international community of states, not merely to refrain from committing such crimes but to co-operate in ensuring their investigation and punishment. Sovereign immunity, based on little more than respect for the dignity of foreign governments, must give way to a legal obligation owed to every member of the international community either to put on trial or to extradite for trial elsewhere any person reasonably accused of violating *jus cogens* by perpetrating a crime against humanity.[28] This is the principle confirmed by the 1993 Vienna Declaration and Programme of Action, which called for states to 'abrogate impunity legislation for those responsible for grave violations of human rights such as torture and prosecute such violations, thereby providing a firm basis for the rule of law'.[29] Most powerfully, of course, it was the judgment at Nuremberg which heralded the removal of the shield of state sovereignty for crimes against humanity:

Crimes against international law are committed by men, not by abstract entities, and only by punishing individuals who commit such crimes can the provisions of international law be enforced . . . It was submitted that . . . where the act in question is an act of state, those who carry it out are not personally responsible, but are protected by the doctrine of the sovereignty of the State. In the opinion of the Tribunal [this contention] must be rejected . . . The principle of international law, which under certain circumstances protects the representative of a state, cannot be applied to acts which are condemned as criminal by international law. The authors of these acts cannot shelter themselves behind their official position in order to be freed from punishment in appropriate proceedings.

And that, in a nutshell, is what did for Augusto Pinochet.

BRING ON THE DIPLOMATS

The concept of state sovereignty produces another class of immunity, namely the inviolability accorded to diplomats and to their embassy premises, and even their diplomatic bags. This privilege, recognized through almost universal subscription to the 1961 Vienna Convention on Diplomatic Relations, is based both on the function of the diplomat in representing his state (which cloaks him in its sovereignty) and on the practical convenience and international public interest of keeping open lines of communication between unfriendly states. There is a dated ring to this rationale in an age of e-mail and video conferencing, but the ICJ insists that diplomacy remains 'of cardinal importance for the maintenance of good relations between States in the interdependent world of today'.[30] This was said in 1980, when condemning the Iranian government for permitting student militants to invade the US embassy in Tehran, where they discovered evidence of spying operations which also breached the Vienna Convention. But there was nothing quite so comical during the Cold War as this Convention, in so far as it established by law 'inviolable' premises which were invariably bugged in every conceivable way by the host state, and were the control centres for spies run by the sending state.

But the Vienna Convention was drafted by thirty-four government lawyers, who were under orders to puff their diplomats up with as much sovereignty as possible: hence they bestowed it *ratione personae*, to cover absolutely every crime and misdemeanour perpetrated during foreign service, whether or not in the course of duty. This may have been appropriate at a time when diplomats were often blackmailed and honey-trapped: without total immunity they could have been framed for serious crime. But it produced the converse result that diplomats could fearlessly engage in serious crime, using their inviolable premises and diplomatic baggage for drug- and gun-running, or to assist terrorists with whom their state was in political sympathy. The most notorious abuse was by the Libyan embassy – or rather 'People's Bureau' – in St James's Square, London, which had a firing range in its basement and at least one 'diplomat' who deliberately aimed and fired at PC Yvonne Fletcher, because it was thought she was not doing enough to stop an anti-Gaddafi demonstration outside. To the chagrin of the murdered policewoman's colleagues, they were required to escort to the airport the Libyan killers, who carried the murder weapon inside one of their untouchable diplomatic bags. Each had been declared a *persona non grata*, which is the worst – indeed the only – thing that can happen to an ambassador, unless his sending state waives the immunity so as to permit his prosecution. The problem, of course, is caused by an immunity which is much wider than is necessary to protect the essential functions of a mission. At street level, abuse is reflected in the host city's unpaid parking tickets and unprosecutable offences of shoplifting: London police reckon that 40 per cent of these crimes are committed by the vehicles or wives of diplomats. (The US, plagued by more diplomats than other countries, has adopted a novel approach to unpaid parking fines: it tallies the penalties incurred by every embassy and deducts the total from that country's foreign aid.)

The Vienna Convention gives ambassadors total immunity, even in time of war, from arrest (Article 29) and from civil and criminal jurisdiction (Article 31). This lasts from the moment they take up their posts to the moment they leave the country. Thereafter, however, they shed that total immunity and wear its undergarment: immunity *ratione materiae*, covering only their actions done in the course of official duties. They may at last be sued for gambling debts and prosecuted for rape committed during their time of duty, if they can be found. This rule for ex-ambassadors has consequences for ex-heads of state – their functions are quite different, but for various reasons they tend to be assimilated in customary international law and in the relevant local statutes. (In Britain, for example, the State Immunity Act applies the incorporated Vienna Convention to 'a Sovereign or other head of State . . . as it applies to a head of a diplomatic mission'.) It follows that a head or acting head of state is totally immune from legal slings and arrows, but an ex-head, whether of state or of mission, is immune only on the restrictive basis, *ratione materiae*, for acts characterized as official functions.

There is, of course, a measure of artificiality about the very concept of 'head' of state, because different political arrangements can allocate this title to ceremonial personages like monarchs, or bestow it upon the actual heads of government. (Thus, Hitler had total immunity when he became Reich chancellor; Tojo remained but partly immune because he was 'under' a hereditary emperor.) None the less, the consequences of shedding absolute immunity can be dramatic, as King Farouk of Egypt discovered to his cost after he blithely ordered eleven expensive dresses for his queen from the Paris salon of Christian Dior. Shortly afterwards he was deposed and all his property confiscated (including the dresses). When the bill arrived he refused to pay, and when sued for the debt relied upon sovereign immunity. But in *Ex-King Farouk* v. *Dior* the Paris Court of Appeal made him pay for his private purchases: for the purposes of trade, there is nothing so ex as an ex-king.

So where does this leave ex-dictators?

American cases on head of state immunity are confused, thanks to the survival of the procedure by which the US State Department may issue a 'suggestion of immunity', which courts accept as binding, whenever attempts are made to sue the former head of a friendly state. This has been used to stop a nuisance writ against Prince Charles (an incipient head of state) while he was visiting the US,[31] and was similarly used to 'suggest' that ex-President Aristide had absolute immunity, during his exile in the US, from an action alleging his responsibility for an unlawful killing in Haiti. Rather than yield its jurisdiction up to the State Department, the court should instead have considered, on the basis that he had only restricted immunity, whether the allegation involved his official conduct during his time as president.[32]

When the Marcos family fled to Hawaii in 1986, America finally had a dictator in residence for whom nobody – except the Marcos family – wanted to suggest immunity. Ferdinand Marcos had for fifteen years in the Philippines personally directed disappearances and what was euphemistically termed 'tactical interrogation' – which meant, for some 10,000 citizens, being asked questions while they were tortured. Victims and their relatives issued an avalanche of writs, and the new Aquino government declined to claim immunity either for Marcos or for his daughter, who was additionally sued for ordering the kidnapping and killing of Archimedes Trajano, the student who had dared to ask her an embarrassing question at a public meeting. In 1992, the Federal Appeals Court held that neither Marcos nor his daughter could claim any sort of immunity: torture and arbitrary killing were contrary to international law, and were not within the legitimate scope of an official's duty.[33] This was confirmed in the class action brought by victims, on the basis that since systematic torture breached a *jus cogens* rule of international law, it could not be considered a legitimate act of state even when authorized by the head of state: 'a lawsuit against a foreign official acting outside the scope of his authority does not implicate any of the foreign diplomatic concerns involved in bringing suit against another government in the US Courts'. This is not always true, of course, but it decided in principle that a ruler loses immunity for unlawful actions breaching *jus cogens*, because they cannot be sovereign acts.[34] Marcos died mid-litigation, and finally in February 1999 his estate was ordered to pay $150 million to his victims out of loot totalling $500 million which had been recovered from his Swiss bank account.[35] The happy ending was undoubtedly conditioned by the fact that neither the friendly Philippines government nor the US felt any diplomatic embarrassment over the litigation, although the case serves as a legal precedent because the court rejected immunity on the grounds that torture could not be an official act.[36]

THE LAW TAKES ITS COURSE

Had Augusto Pinochet chosen to fly to New York rather than London, to take tea with Henry Kissinger instead of Margaret Thatcher, his fate would have been determined by politics rather than law. A 'suggestion of immunity' would surely have issued from the State

Department, to placate the friendly state of Chile. But the General came to Britain, where his dogged pursuer, magistrate Garzón, sought his extradition to Spain, to the fury of the state of Chile. In most countries, this issue would have been decided quickly and politically, in terms of alliances and trading ties and (in the seventy-three countries which still torture) out of fear of creating a precedent which might affect their rulers' retirement plans. But the British government did something which could not have been expected, and which deserves a considerable measure of praise: it let the law take its course. The course that it took – a magical mystery tour through the jungle of sovereign immunity and into the mire of extradition – could not have been predicted, but in the course of the ride international human rights acquired the quality of law: it became, in some small degree, enforceable in the courts of the world. The judges who thought it had no impact against the sovereign state dwindled, from 3–0 at the initial hearing to 2-3, and then lost the last set, 1–6. Four of those judges held that the allegation of a crime against humanity set up an overriding imperative for trial, while five (in the final majority) more narrowly allowed the Torture Convention to override claims to immunity *ratione materiae*. Thanks to the refusal of Britain's home secretary, Jack Straw, to intervene in the legal process, the *Pinochet Case* became the most important precedent for international law since Nuremberg itself, both in law and, importantly, in popular imagination.

The prosecutors levelled a general conspiracy charge accusing the general of using torture throughout his dictatorship as a means of engendering fear and keeping himself in power. Thirty other charges made specific and grisly allegations in respect of particular victims. To take some typical examples:

That you on or about 29th October 1976 being a public official, namely Commander-in-Chief of the Chilean Army, jointly with others intentionally inflicted severe pain or suffering on José Marcelino Gonzalez Malpu, by applying electric current to his genital organs, shoulders and ankles and pretending to shoot his captive naked mother in front of him, in purported performance of official duties.

That you jointly with others intentionally inflicted severe pain or suffering on Irma del Carmen Parada Gonzalez by:

(a) stripping her of her clothes;
(b) applying electric current to her mouth, vagina and breasts;
(c) subjecting her to rape by two men;
(d) putting her hands into chemicals and introducing them into a machine causing her to lose consciousness;
(e) forcing her to eat putrid food and the human remains of her dead fellow captives; in purported performance of official duties.

That you on 24th June 1989 being a public official, namely Commander-in-Chief of the Chilean Army, jointly with others intentionally inflicted severe pain or suffering on Marcos Quezada Yanez, aged seventeen years old, by inflicting severe electric shocks causing his eventual death, in purported performance of official duties.

That you in 1974 being a public official, namely Commander-in-Chief of the Chilean Army, jointly with others intentionally inflicted severe pain or suffering on others by the employment of 'Papi', a man who had visible open syphilitic sores on his body, to rape female captives and to use on them a dog trained in sexual practices with human beings, in purported performance of official duties.

General Pinochet was not accused of participating personally in any single act of torture, but rather with directing them all through his personal command over the DINA, the secret military police who staffed the torture centres in Santiago and elsewhere. The object of his conspiracy with other soldiers and some civilians (including the hooded doctors who attended every session to advise on the level of pain the particular victim could sustain before lapsing into unconsciousness) was to seize and maintain power through terror. That these atrocities were in fact committed was confirmed in 1992 by a commission headed by Senator Rettig, although it was prohibited from 'naming names' and identifying Pinochet and his willing executioners. Prior to his arrest in 1998 the General had never denied responsibility or apologized: he had always boasted of his conduct and occasionally joked that the disappearances had saved bereaved families the cost of coffins. A massive public relations effort was belatedly mounted on his behalf during his enforced stay in Britain, seriously claiming that he had to kill Chileans in order to save them from Cuban-style communism – that they were better dead (or destroyed by torture) than red. His paid propagandists failed to deal with the central allegation, that the conspiracy to terrorize opponents, by torture if necessary, continued until 1990, seventeen years after the fall of Allende – any communist threat having ended, on his own reckoning, by 1978. That was a decade before the torture of Marcos Yanez, a seventeen-year-old youth who campaigned against Pinochet and was arrested by the secret police, who electrocuted him. There were some in Britain, led by former prime minister Thatcher, who believed Pinochet should be rewarded for help he had given during the 1982 Falklands War (by which time he had fallen out with the Argentinians over the Beagle Channel, and permitted some SAS operations from Chile). This was a political consideration: the question of principle was whether he could claim immunity from legal process on the basis that his crimes were committed while he was head of a sovereign state.

A pellucidly clear answer was given by the three-judge majority in the first House of Lords hearing, *Pinochet (No. 1)*. The dictator enjoyed absolute immunity (*ratione personae*) at the time the crimes were committed, by virtue of his position as head of the state of Chile. Once removed from this sovereign position, his immunity metamorphosed: it no longer attached to his person, but only to his acts – and only to those acts which had been properly performed in the course of his duties as head of state. Lord Nicholls said, quite simply, that the Vienna Convention read with the 1978 State Immunity Act

is apt to confer immunity in respect of acts performed in the exercise of functions which international law recognizes as functions of a head of state . . . And it hardly needs saying that torture of his own subjects, or of aliens, would not be regarded by international law as a function of a head of state. All states disavow the use of torture as abhorrent, although from time to time some still resort to it . . . International law recognizes, of course, that the functions of a head of state may include activities which are wrongful, even illegal, by the law of his own state or by the laws of other states. But international law has made plain that certain types of conduct, including torture and hostage-taking, are not acceptable conduct on the part of anyone. This applies as much to heads of state, or even more so, as it does to everyone else: the contrary conclusion would make a mockery of international law.[37]

The court was fully satisfied that this was the law in 1973 when Pinochet seized power. The Nuremberg judgment, that those who commit crimes against humanity cannot invoke state immunity if that state, by authorizing their action, has moved outside its competence in international law, had been unanimously approved as a statement of international law principles in 1946 by the General Assembly.[38] Although the US Supreme Court had said in *Nelson* that acts of torture by police, army and security services are quintessentially 'official' acts, this required further analysis. They are acts by officials, certainly, but they are not legitimate actions for officials to take. Because sovereign immunity is an international law rule, the functions of the sovereign cannot sensibly include behaviour which is contrary to *jus cogens*, and which therefore every sovereign has an *erga omnes* obligation to the international community to forswear. Hitler was acting 'officially' when ordering the Final Solution, but his personal immunity could not subsequently avail him against prosecution for a crime against humanity. A head of state who kills his gardener in a fit of rage, or tortures for the pleasure of watching the death agonies of his victims (Montaigne's definition of the furthest point in cruelty) could always have been prosecuted after his overthrow for these 'private' crimes, because they are outside his retirement immunity, which is restricted to acts related to his official function.

This simple approach was eschewed by most of the seven judges in *Pinochet (No.3)* after *Pinochet (No. 2)* had set aside the first decision because of one judge's connections with Amnesty International. Their long and laborious reasoning is a measure of the complexity and confusion of international law, but there was at least clear agreement that a head of state's personal and absolute immunity ceased, like the diplomat's, on relinquishing that position, and was replaced by a restrictive immunity that attached only to actions that had been performed as an official duty. Thus, there could be no immunity for ex-King Farouk's private shopping sprees, or for murdering gardeners in fits of rage or for enjoying Montaigne's ultimate in torture as a means of personal gratification. (Emperor Bokassa, accused of eating children, could not therefore have immunity in retirement from charges of cannibalism.) Where the law lords parted intellectual company was over whether crimes against humanity were outside the restrictive immunity because they could never be a legitimate function of a head of state, as *Pinochet (No.1)* had held, or whether they were indeed, as the Supreme Court held in *Nelson*, paradigm official acts. If the latter, however, surprise surprise: nobody in *Pinochet (No. 1)* had noticed that the Torture Convention, by defining 'torture' as a crime which could be committed *only* by a person acting in an official capacity, had (for cases of torture) abolished sovereign immunity altogether! Since the Convention defined the offence of torture as an action done by a public official, it logically excluded the possibility of a plea for immunity being based on the fact that the defendant *was* a public official, because 'no rational system of criminal justice can allow an immunity which is co-extensive with the offence'. Otherwise, there would be the self-defeating syllogism:

Only public officials can commit torture.

Public officials are immune from prosecution.

Nobody can ever be prosecuted for torture.

The judges were simply not prepared to credit the diplomatic community with the breathtaking hypocrisy of producing a torture convention with this result.[39]

There was general agreement with the analysis of Sir Arthur Watts, a distinguished jurist who had argued that individuals became subjects of international law when they committed crimes which 'offend against the public order of the international community':

States are artificial legal persons: they can only act through the institutions and agencies of the State, which means ultimately through its officials and other individuals acting on behalf of the State. For international conduct which is so serious as to be tainted with criminality to be regarded as attributable only to the impersonal state and not to the individuals who ordered or perpetrated it is both unrealistic and offensive to common notions of justice.[40]

Where the judges in *Pinochet (No. 3)* differed was over the way to effectuate this insight: most of them thought that lifting the veil of sovereignty required not only an allegation of criminality so serious that it breached *jus cogens*, but in addition the availability of universal jurisdiction, in the sense of a treaty machinery that would permit prosecution in any national, or in an international, court. The better view (that of Lord Millet) is that this follows automatically from the *jus cogens* quality of the rule, but others more cautiously required a convention which imposed a duty on state parties to 'prosecute or extradite'. This practical machinery had been supplied by the Torture Convention, to which Britain, Spain and Chile were parties, which expressly required them to prosecute suspects found within their borders or else extradite them to a jurisdiction which was prepared to put them on trial. The Convention requires all states to outlaw torture, defined as the infliction of severe pain 'by or with the acquiescence of a public official or other person acting in an official capacity'. It follows that the most official person of all, the head of state, could not possibly escape an accountability which fell on the apparatchiks who carried out his orders.

For simplicity and conceptual neatness, the reasoning in *Pinochet (No. 1)*, that immunity is lost in respect of crimes against humanity because these are not state functions, is to be preferred. It was vaguely supported by Lord Hutton and given an interesting twist by Lord Millet, who suggested that any immunity should be confined to acts performed in the 'representative' capacity of the head of state, and not to killings and torture ordered in the capacity of a head of government or army commander or party leader. Warning of the danger of raising the concept of sovereignty to the 'status of some holy fetish',[41] this judge displayed the most accurate understanding of the post-Nuremberg development of universal jurisdiction over crimes against humanity, for which state officers of any rank have no immunity:

The trend was clear. War crimes had been replaced by crimes against humanity. The way in which a state treated its own citizens within its own borders had become a matter of legitimate concern to the international community . . . crimes attract universal jurisdiction if two criteria are satisfied: first they must be contrary to a peremptory norm of international law so as to infringe a *jus cogens*. Secondly, they must be so serious and on such a scale that they can justly be regarded as an attack on the international legal order.[42]

Pinochet (No.3) confirmed the trend. Nuremberg had established liability for crimes against humanity committed in wartime, and later developments had removed the requirement for any connection with hostilities. In the case of torture, the judges confirmed that, as with genocide, the prohibition has been elevated in the hierarchy of international rules to *jus cogens*, signalling 'to all members of the international community and the individuals over whom they wield authority that the prohibition of torture is an absolute value from which nobody must deviate'.[43] The Torture Convention established a regime under which there could be no safe haven – the duty it imposed on all states which found a torturer in their midst was either to try him or to extradite him. Pinochet had been arrested in Britain, which in December 1988 ratified the Convention by passing a local law which made it a crime for anyone to torture anyone else anywhere in the world. It followed that the general could be put on trial at the Old Bailey for tortures committed after that date, or else extradited to Spain to stand trial there.

This conclusion was a striking example of a court taking a treaty not just at its word but (in the absence of express words) at its spirit. The Torture Convention has no reference to any waiver by the parties of sovereign immunity, and there is not a single mention in the *travaux préparatoires* or the literature that any state indicated during the years of drafting that it was prepared to give up this attribute of sovereignty. Indeed, many of the signatories to the Convention are among the seventy-three states which regularly use torture, and their leaders would never have signed it if they had thought it might impact on their retirement plans. None of the lawyers on the anti-Pinochet teams (a number of them QCs or professors of international law, or both) even advanced the argument that the Torture Convention was intended to abolish sovereign immunity, because it wasn't. It was ratified as another exercise in cynical diplomacy, without any belief that it would be enforced. But what nobody could have anticipated is that the English judges would approach this treaty as if it were a contract or a parliamentary statute, without a trace of the scepticism that affects anyone who knows with what hypocrisy these conventions are drafted and ratified, by diplomats who never intend them to have any effect beyond inducing a feel-good factor and a good human rights rating to wave in front of aid donors. The Torture Convention was signed by dozens of states which still torture, by Chile while Pinochet himself was still head of state and could never have intended to provide for his own arrest, and by the government of Mrs Thatcher, the general's most effusive supporter. The general's tactics of objecting to judges who might know about human rights produced an apolitical bench who, with an almost touching naivety, took the Torture Convention to mean what it said. With uncanny, uncynical decency, they proceeded to hoist the old torturer by his own petard.

There was one anxious dissent, from a judge with some international law experience, who feared that an RUC officer on holiday in Florida might suddenly be accused of torture in Northern Ireland. This is a bad example, because a 'suggestion of immunity' would immediately issue from the State Department, just as it had for Prince Charles. But it is not difficult to think of more likely cases, and the objection must be addressed. Some of the majority judges did so, by arguing that immunity is only extinguished by an allegation of torture 'when committed as part of a widespread or systematic attack against any civilian population', i.e. when what is being alleged fits the Rome Statute definition of a crime against humanity. This solution is reasonable, because no doubt there will be politically motivated accusations against former leaders whose conduct is more debatable than Pinochet's (his role as torturer of our time is a matter of historical record). The answer is surely to confine prosecutions to crimes against humanity, and to rely upon domestic legal systems to eliminate charges based on insufficient evidence.

So the law took its course, and on 24 March 1999 the judges ordered the extradition proceedings to proceed – in respect of any act of torture that Spain could show was committed in the final years of the Pinochet dictatorship. In the meantime, he had been forced to greet the millennium under house (well, mansion) arrest in the south of England. His days were spent in the company of lawyers – a form of torture, although defying comparison with that inflicted on his victims. More evidence of his guilt came from freshly opened US National Archives, but this did not deter an international campaign for his release from predictable quarters: Jesse Helms, Dr Henry Kissinger – and even the Pope, who had interceded for Pinochet 'to repeat to the world that at no time can the sovereignty of any state, big or small, be violated, stripping the local government of the power to judge a fellow national'.[44] The most ironic call for Pinochet's freedom came from his mortal enemy, President Fidel Castro, at the Latin American leaders' summit in June 1999, where he declared Britain's compliance with international law 'an affront to national sensibilities'. This outburst – from the region's only remaining leader whose disregard for human rights may have reached criminal proportions[45] – did not help the Pinochet cause.

What did help were a series of strokes and a hasty diagnosis from English medical experts that he had suffered irreversible brain damage and impairment of memory. By this time – March 2000 – Pinochet had been detained for seventeen months and Chile's inability to procure his return was damaging to the electoral prospects of the socialist government. Jack Straw took the decision that his mental condition meant that he was unfit to be tried and therefore (illogically) unfit to be extradited to Spain, the place where his presumed unfitness should have been tested. Straw's decision was politically convenient and certainly justifiable in relation to ordinary crimes: it would be wrong, for example, to put an 83-year-old man with brain damage, mild dementia and bad memory on trial for fraud. But it is not an acceptable standard for letting former leaders off the hook when charged with mass murder and mass torture – as Pinochet demonstrated when he arrived back in Chile, leaping from his wheelchair on the tarmac and waving his walking stick as he embraced his supporters. Most took this as evidence that he had gulled the doctors ('PINOCHEAT!' screamed the English tabloids) but given the number of legal actions brought against him during his absence, this demonstration might well have been evidence of real brain damage. The English Court of Appeal had ordered disclosure of his confidential medical reports, making the important point that *any* claim to avoid charges of crimes against humanity must be decided by 'the highest standards of transparency'.[46] It was richly ironic that a dictator who denied human rights to the thousands he had killed and tortured should at the end of his own life become a pathetic beneficiary of human rights standards.

Like others who have never lost a moment's sleep over their cruelty, Pinochet lived on in Chile, as unlikely to go to prison as to go to heaven, until his death in December 2006. His mental condition and his amnesties were a constant subject of legal argument in the courts of Chile, which eventually approved judicial investigations of many of his crimes, including Operation Condor and the 'Caravan of Death'. His influence drained away after evidence emerged of his corruption and tax evasion. The issue of fitness to stand trial for crimes against humanity remains of importance and there is no doubt that Jack Straw set the standard too low. The question is not whether a defendant has mental impairment (like many criminals) or poor recall (like most octogenarians), it is whether a trial *can* be fair, an issue that must be decided by the court of trial once proceedings have commenced. The trial should go ahead if the prosecution evidence can be properly tested and the defendant's age and disability can be taken into account in mitigation of sentence. Thus the Special Court for Sierra Leone refused to accept the prosecutor's invitation to withdraw charges against an apparently imbecilic Foday Sankoh – the leader of the main rebel faction – and ordered a brain scan to ensure that he really was mentally incapacitated. It is obviously unsatisfactory to allow mass murderers to grow old in the bosom of their families because they are 'unfit to be tried': it would be better first to see whether the prosecution could establish their guilt, and at that point to allow the defence to enter and make out a plea of 'not guilty because unfit to be tried'. Like the plea of 'not guilty because insane', this would mean a discharge to a secure mental hospital and not a return to the family compound. This issue will need to be further considered by the ICC: the real lesson of Pinochet's mental impairment is that there is urgent need to round up the other torturers of the twentieth century while they are still of sound mind.

THE *PINOCHET* PRECEDENT AND THE ICJ

Augusto Pinochet served but one noble purpose in his life: that of helping the world work out how to put tyrants on trial. His case assumes its historic dimension because he was the first to be held potentially liable to prosecution for a crime against humanity committed in peacetime, notwithstanding a cloak of sovereign immunity which the state he headed was determined not to waive. It was symbolic that the ruling in *Pinochet (No. 3)* came on 24 March 1999, the very day that NATO countries began to bomb the sovereign state of Serbia in an effort to stop the atrocities its forces were committing against its own nationals in Kosovo. It was as if the world community had finally decided to obliterate its memory of appeasing Hitler by evolving international law to a position where it could no longer accept that the way in which a state treats its own citizens is purely an internal matter. The point at which interference with sovereignty was justified was when the repression reached such a level of severity that it disturbed world peace. No longer need this be a messy and overly subjective test, because it can now be satisfied by evidence that the state, through officials of its government, is committing crimes against humanity as a matter of policy.

The fallout from the House of Lords decision was immediate and worldwide, as victims formed groups to arraign other torturers, human rights defenders turned into human rights prosecutors, and retired tyrants frantically changed their travel plans. Colonel Mengistu, in Cape Town for a heart bypass, scurried back to the safety of Harare before his operation; ex-President Suharto brought surgeons to Jakarta rather than risk travelling to a hospital in Germany; Pinochet's

Guatemalan equivalent, General Rios Montt, cancelled a holiday in Paris. The fear factor was fanned by arrests of death-squad members in Chile, while in Argentina Videla, Galtieri and their henchmen went back on trial, their amnesties and immunities shredded or circumvented by courts influenced by the *Pinochet* precedent. Several European countries put resident torturers on trial and followed Spain's precedent of issuing extradition requests for Latin American generals who had been complicit in the killing of their nationals. In 1999, Belgium went further than any other state: it passed a pure 'universal jurisdiction' law which gave its courts power to investigate and try crimes against humanity committed by anyone, anywhere – without any necessary jurisdictional link to Belgium other than as the place where the complaint was made. The *Pinochet* precedent stirred the victims of Hissène Habré, who had killed 40,000 and tortured 200,000 during his rule in Chad, to prosecute him at his retirement home in Senegal. When local judges refused to take jurisdiction, his victims complained to Belgium which after investigation issued a warrant for his re-arrest. Even Henry Kissinger had to watch his steps, since they were being watched for him by a website (Kissingerwatch) which tells potential claimants where they may serve their writs for the crimes alleged by Christopher Hitchens in the book and film *The Trial of Henry Kissinger*.

But putting Kissinger on trial is entrancing make-believe and universal jurisdiction, pushed too far too fast in post-Pinochet euphoria, was reined in. The Belgian law was satisfactorily applied to the Hutu nuns residing in Belgium who had lured Tutsis into their church in Rwanda and then helped to incinerate them. It was permitted to breathe down the neck of Hissène Habré, so long as Senegal was prepared to ratify or accept the 'extradite or try' principle of the Torture Convention. But the notion that Belgium – the cowardly country that had allowed the holocaust in Rwanda by pulling out its soldiers – should become the conscience of the world was not easy to accept. Its magistrates became the tool of political activists bent upon misguided courtroom crusades against Israeli prime minister Ariel Sharon, alleging his guilt for the murder of Palestinian refugees in the *Sabra* and *Shatila* camps twenty years previously. This was a foolish case for the court to accept: not only had Sharon been fully investigated at the time and excluded from criminal liability (but not moral obloquy), he had actually sued *Time* magazine in the US for making this allegation, and obtained a retraction. The case was eventually thrown out as a result of the ICJ decision in *Democratic Republic of Congo* v. *Belgium* (see below) that serving ministers retain their immunity. The case which brought Belgium's pretensions to an ignominious end was a complaint by a group of pro-Saddam Iraqis accusing George Bush senior, Colin Powell and General Schwarzkopf of war crimes committed in the course of the 1990 Gulf War. Since that was one of the most justified wars of the twentieth century, and since NATO's headquarters are in Brussels, there was no moral or political justification for accepting this case, other than to provoke the United States and to demonstrate how a 'pure' universal jurisdiction law, vested in a national court rather than an international criminal court, can be open to political abuse. In consequence, the Belgian parliament in 2003 radically amended the law, by requiring henceforth, as a condition of accepting the case for investigation, a substantial link between Belgium and the crime. The only case permitted to proceed under the old law is that against Hissène Habré, the mass-murdering ex-dictator of Chad now living in retirement in Senegal, which declined for many years to put him on trial, despite the government of Chad stating that it will waive any immunity that still attaches to him. The case illustrates a situation where a national court exercising universal jurisdiction may plug the gap which remains when no international court has jurisdiction and it is impossible or impracticable to bring the ex-tyrant to trial in the country he devastated. It also, sadly, illustrates how global justice remains a struggle: in July 2012 the ICJ in *Belgium* v. *Senegal* finally ruled that 'Africa's Pinochet' had to stand trial for breaches of the Convention against Torture: if Senegal continued to evade its obligation in this respect, it must extradite him forthwith to Belgium. Although the tortures for which Habré must be tried are less serious than his 40,000 ethnic and politically related murders, they were particularly obnoxious: prisoners had their mouths forced over the exhaust pipes of running cars, were subjected to 'chopsticks' (the head is wrapped in rope and squeezed by turning two pieces of wood) and were left for weeks in cells with rotting corpses.

The attempt to make Brussels the post-*Pinochet* home of international criminal law had already suffered a reverse in 2002 at the hands of the ICJ, whose judges are appointed to 'represent' their states and tend therefore (with some exceptions) to be wedded to the principle of state sovereignty and to the traditional assumptions of diplomacy. They were gravely disquieted by the actions of a Belgian magistrate in issuing an 'international arrest warrant in absentia' against the Foreign Minister of the Democratic Republic of Congo (DRC) for making speeches which had incited race hatred and possibly led to mass killings. The murderous Kabila government brought a complaint to the ICJ, protesting at this 'affront' to their sensibilities, insisting in the dated language of diplomacy that it had suffered a 'moral injury' from the issue of a warrant by a foreign court against a serving minister.

The Court upheld the Foreign Minister's immunity, and inferred its scope from the nature and work of the ministry in question:

In customary international law, the immunities accorded to ministers for foreign affairs are not granted for their personal benefit, but to ensure the effective performance of their functions on behalf of their respective states . . . The functions of a minister for foreign affairs are such that, throughout the duration of his or her office, he or she when abroad enjoys full immunity from criminal jurisdiction and inviolability. That immunity and that inviolability protect the individual concerned against any act of authority of another state which would hinder him or her in the performance of his or her duties . . . Furthermore, even the mere risk that, by travelling to or transiting another state, a minister for foreign affairs might be exposing himself or herself to legal proceedings could deter the minister from travelling internationally when required to do so for the purposes of the performance of his or her official functions.[47]

This approach is somewhat anachronistic (foreign ministers have no vital need to travel to states where they may be indicted) and it ignored the sensible state practice of reshuffling foreign ministers who run into legal difficulties. In many states, indeed, it is regarded as the minister's duty to stand down and clear himself of a criminal charge before resuming office. At least the ICJ's functional approach confines the scope for immunity to the needs of representative government. It ruled that all political figures were capable of prosecution:

(1) By national courts in their own country for acts committed at any time,

(2) In a foreign national court if their state waives immunity,

(3) In a foreign national court after they cease to hold office, for acts committed before or after tenure or even during that tenure if such acts were committed in a private capacity,

(4) In an international criminal court, for acts committed at any time.[48]

Proposition 3 above relates to the *Pinochet* precedent, and is unacceptably vague. What is meant by saying that a former minister may be prosecuted, e.g. for torture, 'if such acts were committed in a private capacity'? If *Pinochet (No. 1)* and *(No. 3)* established anything, it is the unworkability in criminal law of the distinction between 'public' (or 'official') acts and 'private' acts – a distinction which the Court in *US* v. *Noriega* presciently predicted 'may prove elusive'.[49] It is easy to accept that Noriega's drug trafficking whilst head of the Panamanian government could not constitute public acts done on behalf of the Panamanian state. But compare the charges against Pinochet – his alleged direction of systematic torture by army, police and secret service of his political opponents, and his agreement with other governments to eliminate 'leftists' in the region through 'Operation Condor'. In the view of the two judges in the minority in *Pinochet (No.1)*, it was pellucidly clear that these were acts committed in an official, sovereign capacity which in consequence attracted immunity from criminal process. It was equally clear to the majority (and must be accounted the better view) that such crimes against humanity could never be legitimate exercises of public power, and any immunity attaching to the person of the official who committed them would be lost on his retirement from office. To reiterate the words of Lord Nicholls:

. . . international law has made plain that certain types of conduct, including torture and hostage-taking, are not acceptable conduct on the part of anyone.

This applies as much to heads of state, or even more so, as it does to anyone else; the contrary conclusion would make a mockery of international law.

Thus the 'retirement immunity' referred to in the third proposition in paragraph 61 of *DRC* v. *Belgium* cannot protect against charges of crimes against humanity because the commission of such crimes is outside any official function. In this way (as the concurring ICJ minority explains) the door is opening in municipal law to a jurisdiction based on the heinous nature of the crime rather than on territorial or nationality links. Three of the ICJ's best judges – Rosalyn Higgins, Thomas Buergenthal and Pieter Kooijmans – in a joint concurring opinion, gave the same explanation: crimes against humanity are so heinous they cannot be classified as an official or state action: 'serious international crimes cannot be regarded as official acts because they are neither normal state functions nor functions that a state alone (in contrast to an individual) can perform'.

The final puzzle is what the ICJ means by 'international criminal court'. Its elliptically worded fourth proposition in paragraph 61 reads as follows:

an incumbent or former Minister for Foreign Affairs may be subject to criminal proceedings before certain international criminal courts, where they have jurisdiction. Examples include the International Criminal Tribunal for the former Yugoslavia [Hague Tribunal], and the International Criminal Tribunal for Rwanda [Rwanda Tribunal], established pursuant to Security Council resolutions under Chapter VII of the United Nations Convention. The latter's Statute expressly provides, in Article 27, paragraph 2, that '[i]mmunities or special procedural rules which may attach to the official capacity of a person, whether under national or international law, shall not bar the Court from exercising its jurisdiction over such a person'.[50]

Did this include the Special Court for Sierra Leone, established by agreement between the United Nations and the Sierra Leone government? The issue had to be decided by the Special Court in its first case, an application by lawyers on behalf of Charles Taylor to dismiss the indictment on the grounds that he was President of Liberia at the time it was issued. The ICJ clearly states that no such immunity can bar prosecution in the Hague Tribunal, the Rwanda Tribunal or the ICC, and that these are only *examples* of the 'certain international criminal courts' which may proceed against incumbent high officials 'where they have jurisdiction'.[51] What is not certain, however, is the meaning of 'certain' in that crucial phrase. A sensible reading of paragraph 61 is that the 'certain international criminal courts where they have jurisdiction' denotes courts which are (a) international and (b) possess, by virtue of their statutes, jurisdiction which expressly overrides immunity claims. The Hague and Rwanda Tribunals and the ICC all have this feature in common – a commonality relevantly spelled out by the ICJ's citation of Article 27(2) of the Rome Statute. This citation must be the key to what is meant by the phrase 'where they have jurisdiction' which in turn defines the 'certain' courts, rather than the somewhat throwaway reference to Chapter VII of the UN Charter when describing the origin (but not the jurisdiction) of the Hague and Rwanda Tribunals. This interpretation permits the inclusion of the Nuremberg Tribunal amongst the 'certain' courts, since its charter contained an equivalent provision overriding sovereign immunity and it was established before the UN itself took its formal post-war state.[52] Nobody doubts that it had jurisdiction to override any claim of immunity for Admiral Dönitz (German head of state after Hitler's death), Reich Marshal Göring and the other Nazi leaders. This interpretation of the ICJ's fourth proposition in paragraph 61 of *DRC* does accord with principle and with dicta in other cases such as *Pinochet*, as well as the approach in the opinion of the ICJ concurring minority, who explain that immunity depends not only on the status of the official but also upon 'what type of jurisdiction, and on what basis' the prosecuting authorities seek to assert it.[53] 'One of the challenges of present day international law,' they write, 'is to provide for stability of international relations and effective international intercourse while at the same time guaranteeing respect for human rights.'[54] State practice, as enshrined in treaties, evinces 'a common endeavour in the face of atrocities' by way of a duty to prosecute certain international crimes, such as genocide, torture and grave violations of the Geneva Conventions, which 'open[ed] the door to a jurisdiction based on the heinous nature of the crime rather than on links of territoriality or nationality'.[55] Hence 'the international consensus that the perpetrators of international crimes should not go unpunished is being advanced by a flexible strategy, in which newly established international criminal tribunals, treaty obligations and national courts all have their part to play' in ending impunity for crimes against humanity.[56] Against this background, immunity is an exception to the exercise of a jurisdiction to punish crimes against humanity. As an exception its value must always be balanced against the normative value of ending impunity:

[A] trend is discernible that in a world which increasingly rejects impunity for the most repugnant offences, the attribution of responsibility and accountability is becoming firmer, the possibility for the assertion of jurisdiction wider and the availability of immunity as a shield more limited. The law of privileges and immunities, however, retains its importance since immunities are granted to high State officials to guarantee the proper functioning of the network of mutual inter-State relations, which is of paramount importance for a well ordered and harmonious international system.[57]

This approach is consistent with the fourth proposition in paragraph 61, namely that an international criminal court competently established (whether by treaty or by the Security Council under Chapter VII) may exercise its jurisdiction to override immunities if so directed by its statute; the Special Court for Sierra Leone is so directed, for example, by Article 6(2) of its statute.[58]

The state immunity of rulers, officials or ambassadors derives from the seventeenth century when states were ruled by Divine Right or feudal inheritance, and lacked the facilities for instantaneous communication we now take for granted. Traditional rationales – the indignity of putting a sovereign on trial or the incapacity of judges to determine political questions – carry less weight in the twenty-first century. Even the 'functional' rationale of immunity, based on the need of heads of state and foreign ministers to travel abroad in order to do state business, is less crucial in the age of the e-mail and the video conference. As modern developments call traditional rationales into question, so the attitude towards international crimes has changed. International law now acknowledges the imperative need to end impunity for crimes against humanity, and the logical consequence of this imperative is to end all immunity of state officials, past and present, who are credibly arraigned on such charges by international courts.

Uncertainty still attends the power of national courts to entertain prosecutions of heads of state under municipal law or through the purported exercise of universal jurisdiction: in the latter case, it may be necessary to obtain a waiver by the defendant state of any immunity which still attaches to him, as in the case of Hissène Habré, ex-dictator of Chad, who has been indicted in Belgium with the agreement of Chad (although Senegal still protects him). There can be no immunity, of course, for state torturers and killers: in 2005 Argentinian colonel Adolfo Scilingo was sentenced to life imprisonment in Spain for crimes against humanity – organizing death flights in which dozens of drugged and naked prisoners were pushed out of aircraft over the Atlantic Ocean. Scilingo was a quarry of Baltasar Garzón, whose arrest warrant for Pinochet paved the way for a process by which European courts can claim jurisdiction to try any torturer they can claw from South American states who have been backward in their duty to prosecute.

It does not follow from *Pinochet (No. 3)* that sovereign immunity will no longer bar *civil* actions by victims and relatives against states or their agents who have inflicted torture. Old doctrines die hard, and the basic principle behind immunity – that states are all equal and one state does not sit in judgment on the conduct of another – may still be invoked as it was against Al-Adsani and Scott Nelson, unless (as in the *Marcos* cases) the state to which the immunity belongs decides to waive it, or unless the action can be related in some way to commerce or to the 'private gratification' exception (under this heading, of course, an official who raped a prisoner, even as part of state-sanctioned torture, could be sued for damages). However, it will be open to other courts to follow the logic of *Pinochet (No. 1)* that a crime against humanity can never be part of the functions of a head of state, and so is outside the state's *ratione materiae* immunity. Otherwise, international criminal law will have moved much faster than its civil equivalent, and the right to a remedy – guaranteed in every human rights treaty – will extend only to the satisfaction of seeing the human tormentor behind bars, paying for his crimes but without compensating his victims. This gap makes it important for Britain and other common law countries to legislate an equivalent of the US Alien Tort Claims Act, so that civil claims can be brought when torturers or their assets come within the jurisdiction.

The reality is that states are not equal. There can be no 'dignity' or 'respect' when statehood is an attribute of the governments which presently rule Cuba, North Korea, Syria and Northern Sudan. The dignity of international recognition and even UN membership is denied to the maturing, stable democracy of Taiwan in deference to China's nationalistic pretensions, but is vouchsafed to Somalia, a 'state' without any effective government other than through clan-based militias, and to Bhutan, a Himalayan 'state' completely controlled by India. What sort of respect is owed to the SLORC generals who kept the nation's democratically elected leader, Aung San Suu Kyi, under the lock and key of house arrest for many years, until her welcome release in 2011? The head of the tribal state of Equatorial Guinea murdered his uncle. The Head of the Syrian state authorizes his army to kill thousands of his people. The megalomaniac President Niyazov of Turkmenistan, self-appointed 'father of all Turkmen', made his thoughts the subject of compulsory study in schools, reproduced himself in large statues in every village square, locked opponents in mental asylums and insisted on supervising every PhD thesis. The former prime minister of Antigua, Vere Bird senior, almost went into partnership with the Medellin cartel. It is absurd to kow-tow to people like this, who run governments which claim an 'immunity' from justice on the basis of a dignity they entirely lack. It is dangerous, too, lest rulers follow Machiavelli's advice to do not what is right but what other states do, because the best must emulate the policy of the worst in order to survive. If we could write sovereign immunity on a clean slate, we would undoubtedly confine its operation to ceremonial visits and symbolic actions of the kind expected of kings and aped by dictators, leaving the state and its agents liable, criminally and civilly, for crimes against humanity.[59] This is the way forward, but it calls for amendments to the Vienna Convention and an 'unfreezing' of all the state immunity legislation passed by countries in the 1970s. Reform then was needed for states to be able to trade freely between each other: further amendment is required in order to make them behave with a minimum of civility towards their own people.

9

The Balkan Trials

'When someone kills a man, he is put in prison. When
someone kills twenty people, he is declared mentally insane.
But when someone kills 200,000 people, he is invited to
Geneva for peace negotiations.'

Sarajevo joke, *circa* 1994

Nuremberg was a precedent that the United Nations ignored until the
ethnic cleansing policy of the Bosnian Serbs turned its 'New World
Order' into a joke. The International Criminal Tribunal for the Former Yugoslavia (ICTY) was established by the Security Council on 27
May 1993 as if to stop the world laughing at its impotence, as a substitute for effective military action to stop the war. After catching one
criminal in two years (and a foot soldier at that) the Tribunal finally
lifted a formal finger against the Bosnian Serb leadership on 15 May
1995, by taking over the investigation into their culpability from the
courts of Bosnia and Hercegovina. This step seemed insignificant at
the time (the Bosnian Serb leaders were not under arrest, but on the
contrary were in a position to authorize the arrest of UN peacekeepers, which they did a few weeks later). It marked, nevertheless, the
first time since Nuremberg that an international court had assumed
jurisdiction over the masters of war crimes, towards the close of a
century in which 160 million human beings were slaughtered in war.

At this level, it was a deeply symbolic occasion. Richard
Goldstone, the South African judge appointed as the Tribunal prose-

cutor, assisted by two Australian barristers, stood before a court in The Hague comprising a judge of the Supreme Court of Nigeria, a female judge who was formerly the Minister of Justice for Costa Rica, and a judge who had been Procurator-General of the Court of Appeal for Paris. He sought leave to proceed with an investigation into crimes against humanity allegedly committed by Radovan Karadžić, president of the Bosnian Serb administration and architect of its ethnic policies; Ratko Mladić, commander of its army; and Miko Stanišić, the home affairs minister who unleashed police terror against the non-Serbian population.[1] Goldstone reminded the court of the Nuremberg ruling that 'a plea of head of state immunity will not constitute a defence, nor will it mitigate punishment' and of the salutary 'command responsibility' rule for political and military leaders adopted at the Tokyo trial of General Yamashita and approved by the US Supreme Court:

a person in a position of superior authority should be held individually responsible for giving the unlawful order to commit a crime, and he should also be held responsible for failure to deter the unlawful behaviour of subordinates if he knew they had committed or were about to commit crimes yet failed to take the necessary and reasonable steps to prevent their commission or to punish those who had committed them.[2]

Thus far had we come in the fifty years since Nuremberg, the 350 years since Charles I was tried for tyranny, and the 860 years since the Second Lateran Council which in 1139 forbade the use of crossbows in wars between Christians, thereby imposing the first international law rule against inhumane conduct. It did not seem very far: an empty dock, and cells holding at the time only one Serbian defendant, Duško Tadić. He was not even a soldier, just a freelance torturer – but here he was, the sole representative of those who had instigated or committed the millions of crimes against humanity perpetrated since the end of the Second World War. None the less, it was a deeply symbolic, if not Grotian, moment: the first sign of a seismic shift, from diplomacy to legality, in the conduct of world affairs.

ESTABLISHING THE ICTY

By the simple device of invoking its mandatory powers to preserve the peace, endowed by Chapter VII of the UN Charter, the Security Council in 1993 unanimously established by its Resolutions 808 and 827 the first truly 'international' criminal court. Nuremberg, after all, had been a tribunal set up by four victorious nations, while the ICTY was a subsidiary organ of the Security Council with which all countries were required to co-operate. But the comparison soon pales. The Nuremberg defendants were speedily arrested in a country under Allied occupation and most of them were convicted on overwhelming documentary evidence within the space of twelve months. But the tribunal in The Hague, far away from a continuing and ferocious war, was infuriatingly slow: its first defendant, Duško Tadić, did not arrive until April 1995 and his trial did not commence until 7 May 1996. Much blood flowed under the bridges of the Drina in the meantime: the worst of the Bosnian Serb crimes against humanity, namely the killing of 7,000 Muslim men and boys from Srebrenica, took place in July 1995 while lawyers in The Hague were still arguing their preliminary motions. The decision convicting Tadić of eleven separate crimes against humanity was not handed down until 7 May 1997; incredibly, his appeal did not begin until April 1999. So Tadić's fate (he was given twenty years' imprisonment in January 2000) and that of several Bosnian Serb soldiers who followed him into the dock did not deter the atrocities committed in Kosovo in the years which followed his arraignment. The real problem was that for all the obligations to co-operate with the ICTY which were written into the Dayton Peace Accords after Srebrenica, *realpolitik* was the message of a NATO spokesman widely quoted in the summer of 1996: 'Arresting Karadžić is not worth the blood of one NATO soldier.' The mandate of the 60,000-strong I-For force was 'to detain those indicted persons whom they come across in the course of their duties', so for several years after Dayton, NATO commanders ensured that their duties would make such encounters unlikely.[3] This was not so much a case of dereliction of duty as of correctly divining the real purpose of the Hague Tribunal in the minds of the Security Council representatives who set it up, which was never to put major criminals like Karadžić and Mladić (let alone Milošević) behind bars, but to pretend to an anxious and appalled world that something was being done.

That this pretence was felt to be necessary in respect of Yugoslavia in 1993, rather than in any previous conflict, was due to a combination of factors. Most important were the television atrocity pictures, given added force by the shelling of historical holiday places like the Dalmatian coast and Dubrovnik, which showed the spectre of ethnic cleansing returning to Europe. American television audiences were bewildered that this should be part of the 'New World Order' promised by President George Bush Snr after the defeat of Iraq. There was, too, the futility of the diplomatic soft shoe shuffle, as Vance and Owen solemnly worked out how the aggressor factions should be rewarded, only to produce a plan that failed to assuage their greed. There had been a disastrous failure of sanctions – most ironically of the blanket arms ban, which left Muslims defenceless against the already well-equipped Serbian armies. Then, more television pictures, this time of 'an elegant, cosmopolitan European city, Sarajevo, being systematically pulverized from a safe distance by cigarette-smoking, Šljivovica-drinking gun and mortar crews while they and the snipers leisurely targeted school children, bread queues, housewives doing their shopping, funeral ceremonies and the like'.[4] The United Nations could not be taken seriously unless something was done: the utter failure of diplomacy and sanctions, and the refusal to risk the lives of allied soldiers by armed intervention, made a war crimes tribunal the only face-saving device left. So it was set up fortuitously, but upon its success (everyone started to say) the prospects for an international criminal court, foreshadowed by the Genocide Convention in 1948, would depend.

What, however, is meant by 'success'? Nuremberg 'succeeded' as a trial process because it proved beyond doubt the guilt of most of the Nazi leaders, and acquitted those whose guilt could not be proved. That success derived from the efforts of a thousand investigators and lawyers, with defendants already under arrest, who had complete access to archives and witnesses within the control of an Allied army of occupation. It was 'victor's justice', not in a cynical sense, but because victory brought the power to do justice to some of those who deserved it. Yet there was no 'victory' in Bosnia. The ICTY spent much of 1996 and 1997 concerned with the trial of Duško Tadić, a sadistic freelance thug permitted to torture prisoners at Omarska camp, while the commanders and 'intellectual authors' of the geno- cide remained impervious to its warrants for arrest. Most impervious of all was Slobodan Milošević, who bore a guilt of Göring-esque pro- portions for the entire tragedy, but whose position as head of state and as broker of any possible peace gave him an effective immunity that the Hague prosecutors could not challenge until 1999, when NATO's patience finally snapped.

By 'success', of course, most supporters of the Hague Tribunal mean convictions. True success, however, only attends a tribunal with judges sufficiently robust to acquit wherever there is reasonable doubt. Any court derives its legitimacy from the justice that it does. What the ICTY has had to establish is a capacity to get at the truth while sitting far from the scene of the crime, and its capacity to be fair notwithstanding media prejudice against the defendants and the dif- ficulties their lawyers have in obtaining witnesses and procuring documents (especially security-sensitive material in the hands of the prosecutor).

Many politicians, generals and diplomats view the exponential growth of international humanitarian law with alarm. They have, behind the scenes, accused the ICTY president and prosecutor of irre- sponsibility for demanding that the Dayton Accords include a surrender clause for indicted suspects, and have actually blamed the human rights lobby for causing thousands of deaths by opposing the Vance–Owen compromises with Serbian aggression.[5] What Richard Goldstone and his successors Louise Arbour, Carla del Ponte and Serge Bramnertz have demonstrated, by their willingness to speak out against attempts to marginalize the Tribunal, is the optimistic fact that enterprises of this sort have a tendency to develop a momentum of their own, independent of the concerns of those who create them. The diplomats always fear that international criminal courts will become competing powers in the world, prone to upset the bargains they make with unjust regimes. The ICTY, together with its conjoined tribunal for the *génocidaires* of Rwanda (the ICTR) and the UN War Crimes Court in Sierra Leone, have been teaching them to live with the idea that justice, in respect of crimes against humanity, is non-negotiable.

THE LEGAL BASIS OF THE ICTY AND ICTR

Civil war in Yugoslavia began in earnest in 1991, with the Serb army bombardments of Vukovar and Dubrovnik; by May of 1992, when the Security Council imposed mandatory economic sanctions on Serbia, the atrocities had reached a level Europe had not experienced since the Second World War. Arms embargoes had little impact (imposed on all parties, they had actually tilted the balance towards the well-prepared Serbian army) and in the autumn the United States proposed a war crimes tribunal. There is some tantalizing intercept evidence to suggest that this proposal actually gave pause to the Serbian military commanders – until they realized that any such tribunal would take years to establish.[6] The Security Council began by appointing a commission of experts, eventually headed by Professor Cherif Bassiouni, to investigate violations of international humanitarian law. He faced obstruction from British and French diplomats, who feared that justice considerations would interfere with their peacemaking expedients, and had to raise more than half his initial funding from the Soros and MacArthur foundations.[7] This 'seed money', especially from Soros, was seized upon by Milošević supporters nine years later to allege that the Tribunal must be tainted, although there was no basis for perceiving any judicial bias from such private donations. Bassiouni's commission of experts reported widespread war crimes and crimes against humanity, and proposed an international criminal court – a recommendation endorsed by the UN's General Assembly in December 1992 (a fact which Milošević and his defenders like Ramsey Clark overlooked when they claimed that the Court was unlawful because it lacked General Assembly approval). Bassiouni acted with commendable speed and issued an interim report on 26 January 1993, describing ethnic cleansing, mass murder, torture, rape, pillage and destruction of cultural, religious and private property. That led, on 22 February, to Security Council Resolution 808, determining that the situation constituted a threat to international peace and security, and deciding to establish an international tribunal to contribute to the realization of peace by putting an end to war crimes and punishing their perpetrators. Resolution 827, in May, adopted a report by the Secretary-General which set out the legal and procedural basis for the new institution.[8]

This report serves as the Tribunal's mandate. It accepts that the normal method of establishing a prosecution agency and a court would be for state parties, either through the General Assembly or after special conferences, to draw up a treaty which would then be open for signature and ratification. But that would take years. The need for urgency permitted action under Chapter VII of the United Nations Charter, given that the Security Council had already determined the existence of a threat to the peace. The Tribunal would derive its legitimacy from the fact that it constituted 'a measure to maintain or restore international peace and security'. It would be a 'subsidiary organ' of the Council, albeit a judicial one which would, in the performance of those judicial functions, be independent of the Council or of any political considerations.

In setting up the ICTY, the Security Council acted within its powers under the UN Charter. By Article 24(1), all members 'confer on the Security Council primary responsibility for the maintenance of international peace and security, and agree that in carrying out its duties under this responsibility the Security Council acts on their behalf'.

Article 39 provides:

The Security Council shall determine the existence of any threat to peace or act of aggression and shall make recommendations, or decide what measures shall be taken in accordance with Articles 41 and 42, to maintain or restore international peace and security.

The Security Council had, of course, determined that other local conflicts constituted a threat to international peace: Haiti and Somalia in 1993, Iraq in 1991, the Iran–Iraq War, insurgencies in Lebanon, South Africa and Southern Rhodesia. But in none of those conflicts did it create a court to punish responsible parties. The legality of the Hague Tribunal depended on the scope of Article 41:

The Security Council may decide what measures not involving the use of armed force are to be employed to give effect to its decisions, and may call upon the members of the United Nations to apply such measures. These may include complete or partial interruption of economic relations and of rail, sea, air, postal, telegraphic, radio and other means of communication, and the severance of diplomatic relations.

It is fair to say that the drafters of Article 41 did not have an international criminal court in mind: it is hardly *sui generis* with the examples they chose to give of economic and diplomatic sanctions. But the power is a wide one, and does not *exclude* the imposition of criminal responsibility on persons whose capacity for acts of aggression can only be deterred by the prospect of punishment. Through Resolutions 731 and 748, the Council had already imposed sanctions on Libya in an effort to force Colonel Gaddafi to surrender for trial two of its nationals accused of the Lockerbie bombing; now it was imposing criminal sanctions on individuals more directly. The power of the United Nations to establish courts and tribunals to render binding civil judgments had been upheld by the ICJ in 1954;[9] now it was establishing a court with the power to imprison rather than merely to award compensation. So far as the familiar bogey of state sovereignty was concerned, there was a crucial let-out. Article 2(7), which forbids the United Nations to 'intervene in matters which are essentially within the jurisdiction of any State', expressly commands that 'this principle shall not prejudice the application of enforcement measures under Chapter VII'.

The first, and most significant, decision by the ICTY was to rule itself lawfully constituted by the Security Council. Duško Tadić's preliminary objection that it had no power to put him on trial was rejected by both the Trial and the Appeals Chambers.[10] The Trial Chamber did so on the unsatisfactory basis that the Tribunal itself had no power to review acts of the Security Council, because this would be to enter a forbidden political territory which was 'non-justiciable'. This is a conservative position, much favoured by the late Chinese judge Li, who believed that courts should be subservient to political masters. He denounced the very idea of judicial review of the Security Council as 'imprudent and worthless' because his colleagues were 'trained only in law' and had 'little or no experience in international political affairs'. The appellate majority, however, treated these arguments about 'political questions' and 'non-justiciable issues' as part of the old no-go areas of national honour and state sovereignty. It ruled that legal questions of whether the Security Council had Charter power to act as it did, and whether its action was taken rationally and in good faith, invited legal answers which the judges were qualified and entitled to give, 'particularly in cases where there might be manifest contradiction with the Principles and Purposes of the Charter'.

The first precedent set by the ICTY was therefore to assert the primacy of the rule of law. The Security Council itself could, within a narrow scope, be judicially reviewed, i.e. corrected if it plainly misinterpreted its charter or invented a 'threat to the peace' which demonstrably did not exist. What is heartening about the Appeals Chamber majority is that it was prepared to analyse its own legitimacy by passing judgment on the action of the Security Council, rather than automatically accepting that action as a loyal UN instrumentality. This is an important assertion of independence: international judges are entitled to find that governments, even when they are powerful and unanimous, misunderstand or misapply international law.

The Hague Tribunal set another important precedent in its preliminary ruling, namely that international jurisdiction to punish both war crimes and crimes against humanity did not require proof of an *international* armed conflict – an internecine conflict was enough. The reasoning behind this decision settles an arid scholastic debate, and establishes beyond doubt the competence of the international community, should it wish, to punish rulers who brutally oppress their own people, irrespective of whether their plight directly attracts foreign intervention.

Article 1 of the ICTY Statute empowers it to 'prosecute persons responsible for serious violations of international humanitarian law committed in the territory of the former Yugoslavia since 1991' – a formula which, unbeknown to the UN at the time, would empower the prosecutor years later to investigate allegations of NATO war crimes during the bombing of Serbia. The standard was chosen to avoid any argument about retrospective punishment: the offences would be those clearly established by the time of the outbreak of the Balkan conflict in 1991. By that time the laws and customs of war had been well established, as had the class of 'crimes against humanity' defined at Nuremberg. This precedent, however, related to crimes committed during a period of *international* armed conflict: the Nuremberg judges, notwithstanding the language of Article 6(c) of the Charter, declined to convict the Nazis in relation to crimes committed in Germany against Jews prior to the outbreak of the Second World War. Article 2 empowers the Hague Tribunal to punish 'grave breaches' of the 1949 Geneva Convention (i.e. wilful killing or torture of civilians, wanton destruction of property and ill-treatment of prisoners-of-war and civilians in the course of international armed conflict). Article 3 empowers the Tribunal to punish violations of the laws and customs of war as defined by the 1907 Hague Convention (i.e. use of poisonous weapons, wanton destruction of cities, bombardment of undefended towns, destruction of churches, hospitals or cultural property in the course of armed conflict, whether international or internal). Article 4 empowers it to punish genocide, i.e. attempts to destroy persons because they are members of a national or ethnic or religious group. And Article 5 gives it the jurisdiction to punish crimes against humanity.

It was argued on behalf of Tadić that the Tribunal's jurisdiction was confined under Article 3 of its statute to war crimes committed during international armed conflict, and that the Balkan imbroglio was purely internal. This issue is of import for the future ability to punish human rights violations committed in the course of civil strife, and the Tribunal's broad definition of 'armed conflict' extends customary law to cover the treatment of rebels, at least when they are both 'armed' and 'organized'. The Appeals Chamber found that an armed conflict exists whenever there is resort to armed force between States or protracted armed violence between governmental authorities and organized armed groups or between such groups within a State. International humanitarian law applies from the initiation of such armed conflicts and extends beyond the duration of hostilities until a general conclusion of peace is reached; or, in the case of internal conflicts, a peaceful settlement is achieved. Until that moment, international humanitarian law continues to apply in the whole territory of the warring States or, in the case of internal conflicts, the whole territory under the control of a party, whether or not actual conflict takes place there.[11]

The Appeals Chamber accepted, with some reluctance, that Article 2 (covering 'grave breaches' of the Geneva Convention) could only apply within the framework of international armed conflicts, since the Geneva Conventions themselves were so limited in 1949 when customary law had not advanced far enough to permit the world to put on trial the rulers of a country who chose to put down armed insurrection with inhumane violence. As if to underline the anachronism, the Appeals Chamber went on to hold that most of Article 3 (violation of the law or customs of war) *did* apply to internal armed conflict, because those who conducted it, whether on behalf of the State or on behalf of insurrectionists, were bound by international law to respect 'elementary considerations of humanity' – a conclusion reached by the ICJ in its 1986 decision in *Nicaragua* v. *US*.[12] Since there is a considerable degree of overlap between the conduct condemned by the Geneva Conventions and by customary war law, the distinction drawn by customary law – requiring an international conflict in order to exert jurisdiction over one but not the other – is no longer sustainable. Historically, as the Appeals Chamber points out, there was a 'stark dichotomy' between belligerency – an armed conflict between sovereign states – and insurgency within the territory of a sovereign state. The former was regulated in detail by international law, which turned a blind eye to civil strife so as to avoid encroachment on the sovereignty of a state, i.e. its power to put down its rebels and traitors as it pleased. It was time the dichotomy was abandoned, because a State-sovereignty-oriented approach has been gradually supplanted by a human-being-oriented approach. Gradually the maxim of Roman law *hominum causa omne jus constitutum* (all law is created for the benefit of human beings) has gained a firm foothold in the international community as well. It follows that in the area of armed conflict the distinction between interstate wars and civil wars is losing its value so far as human beings are concerned. Why protect civilians from belligerent violence, or ban rape, torture or the wanton destruction of hospitals, churches, museums or private property, as well as proscribe weapons causing unnecessary suffering when two sovereign states are engaged in war, and yet refrain from enacting the same bans or providing the same protection when armed violence has erupted 'only' within the territory of a sovereign State?[13]

This logic is impeccable, and made irresistible by the overlap between 'war crimes' on the one hand and 'genocide' and 'crimes against humanity' on the other, which are not limited to times of international conflict. This latter category, jurisdiction over which was granted by Article 5, covers inhuman acts directed against a civilian population 'in armed conflict, whether international or internal in character'. The specific examples, ranging from murder, torture, extermination and rape to the lesser offences of deportation, imprisonment and persecution on political grounds, cover most of the crimes punished (but only when committed in international conflict) under the 'grave breaches' regime of the Geneva Conventions. By ruling that it was 'a settled rule of customary international law that crimes against humanity do not require a connection to international armed conflict' or perhaps to any conflict at all,[14] the court effectively side-stepped the limitation of the 1949 Geneva Conventions. State parties had obviously been reluctant in the Cold War era to give foreign states the right (indeed, under the Convention, the duty) to punish any of their nationals for acts of internal oppression and hence the Geneva limitation to 'international' conflicts: now the *Tadić* precedent limits the relevance of this anachronistic distinction and concentrates on the state as internal oppressor as well as external aggressor.

The end result of the Hague Tribunal's exhaustive analysis of customary and conventional international humanitarian law as it had developed by the time of the break-up of Yugoslavia may be summarized as follows:

(1)   Crimes against humanity are inhumane acts of a very serious nature committed as part of a widespread or systematic attack against a civilian population on political, ethnic or religious grounds. They may be committed in times of peace or of war (although the statute of the Hague Tribunal requires them to be linked to armed conflict).

(2)   'War crimes' (i.e. violations of the laws and customs of war, otherwise described as international humanitarian law) cover unlawful methods of warfare deployed against the enemy or civilians in international armed conflict.

(3)   'Grave breaches' of the Geneva Convention are committed by unlawful treatment of certain categories of combatants (the sick and wounded, prisoners-of-war, etc.) and of civilians, but only in times of international armed conflict.

(4)   Genocide, under both customary and conventional law, is punishable whether it is attempted or committed in peace or in civil war or international war.

It was not on the cards that the judges of a tribunal upon which so many humanitarian hopes were riding would abolish themselves at the request of the very first defendant, or be persuaded to limit their own jurisdiction over him. None the less, these appellate judgments were an intellectually impressive beginning, all the more important for emanating from the first truly international criminal court. By defining 'armed conflict' and its temporal and spatial connotations, by severing so forcefully the category of crimes against humanity from any requirement of a connection to international wars, or indeed to any state of conflict, the judgments marked a significant advance in international law. Although the crimes committed in former Yugoslavia were obviously part of an armed conflict, the law which is emerging from The Hague is equally tailored to systematic atrocities committed in states where there is no conflict at all – in America, for example, when hijacked planes were flown into the World Trade

Center and the Pentagon as part of al-Qaida's ongoing conspiracy to mass-murder US nationals.

In November 1994 the Security Council established, as an appendage of the ICTY, a further court with three trial chambers sitting in Arusha – the International Criminal Tribunal for Rwanda (ICTR) – to hear cases arising from the genocide in Rwanda earlier that year (see pp. 98–102). The appeals chamber for both courts is the same body, based in The Hague, thus assuring consistency in the law applied by both tribunals. The ICTR statute does advance international criminal law in one important respect, by imposing individual responsibility for breach of common Article 3 of the 1949 Geneva Conventions. It will be recalled that the 'grave breaches' regime of these conventions imposes criminal liability only for war crimes committed in the course of international armed conflict, and the atrocities in Rwanda were plainly not of that description. The tribal killings had no relation to any inter-state conflict and the only international element in the country – the UN 'peacekeepers' looking on in horror – could not get out of Rwanda quickly enough. Common Article 3, devised in 1949 as merely a minimum human rights standard for states to honour during internal armed conflict, has now crystallized as an international criminal law for the breach of which individuals can properly be punished by international courts.

The Rwanda Tribunal began even less satisfactorily than its big brother in The Hague. There was admitted incompetence and sloth, and some corruption, in its early years and in Arusha in Tanzania this was out of sight and for too long out of mind. However, in the *Kanyabashi Case* (1997), its trial chamber rejected a jurisdictional challenge to the Security Council's exercise of Chapter VII powers in setting it up, ruling that the conflict in Rwanda did indeed pose threats to international peace and security because it unleashed 'a massive wave of refugees, many of whom were armed, into the neighbouring countries which by itself entailed a considerable risk of serious destabilization of the local areas in the host countries where the refugees had settled'. The danger of the conflict spreading to neighbouring states was ample justification for the Security Council's exercise of power.[15]

The Rwanda Tribunal commenced a programme of trials of very significant 'authors' of the genocide, including a number of leading politicians and civil servants ('*bourgmestres*' or district prefects alleged to have planned and organized some of the massacres) and senior executives of the radio station Libre des Mille Collines which broadcast specific incitements to kill more Tutsis (and gave details of their hiding places) during the time of the genocide. It was easier to net these 'big fish' because they had no state in which to hide, and some have been content to co-operate with the Arusha prosecutors and accept a long prison sentence rather than face the alternative of a summary trial followed by firing-squad execution in Rwanda under the new Tutsi-dominated government.[16] In September 1998 came an important breakthrough when the former Rwandan prime minister Jean Kambanda pleaded guilty to genocide. Its alleged mastermind, Colonel Theoneste Bagosora, was put on trial in 2005, and finally convicted in 2010.

The ICTR's most stomach-turning prosecutions charge men (and women) of God with active participation in the genocide. Father Athanese Seromba was deliberately hidden by the Vatican, which gave him a false name and a pleasant parish in Florence: he was eventually exposed by journalists and charged with bulldozing his church so as to crush to death the 2,000 Tutsis he had invited to take refuge inside it. The head of the Seventh Day Adventist church in Rwanda, Elizaphan Ntakirutimana, has been extradited from Texas to face similar charges of complicity in the death of Tutsis who sought the protection of their 'dear Pastor' to whom they wrote: 'we wish to inform you that tomorrow we will be killed with our families'. He replied, according to survivors, 'A solution has been found for your problem. You must die. God doesn't want you any more.'[17]

HOW THE ICTY OPERATES

We have seen that Articles 2–5 give the Hague Tribunal jurisdiction over crimes which in 1991 were accepted in customary international law as attracting individual responsibility, so no defendant could be heard to argue that he had been charged with an offence which did not exist at the time he was alleged to have committed it. Article 6 limits the range of defendants to 'natural persons' (i.e. individuals, excluding organizations or associations) and Article 7 sheets home responsibility to all who 'planned, instigated, ordered, committed or otherwise aided and abetted' the offences. The Nuremberg precedents are repeated: there is no sovereign immunity for heads of state or government agents; commanders are liable for acts of subordinates if they knew of them or failed to take reasonable measures to prevent them; 'superior orders' constitute mitigation but not a defence. The rule against double jeopardy, or being tried twice for the same offence ('*non bis in idem*',) is upheld by giving the Hague Tribunal concurrent jurisdiction with national courts, but a primacy over them which it may take by way of a formal request to any national court to defer proceedings in respect of a suspect and hand him over for trial at The Hague. In this important respect, its *primacy* power, which enables it to wrest jurisdiction from national courts, is much more effective than the *complementarity* power of the ICC which can only insist on taking a case if national law enforcers do not or cannot bring or progress it (see p. 528).

The organization of the ICTY is more extensive. The judges – there are enough for six trial courts (of three judges apiece) and a seven-judge appeal court – are elected by the General Assembly of the UN, 'taking due account of the adequate representation of the principal legal systems of the world' and 'of the experience of the judges in criminal law, international law and human rights law'. The eleven originally selected had a reasonable range of international law experience, but their human rights experience, if any, was obtained in the service of governments accused of human rights abuses, rather than any voluntary service for organizations like Amnesty. More worrying has been the lack of any reference to recent experience of *defending* accused persons, which might be thought the most important qualification for a role which combines the functions of judge and juror, and calls for decisions based on identification evidence and witness credibility. Over the years, the calibre of ICTY/ICTR judges has varied from a number of excellent appointments to other judges who have lacked essential qualities of hard work and reasonable knowledge of the law they are required to apply. Some have been slack, coming into court late, taking time off and relying on their clerks to write their judgments, whilst others have been punctilious and have justified their considerable salary (approximately $180,000) and status (deputy general-secretary level). The UN goes to extraordinary lengths to hide the salaries of its international judges, which many of them collect tax free by virtue of their national laws, but with allowances, perks and pensions, many will be receiving much more than most national jurisdictions would offer. At this rate, the UN is entitled to expect value for money, but there is no institutional check on judicial performance. The judicial appointments arrangements are entirely unsatisfactory: unlike appointments to internal UN judgeships, which are on the recommendation of an expert and independent Internal Justice Council, ICTY judges are nominated by their states and elected not on their merits but by the UN member states where political and regional allegiances determine the outcome. This favours diplomats and lawyers who have served governments (the same problem is encountered in appointing judges to the ICC – Japan has even nominated diplomats without law degrees or legal practice credentials to these judicial positions). The statute says nothing about an age limit for judges: had it been set at seventy, several would have been disqualified.

The prosecutor is an appointee of the Security Council, and Article 16(2) requires that he or she 'shall act independently as a separate organ of the International Tribunal [and] not seek or receive instructions from any Government or any other source'. Despite (or because of) this independence, the appointment of the first prosecutor was a sorry example of UN political horse-trading.[18] Bassiouni was the obvious choice, but the UK feared he would be too aggressive and other states objected either because he was American or because he was Muslim or because he was both. The respected Indian attorney-general Soli Sorabjee was nominated, but of course Pakistan objected vehemently. The first appointee, an unknown (except to Boutros-Ghali) Venezuelan attorney-general, Ramón Escobar-Salom, proved a disaster: he delayed taking up the job for five months, then decided to accept a better offer. His irresponsible behaviour put the whole enterprise in peril: it was only saved by the Australian government making available an experienced deputy, Graeme Blewitt, and then by President Mandela (after Russia had vetoed five further nominees) persuading Richard Goldstone to forgo his seat on the South African Constitutional Court to provide distinguished leadership. None the less, the Tribunal was excruciatingly slow in getting under way: by the summer of 1995, when the Srebrenica massacre took place, it had not commenced a single trial. Judgment in its first case, *Tadić*, was not delivered until May 1997, with the appeal taking a further two years. Delays of this magnitude may have been understandable for a first case, but they continued to plague the Tribunal, notably over the Milošević trial, which began in February 2002 and took three years merely to complete the prosecution case. Confidence began to return slowly in 1998, when NATO forces started arresting some important defendants, including General Krstić, charged with ordering some of the butchery at Srebrenica, and later General Galić, charged with directing the murderous mortar fire into Sarajevo. A welcome breach in diplomatic niceties came when Austrian security police arrested the chief-of-staff of the Bosnian Serb army, who had been invited to Vienna as a conference delegate. He was immediately diverted to The Hague, for trial on charges of ordering massacres of Muslims and Croats in northern Bosnia in 1992. Of course there were ambassadorial protests, but the episode served to emphasize the post-*Pinochet* principle that there must be no hiding place for perpetrators of crimes against humanity.

The Tribunal's main organizational problem has stemmed from Article 11(c), which provides that its registry shall serve both the judges and the prosecutor. Fairness to the defence, and the requirement that justice must be seen to be done, demands a complete separation of the prosecutorial from the judicial function. At The Hague, there has been a very real impression that judges and prosecutors are on the same side: they are housed under the same roof and 'serviced' by the same administration and public relations departments, equally committed to the 'success' of the exercise. This was a problem at Nuremberg, where judges and prosecutors fraternized to the exclusion of the German defence lawyers; regrettably, this history has been allowed to repeat itself to some extent at The Hague. Some recent efforts have been made to 'facilitate social interaction' between judges and defence counsel. What is really needed, however, is proper provision for the defence within the organization of the court. There should be a principal defender, of equal status to the prosecutor, heading up a defence office tasked to ensure that every indictee has a competent and properly resourced advocate. Such an office was first established in the Special Court for Sierra Leone.

The ICTY and ICTR will be judged, at the end of what will be a very long day, by the standards of fairness they are able to demonstrate – by the extent to which they can avoid the dangers of a 'show trial' epitomized by the first *Demjanjuk Case* (see p. 347). The primary reason why Nuremberg commands retrospective respect is that its judges (against the wishes of their Russian brethren) acquitted on many counts and found three defendants to be innocent of all charges on the evidence presented. The presiding judge, Lord Justice Geoffrey Lawrence, was not a great lawyer, but he kept an open mind and gave a scrupulously fair hearing. The first ICTY president, Antonio Cassese, an Italian professor of international law who died in 2011, was a man of outstanding intellectual breadth (as his Appeals Chamber judgments attest) but was frustrated by lack of state support.[19] He appeared at an international conference on the Dayton Accords to urge that Serbia be prevented from participation in the Olympic Games in Atlanta, unless it helped to arrest the 'war criminals' Karadžić and Mladić.[20] The question of whether these men were in fact war criminals was for his tribunal to decide, under a statute which presumed them innocent until proven guilty (Article 21(3)). Ironically, he later presided over the Trial Chamber in the *Kupreskić Case*, convicting three defendants whom the Appeals Chamber in October 2001 ruled should have been acquitted because the trial judges had not properly understood the weaknesses of eyewitness evidence – the kind of problem which sometimes arises when academics with no courtroom experience are appointed as trial rather than as appeal judges. This was an important decision – the first time that convicted men had been released on appeal. The Appeals Chamber insisted that it would not henceforth be a rubber stamp, but would

assess whether or not any 'reasonable tribunal of fact could be satisfied beyond reasonable doubt that the accused had participated in the
criminal conduct'.[21]

The charges against the Serbian, Croatian and Kosovo-Albanian
defendants at The Hague do not infringe the rule against retrospectivity, since they refer to conduct which was at the time contrary to
international law and (for the most part) Yugoslavian law as well –
the latter generally prescribing the punishment of death, which the
Hague Tribunal is not empowered to impose. The rule does not prevent trial by courts or under procedures which did not exist at the
time, so the Security Council (in framing the Tribunal Statute) and the
judges (in drawing up its rules of procedure and evidence) had a free
hand, guided by the basic rules for fair trials reflected in human rights
conventions. The Anglo-American adversary system of trial (as
opposed to the Continental inquisitorial system) was selected as the
model, so the statute and rules generally accord 'equality of arms' to
the defence, including the right to free legal representation both at
trial and during any pre-trial questioning.[22] The accused is 'not to be
compelled to testify against himself or to confess' at the investigation
or the trial stage, and the prosecutor may only question suspects in
the presence of an interpreter after they have been provided with (or
at least offered) legal assistance. They have the right to remain silent,
being cautioned that 'any statement you make shall be recorded and
may be used in evidence', and this 'right to silence' means that no
inference can be drawn against them if they refuse to face cross-
examination. (It might be thought that any innocent man, against
whom there is a *prima facie* case of commanding torture or mass-
murder, would insist on going into the witness box to deny it.)

The rules of procedure and evidence, drafted by the judges, provide a model of 'due process' in criminal courts. The prosecutor has a
duty to disclose all evidence upon which he relies to defendants once
they have appeared for trial: this obligation, reasonably enough, does
not apply in respect of those who remain in hiding. (Radovan
Karadžić's counsel was therefore refused access to the evidence used
to obtain a warrant for his arrest.) Rule 66(c) permits the prosecutor
to approach the Trial Chamber in secret to relieve him from his

disclosure duties in respect of information which might prejudice ongoing investigations or 'may be contrary to the public interest or affect security interests of any State' – a formula appropriate for intercept material and the like. If the prosecution wishes to use it at the trial, it must be disclosed to the defence. In one case, the prosecution was permitted to call, in a closed and highly confidential session, a serving diplomat to repeat information clandestinely obtained by his embassy. There is no rule against hearsay evidence: sensibly, since the trial is by experts rather than by lay jurors, the court 'may admit any relevant evidence which it deems to have probative value',[23] including evidence of a 'consistent pattern of conduct'.[24]

There is one important limit on what is described as 'evidence obtained by means contrary to internationally protected human rights', namely Rule 95, which is couched in these terms:

No evidence shall be admissible if obtained by methods which cast substantial doubt on its reliability or if its admission is antithetical to, and would seriously damage, the integrity of proceedings.

This ambiguously drafted rule gives the court a wide discretion: 'methods [which] cast substantial doubt on . . . reliability' might include confessions extracted by force or threats by soldiers or police, or from witnesses who had been paid by the media for telling their story, or elicited by investigators acting as *agents provocateurs* (see p. 157). Notwithstanding the *prima facie* admissibility of hearsay, one Tribunal judge has invoked the rule to reject second-hand evidence about what eyewitnesses to a crime said to others.[25] The rule would certainly cover identification evidence obtained by methods which have often proved unreliable (confrontations rather than line-ups, for example), or given by witnesses who had only a fleeting glance.[26] It was on this basis – the unreliability of eyewitness evidence – that three convicted defendants were freed on appeal in the *Kupreskić Case*. However, it may not include evidence obtained by surreptitious or unlawful means or by invasion of home or privacy – bugging, telephone-tapping, mail-opening, trespass, kidnapping and burglary are not methods prone to produce unreliable evidence, but rather evidence which is all too reliable. Would the admission of such unfairly or unlawfully obtained evidence seriously damage the integrity of the proceedings? On one level it might be argued that any court of law is compromised if it accepts evidence obtained by violence or other illegality, and on the other that clear evidence of the commission of a crime against humanity should always be admissible, even if obtained as a result of a payment, beating or an illegal bugging. The court has had to elucidate the rule on a case-by-case basis.

One form of surreptitiously obtained surveillance evidence to which no objection should be taken comprises the satellite photographs and electronic intercepts obtained and analysed by intelligence agencies. This evidence can be devastatingly reliable – as the then US ambassador to the United Nations, Madeleine Albright, revealed in August 1995 by showing photographs of mass graves taken by a U-2 spy plane after the fall of Srebrenica. The real problem faced by the prosecutors has been to extract such evidence from secretive intelligence agencies which wish to avoid publicizing their methods.[27] The arguments used by the CIA, MI6 and similar agencies to deny the court timely evidence of atrocities are specious, because there is no secret about the role of electronic surveillance: it has replaced the human spy as the mainstay of modern intelligence-gathering. It was not until April 1999, after the British prime minister had made the indictment of Slobodan Milošević for crimes against humanity a NATO 'war aim', that his foreign secretary personally handed to the Tribunal prosecutor evidence against the Serb leader gathered by GCHQ through signals intelligence.

At Nuremberg, there was no system for appeal. The Hague Tribunal reflects another development in human rights law by providing a right of appeal against errors of law and fact to a five-judge appeals chamber, exercisable by either defence or prosecution. The right of a prosecutor to appeal on questions of fact, however, is unnecessary and oppressive: if two or three experienced judges in the Trial Chamber have delivered a reasoned written judgment in support of a 'not guilty' verdict, it must follow that a 'reasonable doubt' exists. The same mistake was made in drafting the Rome Statute for the International Criminal Court (see p. 544). The Tribunal's second contested trial, over murders of prisoners by Bosnian Croats, resulted in a 500-page judgment which unanimously acquitted one defendant, Zejnil Delalić, but the prosecution immediately announced an appeal. This kept him in prison, when a reasonable doubt obviously existed about his guilt.

One of the most notable achievements of the ICTY has been to identify and to stigmatize rape as a war crime rather than a spoil of war. It did not feature in any of the indictments of Nazi war criminals – understandably, because the worst example of tolerated and systematic rape was during the Russian army advance on Germany through eastern Europe, during which an estimated two million women were sexually abused with Stalin's blessing that 'the boys are entitled to their fun'. The rape of civilians was formally outlawed by Article 27 of Geneva Convention IV, but was signally omitted from the 'grave breaches' regime in Article 147. The systematic rape of an estimated 200,000 Bengali women by Pakistani soldiers in 1971 went entirely unpunished, and although the crime was widely committed by the military and by FRAPH in Haiti under Cedras it was readily amnestied by UN negotiators in 1995. The Hague Tribunal has restored it as a war crime, and as a crime against humanity too, when committed on a widespread scale with a preplanned tactical purpose. In the case of some Serb battalions, gang rapes of Muslim women took place in public in order to terrorize and demoralize the local population by threatening 'to make Chetnik babies'.[28] By indicting Serb police who participated in and oversaw the abuse of Muslim women prisoners in a 'rape camp' at Foca, the Tribunal established the offence as a war crime.

It should be emphasized, however (and this point has been obscured in some Tribunal judgments), that what justifies international condemnation is not an opportunistic act of violation of individual women, but the deployment of rape as a tool of ethnic cleansing. Bosnian Serb militiamen were permitted to rape publicly, so as to humiliate Muslim women in front of witnesses – their village neighbours and fellow camp inmates – in the knowledge that the victims would thereafter carry a cultural stigma. Rape becomes a crime against humanity not because of the act itself, but when it is permitted or committed for political ends – in the Bosnian episodes in 1992, as obscene public exhibitions of the scattering of Serbian seed. The ICTY has been criticized for failing to insist on proper proof of a racist or other political motive when charging rape as an international crime. In the *Celebići Case*, for example, a trial chamber seemed to argue that every rape of a woman (although not, curiously, of a man) was by definition torture, irrespective of motive.[29] This is to blur an important distinction: an act which is wicked in itself becomes especially wicked (that is capable of amounting to a crime against humanity) when deployed systematically and for political ends. Two judges in the *Tadić Case* even ruled at one point that a man could be convicted of rape on the word of an anonymous accuser – a fundamental breach of the right to a fair trial.[30] These mistakes have in due course been corrected, and it does appear that the Tribunal's rape indictments may have had some deterrent effect: the mass rapes which were a phenomenon of the early stages of the Bosnian conflict have not recurred, although this may equally be due to a command perception that the international disgust these atrocities attracted outweighed their domestic value as a measure of ethnic terror.

THE *TADIĆ CASE*

Duško Tadić was forty when he stood in the Hague dock, the first accused to face a truly international criminal court. Born to a prominent Serb family in a small town in Bosnia-Hercegovina, he had excelled at school in karate and made a living teaching it before opening a popular café: the town, and his customers, were mainly Muslims, with whom he had excellent relations until ancient blood hatreds were stirred up in 1990. The nation – Yugoslavia – was fracturing along ethnic lines, as manipulative politicians like Milošević commandeered the media to urge revenge for historic wrongs. There were plenty of those, suppressed for the previous forty-five years by Marshal Tito: the bloody battles with the Turks (i.e. Muslims) over the centuries; the massacre of 250,000 Serbs by the Nazi-supporting Ustashi (i.e. the Croats) in 1941, avenged in turn by the murder of 100,000 Croatians by Tito's partisans (Serbian communists) in 1945. Now the initiative was taken by heirs to the Chetniks – the Serbian nationalist fighters who got it (and gave it) in the neck from all sides during the Second World War. Tadić's father had been one of them, and his mother was a survivor of Ustashi concentration camps.

As ethnic tensions rose, fanned by rabid Serb politicians on radio and television stations which broadcast anti-Muslim and anti-Croat propaganda, Tadić became a typical recruit for Serbian nationalism. His café began to attract like-minded Chetniks from far around: they dressed in paramilitary outfits, gave nationalist salutes, and generally behaved with the puerility and crudity which racist causes throughout the world seem to attract. They supported Serb paramilitaries called 'The Wolves' and 'The Tigers' (fascist killers always seem to identify with ravening animals) and their song, 'We are going to kill all of the *balijas* [an offensive word for Muslims], fuck the *balija*'s mother', was all too prophetic. Tadić began to hero-worship Milošević, to the point of announcing that his next son would be named Slobodan after him. He became at the same time a devout orthodox Christian (the better to hate his former Muslim friends) and went into local politics. By the summer of 1992, he was leader of the nationalist clique which had taken over the town, and was in charge of 'population resettlement' – a euphemism for getting rid of its Muslim majority.

The above facts were found by the court, and there can be no doubt about Tadić's guilt: he was well known locally, and the evidence of witnesses who recognized him from Omarska concentration camp rang true. He took an active part in ethnic cleansing, by detaining Muslim civilians, separating the men and boys from the women and old men, and beating the former then assisting the deportation of the latter. Although he was not a regular soldier (he worked part time, as a traffic policeman), he was allowed the run of Omarska, the nearby concentration camp for Muslim men and boys, where he delighted in arranging severe beatings and grotesque forms of torture (on one occasion, forcing an inmate to chew off another prisoner's testicles and discharging a fire extinguisher into another prisoner's mouth). He was involved in similar brutalities (including rape) at Trnopolje, a prison for Muslim women. In all probability he was a member of the 'shooting parties' which executed Muslims in this period, although the Tribunal, lacking evidence, acquitted him on these charges. Tadić was a licensed thug, a freelance torturer, an enthusiastic participant in the persecution and degradation of hundreds of civilians on account of their religion and their race. His defence to the numerous charges, all alleging instances of brutality and torture, was one of alibi: 'I was not there at the time.' He claimed, for example, never to have visited Omarska, even though the evidence against him was overwhelming. It came from dozens of people who knew him well (some had been to school with him, others he had taught karate) and recognized him at the scene of his crimes: they had no motive to lie about him.

But Duško Tadić was no Hermann Göring. He was a coward – a bullyboy who enjoyed strutting the camps torturing defenceless prisoners in the Serb-dominated summer of 1992, but when in the following year the war became more bloody, he could not face enlistment. He was called up for military service so he fled to Germany, where he lived in Munich at a club run by his brother. Here Tadić was identified in the street by one of his victims, arrested by the German police and in due course transferred to become the first defendant in the Hague Tribunal's cells. His lawyers – an experienced Dutch firm, and some English barristers (who insisted, somewhat comically, on wearing wigs) – were given every opportunity, first to challenge the jurisdiction of the court, and then to cross-examine prosecution witnesses and call evidence to support the defence. The Serbian Republic was reluctant to co-operate with the prosecution, which meant that most of its witnesses were refugees living in the West and had to be brought to The Hague, although later in the trial the court was permitted to take evidence (mainly from defence witnesses) by video link from Banja Luka. On 7 May 1997, the ICTY found Tadić guilty on eleven counts of crimes against humanity; it dismissed eleven further counts of Geneva Convention 'grave breaches' on the technical ground that they had not been proved to have been committed in international conflict and it rejected nine counts – the most serious alleging participation in mass killings – on the ground of insufficient evidence.

This vile man will go down in history as the person whose case settled the principles and scope of international criminal law at the end of the twentieth century. The most interesting question must be whether he was worth it: an ordinary Serb turned into a vicious torturer by two or three years of racist propaganda, but hardly a person with any command authority or ability to influence events. In so far as a virtue may be made of his very ordinariness – he represents a large class of Bosnian Serbs outside the army who 'did their bit' to help with the torture, murder or deportation of Muslims – then he takes on a symbolic capacity, a scapegoat almost, for the community of which he was part. His punishment is less an example of individual responsibility than of collective guilt. This central problem did trouble the Appeals Chamber, when it finally pronounced Tadić's punishment on 26 January 2000. Despite his heinous behaviour, it had to concede that 'his level in the command structure, when compared to that of his superiors, or the very architects of the strategy of ethnic cleansing, was low'. He was given a maximum sentence of twenty years, with a minimum incarceration period of ten.

The trial itself was reassuring, in that it showed that international criminal justice can operate acceptably and effectively, if only the crippling delays can be reduced. The Trial Chamber's three judges were Gabrielle Kirk MacDonald, a no-nonsense American trial judge who later took over from Cassesse as Tribunal president; Sir Ninian Stephen, an outstanding intellect and former High Court judge from Australia; and Lal Chand Vorah, one of Malaysia's more competent jurists. They were working from a shared common-law tradition which required objective findings of fact and evidential rulings that maintained the 'equality of arms' principle of adversary trial. Their 300-page final judgment was a measured and impartial finding of historical fact: the *Tadić Case* decision stands as the most authoritative analysis so far of evidence about the factors which brought such a barbaric war to the Balkans, and about the role of Belgrade in orchestrating the slide into such a war with mindless racism. War crimes tribunals must avoid the show trial danger of propagating one version of history for 'educational' purposes (as in the *Demjanjuk Case*), and must also remember that they are not there to write objective history (the job of historians) but to try, as expeditiously as possible, defendants charged with specific crimes. They should try, however, to lay bare as much of the truth as the evidence reveals about the origins and nature of the particular conflict so as to destroy myths which might arise among future generations. As Nuremberg demonstrates, this is a valuable by-product of an adjudication process which sifts evidence and produces an objective account of what really happened, and the court's judgment in *Tadić* fulfils this important purpose.

The court's principal achievement, however, was to produce a verdict which was demonstrably fair. Tadić was guilty, on overwhelming evidence, of the eleven Geneva 'grave breaches' counts which the court dismissed on the technical legal ground that they had not been proved to have connection with an 'international' conflict (its decision on this point was reversed on appeal). He was probably – although not certainly – guilty of several of the nine counts it rejected for lack of sufficient evidence. Those verdicts displeased the prosecutors as much as the convictions dissatisfied the defence, and both sides appealed. Yet the very care with which the verdicts were reached, and the court's refusal to bend the law against an obnoxious defendant, gave its judgment credibility and impartiality.

In one respect, however, the Tribunal allowed its natural sympathy for victims to override its fundamental duty of fairness to the defendant. It rightly rejected a defence argument that 'one witness is no witness', i.e. that all charges, and especially charges of a sexual assault, require corroboration. However, it wrongly permitted certain prosecution witnesses to remain anonymous, their names and personal details known to the court but not to the defendant or his lawyer. The matter arose because some witnesses who claimed to have suffered assaults were reluctant to testify in public for fear of reprisals. The statute empowers the court to 'order appropriate measures for the privacy and the protection of witnesses, provided that the measures are consistent with the rights of the accused'.[31] To this end, the court could order that their evidence be heard behind closed doors, or by closed circuit television (so that the witness would not be in the same room as the accused) or through technical devices which would distort voices and facial features. This could effectively conceal their identity from all except the defendant and his counsel, whose right to know an accuser's identity is fundamental to the fairness of the trial, as the European Court of Human Rights has repeatedly held.[32] Article 20 of the Hague Statute requires that trials be conducted 'with full respect for the rights of the accused': plainly, justice is neither done nor seen to be done to an accused who is not permitted to know the identity of crucial prosecution witnesses – a point carefully and unanswerably made by the dissenting judge, Sir Ninian Stephen.[33]

The danger of granting anonymity, especially to witnesses whose testimony might be motivated by malice, was dramatically illustrated in the *Tadić* trial itself by the perjury of 'Witness L'. This man – real name Dragan Opacić – had been made available to the prosecutors by the Muslim authorities in Bosnia-Hercegovina, where he had been convicted of serious crime. Entirely on the strength of his proffered evidence, Tadić was accused of executing thirty male prisoners in an orchard adjacent to Trnopolje camp, and with raping twelve of the camp's female detainees. He became the prosecutor's star witness: the court granted him special protection and allowed him to testify to it in secret for three days. The prosecutors were sure he was telling the truth – he had even taken them to where some of the bodies were buried. And Opacić swore he had been present when Tadić killed his father – a sight he would obviously never forget. 'But isn't your father still alive?' the defence asked on day three. Opacić insisted that he had watched him die. 'But this man is your father,' said the cross-examiner, calling to court an old man who rushed to embrace the witness. At this point the prosecution called for an adjournment, then sheepishly returned to ask the court to disregard all that 'Witness L' had said. Denying on oath any knowledge of the father who is embracing you deserves an entry in the Guinness Book of Perjurers. This episode damaged the Tribunal, although not as seriously as it would have had his perjury been uncovered after its judgment. It should serve as a warning to future international courts: no matter how importunate the prosecutor in requesting witness anonymity or secret hearings, publicity is the greatest protection against perjury and should not be discarded, unless there is a real risk that the witness will suffer reprisals.

Jurisprudentially, the *Tadić Case* is important for defining the preconditions for international humanitarian law. There must in the first place be an 'armed conflict', i.e. an intense conflict between organized parties as distinct from 'banditry, unorganized or short-lived insurrections or terrorist activities'. Secondly, there must be a sufficient link established by the prosecution between the conduct charged as a crime against humanity and the armed conflict. Thirdly, where the charge relates to a war crime under the Geneva Conventions, it must additionally be proven that the armed conflict is international in character and the victims were persons protected by the Conventions. The test to be applied under this third element is whether a party to the conflict (in *Tadić*, the Bosnian Serb forces) were co-ordinating and co-operating with a foreign power (Milošević's Serbia) to such an extent that international force was being used against the other party (the Muslim force in Bosnia and Hercegovina). The Trial Chamber had acquitted Tadić because, on the evidence before them, Milošević was not in 'command and control' of the Bosnian Serbs, the test laid down by the ICJ in the *Nicaragua Case*. But the Appeals Chamber ruled that the control test was too strict: a sufficient link was provided by the fact that Milošević trained, equipped and maintained his Bosnian Serb allies. This sufficed to make the conflict 'international' so as to attract the 'grave breaches' regime of Geneva.

Most of Tadić's crimes were contrary to the 'laws and customs of war' which apply to all armed conflicts, whether international or not. These cover all acts in times of civil war which outrage 'elementary considerations of humanity' when inflicted upon civilians, or even soldiers who are placed *hors de combat* by detention or hospitalization. Thus war crimes can be characterized as crimes against humanity whenever committed 'on a widespread and systematic basis, and in pursuance of a policy'. The thrust of this requirement is to exclude from the class of crimes against humanity random atrocities which are not part of a plan or a campaign against the civilian population. However, the *Tadić* court approved the *Vukovar Hospital Decision* that a single act could qualify as a crime against humanity as long as there is a link with the widespread or systematic attack on a civilian population.[34]

The court identifies the rationale for crimes against humanity: they 'so shock the conscience of mankind and warrant intervention by the international community . . . because they are not isolated, random acts of individuals but rather result from a deliberate attempt to target a civilian population'.[35] This presumes there must be a *policy* – to terrorize or discriminate against classes of civilian – and that it will generally emanate, as in Nazi Germany, from the state itself. The policy which makes crimes carried out in its name inhumane need not emanate from *de jure* government: it may be that of 'forces which, although not those of the legitimate government, have *de facto* control over, or are able to move freely within, defined territory'. It follows that, under international law, crimes against humanity *can* be committed 'by a terrorist group or organization' if it is large and powerful, effectively controlling territory without permanently occupying it. The court approves the view of the International Law Commission, whose draft code on crimes against humanity recognizes 'the possibility that private individuals with *de facto* power or organized in criminal groups might also commit the kind of systematic or mass violations of human rights'.[36] This would include the atrocities committed by terrorist gangs if they are systematic and widespread. The bombings of airliners or of civilian shopping precincts by the IRA or the Medellin cartel or the forces of Osama bin Laden may on this view be accounted crimes against humanity, even though they lack one element hitherto thought essential, namely the abuse of sovereign power.

INDIVIDUAL RESPONSIBILITY

The accused, to be convicted, must be proved to have some knowledge of, and sympathy for, the inhumane policy, so as to give him a mental element more culpable than that of the ordinary criminal. This was readily proved against Tadić, from evidence of his racist leanings and his activity in nationalist politics. On this point, however, the Tribunal judgment is unacceptably fuzzy – it seems prepared to convict a defendant who is merely *aware* that his crime is also being committed by others on a widespread basis. But 'awareness' must include some *approval* of the policy. Otherwise, the crucial distinction between ordinary and extraordinary criminals becomes blurred, and the point of individual responsibility is lost if the mental element for the crime is satisfied merely by proof of collective awareness.

The court turned for legal precedents to the Allied Zone trials which followed Nuremberg, although these were conducted by military tribunals over-anxious to convict Nazis and collaborators regarded as 'collectively responsible'. A modern international court needs to be more careful about principles of criminal responsibility than the US military tribunal in the *Mauthausen Case*,[37] which found every single worker in a concentration camp culpable for the gassing of Jews, whether they had any part in it or not; or the French Permanent Military Tribunal, which sentenced to death persons who had informed on members of the Resistance, without having any part in their subsequent torture by Nazi interrogators.[38] The *Tadić* tribunal erroneously approved these decisions, which are really examples of 'victor's justice' (i.e. revenge) imposed without proper consideration of the limits of criminal responsibility. It was on safer ground in approving the approach of the *Zyklon-B Case*, where a British military tribunal ruled that manufacturers of a poison gas commonly used to kill rats were guilty of a war crime if they supplied the gas to the concentration camps with actual knowledge that it would be used to kill humans and not vermin.[39] They became a party to the Holocaust by making and selling the gas for this inhuman purpose, and bore a culpability different in kind, rather than degree, from the concentration camp gardener or cook. These military precedents must be handled with care, although the *Zyklon-B Case* was worth disinterring, as a warning to modern businessmen who may be tempted to supply 'dual use' material to regimes capable of employing it for the worst ends.

Duško Tadić was not employed at Omarska concentration camp; he was a local thug allowed to enter occasionally to torture prisoners. He was implicated, however, in the ethnic cleansing of his village, by 'calling out' Muslim civilians from homes, forcibly separating the women and children and elderly from the men and boys, and dispatching these two groups to their different camps. These acts took place during an armed conflict as part of a widespread and systematic attack on civilians in furtherance of a political policy of racial discrimination with which Tadić sympathized and to which he attached himself as an individual. The court held that this behaviour amounted to a crime against humanity compendiously described as 'persecution', namely repeated inhuman acts of harassment, torment, oppression and discrimination intended to cause suffering and inflicted because the victims belonged to a different ethnic group from their persecutors. There are ample precedents from Nuremberg and the Allied military tribunals for such an offence, although there it tended to be charged against officials of much higher status. The Nazi judges, for example, were convicted of it for systematically bending the law against Jews and Poles and implementing it in an arbitrary and brutal fashion to further Nazi policy.[40] At Nuremberg the rabid anti-Semitic propagandist Julius Streicher was held to have committed a crime against humanity by inciting the murder and extermination of Jews: he was deemed to have persecuted them through his editorship of official and quasi-official publications. Judges and editors are at one end of the spectrum, exercising a power to persuade which foot soldiers like Tadić, at the other end, actually put into practice. All are guilty: their responsibility as individuals may differ in degree, but not in kind.

Tadić's responsibility, however, was at the lower end: he deserved punishment just enough (given the hundreds who deserved it more) to be made an example. But Tadić must be seen as a baseline, a person with a level of culpability below which universal jurisdiction should not be attracted. The judgment on Tadić is the tale of a café in Kozara which changed over eighteen months from a happy multi-ethnic meeting place to a den resounding to the racist obscenities of nationalist thugs. Who was responsible for that sea change? Tadić as an individual bore enough responsibility to go to prison, but the men who polluted and changed his mind – the 'intellectual authors' of the genocide in former Yugoslavia – remained outside the reach of the enforcers of international law, until Milošević was surrendered in 2001.

The first Tribunal president, Antonio Cassesse, argued that criminalization of individuals was necessary to prevent the 'primitive and archaic concept of collective responsibility' gaining hold among future generations. Collective responsibility is not an archaic concept, however, because it is relevant to non-combatants who complicitly or unquestioningly support a government which directs atrocities. This may be unfortunate if it works to perpetuate group hatreds, but it is a consequence of genocide that only time, and not a tribunal, can erase. Tadić is not in himself important; perhaps what really justifies his pursuit and punishment is that he is a representative example of a people the majority of whom actively supported ethnic cleansing. The International Crisis Group reported in 2002 that there were 20,000 war criminals alive and well in Serbia, bitter ex-soldiers and paramilitaries. Crowds filed past the Milošević coffin and mourned at his funeral in 2006. In 2011, their ranks thinned by death and dementia, only a handful turned up to protest against the extradition of Mladić to The Hague. International courts can only punish a few of them, like Tadić, but scapegoats are better than no goats at all. The big question – still unanswered – is whether Serbia can follow Germany and put its own war criminals on trial in its own courts. At least it has made a start, as indictments are being issued by the War Crimes Chamber of the Belgrade Court and a few convictions of Serb paramilitaries have been recorded. There *is* 'collective responsibility' on a people even after its leaders and generals have been individually fixed with responsibility for crimes against humanity: it is the responsibility to continue the prosecution process for as long as it takes to punish all the perpetrators.

The rationale for establishing the Hague Tribunal was that it would assist the peace process by punishing at least some of those guilty of atrocities. The argument is that by so doing, feelings of hatred and resentment can be satisfied to an extent which may make them less likely to erupt in the future. As Cassesse said in his first report to the UN General Assembly in 1994:

How could one hope to restore the rule of law and the development of stable, constructive and healthy relations among ethnic groups, within or between independent states, if the culprits are allowed to go unpunished? Those who have suffered, directly or indirectly, from their crimes are unlikely to forgive or set aside their deep resentment. How could a woman who had been raped by servicemen from a different ethnic group or a civilian whose parents or children had been killed in cold blood quell their desire for vengeance if they knew that the authors of these crimes were left unpunished and allowed to move around freely, possibly in the same town where their appalling actions had been perpetrated? The only civilized alternative to this desire for revenge is to render justice . . .[41]

Many diplomats – especially from France and Britain – feared that the behaviour of an independent tribunal, under its own impetus and uncontrolled by diplomats, might hinder timely peace initiatives by threatening some would-be peacemakers with jail. The evidence does not bear this out: the creation of the Tribunal and its slow progress towards its first trials did not have any damaging effect on the peace process. The indictments of Karadžić and Mladić led to their gradual loss of power and position, and their absence from Dayton did not hamper the peace agreement. Although NATO forces refused at first to make any efforts to arrest them, they gradually slipped from sight, to be arrested many years later in a blaze of publicity and sent for trial. Mladić was in poor health (drinking problems) and had for some years been protected by the Yugoslav army.[42] Karadžić had for many years been on the move, hunted and haunted, a psychiatrist 'well aware of his own paranoia'.

Although the Tribunal's work has inevitably been overshadowed by the problems which dogged the Milošević trial, its achievement in processing and punishing most of the persons responsible for commanding atrocities in the Balkans has been considerable. Biljana Plavšić – Karadžić's vicious deputy during the worst killing years – showed genuine remorse, pleaded guilty and did her best to collaborate with the Tribunal. The Bosnian Serb General Galić, who commanded the siege of Sarajevo (his men pictured in their mountain bunkers as they slugged plum brandy whilst shelling crowded markets and children playing in snow) was jailed for twenty years: the first to be convicted of the Geneva Convention crime of terrorizing a civilian population. General Strugar of the Yugoslav army bore 'command responsibility' for the shelling of Dubrovnik's old town: his eight-year sentence was for failing to take adequate measures to protect a UNESCO World Heritage site or to punish the men who had made it a target. None of these precedents or punishments would ever have come to pass if the nationalist politicians left in charge of Serbia and Croatia by the Dayton Accords had been left to prosecute their own 'heroes'. The Tribunal has avoided the charge of 'victor's justice' by scrupulous fidelity, at appeal chamber level, to the rule of law: several convictions have been overturned because of insufficient rigour in applying the burden of proof. The danger that an over-elastic application of the 'command responsibility' theory will incriminate commanders genuinely ignorant of the unlawful behaviour of men under their command (as in the case of General Yamashita) was avoided in the case of Croatian general Tihemir Blaskić, whose 45-year sentence for atrocities he could not be proved to have ordered was reduced to eight years to punish him for the one crime of which he was certainly guilty, namely directing the inhuman treatment of his prisoners-of-war. Controversially, but correctly, the Tribunal quashed the only conviction for genocide – that of Bosnian Serb general Radislav Krstić, whose men participated in the genocidal killing of 7,000 Muslim men and boys at Srebrenica – because he had not been proved beyond reasonable doubt to have possessed the specific intent necessary for this worst of all crimes. He was guilty, instead, of the lesser offence of aiding and abetting genocide, and his sentence was reduced from forty-six to thirty-five years.

An important event in the transformation of the Tribunal's fortune was the election of the Labour government in Britain in May 1997. Previously, the UK had been cynical about international criminal justice: its diplomats were sympathetic to the Serbs and had taken the lead in the Security Council in pretending that genocide in Rwanda was not genocide. Foreign Secretary Robin Cook's 'ethical foreign policy',[43] with Madeleine Albright's powerful support, required NATO to go on the offensive. Gradually, with the help of SAS 'snatch squads', some big fish were netted – police chiefs, concentration camp commandants, men charged with genocide for giving orders to kill hundreds of Muslims. With their transfer to the Hague cells in 1998–9, joining a group of indicted Bosnian Croats surrendered by Croatia in 1997 after Western economic pressure, the ICTY started to look like a more equal-handed and significant player in the peace process. Then came generals, big fish caught and then convicted. First, Blaskić (sentenced, as noted, to forty-five years initially) and the Bosnian Serb Krstić (sentenced to thirty-five years for aiding and abetting the genocide at Srebrenica). Then Plavsić, Karadžić's successor as Bosnian Serb president, fell into the Tribunal's hands, charged with directing the ethnic cleansing of Muslims she had once described as 'a genetic defect on the Serbian body politic' (she was a botany lecturer and Fulbright scholar before going into politics). She was doubly important – the Tribunal's first ex-head of state and first woman – and was given bail at first, ostensibly because there was no female accommodation at Scheveningen prison but in reality because she had started to talk to the prosecutors in order to obtain a lenient sentence. Several of the Tribunal's targets actually turned themselves in, as if this were the honourable thing to do.

At a work-a-day level there have been problems, however, more in Arusha than in The Hague. The most serious problem is pre-trial delay and then the length of the trial – although defence tactics are sometimes responsible, there has been a tendency for prosecutors to overload indictments by not using enough 'specimen charges'. Defence counsel continue to protest that the court is a 'prosecution entity' because of the fraternal closeness between the court registry and the prosecution, and complain both of delays and of limits on their cross-examination and of the low budget (13 per cent of the court's total) allocated to pay defence lawyers. However, there has been no evidence of routinely unfair rulings or of miscarriages of justice.

The inability for many years to arrest Karadžić and Mladić, the author of Bosnian Serb nationalism and the commander of the Srebrenica genocide, infuriated prosecutors and demonstrated a level of collective guilt and denial in the people who had been hiding them (especially in the Serb Orthodox church, whose vestments disguised Karadžić and whose monasteries welcomed his presence). At one level, it demonstrated the need for an auxiliary crime of harbouring an indicted fugitive from international justice; at a deeper level, it demonstrated (like the crowds at the Milošević funeral) that ethnic hatreds, once inflamed, will not recede quickly. A pragmatic beginning is to support war crime trials through the carrot of foreign investment and aid, and the stick of sanctions and opposition to EU membership. The

Tribunal's third most wanted indictee, General Ante Gotovina, was captured in 2005 when his government, Croatia, gave him away, his support diminished after the European Union made clear that his surrender was a condition of Croatia's entry. The Serbian premier, Kostunica, had been an inveterate opponent of the Hague Tribunal, but in 2005, in order to start negotiations on joining the EU and to receive a US aid package, he delivered sixteen major suspects. In the same year, Haradinaj, the premier of Kosovo, was indicted for supporting KLA war crimes: he made a dignified exit from office, promising to prove his innocence. His people did not protest: the Kosovo Albanians, at least, have learned that 'victor's justice' means justice meted out to victors as well as to the defeated. They had to suffer that lesson in 2011 when Haradinaj, who had been acquitted in 2008 for lack of evidence and had returned to Kosovo where he became opposition leader, was ordered to return for a retrial when the prosecution convinced an Appeal Court majority that there had been a miscarriage of justice when the trial court refused the prosecution's request for more time to receive crucial witness testimony before it threw the case out. The decision was harsh, but it emphasized that in international law, winners can be losers.

THE RWANDA TRIBUNAL (ICTR)

The ICTR was for some years seen as an 'offshoot' of the more important ICTY at The Hague, where, as previously noted, the same appeals chamber dealt with cases sent up from Arusha. There, the familiar problems of overloaded indictments, excruciating delays and massive cost overruns (it has cost over $1,000,000 to defend each prisoner charged with genocide) became more serious matters. By 2012 the Court had convicted sixty-one defendants (seventeen of whom have their convictions under appeal). It had been able to commence transferring cases to the domestic courts of Rwanda after that country abolished the death penalty in 2007. But it had several cases still in progress and was not likely to complete its work until 2015. To this unsatisfactory record must be added evidence of embezzlement by

Court administrators and corruption by a few defence lawyers who had agreed to split the lavish (by African standards) fees with the defendants' families. Several Hutus hired as defence investigators (with access to identities of protected prosecution witnesses) were later found to be suspected themselves of committing genocide. Most damagingly, the Tribunal stood condemned by the Rwandan government, which represented its supposed beneficiaries.

It was that government's initial vengefulness and insistence on inflicting the death penalty on *génocidaires* that originally forced the UN to set the Tribunal in Arusha, far away from the victims whose interests it wanted to serve. There is no 'outreach' from Arusha to Kigali, no sustained television coverage and no regular translation of decisions into the local dialect. Animosity is fanned by stories that HIV-positive defendants are getting expensive anti-retroviral treatment, but not prosecution witnesses – witnesses infected by defendants or by soldiers following their orders.[44] Rwanda held some 80,000 prisoners accused of full-blooded participation in the genocide; despairing of international justice or any other form of regular court process, it tried many of them in *gacaca* ('grass') courts, the traditional clearings upon which community leaders would sit to decide civil disputes. This expedient has produced some confessions and reconciliations through confrontation between perpetrators and victims, but conviction is routine and human rights observers are concerned at the pressure to plead guilty (and obtain a sentence of seven rather than fourteen years) and the lack of due process – or any process at all. These *gacaca* courts at least offer a form of traditional justice, but without analysis of causes or levels of responsibility or proof beyond reasonable doubt. Some cases – rape, for example – cannot be prosecuted, because female victims who might be prevailed upon to testify anonymously in Arusha cannot stand the shame of open hearings on the village grass.

The ICTR has suffered the most serious criticism for the failure of its various prosecutors to commence any serious investigation, let alone prosecution, of members of the French-backed Rwandan Patriotic Front, which under General (now President) Kagame eventually freed the country of 'Hutu power' but in doing so committed massacres itself. Human Rights Watch was particularly critical, pointing out that the ICTY and the Sierra Leone Special Court had been scrupulous to prosecute winners as well as losers implicated in war crimes and that the failure to do so 'jeopardizes the ICTR's long-term legacy'. Many of the RPF assassinations and summary executions took place after it gained control over parts of the country and were undertaken in hot-blooded revenge or to eliminate future enemies and were not justified by the conflict itself. ICTR Prosecutor Hassan Jallow was particularly criticized for transferring for trial in Rwanda a case where RPF (later, the Rwandan army) soldiers had massacred clergy in Kabgayi. The result was a sham trial which shielded RPF officers from criminal responsibility.

Yet for all the criticisms of the ICTR, it can none the less boast some real achievements. In the *Media Case*, where *Radio Libre des Mille Collines* had broadcast incitements to genocide ('The grave is only half full. Who will help us fill it?'), the Court drew a bright line between freedom of speech and incitement to genocide. It convicted Colonel Theoneste Bagosora, who controlled the armed forces at the time of the genocide, and was guilty of murdering a prime minister and a number of moderate politicians, ten Belgian peacekeepers (part of the UN assistance mission) and large numbers of Tutsi civilians. As the Rwandan equivalent of General Mladić, he received a sentence of life imprisonment. The Court has functioned in Africa to end the impunity of genocidal heavyweights – eleven government ministers and a swag of generals and colonels who would have otherwise gone unpunished. Many of them would still be living happily (and some planning more genocide) in other African countries or in the US and Europe, from which they have had to be extradited. The ICTR has, for the first time since Nuremberg, convicted and sentenced for the crime of genocide and it was the first to punish systematic rape as a crime against humanity. Its performance improved with the allocation (thanks to US funding) of more judges and courtrooms, and the arrests (thanks to the US 'rewards for justice' scheme of offering up to $5,000,000 for information) of the major *génocidaires*. The provision of a special ICTR prosecutor (Hassan Jallow replaced Carla del

Ponte in 2004) also helped to speed up cases and make prosecutions more efficient. By the time it completes its last trials and winds up – probably in 2015 it will have punished those primarily responsible for the worst burst of genocide within living memory and done something to assuage the guilt of the great powers on the Security Council which turned blind eyes to the massacres. In Africa, a continent where impunity has hitherto reigned, that may well be accounted no mean feat.

The Hague Appeals Chamber has established some significant benchmarks and persuaded most impartial observers that international criminal justice is here to stay as a measurable contribution to global security. The Court's prosecutors and judges have shown a capacity to get at the truth through the fog of war in complicated and distant countries, and to deal fairly with unprepossessing defendants. Its moderation and professionalism belie the fears about an international criminal court which were whispered by diplomats and then bellowed obsessively by the Pentagon before the Rome Conference (see chapter 10). The UN, which initially starved it of funds, now views the Hague Tribunal as one of the few feathers in its cap. But some indication of trouble in store lay in the behaviour of China and Russia after Louise Arbour's resignation as prosecutor: they truculently refused to accept any chief prosecutor who was a national of a NATO country. Carla del Ponte, a Swiss prosecutor mainly of Italian Mafia members, emerged as a compromise. Her great task was to direct the prosecution of Slobodan Milošević, who was sent from prison in Belgrade, where he was being held on fraud charges, to The Hague on 28 June 2001. His trial began in February 2002; it was ended by his death in March 2006.

THE MILOŠEVIĆ TRIAL

Justice Jackson once remarked, apropos of Nuremberg, that 'courts try cases, but cases also try courts'. The Milošević proceedings were dubbed 'the trial of the twenty-first century' but they now appear more as a test of the fledgling system of international criminal justice.

The case had managed only narrowly to pass that test before the defendant's death in mid-trial stopped it in its tracks.

The arrival of Milošević in The Hague was dramatic and unexpected: he was being held in Belgrade on petty corruption charges when Serbia's government, led by Prime Minister Zoran Djindjić and defying federal Yugoslavian President Kostunica, decided to hand him over – on the eve of a donor's conference which in consequence granted Serbia $1.2 billion in reconstruction aid. There were, however, other factors that made his surrender politically palatable, notably the role played by press freedom. In the weeks before the handover, the liberated local media revealed how Yugoslav army forces had attempted to cover up their killings of Kosovars by bringing the bodies to Belgrade: one mass grave was uncovered outside the city, and a freezer lorry full of corpses was dredged out of the Danube. Public shame about the ex-leader responsible for these crimes meant that protests in the days following his surrender were poorly attended.

When he first appeared in the Hague dock, Milošević opened with the Charles I gambit (see p. 5). Like that first head of state to be charged with war crimes against his own people, he refused to plead on the ground that the court was unlawful. The English presiding judge, Richard May, did not make Cromwell's mistake: he entered a plea of 'not guilty', and in due course appointed an '*amicus*' team to take all legal points that Milošević might take himself had he chosen to instruct lawyers to represent him at the trial. Milošević had no shortage of defenders: in the days after his arrival, The Hague was full of ambulance-chasing defence attorneys eager for a starring role. While they clamoured about the unfairness and oppression of the proceedings, the defendant was being advised by Ramsey Clark (once Lyndon B. Johnson's attorney-general, notorious then for prosecuting Dr Spock for inciting conscientious objection to the war in Vietnam). Clark argued that the Tribunal was unlawful because it had never been ratified by the UN General Assembly – overlooking the fact that it was established by a unanimous Security Council under Chapter VII and requires no ratification, and that in any event the General Assembly had approved its establishment in December 1992. The other legal point taken by Milošević supporters in this period (they took it to the European Court of Human Rights, which held the case inadmissible) was that Milošević had been unlawfully surrendered by the Serbian government, contrary to a ruling of its constitutional court. This too was unsustainable – the punishment of international crimes overrides domestic law. Milošević also muttered about his right to sovereign immunity as a former head of state, but this did not require a reapplication of the *Pinochet* principle because any such claim to immunity is expressly excluded by Article 7(2) of the ICTY Statute.

The Milošević trial began at The Hague on 12 February 2002. Carla del Ponte described the defendant in her opening statement as 'an excellent tactician, a mediocre strategist'. His tactical excellence soon became apparent. His many months of non-cooperation with the court were a smokescreen which had served to obtain him concessions, such as an *amicus* team and an unprecedented opportunity to make an opening statement, which he took to such rabble-rousing political effect that it regained him, temporarily, some heroic status in Serbia. (Vainly did del Ponte plead, 'This is a trial chamber, not a debating chamber': the ghosts of Churchill and Eden, who had warned against international justice at Nuremberg lest it provide a soapbox for the vanquished to rise again, seemed to find vindication in the opinion poll approval of Milošević's opening speech.) It turned out that he had for months been actively preparing for the trial, with a team of Serb lawyers (who sat in the gallery, so Milošević would be better perceived as alone and victimized) and a research unit in Belgrade working up refutations of the prosecution evidence. The prosecution made the mistake of beginning its evidence with witnesses that Milošević, trained as a lawyer, could confidently face down. It was not until Paddy Ashdown testified to the horrific ethnic cleansing he had observed on visits to Kosovo in 1998, and to his personal warning to the defendant that he would end up in the Hague dock unless he stopped it, that Milošević began to falter. He flustered and floundered, and made palpably absurd accusations (the British were guilty of 'ethnic cleansing' in Northern Ireland; NATO countries bombed Serbia because they wanted to annex it); he eventually asked the judges for help in shortening Ashdown's responses. In short, he all too often personified the adage that a man who defends himself has a fool for a client.

The Milošević trial had by the time of his death in March 2006 demonstrated one very positive thing: that international criminal justice could be fair to demonized defendants and that it could provide a true adversarial forum for the assessment of evidence. These two virtues are linked: just as the fairness of the procedures at Nuremberg persuaded Hermann Göring to abandon his initial determination not to participate, so the possibility of vindication offered in The Hague must have been a temptation that Milošević could not resist. His *volte-face* was doubtless a tactical decision, but it reflected an instinctive desire to have his day (in fact, his years) in court. Even at his early appearances after his surrender, when he was refusing to recognize the Court, he could not resist the occasional angry outbursts ('I was defending my country from cruel NATO aggression') and puerile insults ('Don't bother me with charges that are on the level of a seven-year-old retarded child'). At these moments of interruption his microphone was cut off by the presiding judge, whose desk-top switching system served, instead of a gavel, to secure order in the Court. But these boorish outbursts were undermining both of his dignity and of his claim to be taking no part in the proceedings. At some point, he decided that he would be better off entering the arena with a full-blooded defence, whilst striving to maintain his 'victim' posture by defending himself. But for his death, this decision would in the long term have benefited the cause of international justice, because the verdict of the court would have been based on evidence fully tested by an accused armed with a large team of lawyers and researchers, and seconded by a trio of experienced *amici* alert to take all possible legal points in his favour. International criminal law could then have sloughed off the rebuke of 'victor's justice' by the delivery of reasoned verdicts based on evidence heard and assessed in the courtroom without taint from media prejudice or from the national allegiance of the judges.

This positive aspect of the Milošević trial does need to be emphasized, before any analysis of its undoubted mistakes and set-backs. The defendant could (like Charles I) have maintained the logic of his challenge to the court by refusing to co-operate. He could have insisted on his right to remain in his prison cell – since a defendant has a right to be present at his trial, he must have a right to absent himself from it. Alternatively, he could have turned his back on the judges, removed his translation microphones and read a book. If the *amici* counsel had been directed to represent this 'client' against his will, by cross-examining prosecution witnesses without his instructions, the whole event would have been condemned as a 'show trial'. But by entering the arena and contesting the charges with both a defence team and distinguished *amicus* support, Milošević lent credibility to the court by participating in a true adversary procedure for testing the truth of the prosecution allegations.

But the Milošević trial, in American eyes, had, by the time of his death, become something of a disaster. Its massive length speaks for itself: the prosecution case lasted three years, from February 2002 to February 2005, and then there was a six-month postponement to enable Milošević to gather strength for his own defence. The defence case would have lasted at least until 2007 and the court would then have needed another six months to prepare its judgment. The inevitable appeal would have taken several more years. A final result would not have been reached until 2010. In the years before his death, television coverage was fitful and tended to feature the defendant's ups rather than his downs: in consequence, he retained a degree of popularity in Serbia and his political party had considerable success in the 2004 elections. The relaxed detention conditions for unconvicted prisoners in The Hague's Scheveningen prison enabled him to play a continuing role in Serbian politics and to maintain a lifestyle far more comfortable than his victims wished. When hearings took place, Milošević dominated the court, which sat for two days a week to accommodate his illness and allow his right to self-defence. He manifested contempt for the judges and he repeatedly insulted the witnesses and victims. The presiding judge died mid-trial – from causes doubtless aggravated by the defendant's conduct. The prime minister of Serbia, who courageously surrendered him, was assassinated. Milošević, in the months before his death, managed to turn his dock into a soapbox, from which he could declaim remorselessly and without remorse.

In the absence of any verdict, or even of the case for the defence, it is simplistic to ask (as the media did at the time of Milošević's death) whether this is really what fair trial entails for tyrants. If it were, critics could be forgiven for thinking that the international justice game is not worth the candle: leaving them in exile, or festooned with amnesties, might be preferable to a hundred-million-dollar process which permits them to strut and fret for a decade on a televised stage. But the Milošević trial was dogged both by bad luck and bad management and no problem it has thrown up is insoluble. For example, the death of the presiding judge, Richard May, was a serious set-back which required a long delay so that a fresh judge, Lord Bonomy, could 'read himself in' to evidence he had not heard (an expedient less unsatisfactory than commencing the trial all over again). It should have been foreseen as a possibility that had to be guarded against: at Nuremberg, each of the four judges had a replacement ready to step in should he become ill. The judges themselves made a serious error in directing that all three indictments (relating to 'command responsibility' crimes committed in different ways and at different times in three separate regions – Kosovo, Croatia and Bosnia) should all be heard together: the evidence of 300 prosecution witnesses and masses of documents put an enormous strain on the parties and the judges. If the indictment had not been so overloaded, and a first trial had concentrated on the simplest and most recent case (ethnic cleansing in Kosovo) then verdicts might have been rendered within two years. In hindsight, the court was over-indulgent to the defendant by providing him with three distinguished *amici* counsel. When it became clear that he was going to defend himself with a large team of Serbian lawyers and researchers in the background, the *amici* should have been removed. Instead, the court gave two of the Serbian lawyers VIP status, allowing them to sit in 'box seats', i.e. in the press gallery.[45] It was, of course, bending over backwards to be fair and to be seen as fair, a necessary position for international criminal courts at this early stage of their development. But in fact the proceedings could only be as fair as Slobodan Milošević's own behaviour permitted them to be.

The most debilitating feature of the trial was Milošević's continuing ill-health, exacerbated by his insistence on defending himself, despite his high blood pressure – a course which eventually led to his death. The court lost sixty-six full hearing days by 2005 and had numerous early adjournments. It had to resort to a three-day trial week and then allow six months to elapse after the close of the prosecution case in February 2005 so that the defendant could rest before opening his case. Milošević's health problems were so disruptive that at one point the court imposed counsel upon him, against the defendant's wishes and without the defendant's instructions or co-operation. The Appeals Chamber intervened to insist that he must be permitted to take the lead in presenting his case, such as by questioning witnesses and making motions and applications, relying on imposed counsel only to avoid unnecessary delays.[46] This compromise could not work in the case of a defendant who exercised his rights of self-defence with such damage to himself and to the trial process.

International justice displays this tolerance because it is at a very early and unconfident stage of development. Unco-operative defendants who refuse to recognize the court or who disrupt it by defending themselves cannot in future be allowed to hijack their own trial. Fairness in such cases has its limits – or rather, must be balanced by fairness to the victims of the alleged crimes, who have rights as well, and by the imperative of upholding the rule of law. Persons who are indicted for crimes against humanity must take that trial unless they are terminally ill or utterly incapable of giving instructions. If they refuse to plead or to participate, then they should forfeit the right to adversary proceedings and be tried by an inquisitorial process used in many Continental countries and throughout South America, where a judge conducts an investigation and reports to a trial court at which his conclusions may be challenged by the defendant. This is not a perfect solution, but it would ensure that defendants do not hold up the court by refusing to co-operate or by insisting on self-defence in circumstances where they put their health at risk and disrupt the proceedings in consequence. It would also end the professionally unpalatable position of counsel forced to represent someone who does not want to be represented. The adversary trial procedure as developed by Anglo-American jurisprudence offers the best guarantees for the rights of defendants, but they are only entitled to it if they accept the jurisdiction and the rules of the court. If they refuse all co-operation or offer it in a form which entails persistent disruption, they should be made subject to an inquisitorial process whether they like it or not – a process recognized as fair in many countries of the world and which does not depend on the defendant's involvement (although obviously benefits from it).

The prosecution produced no 'smoking gun', although late in its case it was permitted to introduce an amateur video shot at Sre-brenica, showing young Muslims being taken out of a truck by Serb paramilitaries who – after a blessing from a Serb Orthodox priest – then tied them up and murdered them. These grainy, black and white images, so reminiscent of the Second World War film of the SS slaughter of Jews in eastern Europe, did not directly implicate Milošević, but it had a similar impact to the film of concentration camp victims shown at the Nuremberg courtroom, in legitimating the process of sheeting home ultimate responsibility. This served to demolish some nationalist myth-making, and other evidence pointed to his control over Serb paramilitaries. These bloodthirsty groups – 'Arkan's Tigers' and 'Franki's Boys' – were linked to Milošević through documents found on the bodies of their fighters proving they had drawn pay as well as arms and ammunition from the Yugo-slavian army. His long-denied backing for Karadžić was demonstrated by electronic intercepts of conversations between the two, in which Milošević agreed to supply the Bosnian Serbs with arms and equip-ment to attack and extirpate Muslims. The intercept transcripts showed his total sympathy with the forcible removal of non-Serbs and his approval of Arkan's policy to 'take no prisoners' (i.e. to kill non-Serbs who did not flee their homes). Although well aware of atrocities, he never punished or reprimanded the known perpetra-tors. In respect to the deportations in Kosovo, the prosecution evidence showed 800,000 Albanians fleeing from the pillaging, rap-ing and murdering instigated by the Serb forces, who made co-ordinated and planned attacks from village to village and even laid on special trains to take the inhabitants to the border after their homes had been looted and burned. The mass graves yielded up accusing ghosts, of harmless villagers shot in the back by Serb army bullets or herded into mine-shafts to be killed by army explosives. It was a widespread and systematic plan of looting, burning and murdering innocent civilians who fled from Serb soldiers, not from the NATO bombings (which became an excuse to speed up the operation).

Slobodan Milošević deserved to stand trial: he was no brain-damaged Pinochet or cancer-ridden Honecker, but a defendant suffering from high blood pressure he brought on himself by insisting on being his own advocate. He was not an ignorant soldier or an isolated hereditary ruler: he trained as a lawyer and became president of Yugoslavia's biggest bank before becoming president of the Communist Party and of the country. He was the hands-on commander of its army and its police force, which in turn were linked (by pay-slips left behind in barrack-rooms or found on dead bodies) to the paramilitaries who committed so many atrocities. He was the self-confessed architect of the mass extirpation of 800,000 Albanian Kosovars, uprooted from homes where their families had lived for centuries. International law now says that the person in ultimate command is responsible for crimes committed by soldiers, police and paramilitaries if he knows about them yet fails to take necessary and reasonable steps to stop or punish them. Although the Milošević trial ended without a verdict, and many victims felt robbed of the satisfaction they would otherwise have obtained from his conviction and lengthy imprisonment, the very fact that he was put on trial by the international community stands as a landmark in the struggle for global justice. True, there was no written and reasoned judgment to confound those who deny Serb war guilt: they turned up in their thousands to bid farewell to his coffin with their 'Slobo the Hero' banners. But reports depict them as predominantly elderly, and mostly from redneck provinces: their lost leader was denied all state honours and his wife and son stayed away, as did all national and international dignitaries. His chief mourners were fellow indictees, on bail from The Hague, and the release of white doves over his grave provided a surreal, if unintended, promise that his burial might bring peace at last to the Balkans.

The legal post-mortems continue and are identifying mistakes that must not be made again: overloading the indictment, conjoining three separate trials into a massive and unwieldy single proceeding; the lack of an alternate judge; the toleration of disruptive self-defence, and so on. Even at the last the Tribunal faltered, allowing the prosecution (which should have remained silent) to suggest quite recklessly that the defendant might have committed suicide – thus starting a host of conspiracy theories which swirled for days through the media before the conclusive autopsy which established that the cause of death was an all-too-predictable heart attack, suffered unsuspiciously by a 64-year-old man with high blood pressure and cardiovascular disease. Milošević had by this time scarcely begun his defence, but the voluminous prosecution evidence, tested by cross-examination from the defendant, his *amici* counsel and from the court, was available to anyone interested in the truth about his criminal behaviour. The Security Council might have directed the three judges to provide their provisional assessment of the trial in a special report, but no such exercise was contemplated. The same mistake was made by the Sierra Leone court when it declined to render a verdict on Chief Hinga Norman, who died after his trial had ended but before judgment had been delivered. In Anglo-American criminal law, trials must stop for all purposes when the defendant dies, even if his demise comes at the end of all the evidence. Since the evil that great men do lives after them, it would be sensible for international criminal courts in future to combat this by adopting a different rule. Trial judges should issue a report on any proceedings prematurely terminated by the accused's death. This would not be a verdict, but a judicial assessment to assist the verdict of history.

KARADŽIĆ, MLADIĆ AND THE ICTY LEGACY

The most important legacy of the ICTY will be that it paved the way for the ICC by showing that international criminal justice could work. Slowly and expensively, but none the less as a means of providing some justice for victims and some satisfaction for people throughout the world who believe that perpetrators of crimes against humanity should face at least the possibility of punishment. It also served as a template for the moderately successful ICTR in Arusha and the surprisingly effective court in Sierra Leone, and its jurisprudence and some of its personnel have gone into the ICC and into the Lebanon tribunal (which has issued indictments over the Hariri assassination), and the Cambodian tribunal which has convicted the Khmer Rouge's executioner and is currently trying its surviving political leadership.

The ICTY itself is in its mopping-up phase – the last of its 161 wanted suspects, Goran Karadžić was captured in July 2011, after seven years on the run from his indictment for the 1991 massacre of 264 patients and nurses at Vukovar hospital. Importantly, he was arrested by Serbian war crimes investigators, just two months after they had captured Ratko Mladić: a healthy sign that some sections of that nation were willing to accept and requite war guilt. That is more than can be said for many in Croatia, where the jailing (for twenty-four years) of General Ante Gotovina, convicted of ordering 'Operation Storm' which drove 200,000 Serbs out of Krajina and killed thousands of elderly civilians in the process, was met with widespread protest. This sentence was much too long for a 'command responsibility' crime which had, after all, been a reaction to Serb brutality – there were Croatian fears of a repetition of the Srebrenica massacre which had occurred a few weeks earlier. But the conviction of Croatia's war hero was based on evidence that he had approved, and had later taken no steps to punish, the indiscriminate killings of civilians and plunder of their property in the course of a massive offensive by the 150,000-strong Croatian army, which he led (so the trial chamber found) with the specific objective of ethnic cleansing. Gotovina did not help his case by fleeing as soon as he was indicted, evading capture in Catholic monasteries (Catholic authorities, including the Pope himself, refused all co-operation with the prosecutor[47]) and subsequently frequenting holiday resorts ranging from Tahiti to the Canary Islands. The verdict came shortly before the capture of Mladić and Karadžić, and seemed to reassure Serbs that the Tribunal (most of whose indictees had been Serbian) was even-handed. Interestingly, the Court's *Gotovina* decision made clear that Franjo Tudjman, the 'founding father' of non-communist Croatia who died before he could be indicted, was guilty as well: he was the 'elephant in the room' when Gotovina and others planned 'Operation Storm'.

By the beginning of 2012 the trial of Radovan Karadžić was well underway. He had found no difficulty hiding amongst sympathizers (especially Serb Orthodox priests whose vestments clad him and whose monasteries secreted him) and for many years NATO had hardly bothered to hunt for him. But he lived an unhappy existence on the run, unable even to attend his mother's funeral, and he ended up ekeing out a living in Belgrade, bearded and beaded, as a practitioner of alternative medicine. Although he is defending himself, he has learnt from the egregious posturing of Milošević: he has an American lawyer by his side and adopts a respectful, almost scholarly, approach to the Court and to the prosecution witnesses. This strategy might have been dictated by the Court's order that 'should he engage in any conduct that obstructs the proper and expeditious conduct of the trial, he will forfeit his right of self-representation'. Something, at least, had been learnt by the court from its mistaken sufferance accorded to Milošević.

His defence is one of command non-responsibility:

I have been indicted . . . for everything that every crook did on the ground. I am trying to prove that I had nothing to do with the system whatsoever.[48]

He does have a point, in that he (like most other defendants) has been overcharged by the over-zealous ICTY prosecutors, who seem not to mind how many years the trial takes: he has to answer for the siege of Sarajevo (1992–5); ethnic cleansing in Bosnia in the same period and the massacre of 7,000 Muslim men and boys at Srebrenica. It is the latter crime that should have been the only focus of his indictment, based on evidence of the cable he sent to the troops preparing for the Srebrenica offensive, explaining that its aim was to create 'an unbearable situation of total insecurity with no hope of further survival or life for the inhabitants'.[49] (That might confound his claim that 'I had nothing to do with the system whatsoever.') His alternative defence is that the late Richard Holbrooke, President Clinton's special envoy to the Balkans, promised him immunity from prosecution if he agreed to the Dayton Peace Accords. Even if true (Holbrooke robustly denied the claim), it is difficult to understand how any such promise – of immunity from genocide prosecution – could be lawful or binding.

Karadžić was fortunate that the Court did not restart his trial, with Ratko Mladić alongside him in the dock, and both men jointly charged as co-conspirators in one crime against humanity committed at Srebrenica. That would have saved time and money and revealed more as the two would have had to confront their own versions of the crime, and perhaps accuse each other. Mladić's arrest came in May of 2011, and was welcomed throughout Europe – there was little resistance in Serbia to his departure for The Hague. He had kept out of sight for seventeen years, hidden by his friends in the Yugoslav army who dwindled in number as his surrender – the price for European Union entry – became more damaging to the Serbian economy the longer it was delayed. He is generally regarded as the vilest and guiltiest of all the defendants – television footage played in court by the prosecution showed him clearly in charge of the operations and there is no way that he can deny knowledge of what his troops were ordered to do to the men and the boys at Srebrenica. He does not seem to have prospered by evading justice – his daughter, a medical student, committed suicide after reading the allegations against him, and before the helicopter lifted off for Scheveningen he was poignantly permitted a last visit to her grave (a prospect not allowed to the victims of his own mass murders, lying in still-undiscovered mass graves). Both Karadžić and Mladić condemned themselves to miserable years on the run, a form of punishment caused by their own cowardice in refusing to answer the charges brought against them by the international community.

The Mladić trial opened in May 2012, with compelling evidence of guilt provided by his own arrogant television interviews. He was seen strutting around Srebrenica, giving sweets to the boys he was about to kill. He was shown boasting to a Canadian TV journalist that 'Whenever I come by Sarajevo, I kill someone in passing. I could kick the hell out of the Turks – who gives a fuck if you care for them?' His personal diaries have been recovered and provided ample evidence of his plans for ethnic cleansing. His reputation for viciousness was brought home in the courtroom on the first day of the trial, when he made a throat-cutting gesture towards a victim whose husband and son he had ordered to be killed. After a two-day hearing, however, it emerged that the blundering prosecution had not disclosed important evidence to the defence, and the trial had to be adjourned for several months – another example of the way in which overzealous or under-competent prosecutors can make international justice look clumsy and endlessly protracted. Mladić faces far too many counts, and his trial will last far too long. He should have simply been charged with killing 8,000 men and boys at Srebrenica, then quickly convicted and jailed for life.

One high point of the ICTY came on 10 June 2010, when nemesis caught up with the first indictees to be convicted of genocide and other crimes at Srebrenica. Ljubisa Beara, the Mladić henchman who personally co-ordinated the executions and the mass burials with 'a grim determination to kill as many as possible as quickly as possible' was jailed for life (the logical fate of Karadžić and Mladić, if convicted) and others in command of death squads received up to thirty-five years. The Appeal Court had already ruled that genocide was appropriate for 'seeking to eliminate a part of the Bosnian Muslims' and their trial court found that

the scale and nature of the murder operation, with the staggering number of killings, the systematic and organised manner in which it was carried out, the targeting and relentless pursuit of the victims, and the plain intention – apparent from the evidence – to eliminate every Bosnian Muslim male who was captured or surrendered proves beyond reasonable doubt that this was genocide.[50]

For this relief, the ICTY deserves much thanks – without it the worst massacre in Europe since the Nazi concentration camp extermi-nations would have gone unpunished, with its perpetrators left to prop up bars in Belgrade, boasting of their wartime exploits killing Muslim children. Those – and there were many of them, not only in

Serbia – who opposed this 'court without a country' must acknowledge it as a court that has brought a degree of justice to all the countries of the former Yugoslavia.

There can be no doubt, from the hero-worship of Gotovina in Croatia and the Serbian truculence (exemplified by President Kostunica) that few if any of the Tribunal's 161 indictees would have been brought to justice by national law enforcement. At The Hague, by 2012, there had been sixty-four convictions and fourteen acquittals, with other cases either transferred to local courts or with appeals in progress. The court aims to conclude all cases by 2015, with the exception of Karadžić, Mladić and Hadzić. Its achievement has come at a cost – $1.8 billion over its fourteen year existence – although this must be balanced against the taking of so many human lives, the destruction of public buildings, cultural monuments and private property, and the cost of further NATO operations which the Court's contribution to the peace process has helped to avoid. Its greatest failure was to permit prosecutors to overload indictments – when the Karadžić case, for example, was projected to last for five years, the judges were still reluctant to limit the charges. Although the prosecutors have reduced the number of crimes charged in the Mladić indictment from 196 to 106, why is this vicious old man facing 106 criminal charges, at a trial during which he may well die, when he could instead be expeditiously tried and sentenced to life for the crime against humanity which he so obviously commanded at Srebrenica?

As the ICTY's work winds up, scholarly studies are beginning to gather evidence of achievements other than to bring major perpetrators to justice. The ICTY has helped to form attitudes and institutions supportive of democracy in Bosnia, for example, inspiring civil liberty groups determined to carry on its work through local courts.[51] Most notable is the War Crimes Chamber in the Bosnia and Hercegovina State Court (a hybrid court, which sits with international judges and international prosecutors) to which the ICTY has transferred its crime base data, enabling the arrest and trial of 'lesser' war criminals. These number some thousands in Serbia, Croatia (dealt with mainly in the State Court in Sarajevo) Bosnia and Kosovo. The transfer of information to local courts and police has enabled many arrests and as of 2009 had facilitated 140 trials – one hundred in the Bosnian War Crimes Chamber and forty in Croatian and Serbian courts.

The election of pro-ICTY President Boris Tadić in Serbia, to replace the hostile nationalist Kostunica, produced the necessary legal reforms to institute a War Crimes Chamber there, where prosecutor Vladimir Vukčević and his team brave death threats and frequently have their cars smashed up.[52] As well as transmitting data and witness statements and jurisprudence to the national courts, the *ICTY Manual on Developed Practices* has been widely distributed, encouraging the prosecutors and judges to follow best practice in their war crimes prosecutions. There is still much to be done at local level to reduce the scope for political interference and bring to book murderous foot soldiers and middle-ranking death-squad captains. A particular problem has been the 'impunity gap' from the failure of ex-Yugoslavia former states to agree on extradition treaties, and to co-operate with each other's investigators. There is still suspicion, and criticism of 'political' indictments and of the Serbian preference for prosecuting Bosnians and Croats.[53] There will be a need for more EU supervision (and funding) to pursue war criminals once the ICTY completes its last trials and appeals if the impetus is not to be lost – as it was for the prosecutors of Nazi war criminals after completion of the major Nuremberg trials. As for the ICTY legacy, that will surely be secure on the day that a museum opens – in Belgrade and Zagreb and Priština – dedicated not only to commemorate everlastingly the victims of war crimes in the Balkans, but for ever to condemn the brutal nationalist commanders who killed them.

10

The International Criminal Court

'Don't be vague, go to The Hague.'
Slogan of protesters against Kenyan election killings
(2010)

On 17 July 1998 in Rome, 120 nations voted to adopt a statute creating the International Criminal Court – the culmination of a fractious five-week diplomatic conference. Twenty-one nations abstained, but only seven were opposed – although these included the United States, China, Israel and India, representing a massive concentration of people and of power. The Rome Statute is a long and detailed document containing 128 articles: it was ratified by the necessary sixty states (including the UK and France) on 11 April 2002, and its jurisdiction came into effect on 1 July 2002. By July 2012 it had been ratified by 121 nations and the first prosecutor, Argentinian lawyer Luis Moreno Ocampo, and his deputy and then successor, Gambian lawyer Fatou Bensouda, had issued indictments for crimes against humanity in Libya, the Ivory Coast, Uganda, the Congo, the Central African Republic and Sudan. After attempting for several years to subvert the Court, the US in March 2005 allowed the Security Council to refer to it the situation in Darfur, and in February 2011 joined with China and Russia in a unanimous Security Council Resolution to refer the situation in Libya to the ICC prosecutor. The Court had come a long way in what, for international institutions, was a remarkably short time since the Rome Conference.

ROME 1998: THE POLITICS

The Rome Conference was meant to be the millennium moment for a human rights movement which had become fashionable since the Gulf War: the UN worked at breakneck speed to produce an agreed draft of the treaty in only twenty-seven months. Pre-millennium tension played its part, as this Diplomatic Conference of Plenipotentiaries (with hundreds of NGOs cheering them on) made feverish compromises in the days and even hours before the deadline, creating a lowest common denominator court in time for the photo opportunity finish scheduled for 17 July. Cynics thought at the time that even the most enthusiastic states would take years to make the necessary amendments to their national laws and that the necessary sixty ratifications would not be deposited for at least a decade: it was a tribute to the power of the idea (and in some cases, a reaction to America's hostility to it) that the Court came into being and into operation so quickly.

The idea of a world criminal court had received its first concrete shape in 1937, when a draft statute for a court to try international terrorists was produced by the League of Nations. After the Nuremberg and Tokyo Tribunals, the UN made a passing reference to an 'international penal tribunal' in the 1948 Genocide Convention and draft statutes were produced over the next few years by the International Law Commission (ILC). But the project soon went into the deep freeze of the Cold War, and was not brought out again until the 1980s, when Gorbachev suggested it as a measure against terrorism and Trinidad urged it as a means of combating drug trafficking. The General Assembly asked the ILC to resume work, hurrying it along in 1993 after the favourable public response to its creation of a war crimes tribunal for the former Yugoslavia. The ILC draft was delivered in 1994, and the following year the General Assembly set up a 'preparatory committee' to canvass agreement on a text which could be submitted to the Rome Treaty Conference in 1998.

At the commencement of the conference, the delegations fell into three main categories. The 'like-minded' group of forty-two nations, led by Canada and Germany (and joined, since the advent of the Blair government, by the previously hostile UK), wanted a powerful

prosecutor and a court genuinely independent of the Security Council, endowed with universal jurisdiction over war crime suspects
anywhere in the world. They wanted, in other words, a court that
would work. The United States initially wanted a court, but one that
would never work against the interests of the United States. The
model preferred by the US, joined by China and France, was a court
controlled by the Security Council, where they could use their superpower veto to stop any embarrassing prosecutions. The third group
– all the usual suspects, such as Iraq, Iran, Libya and Indonesia – did
not want a court at all. This group had, surprisingly, been led at preparatory committee sessions by India, its motives becoming apparent
shortly before the Rome Conference when it test-exploded a nuclear
weapon.

The Rome Conference was remarkable for the intensity and detail
of the lobbying campaigns mounted by NGOs, led by Amnesty and
Human Rights Watch. Some 175 of these organizations had representatives in Rome, while by the end 800 bodies in all were involved
in pressurizing governments. For human rights campaigners, of
course, the creation of a court to punish human rights violations was
a consummation devoutly to be wished, but what was truly ironic was
their zeal for a court so tough that it would actually violate the basic
human rights of its defendants. Thus Amnesty International, in its
main briefing paper, argued for an all-powerful prosecutor because
'State practice demonstrates that prosecutors are unlikely to bring
cases where the evidence is extremely weak'.[1] Such complacent assertions – the kind that, when made in the past by governments, Amnesty
would devote itself to refuting – were accompanied by a call to do
away with traditional defences. Amnesty argued that the Rome Statute should abolish the defence of duress, the defence of necessity, even
the defence of self-defence, at least unless the defendant could prove
(the burden being on him) that he had 'retreated to the utmost'. Insouciance about the danger of miscarriages of justice was common
among NGOs like Amnesty, which should have been the first to recognize that the danger of wrongful conviction is greatest when the
crime charged is most horrible and unnatural, when the defendants
have for years been tried and convicted in the media and when

prosecutors and judges are trying to carve out careers in a growth profession like international human rights. The Rome Conference was no time to worry about how to prevent defendants from being acquitted: all energies should have been directed to ensuring that at least a few were likely to be put on trial in the first place.

On paper, the Rome Statute is impressive and serves in its definitional sections to consolidate many of the conceptual advances in international human rights law which have been traced in earlier chapters of this book. Crimes against humanity were established as offences which may be committed at times of comparative peace as well as internal or international war, while war crimes, for their part, may be committed during internal conflict: common Article 3 of the 1949 Geneva Conventions became the basis for individual criminal liability rather than remaining an unenforceable promise that states will not devastate their own people. Sexual violence was indelibly identified as a war crime, 'command responsibility' was clearly established as a basis for liability, and (notwithstanding pressure from human rights 'poachers turned gamekeepers') full and in some respects overgenerous provision was made for the rights of defendants. The basic achievement was to turn the Hague Tribunal into a permanent institution, shorn of its power to override national courts but with some improvements in its procedures and personnel, and available for the Security Council to invoke instantly in respect of future genocidal conflicts.

The five-week conference in Rome was not a resounding success, despite its photo-call finish. Concessions were made throughout in an effort to keep the United States on side, and those flaws remained embedded in the Statute at the end after the US had denounced it. Through their naivety, the well-intentioned 'like-minded' group of countries allowed America to weaken significantly a court which, by a policy backflip towards the end of the conference, it decided to oppose. Although the Clinton administration had previously advocated a world criminal court and Clinton himself called for it in his 1998 visit to Rwanda, his personal authority was eroded at the crucial time by the domestic political fallout from his affair with Monica Lewinsky. After her blue dress was taken by the FBI for DNA analysis he capitulated to the Pentagon, which had for some months been briefing the military attachés of its allies that the Court was a danger to soldiers of the Western alliance.² Jesse Helms, chairman of the Senate Foreign Relations Committee, announced that the Rome Treaty would be 'dead on arrival' in Congress if there was any prospect of the indictment of a single American soldier.

Given the traditional Washington stance that the US is above international law, it should have been obvious to diplomats from the 'like-minded' group that America would not ratify the treaty until the Court was operating to its satisfaction. But they tried desperately to placate Senator Helms (with his demand for '100 per cent protection' of American GIs), going so far as to require a state's consent before one of its nationals could be prosecuted in the absence of a Security Council reference. Even this obeisance to state sovereignty was not enough, in the end, to win the American vote, which was lost when the Conference insisted that the Court should have jurisdiction over UN peacekeepers (which could include American soldiers). In principle Blue Helmets should be amenable to ICC justice, and there had been examples in Rwanda of Ghanaian peacekeepers becoming complicit in the genocide and in Somalia of Canadian soldiers being protected by army lawyers from rape charges. However, this has not been a common occurrence, and it was the Conference's insistence on sticking to this particular principle, when so many others had been surrendered, which most inflamed American paranoia. The US delegation rejected the principle of universal jurisdiction over war crimes and crimes against humanity (other than genocide) so vehemently that the US Defense Secretary William Cohen threatened Germany and South Korea with a US troop pull-out if they persisted in their support for its endorsement in the Statute.³

In the end, the Rome Statute gives the Court jurisdiction either by remit from the Security Council acting under Chapter VII of the UN Charter, or by consent of the state of which the defendant is a national or in which the crime was committed. These 'state consent' provisions mean that nobody occupying a position of *current* political or military power in any state (even one which has ratified the Treaty) is likely to be indicted unless (like Colonel Gaddafi) they have alienated all five permanent members of the Security Council. Any retired war criminal who (like Pinochet) retains a power base in his state of nationality will otherwise be safe, since in retirement they are unlikely to constitute a Chapter VII threat to international peace, and their home state will lack the resolve to surrender them to world justice. The class of criminal most likely to be arraigned by their state's consent at The Hague comprises persons who commit barbaric crimes in a cause which has failed or is doomed to failure, in a country which needs help to arrest them or decides to surrender them because it lacks the facilities to try them itself, or simply wants to get them out of the country (as with Laurent Gbagbo in the Ivory Coast). In all other respects, the ICC will become a kind of 'permanent *ad hoc*' tribunal, dependent on references from the Security Council to investigate crimes against humanity in countries where none of the combatants has a superpower supporter.

The Rome Conference was hardly an advertisement for wise global governance. The Vatican (why should this religious enclave count as a state?) took up valuable time by trying to include drug trafficking as a crime against humanity (hardly apt for a court in The Hague surrounded by cannabis-vending coffee bars) and by fears that a definition which made 'forced pregnancy' a crime might justify abortion. India, having led the opposition to the creation of a court at the preparatory sessions, now demanded an extension of the Court's jurisdiction to punish the users of nuclear weapons. This was a hypocritical attempt to deflect criticism over its nuclear test the previous month, and the proposal's defeat provided India with a pretext for condemning the whole enterprise as an exercise in 'European neo-colonialism'. These puerile posturings (from delegates of India's governing Bharatiya Janata Party) were irresponsible enough, but the gold medal for hypocrisy was won by Israel, a state founded by victims of the worst crime against humanity, in whose memory (and, perhaps, for whose future benefit) the movement to create the Court had been inspired. The Netanyahu government voted against it, as a protest after the Conference agreed to make forced settlement of occupied territory a war crime. Israel had settled over 200,000 Jews in the West Bank and the Gaza Strip after the 1967 Six-day War, but since the Statute is not retrospective, Israel's fears that its leaders might be put on trial were nonsense. Forced population transfers can be a potent means of ethnic cleansing, as Serb actions in Kosovo in early 1999 showed, and Israel's decision to vote against the Court merely because its Statute included this as a potential crime was a betrayal of the memory of the Holocaust.

None the less, the Rome Statute was an achievement of sorts: the best deal the human rights movement could do with the *realpolitik* of state power as the twentieth century drew to a close. It would have been sensible to opt for one of the two competing models – either the independent court system preferred by the 'like-minded' nations but operating initially without US support, or else a court controlled by the Security Council which the United States and China would support because they could veto prosecutions of their nationals or allies. This latter model was obviously wrong in principle, because it offered impunity to suspects protected by superpowers, but in its limited area of operation it would have the funding and logistical support necessary to arrest its suspects and to make its decisions stick. Each model offered, in its own way and within its different limits, a coherent and workable international court which might in time and by the force of its performance have overcome its deficiencies. The mistake made in Rome was to erect a compromise with which America would not compromise, and then to close the door on renegotiation by a clause banning amendments until seven years after the Statute enters into force.[4] By the time of the ICC Review Conference in Kampala in 2009, however, the Obama administration had became supportive – the US was virtually an associate member – but it was not until the Gaddafi Resolution (number 1970) in 2011 that the ICC received its imprimatur from all five permanent members of the Security Council voting in favour of a reference to its prosecutor.

ROME 1998: THE STATUTE

The preamble to this first stab at global justice is introduced with these mixed metaphors:

Conscious that all peoples are united by common bonds, their cultures pieced together in a shared heritage, and concerned that this delicate mosaic may be shattered at any time . . .

This dire attempt at literary inspiration moves in meaningless progression from bonds to cultural jigsaws to breakable mosaics, images irrelevant to crimes against humanity, which are generally committed in the name of preserving some culture perceived as incapable of coexistence with others. The preamble continues more prosaically by recalling the 'unimaginable atrocities' (although they are by now all too imaginable) of the twentieth century and then asserting that grave crimes 'threaten the peace, security and well-being of the world' – the factual formula necessary to attract UN intervention under Chapter VII of the Charter. Significantly, the preamble declares it a 'must' – a moral imperative – that 'the most serious crimes of concern to the international community as a whole must not go unpunished', and announces a determination 'to put an end to impunity' by exercising criminal jurisdiction over perpetrators, initially at a national level. The ICC is established as a permanent court with 'complementary' jurisdiction to back up national courts that are non-existent or unable to function.

This language is apt to reflect (although care is taken not to say so in terms) a universal jurisdiction over crimes against humanity, although the preamble hurriedly genuflects to state sovereignty by 'emphasizing that nothing in this Statute shall be taken as authorizing any State Party to interfere in an armed conflict or in the internal affairs of any State', thereby reassuring governments that it is not encouraging humanitarian intervention or cross-border raiding parties bent on snatching indicted suspects and delivering them to The Hague. The preamble confines the Court to jurisdiction over 'the most serious crimes of concern to the international community as a whole' and establishes its back-stop role where national justice systems have failed or broken down. The rationale for the Court's creation is found in the belief that crimes 'that deeply shock the conscience of humanity' threaten world peace, or at least 'the well-being of the world' – this is true, in the sense that our psychological well-being suffers from the sight of atrocities by fellow humans. The Court itself is described as an 'independent permanent international criminal court *in relation-ship with* the United Nations system' – coy phraseology which avoids spelling out the nature of the 'relationship'. Read on, and it emerges that the Security Council is in control: the Court will mainly have jurisdiction over such political leaders as may be thrown its way following intervention by the Council under Chapter VII of the Charter. Without a Security Council reference, there is no power in the Court or in other states to arrest political super-criminals living in a state which refuses to surrender them. Current examples are provided by Colonel Mengistu in Zimbabwe, Hissène Habré in Senegal and Ben-Ali and Saleh in Saudi Arabia.

The Court is established by Article 1 as a permanent institution with jurisdiction to try persons its prosecutor accuses of the most serious crimes of international concern. It is endowed with international legal personality, which means that it has the capacity to enter into contracts and commitments necessary for its purposes. However, it may only exercise its statutory functions and powers 'on the territory of any State Party and, by special agreement, on the territory of any other State'. In reality, of course, states which are civilized enough to ratify the Treaty are unlikely to be run by, or to harbour, persons who have committed crimes against humanity – they will generally live or lurk in states which have not signed up for justice. Such states are unlikely to allow the Court and its prosecutor to operate 'by special agreement' on their territory, at least without intense pressure from the World Bank, the IMF and the United States (which combined in 1997 to threaten Croatia with economic collapse unless it surrendered its indicted suspects to the ICTY).

Article 3 locates the seat of the Court at The Hague – the Netherlands was the only country to volunteer, and was perceived as the natural choice, because it already hosts the International Court of Justice (in a gloomy mock-Gothic mansion) and the ICTY, in a nondescript plaza named after Churchill, who was all for shooting, not trying, the Nazi leaders. The ICC occupies functional buildings which have no aesthetic qualities to compare with London's Old Bailey or the US Supreme Court or the European Court building in Strasbourg designed by Richard Rogers. Architecture has both symbolic and practical significance: countries where justice is valued have distinct and imposing court buildings, while those where it is preordained or seen as an administrative adjunct of the state generally have court-rooms which are indistinguishable from government offices. The idea that The Hague is symbolically suitable because it is 'the capital of international law' sends exactly the wrong message: this is where international law failed to thrive, or to make much of a difference, in the twentieth century.

The International Criminal Court should have been located in an historic or else a specially designed building, home to the judges and the registry, but not to the prosecution. The mistake of Nuremberg (where the prosecutors socialized regularly with the judges to the exclusion of the defence lawyers) and of the ICTY (where both organs are housed under the same roof and are served by the same registry) should not have been repeated. Regrettably, the Rome Statute structures the Court so that it comprises both the judicial and the prosecutorial arm rather than being at length from each other: the court president 'co-ordinates' with the prosecutor (Article 38(4)); the registrar, the president and the prosecutor jointly decide upon staffing matters (Article 44); the prosecutor and registrar must be consulted on court rules and procedures (Article 52); the registry will operate as a press office for both the prosecutor and the judges. Worst of all, the registrar's duties, under Article 43, include the partisan role of running the Victims and Witnesses Unit, which in conjunction with the prosecutor's office arranges counselling and protection for victims who are witnesses – usually for the prosecution. In this clumsy way, court administration has been harnessed to help the prosecutor. These arrangements are much too intimate and interconnected: the principle of impartiality requires a complete procedural and physical separation between prosecutors and judges. Most importantly, there should have been a defence office headed by a principal defender of equal status to the prosecutor. The delegates in Rome, and all those NGOs dedicated to fair trial, overlooked this basic requirement for even-handed justice.

INTERNATIONAL CRIMES

The Court's jurisdiction extends to four offences: genocide, crimes against humanity, war crimes and the crime of 'aggression'. There can, however, be no prosecutions for 'aggression' until after 2017, the earliest date that a majority of states can endorse the definition of the crime agreed at the Kampala Review Conference in 2010. These four categories are described as 'the most serious crimes of concern to the international community as a whole'. The crimes within the jurisdiction of the ICC overlap: genocide, for example, is a crime in its own right as well as a crime against humanity and a war crime, and the latter category includes behaviour which in peace time would be classed as a crime against humanity. As the Appeals Chamber in the *Tadić Case* pointed out, there is now no good reason why the behaviour of nations at war should be judged by rules different from those for internecine conflicts: these legalistic distinctions have preoccupied international criminal law for much too long. It is difficult to understand why this court should not simply have jurisdiction over crimes against humanity, whether committed in war, in times of internecine struggle, in periods of riot and unrest, or at times of utter and seemingly blissful peace. The individuals responsible for any widespread pattern of barbarity, imposed or supported by the state (through its politicians or police or military) or by armed organizations fighting to attain some (or more) power, should be indictable and the charges against them should not depend on technical legal characterization of the nature of the background conflict.

GENOCIDE

Article 6 defines the crime in terms identical to the 1948 Genocide Convention (see p. 325). The essential element which must be proved is an 'intent to destroy in whole or part a national, ethnical, racial or religious group as such'. 'Group' does not include 'social' or 'political' groupings, so General Videla – who infamously ordered babies to be stolen from Argentina's doomed left-wing mothers and farmed them out to loyal army families – could not be indicted for genocide. At the irresponsible insistence of the Vatican, genocidal acts are defined to include 'imposing measures intended to prevent births within the group'. Birth control, even when imposed by law, is hardly a crime equivalent to mass murder – it can only count as genocide if it is imposed by discriminatory measures motivated not for health or population control, but as a means of extinguishing a racial group.

Genocide is not an appropriate term to describe the behaviour of a sovereign state which goes to war with the purpose of annihilating the enemy nation. When Yugoslavia activated the Genocide Convention in 1999 with its claim that NATO bombing amounted to genocide against Serbs, the ICJ pointed out that 'the threat or use of force against a State cannot in itself constitute an act of genocide'.[5] The intention must be to destroy human beings on account of their race – not to discipline, partition or even destroy the state which is persecuting them.

CRIMES AGAINST HUMANITY

Article 7 of the Rome Statute is set out in Appendix D: it contains the authoritative definition of crimes against humanity. The acts themselves are for the most part crimes which cause great and unnecessary suffering – murder, torture, rape and other forms of sexual violence, enslavement, false imprisonment and unlawful persecution or deportation. What gives them their abhorrent quality is that they are committed deliberately 'as part of a widespread or systematic attack [a course of conduct involving multiple acts] directed against any civilian population . . . pursuant to or in furtherance of State or organizational policy to commit such an attack'.[6]

This definition has been criticized as too narrow by NGOs, which preferred the broad sweep suggested by the International Law Commission ('any inhumane acts instigated or directed by Governments or by any organization or group'). The narrower definition at least ensures that the ICC should confine itself to the most heinous offences, carried out systematically rather than on the spur of the moment, and pursuant to a policy conceived either by a state instrumentality (such as the police or the army) or by an organized rebel force or terrorist network, as distinct from a criminal gang. The Article 7(1) definition makes clear that a prosecution may be brought in respect of a single act ('*any* of the following acts . . .') so long as it is known by the defendant to be part of a course of conduct involving multiple atrocities against civilians.

Just how 'organized' the perpetrating entity has to be in order for its members to be subjected to arrest is not, however, clear. There is no requirement that it should be invested with state power, so a structured opposition force, such as the IRA or the ANC in its freedom-fighting days, would seem to qualify: an itinerant guerrilla group, the Lord's Resistance Army, provided the first indictees. Terrorist groups would also appear to come into this category if organized on the scale of al-Qaida which, led by Osama bin Laden, trained thousands of adherents and was in 1998 responsible for the bombings at US embassies in Kenya and Tanzania which took hundreds of civilian lives, followed by its attack on the USS *Cole* and by 9/11. These multiple acts of murder were part of a systematic attack against a civilian population pursuant to an organizational policy to commit such attacks: in common parlance, the bombings were 'crimes against humanity'. Although the Rome Conference rejected jurisdiction over a specific crime of terrorism, this was for the stated reason that, like drug trafficking (the other suggested crime which failed to find sufficient consensus), they were not crimes 'as serious' as genocide and crimes against humanity, and were in any event the subject of other treaties.[7] This is not a bar to ICC prosecution of a terrorist conspiracy which is so well organized and so atrocious as to fit the definition of a 'crime against humanity'. Although on 11 September 2001 the terrorists committed initial crimes of hijacking aircraft (covered by a treaty and not 'as serious' as ICC crimes), this was transformed into a crime against humanity by their kamikaze mass murder, in the cause of al-Qaida's politico-religious agenda for systematic racist attacks on American civilians.

It is now clear that crimes against humanity may be committed by non-state actors (paramilitaries in Yugoslavia; armed civilian bands in Rwanda; guerrillas in a religious mist in Uganda) who have the characteristics of state actors either by affiliation to them or by the ability to carry out a policy through their dominion over territory or people or both. It requires no significant extension to treat members of an international organization like al-Qaida as capable of perpetrating such a crime by virtue of their policy to do so on a widespread or systematic basis: it is this underlying policy which provides international jurisdiction over an atrocity which would otherwise be triable only under the domestic law of the state in which it was perpetrated.[8] Similarly, although drug trafficking was vetoed as an ICC crime, an organized criminal enterprise like the Medellin drugs cartel, in the days when it had a political agenda, might fall within the definition when pursuant to that agenda it systematically assassinated judges, journalists and politicians, and blew up civilian airliners on which prosecution witnesses were travelling.

Included among the acts which may, if carried out systematically, amount to a crime against humanity is the 'enforced disappearance of persons' – defined to mean the detention or abduction of people by or with the acquiescence of 'a State or a political organization', followed by a refusal to acknowledge their whereabouts or fate, with 'the intention of removing them from the protection of the law for a prolonged period of time'. This clumsy wording (most disappearances remove people for ever, by secret execution) was intended to describe the behaviour of a number of South American governments which have allowed death squads to operate in conjunction with the military, and have made no attempt to trace victims. The definition would incriminate those in the squads, or ministers and officials who covered up their activities, and the crime is now supplemented by a 2006 UN Convention for the Protection of All Persons from Enforced Disappearance. Apartheid is re-categorized as a crime against humanity, but is much more carefully defined than in the Apartheid Convention (criticized on pp. 341–2). Henceforth, this crime will require commission of an inhumane offence with the purpose of maintaining the hegemony of a regime of systematic racial oppression.

There are a number of crimes against humanity, as defined in Article 7, which are appropriately charged against political or military leaders, because soldiers and civil servants may implement them without inhumane intent. 'Deportation or forcible transfer of population' is one example, where the object of the policymakers (but not necessarily of those ordered to carry out the policy on the ground) is to breach international law. The crime of 'persecution', defined as 'the intentional and severe deprivation of fundamental rights contrary to international law' committed against an identifiable group by reason of its politics, race or culture, can be deployed against those leaders whose 'ethnic cleansing' falls short of genocide. It will also be appropriate against those who help out – the drivers of the Ford Falcons used by death squads in Argentina; the doctors on hand to regulate the torture of 'subversives' at the Pinochet centres, the lawyers who cover it up, or bring false charges, the judges who take political instruction to refuse *habeas corpus* applications, and so on. It is an essential element of the crime of persecution that the act charged is known by the defendant to have a connection with a crime within the court's jurisdiction (such as genocide or torture or another crime against humanity). After this knowledge, there can be no forgiveness for the 'willing executioner' who prostitutes his or her profession in the service of barbarism. This crime of persecution (defined, confusingly, by overlapping sections 7(1)(h) and 7(2)(g)) will be an important new weapon in the prosecutor's armoury, for use against the lawyers, bankers, propagandists and parasites who use their professional diplomas to wipe the blood of client regimes off their own hands.

The ICTY was the first court to recognize rape as a crime capable of political direction, at which point it can become a crime against humanity. The Rome Statute incorporates this advance – Article 7 duly lists rape, along with sexual slavery, forced pregnancy and enforced prostitution and sterilization, as capable of constituting a crime against humanity if carried out systematically. The idea of raping Muslim women in order that they produce 'Chetnik babies' was not a policy of the Serbian state, but a perverse notion which infected soldiers and their senior officers in a number of Serb battalions – and would therefore still count as an 'organizational policy' sufficient to fall within Article 7. The inclusion of 'sexual slavery' and 'enforced prostitution' provides a belated recognition that the Japanese army's enslavement of 'comfort women' from Taiwan and Korea to service its soldiers during the Second World War constituted a crime against humanity – one that the Allies did not dream of punishing in 1946 and which Japan did not think necessary even to apologize for until 1996. 'Forced pregnancy' means rape followed by 'unlawful confinement' for the purpose of 'affecting ethnic composition'. The Vatican was alarmed that making such monstrous pregnancies the subject of a crime against humanity might justify their termination by abortion, and insisted on the rider that 'this definition shall not in any way be interpreted as affecting national laws relating to pregnancy'. This religious bureaucracy, wrongly elevated to statehood by an unthinking international community, was responsible for including as Article 7(3) the most ridiculous clause in any international treaty ever devised. 'Persecution' had been defined in Article 7(1)(h) to include persecution on grounds of gender. The Vatican, and other homophobic Catholic and Islamic states, insisted on appending clause 7(3):

For the purpose of this Statute, it is understood that the term 'gender' refers to the two sexes, male and female, within the context of society. The term 'gender' does not indicate any meaning different from the above.

This means, presumably, that you can do what you like to transexuals. Persecution is a crime if directed against men as men, or women because they are female, but homosexuals and lesbians may still suffer the thumbscrew and the rack, the 'intentional and severe deprivation of fundamental rights' when this is 'within the context of society', i.e. approved by a gay-bashing government or vicious religion or culture. The inclusion of Article 7(3) is a distasteful but realistic reminder that a majority of states in 1998 still favoured the withdrawal of human rights from homosexuals.

Article 7, otherwise, must be hailed as the high point of the Rome Statute. It crystallizes the concept of a crime against humanity which nations of the world are obliged to punish, and distinguishes it from other crimes by reference to its genesis in the policy of a state or political organization. It is not defined by the gravity of the offence: the lone serial killer may do more widespread damage than the routine police torturer. What sets a crime against humanity apart both in wickedness and in the need for special measures of deterrence is the simple fact that it is an act of real brutality ordained by government – or at least by an organization exercising or asserting political power. It is not the mind of the torturer, but the fact that this individual is part of the apparatus of a state, which makes the crime so horrific and locates it in a different dimension from ordinary criminality. This is why individual responsibility and universal jurisdiction are necessary responses if any deterrence is to be achieved. Just as the eighteenth-century pirate and the slave trader used to be legally untouchable – because on the high seas they were subject to no state's jurisdiction – so the twentieth-century politician and general were invulnerable while they exercised the sovereignty of the state. In the twenty-first century, universal jurisdiction will attach to their crimes against humanity: Article 27 abolishes all immunities for heads of state and members of governments and parliaments. This will apply to states that are party to the ICC Treaty, but it may also have the eventual effect of moving customary international law beyond the position it reached in the case of General Pinochet and in the ICJ decision in 2002 that the incumbent foreign minister of the DRC could not be subjected to a Belgian arrest warrant. Even if this immunity for foreign ministers and heads of state survives to protect them from legal action by other states, it will not save them from arrest on a warrant issued by the ICC.

WAR CRIMES

Article 8 of the Rome Statute contains a lengthy definition of the war crimes over which the ICC shall have jurisdiction, 'in particular when committed as part of a plan or policy or as part of a large-scale commission of such crimes'. These war crimes are defined in four categories, reflecting the historical evolution of the subject by distinguishing between crimes capable of commission only at times of international conflict, and at times of internal armed conflict. There is a substantial overlap and the distinction is no longer necessary, although apparently too embedded in the minds of international lawyers (where it gives rise to endless technical arguments) to be extirpated in the interests of simplicity and comprehensibility.

The first category – Article 8(2)(a) – includes all 'grave breaches' of the 1949 Geneva Conventions (see p. 256). The second category – Article 8(2)(b) – covers 'other serious violations of the laws and customs applicable in international armed conflict within the established framework of international law'. Twenty-six such violations are spelled out, in a subsection which serves to update the limited horizons of 1949. Thus it now includes attacks on peacekeepers or others providing humanitarian assistance under UN auspices (subparagraph (iii)); attacks launched in the knowledge that they will cause disproportionate loss of civilian life or 'widespread long-term and severe damage to the national environment' and are clearly excessive in relation to any military objective (iv); intentional attacks on non-military targets such as churches, schools, museums, hospitals and places of historical or cultural significance (ix); and the use of asphyxiating or poisonous gases (xviii). The behaviour of Bosnian Serbs in deploying captured UN peacekeepers as hostages against NATO aerial bombardment provides the rationale for a new war crime of 'utilizing the presence of civilians or other protected persons to render certain points, areas or military forces immune from military operations' (xxiii). There is another new offence of 'conscripting children under the age of fifteen years' to participate actively in hostilities – an indictment of the recruiters of the 'child armies' of Africa (xxvi) – a section which has already been used by the Special Court of Sierra Leone as evidence of crystallization of a customary international war crime. The ICTY's emphatic condemnation of systematic rape and sexual slavery is repeated: under Article 7 they constitute crimes against humanity; during international hostilities they amount as well to war crimes under Article 8, whether committed as part of a policy or simply to demoralize the populace.

The delegates in Rome deliberately fudged the lawfulness of landmines and nuclear weapons as weapons of international law. The treaty banning anti-personnel mines, concluded in 1997, had been opposed by the United States and China (see p. 283). The

International Court of Justice had delivered an abjectly confused decision over the legality of nuclear weaponry (see p. 269). So the ban in subparagraph (xx) on weapons and methods of warfare 'which are of a nature to cause superfluous injury or unnecessary suffering or which are inherently indiscriminate' (all of which description applies to nuclear bombs and to anti-personnel mines) is expressed 'within the framework of international law' – which does not currently regard them as illegal *per se*. The ban will only apply to them – or to ballistic missiles or other weapons of mass destruction – if they subsequently become subject to a 'comprehensive prohibition' which is then incorporated in the Statute at its seven-year review. If, before that time, some deranged dictator launches a nuclear strike on a military target, or makes use of other modern weapons of mass destruction, he cannot be prosecuted at the ICC for a 'war crime' as presently defined by Article 8, unless his troops fire dum-dum bullets or poison arrows. This staggering omission provides a classic example of the deviousness of international diplomacy: at the Rome Conference, once the major powers had insisted on excluding any specific prohibition of landmines and nuclear weapons, non-nuclear states from the developing world rejected in turn a proposal to incriminate the use of chemical and biological weaponry. In this respect, Article 8 does not develop war law much beyond the nineteenth century.

Article 8 goes on, rather gingerly, to provide jurisdiction over two classes of war crime if committed in 'armed conflict not of an international character'. This class of conflict is clearly distinguished from 'situations of internal disturbances and tensions' such as riots or unrest characterized by 'isolated and sporadic acts of violence'. Crimes committed in the latter period are not 'war crimes' under Article 8, so they must qualify as genocide or crimes against humanity if the ICC is to have any power to punish what will usually be police brutality. As a concession to states beset with internal security problems, the Statute provides that in respect to 'common Article 3 crimes' involving attacks on civilians, 'nothing shall affect the responsibility to maintain or establish law and order in the State or to defend the unity and territorial integrity of the State by all legitimate means'. This provides a wide, albeit question-begging, exculpation for governments fighting secessionist movements and other politically motivated armed groups.

Article 8(2)(c) extends jurisdiction over internecine armed conflicts in respect of all *serious* violations of common Article 3 of the 1949 Geneva Conventions, i.e. inhumane attacks on civilians or sick or surrendered soldiers, including putting them on trials which lack the basic attributes of fairness. To these 'core' crimes Article 8(2)(e) adds a selection of some twelve of the war crimes listed in Article 8(2)(b) as arising in international conflict, notably the use of children as soldiers, or engaging in systematic sexual violence, or attacking UN peacekeepers or historic, cultural and humanitarian targets. These twelve crimes reflect customary international law as it has developed for internal conflicts, which are specially defined as 'armed conflicts that take place in the territory of a State where there is protracted armed conflict between governmental authorities and organized armed groups or between such groups'. This makes it crystal clear that even if terrorist forces or liberation armies fall outside common Article 3 of the Geneva Conventions, their leaders can be brought before the ICC for specific atrocities against civilians. The aimless banditry of a murderous organization like Renamo in Mozambique (before an amnesty gave it a political status to which it had never previously aspired) would henceforth be caught, like the Lord's Resistance Army in Uganda and the Janjaweed militias in Darfur. The leaders of 'Shining Path' in Peru may yet have their moment in the international dock, where their indelibly vicious crimes against women (they have assassinated twelve leading feminists and encouraged widespread rape) would receive a fairer trial than from any court in Peru.

The worst war crime of all – declaring and waging aggressive wars in which millions of combatants and civilians may be killed – is absent from Article 8, because the Rome Conference could not agree on a definition. As a compromise, the ICC was given a provisional jurisdiction over the crime of aggression (by Article 5(1)(d)) which will operate after 2017 when a majority of states accept the definition agreed at the Kampala Review Conference. This is unsatisfactory. Warlike acts of aggrandizement, like Saddam's occupation of Kuwait and Galtieri's invasion of the Falklands, should count as the gravest of crimes, given the multiplicity of international mechanisms available to prevent them through negotiation or arbitration.

As the Nuremberg judgment said, 'to initiate a war of aggression, therefore, is not only an international crime; it is the supreme international crime differing only from other war crimes in that it contains within itself the accumulated evil of the whole'.[9]

CRIMINAL LAW PRINCIPLES

Part 3 of the Statute adopts basic principles found in most advanced legal systems. The prosecution must prove that the criminal acts are committed with *mens rea* (that is, intentionally, and with knowledge of the likely consequences). Defendants will be liable for crimes committed jointly or with a common purpose, for acts of assistance and for ordering, soliciting and inducing crimes and for attempting to commit a crime by taking a substantial step towards its completion. The Statute applies to heads of state, elected representatives and all others who have acted in an official capacity: the plea of 'act of state' will be heeded no longer. The criminal responsibility provisions (Article 25) spell out that guilt of genocide includes the public incitement of others to commit it – a recognition of the role of radio in encouraging the massacres in Rwanda, ('The grave is only half full. Who will help us fill it?') and an override of any free speech arguments in respect of this crime.

Jurisdiction is confined to natural persons – men and women, to the exclusion of governments or corporations or political parties. This was a mistake because reparations cannot be ordered against parties which are not criminally responsible. Why should a multinational chemical corporation not be prosecuted (as well as its directors) for supplying poison gas in the knowledge that it will be used for a crime against humanity? Why should that company, if convicted, not be ordered to pay massive reparations to survivors and to victims' families?

Another questionable exception (in Article 26) is for any person aged under eighteen at the time of the crime. Some appalling atrocities have been committed by 'boy soldiers' whose age should mitigate penalty rather than excuse their crime. In the Sierra Leone Court Statute, they can be prosecuted but not sentenced to imprisonment. Article 8 makes it a war crime to enlist persons under fifteen for an active part in hostilities: those of sixteen or seventeen, old enough to participate in war, should not have been left immune from prosecution.

The Rome delegates sensibly resisted the demands by Amnesty and other NGOs that they should deny to persons suspected of crimes against humanity some of the defences which these organizations had, in the past, urged should be available to political prisoners. Self-defence, duress, mistake which negates *mens rea*, insanity and even intoxication will exclude liability in a proper case.

'Command responsibility' is defined precisely in Article 28: military commanders will be responsible for atrocities committed by their forces if they knew, or should in the prevailing circumstances have known, of the unlawful behaviour of subordinates but failed to take reasonable measures to stop or to punish them. This is an endorsement of the *Yamashita* principle, upon which the ICTY indicted Karadžić and Mladić (see p. 447).

However, the Rome Statute does attenuate one great principle to emerge from Nuremberg, namely that 'superior orders' may mitigate punishment but can never amount to a defence. Article 33 provides that any order – by a military, police, governmental or civil authority – may indeed provide a defence to persons who were under a 'legal obligation' to obey orders (which soldiers and police invariably are) and who did not know the order was unlawful, where the order in question was not 'manifestly unlawful'. Although orders to commit genocide or crimes against humanity are deemed to be 'manifestly unlawful' this will not be the case in respect of military operations amounting to war crimes. Indeed, a bomber crew ordered to drop a nuclear weapon would be under a legal obligation to obey, and that order – (thanks to the ICJ decision analysed in chapter 5) – is not 'manifestly unlawful'. Under Article 33, 'superior orders' may thus constitute a defence – another victory for the Pentagon lobby concerned that soldiers should not be emboldened to disobey military edicts of dubious legality.

Article 29 provides that the Court's jurisdiction must not be affected by any time bar or statute of limitations. This will ensure that complementarity cannot be invoked on behalf of persons suspected of crimes which fall outside time limits for prosecutions imposed by national legal systems. (Many Francophone countries, for example, bar prosecutions after a lapse of fifteen years, even for murder.) Crimes against humanity are of such seriousness that they should be amenable to prosecution for as long as their perpetrators remain alive. However, many national legal systems do provide their courts with power to abort long-delayed prosecutions, at least where the defendant has not been responsible for the delay by evading capture. The ICC has no equivalent power to rule a case inadmissible if there has been unconscionable and prejudicial delay by the prosecuting authorities in preparing it. It is likely that the Court will decide it has inherent jurisdiction to dismiss the case in such circumstances: Article 64(2) mandates it to 'ensure that a trial is fair and expeditious and is conducted with full respect for the rights of the accused', one of which is, under Article 67(1)(c), 'to be tried without undue delay'. Where the delay is both unjustified and has arisen from prosecutorial incompetence, a trial division will be tempted to throw out the case, as it was in *Barayagwiza*, but the better course is to enquire into the cause of the delay and to condemn publicly any incompetence by the prosecutor or registrar, unless the delay has been so prejudicial that the defendant can no longer be fairly tried.

Article 66 enshrines the fundamental presumption of innocence, and places the burden on the prosecution to prove guilt beyond reasonable doubt. Article 67(1) guarantees that the onus of proof or even an 'onus of rebuttal' shall not be imposed on a defendant, although many of the defences adumbrated elsewhere in the Statute (such as 'superior orders' and duress) place precisely such burdens – and reasonably enough – on the defendant. Questions of burden and standard of proof can be crucial in jury trials, although they tend to be academic when verdicts take the form of a reasoned judicial decision: in practice, once the prosecution proves beyond reasonable doubt complicity in a crime against humanity, the onerous task of establishing exculpatory circumstances such as duress or intoxication or mistake will shift to the defendant.

THE COURT

JURISDICTION

The most direct mechanism for triggering the power to investigate and try international crimes is provided under Article 13(b), whereby a 'situation' is referred to the prosecutor by the Security Council acting pursuant to Chapter VII of the UN Charter. This is the method, it will be recalled, under which the ICTY and ICTR were established, by resolutions which asserted that the 'situations' in former Yugoslavia and in Rwanda constituted a threat to world peace. No longer need the UN establish *ad hoc* tribunals: when there is superpower agreement on the need to punish crimes against humanity, committed in peace or war, by or on the territory of any state (whether it is a party to the Treaty or not) then the Security Council may simply resolve to refer the matter to the ICC prosecutor. That action automatically attracts the jurisdiction of the Court over those whom the prosecutor chooses to indict. The first such reference, of a situation in which several hundred thousand people in Darfur had been killed in recent years by militias backed by the government of Sudan, was made in March 2005. The US had characterized such killings as genocide, so despite its opposition to the ICC, it withheld its veto and abstained. Resolution 1970, by which the Security Council unanimously referred the situation in Libya to the ICC in 2011, is now the most important precedent for Security Council action.

In the event of Security Council disagreement or inaction, the position is more complicated. The Court cannot acquire jurisdiction without a Security Council resolution unless, for a start, the conduct in question occurred on the territory of a state which is party to the Statute, or else the suspect is a national of a state which is party to the Statute. Both preconditions were fulfilled in 2004 when Uganda, a party to the Statute, referred the 'situation' within its territory brought about by the Lord's Resistance Army, a guerrilla force comprising Ugandan nationals. However, in the case of political and military leaders engaging in vicious repression of dissident civilians or ethnic groups, it is inherently unrealistic to expect that states run by such persons would ratify the Statute.

This impasse results from a serious split at the Rome Conference. The US, it will be recalled, came to Rome wanting an ICC, but one which had a cast-iron guarantee that no American would ever be indicted. That could best be achieved by a court with jurisdiction triggered *only* by the Security Council, where the US would have a veto, although the US was prepared in addition to let state parties to the Statute have the option of allowing their nationals to be tried (since the US could always decline to agree to the trial of US citizens). Its European allies, led on this issue by Germany, took the 'universal human rights' position: the ICC should have universal jurisdiction, over everyone everywhere, irrespective of their nationality or the state in which the crimes were committed. This position would make the Court a true instrument of international justice, insulated from the superpower politics of the Security Council. South Korea, in an attempt to placate the US, suggested that the Court might at least sidestep the Security Council in respect of crimes committed *on the territory* of a state which was party to the Treaty. Then it added a second possibility – jurisdiction if a state party happened to *capture a suspect who was a national of another state* (just possibly of the US) – and that was when the American delegation threatened both Germany and South Korea with a reduction in US forces unless they withdrew these proposals. The US, said delegation leader David Sheffer, would 'actively oppose' the Court, even if its jurisdiction was based only on the South Korean compromise. The conference was thus bullied into dropping the German proposal for true universal jurisdiction, but it retained a measure of self-respect by insisting the Court have jurisdiction over crimes committed on state party territory. It was partly over this act of defiance that the US, with a show of petulance, voted against the entire Statute.

The state party itself may refer the matter to the prosecutor, providing evidence and requesting a formal investigation which may lead directly to arrests and trials. Alternatively, the prosecutor may initiate investigations '*proprio motu*' (i.e. on his or her own initiative) and seek evidence from states, UN agencies and other 'reliable sources'. But in this case there remains a legal hurdle in the prosecutorial path: a pre-trial division of the Court must examine the evidence, hear any jurisdictional objection, and decide whether to authorize 'the commencement of the investigation'. This clumsy procedure confines the prosecutor's initial investigation to public or volunteered sources: his special investigative powers cannot be engaged unless or until the pre-trial division rules that there is a *prima facie* case, 'a reasonable basis to proceed'.

In short, the politicians and diplomats of the superpowers remain in the driving seat. These provisions were heavily influenced, at Rome, by the desperate need to keep the US onside. The last thing the Clinton administration wanted was a 'superprosecutor' empowered to investigate incidents that they might wish to cover up – in July 1998, they had an example of that close to home, as Kenneth Starr announced an examination of Monica Lewinsky's blue dress for traces of presidential semen. So the 'like-minded' group, against its will, shackled the prosecutor by subjecting him to control by the Court on a matter over which judges should have no say at all, namely who should be investigated as a candidate for prosecution. Although *proprio motu* investigations will be the only way to 'do something' about appalling human rights violations in and by countries which have superpower support:

(1) They will only get under way if it happens to involve the territory or nationals of a ratifying state – and the chances of pariah regimes ratifying the Statute are minimal.

(2) Even if this does happen, the prosecutor cannot 'commence the investigation' unless – from readily available sources and helpful governments – he or she can lay hands immediately on evidence sufficient to satisfy the Court of a 'reasonable case'.

But there was worse to come. The 'like-minded' group had to mollify not only the US, but France and China, which also wanted a court which would be dependent upon the Security Council. So they offered another concession, which appears as Article 16:

No investigation or prosecution may be commenced . . . for a period of twelve months after the Security Council, in a resolution adopted under Chapter VII of the UN Charter, has requested the Court to that effect; that request may be renewed by the Council under the same conditions.

The word 'request' is used euphemistically: the Security Council resolution is mandatory – it stops an investigation or trial dead in its tracks. The order will operate initially for one year, but may be renewed on an annual basis until the evidence is dissipated, the crime forgotten or the prosecutor loses interest. The effect of Article 16 is to give the Security Council ultimate control over the Court, through its power to order a deferral of any particular investigation or prosecution. In other words, the Court operates either by a reference from the Council or (in the event of a reference by a state party or on investigation *proprio motu*) subject to the Council's power to freeze any proceedings it does not like by passing an Article 16 resolution.

COMPLEMENTARITY

The preamble to the Rome Statute emphasizes that the ICC jurisdiction shall be 'complementary' to that of nation states, although the provisions of the Statute itself suggest that 'subordinate' would be a more accurate description of the legal relationship. Article 20 states the fundamental double jeopardy rule, that no person shall be tried twice for the same offence ('*ne bis in idem*') so that there can be no proceeding brought against a suspect in the ICC for conduct in respect of which he has been convicted or acquitted in a national court. This rule is made subject to the reasonable qualification that it does not apply when the national court case was a sham, either because the case was brought there in order to shield the subject from further action, or because it was not conducted with any real intent to establish criminal responsibility. Article 17 applies the same test to the investigation stage: if a suspect is already being dealt with under national law, in a manner which appears genuine and effective, then the ICC must stay its hand, even when local authorities conclude that persons suspected by its prosecutor have in fact no case to answer.

This last exculpation is much too broad, although there are safe-guards: the ICC itself will decide whether it was reasonable for the domestic prosecutor to drop the charges, and may none the less pick up the case if satisfied that the decision was made to shield the suspect or because of a breakdown in local law enforcement.

These double jeopardy provisions impose much stricter limits on the power of the ICC than the equivalent sections of the ICTY Statute. That court has a broad power to intervene at any stage of proceedings in a national court, requesting it to 'defer to the competence of the Tribunal', i.e. stop its proceedings and send the defendant for trial at The Hague. Such a deferral request, which states are obliged to grant, may be made not only when the Hague prosecutor thinks that the local court is biased in the defendant's favour or the local prosecution lacks diligence, but whenever the case is relevant to the ICTY's own work or is appropriate for an international prosecution. This primacy power is necessary to make sense of international criminal justice, so that defendants like Pinochet (who could never be convicted in Chile) and Gaddafi (who would have been convicted automatically in Libya) find a forum where they can be properly tried. But Article 17 of the Rome Statute kow-tows to state sovereignty: the ICC will not be permitted to put anyone on trial who has been 'under investigation' by a national prosecutor and has had charges dropped or the investigation stopped. The only exception will be where the court is convinced that national authorities have been 'unwilling or unable' to carry out a genuine investigation – a difficult allegation to establish, if the burden of proof is placed on the prosecution. Articles 17 and 19 (which provide for state parties and the prosecution to challenge admissibility decisions) are curiously silent about the burden of proof, which in practice will determine many jurisdictional challenges. The normal domestic rule that it falls on prosecutors should be reversed, both to effectuate the Statute's purpose and because it should be up to states to explain why their criminal justice system has failed to put offenders behind bars.[10] If they are not held accountable in this way to the Court, then states will be more tempted to deny the ICC jurisdiction over their nationals by pretending to put them on trial, and the legal chauvinism recently displayed by Libya,

Iraq, Chile, Indonesia and Cambodia, insisting that *their* courts alone must have jurisdiction over *their* defendants, foreshadows how often ICC prosecutors will be robbed of their prey. Although Article 17 was devised to guard against sham prosecutions, in practice it will be more often engaged when states want quickly to kill ex-dictators rather than to offer them up for ICC trial. The issue arose in 2011 when Saif Gaddafi was captured after having been indicted by the ICC, and could not be fairly tried in Libya – which had no extant justice system and could not in any event provide an unprejudiced tribunal. The ICC in such cases must decide whether to release its indictee for local trial under the complementary principle, and the statute is silent over whether it may take into account the likelihood of a death sentence under the local law. Silence does not, however, mean consent and this is a factor the ICC should take into account in favour of trial at The Hague, thus protecting its indictee, if necessary, from a penalty that it is not permitted to impose.

COMPOSITION

The viability of the ICC ultimately depends more on the calibre and experience of its judges and prosecutors than on the fine print of its statute. International appointments systems are prone to throw up mediocrities trusted to toe the line of their nominating government: usually they are selected from within government departments or are in other ways beholden to the state. Often missing are persons of real independence with first-class minds and imagination. Yet one of the main reasons why Nuremberg worked was that the English, French and American judges had experience as criminal *defenders* and not merely as prosecutors; from that experience developed a sense of fairness that infused the proceedings. So what the ICC needed was an appointments system independent of governments, and a set of statutory qualifications which gave weight to those with careers characterized by some criminal defence work. In this respect, the statutory arrangements for appointing the Court's eighteen full-time judges leave much to be desired. They are to be elected by an assembly of the state parties – a recipe for political caucusing – and nominated by respective governments with an eye to such matters as 'equitable geographical representation' and 'a fair representation of female and male judges'. At least half the judges must have 'relevant' criminal law experience, although this may be entirely prosecutorial. Defence experience is not specifically mentioned as a qualification, although nominating states must take into account 'legal expertise on violence against women and children' – a qualification calling, quite arbitrarily, for judges who were formerly prosecutors of rapists and child molesters.

ICC judicial recruitment is problematic because it depends on state examination (often selection is on loyalty rather than merit) and on selection by UN voting blocs (where selection is on nationality rather that merit). This is in stark are contrast with the system for appointing UN administrative judges to positions which are widely advertised: candidates are nominated by an independent body (the Internal Justice Council) which actually sets them a written examination as part of the vetting process. At least the ICC has transparency in its election process, which enables NGOs to comment on the suitability of the candidates. The elections for the first eighteen-judge panel, held in February 2003, saw the defeat of several unsatisfactory nominees – the Chief Justice of Fiji, for example, who had collaborated with a military takeover and the Nigerian 'sleeping judge' whose propensity to doze caused embarrassment at the ICTR. Candidates are required to canvass for votes, by a 'door knock on embassies' campaign or by huddling in whispered conversations with diplomats in the UN's Indonesia lounge. (Candidates should be examined only in public hearings.) Appointments for a non-renewable period of up to nine years, and a substantial annual salary, should encourage judicial independence. The judges elect the Court's president, who chairs the five-judge Appeals Division and is responsible for the administration of the Court. The other judges divide between trial divisions, which comprise three judges, and pretrial divisions, which may be constituted by a single judge.

Rule 103 of the ICC rules of procedure and evidence make provision for *amicus* briefs. This is an important means of acquainting the tribunal with information that may not either be available or of interest to trial counsel. Judges of the Hague Tribunal Appeals Chamber have permitted written and sometimes oral submissions from third parties, most notably in the case of *Washington Post* war correspondent Jonathan Randall, whose successful claim to qualified privilege and source protection was supported by a coalition of media organizations represented by First Amendment expert Floyd Abrams. The Special Court for Sierra Leone has encouraged *amicus* submissions from human rights NGOs like Amnesty and Human Rights Watch, and from universities and the UNHCR on issues of difficulty or complication when 'there is a real likelihood that their submissions will assist the appeals chamber to reach the right decision'. At the same time, it has discouraged *amicus* briefs in trial chambers because of the overriding need to get on with the trial, without disruption and fairly to defendants.[11]

THE TRIAL

PROSECUTION POWERS

Much of the debate prior to the Rome Treaty concerned the power of the prosecutor. As already noted, the US (its president caught at the time in the coils of Kenneth Starr) feared a 'superprosecutor' who might choose to flex legal muscles or play to the non-aligned gallery by investigating as crimes against humanity American attacks on its enemies (such as its cruise missile onslaught being planned at the time on the bases of Osama bin Laden in Sudan and Afghanistan). The NGO lobby and the 'like-minded' nations foresaw the need for a prosecutor with a plenitude of powers, at arm's length from the Security Council. The compromise was to establish a prosecutor whose initiatives would be closely monitored by the judges. Instead of fashioning a true adversary system, with an entirely independent judiciary deciding between a prosecutor with whom they have no close connection and the defence, they gave to the judges sitting in the Pre-trial Division excessive powers to interfere with a prosecution, either by reining it in or unleashing it.

By the time it came to electing the Court's first prosecutor, in

March 2003, a debate of a different kind divided the state parties. Australia had declined to nominate a judge in the expectation that its candidate for prosecutor would be approved. But after a year of enduring the toings and froings of the Milošević trial, many states – especially Latin American and Francophone countries – wanted a prosecutor experienced in inquisitorial procedures. So the post went to Luis Moreno Ocampo, an Argentinian law professor with human rights credentials and a distinguished track record in prosecuting 'dirty war' generals. A foolish objection by certain NGOs that he had also defended priests accused of paedophilia was brushed aside – rightly: some defence experience should be a qualification for every ICC prosecutor. His first few years were spent setting up investigative teams and assessing war crimes in conflicts in eleven countries, and trials began only towards the end of his period in office. The search for his replacement lacked transparency and integrity: it was apparently decided – by whom is not clear – that because most criticism of the Court was coming from African states, the successor should be an African, and preferably a woman. Without any proper advertising for candidates, it was simply decided that Fatou Bensouda, Ocampo's deputy, fitted the bill.

The prosecutor may begin an investigation on his or her own initiative, or as the result of a referral by the Security Council or a state party (see above). If there is insufficient evidence, then obviously no prosecution will ensue. Even where there is 'a case' there may be good public interest reasons not to proceed: victims may be too traumatized to give evidence; the defendant may have a terminal illness; and so forth. The prosecutor's decision not to proceed in such cases will only be effective if it is approved by a three-judge pre-trial division which can, by withdrawing approval, actually force the prosecutor to bring what he regards as unfair or oppressive proceedings.[12] The judges are required in other ways to encroach on the routine investigative work of the prosecutor's office. Under Article 56(3), for example, the prosecutor must apply to them for permission to take a 'unique investigative opportunity' (such as a statement from a potential witness who is about to die) and the judges may even take such measures on their own initiative, against the prosecutor's wishes.

These provisions invite the judiciary to involve itself in the job of prosecuting – an inquisitorial role (familiar in Continental systems) which is incompatible with the Anglo-American adversarial model upon which the Court is principally based.

State parties are bound to co-operate with the prosecutor, who will have to try to make *ad hoc* agreements with non-party states which harbour war criminals. Requests to state parties must be made by the Court through 'diplomatic channels'. State parties are obliged to ensure that their local law procedures permit effective co-operation: by arranging for the execution of ICC warrants; by requiring suspects and witnesses to attend for questioning; by permitting ICC prosecutors to inspect sites and execute searches and seize records and documents and freeze assets. A state party may attach a condition of confidentiality to the security-sensitive information it provides: in such cases the prosecutor cannot turn the information over to the defence, so may use it only as a *lead* to gathering additional evidence, rather than as evidence to be placed secretly before the Court.

The ICC can issue a warrant for arrest if the prosecutor demonstrates 'reasonable grounds to believe' complicity in crime. Suspects who are apprehended in co-operating countries must be transported to The Hague and surrendered into the custody of the Court. Their basic rights throughout the investigation stage are protected under Article 55: they must be informed, prior to questioning, of their rights to remain silent and to have legal assistance free of charge and a competent interpreter if necessary. Article 101 contains the rule of speciality, familiar from extradition law, whereby a person who has been arrested and surrendered to the ICC cannot be proceeded against for conduct other than that referred to in the arrest warrant. In its strict form the rule would tie the prosecutor's hands in the common situation where further and more compelling evidence of involvement in other crimes comes to light after the arrest. For this reason the rule is watered down by a provision which encourages state parties to waive it, at the request of the Court, once notified of the additional evidence. The ordinary costs of co-operating with court requests for evidence gathering and surrender of suspects are to be borne by the state party, although the Court must fund all expenses related to its own personnel and witnesses. There is no provision for prosecution costs to be awarded against convicted defendants, although such a rule would not be unreasonable in the case of wealthy defendants who have profited from their crimes, such as tyrants and high officials who have maintained their positions through oppression. It would be just and appropriate in some cases to order the states in whose name they have committed their crimes to pay for their prosecution.

THE HEARING

The trial will take place at The Hague although Article 3 gives the Court power to sit elsewhere if this is desirable, which it often is, so that victims and witnesses can have easier access to its procedings – subject of course to the following considerations. There can be no trials *in absentia*: the accused must be present, although if disruptive may be removed to a cell video-linked to the courtroom. The trial shall be in public, although Article 68 empowers the Court to move into camera if such a measure is not inconsistent with the fair trial rights of the accused and is necessary 'to protect the safety, physical and psychological well-being, dignity and privacy of victims and witnesses'.

There is no reference in the Statute to televising the trials – a commonplace in America and Europe which is stoutly resisted in the British Commonwealth. The principle that justice must be seen to be done, and the educative force of the medium, argues in favour. In the case of war crimes, the argument is exceptionally strong. There is a special need for truth-telling, for the sake of victims and to combat sanitizing myths gaining credence among the vanquished and to rebut charges of 'victor's justice'. The other side of the coin, of course, is that criminal trials are occasions for lying, and defendants may exploit television coverage to justify their polemic from the dock or witness box. This was Churchill's great fear about Nuremberg, and it was echoed by many in the early days of the Milošević trial, when the defendant was given his platform (an opening speech) which impressed many when shown on Serbian television. But this is a risk that any system of public justice must take in putting a political leader on trial. There was no judicial hesitation about televising the trial of Saddam Hussein, however – the danger of the defendant 'playing to the gallery' was more than counterbalanced by allowing the Iraqi people to see how low the mighty had fallen. Television helps to legitimate legal proceedings and in cases of such importance the world is entitled to see whether or to what extent justice is being done.

The ICTY allows most of its proceedings to be televised without damage to their fairness. It offers victims some satisfaction in seeing at least a few representative perpetrators brought to justice. In fact, such coverage is essential to give the truth an airing in places like the Republika Srpska. In most war crimes trials, the problem is that hearings are not often dramatic – the proceedings are lengthy, slowed down by simultaneous translation and plodding advocacy that has no jury to impress. The ICC has thus far used its inherent powers to permit broadcasting (except for the evidence of witnesses who reasonably object to reliving their experiences of degradation before an international audience), but further thought should be given to producing comprehensible edited versions and encouraging them to be broadcast through media outlets in the defendant's country. The Special Court for Sierra Leone has made television trial coverage a major outreach asset, with edited weekly programmes conveying courtroom scenes in a manner beyond the capacity of local news-sheets. When security advice precluded Charles Taylor from being tried in Freetown and his trial was moved to The Hague, it attracted less interest.

The worst feature of the Rome Statute is that it makes no provision for the defence. It was wrong to perpetuate this Nuremberg failure, especially since the first lesson which should have been learned from the problems of the ICTY and ICTR was the need to provide for competent and non-corrupt defence counsel, preferably (as in the Sierra Leone court) with a principal defender and his defence office to counterbalance the powers of the prosecutor.[13] Instead, Article 67 of the Statute entitles a counsel of choice to those who can pay for this, but leaves indigent defendants merely the right 'to have legal assistance assigned to him in any case where the interests of justice so require'. This means that the registrar has the duty to assign counsel, a task that registrars, who must serve the judges and the prosecutors as well, are ill equipped to perform. The 'registrar's list' system operating in the *ad hoc* courts permits defendants to disrupt their trials by sacking their counsel or demanding the services of unavailable advocates. Incompetent 'ambulance chasers' have battened on to relatives and touted amongst support groups. In 'fee splitting' cases, counsel have made deals to pay the defendant and his relatives a proportion of their fee.[14] A principal defender system can avoid these problems by ensuring that a distinguished independent lawyer is responsible for assigning counsel of competence and integrity. Adversary trials should manifest an 'equality of arms' (i.e. reasonable equivalence of ability and resources between prosecution and defence) and a 'principal defender' system of some kind is necessary to achieve this. It was a poor reflection on the preparatory commission that put the ICC in place that it refused to establish a defence counsel unit – for no better reason than that no provision had been made for one in the Rome Statute.[15] This had been an important innovation by the Sierra Leone court, whose principal defender system was copied by the Lebanon Tribunal (which made its defence office an 'organ' of the courts to balance the prosecution).

Article 67 enshrines the basic rights of the accused, drawn from the 'fair trial' provisions common to all human rights treaties. The accused must have all proceedings translated into a language he understands and speaks, and is entitled to have lawyers and to communicate with them confidentially.[16] He has a right to trial 'without undue delay', but must also have adequate time and facilities to prepare his defence and to cross-examine all witnesses against him and to obtain the attendance of witnesses capable of giving relevant evidence on his behalf. He has a right to remain silent, without having this refusal to explain the prosecution evidence taken as an indication of guilt. It is remarkable how the 'right to silence' is being entrenched in human rights law at the very time it is being rejected by some advanced legal systems, where the view is taken, not unreasonably, that a person confronted with substantial evidence of serious crime has a basic human duty to explain himself, and that failure to do so in these circumstances at trial (as distinct from at the time of arrest) permits an adverse inference to be drawn. It is always wrong to *compel* defendants to answer questions, although the gravity of the charge of a crime against humanity, and above all the interests of victims and relatives to know the truth, would surely justify an incentive to tell it once the prosecution evidence is held sufficient to require an answer. However, the Rome Statute entrenches the right to silence in absolute terms, and goes even further by permitting an accused who declines to testify and undergo cross-examination 'to make an unsworn oral or written statement in his or her defence'. This is a relic of the 'dock statement' permitted to defendants in England in the nineteenth century, when they were not allowed to enter the witness box. It has been abolished in England and in some Commonwealth jurisdictions, and has no rational justification, other than to permit a defendant to make a speech instead of going into the witness box and facing cross-examination. At any event, the Trial Division will have three judges with experience of criminal trials: an accused's failure to testify will in practice be seen as indicating his fear of cross-examination, a fear referable no doubt to his guilt (although this inference will never openly be drawn).

The Rome Statute's provisions on evidence are prefaced by a general power in the Court to admit all evidence which is 'relevant and necessary' – a refreshing change from the complex evidentiary provisions of Anglo/American law which are designed to protect a lay jury from prejudice. The assumption is that experienced judges will not be unduly influenced by learning that the accused has previous convictions, can be trusted to hear hearsay, do not need a corroboration rule in rape cases, and so on. Criticism of this approach by some advocates is misplaced: in deciding liability for crimes against humanity, judges must have available all the information sources a historian would use. They have the power to take 'judicial notice' of facts that either party can establish from secondary sources and which cannot be disputed by the other party.[17] What matters, to the jurist as much as to the historian, is reliability – a quality which the ICTY has described as 'the invisible golden thread which runs through all the components of admissibility'.[18] The reliability of any particular item of relevant evidence will depend upon the circumstances: what matters is the Court's ability to test and weigh it, rather than reliance upon any generalized rule for its admission or rejection. The preparatory commissions which followed the Rome Treaty have provided some draft rules which unnecessarily interfere with judicial discretion in this respect – for example, by according a special privilege to former employees of the Red Cross to withhold evidence from the Court. Customary international law recognizes that Red Cross and Red Crescent officials need to operate under conditions of confidentiality, but duties of confidence must in some specific instances be overridden in the public interest.[19] It would be unconscionable, for example, for the Red Cross to object to an ex-employee offering evidence which could establish the innocence of a defendant.

The ICC is directed by Article 68 to take 'appropriate measures to protect the safety, physical and psychological well-being, dignity and privacy of victims and witnesses' who are given the novel right of separate legal representation to allow their own views to be canvassed. If there is 'grave danger' apprehended to a witness or his or her family, the prosecutor may withhold details of identification or evidence at any pre-trial stage. However, come the trial itself, any measures to withhold identification 'shall not be prejudicial to or inconsistent with the rights of the accused' (Article 69(2)). This formula should ensure that the correct dissenting opinion of Sir Ninian Stephen in the *Tadić Case* is adopted by the ICC, so that we will never have the spectacle of a defendant convicted of a monstrous crime on the word of an accuser whose identity he is not permitted to know.

The defendant is entitled to examine all the evidence upon which the prosecution relies, but this it will have selected from a large body of material collected in the course of the investigation, some of which may point the other way or be helpful to the defence team in its own investigations. The right to disclosure of such material follows from the overriding guarantee of fair trial, and the European Court of Human Rights has ruled that the 'equality of arms' principle requires full defence access.[20] There can be limited exceptions – for example, to protect the names of prosecution informers – but if the information is helpful to the defence, then refusal to disclose means, in European law, that the trial cannot be fair and must be abandoned. The Statute addresses these difficulties in Article 67(2) by imposing a limited duty on the prosecutor to disclose evidence which 'he or she believes shows or tends to show the innocence of the accused, or to mitigate the guilt of the accused, or which may affect the credibility of prosecution evidence'. This approach is unsatisfactory. Disclosure should not hinge on the 'belief' of an adversary party, which will inevitably be coloured by its commitment to prove guilt. Only the defence can judge what will be helpful to the defence. Where material which the prosecution cannot or will not disclose creates a real possibility that the defendant is innocent, then the charge should be withdrawn rather than expose the accused to a trial which carries a significant prospect of unfairness.

The prosecutor may have access to material collected by states through secretive diplomatic channels, and by surveillance and intercept systems which in the interests of their national security they may not wish the prosecutor to divulge to defenders linked with enemy forces. The availability of such material will in any event be known to the prosecutor, who may seek it (as may the defence) under the provisions for state party co-operation. The prosecutor may request evidence from an intelligence officer or security chief of a state which refuses the request on grounds of national security. All such cases can be brought to the Court for resolution under Article 72, which provides for every kind of compromise on disclosure. If a state decides to withhold its 'humint' (human intelligence) or 'sigint' (signals intelligence – i.e. intercepts) on national security grounds, then there is not much the Court can do, except report the unco-operative state to the Security Council. In the meantime, however, the trial will still continue and the Court 'may make such inference in the trial of the accused as to the existence or non-existence of a fact, as may be appropriate in the circumstances'. This is a curiously permissive power: since important evidence is being withheld, the Court should be precluded from drawing any inference adverse to the defence about a fact which hinges on the missing evidence.

Article 69(7) attempts to grapple with a problem litigated more than any other in adversary systems of criminal trial, namely whether and to what extent evidence obtained by unlawful or unfair means should be admitted and used to prove guilt. This is the 'fruit of the poisoned tree' doctrine which relates (for example) to evidence elicited by *agents provocateurs* and confessions obtained by threats or tricks or torture: methods which are objectionable both because such confessions are prone to be unreliable, and because a court's approval of evidence of this sort would only serve to countenance or encourage the ugly behaviour which produced it. The Statute frames the exclusionary rule as follows:

Evidence obtained by means of a violation of this Statute or internationally recognized human rights shall not be admissible if:

(a) The violation casts substantial doubt on the reliability of the evidence; or

(b) The admission of the evidence would be antithetical to and would seriously damage the integrity of the proceedings.

The formulation means that minor breaches of defendants' rights will not lead to exclusion of evidence, and even serious breaches (a confession obtained at gunpoint) may be countenanced unless there is 'substantial doubt' about its reliability, such as if part of it can be proved untrue. The curious phrasing of the alternative part of the rule will call for a value judgment on whether the Court's integrity is likely to be affected publicly by the spectacle of a defendant being convicted on evidence collected in breach of his fundamental rights. If the crime would not have been committed but for the activities of *agents provocateurs*, or the evidence comprised a confession obtained by torture, this would certainly be the case, although there is nothing to stop the prosecutor using such information for the purposes of his investigations. Physical evidence, the whereabouts of which has been obtained by torture, would pass the reliability test. If, however, the torture had been authorized by the prosecutor or his agents, even physical evidence might in those circumstances fail the 'integrity of proceedings' test.

PUNISHMENTS

Article 70 gives the Court a special power to punish, by imprisonment for up to five years, witnesses, lawyers and defendants who deliberately perjure themselves or forge documents for presentation in evidence. State parties must extend their domestic perjury laws to include attempts to pervert justice at the ICC. This provision is necessary: there are notable examples of attempts to frame defendants charged with crimes against humanity. Armand Hammer advanced his commercial interests by presenting Israel with forged documents to secure the wrongful conviction of Ivan Demjanjuk and perjury was committed against Duško Tadić (it is a wise witness who knows his own father – see pp. 474–5), but the first lawyer to disgrace himself before an international criminal court was a Tadić defender, Milun Vujin, who was fined $10,000. He was followed by Florence Hartmann, a French journalist who had been an official spokesperson in the prosecutors' office, who wrote a book which disclosed two of the Court's confidential orders. She was fined €7,000. A very serious case of contempt of the ICC occurred in June 2012, when the Zintan militia holding Saif Gaddafi took exception to the professional behaviour of defence counsel Melinda Taylor, sent by the ICC, and held her in prison for a month. Representatives of the interim Libyan government pretended that the barrister was in the wrong and proceeded to defame her. She was released after a secret deal which doubtless involved promises of no reprisals, but a court with integrity and confidence might in due course insist that the militia leaders responsible for her captivity, and Libyan representatives responsible for defaming her, should be prosecuted for the Article 70 offence (which carries up to five years' imprisonment) of retaliating against an official of the Court on account of duties performed by that or another official.

The gravest crimes call for the gravest penalties compatible with human rights treaties: Article 77 provides that for the worst offences a term of life imprisonment which means 'life' is appropriate. In other cases, sentences may have a length of up to thirty years, and sentences imposed consecutively for multiple crimes may not exceed this maximum. Convicts may additionally be fined, and have property or assets which represent profits from their crimes forfeited. Article 109 requires state parties to co-operate in freezing and seizing assets within their jurisdiction, so whether these financial penalties have any purpose will very much depend on whether Switzerland, Liechtenstein and other havens for 'dirty money' become parties to the treaty. A serious defect in the Rome Statute, which reflects a deficiency in international criminal law, is the exclusion of any jurisdiction over corporations, so only the assets of individual suspects may be attached.

The most notable achievement of the penalty provisions is to eschew the death sentence, following the UN's lead with the ICTY and ICTR. The provisions of the Rome Statute provide further evidence of the movement of international law towards the abolition of capital punishment. States which cling resolutely to it, however, insisted on the insertion of a clause to ensure that the absence of the death penalty from the Rome Statute would not commit them to halting executions of persons convicted of equivalent offences under their national laws.[21] This will have the ironic effect that perpetrators with no place to hide will do their utmost to be tried by the ICC, rather than face execution in their home state. Such a phenomenon has already been witnessed in the early years of the ICTR, where some Hutu leaders were prepared to plead guilty to genocide and suffer lengthy imprisonment rather than face the prospect of trial for the same crime at a makeshift court in Rwanda, swiftly followed by public execution.

There are provisions for ordering reparations to victims of crimes, following the lead in this respect of the Inter-American Court. After any conviction, the Trial Division may hear representations on behalf of victims and their families, and make an order against the convict requiring compensation or restitution of stolen property. Where the convict has no assets, an award will be made out of a trust fund set up by the state parties for this purpose. This is welcome, especially if the trust fund attracts wealthy private individual benefactors, for the prospects of making most convicts 'pay' for their crimes against humanity are remote. The trust fund is run by a board of worthies (Bishop Tutu, Simone Veil and Queen Rania of Jordan are members) but its policies are determined by the assembly of state parties. Most states consider that its funds should go to victims only after someone is convicted for victimizing them, although given the length of time that will be taken in arresting and trying most defendants, it would be more sensible and compassionate to spend the money on the urgent health and counselling needs of ravaged villages and ravished villagers.

The Court may in time deal with a few fallen dictators with millions salted away in Swiss bank accounts, but its focus on individual rather than state responsibility means that the countries and the peoples for whose benefit and in whose service most crimes against humanity are committed will be spared all financial consequences. The Treaty makes no provision for reparations from countries like Serbia where international crimes have had popular support. Were another Hitler to be convicted of genocide, his six million victims would look forlornly for compensation from his personal assets, despite the fact that the collective (or at least governmental) responsibility for the Holocaust would justify reparations. Germany, indeed, has paid out US$60 billion over the last half century to Holocaust victims, and in February 1999 Chancellor Schröder announced a further US$6 billion in compensation for surviving slave labourers, half contributed by guilty corporations. The scandalous failure of the Japanese government and its courts in 1998 to provide reparations to English and Australian prisoners-of-war treated barbarically in its camps provided a topical example for diplomats in Rome: it was precisely because they feared the ICC could embarrass states suffering from human rights amnesia that they declined to allow the Court to order reparations against governments. This omission reflects one of the key weaknesses in the current philosophy behind the international justice movement, which denies the existence of collective responsibility in order to fasten upon the blameworthy individual. Where crimes against humanity are concerned, the two are not mutually exclusive.

APPEALS

The right of a convicted defendant to have both the verdict and the sentence reviewed on appeal – a right notably denied at Nuremberg – is vouchsafed by Article 81, and will take the form of a hearing by a five-judge appeals division. Commendably, there is also provision for a prisoner or (after his death) his relatives to make a later application to review the conviction on the ground that fresh evidence, unavailable at the time of trial through no fault of the defence, has been uncovered which might have resulted in an acquittal if it had been presented at the trial. Victims of a miscarriage of justice may be compensated by the Court, and anyone who has been unlawfully arrested or detained under its process shall have an enforceable right to compensation. The necessity for such provision was demonstrated in 1998 by the case of two Bosnian Serb brothers who were forcibly snatched by NATO forces and immediately transported to prison in the Netherlands, where it turned out, to everyone's embarrassment, that they were not the individuals referred to in the arrest warrant.

Unnecessarily, and indeed oppressively, the prosecution is also given a right of appeal against an acquittal, and the defendant may even be imprisoned pending such an appeal. If the burden of proof 'beyond reasonable doubt' has any meaning, then an acquittal by all or a majority of the experienced judges in the Trial Division, who have had the benefit of seeing and hearing all the witnesses, means as a matter of logic that reasonable doubt *must* exist, whatever the Appeals Division may say.

The Court is controlled by an assembly of the state parties. This assembly meets annually to review the Court's progress and ensure its funding, which comes from contributions the state parties levy upon themselves, funds provided by the UN and voluntary contributions from anyone else. Although the 'voluntary contribution' system is common for UN instrumentalities, it is not satisfactory for criminal courts to entertain any doubts that funding necessary to do justice will be forthcoming. The Special Court for Sierra Leone, the only other international court that defends on voluntary contributions, has warned that 'courts which are so starved of funds that they cannot do justice should close themselves down rather than continue under the expectation that sufficient funding will be forthcoming only if they render verdicts acceptable to the funding body'.[22] If, for example, there is insufficient funding to keep prisoners in humane conditions or to pay for adequate representation for poor defendants, a court thus disabled from acting fairly should wind itself up. Any disputes between state parties over interpretation of the Rome Statute may, under Article 119, be referred to the International Court of Justice. The first Review Conference, held in Kampala in 2010, achieved little other than to define the crime of aggression, but there was such reluctance to imperil the heads of the most aggressive states (i.e. the US and Russia) that its enforcement was postponed at least until after the next Review Conference in 2017. Because the crime cannot be prosecuted until two thirds of the state parties agree, it may not ever come into operation, and even if it does, member states will be entitled to opt out. In this way, the parties to the ICC have funked a universal law against unilateral military intervention. At least this leaves it open for states or regional bodies to take interventionist action on humanitarian grounds without fear of committing an international crime.

ROME 1998: THE AFTERMATH

Much of the support for an international criminal court in July 1998 was governed by the wish to see the great villains of the late twentieth century behind bars. Pol Pot was alive and well through most of the preparatory sessions, with 1.7 million deaths to his discredit. Idi Amin had retired to Saudi Arabia and 'Baby Doc' Duvalier to the south of France; the torturers and death-squad leaders of Latin America clung to the amnesties they had extracted and General Pinochet was preparing to fly first class to take tea with Mrs Thatcher and have his spinal problems attended to by top surgeons in Harley Street. Newspaper articles about the Rome Conference were illustrated by their mug shots – unpaid endorsements of the ideal of international justice. But as the diplomats well knew (even if the journalists did not), these malefactors would all be allowed to escape: the governments of the world would never countenance a court with the power to reach back into history, or even to feel the collars of leaders who were currently in power. The UN insisted from the outset that the Court was a futuristic project, for a 'future generation' of criminals. So obsessed were the diplomats with the need to cast a veil over the past, and indeed the present, that *two* articles of the Rome Statute say so, in terms. Their headings both lapse into Latin, as if trying to cloak their embarrassment. Article 11 (headed 'Jurisdiction *ratione temporis*') emphasizes that the 'Court has jurisdiction only with respect to crimes committed after the entry into force of this Statute'. Article 24 (headed 'Non-retroactivity *ratione personae*') repeats that 'No person shall be criminally responsible under this Statute for conduct prior to the entry into force of the Statute'. The Statute entered into force in 2002, sixty days after it had been ratified by sixty nations.

This global cop-out, dressed up as an application of the well-recognized rule against retrospective criminal prosecutions, was nothing of the kind: genocide, war crimes and crimes against humanity were established in customary international law long before 1998. In principle, the ICC should have been as little bothered by the rule against retroactivity as the courts which tried Eichmann or Barbie or any of the more recently captured Nazis. People like Mengistu and Habré are actually *more* culpable because their crimes were not committed in a world war and they were well aware of the Nuremberg judgment and the conventions which made their actions criminal at the time they were committed. By the devices of Articles 11 and 24, they will not attract ICC attention, although this does not preclude their prosecution elsewhere.

Despite all its compromises and equivocations, the Rome Statute has historic significance. That much is clear from the detailed work which has followed as many (but not all) states have put their domestic legal systems in a position to permit ratification. At the United Nations a well-attended preparatory commission ('prepcom') held eight sessions from 1999 to 2001, providing for the Court's financial framework and the immunities of its staff, agreeing its rules of procedure and further defining its unusual status as 'an independent permanent institution in relationship with the United Nations system'. In the latter respect, significantly, the prepcom has confirmed the possibility, which the US opposes, of prosecuting 'blue berets', whose immunity (under the 1946 Convention on UN Privileges and Immunities) the UN must waive, if (like the Ghanaian 'peacekeepers' in Rwanda) they join in the acts of genocide they are meant to be preventing. The US took an active part in the first six prepcoms under President Clinton who signalled his best wishes by signing the Statute before handing over to George W. Bush. The new administration declined to attend the seventh prepcom, but at the eighth the delegates passed a motion extending condolences to the US over 9/11. So the White House suddenly reversed its position and sent the US delegation rushing back to accept them. It stayed long enough to join discussion about the crime of aggression, but then departed before the final plenary. On 6 May 2002, the Bush administration formally 'unsigned' the Rome Treaty by notifying the UN Secretary-General that the US would not become a party and would accept no obligations arising from President Clinton's signature. In August, the 'bomb The Hague' bill became law: the American Service-Members' Protection Act (ASPA) gave the President power to use military force against any country detaining US soldiers on ICC arrest warrants. It prohibits military assistance to countries which ratify the Rome Statute (except for allies like NATO countries) and prevents US government agencies from cooperating with the ICC. This somewhat puerile legislation, promoted by Jesse Helms and Dr Kissinger (the only 'service member' who might need protection), proclaims in its preamble that the Rome Statute 'could inhibit the ability of the US to use its military to participate in multinational operations including humanitarian intervention to save civilian lives'. This was nonsense: the Rome Statute inhibits the loss of civilian lives by providing for the possibility of deterrent punishment for those who take them lawlessly. The prospect that US service members would ever be prosecuted in the ICC is negligible, because the complementarity provisions of the Statute ensure that the ICC only operates when national courts do not – and the US military justice system normally prosecutes when there is evidence of war crimes.

These antics damaged the US rather more than the Court and ironically they have helped to refute the argument (made by some voices on the European left) that international criminal justice was devised to serve the interests of American hegemony. Ratification has continued steadily, notwithstanding the threatened reprisals, and had reached 121 by mid-2012. US concerns about its nationals being arrested on foreign territory have been met by negotiating 'Article 98(2)' bilateral agreements with many ratifying countries, under which they undertake not to surrender US citizens to the Court, although the legality of such agreements is doubtful. Article 98(2) of the Rome Statute prevents the Court from insisting on the extradition of its suspect if that would put the extraditing state in breach of a treaty obligation to a third state, unless the Court can obtain that third state's consent. It is a provision to protect diplomats and military personnel present under Status of Forces Agreements and was never intended to provide a back door through which state parties, under US pressure, sign a bilateral treaty promising never to surrender any American found in their territory.[23] However, the US antipathy to the Court has dissipated with the Obama administration, which has appointed a former Sierra Leone Court prosecutor, Stephen Rapp, as its Ambassador for War Crimes and has evinced firm support for the Court.

In April 2005, the Security Council referred the 'situation' in Darfur to the ICC prosecutor. That reference was due in part to US action the previous year, when Secretary of State Colin Powell pronounced the g-word – 'genocide' – to describe the killings of African tribespeople by Arab militia (Janjaweed) backed by Sudan government air power. Darfur had first come to Security Council attention in March 2004, on the tenth anniversary of the genocide in Rwanda: over the previous year alone, 100,000 civilians had been killed and twice as many turned into refugees. The Security Council temporized and between March and November 2004 a further 80,000 were killed. But a committee of enquiry headed by Antonio Cassesse reported in January 2005 that Janjaweed and the government had been guilty of crimes against humanity (although they had not committed them in pursuance of a policy of genocide). He recommended an ICC reference and handed to Kofi Annan a sealed list of names of fifty-one suspects, including that of President Bashir. In April, with tacit US agreement (i.e. it abstained rather than use its veto), the historic reference of this 'situation' in Darfur was made to the ICC.

Darfur is proving a difficult test case. The ICC reference came late and partly for 'fig leaf' reasons: the Security Council had done nothing to stop the twenty-year secessionist war in the south of the country and had let the refugee exodus from the western province of Darfur reach a million before it took action. The Sudanese government, implacably hostile to the ICC, at first refused entry to Prosecutor

Ocampo's investigators but then evidently read the Rome Statute and decided to outflank him by announcing that Sudan would conduct its own trials. A few low-level officials were indicted and soon two army corporals were sentenced to death for killing a civilian in Darfur – human offerings to appease the Security Council. These trials do not satisfy the complementarity test, since they are not directed at the main perpetrators.[24]

The International Criminal Court was formally opened on 11 March 2003, when its eighteen judges were sworn in by a Jordanian prince at a ceremony in The Hague delayed by the late arrival of the Queen of the Netherlands. The Dutch prime minister quoted Grotius and invited the delegates to an evening of somewhat tedious ballet in what he termed 'the judicial capital of the world'. It was, none the less, a start and, although nine years and many massacres later the stark fact was that the ICC had only recorded a single conviction, that is not the failure that its critics suggest. It had by the end of this period become an important new player in international affairs, and irrespective of acquittals or convictions, the very decision to initiate an investigation, and certainly any decision to indict, was apt to have momentous consequences.

THE ICC, TEN YEARS ON

For the ICC 14 March 2012 was a red-letter day: its trial chamber found Thomas Lubanga, a Congolese warlord, guilty of a crime against humanity for abducting children and forcing them to serve as soldiers. This was not a significant legal precedent: the Sierra Leone court had already established the illegality at international law of child recruitment and it was not particularly relevant to the Congo, where many worse war crimes had gone unpunished. But this was the first conviction, and it established the ICC's reputation for upholding proper standards of fairness – the prosecution had been seriously reprimanded for failing in its disclosure duties and for using unscrupulous 'intermediaries' who encouraged witnesses to give exaggerated and sometimes false statements.

The evidence of Lubanga's guilt was overwhelming: he was

commander-in-chief of the army and personally encouraged schoolboy recruitment. Conclusive evidence against him was provided by videos showing him speaking to children at a training camp and having several child soldiers in his personal guard. For all that the Lubanga conviction was a formal milestone, the length of the proceedings – six years – for a crime that was relatively easy to prove, was wholly unsatisfactory. There were much worse crimes, and worse criminals, left in the Congo, unaffected by the verdict, notably Bosco Ntaganda, a serving army general accused of widespread atrocities in eastern Congo. But rendered at the very end of the first decade of the ICC's operation, the verdict was an important symbol for the court's first prosecutor, Luis Moreno Ocampo, now succeeded by his deputy, Fatou Bensouda. By this time the ICC had seven countries under investigation and twenty-four indictees, with eleven arrest warrants outstanding.

It is important to recognize that any new court will have procedural teething problems that take some years to work through – the judges must settle rules of evidence and procedure, and the early cases will be marked by uncertainties and delays as novel rules – particularly in a compromise court – are interpreted by trial chamber judges and often re-interpreted by appeal chamber judges before trials can get underway. At the ICC there have been genuine and serious problems in working out a disclosure regime which is fair to the defence and also fairly protective of confidential information supplied by states. This does not, of course, justify the onset of the all-too-familiar expense and delay that have been associated with trial at The Hague, and the failure of the judiciary at this stage to do very much about it. There is not much independent oversight of the ICC – most NGOs that would usually offer criticisms of international institutions tend to be over-supportive of the Court, whilst some commentators, and states run by real or potential indictees, are ideologically biased against it. In August 2011 an expert review by the International Bar Association, 'Fairness at the International Criminal Court', found that it was reasonably fair to both sides in all its pre-trial cases. Whilst contributing states are now getting value for money from the very fact of the Court's existence and capacity to indict mass-murderers, it has yet to deliver justice to their victims.

In 2012, the ICC had this caseload:

Uganda: The Lord's Resistance Army

These crazed jungle fighters, led by Joseph Kony (the self-described mouthpiece of God), aim to rid Uganda of witches and sorcerers and President Museveni, and establish a theocratic state based on the Ten Commandments. They have been fighting the army for twenty years, believing themselves invulnerable when smeared with shea butter and anointed with holy water. They have abducted over 20,000 children for use as sex slaves and soldiers in a barbaric war in which they specialize in mutilation of hands, feet, noses, ears, lips and breasts and indulge in rituals so vile that the details have been redacted from their indictments. Uganda, a state party, referred the case to the Prosecutor in 2004: the following year he indicted Kony and four senior commanders. There can be no doubt of the justification for these indictments – Kony and his crew are among the most disgusting killer gangs operating anywhere.[25] It was the Court's first reference from a state party, and for that reason difficult to refuse, although at first blush it is difficult to see how the complementarity principle could apply: Uganda has an effective court system, and the ICC is reliant in any event on the Ugandan army to apprehend its indictees.[26] The Prosecutor, however, has pointed out that some LRA leaders received an amnesty in 2000, as part of a peace negotiation, and the possibility that this might bar their domestic prosecution meant that the complementarity principle could apply.

The Court has been unfairly criticized for issuing indictments which may interfere with peace negotiations but with someone as unhinged and unreliable as Kony, no agreement can ever be trusted. Typically, he agreed to a peace accord in December 2008 and then refused to sign; within a few weeks his forces had killed 600 people, abducted 400 women and children and caused tens of thousands to flee their villages. The Court has, more convincingly, been upbraided for ignoring allegations of war crimes committed by the Uganda Defence Force, and for allowing itself to be used as a political instrument by Museveni. The Prosecutor could have been more wary at the outset of his request to do Uganda's dirty work, but one compelling reason for seeing Kony in an international court is LRA forays into the Democratic Republic of Congo, Southern Sudan and the Central African Republic which have displaced hundreds of thousands, whilst killing civilians and abducting children. The powers of an international court are appropriately engaged in tracking and arresting leaders of an army which kills and pillages across borders. As the result of a simplistic but viral YouTube attack on Kony, which attracted 90 million viewers in its first week, President Obama made 'special advisers' available to help hunt him down – a token of US support for the ICC in 2012.

DRC: *Lubanga and others*

Again, this was a reference from a state – the Democratic Republic of Congo (formerly Zaire), run by Laurent Kabila. It has a history of internecine warfare that has cost 5 million lives, lost through murder, disease and malnutrition to armies supported by other African states.[27] In due course the prosecutor issued an arrest warrant against Thomas Lubanga, a rebel warlord already in custody, and two of his equally brutal adversaries, Germain Katanga and Mathieu Ngudjolo Chui. Callixte Mbarushimana, a Hutu from Rwanda, is also awaiting trial for DRC crimes. These indictments have been criticized on the basis that they charge crimes committed in the province of Ituri, which has the best-functioning courts in the country (thanks to a $20 million EU grant) where Lubanga was already facing much more serious charges than the single offence levelled at him by the ICC, namely that of recruiting child soldiers.[28] Human Rights Watch and other groups actually wrote to the ICC prosecutor, urging him to add further counts of pillage and rape. Ocampo refused: he was not going to overload the indictment (a lesson learnt from the ICTY) and no doubt he wanted to kick off the ICC's first trial by setting an important precedent on the illegality of recruiting child soldiers (although the Sierra Leone Court had already set that). The ICC's first trial began on 26 January 2009 with a nasty shock for the prosecution – its first witness said he had lied about being a child soldier because he had been coached by a humanitarian aid group. Another witness made a similar allegation, claiming he had been coached by a prosecution intermediary, who then had to be called to explain. A further problem has been caused by the prosecution's approach to disclosure: Ocampo's refusal to provide exculpatory but confidential documents to the defence and to the court itself was described by the judges as a 'serious abuse', although the prosecutor had been concerned to maintain confidentiality with his state source. A more satisfactory disclosure system is now in place. Lubanga was eventually convicted in 2012, and his appeal will authoritatively determine the scope of the crime of child recruitment.

Central African Republic: Bemba

In 2004, the Court received yet another reference from an African state – the government of the Central African Republic, beset by rebel factions, one of which was led by Jean-Pierre Bemba. The difficulties of investigation in an insecure country meant that it was not until 2008 that the prosecutor felt able to apply for an arrest warrant against Bemba, by which time he had fled to Belgium. He was arrested and his trial began in 2010.

Sudan: President Bashir

Arrest has not been possible in relation to any of the Sudanese indictees. President Bashir's response when high-ranking government officials Haroun and Ali Kushab were indicted in 2007 was to promote Haroun to be minister for humanitarian affairs. His reaction to his own indictment, which came in 2009, was to tell the ICC 'you can eat it'. He immediately expelled thirteen international NGOs and stopped humanitarian relief supplies, heedless that his people would suffer as a result of his pique. The African Union expressed 'deep concern about the decision' and demanded that the Security Council suspend the indictment, thereby encouraging Bashir to believe in his invincibility. He has enjoyed strutting around African states, including some that have ratified the Rome Treaty (such as Kenya) and boasting of his impunity. By 2011 he felt confident enough to give interviews to the Western media, claiming that Darfur was 'a traditional conflict taking place since the colonial days' and accusing the ICC of double standards for not prosecuting NATO leaders for their wars of aggression in Afghanistan and Iraq.[29] The tragedy of his continuing at large, and the stupidity of the African leaders who support him, was on display in South Sudan in 2012, a new country against which he was waging war with the same brutality he used in Darfur.

Bashir's public relations offensive has not convinced those who have rationally considered the evidence against the Sudan indictees. The UN estimates 300,000 dead and 1.7 million displaced in Darfur by the actions of Janjaweed militias, obviously supported by the Sudanese army. The Sudanese air force even co-ordinated bombing raids to 'soften up' the refugee camps before they were attacked by Janjaweed cavalry – 'devils on horseback' – later joined by Sudanese soldiers emerging from their Toyota Land Cruisers to join in rape and pillage. The prosecutor's evidence shows that the Janjaweed were trained at Sudanese government camps, armed, paid and supplied with kit and uniforms by Bashir's government. Bashir himself is accused of command responsibility, directing which civilian towns and villages should be the targets of further attacks. The prosecutor argues that this amounts to genocide, by deliberately inflicting conditions of life on Darfuri tribes which are calculated to bring about their physical destruction. But genocidal intention is difficult to prove, and it may be that Bashir has been charged with one of the few crimes for which he is not responsible. Neither the Commission of Inquiry which originally reported to the UN, nor the EU fact-finding mission, was prepared to level this accusation,'[30] and nor was the ICC Trial Chamber when it initially considered the prosecutor's case (it changed its mind after the Appeal Chamber pointed out that it had adopted the wrong test: so long as there was *prima facie* evidence of genocidal intent, that was sufficient for an arrest warrant to be issued, even if, in due course, there might be other reasonable explanations to refute the charge of genocide). This tedious skirmishing is a further example of the futility of charging genocide when the facts provide ample evidence of crimes against humanity, for which in any event Bashir must answer.

Heads of State

The cases of Bashir, Gbagbo and Gaddafi draw attention to the way in which a sitting head of state could – and should – answer an indictment, or challenge an arrest warrant application. The prosecutor is accountable at every stage to the Court: he or she must apply to it for a warrant, and for confirmation of an indictment, and it is not essential at either stage that the defendant be in custody in The Hague. At the latter stage the rules expressly allow an absent accused to be represented by counsel when this is 'in the interests of justice'[31] which it invariably is, and there is every reason in the interests of justice to permit representation by counsel at earlier stages as well. Both Bashir and Gaddafi reacted to their indictments by loudly asserting their innocence and vilifying the prosecutor, but neither had the confidence to instruct lawyers to contest the allegations on the grounds that there was no necessity to issue a warrant or that the evidence did not amount to the crime charged in the indictment. (Gaddafi did approach international lawyers who advised him to take this course, but he preferred to insult the ICC rather than appear before it.) Bashir, by this means, might have successfully delayed the issue of his arrest warrant or refuted the genocide allegation. Alternatively, he could have accepted the prosecutor's offer to postpone the proceedings against him if he sent Haroun to The Hague to be tried first: the evidence against the two of them was the same, and if Haroun was acquitted the Bashir indictment would be dropped.

Bashir was the first ICC indictment of a sitting head of state, and the failure of UN states to support the Court was notable and deplorable. Sudan had a duty to surrender Haroun and Kushab, but the Security Council failed to require it to comply with that duty, which arose specifically under Resolution 1593: when in 2010 the Pre-Trial Chamber issued the ICC's first formal finding of non-compliance against Sudan, the Security Council president merely said after a private meeting that the Council's 'general sense' was that Sudan should co-operate, but that it would not issue any statement or take any immediate action.[32] The Security Council thereafter ignored complaints by the Court about Bashir's visits to other member states.

An Anti-African bias?

This failure to support the ICC, at least until the Libyan reference in 2011, may show that misbegotten criticism of the Court as 'biased against Africa' has had some effect. Much of it has come from Sudanese government propaganda and from nationalists in other African states (some concerned about their own vulnerability to international justice), but it has been repeated in such exaggerated language as *The ICC – Europe's Guantánamo Bay?*[33] Insofar as this criticism is made against international criminal justice, the claim that it is solely focused on Africa is obviously wrong – as courts for the Balkans and Cambodia and Lebanon and Timor attest (together with the demands for prosecutions of Syrians and Sri Lankans). It is true that the ICC has to date concentrated on African states, but that is because, with the exception of Libya and Sudan which were referred by the Security Council, African states have asked it to spend its resources on indicting their nationals. These resources are substantially (60 per cent) paid for by European states, but that is because they have both the money and the commitment to international justice. To claim that the Court 'thereby serves Western political and economic interests in Africa' or (as Paul Kagame puts it) 'colonialism, slavery and imperialism', is as absurd as insisting that African leaders like Paul Kagame (himself the subject of a UN report accusing him of murdering Hutus) should live happily ever after the atrocities they direct.

The first ICC prosecutor, Luis Moreno Ocampo, was open to criticism that in the African states he had been invited to investigate – such as Uganda, DRC, the Central African Republic, Libya and the Ivory Coast – he had turned a blind eye to atrocities by government forces and their allies. To this extent he has created a perception that the ICC is in favour of certain governments, and in the case of the Libyan rebels (whose uninvestigated war crimes include the murder of Gaddafi after he had surrendered), in favour of the side that has Europe's support. It was certainly a mistake for Ocampo to give a joint press conference with Uganda's Museveni, as if to celebrate the president's reference of the Lord's Resistance Army to the Court, and he failed to investigate the DRC government for creating and arming Lubanga's militia, or to indict the Central African Republic generals whose forces have committed most of the war crimes. However, a prosecutor cannot indict if he cannot uncover evidence that will stand up in court, and he has no police force to obtain that evidence or to guarantee the safety of witnesses who would give it. There is a 'catch-as-catch-can' aspect to international criminal justice at this early stage of its development, but member-state governments must be under no illusion that if they refer their 'situation' to the ICC prosecutor, he will not turn around and indict their own members as well as their opponents. When Laurent Gbagbo, the deposed Ivory Coast president, was flown to The Hague in December 2011 to face charges of killing thousands who supported his rival, Alassane Ouattara, Ocampo greeted his arrival by pointing out that crimes were committed by both parties, and Gbagbo's indictment was 'just a beginning'.

The ICC found a new role – although again in Africa – when it was brought in (largely through the mediation of Kofi Annan) to investigate and indict the plotters of the political violence which erupted in the Rift valley of Kenya during the 2008 elections and resulted in 1,300 deaths and hundreds of thousands of displacements. The government had failed to prosecute the main perpetrators – because most of them were government ministers – so the ICC was called in. In December 2010 indictments were unveiled against three each from the two warring factions, including Jomo Kenyatta's son and the deputy prime minister, accused of authorizing excessive force to kill demonstrators and of instructing police to arm a criminal gang for reprisal attacks against the government's ethnic enemies. The ICC has won plaudits for its even-handed investigation, at least in Kenya where its intervention was popular and seems to have curtailed the violence so that the people could peacefully vote for a new constitution. Remarkably, the highly placed indictees all co-operated, attending the Court during its initial reviews (they were allowed bail) and instructing counsel to represent them in challenging their indictments. The case, even in its early stages, shows the utility of having a 'back-stop' international court to hear allegations of crimes against humanity committed in a country where the alleged perpetrators are so involved in its politics that local judges – from their own or opposing tribes – could not be seen as independent.

But who is to decide whether local courts can cope with such trials? The ICC is bound by the complementarity principle, so called by reference to Article 1 of the Rome Statute, which says that the court 'shall be complementary to national criminal jurisdictions'. What this means has to be gleaned from the badly drafted Article 17, which decrees that a case shall be 'inadmissible' (i.e. the Court has no juris-diction to hear it) if it is already being investigated or prosecuted locally, 'unless the state is unwilling or unable genuinely to carry out the investigation or prosecution'. 'Unwillingness' is further defined by reference to the principles of due process, and especially whether or not the local proceedings are conducted independently or impartially, and whether they can be conducted at all if the domestic judicial sys-tem is in a state of 'substantial collapse'.

The incoherence of Article 17 became apparent in respect of the indictment of Saif Gaddafi, who was captured by a rebel band shortly after his father had been beaten, buggered (with an iron bar) and shot by vengeful insurgents. The indictment had come as a result of a Secu-rity Council reference which required Libya to co-operate with the Court, so Libya was under an obligation to convey him to The Hague and abide by the Court's decision as to where and on what charges he should be tried. Instead, it unilaterally announced its intention to keep him and put him on trial in Tripoli. Under Article 17 'the Court shall determine' such an issue, although at first Ocampo unilaterally announced that Libya could proceed, without investigating whether its judicial system was in a state of 'substantial collapse' (it was), or whether it could offer an 'independent and impartial trial' (it could not). The Court then insisted that Saif be taken to The Hague, but Libya asked the Pre-Trial Chamber to permit him to be tried in Tripoli. The question was important, because unless the ICC has the right to decide the place of their trial, some of its indictees will be held by the government (old or new) that they have opposed, and like Saddam Hussein will be subjected to revenge in its courts, which can rarely offer impartial justice after a bloody war. That 'justice' will in most local trials end in a sentence of death – the very sentence which inter-national courts are required to abjure. The Rome Statute does not list capital punishment as a factor the ICC should take into account, although it should be a crucial factor.

11

Justice in Demand

'Al-Assad to The Hague!'

Street chant of Syrian protesters

The first decade of the twenty-first century has witnessed a sea change in the world's responses to crimes against humanity, with concomitant changes in international law to permit trials and punishments – not merely by courts in The Hague but alternatively, and some would argue preferably, by courts applying that law in their own country. The legal buzz-word for this approach is 'complementarity' – the ICC's jurisdiction is co-extensive with that of the country where the crime of mass murder or torture is committed, but a transfer of perpetrators to The Hague is only necessary if local justice – administered by those who have first right to punish because they have suffered the crime – is unavailable or unfair. Any legal presumption in favour of domestic courts is unsatisfactory, however, for the simple reason that local justice is sometimes unavailable and often unfair: the political or military leaders who commit atrocities are either still in power or have tentacles that control the new government (e.g. by having given themselves amnesties, or remaining in control of the armed forces), or else are so hated for their crimes that a fair trial immediately after a revolution is impossible if conducted before local judges, especially if such judges are not independent of the new government.

One way out of this dilemma is to establish a 'hybrid' court, where international judges and prosecutors are in the majority but work together with their local equivalents in the country where the crime has been committed. This has the advantage of permitting justice to be seen by the people at close quarters, giving them a shared sense of retribution and, importantly, helping a post-revolution legal system back on its feet. The best example is the Special Court for war crimes in Sierra Leone, and the worst the Extraordinary Chambers for Cambodia where the 'hybrid' content is reversed and the international judges and prosecutors are in the minority and have often been at odds with the government-appointed majority. There are problems, of course, when the main perpetrators come from an army of occupation which has returned home: in East Timor, international tribunals effectively dealt with local collaborators but prosecutors in Jakarta allowed the real villains from the Indonesian army to slip through their nervous fingers. That has been the case with the impunity allowed the genocidal generals of Pakistan, who commanded the attack on Bangladesh in 1971. This mass murder has always been ignored by the international community, but in 2010 the government in Dacca established a special court to try collaborators – a decision criticized because the defendants are opposition figures, and because of the deplorable decision to subject them to the death penalty. In Lebanon, an international court set up in The Hague to try those suspected of the Harari assassination has been stalled by its inability to arrest its suspects.

The Arab Spring has brought loud demands for justice, and different ways of delivering it. The movement, coming less than two years after the 'Green Revolution' was crushed in Iran, began as a protest against authoritarian rule and its decades of corruption and political and religious oppression, and soon developed into full-blooded demands for democracy. It was fuelled by awareness of how other leaders responsible for crimes against humanity had been called to account – hence the cry of the Syrian protesters, 'Al-Assad to The Hague!'. In Tunisia, where the Spring first blossomed, the thoroughly corrupt President, Ben Ali, escaped with his family to Saudi Arabia, which offers asylum, out of 'Islamic charity', to his ilk. Ben Ali was tried *in absentia* – to Western ears a contradiction in terms – and quickly convicted *in absentia*. In Egypt President Mubarak made the tyrants' mistake of clinging to power for too long after his security forces had killed hundreds of brave protesters in Tahrir Square. He was arrested and put on trial and subsequently sentenced to life imprisonment for ordering the army to shoot at them, and for the corruption that had massively enriched his family and his cronies. Mubarak had disdained to negotiate an amnesty, but Yemeni President Salah removed himself to Saudi Arabia and signed a deal with the main opposition party to resign in return for immunity from prosecution. This amnesty is not valid in international law (see chapter 6) and whether it would hold if he ever returned to Yemen is doubtful: it was met with violent street protests in which thousands of youths chanted 'No immunity for the murderers'.[1] In Bahrain, the King defused some of the outrage at the shooting of protesters and secret military trials by appointing an independent truth commission of respected international lawyers, then accepting their criticisms and promising to implement their reform proposals. These reforms did not extend to democracy or to an independent judiciary, and so low-level protests continue, but the initiative was an innovative use of an international justice mechanism. In Syria, at time of writing, the Assad regime continues to kill opponents (over 9,000 by June 2012) and its truculence has brought a demand from the Arab League as well as the European Union and the United States that it relinquish power, although its superpower support by Russia and China in the Security Council allows it to get away with mass murder.

Saddam Hussein, of course, refused an amnesty offer just before the US invasion in 2003: he suffered trial in a domestic court that delivered revenge rather than justice. This is a perennial and inevitable problem with trials in countries where transition has been violent, and the old regime has harnessed its forces for mass murder of revolutionaries. Their comrades or co-religionists, forming the new regime, want their revenge and resist meddling by other countries or by the ICC – even if, as in Libya, the revolution has been successful only because of international intervention. In such cases a 'hybrid' court offers the most satisfactory compromise, at least for countries where its security can be guaranteed (and even the calm of post-war Sierra Leone was regarded as too dangerous to host the trial of Charles

Taylor). Truth commissions, too, have a place, so long as they are precursors of, rather than alternatives to, criminal trials. Both kinds of justice mechanism may work to reconnect civil society in a nation torn assunder by civil war, and provide means by which the international community may assist the peace process through its legitimate interest in restoring the rule of law and deterring international crimes. Where post-conflict countries are insecure, or unable to give fair trials because of continuing political and religious hatreds, those suspected of committing crimes against humanity should be despatched for ICC trial in The Hague – for their own protection as well, since this will prevent them from suffering the fate of Gaddafi and Ceauçescu. The cases discussed in this chapter demonstrate that the best solution will vary with the circumstances in the particular nation, but it can no longer be maintained, as it was by many at the time of Pinochet's arrest, that international justice is irrelevant or ineffective. Increasingly, the debate in the twenty-first century is whether it is preferable, in a newly liberated nation, to put tyrants and torturers on trial in The Hague, or simply to have them executed by order of the new regime.

LESSONS FROM SIERRA LEONE

Sierra Leone is a West African coastal state which shares a fragile southern border with Liberia. It has had a notable history for centuries of slave-trading, its people plundered by Drake and Hawkins and carried to the United States on ships like the *Amistad*. Its capital, Freetown, was established in 1787 by British abolitionists as a refuge for education and settlement of slaves freed by the British navy on the world's first humanitarian mission. The country was colonized by Britain, which set up an administrative system (memorably described by Graham Greene in *The Heart of the Matter*) and West Africa's first university at Fourah Bay, whilst allowing its diamonds to be exploited by de Beers. After independence in 1961 it went the way of most African states, run down by one-party 'big man' government.

Corruption soon took its toll of elected politicians and a series of army coups were interspersed with raids on the diamond mines by a breakaway Sierra Leone army faction led by Corporal Foday Sankoh, operating from neighbouring Liberia. Styled the Revolutionary United Front (RUF), it recruited gangs of violent, dispossessed youths and armed them with AK-47s for their missions of pillage, rape and diamond heisting. The RUF had no political agenda: its arms and funds came partly from Charles Taylor, Liberia's vicious warlord, but it opposed the UN-sponsored elections of 1996, which returned Ahmed Kabbah, a former UN official. By this time, the RUF had perfected its special contribution to the chamber of war horrors: the practice of 'chopping' the limbs of innocent civilians. It was a means of spreading terror, especially to deter voters in 1996: their anti-election slogan, 'Don't vote or don't write', came true for thousands of citizens, forced to lay their right hand on RUF chopping-blocks after they had chosen to vote. Mutilation worked, as a means of terrifying the population, and so the RUF devised more devilish tortures, such as lopping off a leg as well as an arm, sewing up vaginas with fishing lines, and padlocking mouths. Given their level of barbarism, how could Sankoh and the RUF leadership ever have been invited by Western diplomats to share power?

The UN and the Western countries which had supervised the 1996 elections did not stay around to help President Kabbah, and in 1998 some RUF-inclined officers staged another coup. Kabbah retained a mercenary company, Sandline, to help his return to power, although this was in fact achieved by Nigerian forces acting through a regional OAU grouping (ECOMOG). They arrested Foday Sankoh, who was tried by a jury in Freetown and sentenced to death for treason. In June 1998 the UN passed Resolution 1181 pursuant to which it sent in a token force of 'blue berets' to stabilize the situation, but they were wholly inadequate to stop the renewed fighting between the RUF and the government armies (whose members often swapped sides at night). Discredit for the Lomé Peace Agreement belongs principally to the Reverend Jesse Jackson, whose role as 'comforter and confessor' to President Clinton over the Lewinsky affair had in some bizarre way led to his appointment as presidential envoy to stop the wars of West Africa. Jackson chummed up with Charles Taylor and expressed admiration for the imprisoned Foday Sankoh, describing him as

'West Africa's Mandela' (who is not a psychopath given to mutilating civilians). Jackson's ignorance and moral blindness does not excuse the Western and UN diplomats who agreed to release Sankoh from prison, bestow upon him an apparently valid amnesty, make him vice-president, and hand him the only prize in Sierra Leone worth having – control of the diamond mines. Kabbah signed the Lomé Agreement in July 1999 under intense pressure, his protest symbolized by the companion he brought to the signing ceremony, a child whose arm had been chopped off by the RUF. Kofi Annan, feeling queasy about the amnesty, telephoned his representative at the last moment asking him to make one reservation, to the effect that it would not cover crimes against humanity.

The Lomé amnesty purported to cover crimes Sankoh and the RUF committed under Sierra Leone law, like murder and grievous bodily harm (i.e. mutilation). It did not cover the same offences when characterized – through their widespread and systematic nature – as crimes against humanity, as the Special Court subsequently held. The RUF, programmed to kill and pillage and mutilate, continued to do so after Lomé, so in any event the amnesty was invalidated under national law, because he had not kept an essential condition of granting it.

The UN had to send in another 'peacekeeping' mission, a ragtag army of Zambians (they arrived without kit), insubordinate Jordanians and disorganized Kenyans, and put them all under the command of an unpopular Indian major general, whose orders they routinely disobeyed. After Sankoh's forces had taken 500 Zambian hostages and were about to overrun Freetown, it was Britain that saved the day. It did not, sensibly enough, rely on any UN mandate, but intervened at the invitation of the elected (although partly ousted) government and for the initial purpose of safely evacuating British nationals from Freetown. The continuing presence of British forces proved necessary to provide some stability and to frighten the RUF (when one of its gangs kidnapped British soldiers, the ensuing SAS rescue wiped out twenty-four gang members). British/UN occupation of Sierra Leone ended a ten-year civil war which lost over 100,000 lives, hundreds of thousands of limbs and created one million refugees.

During its course, many thousands of children were abducted and forced to become drug-crazed child soldiers or sex slaves. The rules of the Geneva Convention were replaced in some areas by the ju-ju belief in obtaining your enemy's strength by eating his heart, preferably raw.

In due course a large UNAMSIL contingent took control and supervised fresh elections in 2002 that returned President Kabbah. The ten-year toll of death and destruction had reduced this diamond-rich nation to the poorest country in the world: it had the lowest level of life expectancy and adult literacy. Now it had a million refugees to resettle and a million scores to settle after all the murders and rapes and maimings and lost childhoods.

This war had ravaged a small state that could have been saved had the Security Council acted forcibly to protect voters in the 1996 elections and to defend the democratically elected government. Instead, as its panel of experts headed by Lakhdar Brahimi concluded in their millennium summit report, its fundamental peacekeeping failure had been its 'reluctance to distinguish victim from aggressor'. Adherence to the shibboleth of neutrality had once again – as at Kigali – resulted in 'complicity with evil'. The Blue Helmets' mandate and mantra – 'Use force only in self-defence' – meant turning a blind eye to atrocities, 'keeping the peace' only in the sense of protecting the privileged lives of the peacekeepers. In the UN's new department, its 'Lessons Learned Unit', Sierra Leone was no end of a lesson.

More positive, however, has been the result of the UN's work to establish a war crimes court. Security Council Resolution 1315 in August 2000 had declared that the situation in the country constituted a threat to international peace and directed the Secretary-General to set up a 'strong and credible special court' by an agreement with the president of the country. This was a new way of dealing with impunity: Nuremberg had been a military tribunal set up by the victors; the ICTY and ICTR were creatures of the Security Council alone, and the ICC was the result of a treaty between states. The Special Court for Sierra Leone (SCSL) was established by a bilateral agreement between the UN and the Sierra Leone government. It is funded by voluntary state contributions and thus is placed outside Security Council control. It is 'accountable', for its management policy and its use of funds, to a management committee comprising representatives of those states which fund it and the UN legal department. These constitutional arrangements are acceptable to the United States, since they come with the blessing of the country whose nationals are to be tried, and the US has been a major donor to the Court along with the UK and the Netherlands. The SCSL is by this arrangement independent both of the United Nations and of the Sierra Leone government: it has no connection with the Sierra Leone legal system, differing in this respect from the Iraqi special tribunal and the Cambodian Extraordinary Chambers, both of which were embedded in their dysfunctional domestic legal system, and from the war crimes tribunal in East Timor, which was an administrative unit of the UN. The Court operates only in the sphere of international law, and is thus unaffected by the Sierra Leone constitution (which would otherwise have required a referendum to establish it) and from local political pressures. It applies and develops international human rights law as that has emerged from Nuremberg and The Hague and Rwanda Tribunals, and it has made its own contributions to that developing jurisprudence in respect of such issues as the legality of child recruitment, of forced marriages, of amnesties and of presidential immunities.

The SCSL is described as a 'hybrid' court, because the majority of its judges (three out of five in the Appeals Chamber and two out of three in the Trial Chambers) are appointed by the UN and the others by the government of Sierra Leone. The prosecutor and registrar are UN appointees, but they have local deputies. This maintains the 'international' image of the Court (the more so as a number of government appointees are also international lawyers) and operates as a safeguard: there is never a majority of judges vulnerable to domestic or factional pressures. This is to be contrasted with the Iraqi special tribunal, where all judges are locals who have suffered under the rule of the defendants they are attempting to try, and also the Cambodian genocide court, where government-appointed judges are always in the majority.

There are a number of further distinctions between the SCSL and other international criminal courts. Its statute limits jurisdiction to those alleged to 'bear the greatest responsibility' for crimes against humanity and war crimes, so the Court does not bother with foot soldiers of the Tadić variety. It sits in Freetown (other than for the trial of Charles Taylor) doing justice at the scene of the crime rather than in courtrooms thousands of miles away from the affected community, and its hearings in a specially built modern court (to be donated to the nation on completion of its work) have been attended by local people and covered by local press and television. It has an outreach programme, which involves court officials travelling around the country to explain its work through lectures and public meetings, and a public affairs unit that trains local media and produces audio and visual summaries of the Court's work. By involving local lawyers in prosecution and defence teams and registry staff, it has helped to build up professional expertise in a society where many lawyers were killed in the fighting or fled abroad. The SCSL has made a number of well-received innovations, most notably an office of principal defender (the defence office) which ensures high-quality representation for indigent defendants and has prevented corrupt practices like 'fee splitting' that have disfigured justice elsewhere. Its witness protection programme has supported several hundred witnesses both for the prosecution and the defence. Human Rights Watch concluded that 'the court's judicial operations, combined with its outreach programming, [are] helping to leave an important legacy by strengthening respect for the rule of law in Sierra Leone. Through employment and training of Sierra Leonean staff, the court is also building local professional capacity. The office of the principal defender (defence office) continues to serve a critical function in helping to protect the rights of the accused and represents an unprecedented and important innovation for international and hybrid tribunals.'[2]

That said, 'justice in motion' in the SCSL has too often been justice in slow motion. The Court began with exceptional swiftness: the prosecution and registrar started work in August 2002 and most of the indictments were handed down in March 2003. The Court, noting the delays (running into years) in other tribunals in having preliminary jurisdictional motions decided first by the trial court, 'fast-tracked' them direct to the Appeals Chamber. The Appeals Chamber sat to hear all preliminary jurisdictional motions in November and these were decided by the time the court buildings were opened in March 2004. Then trial delays set in, partly caused by the United Nations, which failed to appoint a second trial chamber until the following year. This meant that the first trial chamber had to hear two cases, involving defendants from rival factions, in alternate six-week sessions. The early hope that the Court could complete its work within three years has been dashed although the trials of leaders of the three main factions were completed within five years of its announcement, and by mid-2012 only the Charles Taylor appeal proceedings remained. But the delay of thirteen months in giving the verdict on Taylor was unacceptable. At least the Sierra Leone experience does suggest that, with proper resources and competent judges and prosecutors and an effective defence office, it is not impossible for a modern war crimes court to produce indictments within six months, for trials (if the indictees are in custody) to begin six months later, with verdicts following within fifteen months and completion of appeals within a further nine months. This three-year window should be the eventual object of the ICC and any other international criminal court. Unless it can be achieved, and at reasonable expense, the international criminal justice project will falter: already, it is effectively confined to those bearing 'greatest responsibility' for atrocities.

Lessons from Sierra Leone are being studied as this war-ravaged and impoverished country slowly begins to offer a decent way of life to its people. It shows that reconciliation and retribution can go hand in hand: a truth commission was in session while the Special Court was gearing up for its trials, complementing rather than competing with the justice process. Its developments in criminal jurisprudence have been of particular value to the ICC, as precedents for punishing child soldier recruitment and for dealing with internecine conflicts in African states involving factional fighting, replete with amnesties and immunities and peace agreements. In principle, the Sierra Leone 'hybrid' model would serve wherever there is international consensus that war crimes in a particular state should be prosecuted and where the government of the state is willing to accept international assistance to do so effectively and fairly. The ICC itself has power to sit outside The Hague, and would be well advised to do so given the importance of delivering justice near the scene of the crime and inter-acting with the community that has been victimized. These are real advantages that come from locating the court in the country where the conflict took place.

Establishing a war crimes court in a war-torn country so soon after the end of the conflict carries obvious risks, however, especially for its personnel. The security situation has necessitated that a very large slice of the budget – over 20 per cent – is devoted to security, both of the court officers and more particularly to protect witnesses during the trial and post-trial phase. In mid-2005, the witness and victim sec-tion was taking care of an overall total of 123 witnesses and defendants, in separate 'safe houses' and in the Special Court's secure detention facility. The living conditions for foreign staff were fairly basic and personnel were vulnerable to equatorial diseases, especially malaria. Operations in Freetown were logistically challenging, but the advantages of delivering justice when and where it matters – where it can be seen to be done by those who need it most – are very impor-tant. Not only did the presence of the court in Freetown symbolize the nation's emergence from the moral and physical degradation of the war, but the process of prosecution and punishment of those centrally responsible has permitted some sense of closure for living victims. In the end, the country's return to legality will advance the broader goal of a sustainable peace, whilst the advance of international criminal justice may deter military and political leaders in the future from returning to atrocities.[3]

The Court was established to try those alleged to bear greatest responsibility. Foday Sankoh, the RUF leader, died in its custody from a brain tumour which had affected his wits by the time he appeared in the dock. The Court did its best to keep him alive and tried to send him abroad for brain scanning (facilities did not exist in Freetown), but not even donor countries would admit him. Chief Hinga Norman, leader of the rival faction which fought for the government, was home affairs minister at the time of his arrest as he was making his way to a cabinet meeting. His trial raised important questions as to the 'rea-sonableness' of the force that can be used to put down a brutal insurrection, but he died before judgment could be delivered and the

Court, despite the request of his family, refused to deliver any decision.

The Court took on a new importance when Charles Taylor appeared in its dock. He had been indicted back in March 2003, when he was still President of Liberia. In June of that year this indictment was transmitted to Ghana, where Taylor was making a presidential visit, but that government refused to arrest him. Later in the year, he left Liberia and was given sanctuary in Nigeria, which came under mounting pressure to surrender him once the SCSL appeals court had held that his head-of-state immunity did not prevail over an indictment for crimes against humanity. President Obasanjo resisted these demands – made by the US as well as many other nations – until the new Liberian government, led by Ellen Johnson-Sirleaf, asked him to transfer Taylor to Sierra Leone. Mr Taylor made his first appearance in the court at Freetown on 5 April 2006. It was a truly international forum: the judge, Richard Lussick, was a Samoan trained in Australia, the prosecutor an English silk born in Guyana, and the public defender a Nigerian, while the defendant himself had been to school and to prison in the US. Ironically, given the plaudits this court has received for doing justice on the front line, its president requested the Security Council to move the Taylor trial to The Hague because of security concerns, and the Netherlands was prepared to make available to the US-backed SCSL the building and facilities reserved for the ICC.

There, the trial proceeded at the inevitably slow pace – it took over three years, and then the judges, quite unconscionably, took a further thirteen months to produce a 2,500-page verdict. The prosecution alleged that in order to gain a share in Sierra Leone's diamonds, Taylor conspired with Foday Sankoh's Revolutionary United Front to wage Africa's most brutal war against a democratically elected government, after having trained in Libya at the invitation of Colonel Gaddafi (an 'unindicted co-conspirator'). Much of the evidence against him was stomach-turning, but the question for the Court was whether he was involved in a joint criminal enterprise with the RUF – he had never set foot in Sierra Leone and the prosecution had to rely on evidence that he had been in communication with RUF leaders and was their *de facto* commander – their 'godfather'. But such contact was necessary, said Taylor, to perform his UN-accredited role as peacemaker. The prosecution claimed he was directing his RUF proxies, and in return for diamonds was arranging to supply them with weapons, military personnel and safe haven at the Liberia/Sierra Leone border. It called thirty 'insider witnesses', ex-RUF fighters (discreditable characters who had been paid 'expenses' by the prosecution and were an easy prey for cross-examiners), who testified to his role in supplying guns and receiving diamonds.

The trial itself was notable for the fact that Taylor, unlike other defendants and many defendants in other courts, played the justice game. He hired a senior British counsel, capable of admonishing the judges with much greater effect than a whining self-defendant, and not above giving interviews to complain of the prosecution-friendly nature of international justice. Ironically, the more aggressive his QC, the more the trial gained legitimacy. This particular trial received more publicity than any other when super-model Naomi Campbell and actress Mia Farrow stepped into the witness box to tell of receiving rough-cut diamonds from Taylor after a dinner with Nelson Mandela, an extraordinary story which turned out to be at least partly true when the diamonds were recovered from a charity worker to whom Campbell had entrusted them. The appearance of these public figures in the witness box showed the world – on television – that justice was being done, and that even the wealthiest could not evade it when called on to assist (Campbell, initially reluctant, agreed to attend when served with a subpoena).

The verdict, delivered in March 2012, found Taylor guilty of aiding and abetting eleven war crimes and crimes against humanity, ranging from terrorism, rape and murder of civilians to recruiting child soldiers and child sex slaves. He was, however, acquitted of two sets of charges at more serious levels, namely of responsibility for ordering these crimes, and for 'joint enterprise' – conspiring with rebel groups in Sierra Leone to carry them out. The prosecution failed to prove beyond reasonable doubt that he had a position of 'superior responsibility' over the armed groups, or that he had 'effective control' over them, which the court defined as 'material ability to prevent or punish the commission of the offence'. So the prosecution lost its claim that Taylor was 'godfather' to these mass-murdering and mass-mutilating groups, whose barbarity was uncontested, and set out in the judgment in blood-curdling detail. But he was none the less found to have supplied them with arms and ammunition and money (and even with herbs that the child soldiers were told to rub on their bodies to protect them from bullets) in return for a share of the spoils, namely uncut diamonds. What fixed him with criminal liability for 'aiding and abetting' the crimes was simply that he provided assistance at the time he knew they were being committed – knowledge he had gained from reading the newspapers and from confidential ECOWAS reports that were supplied to him as the president of Liberia. His defence that he was merely helping the international community by brokering a peace between the elected government and its insurgents backfired: this was regarded as the most despicable aspect of his behaviour because of the breach of trust involved in exploiting his position as peacemaker, while secretly assisting the most violent group (the RUF) to continue fighting and sending him the diamonds.

The Taylor verdict will have most consequence as a 'mind how you go' warning to other political and military leaders who send assistance to brutal factions in a civil war. President Reagan's arming of the Contras in Nicaragua would be an example of conduct that could now constitute an international crime of 'aiding and abetting', and any national leader who sends money or arms to Assad's brutal forces in Syria, might still be prosecuted on this basis. The Taylor precedent will be important for the conviction of Bashir and his indicted ministers, when or if they stand trial at the ICC: there is ample evidence that they provided 'material support and assistance' to the murderous Janja-weed militia. Of course the Taylor decision is under appeal by both sides and the convictions may not be upheld – some of the eleven verdicts were questionable because they relate to crimes that require specific intent (such as rape and terrorism) and it is difficult to see how Taylor could be convicted of a sufficiently specific intention to aid and abet particular rapes or terror attacks merely by helping to provision an army in the knowledge that its troops were prone to commit this crime. Once again, the decision highlights the vital role of media in reporting war crimes: their publication of such reports may provide the basis for proving the culpable mental element of those defendants who have read them yet continued to provide help to perpetrators.

THE KILLING FIELDS OF CAMBODIA

The worst atrocity since the Holocaust was played out on the killing fields of Cambodia, as 1.7 million lives were sacrificed to the perverse dream of a return to a pure primitive agrarian society which had struck the young Pol Pot when he was waiting on tables in Paris. He and his principal lieutenants – Ieng Sary, Khieu Samphan and Nuon Chea – conspired to inflict their orgy of mass murder and slave labour upon an unwilling population, ironically driven into their arms by the US carpet-bombing of Cambodia which killed tens of thousands of Cambodians, and by US support for the utterly corrupt government of Lon Nol. The Khmer Rouge army entered Phnom Penh in 1975, executed all Lon Nol's officials, turned back the clocks to 'year zero'. ordered all the people to go to work in the countryside and then sealed the nation so that no news of their crazed massacres would reach the outside world other than from refugees who were not at first believed, because of the incredible horror of their stories and the suspicion that they were exaggerating so as to claim asylum. But winding back the clocks had involved annihilating all those who had mattered as individuals, and turning the country into an ethnically pure, work-worshipping agrarian collective, devoid of private property, religion, memories, or contact with the outside world. All 'class traitors' were eliminated – which meant anyone with tertiary education or who had followed 'individualistic' or professional pursuits, and anyone who belonged to a 'different' rural or ethnic group. All Vietnamese were murdered, 300,000 out of half a million Muslims were killed and of the 60,000 Buddhist monks, only 1,000 survived. This was a form of genocide – the deliberate elimination of all or part of racial and religious groups – but most of the killings were of class enemies, slow workers and those suspected of disliking the regime, so might more accurately be termed 'politicide'. That was certainly the case at Tuol Sleng Examination Centre ('Office 21') where 'Duch' presided over the torture (by *bastinado* or electric shock) and execution (bullets were scarce, so gardens tools were used to hack victims to death). Meticulous records and photographs were kept, showing that of 15,000 prisoners, only five came out alive.

This monstrous regime was only overthrown by Vietnam, which invaded Cambodia in 1979. Hypocritical Western statesmen – in particular from the Carter administration – condemned the incursion on state sovereignty, although if ever an invasion were justified on humanitarian grounds, this was it. Vietnam installed a Khmer defector, Hun Sen, who in due course built up a Cambodian People's Party machine which included some other ex-Khmers. The new government, backed by Vietnam and the Soviet Union, was opposed by China (sponsor of the Khmer Rouge) and by the US as part of Nixon's rapprochement with China. In 1981 the UN, to its lasting disgrace but under American pressure, gave Cambodia's seat to the Khmer Rouge (represented by Ieng Sary) and any prospect of retribution for their massive crime was blocked – it was not until 1985 that a British MP who chaired an obscure UN subcommittee on Protection of Minorities was able to launch an investigation. Ben Whitaker described the Khmer atrocities as 'the most ferocious that had occurred anywhere in the world since Nazism'.[4]

The idea of putting the architects of the killing fields on trial came to the Clinton team at the State Department in 1997, as these mass murderers emerged from their hideouts on the Cambodia/Thai border. Pol Pot was there (it was reported that he was making occasional forays across the border to have his haemorrhoids treated in a Thai hospital) and his trial would make the exercise worthwhile. It caught the imagination of Secretary of State Madeleine Albright, and her War Crimes Ambassador, David Scheffer, was tasked with negotiating a suitable procedure. The Cambodian government, noting the UN money that was flowing to the Rwanda Tribunal, was not averse to receiving a similar hand-out, and there was some support at the UN either for expanding the jurisdiction of the ICTY to include a Cambodian Chamber (the simplest and in retrospect the best option), or to establish a separate *ad hoc* tribunal to sit in Cambodia. The problem with extending the jurisdiction of the ICTY or creating a special court was that this would have to be done by the Security Council under its Chapter VII power 'to maintain or restore international peace and security', and some states – Russia and China in particular – pointed out that no threat to international peace currently existed in Cambodia. Scheffer argued that continued impunity for the Khmer Rouge leadership could well destabilize the country in the future and draw other states into a renewed international conflict,[5] but the urgency of his mission was dissipated in 1998 when Pol Pot died in mysterious circumstances, and the unreliable King Sihanouk purported to grant amnesties to Khieu Samphan and Nuon Chea (whilst at the same time saying that an international tribunal had a 'perfect right' to deal with crimes against humanity in Cambodia).

In 1999 a UN commission of experts urged that the Security Council deploy its Chapter VII powers to set up such a tribunal, because the Cambodian legal system was dysfunctional: its judges were not independent or trained for the task and had no respect for due process. This became the entrenched position of the UN Secretary-General, Kofi Annan, and his counsel Hans Corell: in the years of negotiation that followed they insisted upon a 'hybrid' court on the Sierra Leone model, with international judges and prosecutors in the ascendancy. But Hun Sen was intransigent: he adamantly refused to accept a court that he could not control, because it might delve into his own role and that of his political allies, former Khmer lieutenants, in carrying out the barbaric orders of Brother No. 1 (Pol Pot) and No. 2 (Nuon Chea). He claimed that 'these trials were meant for the Cambodian people'[6] in which judges and prosecutors appointed and influenced by his government must have the final say. His intransigence wore down the UN officials: under pressure from France and Australia, they finally conceded primacy to Cambodia. In June 2003 they signed an agreement to set up the Extraordinary Chambers in the Courts of Cambodia for the Prosecution of Crimes Committed during the Period of Democratic Kampuchea (ECCC). It took another sixteen months for Cambodia to ratify the agreement, which entered into force in April 2005.

The trial and appeals courts of the ECCC have built-in Cambodian majorities (three out of five trial judges and four out of seven appeal judges) but decisions require a 'super-majority' of four judges at trial and five at appeal – meaning that at least one international judge will need to assent in every final decision. Cambodia appoints the prosecutor and registrar, with their deputies supplied by the UN – the reverse of the Sierra Leone arrangement.

Otherwise, the court mirrors international criminal courts in abjuring death sentences and having no jurisdiction over corporate or political entities. One valuable addition to the Court's jurisdiction is the crime of 'destruction of cultural property' comprising theft or damage to historical buildings, archaeological sites, museums, works of history of art, important collections of books or libraries. These heritage treasures were deliberately destroyed by the Khmer Rouge as part of their effort to turn back the cultural clock to 'year zero'. The cost of the whole exercise is being met from voluntary contributions, notably from Japan (a new convert to international criminal justice) with France, Australia and the UK as the other major donors. Although the court will apply international criminal law, as well as Cambodian law against murder and torture, it is questionable whether it can be classified as an 'international court' under the *Democratic Republic of Congo* v. *Belgium* test (see p. 437) given the degree of Cambodian government power over its personnel and procedures.

In some respects these procedures – settled after a whole year of sometimes bitter argument between the international and Cambodian judges – depart from the adversary model in other courts, as they are based on French civil procedure. There are two 'Co-Investigating Judges' whose office collects and collates all evidence in a 'case file' which is presented to the trial court together with the indictment, and is a massive collection of material (books written about Cambodia, for example) much of which is irrelevant. Vast amounts of time and energy are expended on translating almost every document into three languages (Khmer, English and French). Because the proceedings are in part investigatory, neither prosecution nor defence can initiate particular lines of investigation – they must ask the office of the Co-Investigating Judges to do so. Nor, at trial, can they cross-examine witnesses; this is done by the judges, to whom they may suggest questions.[7] These procedures were not unfair to the first defendant,

'Duch', who gave evidence and effectively admitted his guilt. In the second trial, however, where the four defendants (Nuon Chea, Khieu Samphan, Ieng Sary and his wife) are contesting the charges, these limitations on defence rights available in other international courts may give rise to complaints. It was a mistake – as it has been in the ICC and all other courts – to enshrine the right to silence (which all defendants in the second trial have claimed). This relic of primitive English trial procedure, now abolished in the UK, means that judges cannot draw the obvious inference from a defendant's refusal to give evidence after the court has ruled that there is substantial evidence, which should be answered, of his guilt of torture or even murder. There is no inducement for defendants to face examination, so the trial is denied important evidential material and the victims are denied the satisfaction of seeing them explain or answer for their conduct.

Victims are given what is termed 'civil party participation', a Cambodian law import which allows them to testify in court without being called by either party. It caused delays in the first trial, although it did give the proceedings the flavour of a truth commission as victims spoke dramatically of their sufferings, and the public impact was considerable. But this is a show trial dimension which has no place in a justice procedure, and the court took steps to limit it in the second trial after 4,000 victims claimed the right to participate. Two lawyers have been appointed to represent their interests, in the hope of reducing the time which would otherwise be spent on irrelevant testimony. The mistake was to give victims any right at all to intervene in the trial itself other than as witnesses for either side: the proper time for them to be heard is at the sentencing stage, when their testimony cannot prejudice the verdict but can assist the court in determining the length of sentence that retribution requires. The rules also give them a right to 'moral and civil reparations' against defendants, which is pointless if (as usual) the latter have no money, although awards may be made from donated funds if they are forthcoming and may take a collective form – e.g. an order to build a museum or a monument (after the first trial, the court unimaginatively ordered merely that the defendant's confession and apology should be placed on its website).[8]

The ECCC has, more importantly, become the focus for valuable

NGO and outreach work that would not have taken place without it. School textbooks have been produced to educate both children and teachers about the country's unpardonable past, and many local learning centres and legacy projects have been set up. The result of the first trial, although forgone, did seem cathartic to many survivors. Although evidence of the court's value is mainly impressionistic, there is no doubt that it is providing a role-model for a legal profession which is slowly recovering after all judges and lawyers were exterminated as 'elitist' under Khmer rule. To this extent, like the Sierra Leone Special Court, the model of a 'hybrid' court sitting at the scene of the crime and engaging the local community both in its proceedings and in the wider issues of memory and reconciliation, is preferable to siting a war crimes court in the far-away Hague.

The ECCC has suffered both from corruption (endemic in Cambodia) and from political interference (inevitable when Hun Sen can manipulate the majority of its judges). Cambodian staff at the court were required to hand over part of their salary to the court administrator and the Cambodian judges have vetoed the attempts of the international judges to investigate suspects who had political connections with the regime. Cambodia is a semi-authoritarian country and the UN should not have yielded it primacy: the compromise of a 'super majority' voting principle, requiring four out of five judges to support a court decision and thus preventing the three Cambodian judges from outvoting their international colleagues, has not worked. It has simply meant that any consequent 3–2 split means that no decision is reached, resulting in deadlock and permitting the Cambodian judges to frustrate the Court's progress. Never again should an 'international' court be controlled by local judges, with local politicians pulling their strings. Kofi Annan, Hans Corell and the commission of experts were right about Cambodian justice, and the Court's much publicized problems have stemmed largely from this source. There have been delays as international judges argue with their dominant Cambodian counterparts. The first trial, that of Kaing Guek Eav (a.k.a. Duch), the commander of Prison S-21 where 15,000 were tortured and killed, lasted several years despite his confession (he was jailed for thirty-five years, reduced to nineteen because of time he had already served). The second trial did not start until November 2011 – a five-year delay – and is already proving unmanageable, with a 700-page indictment and a case file of many thousands of pages (and hundreds of witnesses). The judges have sensibly chosen not to start with the genocide charges, but they will need to do a great deal more trimming of the indictment if the case is to conclude before one or more deaths of defendants aged between eighty and eighty-six.

There are significant legal issues as well: the validity of the Royal pardons (the simple answer is that they bar a Cambodian, but not an international, prosecution); the double jeopardy arising from a 'show trial' held by the Vietnamese back in 1979 (the simple answer is that a trial *in absentia* is not a trial at all) and the mental fitness to stand trial of Madame Thirith (the simple answer being that if she can understand what she is being accused of, the case should proceed). But thanks to lawyers on all sides no answer is simple, and the trial (and inevitable appeals from the trial court's decision) will continue for some years so long as donors can be found to support an exercise that by 2012 had cost $200 million. There is concern at the behaviour of local judges in cases no. 3 and no. 4. These are at an investigative stage and may go no further because Hun Sen wants no more defendants, because they might include his friends in the ruling Cambodian People's Party, or even himself. In 2012 'his' judges, to the fury of the international jurists, were making rulings that may not allow further investigations to proceed. For the present, the ECCC is partly filling its 500-seat courtroom because of continuing interest in trial no. 2: the good that it has done locally, however, must be weighed against the damage to international justice, if this particular model cannot provide justice to victims because of political interference.

LONG AGO AND FAR AWAY: BANGLADESH

The Cambodian court, at least, does not pretend to be 'international': its name (insisted upon by Hun Sen) identifies it as 'the Extraordinary Chambers in the Court of Cambodia'. The opposite is true in

Bangladesh: it has an 'International Crimes Tribunal' established under the International Crimes (Tribunals) Act 1973, about which there is very little that is international. There are no foreign judges, and lawyers from overseas are banned from representing its defendants and, in some cases, from even entering the country. Its law (passed in 1973) is severely out of date and its procedures do not reflect the 'best practice' of the ICTY. Defendants, all drawn from the losing side of the 1971 war, are disabled from challenging the law on constitutional grounds, and at least one of its judges was a member of a 'People's Inquiry Commission' which convicted the defendants *in absentia* some years ago. The defendants currently on trial are members of an Islamist political party (the government is predominantly Hindu), which is one of the main opposition groups and was previously part of a coalition government. To black cap it all, and unpardonably, those convicted may be sentenced to hang by the neck until they are dead.[9]

That said, it must be recognized that the invasion of East Pakistan (now Bangladesh) by the army of West Pakistan (now the Pakistan army) with the support of local Islamic parties (whose elderly leaders are now going on trial), is perhaps the oldest example of a genocide that still demands a reckoning. It arose from the secessionist demands of East Pakistan, led by Sheik Mujibur Rahman of the Awami League, made against the military government which had controlled the whole country since the collapse of Pakistan democracy in 1958. After an Awami-led general strike in March 1971, the Pakistan army was mobilized by the President, General Yahya Khan, to strike back. On 25 March 'Operation Searchlight' began a nine-month reign of terror. The army attacked Dacca and massacred university students and professors and an estimated 1,000 other intellectual leaders of the Bengali people, killing tens of thousands of the poor as well, burning their homes and calling it 'slum clearance'. Then the army began killing as many as it could find of the country's 10 million Hindus, with the fanatical assistance of local Muslim groups such as Al Badr, the army wing of the Jamaat-e-Islami, and the Razakars, mainly Bihari Muslims who had been violently attacked by Bengali militias and so, when protected by the Pakistan army, responded even more viciously. There is no doubt that hundreds of thousands of Bengali citizens were killed – the government puts their number at 3 million (which is too high), with an estimated 200,000 rapes (which may not be too high). The impregnation of Bengali women was deliberately planned to affect the ethnic balance, and at least 25,000 pregnancies were said to have resulted.

The scale of the atrocities led to allegations of genocide, supported by evidence of the targeting of Bengali intellectuals and future leaders, by the ethnic rape programme and by the efforts over the nine-month civil war to wipe out the Hindus. But the main object of the atrocities was to stop the nation obtaining political autonomy, and this cannot constitute a genocidal intention: it would be much less complicated (as a report by the International Commission of Jurists concluded in 1972) to prosecute perpetrators (not all of them on the Pakistani side) for horrific crimes against humanity. That was not possible: the main perpetrators were army officers safe in Pakistan after India had intervened and driven them out of what would soon be called Bangladesh. Several thousand of their local collaborators were put on trial under the 1973 Act, but these proceedings were abandoned after the assassination of Mujibur Rahman in 1975. The Bangladesh army generals, who have held power for most of the time since, did not want to continue the trials (some of them, too, had been complicit) and Jamaat-e-Islami had become a mainstream political party. But that party and its allies were trounced in the 2008 elections by the Awami League, whose promise to 'bring back war crimes trials' proved immensely popular among people who had lived all their lives with fearful memories or stories of the unrequited horrors of 1971.

There can be no doubt about the legitimacy of the war crimes court. Some of the incidents – especially the organized torture and bayoneting to death of university professors – were as barbaric as the behaviour of Nazi storm-troopers, and were carried out by trained army officers at the beginning of the war and by Jammat-e-Islami members at its end. There can be no prosecution in this Bangladeshi court of the main Pakistani perpetrators, but that is not a reason to stay the hand of local justice from collaring collaborators who can be proved to have committed crimes against humanity, even if they happen to be leading members of the political opposition. In this respect, much of the criticism of the court is misplaced. There is, however, no doubt that the international community would have been willing to co-operate with personnel and funding, as it did with Sierra Leone and Cambodia, had the government of Bangladesh been prepared to accept a 'hybrid' court with international judges and prosecutors in the majority, or at least abjure the death sentence. This cringingly poor country passed up valuable offers of international assistance, and can afford only a derisory budget of $1.4 million for the court. This does suggest that it wants to control the court and hang the defendants – or, at least, those who are opposition leaders. Inevitably, the court has had a bad press, but the government has dug its grave by insisting on the death penalty, and betraying the victims by declining international assistance that is needed for educational and outreach programmes that would otherwise have been forthcoming. It might even have been possible to establish by agreement an international court that could summon retired army officers living in Pakistan or other countries, but this prospect was passed up as well.

Bangladesh has taken in some ways a brave decision to reopen this process, and it has no reason to thank the United Nations which took no action at the time and has taken no action in the four decades since. Nonetheless, as the case of Saddam Hussein shows (see chapter 13), without UN involvement trials of mass atrocities can go very wrong, delivering neither justice nor reconciliation and serving only to reinforce impunity and revenge. There is undoubtedly a genuine desire throughout this populous country for some accounting for the murder of martyrs who died to found their nation, but this cannot be achieved by rushing through a process that targets only their current political enemies. (Some Awami League fighters who are still alive also perpetrated atrocities but the court has no jurisdiction to try them.) The case of Bangladesh is best used as an example of the depth and persistence of a community's need for eventual justice on atrocity perpetrators and as an argument for making such courts scrupulously impartial. In early 2012 protests swept Bangladesh demanding speedy trials for the arrested war criminals. It would be good to think they were spontaneous, and reflected a deep-seated desire for expeditious justice and for the educative and historical value of a war-crimes trial. It would be less good if they had been orchestrated by the Awami League to pressure the court to convict and hang some of their opponents, before both sides face re-election.

THE CASE OF EAST TIMOR

Timor was carved up, centuries ago, by colonial powers. The western part of the island was occupied by the Dutch, who yielded it up in 1949 as part of Indonesian independence, but the east remained a province of Portugal until the fall of the Caetano dictatorship in 1974. The new Portuguese government wanted to wash its hands of the encumbrance as soon as possible, and proposed self-determination after a direct parliamentary election scheduled for 1976. Fretilin, the Revolutionary Front for an Independent East Timor, was front-runner: it was opposed by an 'anti-communist movement' backed by the US, which wanted integration with Indonesia. The brutal Cold War diplomacy of the era was epitomized by the visit Dr Kissinger and President Ford paid to Indonesia in December 1975: the moment they left, after secretly approving Indonesian aggression because the US did not want an independent East Timor under Fretilin ('another Cuba'), the Indonesian army invaded and occupied what was still, at the time, a part of Portugal. It was a swift war of annexation: a few months later an unelected puppet assembly resolved that East Timor should become the twenty-seventh state of Indonesia. Diplomats from East and West covered up war crimes (the UK ambassador pretended that a team of British and Australian newsmen butchered by the advancing Indonesian army had been accidentally 'caught in crossfire'). They urged recognition of this *fait accompli*, notwithstanding that it breached two rules of customary international law, namely

(1) that colonial peoples must, at the end of their colonial status, have the opportunity freely to determine their political future at a plebiscite;

(2) that peoples whose territory is occupied by a foreign power have a right to self-determination.[10]

The Security Council buckled under US pressure and declined to condemn the invasion either as aggression or as a plain breach of Article 2(4) of the Charter. Indonesia was vital to Western interests in Asia and in the wake of its Vietnam débâcle the US would do anything to prevent a socialist toehold in Timor (a position that had already led it to support Indonesia's efforts to crush the independence movement in West Papua). So Fretilin became the more broadly based Falintil and went underground to continue the struggle through the next twenty-five years of Indonesian occupation. Indonesia invested heavily in infrastructure for East Timor, previously lamentably ignored by the Portuguese, but its army put down sporadic pockets of opposition with ferocity. Tens of thousands died in these bloodbursts over the quarter century: for example, the entire village of Kraras was wiped out in 1983, and in 1991 there was a notorious massacre of protesters at Santa Cruz cemetery, followed by another massacre later the same day as soldiers dragged wounded protesters from hospital beds and executed them. Those and other atrocities were committed by the élite Kopassus force, trained in the US and Australia and commanded in some periods by Lieutenant-Colonel Prabowo. He was the son-in-law of Indonesia's massively corrupt President Suharto, who had come to power in 1965 in a military coup which led to the killing of over a million citizens, ostensibly because they were communists but essentially because most were Chinese. The UN, while it never formally recognized East Timor's annexation, turned a blind eye to all these outrages, although the Santa Cruz killings were captured on video and did much to alert human rights groups to the East Timor issue.

If the right of self-determination means anything – and its constant invocation by the General Assembly as the rationale for decolonization has made it a rule of international law – then the East Timorese were certainly entitled to it in 1975, just as the West Papuans are entitled to it today. They were ethnically, religiously and culturally distinct, forming in a discrete territory an overwhelming majority to throw out the Portuguese administrators and to vote to determine their own future – be it independence as a sovereign nation or integration or association with Indonesia. The Indonesian invasion in December was an unlawful act of aggression intended to destroy the right of self-determination just as it was coming to fruition. The occupation was condemned by the General Assembly as a blatant breach of the 1960 Declaration on the Granting of Independence to Colonial Territories and Peoples – an important stage in the elucidation of the right as requiring a free and genuine expression of the will of the peoples concerned.[11] This declaration condemns 'all armed action or repressive measures' against a dependent people aimed at preventing free and peaceful determination of political status (paragraph 4). In the short term Indonesia 'got away with it', but it follows in principle from the *erga omnes* nature of the right to self-determination that military occupation which defeats it continues to be illegitimate.

But in 1995 the ICJ failed the East Timorese by ducking this issue in a case brought on their behalf by Portugal over a treaty Australia had signed with Indonesia to carve up the oil-rich Timor Gap. Portugal, exhibiting a concern for the East Timorese which it had never shown during its colonization of the country, took Australia to the world court, claiming that the treaty had failed to respect East Timor's right to self-determination. Australia argued that 'there is no binding international legal obligation not to recognize the acquisition of territory that was acquired by force'[12] – a crude contention (that might makes right after about fifteen years of wrong) which the court should have emphatically refuted. The ICJ portentously declared that 'the right of peoples to self-determination has an *erga omnes* character and is one of the essential principles of contemporary international law'[13] But all the *erga omnes* force in the world would not move its judges to condemn Australia's behaviour, lest this 'imply an evaluation of the lawfulness of the conduct of another state which is not a party to the case'. Australia had made an 'optional clause' declaration of submission to the ICJ, while Indonesia of course had not, so in its absence the Court declined to state the obvious – that Indonesia's annexation had been, and still was, unlawful.

The *East Timor Case* was a jurisprudential cop-out. Indonesia was in effect rewarded, both for its continuing illegal occupation and for its cynical refusal to accept international justice, by a ruling that its non-consent operated to prevent even indirect criticism by the world court. There could be no greater inducement for states to refrain from signing the Optional Clause (only sixty-five have done so thus far) than the assurance that they will be damned if they do, but not damned if they don't. Indonesia's refusal to submit to ICJ jurisdiction should have been interpreted as a waiver of its right to defend its invasion of the island – for which, incidentally, no legal justification has ever been offered. Alternatively, the Court could have assumed the illegality of Indonesia's invasion (since this was admitted by Australia) and gone on to decide the vital question of whether lapse of time meant that the annexation could be treated as a lawful *fait accompli*. But many ICJ judges fear to apply the letter of the law they so confidently enunciate (e.g. self-determination has an *erga omnes* character) to any factual situation where the correct result would be to embarrass states, especially their own or those in alliance with them. So, until 1999, the 800,000 East Timorese proved inconvenient and insignificant, not only in the political arena where states wished to trade with and befriend Indonesia, the fourth largest country in the world, but at the bar of international justice as well. The judicial custodians of international law refused to apply one of its established principles – that acquisition of territory by force has no legal effect – because to do so would embarrass Indonesia, notwithstanding that its army was engaging with apparent impunity in sporadic massacres of East Timorese.

International law aside, the problem of the Indonesian army in East Timor was in microcosm the problem of Indonesia under a neo-dictatorial political system in which the army ruled 210 million people spread through eighty islands and its officers thrived on the corruption consequent upon this power. Military governors cracked down viciously on dissent, notably on democracy and human rights campaigners in Jakarta, and on the separatist movements not only in East Timor but in the Muslim province of Aceh and in West Papua, annexed by Indonesia after a bogus 'Act of Free Choice' in 1969.

In 1998, President Suharto was forced to resign by mass demonstrations – initially put down by the army with lethal force, but eventually unstoppable. His short-term replacement, President Habibie, had to cope with economic ruin as he nursed the unstable nation through its transition to democracy. Like most Indonesian civilians, he viewed the East Timorese as ungrateful and disposable: in January 1999, without consulting the army, he announced a UN-sponsored referendum for the province, giving its citizens the choice of becoming either an autonomous province of Indonesia or an independent country. His decision was astonishing, and its wisdom may be questioned in terms of the suddenness of the transition it envisaged, but the UN's role in this double decolonization delighted human rights NGOs. Those with any knowledge of the country cautioned that a UN peacekeeping presence would be necessary in the run-up to the referendum, and especially thereafter. However, Habibie optimistically insisted that the Indonesian army could keep control, and neither the UN nor the US (vital in keeping his economy afloat) demurred. But the army was furious about the referendum, because independence would mean loss of face as well as loss of power. In February, some army leaders conspired to intimidate the population before the vote, agreeing to set up and arm militia groups in each of the thirteen provinces: their object would be to threaten havoc unless the referendum was lost. The chief conspirators were intelligence chiefs in Kopassus special forces who reported to General Zacky Anwar, together with East Timor's military governor (Abílio Soares) and militia leader Eurico Guterres.[14] The collaboration between the Indonesian military and the freelance militias was obvious to all observers in the months before the ballot: they worked together quite brazenly, and bore joint responsibility for attacks on pro-independence families, such as the massacre at a Liquica church on 6 April in which sixty-seven people were shot or hacked to death. The purpose of the terror was to spread the militia's message: what is the point of voting for independence if you are going to be killed the next day? There could be no doubt about the certainty of a bloodbath after a 'Yes' vote unless the UN insisted upon having troops on the ground to prevent it.

The referendum was held on 30 August, and attracted an amazingly high turn-out of 98.6 per cent. On 4 September, in the face of expert warnings that this would trigger a militia uprising, the UN announced the result: 78.5 per cent in favour of independence. Overnight, the militias and sections of the Indonesian army began systematically to kill, loot and scorch the earth. It would be wrong to say that they ran amok: there was method in their madness. Typically, the Falintil intelligentsia and its supporters in the professions were the first to be rounded up and murdered. Several thousand of them died over the fortnight before the Australian force landed. The scorched-earth policy of the rampaging militias forced 500,000 East Timorese to flee into the jungle in fear of their lives, while 130,000 were forced at gunpoint across the border to West Timor. Fourteen Catholic priests and nuns were murdered in Dili, as well as the head of the Protestant church. The UN mission which had supervised the referendum quickly evacuated itself to Darwin, where survivor accounts of killings were difficult to bear for the simple reason that this was all the UN's doing. By going ahead with the referendum in the absence of reliable military protection, they had in effect lured the East Timorese into a trap: their vote for independence was the cue for them to be butchered by the Indonesian army. Failure to rescue them from a graveyard of good UN intentions would be unconscionable, and everyone connected with the UN knew it.

For that reason, the UN's diplomacy was more desperate than in any other crisis: five UN ambassadors immediately rushed to Jakarta to ask the government's permission for an international force to enter East Timor. 'Don't lecture us,' the country's foreign minister shrieked at them, in public. As hundreds were being slaughtered, Indonesia's obsession with its own sovereignty held up any rescue mission for eight days. 'We cannot stand by and allow the people of East Timor to be killed,' said Kofi Annan, described as 'visibly shaken', on day five of the massacres. 'Because we bombed in Kosovo doesn't mean we should bomb in Dili,' snapped back Sandy Berger, President Clinton's national security adviser, who talked in Kissinger-esque terms of America's national interest, to which East Timor was insignificant besides the importance of Indonesia's transition to democracy.[15] The UN Security Council simply froze for those eight shameful days, as America waited vainly for Indonesia's defence chief, General Wiranto, to restore discipline among its troops, and China made it clear it would veto *any* armed intervention under Chapter VII which did not have Indonesian approval. Meanwhile, the militias and supporting

Kopassus troops took their revenge on the 'Yes' voters (some of whom had signed their death warrants by answering irresponsible Western TV journalists who asked how they had voted). The slashing and burning spree developed a momentum of its own, fuelled not only by hatred of the East Timorese but by a more general frustration at the army's loss of power and prestige after the fall of Suharto.

As the death toll mounted, Australia and New Zealand called for a 'coalition of the willing' to go in, Kosovo style, but answer came there none. Indonesia unhelpfully announced that it would not permit foreign troops to enter until November, after its new parliament met to ratify the independence vote.[16] (By then, of course, there would be very few East Timorese alive to be independent.) At last, on 12 September, President Clinton acted as he should have from the outset and threatened President Habibie with the loss of billions of dollars in loans and aid unless he permitted a UN peacekeeping force to enter East Timor. Habibie yielded, and the 7,000-strong Australian-led force was gathered and prepared. By the time it came ashore a week later, East Timor lay in ruins – its buildings torched and earth scorched by the Indonesian soldiers who then exited in surly silence, while the militias slunk across the border to West Timor. It took many more weeks before the majority of the East Timorese felt enough trust in UN protection to come down from their hiding-places in the hills, most of them suffering from diseases that would spread with the onset of the rainy season. Their one joy was that the referendum result was ratified by the new Indonesian parliament and, on 25 October 1999, East Timor was formally handed over to the UN by Habibie's elected replacement, President Wahid. It was not until February 2000 that the UN Transitional Authority in East Timor (UNTAET) was able to establish a proper relationship with Indonesia, following an historic visit by President Wahid when he was welcomed to this nation-in-waiting by Xanana Gusmão, the Fretelin leader who had, Mandela-like, spent many years in jail in Jakarta. The UN thereafter helped the East Timorese to prepare for civil society and self-government under a new constitution, taking care not to impose its own solutions over the sometimes unfathomable preferences of local leaders (such as their sentimental choice of colonial Portuguese as the official language). In

April 2002, Gusmão was democratically elected as the country's president. Kofi Annan still regards East Timor as the UN's finest hour, which is probably true – notwithstanding its unfinest first quarter.

In due course, the occupying force began to excavate mass graves and to take witness testimony after the UN Human Rights Commissioner, Mary Robinson, claimed there had been 'a well-planned and systematic policy of killings, intimidation, displacement and destruction of property'. Yet the Human Rights Commission, at an emergency meeting in Geneva, split on whether it should bother to mount an investigation: most Asian countries (including Japan, China, India and even the Philippines) were prickly and opposed to embarrassing Indonesia with further evidence of the misdeeds of its army. Although the obvious solution was for the Security Council to establish a war crimes tribunal for East Timor, under the Hague umbrella which already covered former Yugoslavia and Rwanda, China made clear that in defence of Indonesia's sovereignty it would veto any such proposal – so none was made. Eventually it did set up an inquiry (with no power to bring anyone to trial), but Indonesia refused to grant visas for its members to enter West Timor or Jakarta to interview witnesses.

In 2000, the United Nations set up the Special Panels of the Dili District Court (more commonly known as the East Timor Tribunal). This was a 'hybrid' tribunal (each of the three panels had two international judges and one East Timorese judge) established to try 'serious criminal offences' which took place during 1999. As expected, the Tribunal's work was hampered by Indonesian non-cooperation, resulting in only eighty-eight of the 400 indictees (i.e. those collaborators left in East Timor rather than Indonesian army officers who had returned home) facing justice for crimes committed in the course of the conflict. This record was satisfactory enough in the circumstances: eighty-four were convicted, but most were foot soldiers who had not been responsible for international crimes committed before and after the UN referendum: the main perpetrators were Indonesian army officers and the Indonesian government refused to make them available to any UN court. Chronic underfunding of the Tribunal was an issue, and trials were delayed due to a lack of support staff and insufficient numbers of qualified interpreters. Eventually, the United

Nations suspended the Tribunal in 2006. As a result, some cases of murder, rape and torture went unpunished. However, these were not international crimes: and the tribunal functioned in effect as a court imposed on a dysfunctional justice system in order to try a backlog of criminal offences.

However, in Jakarta, transition to democracy in late 1999 brought a popular demand for human rights and an initial resolve, in the new parliament, to investigate and punish military transgressors in East Timor, as well as in other parts of Indonesia. Parliament established a civilian human rights commission which soon uncovered evidence of massacres in East Timor and of how bodies of victims were transported across the border for secret disposal in West Timor. It called in and cross-examined senior generals and uncovered the conspiracy to form and arm the militias, and to fund them from the budget of East Timor's civil administration. Its report, in January 2000, accused thirty-three leaders of crimes against humanity and demanded their prosecution: 'command responsibility' was fixed on the former military chief, General Wiranto, five other generals and a number of senior officers, together with the militia commanders and the former civilian governor of East Timor, Abílio Soares.[17] The UN Human Rights Commission inquiry reported at the same time with broadly similar conclusions, except that it recommended an extension of the Hague Tribunal, including judges from Indonesia, to try the accused.

The Indonesian government rejected this affront to its sovereignty, but renewed its promise to bring the suspects to justice – although the approval for trials of Soares and some junior officers was not given until late 2001 by President Megawati, under strong international pressure, and amid serious doubts about the capacity of local judges to manage them. The trials began in Jakarta in March 2002 before a special human rights tribunal: eighteen military officers and militia leaders were accused of a crime against humanity by permitting widespread and systematic militia attacks on civilians, 117 of whom lost their lives.[18] General Wiranto, the overall commander, was allowed to resign from cabinet in return for an agreement not to prosecute, and the attorney-general lacked the courage to indict Zacky Anwar and the other senior army officers implicated in the killings.

The Jakarta trials were, like the Leipzig trials after the First World War, an example of 'loser's justice'. They failed, not because of the specially trained human rights judges in the trial court, who displayed courage and fairness, but because of a cowardly and incompetent prosecution and a corrupt appeals court. Eighteen suspects were tried, but only six were convicted in the first instance – they were acquitted not because they were army officers but because the prosecutor, perhaps deliberately, presented insufficient evidence for the court to convict them. Indeed, the main defendant, Major-General Adam Damiri, the army commander of the East Timor region, was convicted (after the craven prosecutor had begged for his acquittal) by brave judges who suffered serious abuse from Damiri and the army afterwards.[19] The six convicts were permitted bail – Damiri led Indonesian army onslaughts on Aceh separatists while another officer taught ethics at the army college – and then the appeals court acquitted them all. That left only two East Timorese civilians facing prison – Guterres, a militia commander (five years), and the ex-governor Abílio Soares (three years). They were freed on bail pending appeal but this was a fraudulent constraint – the government never intended to punish them, or anyone else. Soares died in his bed in 2007, and Guterres had his sentence quashed in 2008. The Jakarta war crimes trials provide a very good example of the kind of sham prosecutions which the International Criminal Court is entitled to disregard under its complementarity principle.

The successful battle by Indonesian generals to avoid international justice was illuminating in one respect. They made no secret of their fears of suffering the fate of Pinochet, or of the indignity that would attend their appearance in uniform in the Hague dock.[20] What exercised them most was the humiliation of being tried in another country, under the world's gaze, rather than in their own courts. This fear of suffering the *indignity* of international criminal justice seems widely shared in military circles (it has caused generals like Mladić and Gotovina to take the coward's path of avoiding trial), and it infects political leaders as well. It follows that the prospect of trial at The Hague can have a real deterrent effect. The army and the militias behaved like nervous murderers, transporting the corpses, at great inconvenience, long distances to bury them across the West Timor border. The advent of international criminal law, for all the pot luck of its enforcement, had at least made them afraid of retribution when their victims are disinterred.

Kosovo and East Timor were both depicted in the media as 'ethnic conflicts' underlain by blood hatreds between races and religions: the Catholic Serbs against the Muslim Albanians; the Catholic East Timorese against the Muslim Indonesians. This analysis is simplistic, and essentially false. As historian Noel Malcolm points out in respect to Kosovo, 'It ignored the primary role of politicians (above all, the Serbian nationalist-communist Milošević) in creating conflict at a political level . . . between low-level prejudices on the one hand and a military conflict, concentration camps, and mass murder on the other, there lies a very long road: it was the political leaders who propelled the people down that road, and not vice-versa.'[21] The East Timorese have never hated the Indonesians as a people or as Muslims: leaders like Gusmão and Ramos-Horta always talked of both peoples sharing a common enemy in the form of the corrupt para-political generals of the Indonesian army. What emerges starkly from both situations is the criminal responsibility of political and military leaders for preparing and permitting crimes against humanity. The actual killers were soldiers and mad-dog militias, but criminal responsibility lay indelibly with commanders who had long before built their power upon racism and nationalism, in the course of which they offered impunity to the killers they inspired. Milošević and Suharto, and their respective army commanders now in boltholes in Belgrade and barracks in Jakarta, provide a convincing argument in favour of developing a system of international criminal justice which has power to humiliate as well as to incarcerate the military commanders of crimes against humanity.

The Jakarta trials were condemned in 2005 by a UN commission of experts, which described them as 'manifestly inadequate, principally due to a lack of commitment on the part of the prosecution'.[22] It recommended that Indonesia be given a second chance to investigate properly, under international supervision, failing which a special UN court should be set up to try them. Although welcomed by NGOs, this report has gathered dust: Indonesian law enforcement in the wake of the Bali bombings is devoted to dealing with Islamist terrorist organizations and keeping peace in tsunami-devastated Aceh, and the international aid forthcoming to cover these crises is not being made contingent upon the country addressing issues of impunity. One consequence of Indonesia's failure in this respect is that its army commanders continue persecution in West Papua; boatloads of refugees that occasionally reach Australia are given asylum, to the outrage of the Indonesian government.

TRIALS OF THE ARAB SPRING

The year 2011 saw rebellions in the Arab world which overthrew dictatorial regimes in Egypt, Libya, Tunisia and Yemen, produced bloodshed in Syria and wrought some political changes in Bahrain, Morocco and Jordan. They had in common a demand for democracy, and were begun by street protests against decades of repression by state security forces and against the endogenous corruption of the ruling elites. The demand for 'justice' was another common factor, meaning restoration of a rule of law which had been effortlessly bent or broken by the dictators, their brutal security forces and their corrupt wives and families, and also accountability – retribution not only for the extortion and torture in the past, but for the killings and beatings of the young protesters whose courage was bringing these regimes to their knees. A factor inflaming the protest was the electronic availability, via Al Jazeera or Wikileaks cables, of reliable information of a kind which state-owned radio and television would never dare to publish, revealing the truth about corruption in ruling families and secret co-operation with the US to facilitate torture and to support Israel. In terms of accountability, the Syrian banners calling for 'Al-Assad to The Hague,' crystallized the demand for justice on those who had perpetrated crimes against humanity. The publicity given to precedents set by international courts had created an expectation that the old regime's torturers and murderers were amenable to punishment. For all the criticism of international justice, and cavils at its costs and delays, its achievement has been to engender a belief on the Arab street that tyrants deserve to be put on trial for their crimes against civilians.

The fall of Saddam in 2003, although brought about by unlawful and unjustifiable foreign intervention, had been popular in Iraq, and his trial, however flawed, had been welcomed by the people he had so cruelly misruled. The 'Green Revolution' in Iran may have failed in 2009, but the very brutality of its repression had created martyrs from and for an interconnected Arab youth: the death of Neda Agha-Soltan, at the hands of Iran's part-time thugs, the Basij militia, was remembered in Tahrir Square: it gave Egyptians the strength to resist Mubarak's equivalent, the Baltagi militia, and to jeer whenever Iran's supreme leader, Ali Khamenei, appeared on the TV screen. One common factor in all the successful revolts was the simple demand for human dignity: this had been the spark which first ignited the 'Jasmine Revolution' on 17 December 2010, when a Tunisian street vendor named Mohamed Bouazizi set himself alight after being humiliated by policemen who arbitrarily confiscated his cart. They had unfairly taken his livelihood – why not take his own life? Demonstrations against abuses of power by police brutality and extortion, and against the massive corruption of President Ben Ali and his family and cronies (verified by the Wikileaks cables) spread spontaneously throughout the cities of Tunisia, and were soon backed by professional associations and trade unions: crucially, the army refused to attack the protesters. Ben Ali and his family took off for Saudi Arabia on 14 January, an event that inspired the demonstrators in Egypt's 'day of wrath', 28 January, against Mubarak's authoritarian rule.

Further excitement was caused earlier that day, when the regime cut all Internet links and international telephone lines – a sign of panic from the hated security services. In Tahrir Square, young men distributed tissues sprinkled with vinegar ('a tip from our Tunisian friends'). Soon the teargas arrived. Then snipers' bullets ripped into the crowd and secret police drove trucks at and over groups of protesters.[23] Just eighteen days, but 850 deaths later, Mubarak was history. It had been eighteen days of lies by the state's media ('Everything is calm'), whilst the truth could be seen by anyone tuned to Al Jazeera, where they could witness the brutality by the Baltagi militias and realize that the liberals and leftists, who led the protests, were being joined by younger Islamists from the Muslim Brotherhood (which stayed officially aloof). They could watch Muslim and Christian groups protecting each other from Baltagi attack whilst at prayer in the square and hear interviews with human rights lawyers on their way to courts to obtain orders from independent judges. Mubarak promised reform but his promises were contemptuously rejected; he tried to appeal to America through a CNN interview warning that the alternative was Islamic extremism, but Hillary Clinton told him to 'listen to the street' and step down; eventually on 11 February 2011, he resigned and transferred all his powers to the Supreme Council of the Armed Forces (SCAF).

A few days later, the protests began in Benghazi; Gaddafi and his son Saif reacted by killing some civilians and issuing bloodthirsty threats to kill many more. It took only a few weeks for the Security Council to intervene, first by referring the situation to the ICC Prosecutor (Resolution 1970, 26 February 2011) and then by empowering NATO to use 'all necessary measures' to protect civilians (Resolution 1973, 17 March).

By this time protests had erupted in Bahrain against King Hamad: police killed some protesters and order was restored only with the help of Saudi Arabian forces and the promise of an independent international investigation. Protests in Yemen began after Ben Ali fled from Tunisia and increased after Mubarak's resignation; the day following NATO's first attack on Libya, sixty were shot dead by police and army snipers. President Saleh promised some reform, but it was too little and too late. After being injured in a bomb attack he left for Saudi Arabia, where an uneasy amnesty was brokered. In Morocco and Jordan, rulers offered reforms before protests took hold. In Syria, street protests against the Al-Assad regime began in March, after NATO's intervention in Libya; they were ruthlessly repressed and over 5,000 demonstrators had been killed by February 2012, when a fairly mild Security Council Resolution, which did not call for intervention or even ICC referral, was none the less vetoed by both Russia and China. China has a long-standing objection to any form of intervention (other than its own) in the sovereignty of states, and Russia, with brutal opportunism, wished to preserve its extremely lucrative ($3.5 billion) arms trade with the Assad regime. But an additional reason for vetoing this milksop motion may well have been the realization of how ambiguous the English language can be, or can be made, because allowing NATO to take 'all necessary measures' to protect civilians in Benghazi had meant, obscurely but inevitably, empowering it to take the only measure that would guarantee their protection, namely regime change.

The causes of the Arab Spring were legion: poverty, unemployment among educated youth, brazen cronyism and corruption, long-time repression and torture of dissidents by the secret police, arbitrary detention and banning of political parties, nationalist and Islamist sentiment – all factors which played a part in the demands for democracy and justice, free speech and due process. Wikileaks became the unauthorized provider of CIA-based information, broadcast through Al Jazeera which provided round-the-clock coverage which its sponsor government in Qatar had refused to censor (despite pleas from Mubarak and Ben Ali). Social media – Twitter, Facebook and mobile phones – were universally used to organize and energize. Human rights was not only a demand, but a form of deliverance as human rights lawyers worked to keep protesters safe in Cairo, and the Bahrain Centre for Human Rights played a vital role in keeping the army at bay.[24] This provided important evidence for the 'universality' debate; Arab leaders had always supported Asian despots who insisted that human rights were 'Western' inventions, but when push came to shove on the Arab streets in 2011, it was these 'Western' values that people wanted, despite hostility to America in places (such as Egypt) where it had been close to the old regime, and universal hostility to Israel, especially over its Gaza attack. But as these revolts were demands for justice, how much justice did they do to the regimes they overthrew?

Ben Ali was the first to flee, and was refused asylum in France before landing in Saudi Arabia, home to retired tyrants. Whatever possesses this country, in the name of 'Islamic charity', to harbour mass murderers like Idi Amin it has never made clear. In time, it should be put under pressure to disgorge Ben Ali for a proper trial. He received an improper trial *in absentia,* lasting less than one day in the Tunis Criminal Court. The prosecution called its evidence, which was undisputed (because there was no defendant or lawyer to dispute it), that $27 million in jewels and public funds had been found secreted in one of his palaces. The judge then retired for six hours during which time he persuaded himself beyond reasonable doubt that Ben Ali and his wife were guilty of embezzlement and sentenced them to thirty-five years in prison. There were tears of happiness and cheers of jubilation from the crowd outside the court, although Ben Ali, if ever extradited, can ask for the proceedings to begin again. This was a case where justice could only be said to have been done in a symbolic sense: Ben Ali had openly boasted about using the judiciary as his 'right arm', and in this case his right arm was firmly around his own neck.

Hosni Mubarak was brought to court in person, although on a hospital stretcher, just six months after stepping down and disappearing into his villa at Sharm-el-Sheikh. It had been widely thought that the army would arrange a Saudi exit for the 83-year-old ex-president, but the continuing demonstrations in Tahrir Square (especially against military courts which were handing out prison sentences to protesters) put the army under pressure to prevent violence before the November elections. So it abandoned Mubarak to the public prosecutor, who charged him and his interior minister with 'intentional and premeditated murder of peaceful protesters' and with corruption charges based on lavish bribes they had received from land developers. (His two sons were charged with corruption by illegally using their public position for profit.) The appearance of this once-mighty figure, now an old man lying on a hospital bed in a cage with steel bars and wire mesh, certainly shocked the millions who saw it on television. The early stages of the case were fair: the civil court judge selected to try it had a reputation for independence (earned by releasing banned members of the Muslim Brotherhood). He allowed Mubarak to reside at a nearby hospital during the trial, where his health could be monitored. The ex-president, defended by a competent legal team, appeared fully capable of following the proceedings and with a politician's enduring vanity he dyed his hair for court appearances.[25]

The verdict in the murder trial was not a foregone conclusion and the court heard from highly placed army witnesses that Mubarak gave no orders to shoot. Lawyers for the families of victims even complained that the security authorities were protecting Mubarak by not producing evidence of his guilt. There was no overt indication of unfairness, or that the anger expressed in Tahrir Square would prejudice the verdict. The fact that Egypt had a well-respected legal system, which Mubarak had interfered with but had not replaced, meant that with security under control by the army, there were no inherent difficulties in this domestic prosecution for a crime under national law of premeditated mass murder, even though as a matter of international law, the repeated killing of protesters would amount to a crime against humanity. The result was reasonably fair. Mubarak received a life sentence, and his sons were acquitted.

For President Saleh of Yemen there would be no trial. His sclerotic and increasingly brutal thirty-three year regime ended in November 2011 when the Gulf Co-operation Council (essentially Saudi Arabia and the UAE) brokered an amnesty deal by which he agreed to hand over power to his deputy, who in turn undertook to allow some participation by the opposition. As Saleh set off for medical treatment in the US, tens of thousands of protesters turned out to deride his pardon with the chant 'Signed or not, martyrs will not be lost'.[26] Hundreds had been shot and thousands wounded by government troops, evidently acting under orders from the president, who as a matter of international law cannot rely on an amnesty for a crime against humanity, in so far as it comprises his command responsibility for repeated and systematic killing of civilian demonstrators. Western diplomats supported this amnesty, despite its invalidity in international law and the fact that it may not even stick locally, where there is anger not only at Saleh's escape from prosecution but because it leaves his relatives in their leading and lucrative positions in the government of Yemen. Diplomats always favour amnesties, but by delaying the prospect of justice for people whose children have been murdered at the order of the beneficiary, they make it more likely that protests – and the killing of protesters – will continue. An amnesty would probably have been offered to Colonel Gaddafi, had he shown any sign of accepting it, but he fought with manic confidence: by the time he was torn to pieces by rebels his only way out was a plea bargain – he had already been indicted by the ICC. His government officials contacted international lawyers and were advised to contest the indictment at the ICC: his appearance there, even through a legal representative, might have led to a negotiated end to the war. But, in the end, he decided not to acknowledge the court.

The Arab Spring was sprung by liberals and leftists, leading the educated but unemployed youth and the more cautious unions and professional classes to demand an end to unbenign dictatorships. Only later did the Islamists join in – but when they did, in time for elections, it was to fight them with party organizations that had been operational for many years, and capable of reaching the villages and the peasantry who were not a party to the spirit of Tahrir. Tunisia, which had been vouchsafed its first elected parliament since the 1950s saw moderate Islamists win in a landslide, and with 24 per cent of the seats held by women. In Egypt, the liberals should have insisted on first reaching agreement over a new secular constitution, which would have given them time to organize for the elections: instead, fear that the military might hijack the revolution tipped them into agreement to early elections. These resulted in the Muslim Brotherhood winning 47 per cent of the seats and the Salafists – Muslim extremists who demand literal adherence to Sharia law – taking a further 18.5 per cent. The Egyptian people have freely chosen the very people whom Mubarak had tried to suppress – the Muslim Brotherhood and the Salafists – to govern them in his stead, and only the army stands in the way of the Islamist agenda – the very army that has dismayed the liberals by censoring the media and subjecting civilians to secret military trials.

It would be ironic if, in years to come, these 2011 revolutions against authoritarian rule were to produce states governed by Islamist majorities which deny freedom of speech and refuse to tolerate apostasy, homosexuality or the rights of Christians, Marxists or secularists, and which compel women to wear veils and disallow them work and education. However, the immediate electoral appeal of moderate Islamist parties could be put down to their better organization, their welfare services in the provinces and their decades-long hatred of the extortion and nepotism that had characterized secular Arab governance.[27]

Al-Qaida was largely irrelevant to the Arab Spring: it was neither an intellectual inspiration nor a fighting force. Democracy has brought moderate Islam to power, and it will be a struggle for the future to ensure that it exercises it with due respect for the rights of women and of minorities.

THE LEBANON TRIBUNAL

The Arab Spring did not bud in Lebanon, although its influence was felt in the election of a Hezbollah coalition in June 2011, replacing the government which had been led by the son of Rafik Hariri, the prime minister murdered (along with twenty-two others) in a massive Beirut truck bombing in February 2005. The finger of suspicion had pointed at once towards Damascus, because the Syrian regime had fallen out badly with Hariri, and Al-Assad was known to be ruthless. This explains why George W. Bush, although fervently opposed to the ICC, urged the establishment of a new tribunal, based on the international court model, to try what was not exactly a crime against humanity but a very serious crime against democracy in Lebanon. His support (and US funding) was enough to get the new tribunal off the ground without too many questions being asked about its logic: it would be an international court, sitting in The Hague but empowered to investigate and punish a crime of murder committed within a sovereign state. The UN's Charter VII powers were used, on the basis that crimes of this sort – assassinations of elected prime ministers so carefully planned as to indicate the involvement of a foreign state – imperilled world peace and could lead to international conflict. This might have been thought to be 'mission creep' for international criminal justice, given that a one-off assassination, even with collateral casualties, cannot amount to a crime against humanity. But with funding and enthusiasm from the Bush administration, the Lebanon Tribunal quickly set up shop with expert prosecutors, independent judges and the most up-to-date rules and procedures, drawn to a large extent from the most recent war crimes court in Sierra Leone. The UN's finest court administrator, Sir Robin Vincent, was made its Registrar, and he insisted on an important Sierra Leone innovation, namely a 'principal defender', to run an office that would be an 'organ' of the court, counterbalancing the organic power of the prosecutor, which has tipped the balance against the defence in other courts. Ironically, the Lebanon Tribunal offered the best facilities for defendants, but has had no defendants to enjoy them.

The prosecutors had begun, back in 2006, by believing like everyone else in the guilt of Syria. That was the conclusion a preliminary UN investigation jumped to in a report a few months after the killing. Syria certainly had the opportunity – its troops were stationed in Lebanon at the time – and it had the motive, in the sense of wishing to remove the most prominent and effective critic of its influence in the country. Suspicion deepened when three senior Syrian security officials separately met violent but mysterious deaths: was this the elimination of potential witnesses who could link to President Assad the order to kill Hariri? It came, therefore, as some surprise when after a five-year investigation, the prosecutors finally unveiled their indictments – of senior Hezbollah officials. They included Mustafa Badreddine, who had previously been jailed in Kuwait for ordering bomb attacks against Western targets. Hezbollah, a Shia Muslim group, is backed by Iran and Syria, so the fact that it carried out the bombing – if it did – leaves open the question of whether it was acting at Assad's request. But the Tribunal's practical difficulty, now that Hezbollah dominates the government, is to ensure that Lebonan continues to adequately fund the Tribunal (it is meant to pay 50 per cent), and to obtain its co-operation to arrest the suspects.[28]

SYRIA – LETHAL FORCE AND THE RIGHT TO PROTEST

The Assad regime had come to power in Syria in 1970 by way of a military coup led by the father of Bashar Al-Assad, who returned from an ophthalmology practice in England in 2000 to succeed him. He inherited the leadership of a Ba'ath Party which closely controlled political and social life through a cruel and sinister security network, the Mukhabarat. In 1982, his father had massacred 25,000 civilians in the city of Hama in order to put down an uprising by the Muslim Brotherhood. The majority (74 per cent) of the population are Sunni Muslim, but the Assad family and its henchmen – and the chiefs of its military and security apparatus – are all members of the Shi'ite Alawite sect, a 10 per cent minority. The President's brother, Maher Al-Assad, commands the elite army force which did most of the killing, as the Arab Spring turned into a Syrian winter.

The first demonstrations, in February 2011, were peaceful, with familiar demands for free speech and greater respect for human rights, but one consequence of long-time repression is that even peaceful protest appears dangerously subversive to those unused to it. The tipping point came in mid-March, when the security forces fired on a funeral procession and tortured some young children caught spraying anti-government graffiti; later, furious protests were met with army fusillades against the protesters. From then on the death toll mounted by about fifteen to twenty each day, with dead bodies left to rot in the street so their sight and stench would deter others. Demonstrators were killed by snipers stationed on the roofs of public buildings with orders to fire at protest leaders and at any civilian observed (as many were) taking pictures of army brutality on hand-held cameras or mobile phones (there was fear that the images might end up in an international courtroom). By mid-May, there were 800 dead, and 7,000 being tortured in prison, with many more wounded and bleeding in their homes because any doctor who treated a dissident in hospital was put under arrest. Soldiers started to use machine guns to cut down protest marches and 'blacklists' were being circulated carrying the names of dissidents they were ordered to shoot on sight. At this point, there was sufficient evidence that Assad was guilty of a crime against humanity, and that conclusion became compelling to the UNHRC Commission of Experts in November, by which time 3,500 had fallen. By February 2012, when China and Russia vetoed a mild Security Council Resolution calling upon Assad to step down, the toll stood at more than 5,000.

The conflict became a civil war, as some army defectors set up a 'Free Syrian Army' to fight back. When the UNHRC in September asked that its Committee of Experts be allowed entry, Assad refused:

from an early stage he had banned all media, a strategy that had worked well for the Sri Lankan government in 2010, when it kept the world from knowing how its army was massacring Tamils. The US and the European Union imposed some half-hearted sanctions and travel bans on a few of Assad's cronies, which did nothing to stop the killing, and imposed an arms embargo which actually helped the Syrian forces, already armed to the teeth with Russian weapons, by denying weapons to the Free Syrian Army. The West was reluctant to ask Assad to stand down because it feared what might follow, but as the casualties mounted it became clear that anything that followed would be better, in the long term, than further rule by Assad. The Security Council abandoned its new-found 'responsibility to protect', at least by its failure to refer the situation in Syria to the ICC prosecutor as it had done with Darfur and Libya. Although there was no wish for 'boots on the ground' in Damascus – Assad's opposition had no credible leaders or organization – the ICC reference should have been made once Assad could reasonably be suspected of perpetrating a crime against humanity, i.e. in late November 2011, when a UN Expert Commission came to that conclusion. An ICC reference would have put pressure on the regime to reverse its 'shoot to kill' policy. With an indictment in the offing, Assad may have hesitated to add to its counts.

This raises an important legal issue which was common to all Arab Spring countries, namely the point at which demonstrations might lawfully be dispersed by the use of lethal force. This decision is within a government's prerogative – Bloody Sunday (when British paratroopers notoriously killed thirteen Irish republican demonstrators) was not an international crime. But a year of Bloody Sundays – the like of which in Syria had produced 9,000 dead – is a different matter. A persistent brutal crackdown on a protest movement does amount to a crime against humanity, contrary to Article 7 of the ICC Treaty, if multiple acts of murder or persecution are committed, pursuant to state policy, 'as part of a widespread or systematic attack against any civilian population'. The deliberate decision to use tanks, machine guns and snipers against unarmed crowds repeatedly over a period of months is clear evidence of the commission of exactly such a crime. Assad was not a would-be reformer boxed in by hardliners (the initial view of the UK Foreign Office and US State Department). Nor was he 'the blind ophthalmologist' carried along by events. He made the decision to stop the protests by lethal force in order to protect his family's power and wealth from democratic challenge. His younger brother Maher, who commands the army division which committed many of the atrocities, is another prime perpetrator together with relatives who run his brutal secret police, and others from the minority Alawite sect who are part of his inner circle. Even Bashar's wife, Asma, the fragrant graduate of London's exclusive Queen's College, deserves to be investigated as part of that circle. Credulous journalists at American women's magazines had extolled her charity and compassion, but she remained publicly supportive of her brutal husband at the height of the killing and was more concerned (as her leaked emails revealed) with luxury shopping in Europe. In international criminal law, Caesar's wife is not above suspicion, especially when she behaves like a mass murderer's moll.

The rules on the use of force and firearms during civil unrest were settled by the UN in 1990. Armies and police must only resort to lethal force when 'absolutely necessary' in defence of themselves or others against the threat of death or serious injury. They have a duty to act proportionately, i.e. to equip themselves with non-lethal incapacitating weapons such as water cannons and to use these first. They must respect and preserve human life – e.g. by ensuring immediate medical treatment for the injured and by punishing any official guilty of arbitrary killing. 'Internal political instability may not be invoked to justify any departure from these basic principles,' say the UN rules, and they apply 'in the dispersal of assemblies that are unlawful but not violent'. Even in the case of violent demonstrations, lethal force may be used only 'when strictly unavoidable in order to protect life'.

The UNHRC Commission of Experts, which, although refused entry into Syria, was able to interview many victims and witnesses of human rights violations, concluded:

The scale of these attacks against civilians in cities and villages across the country, their repetitive nature, the levels of excessive force used consistently by units of the armed forces and diverse security forces, the coordinated nature of these attacks and the evidence that many attacks were conducted on the orders of high-ranking military officers all lead the commission to conclude that the attacks were apparently conducted pursuant to a policy of the State. Multiple witnesses indicated that, on different days and in different locations, officers at the level of Colonel and Brigadier General issued orders to their subordinate units to open fire on protestors, beat demonstrators and fire at civilian homes. The commission received credible evidence that it is unlikely that the officers issued these orders independently given that the Syrian military forces are professional forces subject to military discipline. The commission therefore believes that orders to shoot and otherwise mistreat civilians originated from policies and directives issued at the highest levels of the armed forces and the Government.[29]

The case of Syria, 2011–12, shows the limit of the UN's 'responsibility to protect' doctrine. It works well enough in relation to a small (population 6 million) pariah state like Libya, run by a half-crazed dictator who has insulted and embarrassed the statesmen of all significant states and has been left with no ally amongst the 'big five' powers on the Security Council. It does not work in respect of a larger (population 22 million) country like Syria, which has one proactive big-power protector (Syria is Russia's closest ally in the region and provides the harbour for its fleet). Moreover, Assad was predictable in geopolitical terms – until 2011 his quiet repression through the Mukhabarat had guaranteed a quiet life (Damascus was regarded as one of the world's safest cities) and despite his destabilization of Lebanon and support for Hezbollah, he was a potential conduit for the West to a nuclear-armed Iran. By the time it was clear he had to go, there was still no alternative: unlike in the case of Libya, his opposition was neither organized nor tribal, and unlike in Tunisia and Egypt, the army was not a neutral force that could 'hold the fort' until democracy could be introduced. The very fact that Russia could and did block even the mildest Security Council criticism of Syria exposed the flaw in the 'responsibility to protect' doctrine, when one or more of the 'big' five members is not prepared to shoulder any responsibility.

12

Terrorism: 9/11 and Beyond

> 'Military Justice is to justice what military music is to music.'
>
> Georges Clemenceau

On 10 September 2001 it might have been said with some confidence that the third age of human rights, that epoch in which basic humanitarian norms will achieve some level of enforcement, was underway. Forty-two states, including Britain, France and Russia, had ratified the Rome Statute, and the ICC was expected to open its doors by late 2002. Milošević was in the Hague dock, while Theoneste Bagosora (alleged architect of the Rwandan genocide) awaited trial in Arusha. A war crimes court had been agreed for Sierra Leone and a similar tribunal to try Khmer Rouge commanders was being negotiated between the UN and Cambodia. There was a court in East Timor and a promise from the new Indonesian president that some accused officers would go to trial in Jakarta. The old amnesties in Latin America were being overturned, and in Africa there was increasing international resolve to confront the oppressive behaviour of Robert Mugabe. The Libyan leopard seemed to have changed its spots en route to Lockerbie, and even the government of Iran wanted rapprochement with the West. After the peace settlement in Northern Ireland (accomplished with considerable US assistance), the major intractables were Iraq (where UK and US bombing forays were becoming counter-productive) and Palestine. The advancement of civil and political rights in the world seemed sufficiently assured for the two leading NGOs – Human Rights Watch and Amnesty International – to switch their spotlights to the economic and social rights they had hitherto neglected.

Then, quite literally out of a clear blue sky, came the kamikaze attacks on the World Trade Center and the Pentagon on 11 September. The generation who could still remember where they were when they heard the news that Kennedy had been shot was replaced by a generation who will forever live with the freeze-frame in their minds' eyes of the passenger jets exploding their fuel tanks on the buildings that served as the buck-teeth of New York. If there was any silver lining in the black cloud which hung for weeks over Manhattan, it was the message to Americans that their ultimate safety lies in engagement with international law and co-operation. But injured pride and emotional chauvinism meant new bursts of isolationism in the world's most powerful and prosperous nation. In the weeks after 9/11 Tony Blair, playing Cicero to George W. Bush's verbally dyspraxic Caesar, spoke movingly about putting the world to rights, but Donald Rumsfeld's asides hinted at a simpler desire – to nuke the enemy, then go home and turn on the 'star wars' security system. On the evening of 11 September, when the president came down from his flying bunker (he had been sent aloft in Air Force One for his own safety) he faced the TV cameras and said 'Freedom itself was attacked this morning by a faceless coward' and later ventured the afterthought, as if a light-bulb had flashed a caption above his head, 'this could be . . . an opportunity'. This chapter will examine how the US took that opportunity, firstly to expand the dangerous right to use force in self-defence and then to weaken the Geneva Convention protections for humane treatment and fair trial of prisoners of the war on terror, whom it renamed 'unlawful combatants'. It will consider the extent to which the Obama administration has renounced these excesses, whilst developing new methods of 'targeted killings' by unmanned drones, and how in 2011 it hit the highest-value target of all, Osama bin Laden.

ENEMIES OF HUMANKIND?

The Russians withdrew from Afghanistan in 1989, beaten by the brave fighters of the Mujahidin, an Afghan army which had been bolstered by 30,000 radical Muslims from the Islamic diaspora, mainly Pakistan, Saudi Arabia and the Gulf states. The subsequent emergence of the Taliban, like the recruitment of the 'Afghan Arabs', had been sponsored by the US, whose policymakers had not heard the parable of the dragon's teeth. ('What was more important in the world view of history?' scoffed Jimmy Carter's former National Security adviser Zbigniew Brzezinski. 'The Taliban or the fall of the Soviet Empire? A few stirred-up Muslims or the end of the Cold War?') The 'stirred-up Muslims' spent a few years fighting viciously along tribal and warlord allegiance lines, until Mullah Omar and his zealous students from *madrassas* (colleges which study nothing but the Koran) won a string of victories and in September 1996 captured Kabul. There lived Mohammed Najibullah, the country's president from 1986 until 1992 when he had taken refuge in the UN compound, protected by an international law which other Afghan factions had respected. The Taliban's first act in Kabul was to violate the UN's immunity by seizing and torturing the former president, then castrating him and dragging his body behind a jeep before hanging it from a lamppost.

This premeditated barbarism by men who came in the name of religion gave fair warning of their approach to human rights. As the Taliban, who were mainly Pashtuns, battled the Tajik forces of Ahmad Shah Masoud and the Uzbek forces of General Rashid Dostrum and the Southern command of Gulbuddin Hekmatyar over the next few years, they behaved with a calculated ferocity – Mullah Omar personally authorized the massacre in August 1998 in the town of Mazar, for example, which left 6,000 civilians, many of them women and children, dead in the streets.[1] It is no excuse that their opponents behaved in kind, although America's post-9/11 allies, especially warlords like Dostrum and Hekmatyar, certainly did. The world simply looked the other way – Afghanistan was a 'basket-case', in a too-hard basket – until Madeleine Albright noticed that the Taliban were refusing to allow women to work or to be educated, and she described them as 'despicable'. But the repression instituted by the Taliban through its 'Ministry for the Prevention of Vice and the Promotion of Virtue' – brutal public executions, often for 'crimes' of apostasy or adultery (homosexuals were crushed to death under walls); bans on television, music and sport; its disruption of UN aid supplies and massacres of opponents – all went uncondemned. The CIA had been pumping billions of dollars to the ISI (Pakistan's intelligence service) in full knowledge that the lion's share was being distributed to arm and equip the Taliban: they were, after all, taking over the country, and their backing would be necessary, amongst other things, for the US company Unocal to carry through its oil-pipeline project.[2] What made the world, and the US in particular, first take serious notice of this monstrous regime was its association with Osama bin Laden, 'the man who declared war on America'.

Bin Laden was a charismatic Saudi endowed with great wealth from a family construction business. He had fought on the front lines and helped to fund Mujahidin fighters in the war against Russia: he built *madrassas* and 'guesthouses' over the border in Pakistan where 'Afghan Arabs' were trained before going into battle. In 1988 he formed al-Qaida ('the base') initially as an organization to keep in touch with his fighters, but after the Russian withdrawal, its members were required to take a secret oath (*bayat*) to continue the holy war beyond Afghanistan.[3] America became their target after it committed the sacrilege (in their eyes) of stationing troops in the holy land of Saudi Arabia during the Gulf War. Bin Laden spent some years nurturing al-Qaida in the Sudan, making another fortune in the meantime on construction projects delivered by its government, until he moved back to Afghanistan at Mullah Omar's invitation in 1996. There, from the Hindu Kush mountains, he issued his first declaration of jihad against Americans, recorded on audiotape and distributed to al-Qaida supporters in forty different countries. In February 1998 he delivered a widely published and full-blooded *fatwah* calling upon Muslims to kill Americans, including civilians, wherever they could be found. On 7 August 1998 his operatives exploded truck bombs outside the US embassies in Kenya and Tanzania, killing 234 (twelve Americans) and wounding 5,000. Two weeks later President Clinton authorized cruise-missile attacks which destroyed a chemical factory in the Sudan (which turned out to have nothing to do with bin Laden) and one of his several bases in Afghanistan. The Security Council, in December, finally passed a resolution condemning the Taliban for harbouring terrorists and violating human rights.

By this time, al-Qaida was an organization rather like a multinational company, with some 6,000 members, several hundred million dollars (funnelled through Saudi banks, mainly 'Zakat' donations to bogus charities), training camps and quarters throughout Afghanistan and cells in at least thirty-five other countries. Its first attack on an American target had been as early as 1992 – a hotel bomb in Aden, intended to kill US troops on their UN mission to Somalia. The 1993 bomb at New York's World Trade Center was made by an al-Qaida operative trained at a bin Laden guesthouse in Pakistan. The killing of eighteen US servicemen that year in Mogadishu – the event which gave rise to the 'Mogadishu factor' – has been attributed to al-Qaida trainees, and in 1998 a grand jury actually indicted bin Laden for procuring those Somalian murders. Al-Qaida links were uncovered in bombings which killed Americans in Saudi Arabia in 1995 and 1996 (at the Dohor Towers), and in the following years there were a number of operatives caught 'red-handed' before they could hit various American targets. Several possessed al-Qaida 'training manuals', instruction-books in terror.[4] On 5 October 2000 the USS *Cole*, anchored off Yemen, was attacked in a suicide bombing which killed seventeen American sailors, and prompted the Security Council to pass Resolution 1333 (December 2000) prohibiting military assistance to the Taliban until it handed bin Laden over to face the indictments that had accumulated against him in New York.

Against this background, the most astonishing thing about 9/11 was that Western intelligence did not see it coming. By that time, there can be no doubt that bin Laden and al-Qaida had an organizational policy of committing multiple murder of civilians, as part of a widespread and systematic attack directed in particular against Americans. That, of course, precisely satisfies the definition of a 'crime against humanity' in Article 7 of the ICC Statute. This characterization of the 9/11 atrocities meant, on the precedent of NATO's attack on Serbia, that the international community would be entitled to override sovereignty in order to punish the crime, so long as the sovereign state to be invaded bore responsibility for it in international law.

Whether the sovereign state of Afghanistan could bear such responsibility depended upon the relationship its Taliban government had forged with bin Laden and al-Qaida. A British embassy official watched that relationship develop symbiotically: they became 'two sides of the same coin: Osama cannot exist in Afghanistan without the Taliban and the Taliban cannot exist without Osama'.[5] Mullah Omar was a close friend who knew what he was doing when he invited bin Laden to relocate al-Qaida in the Hindu Kush in 1996, with thousands of trained 'Arab Afghans' who would fight alongside the Taliban army in its civil war against the Northern Alliance. Bin Laden became, in effect if not in title, a Taliban general, commanding special (and specially motivated) forces in much the same way as Himmler commanded the SS divisions alongside the regular German army. Mullah Omar and his ministers knew and approved of bin Laden's conspiracy to kill American civilians: his propaganda videos and his 'fatwahs' in 1996 and 1998 were widely publicized, and the Taliban permitted him to construct and run training camps not far from their capital of Kandahar: the 'eagle's nest' of tunnels through the mountains behind Tora Bora was the country's largest military complex. There are hundreds of recorded instances of al-Qaida's fighters serving the Taliban, whether integrated with its army (carrying out civil war massacres and jointly running training camps for Kashmiri militants) or in special kamikaze operations (such as the suicide bombing by operatives posing as a news team which killed Northern Alliance leader Masoud two days before 9/11). After the fall of Kabul, evidence of the interdependence of the Taliban and al-Qaida and of their close co-operation in projects to develop weapons of mass destruction was found in abandoned 'safe houses'.

The Taliban, in other words, knew that bin Laden was the linchpin of a continuing conspiracy to murder Americans, whether civilians or diplomats or soldiers, conducted systematically and pursuant to a racist policy. With that knowledge, they gave him assistance, ranging from physical protection to the use of state facilities. The Taliban leaders would not have known precisely the time or nature of the 11 September attacks, but they obviously knew that a crime of this dimension was on the cards, and they deliberately assisted, and politically and ideologically approved. There is a case for the Taliban leaders to answer for aiding and abetting the crime against humanity that was perpetrated on 11 September.

MAKING WAR MEANS MAKING LAW

On 11 September 2001, two hijacked American Airlines 767 passenger jets were flown into the Twin Towers, a third into the Pentagon while a fourth (United Airlines flight 963, probably aimed at the Capitol building) crashed after its courageous passengers had tackled the hijackers. In all, 2,973 civilians lost their lives, mostly American, although there were casualties from many countries and creeds. The nineteen hijackers were Arabs, fifteen from Saudi Arabia, some university educated: they had steeled themselves for this kamikaze operation through an interpretation of the Koran which required them to accept the religious duty of jihad – a holy war on infidel America, in which the moment of a martyr's death would see him translated into a parallel universe. Judging from the jottings of team leader Muhammed Atta, they would have torn off their shirts and puffed out their chests to meet the moment of impact, entrusting what was left of their bodies to 'the women of paradise, waiting and calling out "come hither"' (it is one of the blacker ironies of al-Qaida's extremist jihaderie that condemnation of pornographic films in life is rewarded, in death, by stepping into one). This is not offered as a cheap aside, but as evidence that their actions were motivated by a superstitious belief system that must qualify (however grotesque) as religious. They were members, however, of an organization with political objectives: the purpose of the jihad was, by humbling America, to force its troops out of Saudi Arabia, to undermine its traditional support for Israel and to stop its bombing of Iraq. These were the three declared aims of Osama bin Laden, to be advanced through a policy of widespread and systematic killings of American citizens.

In the weeks following 9/11, evidence accumulated which pointed convincingly to bin Laden's overall responsibility. Although President Bush spoke in Wild West language of wanting him 'dead or alive' and preferring his 'head on a plate', the British government thought it necessary to justify the impending attack on Afghanistan by publishing a summary of the case against him,[6] which demonstrated in blood-curdling detail that bin Laden had consistently incited the murder of Americans, had confessed to involvement in the 1998 bombings of the US embassies in Kenya and Tanzania (which killed several hundred civilians) and had subsequently ordered the attack on the USS *Cole*. Although some critics tried to dismiss the evidence as 'circumstantial', this missed the point: in proving conspiracy, as every criminal lawyer knows, circumstantial evidence is often more credible than fallible human testimony. The case became more compelling when further evidence for his guilt was subsequently uncovered in al-Qaida quarters in Kabul: on a videotape bin Laden is heard giggling with delight as he recalls how the damage to the towers was beyond his expectations ('we calculated in advance the number of casualties from the enemy . . . I was the most optimistic. Due to my experience in this field, I thought the fire from the petrol in the plane would melt the iron structure of the building'). This all amounts to *prima facie* evidence of guilt, although whether it would remain so after being fleshed out in a courtroom and tested by cross-examination and forensic science is another matter – the point is that even prior to any US incursion on Afghan sovereignty, Osama bin Laden had been shown to be at the hub of a conspiracy to commit mass murder.

But that was not all that the evidence eventually proved. Bin Laden was not, as seemed at first, a peripatetic gang leader – a modern pirate, owing no state allegiance and receiving no state assistance, temporarily moored somewhere in the Hindu Kush. As the Taliban government unravelled, it became clear that bin Laden and his 'special forces', the Afghan Arabs, motivated by religious zealotry, were a part and parcel of that government. He was not a 'guest', as the Taliban pretended, who was owed hospitality under Pashtun tradition: he was a significant part of Mullah Omar's apparatus of control and repression. Exactly what part defies any sensible democratic comparison, but his roles included intelligence chief, commander of an 'Arab SAS' attached to the Taliban military forces, and a general in charge of conducting foreign offensives. The legal significance of identifying him as a state actor rather than a casual resident was that Mullah Omar and his ministers were individually and collectively responsible for those of his actions of which they approved. Since they must have known that his plans were to murder US citizens, as well as of his preparations to carry this out, they were guilty of aiding and abetting his preparations for this genocidal jihad against Americans (and anyone else who happened to get in the way).

This characterization of bin Laden's role in the Taliban government is crucial to the legitimacy of turning a hunt for a terrorist into a war against Afghanistan. The Taliban, although fighting a civil war, constituted the government of Afghanistan under the current declaratory theory of recognition,[7] since they effectively administered 90 per cent of the country, in many parts of which their repressive 'law and order' had been welcomed as a 'last resort' alternative to the anarchy of marauding criminals and pillaging warlords. Pakistan had been permitted by the West to sponsor the Taliban, and much of its initial funding had come (via ISI) from the CIA. Without doubt, it 'harboured' al-Qaida, but what danger did that carry, in international law, to its own claim to the immunities of sovereign government?

The International Court of Justice had declared in 1949, in a ruling sought by Britain after its ships in the Corfu Channel struck mines laid from Albania, that every state has a duty to prevent its territory being used for unlawful attacks on other states.[8] In 1980, after the hostage-taking saga at the US embassy in Tehran, the same court ruled that Iran was responsible at two stages – initially for a failure in 'vigilance' by not controlling the militants, and subsequently by tolerating their occupation of the embassy which amounted to adoption and approval of the terrorist acts.[9] There is much in the ICJ decision in the *Nicaragua Case* to the same effect, although it made a crucial distinction between controlling forces which performed the unlawful act (America was thus responsible for the acts of its navy in mining Nicaraguan harbours) and merely training and equipping them (the US was not liable for crimes of the contras).[10] In the case of an attack by an arm of government, civil liability is strict, permitting no defence of mistake or ignorance: France admitted responsibility and paid compensation to New Zealand when its secret service destroyed the *Rainbow Warrior*,[11] and the Soviet Union was accountable for the wrongful action of its air force in shooting down Korean Airlines flight 007.[12] However, when the unlawful attack is by non-government agencies or groups – the militant students in the *Tehran Embassy Hostages Case*, or the contras in the *Nicaragua Case* – the test is effective control, and 'What really matters . . . is the amount of control *which ought to have been exercised* in the particular circumstances, not the amount of actual control.'[13] Afghanistan's duty imposed by international law was, in effect, to exercise due diligence: to take whatever steps were reasonable to stop al-Qaida furthering its conspiracy by launching attacks on Americans, or to arrest them as soon as there was reason to suspect that they had launched such an attack.

It follows that as a general principle of international law one state may not attack another, whether by sending its own air force to bomb the World Trade Center or by achieving the same result through the criminal actions of terrorists condoned by an arm of its government. In the latter case, so the ICJ held in *Nicaragua*, the actions of such 'irregulars' can constitute an armed attack of such a scale that would distinguish it from a 'frontier incident' and was of a kind which might be committed by regular forces.[14] Responsibility is imputed by international law if the state could and should have controlled the irregulars, but chose not to do so. Just as France was responsible to New Zealand when its secret service sank the *Rainbow Warrior*, so Afghanistan was responsible to the US when its 'SAS' (bin Laden's 'Special Arab Services') hijacked passenger planes and used them to demolish the Twin Towers. The US was not only entitled to demand the extradition of bin Laden, but to hold to account the government which he served. Legal proceedings in the ICJ would have been idle (for a start, neither the US nor Afghanistan accept ICJ jurisdiction) but on what basis did international law permit the extravagant alternative of overthrowing that sovereign government?

An armed incursion cannot be justified merely because the state refuses an extradition request, nor could the overthrow of the Taliban ever be defended as revenge for 9/11. One of the few crystal-clear international law rules is that 'states have a duty to refrain from acts of reprisal involving the use of force'.[15] It is premature to postulate a general right to overthrow a state when its crimes are not against humanity but amount to lesser breaches (however outrageous) of human rights standards. The Taliban deprived the Afghan people of many civil, political, economic and social rights – freedom of speech and choice of religion, fair trial and (in the case of women) of an education. This amounts to a tyranny which may at some future time be held to justify armed intervention, but it does not breach the barbarism threshold so as to amount to genocide or any other crime against humanity that the world community is entitled (if not obliged) to bring to an end. The voguish 'responsibility to protect' principle would not be engaged, because thus far it has been confined to a state's responsibility to protect the lives of its own people, by not killing them unlawfully. The Taliban, however cruel their regime, was not as bad as that.

But the acts of 9/11, together with the African embassy bombings, and the other atrocities committed or attempted pursuant to al-Qaida's policy, amounted precisely to a crime against humanity: they were 'multiple acts of murder committed as part of a widespread and systematic attack against a civilian population'. It was to punish such crimes in Kosovo that NATO breached Yugoslavian sovereignty, and the same principles might be applied to Afghanistan if its government had aided and abetted al-Qaida to such an extent that it bore some responsibility for the horrors of 9/11. (It had, after all, done more for al-Qaida than Charles Taylor had done for the RUF, whose crimes against humanity he would be convicted of aiding and abetting.) On this basis, going to war to overthrow the Taliban would be legitimate, so long as the ten preconditions for human rights intervention by way of a just war (set out in chapter 14 at pp. 755–6) were met. But this was not the approach of the Bush administration, which relied throughout on its right of self-defence in customary international law. Was the first war of the twenty-first century really an exercise in anticipatory self-defence – in which case, how many other states, Iraq being the first, are to be laid to waste when superpowers anticipate attacks which might never come, or can it be brought within the emerging but limiting notion of a human rights offensive to prevent crimes against humanity?

SELF-DEFENCE: THE IGNOBLE ART?

The right to use force in self-defence is expressly preserved by Article 51 of the UN Charter, although in terms which make its exercise subject to Security Council oversight. The fundamental Charter obligation on members to 'refrain in their international relations from the threat or use of force against the territorial integrity or political independence of any state . . .' may be overridden by the Chapter VII powers of the Security Council and (as argued above) by the right to stop commission of crimes against humanity, and by the 'inherent' (i.e. customary law) right described in Article 51:

Nothing in the present Charter shall impair the inherent right of individual or collective self-defence if an armed attack occurs against a Member of the United Nations, until the Security Council has taken measures necessary to maintain international peace and security . . .

As an exception to the general duty to respect sovereignty, Article 51 should (like all exceptions) be strictly construed, i.e. limited to its scope in customary international law and available only so long as the Security Council does not act to take control of the situation (although the self-defender must have some latitude in deciding whether Security Council actions are likely to be effective). But the severest limits on the right are imposed by customary law itself: since it is grounded in necessity, the counter-attacks must be solely and immediately designed to remove the threat, and must remain proportionate to that objective. The key precedent derives from a rebellion against British rule in Canada in 1837: the rebels ('terrorists' in British eyes) had many American supporters across the Niagara who supplied their base (an island on the Canadian side of the river) from the US steamboat *Caroline*. In response, British soldiers boarded the steamer in an American port, fired it and set it on a course over Niagara Falls: two

American citizens were killed. The US and British governments engaged in pointed correspondence about the latter's claim to be acting in self-defence, culminating in British acceptance of Secretary of State Webster's formulation of the principle that states claiming the right must 'show a necessity of self-defence, instant, overwhelming, leaving no choice of means, and no moment for deliberation'. There must be 'nothing unreasonable or excessive, since the act, justified by the necessity of self-defence, must be limited by that necessity, and kept clearly within it'.[16]

The *Caroline Case* was endorsed as a correct statement of the law by the court at Nuremberg.'[17] It was relevant to the US response to 9/11 since the British were claiming self-defence against non-state actors (the Canadian rebels) who were 'harboured', quite literally, by the Yankees on the shoreline. It would justify a counter-attack on terrorists in the state that shelters them, even unwillingly (the American authorities had tried without success to stop local support for the rebels). So there is no doubt that the US and its allies were entitled to bomb bin Laden's training camps and terrorist infrastructure within Afghanistan, so long as 'extra-territorial law enforcement' was the object of the expedition. Some text-writers (and the ICJ in the *Nicaragua Case*) appear to think the right to use force only arises when the target state has itself been involved in the attack, although this is wrong (in the *Caroline Case* the US was not supportive of its citizens who aided the Canadian rebels) and for present purposes is beside the point, given bin Laden's approved position within the Taliban government. The real question is whether it was legitimate for the US and its allies to turn a defensive attack on bin Laden's lairs into an offensive war to overthrow the Taliban.

Precedents provide no support for an exercise of self-defence which begins as a specifically and proportionately targeted response to an atrocity directed from a sheltering state and then changes course to obliterate that state's government. The paradigm American exercise of 1916, when President Wilson sent troops into Mexico in hot pursuit of bandits who attacked across the Rio Grande, was justified on the basis that the Mexican government was too weak to maintain order: the US was enforcing the law, doing the Mexican government's duty but not seeking to supplant it.[18] By capturing or killing the bandits, and destroying their hide-outs, the US was acting proportionately, doing exactly what was necessary to secure its borders against a continuing threat, without incongruously lashing out in a revenge sortie that killed innocent civilians or overthrew the incompetent national regime. The US strike against Libya in 1986, some ten days after a disco bombing in West Berlin had killed an American soldier and injured fifty more, was also (at least, ostensibly) targeted at terrorist infrastructure: the US rejected claims that this was a revenge attack with the real intention of killing Gaddafi. Secret intelligence, it said, showed the Libyans to be imminently planning further anti-American atrocities, so the measure was 'anticipatory self-defence' not directed to the overthrow of Gaddafi's regime.[19] This is questionable – force may be used to intercept any attack, but not to pre-empt an attack that is merely possible. The US would have been entitled to sink the Japanese fleet in 'anticipatory self-defence' the moment it set sail for Pearl Harbor, but not to demolish it beforehand merely on the grounds that it had the capacity to carry out such an attack. In any event, under the doctrine of proportionality, 'it would be utterly incongruous to permit an all-out war whenever a State absorbs an isolated armed attack, however marginal. A war of self-defence is the most extreme and lethal course of action open to a State' – especially the United States – 'and access to it must not be allowed on a flimsy excuse'.[20]

The question of proportionality in the permitted US response to 9/11, however, must take into account the fact that bin Laden had been the cause of US attacks on his Afghan hosts before: two weeks after the embassy bombings in 1998, cruise missiles struck a training camp in Afghanistan where al-Qaida was believed to be holding a top-level meeting. Then, America also pleaded self-defence[21] – its armed response served at least as a warning to the Taliban about tolerating bin Laden, who was indicted in New York for the embassy bombings shortly afterwards. But like the strike on Libya, it was a fairly immediate response to a specific act of terrorism, that act not of itself amounting to a crime against humanity. It served as a warning of 'more to come' if the terrorist act was repeated. It had no wider purpose – certainly not the overthrow of the Taliban. These embassy bombs had killed twelve Americans and over 200 Africans: was it merely the much larger number of Americans killed on 9/11, and the fact that the attack occurred on American soil in circumstances of peculiar horror and spectacular symbolism, that justified a war to topple a sovereign government?

A difference in kind, rather than degree, can be found not in the horror or the casualty figures, but in the fact that 9/11 assumed the character of a crime against humanity, while the embassy bombings – at the time, more routine terrorist incidents – did not. The 9/11 attacks came as part of a policy calling for widespread and systematic assault on innocent civilians, not confined to diplomatic or military targets, adopted by a network which had by that time plainly developed the necessary political and organizational clout to rank as a perpetrator within the Rome Statute's definition. It is true that the fact that 9/11 counts as a crime against humanity gives the US more latitude for self-defence – the 'proportionality principle' would permit this counter-attack to be more ferocious and long-lasting, i.e. to be proportionate to the seriousness of the original attack. But the customary law requirements of necessity and immediacy must still come into play: pounding the Taliban into the dust three months after 9/11 satisfied neither. That is why the alternative rationale for 'Operation Enduring Freedom', as an example of the right to punish and prevent more crimes against humanity, is to be preferred since it is limited by neither requirement, although it does attract the Kosovo preconditions which are restrictive in a different (but more logical and humanitarian) way (see pp. 755–6). These include a duty on the interveners to make good the civilian damage and to bring leaders of the defeated government to trial before an international court.

The argument that Article 51 of the UN Charter justified the overthrow of the Afghan government after the legitimate destruction of bin Laden's terrorist infrastructure depends upon whether further threatened attacks were 'imminent'. Having shown no regret for harbouring al-Qaida, the Taliban if left in charge of the Afghan state might harbour it again. The threatened attacks would come from a regrouped al-Qaida, of course, and not from the Taliban, but it was legitimate under Article 51 for the US to dismantle whatever capacity the Taliban had to assist al-Qaida in the near future. In deciding to overthrow the Taliban, the US took the position that it remained under imminent threat of attack so long as that organization had *any* part in the government of Afghanistan. That was difficult to square with the *Caroline* rule. By the time (mid-October) that the US switched to this new and broader objective, at first by acting as the air force of the Northern Alliance (B-52 bombing enabled its advance to take Mazir-al-Sharif and Kabul) and then by joining in the assault on Kandahar, it could not seriously be contended that America was in any imminent danger from which it had to be rescued by the forcible overthrow of the Taliban. There was no evidence of the degree of urgency and immediacy required by the *Caroline* doctrine.

In any event, Article 51 assumes that the counter-attacks will be short-lived, until the Security Council is able to take charge, and the self-defender must respect the Charter duty in Article 2(3) to resolve disputes by peaceful means 'in such a manner that international peace and security, and justice, shall not be compromised'. The US had at the outset notified the Security Council of its reliance on self-defence, as Article 51 requires, and the Council had by Resolution 1368 (passed on 12 September) recognized the applicability of the right and called on all states 'to work together urgently to bring to justice the perpetrators, organizers and sponsors of these terrorist attacks', stressing also that those responsible for 'aiding, supporting or harbouring' the perpetrators would be held accountable. A second resolution, 1373 (passed on 28 September), directed all members to 'take the necessary steps to prevent the commission of terrorist acts' – an explicit recognition of the need for preventative action, but providing no direct mandate for overthrowing the Taliban government. Neither resolution authorized the use of force against Afghanistan, because the US was not asking for any such authorization and nor did it even rely on 1373 as justification for its wider war. Its NATO partners had invoked Article 5 of the North Atlantic Treaty – 'an armed attack against one or more of them in Europe or North America shall be considered an attack against them all' – and notified the Security Council that they were exercising the regional right of coming to America's assistance. Other countries which offered armed support, like Japan and Australia, came within the 'collective self-defence' umbrella permitted by Article 51: the basis of the coalition, however, was that it was acting in support of America's right rather than asserting its own. Most of these countries did, at least for domestic consumption, assert that they were also at risk from terrorist attack, although their logic was circular, since that risk derived from the fact that they had joined up to the US military campaign.

The UN made no attempt to take charge of the situation. There were some vain attempts at negotiations in early October shortly before the US bombing campaign switched to support the Northern Alliance, and Taliban spokesmen variously offered to look at the evidence or to surrender bin Laden for trial in an Islamic state. These offers (and it was never clear that they were serious) fell on deaf ears, i.e. those of President Bush, who responded, 'when I said no negotiations, I mean no negotiations. We know he's guilty, turn him over.'[22] This ultimatum, six weeks after the original attack, was certainly not the language of self-defence. It was a gunpoint demand to extradite America's public enemy number one. (Purists may decry the lack of extradition formalities, although it is fair to point out that America had on several previous occasions asked the Taliban for bin Laden's surrender over the embassy bombings, and by 14 October his involvement was well established: he had virtually confessed as much on tapes sent to supporters.) When the Taliban did not immediately respond, the B-52s began bombing their front line in earnest. The Northern Alliance went in, as America's surrogate ground force, to mop up all the way to Kabul, at which point American marines joined them for the attack on Kandahar, which fell in early December.

By this time, indeed by late October, the legal basis for the bombing as self-defence under Article 51 was becoming doubtful. It would fail all three tests – of necessity, proportionality and immediacy – which the customary law doctrine requires, unless al-Qaida were to be regarded as an inseparable part of the Taliban government, which had become almost a household word for cruelty. Its overthrow *could* be justified as an intervention to punish and prevent crimes against humanity and (more doubtfully in law) as an intervention to overthrow tyranny and restore democracy and fundamental human rights. But it was in fact justified at the time as a legitimate Charter exercise of 'anticipatory self-defence', a justification which strained the *Caroline* doctrine and if generally accepted would dangerously expand the power of any state to go to war whenever it felt threatened (a danger that came to pass in 2003 when the US used this expanded definition as a justification for its invasion of Iraq).

It could be said – it was certainly felt, by Americans – that 9/11 was so horrendous that it justified annihilation of bin Laden's Taliban sponsors and supporters. That cannot be allowed, however: twice as many human beings were exterminated at Srebrenica, and using 9/11 as a warrant to wipe out a government is simply to invest American lives with an importance above all others. The doubtful doctrine of 'anticipatory self-defence' was the basis upon which America notified the Security Council pursuant to Article 17. It spoke of 'the ongoing threat to the US and its nationals posed by the al-Qaida organization . . . made possible by the decision of the Taliban regime to allow the parts of Afghanistan that it controls to be used by the organization as a base of operation . . . From the territory of Afghanistan [it] continues to train and support agents of terror who attack innocent people throughout the world and target US nationals and interests . . .'[23]

This is plainly a complaint that Afghanistan was 'harbouring' terrorists and it lays the legal ground for an exercise of self-defence to destroy al-Qaida and its bases and training camps. But it shows no immediate threat necessitating the Taliban government's overthrow. If US and allied action in Afghanistan and subsequently Iraq is to stand as a precedent for the legality of 'anticipatory self-defence', it will dangerously twist customary law, to the point where it becomes a vigilante's charter, a *carte blanche* for Israel or China or any other aggressive country to respond to a transborder terrorist attack by force designed to overthrow the state from which it is launched, for so long as the Security Council (which may be immobilized by one permanent member veto) forbears to act.

This danger was demonstrated ten days after the US notification, when Israel retaliated for the killing of a former government minister by invading several towns within the Palestine National Authority: it explained that it was acting against that Authority 'in the way currently accepted by the international community to act against a leadership that supports terror'.[24] In the years which followed, Israel interpreted the George W. Bush doctrine of self-defence as 'two eyes for an eye, a row of teeth for a tooth', meeting each Palestinian suicide-bombing with a revenge sortie, culminating in the wilfully disproportionate attack on Gaza in 2009–10. The government's claim to 'self-defence' included defending itself against those who might hold it to international law standards: it refused entry to Mary Robinson, and to Richard Goldstone's Commission which had been tasked by the Human Rights Council to investigate the Gaza attack. In mid-December, India threatened to invoke the Bush doctrine after a suicide-bombing at its parliament by a Kashmiri liberation group 'harboured' by Pakistan cost thirteen lives. The spectre of nuclear weapons being used in 'self-defence' by two irresponsible powers which possess them demonstrates the danger of easy recourse to 'self-defence' in answer to terrorist provocation. Although international law forbids reprisal attacks, they will always be justified under Article 51 if 'self-defence' can be automatically engaged by an atrocity.

Self-defence, in international as in domestic law, is a blunt and somewhat primitive doctrine, difficult to distinguish from revenge. It is, moreover, excessively dependent on the subjective assessment of a wronged self-defender. If international law is to permit a response to terrorist attack which involves the overthrow of the state from which it is launched, then justification is better found in the obligation of the world community to punish a crime against humanity than in the self-assessed defence exigencies of the state which has been attacked. In the latter case, the attacked state is always likely to judge that its defence requires the destruction of a government which has 'harboured' the terrorists, in the sense merely of permitting them to reside, without any proof that high government officials have known and approved of their plans. The self-defender may attack the rogue state without accepting any duty to pick up the pieces or to prove the guilt of its leaders before an impartial court. When the self-defender is the US, or China or Russia, permanent members who can paralyse the Security Council, then its subjective judgement cannot be called into question in that forum, which in any event is political and not judicial. Nor can these most powerful states be called to account in the ICJ, because they do not accept its jurisdiction and in any event its procedures take years. Yet some forum for assessing the legality of the self-defence claim is essential, as the Nuremberg court pointed out when rejecting Göring's argument that Germany alone could decide whether to go to war in self-defence: 'whether action taken under the claim of self-defence was in fact aggressive or defensive must ultimately be subject to investigation and adjudication if the international law is ever to be enforced'.[25]

The 'crimes against humanity' approach, which requires proof (which may be tested at a subsequent international trial) of the accused state's complicity with a terrorist crime of that magnitude, parallels the test for state accountability in public international law for terrorist acts. In the *Nicaragua Case*, the ICJ found that the US could not be held accountable for the 'terrorist' acts of the contras while they made transborder attacks on Nicaragua. Although America had helped to finance, equip and train the insurgents, this degree of involvement was not so great as to impute their atrocities to the US for the purposes of ordering compensation. State accountability for terrorist acts, the Court decided, depended on whether it exercised 'effective control' over the wrongdoers so as to be 'substantially involved' in their crimes.[26] Although Security Council resolutions, and the ICJ in the *Tehran Embassy Hostages Case*, condemn states for 'tolerating' or 'encouraging' terrorism, more is needed for liability in public international law. But where 'effective control' or 'substantial involvement' does exist, that will mean that officials in the political or military hierarchy knew and approved of the terrorists' conduct. They will thus be guilty, in international criminal law, of aiding and abetting such conduct when it amounts to a crime against humanity.

This would have provided the US and its allies with a more persuasive legal justification for the use of force to remove the Taliban. To sum up, that government had not merely 'encouraged' or 'harboured' al-Qaida: the terrorist organization trained and equipped a special force of more than 6,000 men, which used army facilities and placed itself in battle under the general army command. When the Taliban army broke ranks, the Arab fighters were used to shore them up. Their role in the oppressive Taliban state was as a security and intelligence service, available to kill enemies of the regime, ranging from dissident shopkeepers to the much-feared head of the Northern Alliance, General Ahmad Shah Masoud, assassinated by two of bin Laden's suicide bombers (posing as a TV crew who wished to interview him) just two days before 11 September. The evidence which emerged from Kabul showed that Taliban leaders were aware of al-Qaida's preparations for major terrorist offensives, probably including their plans for use of chemical and nuclear weapons, and they were of course aware that they were holding terrorist training camps. At the highest level, the government knew of bin Laden's role in the 1998 crimes and of his continuing, murderous jihad against Americans. Notwithstanding this knowledge, they integrated his forces with theirs, assigned him special projects (like the killing of Masoud) and operated a pact of mutual protection – being well aware of what he was up to (a course with which they showed every sympathy). The case for 'effective control' can be made out against the state, and the case for aiding and abetting a crime against humanity can be levelled individually against Mullah Omar and his ministers. But the war was only 'just' to the extent that its objective was to capture them and put them on trial – as it wore on, its objective became that of killing more Taliban. And vice-versa.

THE ROAD TO GUANTANAMO BAY

The immediate and rightful response of the United States to the atrocity of 9/11 was to demand 'justice', although that word sounded, in many powerful mouths, like the cry of the lynch mob for summary execution, assassination squads and Osama bin Laden's 'head on a plate'.[27] The confusion over the meaning of the word 'justice' became acute when the Pentagon chose 'Operation Infinite Justice' as its first brand name for the bombing of Afghanistan. This made no philosophical sense, because human justice is both finite and fallible. More importantly, it begged the question, which Western leaders so notably and for so long failed to address, of exactly what forensic procedure they proposed to adopt to persuade the rest of the world that their cause was right. What court, if any, awaited bin Laden and his lieutenants, or indeed Mullah Omar and his ministers?

The last thing Western leaders wanted was for Osama bin Laden to come out with his hands up. Bill Clinton claimed to have secretly authorized a CIA assassination after the embassy bombings, and President Bush and his advisers made it clear that they preferred him dead rather than alive. This preference the Obama administration shared: its Navy Seals were tasked to kill rather than capture (see chapter 14). Ironically, this was the consummation bin Laden himself would devoutly have wished: in his belief system, attaining a fast track to paradise required him to die mid-jihad, and not of old age on a prison farm in upstate New York. It did not occur to the presidential policymakers, who produced the plans for a 'military commission' to convict and speedily execute the al-Qaida leader in the regrettable event that he were taken alive, that this would ensure his earthly martyrdom and (if only in his own mind) his transport to paradise. But suppose he were to be captured and interrogated, and later sit for some time in a criminal court dock and then, after a reasoned judgment, be locked for the rest of his life in a cell in Finland? Surely this would greatly assist the work of demystifying the man, debunking his cause and de-brainwashing his many thousands of followers. A fair trial before an independent court might serve this practical purpose, and besides, it was also what international law required.

There can be no warrant for the cold-blooded execution of a surrendered terrorist. Although at one point in history it was common to hang captured pirates, terrorists of the high seas, instantly from the yard-arm, the better practice (at least of the British navy) was to return them for trial at the Old Bailey. Summary execution of terrorists is tempting to law enforcement agencies, because it avoids the danger of exposing informers or secret intelligence at a trial, and it pre-empts further terrorist hostage-taking by their comrades in efforts to free them. The temptation has not always been resisted, and even in Europe secret-police squads have been accused of assassinating Basque, IRA and Baader-Meinhof cadres. But the right to life, or at least the right not to have life extinguished by the state without due process, is fundamental even in war (with the possible anachronistic exception of spies and mercenaries). From the moment that America and its allies intervened on the side of the Northern Alliance in its civil war with the Taliban, the Geneva Conventions of 1949 applied, requiring humane treatment for all combatants who surrender and no punishment without some form of fair process.

This was not, however, accepted by Donald Rumsfeld, who maintained that the US was under no obligation to treat either Taliban or al-Qaida fighters as 'prisoners-of-war' under the Geneva Convention when they were transferred to 'Camp X-Ray' at Guantanamo Bay in January 2002. His British and French allies disagreed – the first significant split in the 'coalition against terror' – and so did the Red Cross and the UN's Human Rights Commissioner, Mary Robinson. This legal issue is important, not only because the Geneva Convention guarantees humane treatment for POWs (by now, this has become a rule of customary international law for all captured fighters) but because of its rule against coercive interrogation and its requirement that any trial of POWs be conducted fairly, before an independent and impartial tribunal.

Article 4(1) of Geneva Convention III, 'Relative to the Treatment of Prisoners of War', extends that status to members of the armed forces of parties to the conflict, and to 'members of militias and volunteer corps forming part of such armed forces'. There can be no doubt that Taliban fighters fall within this definition: they were the army of the Taliban government. There is some doubt about the 'Afghan Arabs' of al-Qaida, but since they formed a volunteer militia which fought in cahoots with the Taliban army from the outset of the war, the better view is that they too deserved POW status. Their symbiotic relationship was the UK government's justification for attacking both without distinction, and on the battlefield no differentiation was made (or was possible to make) until the closing stages when fire was concentrated on al-Qaida units at Tora Bora. In these circumstances, it is unrealistic to draw any distinction between the two groups for the purposes of the Geneva Convention.

The US position is to deny that the Convention applied to either group: it labelled them 'unlawful combatants' or 'battlefield detainees' rather than POWs. The reason offered was that they fought without wearing military uniforms – but since when have Mujahidin sported regimental braid? Article 4(1) does not require a distinctive insignia and any such requirement would be unreal in many Third World wars. The requirement for a 'fixed distinctive sign recognizable at a distance' (along with open carriage of arms and some form of command structure) is a requirement under Article 4(2) for paramilitaries and resistance fighters, who do not form part of a government's armed forces but who seek POW status when captured. The thrust of the requirement is to distinguish those who fight in the open (as did the Afghan Arabs) from spies, saboteurs and other disguised or clandestine operatives. The al-Qaida fighters, with their beards and their AK-47s, were certainly 'recognizable at a distance' – even at the distance between Afghanistan and Florida, where the US command centre that targeted missile attacks on them was located.

Tellingly, the Northern Alliance fighters – the US surrogates – had no distinctive uniform, and nor of course did the CIA 'special forces'. The Soviet Union was never permitted to use this pretext for avoiding the Convention when it captured Mujahidin fighters in the 1980s: when the same men (or their sons) in the same clothes were captured twenty years later fighting for the Taliban, it was illogical to pretend that their status had changed. There was some suggestion that al-Qaida prisoners might be regarded as 'mercenaries' under the 1977 Geneva Protocol (which neither the US nor Afghanistan had ratified) but that category is limited to persons 'motivated to take part in the hostilities essentially by the desire for private gain' and promised substantial 'material compensation'. The Afghan Arabs, motivated not by money but by the prospect of a fast track to paradise, fall outside this definition. What made the US position plainly untenable was Article 5 of the 1949 Convention, which declares that if there is any doubt about the POW status of detained combatants, 'such persons shall enjoy the protection of the present Convention until such time as their status has been determined by a competent Tribunal' – and not by Donald Rumsfeld.

That the US have attempted to wriggle out of the Geneva Conventions is ironic, given that many of the lives they have saved or made bearable over the past half century have been those of American soldiers and airmen captured during the wars in Korea and later in

Vietnam. Then, it was China and North Vietnam who tried to wriggle out of the Convention with pettifogging legal arguments (for example, China's refusal to admit that there was a 'war' in Korea, and hence its claim – condemned by the UN – to execute captured US pilots as spies). The Geneva Conventions of 1949, ratified by the US, are a monumental achievement in universalizing civilized values – even Saddam Hussein felt obliged to permit the Red Cross to visit American POWs as he was being bombed into submission during the first Gulf War. The US position on their inapplicability to the 'Camp X Ray' detainees was therefore dangerous as a precedent, particularly for its own forces in the future. It was also wrong in law, as the US Supreme Court eventually decided in the 2006 case of *Hamdan* v. *Rumsfeld*, ruling that common Article 3 applied to all prisoners held at Guantanamo.

So what was the point? It was not that the US wished to deny them humane treatment, monitored by the Red Cross. The provisions about coercive interrogation are often misunderstood: a POW is only *bound* (under Article 17) to give 'name, rank and number' and date of birth, in the sense that this is the only information he may be punished for withholding: the Convention does not preclude him supplying further information, so long as this is not elicited by threats or force. The reason why the US was so determined to deny POW status was its objection to the Convention requirement in Article 3(1)(d) that POWs cannot be sentenced or executed 'without previous judgment pronounced by a regularly constituted court affording all the judicial guarantees which are recognized as indispensable by civilized peoples'. This requirement is re-emphasized by Article 84: 'In no circumstances whatever shall a POW be tried by a court of any kind which does not offer the essential guarantees of independence and impartiality as generally recognized.' The Geneva Convention specifically permits POWs to be placed on trial for war crimes and crimes against humanity, and even for acts that are forbidden by the domestic law of the detaining power at the time of their commission (Article 99): what it demands is that the court of trial must be fair in procedure and independent of military or political authorities.

The prisoners at 'Camp X-Ray' were held under the Geneva Conventions (as the Supreme Court eventually ruled) and their detention should have ended either by repatriating them, under Article 118, to their country of nationality (which might try them in regular courts for offences against its laws) or by putting them on trial in their place of detention. That trial, to be in accordance with the 1949 Geneva Conventions, would have to be fair, and conducted by independent and impartial judges. Even if the prisoners were unlawful combatants rather than POWs, customary international law still requires fair process and an unbiased court, since it has come to reflect the norm expressed in Article 75 of the first 1977 Protocol, namely that all captured combatants have the right to trial 'by an impartial and regularly constituted court' with the presumption of innocence and 'all necessary means of defence'.

Since the legal system in Afghanistan was in chaos, there could be no objection to transferring suspects to the US – hooded and sedated if necessary for security in transit – and for putting them on trial under international or American law. It was objectionable, however, to take them to Guantanamo Bay in order to deny them any trial at all. That was the intention of the Bush administration, in the apparent belief that they could in the twenty-first century get away with the devious ploy by Charles II in the seventeenth, who detained republicans on Jersey and other offshore islands where *habeas corpus* could not reach. The beauty of Guantanamo was not its beach and wildlife but the fact that it was not US sovereign territory. It had been permanently leased from Cuba in 1903 for use as a US naval station, at a nominal rent of $5,000 per year (Fidel Castro refuses to cash the rent cheque but has not sought to cancel the lease). Judges at first instance and in appeal courts upheld the fiction that Cuban sovereignty made the base a 'legal black hole', where men could be indefinitely detained as 'unlawful combatants' and subjected to regular interrogation, deprived of lawyers or Geneva Convention protection. Detainees have claimed that they have been the victims of torture: whether or not this is true is known by the Red Cross, which has an office at the base (closed throughout August, a Swiss holiday), but they have bound themselves to silence. What can be said is that until June 2004, when the Supreme Court ruled in *Rasul* v. *Bush* that due process applied to Guantanamo, all its detainees suffered a form of mental torture – of not knowing why they were being held or if or when they would be released. The true cruelty of the Guantanamo concept was not the shackling and hooding and orange boiler suits and cages behind barbed wire (Camp Delta, built by Halliburton subsidiary Brown & Root to replace the ramshackle 'Camp X-Ray', is comparable with many US high-security prisons), but the trauma that comes from having no legal hope at all. It was ended when the Supreme Court declared in mid-2004 that detainees had the right to challenge their detention, although the only means the government is even now prepared to allow to effectuate that right – a 'special military commission' – is so lacking in fairness that Guantanamo Bay remains a symbol of disregard for international law.

The treatment of aliens is probably the most distasteful aspect of US law: foreigners in the 'land of the free' are neither entitled to be free nor, in Guantanamo Bay, were they even regarded as being in the land itself. That should not, of course, have denied anyone held there by US power the right to challenge the lawfulness of his detention, but in the wartime case of *Johnson* v. *Eisentrager* the US Supreme Court denied that right to Nazi prisoners convicted by US military courts in Germany, on the basis that to allow 'the great writ' to enemy prisoners taken in foreign countries would hamper the war effort.[28] This may be reasonable enough in wartime or in relation to convicted prisoners who have a right of appeal, but it cannot apply after hostilities are over, and when indefinite detention by the US army is unlawful. In *Rasul* v. *Bush* the Supreme Court decided that the Guantanamo detainees were entitled to challenge the legality of their detention in US courts: *habeas corpus*, 'an integral part of our common law heritage' since Magna Carta, 'does not act upon the prisoner who seeks relief, but upon the person who holds him in what is alleged to be unlawful custody' – and the ultimate custodian was George W. Bush, a resident of Washington DC, not of Cuba. It followed that the detainees could seek due process in any federal court that had jurisdiction over the president, despite the technicality that they were not held on sovereign soil.[29]

In an associated case, *Hamdi* v. *Rumsfeld,* the Court indicated that the US constitution does not permit suspected enemy combatants to be held indefinitely: they must sooner or later be tried as civilians or treated as prisoners-of-war with Geneva Convention rights to fair trial. The Court accepted that Guantanamo detainees might, under the laws of war, be held until the end of hostilities, but in the meantime they had a right to counsel and to rebut the government's claim that they were enemy combatants – they were entitled under Geneva Convention III to a 'competent tribunal' to decide their status – to 'a fair opportunity to rebut the government's factual assertions before a neutral decision maker'. In response, the Pentagon in July 2004 did what it could and should have done in February 2002 and set up a 'Combatant Status Review Tribunal' to decide whether the men it was keeping in Guantanamo as 'enemy combatants' had done any fighting at all. The decision-makers were not neutral (three army colonels), the proceedings were not fair (the burden of proving non-combatant status was on the detainee) and no counsel was permitted (the detainees were allocated 'personal representatives' by the Pentagon). Since the Pentagon, which employed the Tribunal members, had already decided that the first 230 applicants were 'unlawful combatants', it is unsurprising that only two of them were able to persuade the Tribunal that they were not. Some detainees were later released – notably nationals of Western allies such as the UK – and in 2007 the only white man in the camp, the Australian David Hicks, obtained his release by the expedient of pleading guilty. His government had shown such lack of interest in his welfare that after six years in Guantanamo his release had become an election issue, which it sought to defuse by an arrangement with the US whereby he would be transferred to freedom in Australia after he pleaded guilty to a charge of which he (and most legal experts) believed he was innocent. This cynical deal between the US and its most fawning ally demonstrated what Wikileaks' revelation of detainees' records in 2011 was to prove, namely that far from being 'the worst of the worst', as Bush and Cheney had alleged, 92 per cent of inmates were unconnected with al-Qaida: most were low-level camp followers of the Taliban, many turned over by malicious informants in return for US bounties.

On the day after his inauguration in January 2009 President Obama signed an order requiring Guantanamo to be closed within one year. But this was not to be. Whilst many were released 179 remained three years later. An irrational fear descended on the 'land of the brave' at suggestions that any terrorist suspect – even the harmless ethnic Uighurs from China – might set foot on the mainland, if only in a maximum-security prison. Congress voted to refuse funding for any such transfer and proceeded at the end of 2011 to pass another bill allowing detention without charge, notwithstanding the likelihood of its eventual rejection by the Supreme Court. The Attorney-General had confidently announced that Khalid Sheikh Mohammed and other inmates against whom there was real evidence (as opposed to evidence obtained by torture) would be tried by Federal Court juries in New York, but again the irrational fear descended (that they might actually be acquitted) and the president was, once more, forced to eat his Attorney-General's words and revive the discredited military commissions, which have managed, since the camp opened, to convict only six of the 779 detainees held in that period. It is significant to note that of the first fifty-seven *habeas corpus* applications brought by inmates the government was found to lack sufficient evidence to detain in thirty-eight cases. There has been an increased use of the detention centre at Bagram air base in Afghanistan, where *habeas corpus* petitions have been blocked on the pretext that it is in a conflict zone.[30]

CAMP JUSTICE: THE TRIAL OF KHALID SHEIKH MOHAMMED

The trial of the much waterboarded alleged mastermind of 9/11 began in May 2012 at Camp Justice, the absurdly named new court complex at Guantanamo Bay. The Obama administration had seemed to recognize that no military tribunal could be independent and impartial when it promised to have the Khalid Sheikh Mohammed (KSM) case heard by a real judge and a civilian jury in New York. But this caused political panic, both from fear (stirred by Mayor Bloomberg) of having the defendant physically present on the US mainland and from the fears of Republican congressmen that a fair trial might result in an acquittal. The Attorney-General reversed the decision, so a military commission comprising army officers, who are soldiers employed by the same department of state as the military prosecutors, will be his judges and jurors. These officers could hardly be perceived as impartial towards a declared enemy in the dock, a member of an organization which tried to kill their comrades in Iraq and Afghanistan, where the presiding officer has served.

The pity of this trial is that there are real issues of guilt or innocence that demand impartial judgment. The confessions of KSM are doubtful, not only because they have been procured by torture but because he is a liar prepared to admit to anything (including the murder of journalist Daniel Pearl) in order to achieve his express wish for martyrdom. He and his co-defendants originally wanted to plead guilty before a jury and become martyrs as quickly as possible, but military trial at Guantanamo has given them the opportunity to discredit the proceedings. They have adopted the 'Charles I gambit' of not recognizing the court, although their lawyers recognize it all too well and are raising pre-trial points that will take years to resolve. This spectacle will not bring closure for relatives of the 2,969 victims of 9/11, of whom a few (chosen by lottery) have been permitted to attend, while the others can only watch the forensic tedium on closed-circuit television at US army bases.

There can be no doubt that the lawyers and officials involved in this military exercise will do their best to be fair and will wrestle with questions about the admissibility of torture and hearsay evidence (their new rules prohibit the admission of a defendant's confession obtained by torture, but not of any other evidence – even from co-defendants – obtained by torture). The presiding officer, Colonel James Pohl, presided over the military proceedings against the soldiers who tortured Abu Ghraib prisoners, and has tried to look fair by allowing the five defendants to have prayer mats, and regular adjournments so they can genuflect towards Mecca. But the crowning irony comes from America's obsession with the death penalty. These defendants want nothing more than to be killed by American soldiers, because they believe that this provides their fast track to Paradise. The ultimate absurdity of Camp Justice is that, at serious cost to America's reputation, the country is in the process of giving its worst enemies exactly what they want.

Guantanamo Bay carries on, a symbol of America's double standards – due process for its own citizens, but arbitrary imprisonment (with the prospect of execution) for aliens it suspects may be its enemies. Conditions in the prison have certainly improved, with soccer pitches and education classes, and to Obama's credit torture techniques are no longer practised (a number of Algerian prisoners have actually demanded to remain in the camp, for fear of torture if sent home). However, there have been no prosecutions, either of the lawyers who perverted the law by drafting the torture memos or of those who did the torturing. No longer a gulag, Guantanamo remains an iconic example of America's inability to come to terms with international law. Defence lawyers derive a certain black humour from having to fly on army planes to the island's motel, where after a night of exposure to pornography on the army TV channel they breakfast at a dockside MacDonald's and watch soldiers saluting their officers – 'Honour bound, Sir', to which the reply is 'Freedom, Soldier'. After these magic passwords, they are escorted through the barbed wire into a world where iguanas, a protected species, have more rights that human detainees.[31] They then appear in military commissions where the so-called judges lack any independence from the prosecuting and detaining authorities. That means they are not courts at all, but star chambers, creatures of the executive – in this case, of the US defense department. It would have been so easy and so obviously right to give these men on trial for their life a jury or a tribunal of real American judges, perhaps with a few international jurists, but where terrorist suspects are concerned Americans are not prepared to take the risk of an occasional acquittal.

Guantanamo Bay has been a public relations disaster, precisely because its constitutional basis has been constructed by 'Bush lawyers' – doctrinaire professionals who have given the Bush administration convenient rather than correct advice about the US constitution and the Geneva Conventions and the laws relating to war and torture. It was not wrong to transfer men captured on Afghan battlefields to a holding prison where they could be interviewed and if necessary detained until the war was over or tried for war crimes before an independent and impartial court. But the Bush lawyers hit on the ruse of holding them in a legal limbo-land, advising the government that on Cuban sovereign territory they would be immune from the rule of US and international law. The idea was to hold them indefinitely, without trial or any other due process, without access to counsel or family and with only the Red Cross as an observer with its lips sealed. The men have been held long after the war in Afghanistan in which they were captured was ended – on the basis that the 'war' in question was that on terror and may be never-ending. They were either Taliban foot soldiers (unarguably 'prisoners-of-war' for Geneva Convention purposes) or else members of al-Qaida brigades fighting with the Taliban and entitled at least to humane treatment. Yet some have been held for ten years virtually incommunicado as 'unlawful combatants' without any charge that specified the law they were meant to have broken.

There is mounting evidence that, allegations of beating and torture and Koran-abusing aside, the conditions in which they have been held for that period have deeply affected their minds and personalities, reducing them to states of 'learned helplessness' and despair. There are serious ethical questions about the doctors and psychiatrists who are employed in the Camp Delta regime, both to assist interrogation and to force-feed prisoners on hunger strike. Credible and mounting evidence indicates that 'in depth' interrogation techniques were regularly used: cacophonous and stress-inducing sounds (infants wailing, cats meowing and Yoko Ono singing), hooding, phobia-exploitation (especially fear of dogs when naked), sexual humiliation and sleep deprivation. Such techniques were regarded as legitimate under the 'Bush lawyer' definition of torture supplied by Assistant Attorney-General Jay S. Bybee (pain comparable to 'physical injury such as organ failure, impairment of bodily functions or even death'). There has been no legal come-uppance for the Bush lawyers who perverted legal doctrine so that their political masters could authorize torture with a clear conscience: Bybee became a Federal judge, Yoo a law professor at Berkeley. The CIA torturers will not be prosecuted, says Eric Holder, as his Justice Department devotes more and more resources to the prosecution of Bradley Manning and the Grand Jury proceedings to hunt up evidence against Julian Assange.

TARGETED KILLINGS

In war, it has for centuries (if not for millennia) been lawful to kill enemy commanders, even if they are Kings or Popes. As Alberico Gentili, Regius Professor of Civil Law at Oxford in the time of James I, pithily put it, 'A man who is dead renews no war.' This jurist, more humane than others of his time, reluctantly accepted that commanders might be killed if by so doing more lives could be saved, e.g. if they were implacable enemies incapable of trustworthy negotiation: 'even Caesar thought it folly to spare one who had more than once figured as his opponent'. These thoughts ('Stone dead hath no fellow') comforted Cromwell and the judges who sentenced Charles I to death for instigating two civil wars and planning a third: the incorrigibility of a commander who is at liberty always provides a utilitarian rationale for 'termination with extreme prejudice'.

In 1943 Roosevelt personally approved the assassination of the Japanese Admiral who commanded the Imperial Fleet, and the British launched an unsuccessful commando raid to kill General Rommel. But in the great wars there was a reluctance to resort to treacherous tactics or to target political and military leaders: the concern, which continued throughout the Cold War, was that this would unite the enemy's people and – more worryingly – provoke reprisal assassinations. In the 1970s, US Congressional Committees exposed comical CIA plots to murder Fidel Castro – sending him exploding cigars and poison pens – and the outcry led both Presidents Ford and Reagan to ban political assassinations by way of Executive Order 12333: 'no person employed by or acting on behalf of the United States Government shall engage in, or conspire to engage in, assassination'. This comports with the Fifth Amendment to the US Constitution, which protects 'any persons' (not just US citizens) from being 'deprived of life . . . without due process of law'.

Until 9/11, the legal position was clear: in war, active combatants could kill and be killed, subject to rules about surrender and prohibitions on taking life by treachery, perfidy, poison and so on. The paradigm was a conflict between opposing armies simultaneously and legitimately invoking the right of self-defence. Otherwise, when not engaged in conflicts of international or non-international nature, the Geneva and Hague Conventions were inapplicable, and confrontations with insurgents, rioters and terrorists were not matters for international humanitarian law at all: they were to be governed by local law which generally allows police to use reasonable force to apprehend criminals and protect the public. After the US embassy bombings in Lebanon, the CIA was advised – correctly – that Order 12333 would not bar them from killing a terrorist whom they knew to be driving a truck full of explosives towards a US embassy, if this were the only way to stop him.[32] In these circumstances, it could hardly be contended that lethal force was unreasonable. But like the 'ticking time bomb' scenario, it is also unrealistic: when three IRA bombers were shot dead on Gibraltar by British security forces who honestly believed they were about to activate a car bomb, it turned out that the belief had been induced by completely false information – the three were unarmed and harmless, at least at the time they were shot. The European Court of Human Rights, in a narrow decision, found that the UK had denied them the right to life because its intelligence services had jumped to over-hasty and mistaken conclusions.[33] In the case of known members of terrorist organizations, security services will always want to be safe rather than sorry, but the 'reasonable force' requirement exercises a necessary and humane restraint over their trigger-happiness. This is exactly why it has suited the US, Russia, Israel and Iran to reconfigure international law, so that the rhetoric about a 'war on terror' is taken seriously enough to engage International Humanitarian Law (IHL) – the law of war, which (unlike the rule of reasonable force) allows terrorists (aka 'enemy combatants') to be killed without much compunction.

'Targeted killing' has been defined as 'the intentional premeditated and deliberate use of lethal force, by states and their agents under the colour of law, or by an organised armed group in armed conflict, against a specific individual who is not in the physical custody of the perpetrators.'[34] Such killings will often violate the right to life. Although they are lawful in certain circumstances if the target is an enemy combatant at a time of armed conflict, in times of peace they will be unlawful unless the force used is reasonable to prevent crime or apprehend criminals. Otherwise, they amount to extrajudicial killings in breach of human rights law. Notwithstanding this, Israel has frequently targeted Palestinian leaders (one recent assassination team in Dubai made use of British passports and this caused a diplomatic furore, unlike the assassination itself, even though it was of a Hamas leader at a time he was engaged in diplomacy rather than war). Mossad is almost certainly behind the drive-by murders of nuclear scientists in Tehran. Russia in 2006 passed a Federal law (No. 35-FZ) allowing the president to authorize Security Service killings of those with 'an ideology of violence' and Chechnyan separatists have duly been killed. However, as the Special Rapporteur on extra-judicial killings pointed out in 2010, the lack of transparency on the subject from all states makes accountability impossible:

'To date, no state has disclosed the full legal basis for targeted killings. Nor has any state disclosed the procedural or other safeguards in place to ensure that killings are lawful and justified. This refusal . . . violates the international legal framework that limits the unlawful use of lethal force against individuals . . . a lack of disclosure gives states a virtual and impermissible licence to kill.[35]

This is particularly unacceptable because states which claim the rights of belligerents in conflict with terrorists, and hence the legal right to target enemy commanders, usually do so through civilian operatives – the CIA and Mossad – rather than using their military forces which are familiar with and accountable to the law of war. As UN Rapporteur Philip Alston has pointed out, intelligence agents who directly participate in hostilities may themselves be lawfully targeted and killed. But because CIA agents do not have the immunity generally accorded to soldiers on active service, they could be prosecuted for murder in any country where they have been active in planning assassinations or in providing information that leads to killings by the predator drones which are fast becoming the state assassin's weapon of choice.

The states that deploy targeted killing methods argue that they are at war with those they are, in self-defence, entitled to target. As Harold Koh, US Solicitor-General, puts it:

As a matter of international law, the US is in armed conflict with Al Qaeda, as well as the Taliban, in response to the horrific 9/11 attacks and may use force consistent with its inherent right to self-defence . . . including by targeting persons such as high level Al Qaeda leaders who are planning to attack us.[36]

But this bold statement begs many questions. How can you have an 'armed conflict' ten years after a terrorist atrocity unless there is some organized enemy, rather than a random collection of terrorist groups? What actual criteria are used for putting names on the secret death list: is it enough to be sympathetic to terrorism, or married to a terrorist, or to be anti-American or to provide shelter or funds to terrorist groups? What is the required degree of proof (is it enough that guilt is likely, or on the balance of probabilities, or beyond reasonable doubt)? There are no accountability mechanisms – no inquests, sometimes not even a casualty list, although the US usually announces – and celebrates – when it hits a high-value target. There is, of course, no fairness or due process to enable the potential victim or his relatives or any outside body to challenge the accuracy of the information on which the targeting decision has been made, or the decision – by shadowy intelligence operatives – to place him on the target list. The lack of proper criteria was revealed by the Senate Foreign Relations Committee in 2009, when they reported that the Pentagon's approved list of 'prioritized targets' contained 367 names and had been expanded to include fifty Afghan drug lords suspected of donating money to the Taliban. Suppose the suspicion was unreasonable, or the donation had been at gunpoint, or had been of a negligible amount. What the Pentagon is doing is secretly sentencing people to death, for an unproven crime.

The Israeli Supreme Court is the only tribunal to have confronted the legality of targeted killing, in a country where the UN Special Rapporteur has counted 387 deaths from this mode of execution in the six years between 2002 and 2008 (234 were targeted members of Hamas and the other 153 were civilians who got in the way).[37] The Court contented itself with general comments about the categories of targets (dangerous and dedicated terrorists) and gave out some

Polonius-like precautionary precepts: 'well-based information is needed'; 'innocent civilians are not to be harmed'; 'in case of doubt, careful verification is needed before an attack is made'. The reality is that innocent civilians very often are killed, and that verification always seems 'careful' to the mind of the targeters. The Israeli judges and officials appear morally content to risk civilian lives: one enquiry merely found 'shortcomings' in the evaluation of information after a one-ton bomb was dropped on a building in Gaza City. It had killed many civilians (a result that was obviously foreseeable) in order to assassinate Salah Shehadeh, a Hamas military leader. This was plainly a case of manslaughter by gross negligence. The Israeli defence force said that lessons had been learnt, but not about civilian casualties – later when it executed by missile Sheikh Yassin, the wheelchair-bound Hamas spiritual leader, it killed eight others outside his mosque. In similar vein, the CIA's anxiety to kill al-Qaida leader Al-Zawahiri led to a drone attack on a village in Pakistan where he was mistakenly thought to be hiding, and eighteen civilians were killed. There was no explanation, no accountability and no compensation, for what the CIA calls a 'decapitation strike'. The more valuable the target, the less care is taken about civilian casualties: in March 2003 the US openly made a number of 'decapitation strikes' on suspected hiding places of Saddam Hussein in Baghdad, using cruise missiles and 2,000lb bombs.

All this is justified – by the Obama administration more fervently than by its predecessor – as an exercise in self-defence under Article 51 of the UN Charter. But this Article grants the right only against attacks (or imminent attacks) by other states. Terrorists, and politicized groupings like the Taliban, are non-state actors against whom the right of self-defence can only arise – if at all – under customary international law. If it does arise, which is doubtful, it can be triggered only by an 'armed attack' which the ICJ has repeatedly held must be of considerable scale;[38] 9/11 would qualify, but that was over a decade ago and terrorist atrocities by al-Qaida since have been sporadic and low intensity. Harold Koh, by speaking of 'high level al-Qaida leaders who are planning to attack us' invokes the Bush doctrine of anticipatory self-defence, and applies it to what seems to be wishful thinking on the part of hypothetical 'high level al-Qaida leaders'. The customary law *Caroline* doctrine, that the need to kill in self-defence must be 'instant, over-whelming and leaving no choice of means' against a threat that is real and imminent, would certainly justify the CIA's right to assassinate the driver of a suicide truck, but would not legitimize summary execution merely of suspected al-Qaida operatives, or Taliban commanders when not on active operations.

Whether or not the customary law right of self-defence arises depends on whether the targeted killing can be described as having been committed in the course of an 'armed conflict' – a phrase unde-fined in the Geneva Conventions, which unnecessarily divides 'conflicts' into those which are 'international' (i.e. involving two or more states) or 'non-international' (i.e. between a government and rebels). The irritating distinctions between the two, for the purposes of war law and human rights law, are being eradicated (see the *Tadić* judgment earlier, p. 469) but neither concept is really appropriate for asymmetric warfare, where terrorist flashpoints occur across many countries. The assumption that international humanitarian law applies creates further legal controversy: who may be targeted as a belligerent, and over what period? The Geneva Conventions permit civilians to be targeted if they are taking a 'direct part in hostilities' which would seem to exclude funders of and sympathizers with ter-rorists, or leaders of a 'political wing' (the role Gerry Adams and Sinn Fein played in relation to the IRA). It does not, and certainly should not, exclude the 'farmers by day, fighters by night' who are so familiar in rebel militias, or indeed the 'soldiers by day, fighters by night' who defected at evening from the forces of corrupt governments to join bloodthirsty insurgent groups in the West African wars. All these dif-ficulties arise from trying to justify targeted killings of suspected terrorists under the laws for war between great states.

There is one further problem, which appears to have gone unno-ticed. If the fight against terrorism is squeezed into a war-law paradigm, then the Geneva Conventions and customary rights and protections must apply to terrorist and to law enforcer alike. If it is lawful to kill bin Laden, Al-Zawiri, and other Hamas and Taliban commanders, then it must equally be lawful for them to kill their opposite numbers – the US commander-in-chief, his generals, his secretaries of state and his allies (even the Queen of England, as head of state of a US ally, may qualify as a legitimate target: 'her' soldiers, belonging to 'her' regiments, take their oath of allegiance to her as their commander-in-chief). Certainly President Obama, as an operational commander-in-chief who says he approves each drone strike, would be a legitimate target of those groups to whose leaders he authorizes the despatch of lethal missiles. The president would be classed as a 'combatant' under the very law that his Solicitor-General applies to leaders of the Taliban and al-Qaida, thereby dignifying them to a degree which is both unreal and unacceptable. Gangsters who deliberately take the lives of innocent civilians in order to spread terror deserve to be treated like dangerous criminals and shot down whenever necessity requires, and not treated in law as if they were warriors matched in combat with great states.

These states – notoriously the US, Russia and Israel, with more likely to follow if the practice goes unchallenged – demean themselves and their claims to legality by secret assassinations. President Obama, in accepting the Nobel Peace Prize, boasted that 'even as we confront a vicious adversary that abides by no rules . . . the United States of America must remain a standard-bearer in the conduct of war'. That standard he certainly raised by ending torture and downsizing Guantanamo, but then lowered it again by approving hundreds of targeted assassinations. These killings are summary executions, the punishment of Alice in Wonderland's Red Queen ('sentence first, verdict afterwards'), which deny the right to life, the presumption of innocence and the right to a fair trial. No one can question the right of law enforcement officers to kill cornered terrorists or those who are caught in the act of taking or preparing to take innocent lives, but not when there is an alternative non-lethal solution – when capture is possible or surrender is on the cards. Targeted assassination amounts to the premeditated murder of suspected criminals, and the more imprecise the target – in the sights of a drone rather than a soldier's rifle – the more likely that it will amount to the manslaughter of unsuspected civilians.

What is the position under human rights law? The UN Rapporteur argues that 'a targeted killing in the sense of an intentional, premeditated and deliberate killing by law enforcement officials cannot be legal because, unlike in armed conflict, it is never permissible for killing to be the *sole objective* of an operation'. But it does not follow that premeditated targeting has the sole objective of sentencing a suspect to death without trial – the purpose may be to save lives, by removing gunmen or suicide bombers as they prepare for their assaults. It would obviously be a breach of the right to life if terrorist sympathizers were targeted to deter others, or if anyone was killed in circumstances where it was reasonably possible to arrest them. Judgments under human rights principles depend on all the circumstances, applying Article 6 of the ICCPR, namely that 'no one shall be arbitrarily deprived of his life'. There are circumstances where a utilitarian calculus would justify killing terrorists hell-bent on missions to blow up civilians, so long as the shooting does not endanger other civilians in their vicinity. The record of drone attacks demonstrates that frequently individuals are targeted when they pose no clear or imminent danger, and whether they do or not, strikes are often launched which foreseeably cause the deaths of civilians.

For all that human rights lawyers may complain, targeted killings are undeniably popular. The president's ratings shoot up whenever a terrorist suspect is shot or bombed: for the public and its popular news providers, 'suspicion' might as well mean 'proven beyond doubt'. The Israeli revenge attacks after the massacre of its Olympic athletes by the Palestinian group 'Black September' in Munich were widely regarded as 'justice', even though a number of victims are now acknowledged to have been innocent of any complicity.

There is a sense here in which international law has failed: neither the UN Charter nor the Conventions nor the customary norms of the courts have provided intelligible and satisfactory guidance for waging asymmetric warfare. Hence the silence of states on the subject, whilst the UN Rapporteur, a voice in the international wilderness, condemns many targeted killings as murder and inferentially invites the accusation against the US, Israel and Russia that they are committing a crime against humanity by widespread and systematic killing of individual suspects. The way forward may in fact be to find a way back – to the principles of reasonable force and proportionality which govern most domestic laws dealing with treatment of violent criminals, which would be applied to terrorist groups but not to armed political forces like the Taliban (which did once form a government and may be open to negotiation through its offices in Qatar).

SEND IN THE DRONES

The abiding American fear of the sight of black body bags returning from some foreign field – Vietnam, and later Iraq – has led to the anxious development of methods of waging wars without human casualties – on the US side, at least. Bombing from 15,000 feet over Kosovo caused no loss of American life, although on the ground unarmed Kosovars died as a result of imprecise targeting. The drone, originally a reconnaissance and surveillance craft, has lately been armed with hellfire missiles and laser-guided bombs and is 'flown' – in fact controlled – by a large team of operators up to 12,000 miles away. There has been an exponential increase in their use for targeted killings since drones came into service for that purpose in 2005: the Obama administration has authorized their use – over Pakistan in tribal areas, Afghanistan and Yemen – ten times more often than President Bush. Their 'buzz of death' – like a lawnmower in the sky – is routinely heard over Gaza, helping Israeli forces as they try vainly to distinguish, from above crowded residential neighbourhoods, between civilians and militants.[39] There are now more hours flown by CIA-controlled drones than by the US Air Force, and more 'pilots' are being trained for unmanned aircraft than for conventional war planes.

One problem with the operation of drones by the CIA is that the intelligence services are not 'combatants' for the purposes of war law, even though they are now so much a part of a nation's defence apparatus that it is absurd to regard them as akin to the 'spies' who were exempted from war-law protection in past centuries. The fact is that the CIA does not have the transparency and accountability obligations of the other branches of government, and therefore it is impossible to discover with any certainty the number of casualties caused by drone strikes, or the extent to which they hit their targets and/or hit civilians. In May 2010 US officials claimed that drones had killed 500 combatants and only thirty civilians, but a report in late

2011, based on front-line investigations, claimed 385 civilian deaths, including 168 children. Other surveys have suggested several thousand deaths thus far, about 20 per cent of them being civilians.⁴⁰

Drone killings in the tribal areas of Pakistan and in Yemen have been widely reported. In some cases targets appear to be armed and involved in conspiratorial meetings and councils of war, but in others they have been attending weddings and funerals or are emerging from hospitals or mosques, and the lethal missile has taken its toll of family members, mourners and bystanders.⁴¹ Targeting is not always precise: in Pakistan there have been cases where pro-government leaders, their families and children, and even army soldiers, have been killed by mistake in drone attacks that have seriously damaged US relations with a politically tense, nuclear-armed nation that is not at war with the US.⁴² The Obama administration carries out these attacks, which it believes are helping it win the 'war on terror', with insouciance, and there was a lack of protest in the US until a drone strike in Yemen targeted an American citizen, Anwar Al-Awlaki, rumoured to be al-Qaida's operational leader in the area.

For this assassination the US government at least took counsel's opinion, which it subsequently refused to release, no doubt to avoid comparisons with the perverse 'torture memos' of the Bush lawyers. It is said to have concluded that Al-Awlaki's killing would be lawful if the Yemeni government consented to the attack and to the use of its airspace (it did) and if there was no possibility of arresting him – a question that does not appear to have been considered by US or Yemeni authorities. The rockets were fired at his pick-up truck, in which he might have been picked up rather than bombed to pieces (with several others who may or may not have been terrorists). The 'drone memo' apparently concluded that Executive Order 12333 did not prevent the killing of a suspect in an armed conflict between the US and al-Qaida, and that notwithstanding the Fifth Amendment's prohibition on the arbitrary deprivation of life, this constitutional right could not avail a US citizen who joined an enemy force.⁴³ This last point is correct as far as it goes, but the Fifth Amendment must entitle a citizen or his family to know whether he is on a death list and to apply to have himself taken off it. But when Al-Awlaki's father sought judicial review of the secret policy that had authorized the killing of his son, the judge told him he did not have standing. If the victim's father does not have standing to challenge a targeted killing, who does? In the UK he would have been entitled to an inquest, as would the family of the website editor killed with him, and international courts have repeatedly held that the 'right to life' implies a right to an inquiry whenever a life is violently taken by a government agency.

In this respect the Obama administration seems to have given the CIA *carte blanche* to choose targets for execution and to carry out these executions without answering for, or even admitting, that they have taken place or that they have caused civilian casualties. Under the international humanitarian law (IHL) paradigm, civilians who are suspected of terrorism cannot be lawfully targeted: the test of whether they are 'directly participating in hostilities' means they must be carrying arms or, in the case of suspected suicide bombers, there must be evidence that they are concealing explosives.[44] It would appear that the CIA does not bother with combatant/civilian categories: Yemen, for example, is not a war zone; many suspects fall into the 'civilian' class, being preachers and sympathizers and friends; those who press the hellfire buttons in Nevada do not pause to consider whether their targets are engaged in combat missions or not. However, there is no point speculating about the criteria for listing or executing: these are secret CIA prerogatives, beyond the jurisdiction of the courts or the disclosure provisions of the Freedom of Information Act.

The battlefield utility of drone technology – currently available to forty nations – means that it will be widely used in future conflicts, and by states even less scrupulous than the US and Israel. Drones will become more compact, and more difficult to detect or shoot down – already there are plans for bird and even insect-size drones, capable of crawling inside homes or squatting on window ledges to listen and send 'kill' messages to their bigger brethren without the need for any 'pilot' in Nevada to press a button. This prospect emphasizes the need for the US to make its drone operations more principled and transparent in the following ways:

1) By acting consistently with its own IHL paradigm and moving overall responsibility from the CIA to the Department of Defense,

which is more accountable and more likely to recognize the rules of international law.

2) There must be transparency both in respect of the target list and the criteria for listing, and an opportunity for those listed – however infrequently they will take it – to surrender or to seek (through friend or father) a judicial review of whether the evidence against them proves that they are the sort of active terrorist or combatant who belongs on the list.

3) Rules of engagement must exclude any killing if civilians are likely to be present.

4) Rules must prevent killing of a target who can be neutralized in other ways (e.g. if there is a reasonable prospect of capture or arrest).

Unless such steps are taken, drone killings will be correctly characterized as summary executions, and approval of them *en masse* may turn out to be Obama's Guantanamo. As William Shawcross has pointed out, after Bush era mistreatment of suspects ended, 'instead, Obama killed them . . . the widespread public acquiescence (in both the US and Europe) to aerial killing by President Obama was a powerful demonstration of the way in which political and 'moral' judgements can be driven by perception of personality and politics'.[45] The 'decapitations' credited with weakening al-Qaida may in the long run weaken the influence of the US, certainly in Pakistan, where collaboration is essential if Islamic extremism is to be successfully combated. The White House does not seem to get this: at its 2011 Correspondents' Ball, Obama joked about his advice to boys with designs on his daughters – 'I have two words for you . . . Predator drones. You will never see it coming.' The laughter, from White House correspondents who have long ignored the scandal of targeted assassinations, was not shared in Pakistan. Aziz, a sixteen-year-old boy who attended a conference organized by a British charity about the danger of this kind of Nintendo warfare, was killed by a drone a few days later – targeted, so many believe, because he attended the conference.[46]

EXECUTING BIN LADEN

On a May morning in 2011 the United States resembled the land of
the munchkins, as its people celebrated the death of the Wicked Witch
of the East. Their joy was understandable, given the terror and torment which bin Laden had freely and frequently confessed to having
put them through. The president and his generals, photographed
hunched around a White House situation room computer screen
awaiting the 'Geronimo' moment, look like witnesses at an execution.
That was what happened, when Navy commandos entered bin Lad-
en's bedroom. They shot his wife, who was shielding him, in the leg,
so as to disable her, then blasted the unarmed and unthreatening bin
Laden in the face and chest, before radioing the president: 'For God
and Country – Geronimo, Geronimo, Geronimo.' Obama turned and
said, 'We got him.' They celebrated with turkey pita wraps, cold
shrimps, potato chips and soft drinks, and notified security that tours
of the West Wing, cancelled earlier that day, could begin again. The
president told the world that 'justice was done', although as a former
law professor he knew the absurdity of that statement. What was
done, by his authority, had nothing to do with justice: it was a cold-
blooded execution of public enemy no. 1.

President Clinton claims to have secretly authorized bin Laden's
assassination after al-Qaida's truck bombings of US embassies in
Kenya and Tanzania in 1998. After 9/11, when President Bush had
called for his 'head on a plate', a US $50 million bounty was put on
that head. It produced no intelligence, and nor did torture of his associates, contrary to opportunist claims by Bush loyalists after the
killing. The water boarding (183 times) of Khalid Sheikh Mohammed
produced only the false information that a courier called Al-Kuwaiti
was 'retired' and of little significance, whereas Al-Kuwaiti was in fact
of enormous significance and his car was tracked by Pakistani investigators (hired by the CIA). It led them to a large compound behind
barbed-wire-topped high-security walls in Abbottabad, near Pakistan's leading military academy. The CIA sent stealth aircraft to
photograph it from the air and spies took a safe-house nearby and
photographed it from the ground; telephone calls were intercepted
and after several months of surveillance, the shadowy male figure in

the compound was identified.[47] It was extraordinary that bin Laden had hidden safely for years under the very noses of the Pakistan military – so extraordinary that it gave rise to the inference that he must have been protected by elements of the ISI (Pakistani intelligence). Reasonably enough, the US on this basis ruled out any joint operation with Pakistan. (There has never been any corroboration of the inference that bin Laden was being protected, and cock-up being more likely than conspiracy, he doubtless survived precisely because no one would ever think of looking for him in Abbottabad.) But the rejection of any form of co-operation with Pakistan did reduce US options for dealing with him, either to a strike by heavy B-2 bombers, which would obliterate the compound, or a helicopter assault with highly trained commandos. The bombing option was ruled out, not because it would kill everybody but because there was a danger that the Pakistani armed forces would detect the bombers and shoot them down in the belief that they were an Indian air force attack. That left the commando raid, in low-flying, under-the-radar helicopters.

Was the invasion of Pakistan's airspace, as its government complained, an unlawful incursion on its state sovereignty? An invasion it certainly was, but the legality depended on the reasonableness of the belief in Pakistani complicity. Bin Laden had been indicted in the US for terrorist mass murders and there was overwhelming evidence that he was a major international criminal, whom it appeared that Pakistani authorities were harbouring. The US was entitled to apprehend him, and to do so in the only way that would be likely to succeed, i.e. by keeping its operation secret from the sovereign state. Although it now turns out that Pakistani agents were probably not complicit in hiding him, it looked at the time as if they were. Just as Israel was entitled to invade Uganda's sovereignty to free the Entebbe hostages, and to kidnap Eichmann without notice to Argentina, so the US was justified in its stealthy snatch mission – always supposing that its objective was to capture bin Laden if possible and to kill him only if necessary.

It is this question which really matters. The White House first put out a false story about his death occurring in a 'firefight', and when this did not wash they said the president had ordered a 'capture or kill' operation – although that presidential order has never been produced. Subsequently one national security official has admitted that there was never any intention of capturing bin Laden alive, and that the Navy SEAL team was told, 'We think we found bin Laden, and your job is to kill him' – to which the commandos responded with cheers.[48] There was a quick shuffle of military personnel over to the CIA because the US was not at war with Pakistan, and this had to be a covert civilian operation, so despite its use of Navy commandos, it was conducted under CIA statutes. There was some shooting of other people in the compound: Al-Kuwaiti and his brother, and bin Laden's son were killed but only one of them was armed. Bin Laden was unarmed, and although there was an AK-47 and a pistol in the room, he had not reached for them and they were not found until after his death. He would seem to have been killed without being given a chance to surrender, or time to take any action at all. He was buried at sea, in order that his tomb would not become a shrine, without the post-mortem or inquest that Pakistan's domestic law requires. Photographs of his cleaned-up body on a mortuary trolley have been withheld by the White House so they would not become iconic, like Che Guevara on the slab. The US simply refused to accept the human rights rule that the right to life requires a public inquiry whenever violent death occurs from government or police action.

It is fairly clear that any such inquiry would have revealed that bin Laden was executed without having been given any opportunity to surrender, in circumstances where he could simply have been disabled (like his wife), by being shot in the leg. The law permits criminals to be killed in self-defence, if they or their accomplices resist arrest in ways that endanger those striving to apprehend them. They should, if possible, be given the opportunity to surrender, but even if they do not put up their hands or wave a white flag they should be taken alive if that can be achieved without risk, and their captors are entitled to disable them if necessary to reduce that risk. Much would depend on whether the Navy SEALs thought there was such a risk to themselves that they could eliminate it only by killing their target, but the circumstances suggest that a commando of reasonable fortitude would not have hesitated to capture bin Laden if his instructions had required it – another reason for believing they did not. By killing him, of course, they precluded any intelligence benefits that might have accrued from his interrogation: had he been broken or 'turned' or simply told the truth from boastfulness or in the hope of a plea bargain, his information might have helped to destroy al-Qaida. They also gave him the consummation he most devoutly wished, namely a fast-track to paradise. His belief system held that the perfect death was mid-jihad, from an infidel bullet.

The security problems that would have arisen at any trial should not be minimized nor the danger of it ending up as a squalid circus like that of Saddam Hussein. But the notion that any form of legal process would have been too hard must be rejected. Khalid Sheikh Mohammed, also (and confusingly) alleged to be the architect of 9/11, faces a trial of sorts (a military commission) and had bin Laden been captured he could have been put in the dock alongside him, so that their joint or separate responsibility could have been properly examined.

Bin Laden could not have been tried for 9/11 at the International Criminal Court – its jurisdiction came into existence only on 7/12, nine months later. But the Security Council could have set up an *ad hoc* tribunal in The Hague, with international judges (including Muslim jurists) to provide a fair trial and a reasoned verdict that would have convinced the Arab street of his guilt and his unworthiness. This would have been the best way of demystifying this man, debunking his cause and de-brainwashing his followers. In the dock he would have been reduced in stature – never more to be remembered as the tall, soulful figure on the mountain, but as a hateful and hate-filled old man, screaming from the bar or lying from the witness box. Since his videos exult in the killing of innocent civilians, any cross-examination would have emphasized his inhumanity. These benefits that flow from real justice were forgone by the choice of summary execution.

It was not always thus. When the time came to consider the fate of men even more steeped in wickedness than Osama bin Laden – namely the Nazi leadership – the British government wanted them hanged within six hours of capture. President Truman demurred, citing the conclusion of Justice Robert Jackson that summary execution 'would not sit easily on the American conscience or be remembered by our children with pride ... the only course is to determine the innocence or guilt of the accused after a hearing as dispassionate as the times will permit and upon a record that will leave our reasons and motives clear' (see p. 308). He insisted upon judgment at Nuremberg, which has confounded Holocaust-deniers ever since its delivery. Killing instead of capturing Osama bin Laden was a missed opportunity to prove to the world that this charismatic leader was in fact a vicious criminal, who deserved to die of old age in prison after years of mental suffering, rather than instantaneously, as a martyr to his inhuman cause.

FAIR TRIALS FOR INTERNATIONAL TERRORISTS?

The question of how to process 'terrorist' prisoners captured in battle should be answered by reference to the Geneva Conventions, which require them to be released to their home state or be put on a fair trial. The purpose of such trial would be to assess their guilt of any war crime that could be alleged against them, and to decide whether they were in fact 'terrorists' who had conspired to commit a crime against humanity. Since it was not a crime to join the Taliban, or even al-Qaida if the intention was to train for service in the KLA in Kosovo, for example, guilt in the case of captured fighters would hinge on their knowledge of or participation in al-Qaida's wider objective to massacre Americans. In all cases, the need is to find a court which can offer defendants a fair trial.

SPECIAL MILITARY COMMISSIONS

The perpetrators of 9/11 'don't deserve to be treated as prisoners of war', declared Vice-President Cheney, announcing the President's Executive Order, signed by President Bush on 13 November 2001, to provide an alternative method of trial for 'unlawful combatants'. 'They don't deserve the same guarantees and safeguards that would be used for an American citizen going through the normal judicial process.'[49] Instead, they deserved to be 'executed in relatively rapid order' like a team of German saboteurs tried in secret during the Second World War by a 'special military commission'. This is a presidentially ordained tribunal last used to convict General Yamashita, one of the few Japanese generals whom historians now believe was innocent. The US proposed such a court to Scottish law officers as a model for Lockerbie, but they emphatically rejected it because of its palpable unfairness. It is important to understand that a 'military commission' is not the same as a court martial – a genuine court in the Anglo-American adversary tradition used to try members of the armed forces and familiar from movies like *A Few Good Men* (in which Tom Cruise and Demi Moore proved that 'military justice' is not a contradiction in terms). A 'special military commission' comprises a group of officers ordered by the president, their commander-in-chief, to sit in judgment on certain defendants according to rules set out in the presidential order.

The President's order of 13 November was premised on a state of emergency which made it inexpedient to apply 'the principles of law and the rules of evidence generally recognized in the trial of criminal cases'. The order applied to all non-US citizens whom 'I determine from time to time in writing' are reasonably believed to be members of al-Qaida, or else have aided and abetted acts of terrorism (or have 'knowingly harboured' individuals preparing for such acts) which are designed to affect adversely 'the US, its citizens, national security, foreign policy or economy'. All suspects shall be placed at the disposal of the Defense Department, which shall detain them 'humanely' until their trial. This was to be by a 'military commission', i.e. a body of military officers, paid and promoted by the Defense Department, commissioned by the president to try terrorist suspects. The commission shall admit any evidence which its presiding officer thinks would 'have probative value to a reasonable person'. The military commission is given exclusive jurisdiction over these suspects, who shall not

be privileged to seek any remedy or maintain any proceedings, directly or indirectly, in

i)   any court of the United States,
ii)   any court of any foreign nation, or
iii) any international tribunal.

These military commissions would, as *The New York Times* editorialized, be 'a breathtaking departure from due process'.[50] When first announced, they were to sit in secret, without any presumption of innocence and no provision for appeal. Pressure from allies and human rights organizations forced the Defense Department to abandon these unfair provisions under rules revised in March 2002 which required unanimity in passing a death sentence and promised some form of 'review' by civilian lawyers. But the commissions still fail abjectly to conform with the fair-trial guarantees under the European Convention, a matter which would prevent the extradition to the US of terrorist suspects captured in Europe if there is a prospect that they would be subjected to commissions of this kind.[51] A trial of al-Qaida members or Taliban leaders before such a military commission, especially if followed by executions 'in relatively rapid order', would provoke anger throughout the world, much of it from US allies and supporters. The principal objections would be:

1.   The commission, and the body of military officers who will review its convictions, are not independent or impartial, as required by Articles 3 and 84 of Geneva Convention III and by customary international law (reflecting Article 75 of the Geneva Protocol). The army officers who act as 'judges' are paid and promoted by the Defense Department, an arm of the government which has alleged the guilt of the defendants and which acts in any event as their detaining power.[52] These officers are commissioned to sit as 'judges' by the president, their commander-in-chief, who has 'determined in writing' that the defendants should be prosecuted and who thus has a vested interest in their conviction.

2.   The president or his nominee, the defense secretary, cannot be impartial in deciding whether to commute the sentence because it will have been imposed by his own tribunal.

3. There are no normal evidentiary rules or safeguards – evidence is admissible if the presiding officer thinks it would have 'probative value to a reasonable person', i.e. to himself. A distinguished US judge who made a study of the records of military commissions in Japan after the Second World War concluded that they 'provide a stark example of the potential for abuse when rules of evidence are so flexible as to be non-existent'.[53] General Yamashita's commission hearing was aptly described by a dissenting Supreme Court justice: 'a more complete abrogation of customary safeguards relating to the proof . . . hardly could have been made . . . the directive made the commission a law unto itself. It acted accordingly . . . [it] consistently ruled against the defense . . . Every conceivable kind of statement, rumor, report, at first, second, third or further hand, written, printed or oral, and one 'propaganda' film were allowed to come in.'[54]

4. Prisoners have no access to civilian courts. Death sentences will be imposed by the unanimous vote of a 'jury' of army officers who give no reasons for conviction or sentence. There will be no appeal on the merits but rather an application to a group of senior lawyers who will 'review' the conviction – i.e. recommend that it be quashed if it is irrational, but not if there remains a lurking doubt over guilt.

The 'special military commission' has been much vilified – usually as a 'kangaroo court' (a description disliked by Australians, who cannot understand how these lovable marsupials ever came to be associated with injustice), but in truth it is not a court at all. It is an extension of the executive power of the president, a prerogative body as unacceptable today as the Star Chamber of the Stuart kings was unacceptable, in the dawn of modern democracy, to the Long Parliament. The procedures of the special military commission have been improved since that original executive order of November 2001, both in the latter stages of the Bush presidency and under Obama, but the basic objection remains – it is not a court, it is a panel of five military officers, employees of the same authority that detains and prosecutes the defendants. The commission's first hearings at Guantanamo in August 2004,[55] were comical. It turned out that only one member – the presiding officer, Colonel Brownback – was legally qualified. How did he get the job? Because, he explained, he was a close friend of the major-general who is supervising the whole tribunal and who is head of the appointing authority that appoints the prosecutor as well. They are such close friends that they 'roasted' each other at their retirement parties. Colonel Brownback admitted in answer to defence questions that he had let his law licence lapse and he would need to take some refresher courses before he could recommence practice.

The presiding officer combines the role of judge and juror. He makes the legal rulings, then he participates with the other four officers in deciding the facts and bringing the verdict, like a judge who retires with the jury. One of the officer/jurors admitted at the 2004 hearings that he had been in charge of the logistics of bringing the detainees from Afghanistan to Guantanamo – rather like the prison guard who escorts the prisoners to the court, then takes a seat in the jury box. Another officer/juror was the senior intelligence officer in Afghanistan, in the manner of an FBI agent who sits as a juror on a case brought by the FBI, having helped to generate the intelligence that led to the arrest. Most of these officers have no previous experience passing judgment or making legal determinations. This qualification is essential, because the rules of evidence are so vague (anything is admissible that 'would have probative value to a reasonable person') and it does require forensic experience to understand, for example, the fallibility of 'fleeting glance' identifications, of induced prison-cell confessions and of hearsay statements untested by cross-examination. The panel members have no expertise in sentencing – which is entirely at their discretion and may include a death sentence. The special military commissions have had a bizarre history, their make-up and procedures going back and forth between Congress and the Supreme Court. After they were declared non-compliant with the Geneva Conventions in the 2006 case of *Hamdan* v. *Rumsfeld*, Congress made some cosmetic changes, having previously passed an Act that denied detainees any opportunity to challenge their continuing incarceration or the decisions of the military commission by way of *habeas corpus*. This law was struck down by the Supreme Court in the 2008 case of *Boumediene* v. *Bush* because it effectively removed the right of *habeas corpus*. Fearful of another successful challenge to the special military commissions, Congress made some further minor amendments in 2009. At that point, of course, Obama's Attorney-General, Eric Holder, was still promising to close Guantanamo and to have those serious criminals, against whom they could bring evidence untainted by torture, tried by juries in Federal courtrooms in New York. These promises were negated by a public and Congressional outcry: Americans were simply not prepared to have Guantanamo inmates on their soil. As matters stand, various cases challenging the constitutionality of special military commissions are wending their way, once again, towards the Supreme Court.

The basic problem is that these commissioners lack the *appearance* of impartiality, and more importantly they lack independence. The appointing authority is a section of the Defense Department, which is responsible for selecting the prosecution charges and is supervised by the Defense Secretary. So, in effect, the Guantanamo panels are emanations of the Defense Department, the same department which employs the prosecutors and the lead defence attorneys, all of whom are military officers and who have been imposed on the defendants, who will not, it seems, even under Obama, be allowed to defend themselves. They will be permitted to hire at their own expense private attorneys to assist those army lawyers imposed upon them, so long as those attorneys pass a security clearance. Most unacceptably, communications between defendants and counsel will be monitored, so there is no attorney–client privilege. The prosecution can withhold evidence – even 'potentially exculpatory' evidence – from the lead defence counsel, even though he or she will be an army officer. At least there is the possibility of review by four respected civilian lawyers, but they do not form a court of appeal, and they are not required to hold hearings.

These commissions do not satisfy the fair-trial standards in the Geneva Conventions or in the Civil Covenant, both ratified by the US which is thereby bound by Article 2 to extend Convention rights

'to all individuals within its territory and subject to its jurisdiction' –
i.e. to Guantanamo Bay, after the decision in *Rasul* v. *Bush*, and they
will not be perceived by the rest of the world as satisfying those standards. The American Bar Association was among the first to condemn
the process, on the basis that the US military is captor, jailor, prosecutor, defender, judge of fact, judge of law and sentencer with no appeal
to an independent judicial body. American judges have been more
restrained, although in the *Hamdi* v. *Rumsfeld* case decided with
Rasul, the US Supreme Court majority stated: 'We have long since
made clear that a state of war is not a blank cheque for the President
when it comes to the rights of the nation's citizens.' US citizens, of
course, are constitutionally guaranteed a fair trial, so 'unlawful combatant' John Walker Lindh was quickly liberated from Guantanamo
to face a fair jury trial in a US district court – an admission (if one was
needed) that what other detainees are receiving is not 'justice' at all.
The UK's attorney-general has made this clear, following British judge
Lord Steyn's condemnation of the special military commission as a
'mockery of justice'.[56]

A proper trial for the Guantanamo detainees looks unlikely. It
would have been so easy to call upon real and independent judges to
do the job, much more expeditiously and effectively than military
officers who, for all their wish to be fair, cannot disentangle themselves or their appointments from the US military authority that
brings the prosecution. The 'special military commission', if allowed
to proceed after the spate of appeals currently besetting it, will be
perceived as 'victor's justice', as summary as the US Defense Department can get away with, at a time when the American public does not
protest very loudly about denial of constitutional rights to aliens. It
marks an historic *volte-face* from the position of Truman and Jackson, who rejected the military commission model when it was
suggested for Nuremberg. There were, of course, alternatives. If credible evidence exists against any Guantanamo detainees of complicity
in 9/11 or in any other al-Qaida conspiracy to kill Americans, they
could have been brought to trial in New York. Zacarias Moussaoui,
the French citizen charged with being the twentieth hijacker in the
conspiracy behind the 11 September attacks, was afforded trial by a

jury in Virginia (he was arrested on immigration charges in August whilst learning to fly).

JURY TRIAL

However, jury trial in the US has drawbacks. A New York jury, literally 'twelve angry men', might be too emotionally involved in the events of 9/11 to consider the evidence dispassionately. One word – 'guilty' – from the jury foreman would not be calculated to convince in the mosques of Pakistan or the universities of Europe: what is needed for this purpose is a closely and carefully reasoned judgment, joined by Muslim jurists, setting out an incontrovertible, 'beyond reasonable doubt', case for guilt. Moreover, upon conviction, the jury would hear evidence to decide the punishment, and given the casualties of 9/11 some death penalties would be a foregone conclusion.

The outcome of the Moussaoui trial might be seen as a vindication of the American jury in that it resisted the prosecution's outrageous attempts to inflame it into a death sentence decision by playing tapes from the cockpit voice recorder of the last minutes of the brave passengers on the hijacked UA flight 93. The six-week trial certainly did not glamorize the defendant or provide him with a political platform – he screamed abuse at Americans and wildly exaggerated his role in an obvious ploy to secure a death sentence (and consequent martyrdom). In fact, this case called for the most careful and reasoned analysis of the defendant's true role and of the failures of law enforcement agencies to uncover it, but such judgments cannot emerge from the evidential free-for-all of a jury trial.

A jury trial is at least a full-blooded adversary affair in which the defendants could, if they chose, be aggressively defended and the government evidence can be tested for all to see its truth or its falsity. The fear that a trial might be exploited to provide a soapbox for enemy philosophy was short-lived in the case of Moussaoui whose interventions only served (as they were intended) to condemn him. The issues at a criminal trial concern what the defendants did, and what knowledge they had of what their accomplices were doing:

their political and religious beliefs are irrelevant. There is no forensic basis for permitting speeches or evidence to justify the crime.

THE LOCKERBIE ALTERNATIVE

An appropriate precedent for trying foreign nationals on charges of international terrorism is an especially convened, but none the less independent and impartial, judicial tribunal. A special court was established by the US and UK to try the two Libyan intelligence officers accused of placing a bomb on board Pan Am flight 103, which had exploded over Lockerbie in Scotland on 21 December 1988, killing 259 passengers and crew. The court, which convicted the senior officer, Abdul Basset Ali Al-Megrahi (his conviction was confirmed on appeal in March 2002), reflected territorial jurisdiction (the offence having been committed in Scotland) by comprising three Scottish judges, applying Scots law and giving audience only to Scottish advocates. It sat at Camp Zeist – a disused American airbase in the Netherlands, which had been placed under UK sovereignty for the purpose of the trial. The charge was conspiracy to murder, rather than to commit a crime against humanity, but the international justice principle that such crimes required a reasoned verdict was adopted, removing the jury and allowing the judges to determine facts as well as law. An international flavour also came from the fact that the prosecution was a joint operation, the evidence having been worked up over twelve years by US as well as Scottish law enforcement agencies.

The Lockerbie model, although the outcome of many years of US pressure and UN sanctions, offered an alternative mode for trial of any detainees suspected of complicity with al-Qaida, or for those on CIA 'suspect' lists who are captured before they can be killed by drones. It could take the form of three independent professional American Federal judges, sitting in a neutral location but operating under and applying the law of the state of New York, delivering a reasoned written decision in lieu of a jury verdict, with a normal right of appeal.

Lockerbie may be a 'one-off' situation: it reflected a bargain under which Colonel Gaddafi obtained relief from economic sanctions and the possibility of his own indictment (since he must have approved the terrorist plan) in return for handing over intelligence officers suspected of planting the bomb and exposing his country to compensation demands (in 2005 Libya paid $2.7 billion to victims' relatives). He had, of course, offered to try the suspects in Libya – a ploy that was flatly rejected, given that state's evident complicity – and then to surrender them for trial by the ICJ (inappropriate) or an international jury (cumbersome, and no reasoned verdict).

The importance of the trial was that it established, to the satisfaction of three experienced Scots judges (and five more on appeal) that the bomb was planted by an agent of Libya, not by terrorist groups supported by Iran or Syria. The open and adversarial nature of the proceedings also served the interests of truth – in particular by subjecting the CIA's star witness to a cross-examination which comprehensively destroyed his credibility,[57] and through painstaking forensic science, which found tell-tale clues in tiny fragments which fell from 31,000 feet (the 'made in Malta' label from the Babygro jumpsuit covering the suitcase bomb). The reasoned verdict proved important, not least because it has informed subsequent debate over the correctness of Al-Megrahi's conviction.

Lockerbie stands as an important acknowledgement in state practice of the overriding importance of bringing terrorists to justice. It also provides a good example of why international criminal courts should abolish the so-called 'right of silence'. Al-Megrahi was too craven to enter the witness box to face cross-examination, later claiming that his lawyers advised him to remain silent. This may well have been because they feared his guilt would have been exposed had he done so, but as a matter of morality, whenever a court holds that the prosecution has established a *prima facie* case of mass murder against the defendant, the relatives of victims and the public should be entitled to an explanation. If he refuses to take the opportunity to testify, his refusal should be a factor in the assessment of whether he is guilty. Al-Megrahi's supporters who claim that 'he always asserted his innocence' overlook the fact that he failed to assert it at the appropriate time, namely in the witness box at his trial.[58] The 'right to silence' is a valuable protection to suspects against being forced to incriminate themselves in police stations after their arrest but is inappropriate at the trial, by which time they will have had years of legal advice to prepare themselves for cross-examinations. The so-called 'right' has been abolished in England, where it originated, but not in any international court.

A UN TRIBUNAL

The Security Council could be requested, for the trial of suspected major terrorists, such as those accused of planning an atrocity like 9/11, to use its Chapter VII power to establish an *ad hoc* tribunal, as it had in The Hague for former Yugoslavia and in Arusha for Rwanda. The Council would readily have acceded to such a request, given its unanimous support for the US after 9/11, which it had characterized in two September 2001 Resolutions as a threat to international peace (the precondition for exercise of Chapter VII power). There would have been no difficulty about appointing a high-profile American prosecutor, and judges, including Muslim jurists, could have been appointed from coalition countries. The Hague Tribunal rules of evidence and procedure afford basic rights to defendants whilst permitting the reception of all relevant and reliable evidence, with protocols for evaluating the kind of hearsay evidence which may be necessary to prove terrorist conspiracies and which protect from public disclosure on national-security grounds the identity of informers or evidence from electronic intercepts and other means of secret intelligence-gathering. A trial of top terror suspects would be most appropriately held in The Hague, away from local pressures and prejudices in America or Afghanistan.

It has been argued that 'it is hard to say the US owes foreign terrorists a higher standard of justice than it affords its own troops – which is, after all, military justice too'.[59] This is misconceived, because there is a qualitative difference between military justice administered to US troops through the court martial system, and the 'special military commissions' which are not 'courts' in any meaningful sense. Foreigners suspected of terrorism, and foreign government officials charged with complicity and captured in their own state, are entitled to a trial which accords with the minimum standards of international criminal justice – which a special military commission does not meet.

Although an international court was first proposed by the League of Nations in 1937 to deal with terrorist crimes, and the idea was revived in 1987 by President Gorbachev for the same purpose, today cynical diplomats and nervous politicians raise spectres of terrorists who will be permitted to justify their crimes from the witness box, or guilty men who will walk free on legal technicalities or by retaining clever defence counsel. But this has not been the UK's experience in bringing IRA bombers to justice (the gravest danger has been of prejudiced juries and wrongful convictions) or of the US in trials of violent radicals of the 1960s and 1970s. There is no reason why an international court cannot perform as well as a local court in this respect (with the added presentational advantage over a jury of producing a written and reasoned judgment). In judging political and military leaders, the international court has the advantage of impartiality, and can apply 'command responsibility' principles. 'Heroic' terrorist leaders would be subject to a demystifying process which confronts them with evidence of the moral and physical squalor in which they have operated, with their hypocrisies and cruelties, and with the barbaric results of their rhetoric and theology. Any cult status they have acquired must dissipate with the evidence that their savage God has failed. Their promises to credulous followers of triumph, or of a martyr's glorious death, will be refuted by the simple fact that these leaders are now neither in power nor in paradise, but in the dock.

This is one reason, of course, why many al-Qaida members refused to come out with their hands up. Their choice of suicide rather than surrender derived from the superstition that by dying mid-jihad they would be transported into paradise, but there was also a recognition among the leadership that capture, followed by trial, would damage the cause. That is because a criminal trial would strip bare its philosophical basis and reduce it to one essential element: the *mens rea* for commission of a crime against humanity. The hateful and hate-filled mind thus displayed – through prosecution evidence and the optional addition of the defendant's testimony (confined to the issue of whether he really did intend to kill innocent civilians) – would not inspire love or respect or emulation. Logic has its limits in persuading people bent on glory through death: fanatical minds cannot be prised open by rational argument, and terrorism of this nature self-evidently will not be deterred by the death penalty. But since their belief is essentially mystical, a process of demystifying its apostles is necessary: a fair trial of al-Qaida leaders might serve to start the deprogramming process.

THE CRIME OF TERRORISM

The first fundamentalist 'suicide bomber' to terrify London was Guy Fawkes, caught quite literally 'bang to rights' with matches and explosives in a cellar under the House of Commons. That was exactly 400 years ago, since when the killing of innocent civilians has been a tactic variously of Fenians, Narodniks, Weathermen, Malaysian communists and IRA bombers, well before the terrorist incidents that trouble today's world. After the New York aeroplane attacks of 9/11 (2001) and the London tube and bus bombings of 7/7 (2005) came the disco in Bali, the train in Madrid, the cafés in Israel, the theatre in Moscow, the school in Beslan and the hotels in Mumbai – repeated and fearful reminders of the calculated cruelty of fanatics. Their object is to provoke responses so repressive that they will encourage recruits and supporters who would never otherwise help their cause. If any lesson could be drawn from the previous history of terrorist alarums and excursions, it was not to overreact: abandoning basic human rights was not only a form of surrender, it was calculated to give the terrorists exactly what they wanted. The 'propaganda of the deed' derived from reprisals – from tortured suspects, from internment, and from over-hastily convicting the innocent. Today's Islamic terrorism, for example, may be traced back to the torture of the Muslim brotherhood in Nasser's Egyptian jails, via Israeli ill-treatment of Palestinians. The smartest counter-terrorism does not deal in *lex talionis* – an eye for an eye – and nor does it use the inflated rhetoric of war: it treats terrorism as a very serious crime to be combated by better intelligence gathering and more effective police work, together with close international cooperation. As the 9/11 Commission put it: 'The US government should offer an example of moral leadership to the world, committed to treat people humanely, abide by the rule of law, and be generous and caring to our neighbours.'[60]

Inevitably, however, the impact of 9/11 and 7/7 and the other terrorist atrocities has been to cause damage to civil liberties in some domestic jurisdictions, most notably the US and UK, which have cut back *habeas corpus* as a protection for aliens (who may be residents of many years' standing): under new 'anti-terrorism' legislation they may be held without charge and without limit of time if suspected of terrorist associations. This is a breach of Articles 8 and 9 of the Universal Declaration, which guarantee an effective remedy and prohibit arbitrary arrest and detention. These oppressive measures have been justified by reference to a 'state of emergency', although this is not an excuse the Universal Declaration admits: it allows states to punish such exercises of its freedoms as are incompatible with UN principles (Article 29(3)), or are aimed at destroying the rights of others (Article 30) but not by unfair procedures. Even if customary law provides a 'state of emergency' exception, like the European Convention, this refers to situations that temporarily 'threaten the life of the nation'. Islamic terrorism threatens to take lives, from time to time, in Western nations, but not to impair state functions or cause more than temporary inconvenience. In 2004 the House of Lords stopped indefinite detention of aliens (mainly Algerians) suspected of terrorism in the UK because this amounted to discriminatory treatment, contrary to Article 14 of the European Convention. It should have decided that indefinite detention for anyone, alien or not, was contrary to Magna Carta and common law and that no 'state of emergency' – by definition, a temporary state – could justify *indefinite* detention for anyone. Similarly, attempts to stop radical preachers by inventing new hate-speech crimes are doomed to failure. It is an offence in most jurisdictions to incite violence or incite others to commit murder or to bring about civilian deaths recklessly: not even the First Amendment to the US constitution protects those who shout 'fire' in crowded theatres. But criminal restrictions on speech create martyrs or drive terrorist recruiters underground (at one stage, the UK proposed a law against 'glorifying terrorism' so wide it would have banned a sympathetic biography of Robespierre).

The wartime jurisprudence of major countries abounds in statements by nervous judges that their review powers must be surrendered to the executive because the existence of the country is imperilled ('the constitution is not a suicide pact'). This is a counsel of timidity rather than logic, since there is no rational basis for the belief that availability of judicial review could force a surrender or seriously handicap the exercise of defence powers, much less so in a situation where the 'war' is not being fought against a powerful state but against ill-defined 'terrorists'. Since 'necessity' is the touchstone, detention of suspected terrorists may be justified, but not without provision for judicial scrutiny to ensure that there is some basis for the suspicion and access to lawyers to argue that there is not. Allowing civil liberties to be determined solely by the executive or the military because there is an emergency is to commit the fallacy exposed by Justice Douglas when the Supreme Court prevented the president from using the Korean War as an excuse to order the nationalization of a steel mill without putting legislation through Congress: 'while an emergency does not create power, emergency may furnish the occasion for the exercise of power'.[61] Just as an emergency cannot justify depriving Congress of legislative power, nor can it deny the courts their constitutional function of ensuring that the legislation is valid: 'True it is that an emergency may be the occasion which calls for the legislation, but it is the nature of the legislation itself, and not the existence of emergency, that must determine whether it is valid or not',[62] and whether it has been properly construed and applied in a particular case. The *erga omnes* obligation of every state under international human rights law precludes, even in times of terrorism, the summary execution of suspects, or their punishment by non-independent, unjudicial tribunals, or their arrest and detention in a manner which is arbitrary because it permits of no legal challenge.

The long-term legacy of bin Laden and the Taliban will be to cut back the second of President Roosevelt's 'four freedoms', that of religion. The framers of the Universal Declaration did not envisage 'holy war' theology – the salvation of one's soul through calculated slaughter of innocents, when they drafted Article 18, which guarantees the freedom '. . . in community with others and in public . . . to manifest religion or belief in teaching, practice, worship and observance'. If 9/11 was a manifestation of the religious duty of jihad by practice and observance – as undoubtedly, for its supporters, it was – then this is a kind of freedom that has no place in any human rights treaty. (It is, of course, denied by Article 30 since it involves an act aimed at the destruction of the right to life guaranteed to others.) Similarly, Article 20 of the International Covenant on Civil and Political Rights, which calls upon state parties to introduce laws against advocacy of religious as well as racial hatred, will require more careful consideration. The religious hatred to be outlawed must 'constitute incitement to discrimination, hostility or violence', a formula which would cover an exhortation to a jihad against Christians. But looking at the other side of the coin, it should not be unlawful to incite loathing for any religion which violates human rights as excessively as that form of Wahhabism practised by the Taliban, or to incite hostility against those hate-filled extremists who kill civilians of other faiths in the name of religion. One man's blasphemy is another man's bedtime reading: Article 20's attempt to protect religion is objectionable because, unlike race, religion is – or should be – freely changeable and hence open to the fiercest polemic or satire.

The greatest challenge of 9/11 to national law and policy will be to reach universal agreement on the definition of terrorism, or at least (since 'terrorism' is really a description of a technique for committing crimes of violence) on the kinds of terrorism that should attract international action and punishment. There are no less than twelve UN conventions which refer to terrorist acts such as hijacking and hostage-taking, but none offers a generic description. One formula that the UN offers came from its Sixth Committee in December 1994:

Criminal acts intended or calculated to provoke a state of terror in the general public, a group of persons or particular persons for political reasons are in any circumstances unjustifiable, whatever the considerations of a political, philosophical, ideological, racial, ethnic, religious or other nature that may be used to justify them.

This is so broad as to be meaningless – because most serious criminal acts are intended to provoke terror in particular persons. A better definition is to be found in Article 2 of the International Convention for the Suppression of the Financing of Terrorism (1999), which focuses upon the targeting of civilians and is notable (in Article 5) for extending complicity to artificial entities, such as banks and finance companies whose officials deliberately or recklessly allow transfers of funds to dubious customers. But the Convention does not create a crime of terrorism and it leaves to sovereign state parties' discretion to regulate rather than prosecute the offending corporations. For all our talk of terrorism, there is still no 'international crime' and no universally agreed definition. The best this Convention can offer is the following:

Any other act intended to cause death or serious bodily injury to a civilian, or to any other person not taking an active part in the hostilities in a situation of an armed conflict, when the purpose of such act, by its nature or context, is to intimidate a population, or to compel a government or an international organization to do or to abstain from doing any act.

Attempts to formulate a legal definition have always foundered, in drafting of conventions and debating General Assembly resolutions, on the inconvenient fact that one person's terrorist is another's freedom fighter, so that the label of 'terrorist' is merely a pejorative description of the insurgents whose aims we do not like (or whose enemies we do). Terror tactics, as developed by the Narodnik opponents of the Tsar in the late nineteenth century, were calculated to provoke savage, disproportionate reprisals which would prove counter-productive by rallying popular support against the repressive regime. Al-Qaida is not unique in its use of terror techniques: before it began in earnest, each year between 1990 and 1996 brought 4,300 terrorist attacks in the world, with eight civilian casualties for every soldier who fell. It is this propensity, and often intention, to produce civilian deaths that makes terrorism unconscionable in the twenty-first century, no matter how justified its political objectives. States which fight are bound by the Geneva Conventions to avoid civilian casualties if at all possible: there can no longer be any reason not to hold insurgents, who aspire to run states, to the same standard. Freedom fighters must not be supported – they should, on the contrary, be arrested – if mass murder of civilians is part of their record or the inevitable result of their policies. This means something that Arab states wilfully refuse to understand, namely that when Hamas finances, approves and directs a suicide-bombing campaign, its leaders are guilty of perpetrating a crime which is against humanity, as well as against Israelis. But this does not give Israel a 'self-defence' mandate to kill Palestinians, let alone to conduct an operation like the 2009–10 attack on Gaza which targeted civilians and their homes. International criminal law attempts to square a vicious circle by condemning both terrorists and states that respond with needless or disproportionate force.

Those leaders who promote either terrorism or lawless anti-terrorism as a consistent act of policy have become, at least in theory, vulnerable to ICC jurisdiction in respect of acts committed after 1 July 2002. The concept of the crime against humanity is neutral: it makes a crucial distinction, which hinges not on the politics of the perpetrator but on the horrendous nature of the deed. Individual terrorist acts that cause 'collateral damage' may stay beneath the severity threshold, and remain for domestic law to prosecute and punish. But terrorist conspiracies which envisage widespread or systematic attacks to mass murder innocent civilians are a breach of international criminal law just as much as needless army killings of civilians. They should attract universal jurisdiction and when domestic prosecution is unavailable, the conflict should be certified by the Security Council as fit for investigation and trial by the ICC.

This is the answer to the US claim that it is 'at war' with terror and with terrorists. This claim is mere rhetoric, invoking by sleight of language that vast body of law applicable to wars between nations, but not to battles with criminals. War law entitles armies to kill enemy combatants and commanders in the ordinary course of operations, whilst criminal law requires treatment of gang members with force that is reasonable in the circumstances. The US and Israeli preference for summary execution of suspects – by drone attacks or 'kill operations' of the kind that took out bin Laden – presupposes that al-Qaida is a state. It is, on the contrary, an exceptionally dangerous criminal gang which takes no prisoners or, if it does, refuses to acknowledge that it is bound by law to treat them humanely. The international scope of its operations, and its utter disregard for human life, brings its widespread and systematic operations within the definition of crimes against humanity, although they cannot be characterized as war crimes. That means the ICC has jurisdiction to investigate and to prosecute, if they are nationals of a ratifying state or have committed crimes on its territory, or if a 'situation' where they have committed crimes is referred by the Security Council. Usually, terrorists should be tried in the country where they are captured, or else extradited for trial in the domestic courts of the country where they have done damage. But the ICC is an appropriate court of last resort for a trial of terrorist leaders who cannot receive justice in states that have already declared them guilty. Bin Laden and Tamil Tiger leader Velupillai Prabhakaran had their lives been spared, and Öcalan (the Kurdish nationalist leader) and Guzman ('the Shining Path' leader in Peru) provide examples of guerrilla heads who could, under this analysis, be tried by an international court, as could Pablo Escobar, General Noriega and other crime bosses who give orders to kill, at random, across state lines. This is not to say that they should face ICC justice, only that it would be available to deal with them in appropriate "fall back" circumstances. The court has the power to indict Kenyan politicians for organizing or encouraging large-scale political killings and it could similarly take jurisdiction to deal with gangmeisters whose power is such over their domestic justice system that they have become untouchable for widespread and systematic crimes of murder and torture.

There is a sense in which terrorism, in Walter Laqueur's words, is 'the weapon of the weak', but suicide-bombing is usually a weapon used against the weak, those ordinary citizens blown to pieces whilst going to work in trains and buses or relaxing in crowded cafes and discotheques. What is owed to these victims is not a 'counterterrorism' in which uniformed men in tanks and planes inflict the equivalent grief on people in the communities which the terrorists wish to make stronger: that simply locks the vicious cycle. Courage is required to counter the fear which terrorism spreads, and that courage comes from belief in the value of liberal democracy and – most difficult, this – a willingness to address the real grievances that terrorists so cruelly and criminally protest about. It does the dead a disservice to call their killers 'evil' or 'cowards' or to otherwise dehumanize them by perceiving them as aliens: the point surely is that they are fellow human beings and that their actions morally diminish us all – to a level that our own reactions must strive to rise above. Treating terrorist onslaughts as crimes against humanity when they systematically mass murder civilians, and responding to them within the limits fixed by the 'just war' preconditions (see chapter 14) not only serves to limit the collateral damage but brings the 'war on terrorism' within the framework of international human rights law. One important consequence of that development will be to insist that state coalitions which choose to wage wars in the twenty-first century must no longer conquer the enemy on the battlefield: they must be prepared, subsequently, to prove the enemy's leaders guilty of crimes against humanity, in an international courtroom.

13

Toppling Tyrants: The Case of Saddam Hussein

'The use of force to avert overwhelming humanitarian catastrophe has been emerging as a further, and exceptional, basis for the use of force . . . I know of no reason why it would be an appropriate basis for action in present circumstances.'

UK Attorney-General on the legality of invading Iraq,
7 March 2003

Saddam Hussein ruled Iraq for almost a quarter of a century, in the course of which he murdered political opponents, disobedient villagers, and ethnic enemies like Kurds and unruly Shias. He started a five-year war with Iran that left a million dead – thousands from mustard and nerve gas. In 1998 his army, led by Ali Hassan al-Majid ('Chemical Ali'), killed 5,000 Kurds in Halabja in one poisoned-gas attack, part of the genocidal Anfal campaign to eliminate the rural Kurdish opposition by razing villages and rounding up males over fifteen for mass execution. In 1990 his invasion of Kuwait was so blatantly in breach of international law that most nations of the world joined a US-led 'coalition of the very willing' in a counter-attack that stopped short of Baghdad. Let off the hook, Saddam vengefully slaughtered and starved Kurds and Shia Arabs who had risen at the hope of liberation, and he later attempted an assassination of George Bush senior, who had encouraged them. The Gulf War produced irrefutable evidence of Saddam's obsession with weapons of mass destruction – his quest for nuclear bombs, his craze for ballistic missiles, his laboratories where every noxious gas or poison was keenly cultivated, ranging from deadly VX (a drop of which kills within the hour) to vats of a virus that produces camelpox, an unpleasant disease that he had fantasies of inflicting on an America that lacked experience with camels.

Over the ensuing twelve years, Iraq's refusal to comply with the strict terms of the 1991 ceasefire contained in Security Council resolution 687 led to sanctions, which crippled the economy and lost vast numbers of lives – especially the lives of babies and young children denied medicines and food, despite the UN's 'oil for food' programme from which top Iraqi officials corruptly enriched themselves. Saddam Hussein modelled himself proudly upon Stalin: his Ba'athist party was a totalitarian regime which suppressed all opposition at home and lied relentlessly abroad. At Abu Ghraib and other prisons, thousands were executed each year without trial, whilst lesser punishments included Star Chamber practices of mutilation (albeit with electric drills), branding and cutting off ears. Women prisoners were allowed a more decent death by beheading, usually after repeated rape by guards. Uday, the dictator's son and heir, had his own private torture chamber and was fond of executing dissidents himself and shooting women who refused his advances. Saddam and sons even killed some forty members of their own family, including insubordinate women and children. Since his accession to power in 1979, the files of Amnesty International and Human Rights Watch bulged with evidence of his barbarity. If ever a tyrant deserved to be toppled, it was Saddam Hussein.

This consequence was achieved by another US-led invasion in March 2003. President George W. Bush, principally supported by Tony Blair, took the military action necessary to overthrow the regime, replacing it in due course by an elected government. But democracy was produced at an appalling cost: by March 2006, over 2,000 American soldiers had been killed and 20,000 wounded, together with over 100,000 civilians, all at an expenditure estimated eventually to reach US$2 trillion. Iraqis had initially reacted with some joy at the fall of

Saddam, but there followed an orgy of looting and destruction, and before long US occupation provoked a devastating insurgency, initially from Saddam's followers and some opportunistic al-Qaida operatives, then and increasingly from a minority Sunni community humiliated and provoked by the US 'invaders', and separately from some fundamentalist Shi'ite groups. The assault on Iraq had been undertaken without UN Security Council approval, and could be justified on no traditional doctrine of international law. The belligerents were not under imminent threat from Saddam, and neither the US nor the UK claimed to be acting pursuant to any right of humanitarian intervention to stop civilians being mass (or even individually) murdered. The invasion had no rational connection to the war on terror – indeed, al-Qaida was revived and strengthened by the propaganda opportunities which followed the occupation. Israel benefited, of course, but so did its powerful enemy Iran, which looked forward to influencing its newly liberated co-religionists, the Shia majority in Iraq. The Iraqi Kurds were the big winners but the Sunni minority, so suddenly reduced to pariah status, was angry and armed. As the death toll in what was indubitably a civil war continued to mount, the question 'Was it worth it?' received an increasingly negative answer, especially (and ironically) from the human rights organizations whose research was used for propaganda in favour of the war in the first place.

It is, for this reason, important to clarify the grounds upon which the US and UK put their case for the lawfulness of 'Operation Iraqi Freedom'. Although they plundered and publicized the files of Amnesty and Human Rights Watch to denounce Saddam as evil – a 'monster' and 'another Hitler' of whom the world would be well rid – they never suggested that his human rights record would make 'regime change' lawful. That was a slope down which the Bush administration refused to slip, lest it create an uncomfortable precedent. It was relevant only to his propensity for evil-doing: a man this bad would be more likely to attack the US with the weapons of mass destruction he was presumed to possess or to be in the process of obtaining; he would be more likely to link up with al-Qaida's plans to kill more Americans; he would at the very least be certain to mislead the UN and deceive its 'Inspector Clouseau', the plodding Mr Hans Blix. What the US government proclaimed instead was its right to go to war, irrespective of the UN, whenever it intuited that its national security was at risk. This is the 'Bush doctrine' of the right to preemptive (in fact, 'preventative') use of force, an alarming expansion of the international law right to self-defence.

It alarmed the UK, which refused to accept it. Instead, Tony Blair found legality for the invasion in the text of Security Council resolutions before and after the first Gulf War in 1990. 'All necessary means' had then been vouchsafed to coalition partners prepared to put Saddam back in his box, and this blank cheque could be 'revived' if he failed to honour the undertakings given in the ceasefire agreement, namely to abandon WMD and to permit UN inspections to prove that he had abandoned them. It was an argument more of contract than of international law, but its validity could only be put beyond question by the Security Council itself, passing a second resolution specifically authorizing the use of force. When this did not eventuate (thanks to vetoes threatened by France, Russia and China, and opposition from most non-permanent Security Council members), the British attorney-general, Lord Goldsmith, nevertheless decided it was 'reasonably arguable' that the US and UK could invade alone – on the assumption, indeed the assurance, that Saddam Hussein was actually in possession of WMD, the existence of which he was hiding from inspectors. It was upon this 'fact', confirmed by unidentified 'intelligence sources', that the governments of the US and the UK built their different arguments for the lawfulness of the invasion of Iraq. Most international lawyers disagree with these arguments, for reasons that this chapter will explore. It will not seek to answer the more interesting question of why the 'fact' was entirely false – Iraq had no WMD, having obediently destroyed its stockpile after the first Gulf War – but it will address a question more interesting still: irrespective of WMD, is there a basis in international law for extirpating a tyrant who mass murders his own people?

The invasion led to the prosecution of Saddam Hussein for crimes against humanity. Although this allegation seems easy to prove (the photos of women and children lying gassed on the streets of Halabja, for example), refutation is none the less possible. 'Halabja?' said the defendant, shaking his head when the allegation was first mentioned in court. 'Yes. I read about that in the newspapers.' Any prosecution would have to establish that Saddam knew and approved, and it would also have to disprove any defence – one unlikely suggestion from his supporters was that the poison gas came from Iranian air force jets. The allegation meant that an independent and impartial court should have been found to try him. That ruled out a court in Iraq, where newly elected politicians were baying for his blood and it was not possible to find an Iraqi jurist personally unaffected by his rule, and where a fair trial was in any event impossible because defence lawyers were being killed. Moreover, since genocide is an international offence – a crime against every human being, not just Iraqi victims – it would have been appropriate to establish an international court to try Saddam and his henchpersons. Regrettably, this option was rejected by the US in favour of a local court that could be relied upon to order that the main defendant be hanged by the neck until he was dead. Those who argued that the war was morally justified by the prospect of Saddam on trial should have gone on to examine what sort of trial he would be on and whether it really would have any connection with the legacy laid down by the tribunal established by occupying forces at Nuremberg.

Any nation that proclaims its mission to rid another country of crimes against humanity cannot countenance the commission of such crimes by its own forces. But Abu Ghraib prison, where so many of Saddam's own critics were put to death, became an interrogation centre where civilian internees, the vast majority of them innocent of any crime, routinely suffered inhumane treatment and torture. The Red Cross warned US commanders, who took no notice because its reports were secret, until photographs were published of guards using their prisoners for obscene sport. James Schlesinger's comment – '*Animal House* on the night shift' – may have been an apt description of the behaviour of convicted prison guards Charles Graner and Lynndie England, but that behaviour was an all too predictable consequence of the state of mind prevailing at the very top of the US administration: the Geneva Conventions were obsolete and now 'the gloves must come off'. Although the night-shift sadists were jailed, nothing could repair the damage of pictures worth more than a thousand words: they became recruiting posters for al-Qaida, snapshot proof for every paranoid Islamist of what American 'freedom' really meant. 'We do not do torture,' insisted President Bush, but the device of 'extraordinary rendition' allowed other countries to do the torture for them and in any event he boasted in his autobiography, published in 2010, that he did authorize water boarding. The rule that systematic maltreatment of prisoners – whether or not captured in war – counts as a crime against humanity requires reassertion, at a time when failure to respect basic human rights only gives encouragement to terrorists.

GIVE WAR A CHANCE

On 9 September 2001, George W. Bush convened a White House meeting to consider Iraq's refusal to comply with UN disarmament requirements despite sanctions which had beggared the country. The decision was merely to make these sanctions 'smarter',[1] and it was in line with the intelligence of the time. US Secretary of State Colin Powell had recently announced that Saddam 'has not developed any significant capability with respect to weapons of mass destruction . . . the US policy of containment has effectively disarmed the Iraqi dictator . . . America has been successful in keeping him in a box.'[2] Condoleezza Rice had just referred to Iraq as weak and defenceless: 'We aim to keep his arms from him. His military forces have not been rebuilt.'[3] When the White House meeting reconvened a few weeks later, the post-9/11 mood was very different: it was impossible for the president to believe that there was no connection between that atrocity and the man 'who tried to kill my dad' (by a car bomb planted by Iraqi agents when Bush senior visited Kuwait).[4] In January 2002, in his first State of the Union address, the president placed Iraq alongside Iran and North Korea on the 'axis of evil'. In February, he began to redirect US forces from Afghanistan to the Gulf, and the following month he made his intentions plain at a private meeting with senators: 'Fuck Saddam. We're taking him out.'[5]

Planning for war began in the Spring of 2002, although it was not until September that the 'Bush doctrine' was enunciated to justify it, in a paper entitled *The National Security of the USA*: 'We will not hesitate to act alone, if necessary, to exercise our right of self-defense by acting pre-emptively' against 'rogue states and terrorists who rely on weapons of mass destruction – weapons that can be easily concealed, delivered secretly and used without warning.' Iraq was a rogue state and Saddam a rogue statesman. If he *was* concealing WMD, there was every reason to believe, given his history and psyche, that he was capable of delivering them ready for use into the hands of terrorists. This was the spectre that motivated Tony Blair too, as he mulled over revelations about the corrupt Pakistani nuclear scientist AQ Khan, who had been selling nuclear enrichment secrets to anyone who paid him, specifically to Iran, North Korea and Libya, although not to Iraq. Bin Laden had announced that Islamists had a 'duty' to obtain and use nuclear weapons: surely the time had come to eliminate any regime that could, and might well, supply them? Unlike Bush, Blair accepted that 'regime change' could not be justified by a mere possibility as distinct from an imminent threat. But Saddam had repeatedly breached UN inspection obligations imposed by the ceasefire agreement after the first Gulf War. Security Council members could still use 'all necessary means' to enforce them, and the only surefire means to produce Iraqi compliance was the forcible removal of Saddam.

The US pre-emption doctrine and the UK 'all necessary means' approach both hinged upon a factual finding that, contrary to Colin Powell's confident assertion in 2001, Iraq was in fact in possession of weapons of mass destruction and was concealing them from UN inspectors. All decision-takers, including the French, Russian and Syrian governments, were inclined to believe that Saddam did possess WMD, and the Security Council in November 2002 passed Resolution 1441 because of the unanimous view that he was therefore in breach of obligations arising from the 1991 ceasefire resolution. In February 2003, Colin Powell gave the Security Council the CIA's hair-raising forensic picture of Saddam's 'arsenal': evidence that he 'had never accounted for vast amounts of chemical weaponry: 550 military shells with mustard gas, 30,000 empty munitions and enough precursors to increase his stockpile to as much as 500 tonnes of chemical agents'. The CIA's elementary mistake was to confuse 'unaccounted for' with 'still possesses' (it later turned out that these stocks were 'unaccounted for' because they had all been destroyed). But Powell's claims sounded chilling. 'Our conservative estimate is that Iraq has enough chemical agent to fill 16,000 battlefield rockets . . . causing mass casualties across an area nearly five times the size of Manhattan.'[6]

In similar hyperbolic vein was the 'evidence' published a few months previously by the UK government in what is now described as 'the dodgy dossier'. Its headline claim – that Saddam's ballistic missiles could descend on Europe 'within forty-five minutes of an order to use them' – was false, or at least 'sexed up' (this allegation came to the BBC from a government scientist, Dr Kelly, who committed suicide when revealed as the source). The Prime Minister, in his foreword to the dossier, pronounced himself satisfied that the 'intelligence established beyond doubt that Saddam has continued to produce chemical and biological weapons, that he continues in his efforts to develop nuclear weapons, that he has been able to extend the range of his ballistic missile programme . . . Faced with someone who has shown himself capable of using WMDs [cue photographs of women and children on a Halabja street], I believe the international community has to stand up for itself and ensure its authority is upheld.' The dossier made a compelling case for taking 'all necessary means' to bring Iraq into compliance, especially when accurate descriptions of Saddam's record for internal repression and international deception was set forth, laced with heavy (and later discredited) hints about his efforts to obtain weapons-grade uranium from Niger and his development of a new generation of Scud missiles capable not only of hitting Israel, but Greece, Turkey and the British bases in Cyprus. The message was that if the UN was to play any credible part in securing a peaceful future, it must begin by enforcing its own resolutions against Iraq. If it could not, because of power plays within the Security Council, then the US and UK should enforce them for it.

If (and only if) the intelligence was correct, this was not an unreasonable or unlawful proposition. What makes it now appear so naive – or, worse, devious – is the astonishing series of mistakes made by Western intelligence services, notably the CIA and MI6, in feeding to political leaders wildly inaccurate assessments and allowing their reproduction, suitably 'sexed up' but bearing their imprimatur, in public documents. Some commentators argue that the CIA was actually 'suborned' by the White House to 'exaggerate, distort and misrepresent intelligence findings',[7] and this allegation receives some support from the language of the 'Downing Street Memorandum', a note by MI6 chief Sir Richard Dearlove of a meeting at the White House in July 2002:

Military action was now seen as inevitable. Bush wanted to remove Saddam, through military action, justified by the conjunction of terrorism and WMD. But the intelligence and facts were being fixed around the policy. The NSC had no patience with the UN route and no enthusiasm for publishing material on the Iraqi regime's record. There was little discussion in Washington of the aftermath after military action.[8]

Intelligence officials, like other public servants, are amenable to the mood of their political masters and may have helped to 'fix' the facts, although whether in the sense of 'relevantly gathered' or 'rigged' Sir Richard has not condescended to say even to the Chilcot Inquiry. A less conspiratorial explanation is that, until the first Gulf War, Saddam's WMD capacity was precisely known to Western intelligence – for the simple reason that they were debriefing executives from the Western companies which supplied the wherewithal for it. MI6, for example, would recruit businessmen who were supplying Saddam with 'dual use' machinery for bomb manufacture – business they had been secretly encouraged to obtain by Thatcher government ministers. They were given copies of Kanan Makiya's book *The Republic of Fear* – a devastating exposé of Saddam's cruelty – to persuade them to act as spies during their period of privileged access to his arms and chemical weapons factories outside Baghdad. But after the Gulf War, when the UK government tried to conceal its role in arming Saddam by having these businessmen prosecuted at the

Old Bailey, the cover-up backfired and the 'Iraqgate' scandal was exposed.[9] The result was that most Western businessmen no longer went to Baghdad – and those who did never reported back to MI6. Its only 'intelligence' about arms procurement came from highly suspect sources: defectors with an axe to grind against the regime or an incentive to gain asylum by exaggerating its arsenal, and Iraqi exiles prepared to say anything to support the case for invasion. What made their claims so credible was the irrefutable evidence from 1990 that Saddam was trying to go nuclear, and was stockpiling chemical weapons. Could this leopard really have changed his spots? He had thrown out UN inspectors in 1998, and suffered economic sanctions as a result. From this action, Western intelligence services, using their intelligence, deduced that he must have something to hide – and that 'something' had to be weapons of mass destruction. Their logic was impeccable – except that it attributed a rational Western mind to the dictator of Iraq.

So it would be wrong to impute downright dishonesty to the intelligence officials, much less to policymakers who relied on their assessments: the Hutton Inquiry in the UK, for all its shortcomings, was correct in that finding. However, it never went on to examine the 'unidentified sources' in Iraq who supplied MI6 – presumably for reward – with false information (about the 'forty-five minutes', for example), or to explain how the assessments came to be so comprehensively wrong. This provides a powerful argument against the Bush doctrine of pre-emption, when based on subjective and secret assessments of the nature of the threat that needs to be pre-empted. It also provokes the ironic reflection that Saddam's own secrecy and duplicity contributed in large part to his downfall. Out of pride, out of a reluctance to be seen to be obeying the UN, out of a desire to be thought (especially by Iran) as a feared and baleful and heavily armed enemy, he refused to admit (or to admit inspectors to discover) that he had meekly destroyed his chemical arsenals and torn up his nuclear plans – soon after the ceasefire agreement had required him to do precisely that. His regime was liable to overthrow not because it was dangerous, but because he had so convincingly *pretended* that it was dangerous.

The crunch came in November 2002, when the Security Council unanimously called his bluff. Resolution 1441 held him in breach of the ceasefire resolution and set up a new inspection regime – the United Nations Monitoring, Verification and Inspection Commission (UNMOVIC) – which he would disallow or obstruct at his peril. So far, one might say, so good: Iraq had blatantly disobeyed previous UN directives (no inspectors had been permitted since 1998) and an ultimatum was long overdue. Saddam's old habits of deceit and obstruction died hard, however, and the anxiously awaited report by Hans Blix and Mohamed ElBaradei (head of the IAEA, the nuclear inspectorate), when tabled at the UN on 28 January 2003, severely criticized Iraqi non-compliance. But Blix had as yet found no WMD, and asked for more time to search for weapons that (privately) he believed he would find. The US and UK could not wait – for severely practical, operational reasons, the president insisted that the war had to begin in March, so it could be over before the searing heat of the Gulf summer required its postponement until October. In early February, the UK published *The Infrastructure of Concealment, Deception and Intimidation* – an even dodgier dossier, since part of it turned out to have been plagiarized from a thesis written twelve years previously by a Californian graduate student. But on 5 February, Colin Powell confronted the Security Council with 'irrefutable and undeniable' evidence that Saddam was concealing weapons of mass destruction. The following week, Dr Blix gave what was, for Americans hell-bent on war, an infuriatingly unhelpful interim report: no WMD yet, but many prohibited weapons still 'unaccounted for'. Given the CIA 'evidence', credible because it chimed with Saddam's conduct a decade previously, it seemed only a matter of time before the WMD would be discovered . . . but how much time?

As anti-war demonstrations took place throughout the world (attracting in London over one million protesters), Dr Blix's wild goose chase continued: on 7 March he asked again for more time (much of it, so far, he had spent travelling back and forth to the UN). Britain – prompted by the US military deadline – offered only ten days, and began an intensive lobbying campaign to persuade non-permanent Security Council members to vote for a second resolution which would put the legitimacy of invasion beyond dispute. For all the deadly seriousness which attended these last desperate days, it is comical to think how the waging of a war could turn on the 'swinging six' – such paradigms of morality as Guinea, Cameroon and Angola, together with Pakistan, Chile and Mexico. The French somewhat spoilt the diplomatic tea dance when President Chirac announced that they would veto the 'second resolution' without bothering to hear further argument, and television honours in the ensuing Security Council debates went to his suave and smirking foreign minister, Dominique de Villepin, a man with impeccable grooming and offering the impeccable argument that since Resolution 1441 was an ultimatum to permit a full and complete inspection, hostilities should not commence until Dr Blix had completed a full inspection. On 16 March, Messrs Bush and Blair and a small Spaniard (Prime Minister José Aznar) who reminded everyone of the waiter in *Fawlty Towers* decamped to an island in the Azores normally frequented only by planes which lose engines over the Atlantic and held a last-ditch council of war. Dr Blix and his UNMOVIC team hastily left Iraq, and at daybreak on 19 March, 'Operation Shock and Awe' hit Baghdad.

In those final frenetic weeks, the Security Council debate over whether to go to war diminished into the narrow issue of whether to give the inspectors more time to find the WMD that most – including the inspectors – believed to exist. The question, of whether war could be justified against an unpredictable ruler who refused to disarm, was Iraq-specific in the sense that this rogue state had been put on probation by the Chapter VII ceasefire resolution back in 1991 and was therefore bound by UN obligations that did not shackle states like Iran and North Korea. But deterring them from irresponsible actions was part of the rationale behind the Bush doctrine (and is currently echoed by those who favour an attack on nuclear-capable Iran): the US would not hesitate to use its fire power, unilaterally, against any country that stockpiled WMD and manifested an inclination to use them (or to make them available for terrorists to use) against the US or its interests (in particular, its tacit interest in supporting the state of Israel). The UK did not accept that US and global interests were identical, as Tony Blair explained: 'Regime change alone could not be and was not our justification for war. Our primary purpose was to enforce UN resolutions over Iraq and WMD.'[10] Sir Jeremy Greenstock later articulated another unspoken reason that was much in British minds: 'There were compelling reasons for staying with the US in this complex operation, not only because Britain had something valuable to offer (a passport to other support, military incisiveness, historical perspective and experience) but also because the damage to world diplomacy if America went solo was too awful to contemplate.'[11] This sniffy cultural superiority came easily to British diplomats, but it was widely (and less elegantly) promulgated to keep Labour Party stalwarts in line: 'The bloody Yanks are going in anyway and we have to be with them to exert a restraining influence.' There is scant evidence to support this pretension, but it maintained Blair's majority in his own party.

Although none of these justifications for war had any direct connection with human rights, it was the moral argument for toppling a tyrant that persuaded more people than US 'pre-emption' or the UK's picayune textual exegesis of UN resolutions. It had first, and most memorably, been made by Kanan Makiya in *The Republic of Fear* – a brilliant analysis of Ba'athist totalitarianism as seen from Harvard, published back in 1989. Makiya was an academic who had never ventured to Iraq during Saddam's reign, although he became the intellectual force behind Ahmed Chalabi and the Iraqi exile group and was trusted by the White House as a sure guide to what the people in Iraq wanted. 'He's written great books about the subject, knows the country intimately,' explained Vice-President Dick Cheney on *Meet the Press*. Makiya assured Bush that war would lead the Arab world to democracy: 'People will meet the troops with sweets and flowers.'[12] But Makiya was a coffeehouse intellectual, like many exiles whose smooth talk beguiled Western liberals – and their liberalism was a world removed from the mindsets in the mosques of Falluja and Basra. On 31 January 2003 George W. Bush, encouraged by the halcyon predictions of Iraqi exiles, assured Tony Blair that the US anticipated no internecine warfare between the different religious and ethnic groups after his invasion.[13]

Human rights considerations had previously played no part in

Western policy towards oil-rich Iraq. The Reagan administration had welcomed Saddam's war with Iran, its mortal enemy after the fall of the Shah and the embassy hostage crisis in Tehran. Donald Rumsfeld had conveyed the warmest of greetings to Saddam on behalf of President Reagan on visits in 1983 and 1984. Halabja was hardly noticed: European and US companies were encouraged by their governments to scramble for contracts thereafter until Saddam's invasion of Kuwait brought on the first Gulf War. George Bush senior stopped the 'yomp' to Baghdad for fear of upsetting the Saudis, but then irresponsibly encouraged Kurds in the north and Shias in the south to revolt: they did so, expecting US support, and were massacred when it was not forthcoming. 'No fly zones' staunched this bloodletting, but for many they remained a memorial to the equivocation of the first President Bush. Another unforgiven memory was of Saddam's Scud missiles, fired gratuitously at Israel – his removal would be a boon to that country's security. This prospect was earnestly taken up by 'neoconservatives' – utopians on the right wing of the Republican Party who rejected both isolationism and the *realpolitik* of Dr Kissinger, and actually thought the world could be reshaped in America's image by American force. Some of these ideologues were associated with Israel's Likud party, although, ironically, the one thing they all had in common was that they had avoided service in Vietnam. They did not apprehend the parallel with Vietnam-era thinking and saw no oxymoron in their slogan, 'a stable democratic Iraq'. By 1998 their campaign had produced the Iraq Liberation Act, a provocative Congressional measure which promised money and guns to Iraqi oppositionists. These 'neocons' were intellectually active in the Bush administration and responsible for its naively optimistic notion that democracy would instantly transform the Arab world. But they were certainly not human rights warriors: that role was taken by liberal journalists like Christopher Hitchens (disarmingly writing 'as one who could not easily name a mistake that the Bush administration has failed to make'), Michael Ignatieff and William Shawcross ('Hussein has started a new nuclear bomb programme with new methods of concealing it . . . We cannot walk away yet again while this man conspires to build weapons which he trusts will make him untouchable and with which he could kill millions of people.')[14] The pro-war *Economist* told tales of Saddam's massive but concealed arsenal,[15] whilst leading neocons like Richard Perle and Kenneth Adelman predicted that the invasion (dubbed 'Desert Storm II') would be a 'cake walk': 'Dancing in the streets of Baghdad will be even more joyous . . . Saddam's relentless drive for nuclear weapons poses a dire threat to civilised nations.'[16] They derided opponents as 'appeasers' in the tradition of Neville Chamberlain – although the Second World War was no 'cake walk', and attacking Hitler after Munich would not have been pre-emptive: by then, he had already invaded the Rhineland, Austria and Czechoslovakia.

Opponents of the war had to acknowledge the ruthless cruelty of Saddam and his regime – a forensic handicap for most, although one that did not bother the *realpolitik* school of Dr Kissinger and Brent Scowcroft, concerned that the new Bush doctrine would alienate allies and would be adopted by other states with disastrous results (such as by India, with a pre-emptive strike on Pakistan). The better argument was Kofi Annan's – on the need to respect UN procedures, dilatory and exasperating though they were, rather than to undermine the organization by circumventing its charter (although by electing Libya to chair the UN Human Rights Commission, the UN was at this point doing a good job of undermining itself). Democrats like Edward Kennedy detected in the demand for pre-emptive regime change an imperial aspiration, and urged their country to act in good faith through international agencies to avoid war. They invoked John F. Kennedy, who had rejected military advice to invade Cuba in a pre-emptive strike that could have caused a third world war: instead, he obtained Security Council support for the blockade which soon secured the removal of the Soviet missiles.[17] But George W. Bush was no John F. Kennedy. The leader who had been most successful in containing Muslim extremism, Malaysia's Dr Mahathir, warned the US that an invasion would infuriate the Islamic world: 'There will be more willing recruits to the terrorist ranks.'[18] The Archbishop of Canterbury denounced the impending war as unjust, by reference to Thomas Aquinas, who had insisted that just wars must have good intentions, good legal authority and proportionate ends. America, he preached, had lost the power of self-criticism and had become trapped in a 'self-referential' (or was it 'self-reverential') morality.

The most astute critics were those prepared to agree that the world would be a better place without Saddam, while pointing out that war was always hell (especially for civilians and children) and there was no clear evidence of his present dangerousness. There was no evidence at all, other than in Dick Cheney's musings, that Saddam had any truck with al-Qaida. (On the contrary, bin Laden had repeatedly condemned Saddam and his secular regime.) With the 'war on terror' yet to be won, it was foolish to open another front that could only drive Ba'athists and terrorists into an unholy alliance. Iraq was, like Palestine and Kashmir, another impossible legacy from the British Empire: its 25 million people were (approximately) 60 per cent Shia, 20 per cent Sunni and 20 per cent Kurds, within which categories were tribal, political and religious divisions and enmities. It was Saddam's very ruthlessness that had kept these fractious factions in some kind of unity – if he were toppled and no clone of General Musharraf replaced him, the centre could not hold. Given the man's own aggression, instability and stupidity, he could not be trusted with any nuclear weapon: but the point at which he was about to acquire one was the point which would justify invasion on the classic test for self-defence.[19] There was no evidence at all that this point had been reached, and on 31 January 2002 President Bush privately admitted that the US would invade 'whether WMDs were found or not' – in which case the war would be *preventative*, to overthrow a malign dictator who might one day acquire weapons of mass destruction, rather than *pre-emptive*, to stop him using or transferring to terrorists the weapons already in his possession.

THE BUSH DOCTRINE AND BEYOND

The war's legality was central to the debate in Britain, Australia and Europe. The newspapers were full of feature articles, letters and petitions from professors and practitioners, mostly calling for a second Security Council resolution or rejecting the Bush doctrine of pre-emption as incompatible with international law. Curiously, this dimension did not much feature in the US media: *The New York*

Times, its reporters being fed false stories about Saddam's arsenal by Dick Cheney's cronies, declined to publish a petition from a galaxy of New York academics, warning that if 'the US rides rough shod over international law today, we will create precedents that will surely come back to haunt us when invoked by our enemies in the years ahead'.[20] This phenomenon was in part cultural: for Americans, going to war meant a presidential political judgement based on the national interest, to which international law was a marginal consideration. Opponents of war in the Security Council focused on the lack of 'automaticity' in Resolution 1441 and the need to give the inspectors more time: the Bush doctrine of pre-emption, the right of any state to use force against a threat which it alone apprehends, did not appear uncongenial to France, Russia or China, countries that have acted upon that principle in the past (in France's case, by sinking a Greenpeace protest boat in New Zealand). This may explain why there was no groundswell in the General Assembly to request an advisory opinion from the ICJ on the legality of military action (the route by which the legality of nuclear weapons was tested). The world seemed gloomily to accept that unipolarity of power resided in the US.

That undoubted fact cannot permit the Bush doctrine to stand as an acceptable update of the right to use force in self-defence, set out in Article 51 of the UN Charter, which allows force to be used only 'if an armed attack occurs'. Purists argue unrealistically that this means that no state can use force unless actually under hostile attack, but the *Caroline* doctrine must be implied, which permits states to use force to avoid the threat of an *imminent* attack (see p. 619). This doctrine of 'anticipatory self-defence' means there must be a real and credible threat of attack, not a threat that has yet to emerge, and it must be of an actual attack on the self-defending state. Moreover, there should be no non-military alternative to the proposed course of action that would be likely to be effective in averting the threat or bringing an end to the attack.[21]

It is reasonable to recalibrate these rules in a post-9/11 world where terrorists (whether state-supported or not) might cause vast damage by attacking with weapons of mass destruction. States must be entitled to a more flexible interpretation of 'imminence' than that concept connoted at a time when armies and battleships took weeks to move into position. If a nation, acting in good faith on evidence that is convincing and can be made public, uses force to attack a secret facility which is preparing for use nuclear bombs or chemical weapons, or if it attacks a terrorist training camp or invades a state which actively sponsors a terrorist movement, it lawfully deals with an active threat which is 'imminent'. On this basis, the action against al-Qaida in October 2001 lawfully encompassed an attack on the Taliban government of which it was an adopted part, although a different and better justification is available (see pp. 627–8). In the case of Iraq, of course, there was no evidence of its support for international terrorists. It was not clear whether Saddam actually possessed WMD and highly doubtful that he had nuclear capability: these would indeed be 'threats' but they had not emerged as such by March 2003, although Dr Blix was leaving no stone or grain of sand unturned. Discovery might in many minds have been 'imminent', but until it was made the 'threat' had not emerged. The Bush doctrine of 'pre-emption' (in reality, 'prevention'), which claimed the right to respond forcibly to a threat which had not yet crystallized but might materialize at some time in the future, did not accord with international law and could not be brought within it by any flexible development of the concept of 'imminence'. The fatal flaw in the doctrine is that 'it excludes by definition the possibility of *ex post facto* judgment of lawfulness by the very fact that it aims to deal in advance with threats that have not materialized'.[22] That, of course, is its great advantage for aggressive statesmen – they can never be proved in retrospect to have acted unlawfully.

Saddam had no weapons of mass destruction, but back in March 2003 there was a real prospect that he was hiding them and might use them or supply them to terrorists. The National Security Statement of September 2002 purported to adopt the traditional argument of 'imminence' to deal with that scenario, by the 'option of pre-emptive action to counter a sufficient threat to our national security . . . the US cannot remain idle while dangers gather'. This is not anticipatory self-defence against an imminent threat: it signals the unilateral right to use force against states which might possibly develop WMD and then might possibly use them or deliver them to terrorists. It is neither an 'adoption' nor an 'adaption' of international law, but the announcement of a new rule of entitlement to go to war whenever a 'sufficient' danger to US security is intuited, the sufficiency of the threat to be judged by the US alone. If this is to become a rule, then other states are entitled to apply it. If it is not, then it is simply an opportunistic entitlement exercisable by the most powerful nation in the world, which may not always be the US. It is a feature of the lawless world described by Thucydides, in which the strong do what they wish and the weak what they must.[23]

The Bush doctrine was studied with mounting apprehension by the UK and rejected in terse legal phraseology by its attorney-general:

I am aware that the USA has been arguing for recognition of a broad doctrine of a right to use force to pre-empt danger in the future. If this means more than a right to respond proportionately to an imminent attack (and I understand that the doctrine is intended to carry that connotation) this is not a doctrine which, in my opinion, exists or is recognised in international law.[24]

On what legal basis then, would the UK join the invasion? Lord Goldsmith hummed and hawed through a lengthy examination of the 'revival' theory, i.e. that Resolution 678 (in 1990) permitted 'all necessary means' to be used to restore peace to the Middle East after the invasion of Kuwait and any breach of the ceasefire agreement (Resolution 687) revived that power in any Gulf War coalition partner which wished to exercise it. This had been the basis for bombing Saddam in 1993 and again in 1998 ('Operation Desert Fox'), but the problem was that 'revival' was contingent on a Security Council finding of breach. Resolution 1441 had certainly made that finding, but at the same time had created UNMOVIC to give Saddam one last chance. Lord Goldsmith admitted that 'the safest course would be to secure the adoption of a further resolution to authorise the use of force', but 'a reasonable case can be made that resolution 1441 is capable in principle of reviving the authorisation in 678 without a further resolution'. He worried that 'a reasonable case does not mean that if the matter ever came before a court I would be confident that the court would agree with this view . . . It might well conclude that . . . a further Council decision [was required].'

This was hardly a ringing endorsement for legality. It was an opinion couched in the circumlocutions familiar to English Queen's Counsel: 'a reasonable case' usually decodes as 'I will with pleasure take your money to argue this point with a straight face. It might – but probably will not – succeed.' Lord Goldsmith did not give a gambler's odds for success, which were at most 20 per cent (lower, if professors of international law comprised the court). He consoled his client, the prime minister, by reminding him that the legality of the war over Kosovo in 1999 'was no more than reasonably arguable' (i.e. 'you got away with it that time'), and concluded with an important caveat that action may be taken 'to remove Saddam Hussein from power if it can be demonstrated that such action is a necessary and proportionate measure to secure the disarmament of Iraq. But regime change cannot be the object of military action.' This distinction made no impact on President Bush, for whom regime change was the avowed object.

The revival argument hinged on whether Security Council resolution 1441, by holding Iraq in material breach of its ceasefire obligations, had thereby implicitly revived the right of one or more coalition partners to use 'all necessary means'. The object of 1441 was 'to afford Iraq a final opportunity to comply with its disarmament obligations' and so 'to set up an enhanced inspection routine with the aim to bring to *full and verified completion* the disarmament process'. To this end, the Security Council established UNMOVIC and resolved to reconvene 'to consider the situation' after its report, recalling that 'the council has repeatedly warned Iraq it will face serious consequences as a result of its continued violations'. Resolution 1441 was an ultimatum, but its finding of 'material breach' did not automatically trigger a right to use 'all necessary means', a right contained in a resolution passed in a different context twelve years before. It plainly envisaged that the inspector's report (called for within thirty days) would be considered by the Security Council: 'serious consequences' might well ensue if there was then a consensus in favour. The problem was that Dr Blix needed more time to produce a 'full and verified completion' report and the US had no time to spare: invasion had to be in March or else lapse until October. And (a point in favour of 'revival') the US had made it their sticking point in negotiations at the UN over drafts of Resolution 1441 that it should *not* concede the need for a second resolution approving force, which is why 1441 did not expressly refer to any such second resolution. What it did refer to, however, was the Security Council reconvening on receipt of the UNMOVIC report 'to consider the situation', a consideration which, if it were to produce 'serious consequences', would seem to require a resolution to that end and not merely a polite discussion. There was nothing to show that France, Russia and China were voting only for a discussion, and a number of non-permanent members – Mexico, Ireland and Syria – said in terms at the time it was passed that Resolution 1441 had 'no automaticity' and a further resolution would be required before force was used. In other words, the diplomats had deliberately made the resolution ambiguous, so that the US and everyone else could sign it. 'Paltering in a double sense' may be the black art of diplomacy, but the fundamental rule is that the Security Council itself is the sole and authoritative interpreter of its own resolutions. The majority of Security Council members, it turned out, were not prepared to endorse the US/UK interpretation.

For this reason, the preponderance of international jurists conclude that the invasion of Iraq was a breach of Article 2(4) of the UN Charter because it had not been approved by the Security Council under Chapter VII powers and it could not be justified under Article 51 as self-defence against an imminent threat, or else as a humanitarian intervention. It was barely arguable that the exercise could be justified by the 1990 resolution as revived by the Resolution 1441 finding of 'material breach', but the odds were against any international court accepting such an argument. The very fact that it was arguable, however, permitted the UK and the US to maintain that the war, which they considered just, was not necessarily illegal, a claim they knew could not be challenged in court. The International Criminal Court Statute expressly postponed jurisdiction over the crime of aggression unless and until a definition could be agreed at a 'Review Conference' listed for 2010. Bush and Blair were not war heroes, but they were not war criminals. They faced increasing criticism when WMD proved chimerical and casualties mounted, so they fell back in their rhetoric on the objective they had previously disavowed, namely to punish Saddam for his monstrous human rights record. Their case for war, in retrospect, became the case for tyrannicide. But, as the noble Romans recognized, that case is arguable so long as it is only the tyrant who gets it in the neck.

REGIME CHANGE

On 30 January 2002, when Bush and Blair met at the White House, the president hinted darkly at the possibility of assassinating Saddam. This might have been accomplished by some undercover agent, highly enough placed to recognize a double of the Iraqi president when he saw one, and funded by a secret subvention under the Iraq Liberation Act. It would not have worked: Uday, the heir apparent, was even more malevolent and unstable than his father and there were plenty of generals ('Chemical Ali' for one) available to lead what would remain a Ba'athist police state. As a last and desperate alternative, the US made an amnesty offer to Saddam (repeated on 17 March, with a condition that he and his sons leave the country within forty-eight hours). War would have been averted, at least for a time, by an indulgence that Saddam and sons, obsessed with their own power, refused even to consider. The very fact that this amnesty was offered, at a time when Saddam's crimes (real and alleged) were on magnified display, provides a further example of the traditional reluctance of states to bring powerful perpetrators of crimes against humanity to justice. It demonstrates, too, just how irrelevant to the motives for war were his endless human rights violations, all of which President Bush would forgive if Saddam agreed to be golden-parachuted into exile in the south of France where he could spend his rake-off from the 'oil for food' programme. There would be no retribution for the genocide at Halabja or the starvation in the marshes: the mass graves would remain unopened. The Ba'athist government could continue as usual, preferably under a strong general in the Musharraf mould. How much more respectable was the option of putting him instead on trial in The Hague for crimes against humanity?

Philip Bobbitt was one of the few commentators in favour of regime change who recognized the need to justify it by a development in international law, which would respond to a permanent change in the strategic environment. He shunned the 'might makes right' arrogance of the Bush doctrine, and argued that war against Iraq, in the context of the wars over Kosovo and Afghanistan, represented the beginning of a new international norm:

It would strengthen the emerging rule that regimes that repudiate the popular basis for their sovereignty – by overturning democratic institutions, by denying even the most basic human rights, and by practising terror against their own population – jeopardise their rights of sovereignty, including that of seeking whatever weapons they choose.

This was the best – indeed, the only – legitimate basis for 'regime change': tyranny (at least to the extent that had been practised by Saddam) forfeits sovereign rights. The argument had been advanced by John Cooke at the trial of Charles I (see p. 5), but despite this Puritan pedigree it did not appeal to the White House, which had an abhorrence of any international law rule that might fetter its self-interested determination of the need to use force in the interests of the US.

But the Genocide Convention, ratified by President Reagan, required state parties to set up an international process to bring Saddam & Co. to justice for genocide – which meant indicting him for the Anfal campaign against the Kurds in 1988, and for his destruction of the lives and the livelihood of the marsh Arabs (by draining their marshes) in 1991. Despite the Convention, world leaders and their diplomats have not been capable of thinking this way until very recently, when some have acknowledged the obligation to punish crimes against humanity committed by heads of state. But could that obligation justify a war against a sovereign state to capture its indicted leader? An Eichmann-style kidnap or a military 'snatch' would be proportionate to achieving the objective, but a war which caused tens of thousands of deaths and destroyed the national infrastructure would seem a case of burning the house to roast the pig. But if the indicted tyrant *did* possess WMD and especially a nuclear capacity, the indictment itself would be sufficient to establish his (or her) danger to global security. If the 'Big Five' on the Security Council could not unanimously agree to take action, invasion by a coalition of states would then be justifiable, whether or not the strict 'imminent danger' test for self-defence could be satisfied. So on what international law basis might such an invasion be premised? The developing right of 'humanitarian intervention' was pooh-poohed by the British attorney-general and never asserted by the US, and had hitherto been confined to cases such as Kosovo where crimes against humanity are ongoing. But when President Bush addressed the UN on 12 September 2002 on the reasons why the world must hold Saddam to account, the first reason put forward was Saddam's human rights record, not his presumed acquisition of WMD:

Iraq continues to commit extremely grave violations of human rights and the regime's repression is all-pervasive. Tens of thousands of ordinary citizens have been subject to arbitrary arrest and imprisonment, summary execution, and torture by beating and burning, electric shock, starvation and rape. Wives are tortured in front of their husbands, children in the presence of their parents – and all of these horrors concealed from the world by the apparatus of a totalitarian state. His regime once ordered the killing of every person between the ages of 15 and 70 in certain Kurdish villages in northern Iraq. He has gassed many Iranians and 40 Iraqi villages.[25]

But Bush was not moved, even by his own words. All this was not enough to justify regime change and the president never claimed that it was – as a matter of law or as a matter of America's superpower right to act as its national security interests required. He demanded weapons inspectors, but never thought of asking for human rights monitors. He invoked the ceasefire resolution 687, banning acquisition of WMD; not Resolution 688 requiring an end to internal repression. Tony Blair, too, accepted that a state's repression of its own people could not, without Security Council agreement, justify intervention, although he did so through gritted teeth:

It may well be that under international law as presently constituted, a regime can systematically brutalize and oppress its people and there is nothing anyone can do, when dialogue, diplomacy and even sanctions fail, unless it comes within the definition of a humanitarian catastrophe . . . This may be the law, but should it be?

His question was rhetorical; it would have been more interesting to ask whether it might become the law, either through attachment to the emerging doctrine of humanitarian intervention, by way of the responsibility to protect principle or through a new and free-standing rule of the kind anticipated by Philip Bobbitt. Most of the ten preconditions for a lawful humanitarian mission without Security Council support (set out at pp. 755–6) were satisfied (or could have been satisfied) in the case of Iraq in early 2003:

(1) There was convincing evidence of the commission of crimes against humanity, although these were mainly in the past, and overlooked at the time by the international community. There can be no statute of limitations on such crimes and nor can other states waive, through inaction, the duty to prosecute them. Human rights groups alleged that torture and persecution were continuing, albeit not on a scale that could be described as 'catastrophic' or as amounting to an 'emergency' which would justify immediate action.

(2) Security Council resolutions had consistently identified Iraq as a threat to world peace and had imposed sanctions which were ignored.

(3) The proposed intervention did not have the stated purpose of punishing these crimes, although that was the reason why many supported it.

(4) The armed response was collective, in the sense that the US eventually gathered the support of forty states, although their contribution (with the exception of the UK) was minimal. It failed, however, to gain the support of the majority of Security Council members.

(5) On the basis that Saddam did possess nuclear weapons,

regional blocs and the European Union wanted them destroyed.

(6) The US did stand to profit in the sense that its corporations gained further access to Iraqi oil, although this was offset by the massive cost of the intervention, the brunt of which was borne by the US.

(7) The method of warfare generally complied with the Geneva Conventions, which the US accepted on this occasion must apply to its invasion and its period in occupation. The question of proportionality is more difficult (see below).

(8) Given Saddam's recalcitrance and determination to hang on to power, invasion was the only way to achieve any improvement in the human rights of the Kurds and the Shia majority, or of realizing their demands for self-determination.

(9) The US was woefully unprepared for occupation. It did not envisage any insurgency. It has reluctantly shouldered the burden, in lives and money, of providing security, democracy and a trial process, and was prepared to allow the UN a limited role in assisting the return of the country to normality.

(10) Saddam was taken alive rather than shot in his bolt hole, but the decision to hand him over to the Iraqis for trial and inevitable death sentence, rather than take him before an international tribunal was a serious mistake.

'Humanitarian intervention', therefore, was not out of the question as a justification, although there was no continuing or threatened persecution on a scale that could call forth emergency action. Intervention on this ground would have failed the test of proportionality – an essential component in a just war ever since its definition by Thomas Aquinas. Wars of any kind take an appalling toll on civilians and soldiers alike, much heavier than the toll on human life that was being taken by Ba'athist repression, even when the lives lost by sanctions are taken into account. Proportionality had been a problem, too, in the case of Kosovo. There it was resolved by reference to the will of the Kosovo Albanians, who were prepared to take the casualties (and about 1,000 of them became 'collateral damage') as a price they stoically agreed to pay in return for freedom from Serb oppression. The

Iraqi exiles – several million of them – were overwhelmingly in favour of invasion, but they would not be in the firing line. The Kurds, who had the long-term agenda (which may yet come to pass) of self-determination, were likewise in favour. The Sunni minority, of course, were implacably opposed, and although some have been prepared to vote in subsequent elections, they have provided most of the resistance fighters. The Shia majority were beneficiaries of the war and victims of its immediate aftermath – they welcomed the fall of Saddam but not the US occupation that followed.

Proportionality is an objective measure and, in using force without Security Council cover, the desire of peoples for liberation must be weighed with their potential suffering, as well as with further imponderables such as the cost in the lives of troops on both sides, the empowerment of Iran, the belittling of the UN, the encouragement to terrorism, and so on. Iraq was a country at peace, albeit the peace of the mass grave: war can only be proportionate and 'humanitarian' if it can confidently be predicted to reduce, eventually, the overall body count. In March 2003, this question was moot: there was no serious attempt to consider whether invasion, with its inevitable toll in human lives, would be a proportionate response to the threat of WMD, much less to calculate whether the lives saved by removing Saddam and lifting sanctions would amount to more than the lives lost in the process.

The way the world should have proceeded against Saddam Hussein was to invoke the Genocide Convention, with its requirement that leaders credibly accused of the worst of all crimes must be brought before an international tribunal – if no national court is available – to account for their actions. This was a procedure as available in 2003 as it was after Halabja, in 1988. Ceasefire resolution 688 had imposed basic human rights standards on Iraq, which were immediately breached by the starvation and mass murder of the marsh Arabs. Had parties to the Genocide Convention established an international court to consider indicting Saddam and his henchmen, followed by a Security Council regimen that dispatched human rights inspectors to gather evidence and to examine his prisons, police cells and court systems, Iraqi disobedience would have been more difficult for France and Russia and Germany to overlook. This is make-believe, in the sense that nobody had ever suggested it in the fifteen years since 1988, although it offered a way forward that may have produced 'regime change' that was altogether less bloody and certainly more legitimate.

The Kellogg–Briand Pact had outlawed war as an instrument of national policy. The United Nations Charter, drawn up after the world's worst war, had not gone so far: it sought to subject the use of force to the rule of law. After many failures and fissures, it seemed by the century's turn that it had more or less succeeded: without Security Council approval, force could only be justified in order to oppose an armed attack or an imminent threat thereof or to avert a humanitarian crisis. But in March 2003, these legal rules were swept aside: the question for nations deciding whether to support an invasion of Iraq was not whether it was lawful, but whether it was wise.[26] International law was marginal to this judgement: the only belligerent to take it seriously was the UK and then mainly as an insurance policy – a 'reasonable', rather than a compelling, argument to cover its back if hauled before the ICC or the ICJ. After the occupation had gone badly wrong, Kofi Annan unequivocally declared that the invasion was unlawful. He might more accurately have said that the arguments advanced for the invasion were inconsistent with international law as it presently stands. It was perfectly consistent with his own statement at the UN Millennium Summit about the 'need to forge unity behind the principle that massive and systematic violations of human rights – wherever they take place – should never be allowed to stand'.[27] The UN has notably failed to forge that unity: rulers of African and Arab states fear that their own violation of 'Western values' might provoke an American-led intervention, while for the Bush administration, massive violation of human rights could never be a reason for intervention unless US security interests were also threatened. What hope then is there for a future in which the use of force by great nations is subject to the rule of law?

The Millennium principle that massive and systematic violations of human rights must not be allowed to stand means inevitably that the use of force cannot be limited to the sclerotic categories written into the UN Charter in 1945. Wars are not necessarily 'unjust' because Russia or China oppose them, or coincidence brings states like Cameroon, Guinea and Angola to non-permanent membership of the Security Council at the time of the vote. The justification for self-defence under Article 51 does not permit the use of force against states where ethnic or dissident groups are mass murdered or tortured, or states which insist on developing a nuclear weapons capacity in a way which endangers the world. The latter problem the UN can try to deal with through the IAEA, as it is doing without great success with Iran, but outside the 'emergency' which calls forth humanitarian intervention, the former states remain a scar on a world that has yet to appreciate the need for a norm against tyranny. That is why some brutal dictators still live happily ever after, whilst others strut their local stage. Running a despotic government which commits widespread human rights violations is not currently condemned by the law of nations: the Taliban would still be the lawful government of Afghanistan if it had not made the mistake of harbouring Osama bin Laden. However much Kofi Annan has talked about the need to end impunity, tyranny still rules OK – ish.

The ultimate goal of the modern human rights movement must be to eliminate rulers, be they hereditary monarchs, military dictators, high priests or political despots who comprehensively violate the fundamental liberties of their subjects. That can only be achieved by a UN convention against tyranny, which would invalidate provisions in national constitutions preventing the prosecution of leaders for crimes committed while in office, and would nullify, once and for all, amnesties and immunities traditionally accorded to those who wield the power of the state. It might establish an international tribunal empowered to examine the record of particular governments to decide whether their violations of fundamental rights are so systematic and widespread as to justify a finding of tyranny. That finding, when transmitted to the Security Council, would serve both as a warning and as a warrant – a warning to such governments to change, or else face the prospect of regime change, by a war the legitimacy of which could not be in doubt. The moral rightness of overthrowing Saddam Hussein and the wrongfulness in law of the means used to accomplish it, serves to emphasize the urgency of devising a procedure for removing the protective veil of sovereignty from regimes and rulers who so grossly abuse it.

THE OCCUPATION OF IRAQ

The invasion of Afghanistan was entitled 'Operation Enduring Freedom', and next came 'Operation Iraqi Freedom'; the first proclamation of the US occupation authority was called 'Freedom Message No. 1' (Comedian Jon Stewart's British audience could be forgiven for taking him seriously when he explained: 'We Americans don't do torture. We do freedom tickling'). In Afghanistan, the Bush administration denied that men it captured on the battlefield were prisoners-of-war under the Geneva Convention, but in Iraq it conceded that the Conventions applied – in battle, during occupation and in prisons like Abu Ghraib. The battle itself was over quickly, in three weeks, with few allegations of war crimes. There was 'collateral damage' – killing civilians – especially from the missiles targeted on Saddam's possible hiding-places throughout Baghdad. Notoriously, there was an attack without warning on the office of Al Jazeera which killed its correspondent, despite the fact that the television company had supplied the co-ordinates of its office to the Pentagon at the start of the war. Al Jazeera is a beacon of progress in the Arab world, where undemocratic governments have been the first to complain about it telling unpalatable truths. Any deliberate attack would be a war crime, and the US refusal to conduct an enquiry inflated what was in all probability a targeting error into an alleged plot against the 'non-embedded' journalists and the Arab press.

Under Geneva Convention IV, the US and UK as 'occupying powers' had a duty to maintain peace and public order, punish crime and protect civilian lives and property.[28] The US had been planning this invasion for over a year but had not made adequate preparation for these duties – as its failure for many months to restore water, sewerage and electricity services to Baghdad demonstrated. That newsworthy moment of joy as Saddam's effigy bit the dust was short-lived, followed by looting which convulsed and desecrated the city: marines stood idly by as human locusts emptied the National Museum of treasures that belonged as much to the world as to Iraq. The looters were replaced by criminal gangs (led by hardened psychopaths newly released from prison and mental asylums) and then by militias specializing in revenge killings and kidnaps of professionals and Westerners. 'Operation Iraqi Freedom' turned into 'Operation Iraqi Anarchy' as every art gallery, museum, cultural centre and civic and political institution of the Iraqi state was gutted. There were not nearly enough US soldiers on the ground: the army had asked for three times the number that Donald Rumsfeld grudgingly vouchsafed, as he complacently minimized the consequences: 'Stuff happens . . . and it's untidy, and freedom is untidy, and free people are free to make mistakes and commit crime and do bad things.' Those who choose to liberate others by war, however, have a responsibility under Geneva Convention IV to stop them doing bad things – and this was one of the legal responsibilities that the US Defense Department culpably refused to shoulder. Had it done so, the occupation may have proved less problematic, and the resulting insurgency less severe.

International law limits the use of force to its lawful objective. Since the UK was relying on the 'revival' of the 'all necessary means' resolution of 1990 (Resolution 678), it followed that the interim administration established by the coalition had to be proportionate to achieving Iraqi disarmament. 'The longer the occupation of Iraq continues and the more the tasks undertaken by an interim administration depart from the main objective, the more difficult it will be to justify the lawfulness of its operation' advised its attorney-general.[29] Lord Goldsmith pointed out that Geneva Convention IV expressly forbids any alteration of the status of public officials or judges or the imposition of major structural or economic reforms. The occupying power is not meant to replace the government of the country, which is merely in abeyance until the temporary occupation ends. The US would have none of this: its real objective, 'regime change', required an utter transformation of Iraqi government and society. So as soon as the main battle was over, the US proclaimed a new government which it called the 'Coalition Provisional Authority' (CPA). Its head, Paul Bremer, had the powers of a satrap and he used them to achieve an economic and political revolution, replacing socialist structures with free enterprise, sacking a host of Ba'athist judges and officials and training a 'shadow' Iraqi government that took over for six months prior to the elections (which it lost) in January 2005. There were, after all, no WMD to be disarmed, but there were countless conventional weapons in dangerous hands: the CPA had no programme to confiscate them or to induce their surrender. Bremer's worst blunder was to disband the Iraqi army, which destroyed the only effective local enforcement authority and laid off many thousands of angry and armed Sunnis. Almost as damaging was his 'de-Ba'athification order', which at a stroke removed capable officials from civic institutions and from the courts. Almost one million Iraqis had joined the Ba'ath party, mostly as a good career move: their removal from public offices without any finding of complicity in the crimes of the regime denuded the country of talent and experience at a time when these qualities were desperately needed.

It is easy to be wise after the event, although Colin Powell's State Department was wise enough before it on most of these issues: President Bush and Vice-President Cheney preferred the myopic advice of the Pentagon and the naive triumphalism of neocon ideologues at Defense, who believed (with that dangerous mixture of utter sincerity and total ignorance) that 'freedom' would instantly produce a united and peaceful Iraq. It was at their insistence that the country did not become the subject of a UN mandate, like Bosnia and Kosovo: the UN was suspect, since it had failed to stand by the US, and the Security Council had first to pass a resolution supporting the CPA before it was invited to assist in the difficult task of putting the state back together again. Kofi Annan could well have taken the position that he was not going to hazard his staff, but humanitarian instinct and a desire to rebuild bridges with the US prevailed. Sergio de Mello, the UN's Human Rights Commissioner, who had overseen East Timor, was soon killed in a suicide-bombing of the UN headquarters. It ushered in a time when humanitarian work in the country would become almost impossible.

ABU GHRAIB: SADISTS ON THE NIGHT SHIFT?

The period of US occupation of Iraq will be worst remembered for the obscene pictures of American soldiers enjoying themselves by subjecting detainees at Abu Ghraib to violence and degradation. An army investigation found numerous instances of 'sadistic, blatant and wanton criminal abuses' and the soldiers received prison sentences ranging from three (Lynndie England) to ten years (Charles Graner). Their behaviour mimicked the more juvenile obsessions of American pornography: victims were forced to masturbate and have sex with each other whilst leering GIs taunted and humiliated them. More serious were the torture pictures – of hooded men hanging from hooks and naked Arabs screaming as Alsatians growled at their genitals. More serious still were pictures of two corpses wrapped in cellophane and packed in ice, in cells plastered with blood.

These torture pictures proved a disastrous own goal for the war on terror, because they became recruiting posters for al-Qaida throughout the Middle East. The pretence that they merely depicted the doings of a few rotten apples in an otherwise wholesome US military barrel was soon belied – not only by the official Schlesinger report into Defense Department operations, but by a paper trail which showed first how Bush administration lawyers had wilfully misinterpreted the law to approve the use of inhumane interrogation techniques for Guantanamo detainees, and secondly how these techniques had 'migrated' to Iraq, borne by military intelligence officers who naturally assumed that they could get away in Abu Ghraib with what had been approved in Guantanamo. Although the inhumane techniques they had been taught did not extend to forcible sex or harsh beatings, the lessons had left an expectation that the Geneva Conventions were irrelevant and that prisoners could be cruelly treated so long as they were not caused permanent physical injury.

The sad story began in the office of counsel to the US Department of Justice, where in the months after 9/11 a group of clever, casuistical lawyers decided that international human rights law must be reinterpreted to deny certain rights to 'war on terror' suspects. Having dreamt up the legal fiction that *habeas corpus* could not extend to an island in Cuba occupied but not owned by the US, their next trick was to explain why the Geneva Conventions did not apply to its detainees either, even to those who had been enlisted in the forces of the government of Afghanistan. It applied only to those who fight for state parties, they said, and although Afghanistan was a state party, it was none the less such a 'failed state' that it lacked the capacity to remain a party to the Conventions. This argument was devised by Jay Bybee (now promoted to a Federal judgeship) and approved by Attorney-General John Ashcroft, who duly advised the president that Taliban combatants 'were not legally entitled to Geneva Convention protections as prisoners-of-war because during the relevant time of the combat, Afghanistan was a failed state. As such it was not a party to the treaty and the treaty's provisions do not apply.'[30]

This advice was legal nonsense, as lawyers in Colin Powell's State Department forcefully pointed out:

The President should know that a decision that the conventions do apply is consistent with the plain language of the conventions and the unvaried practice of the United States in introducing its forces into conflict over fifty years. It is consistent with the advice of Department of State lawyers and, as far as is known, the position of every other party to the conventions. It is consistent with UN Security Council resolution 1193 affirming that 'all parties to the conflict in Afghanistan are bound to comply with their obligations under international humanitarian law and in particular the Geneva Convention' . . . from a policy standpoint, a decision that the conventions apply . . . demonstrates that the United States bases its conduct not just on its policy preferences but on its international legal obligations . . . A decision that the conventions do not apply . . . weakens the protections accorded by the conventions to our troops in future conflicts.[31]

On 7 February 2002, President Bush rejected that indubitably correct advice, and decided that the Geneva Conventions did not apply to any detainees at Guantanamo. It occurred to Bybee that since that was now the case (the president had said so), there was no need to establish tribunals to determine whether these detainees were prisoners-of-war or not.[32] (This opportunistic advice would later be overruled by the Supreme Court.) Having persuaded the president to dump the Geneva Conventions, the Bush lawyers turned their mean minds to the Convention against Torture. In August 2002, they redefined torture as 'physical pain equivalent in intensity to the pain which accompanied serious physical injury, such as organ failure, impairment of bodily function, or even death' – a definition which would exclude pulling fingernails, burning with cigarettes and most electric shocks. In his memorandum to presidential counsel Alberto Gonzales, Bybee drew a distinction between acts of 'torture', for which the Convention required criminal penalties, and acts of 'cruel, inhuman or degrading treatment or punishment', which it merely condemned. Although Article 16 of the Convention requires state parties to 'undertake to prevent ... other acts of cruel, inhuman or degrading treatment or punishment which do not amount to torture as defined in Article I', Bybee managed to turn Article 16 on its head: if it wasn't torture (which he too narrowly defined as 'excruciating and agonizing physical pain'), the US was free to indulge as much as it liked.[33] Its treatment could be as cruel and inhuman and degrading as it was possible to make it, so long as it didn't cause pain equivalent to the pain of organ failure or death.

The Department of Defense drew up three categories of cruel conduct that could in consequence be unleashed on Guantanamo detainees:

(I)   These were the 'Mutt and Jeff' routines familiar in police stations throughout the world. The detainee could be rewarded with cookies and cigarettes for useful answers, and be yelled at, if uncooperative. Deception could be used, especially to produce fear of torture. The interrogator 'may identify himself as a citizen from a country with a reputation for harsh treatment of detainees'. So prisoners could be told they were about to be tortured, so long as no actual torture took place.

(II) Permitted was 'the use of stress positions' and 'the use of falsified documents or reports' (including death certificates for family members). Solitary confinement could last up to thirty days, accompanied by 'deprivation of light' (darkness) and by 'auditory stimuli' (loud and unbearable noise). Interrogation could take place in a 'non-standard environment' – whatever that sinister euphemism may mean (and it could in theory mean a shark tank). Interrogations could last for twenty hours without a break; all religious and other 'comfort items' must be removed; prisoners could be starved and stripped naked. Other Category II techniques for Arabs included shaving of beards ('forced grooming') and 'using detainees' individual phobias (such as fear of dogs) to induce stress'. The Abu Ghraib photographs starkly showed the latter method of stress induction.

(III) The following techniques were approved for uncooperative detainees:

(1) The use of scenarios designed to convince the detainee that death or severely painful consequences are imminent for him and/or his family.

(2) Exposure to cold weather or water.

(3) Use of a wet towel and dripping water to induce the misperception of suffocation.

(4) Use of mild, non-injurious physical contact such as grabbing, poking in the chest with the finger, and light pushing.

This gave licence for 'water boarding', in which the 'misperception of suffocation' was used in a 'non-standard environment' (submersion in a tank) to make detainees believe they were drowning. This was certainly a scenario designed to convince them that death was imminent, and it appears from the pictures of the cellophane-wrapped corpses at Abu Ghraib that occasionally it was.[34]

The interrogation techniques in categories II and III were undoubtedly cruel and inhuman, and hence prohibited by the Geneva

Conventions and by customary international law when applied to prisoners-of-war and civilian suspects. They were all capable of amounting to 'torture' in certain circumstances – when applied routinely to detainees, for example, in a manner calculated to cause severe pain or lasting psychological damage. They should never have been authorized for Guantanamo detainees: the Bush lawyer argument that Afghanistan was a 'failed state' and so its supporters were outside the Convention was bogus, as the State Department lawyers so forcibly pointed out. It should have been obvious that, once authorized, these cruel techniques would become institutionalized and availed of wherever 'intelligence' needed to be extracted from detainees. This was the experience of the British army, which developed 'in depth' interrogation techniques in Aden and Oman in the 1960s and used them on internees in Northern Ireland until they were declared contrary to common law and to the European Convention on Human Rights. Such techniques do not 'migrate' like swallows in summer – once taught, they accompany an army wherever it plants its flag. Since they are cruel and inhuman, they dishonour that flag and produce widespread disaffection amongst communities whose members are subjected to them, especially if – as in Northern Ireland and Iraq – most internees are innocent of any involvement in terrorism.

What is so strikingly absent, in all the thousands of pages of legal memoranda generated in the US Justice Department to justify harsh interrogation, is any sense of how deeply entrenched in Anglo-American common law is the prohibition against torture – a degrading and dishonourable practice yielding unreliable results which English common lawyers as early as the fifteenth century despised as 'something done by the French'.[35] Its use by the King's Star Chamber against Puritan preachers in the 1630s was a potent grievance for those early republicans who fled to Massachusetts. In 1641, Parliament ended torture when it abolished the court of Star Chamber as a preliminary to fighting the civil war to end the 'tyranny' of Charles I. Thereafter, the highest courts in Britain, America and the Commonwealth have refused to admit into evidence confessions obtained as a result of inhuman treatment on the principle that, as Justice Frankfurter put it, 'States in their prosecutions respect certain decencies of civilised conduct'.[36] International human rights law treats the law against torture and inhuman or degrading treatment as absolute and nonderogable.[37] The rule has a *jus cogens* quality: the House of Lords in *Pinochet* and the ICTY in *Furundžija* endorsed Judge Kaufman in *Filártiga* v. *Peña-Irala:* 'The torturer has become, like the pirate and the slave trader before him, *hostis humanis generis*, an enemy of mankind' (see p. 334). In 2005, the House of Lords declared in the case of *A* v. *Home Secretary (No. 2)* that the common-law prohibition against the reception of evidence obtained by torture was still absolute, and applied to all court proceedings (including special 'terrorist' courts): interrogation evidence from abroad was inadmissible if the defence could show that it had been procured by torture.

The law lords refused to gloss or underestimate the definition of torture: it was, in the words of Article 1 of the Convention, any act 'by which severe pain or suffering, whether physical or mental, is intentionally inflicted by or at the instigation of public officials . . . It constitutes an aggravated and deliberate form of cruel, inhuman or degrading treatment or punishment.' But they warned that the standard of what amounts to torture was not immutable: whether 'inhuman treatment' qualifies 'depends on all the circumstances of the case, such as the duration of the treatment, its physical or mental effects, and in some cases, the sex, age and state of health of the victim'.[38] What was originally classified as 'inhuman and degrading' might later amount to 'torture' as higher standards and scientific evidence about its effects become accepted. Lord Bingham conjectured that category 2 and 3 techniques 'may well' fall within the Convention definition of torture.

The simple fact, for all the twisting of legal rules to distinguish between 'torture' and 'inhuman treatment' and between 'prisoners-of-war' and 'unlawful combatants', is that international law requires all states to prohibit officials from treating prisoners brutally: the full title of the Torture Convention is the Convention against Torture and Other Cruel, Inhuman and Degrading Treatment and Punishment. The distinction may be relevant to extradition treaties or to the size of damages awards, and a charge of committing a crime against humanity may require proof of 'torture' under Article 7(1)(f) of the Rome

Statute – in which case proof of cruel treatment will not suffice unless the physical and mental suffering can be described as 'severe'. But as the Abu Ghraib record demonstrates, interrogation that begins with calculated cruelty and degradation – nudity, dogs, stress positions, solitary confinement, and so on – can readily reach the severity threshold when practised daily or when other techniques are added for cumulative effect. Category III 'water boarding', for example – where the prisoner suffers virtual drowning – is without question a torture technique, used, as '*il submarino*', for decades in the torture chambers of South America and in Algeria and Egypt.

After publication of the photographs from Abu Ghraib, approvals for 'non-Geneva' interrogation methods were rescinded. Intelligence agencies circumvented the prohibition by the process of 'extraordinary rendition' – secretly flying 'high value' detainees to prisons in states like Egypt, Syria, Uzbekistan and Yemen, in the hope that torture would elicit information that could be passed back to the CIA. 'Extraordinary rendition' is a lawless operation which is expressly prohibited by Article 3 of the Torture Convention: 'No State party shall expel, return or extradite a person to another State where there are substantial grounds for believing he could be in danger of being subjected to torture.' In pretended compliance with Article 3, America and European countries seek what is termed a 'diplomatic assurance' from the receiving country that a deportee (usually a failed asylum seeker) will not be tortured. These assurances are not worth the paper on which they are faxed. They are 'diplomatic' (i.e. likely to be deceptive) because no state will admit that it tortures. Since they are only sought from states which have a record of permitting torture, they are obviously untrustworthy and some have been proved false.[39] The 'diplomatic assurance' is a practice that should stop, whether in asylum or terrorist deportations or 'extraordinary renditions'. Under the rule in *A* v. *Home Secretary*, a diplomatic assurance should never be accepted by courts as a licence to introduce interrogation evidence from states known to permit torture, and the European Court, in the 2012 *Al Qatada case*, firmly endorsed this principle. It refused to allow the UK to return a suspect for trial in Jordan because of the likelihood that he would face evidence obtained from witnesses by torture.

The rationale for the rule against torture is not only that it dishonours the state and the legal system that permits it, but that it is counter-productive: much of the evidence elicited will be unreliable, and public sympathy will swing behind victims and their cause. Why then was the Bush administration so keen to permit it and so insouciant about criticism – which Donald Rumsfeld dismissed as 'isolated pockets of international hyperventilation'?[40] There was certainly a post-9/11 feeling that the Geneva Conventions were obsolete in this 'new' war on terror, where information might have to be obtained quickly from captured suspects in order to foil bombings and other atrocities. The 'ticking time bomb' scenario was always quoted, involving a suspect who knows where the bomb is hidden and is not prepared to give the vital information voluntarily. Is it justifiable to torture it out of him in order to save lives – a moral end which would justify unlawful means? The problem with the hypothesis, of course, is its unreality: fanatics privy to such knowledge either stay silent because they welcome torture and death as martyrdom, or are sufficiently hardened or pain-wracked to supply false information, which distracts police while the time ticks away. The official who orders the torture may think his judgement is moral when in reality it is perverse. James Schlesinger posited a 'minimum harm rule' for the interrogator: do not inflict more pressure than is necessary to get the desired information, but never cause permanent damage and always be prepared to take the consequences. The danger of a minimum harm rule, however, is that interrogators will always ratchet up the pain if they do not get the desired answers. Schlesinger recommended a professional ethics programme to equip military leaders with a 'sharper moral compass for guidance in situations often riven with conflicting moral obligations'.[41] While ethics education is always welcome, an education in legal obligations, explaining why the law prohibits torture and cruel treatment, would be more appropriate.

Certain forms of torture often work, especially the kind practised by Pinochet and Saddam where spouses, parents and even children were maimed and violated within the sight and hearing of suspects with information their interrogators wanted to extract. But torture of this kind is so bestial that a Western state could never sanction it: the only torture that US officials could authorize – 'stress positions', exploitation of dog phobias, and Category III techniques – will not terrify the real terrorist, and top commanders in Iraq have admitted that they learned little about the insurgency by using these techniques. This kind of inhumanity produces any amount of unreliable leads and rumours from detainees who will say anything to stop it: if truth from prisoners is wanted, interrogators would do better to offer money or freedom. In Iraq, the Red Cross estimated that 75–90 per cent of the detainees had no connection with the insurgency and no useful information to offer in any event. Yet every Iraqi subjected to ill-treatment had a dozen or so relatives – sisters, brothers, parents, wives and children – who became in consequence committed to a blood feud against 'the invaders'. Multiply this number by the number of prisoners ill-treated and the number of Iraqi civilians shot accidentally or through 'pre-emptive' action in Falluja and other flashpoints, and the reason why so many Iraqis who were well disposed to the overthrow of Saddam came to oppose the US military can readily be appreciated. The most significant intelligence tip-off – the whereabouts of Saddam Hussein – came from treating an internee kindly.

The effect of torture on the weak, the innocent or the mere sympathizer cannot be underestimated. It can produce amazing results – false admissions to crimes carrying life imprisonment or even death. In the 1930s, Stalin's show trials fooled the world because every defendant's confession was word perfect, but we now know that before the trial opened, they spent months on 'the conveyor', a disorientation technique in which denial of food and sleep produced suggestibility and acquiescence in the fantastical script written by the prosecutor. They were told at rehearsal that if they changed their lines in the public courtroom, their wives and children would be killed – and they knew that Stalin's willing executioners were not bluffing. The 'conveyor' has been followed, in the grim argot of state sadism, by the 'parrot's perch', the 'telephone', the 'aeroplane', 'water boarding' ('the submarine'), not to mention old standards like the cattle prod, the cigarette burn and the electrode attached to the genitals. The Schlesinger report admitted that there were 'five cases of detainee deaths as a result of abuse by US personnel during interrogations. There are twenty-three cases of detainee deaths still under investigation' – a roundabout way of admitting that at least five and perhaps as many as twenty-eight Iraqis were tortured to death by US intelligence personnel.

Abu Ghraib may have been characterized by James Schlesinger as '*Animal House* on the night shift', but on the day shift, in interrogation rooms, it was institutionalized ill-treatment, approved at the very top by the Secretary of State for Defense. The Americans may have learned little about the insurgency, but would-be insurgents certainly learned something about Americans. As one popular (and initially pro-US) Shia preacher put it in mid-2004, at Friday prayers:

It was discovered that freedom in this land is not ours. It is the freedom of the occupying soldiers in doing what they like . . . abusing women, children, men and the old men and women who they arrested randomly and without any guilt. No one can ask them what they are doing, because they are protected by their freedom . . . no one can punish them, whether in our country or their country. They express the freedom of rape, the freedom of nudity and the freedom of humiliation.[42]

The rhetoric was provocative, but it drew corroboration from the torture pictures from Abu Ghraib, ironically supporting the message that Iraqis had to fight for their own freedom, against their own liberators. President Bush rightly said that the Abu Ghraib photographs 'do not represent America', but they caused America a massive loss of respect and moral authority.

The Schlesinger report explained how the ill-treatment permitted for Afghan detainees in Guantanamo Bay had 'migrated' to Iraq, where the Geneva Conventions applied with full force. The 'message in the field' was that no distinction should be drawn on grounds of geography: intelligence personnel trained to terrify Arabs in Guantanamo used the same techniques to terrify Arabs in Iraq.[43] But the Schlesinger report never grappled with the real problem, which was why it had been necessary to depart from the Geneva Conventions at Guantanamo in the first place. It must have been obvious to those who recommended this course to the president (misstating legal doctrine in the process) that military intelligence officers trained to use inhumane techniques in one war would use them in the next. The Schlesinger report frankly admitted that the 'brutality and purposeless sadism' extended beyond ordinary soldiers to military intelligence personnel and occurred during interrogation sessions and not only at Abu Ghraib. There was 'both institutional and personal responsibility at higher levels', although the person most responsible – Donald Rumsfeld – had his resignation offer refused by President Bush.

Soldiers and their commanders, under pressure and under deadly threats, will always be tempted to break rules to get results. This 'stuff' always happens in wars and in countries where the occupiers are resented. The only satisfactory deterrent is to prosecute those with 'command responsibility', or at minimum to require their resignation, although the only senior officer prosecuted over Abu Ghraib was Janis Karpinski, who was in charge of the prison. Charges against interrogators should have followed, but they did not. International human rights law can lay down rules but it cannot at this juncture require their enforcement against an occupying power. Its only safeguard is the Red Cross, mandated under the Geneva Convention to inspect prisons and report to the detaining authority. Its record at Abu Ghraib was estimable: within a few months of the invasion, its reports were highlighting the systematic use of 'methods of physical and psychological coercion' to obtain information, and 'excessive and disproportionate use of force against persons deprived of their liberty, resulting in death or injury', described in sufficient detail to alert any responsible authority to the need for urgent action.[44] Schlesinger was particularly critical of 'the failure to react appropriately' to this report. What happened to it? A Senate inquiry was subsequently told by army generals that 'it became lost in the Army's bureaucracy and was not adequately addressed', although it later emerged that ICRC reports had indeed been addressed – by an attempt to stop the Red Cross from making on-the-spot inspections.[45] The main ICRC report, in February 2004, was passed by Paul Bremer to the top British diplomat, Sir Jeremy Greenstock, who forwarded it to the military brass in London: they in turn decided not to alert government ministers because the report mainly concerned US forces.[46] It was only through a leak of the ICRC report to the *Wall Street Journal* that the Abu Ghraib scandal became public knowledge – at which point the Red Cross was prepared to state publicly that it had 'repeatedly made its concerns known to the Coalition forces'.

The episode proves the point that Red Cross inspections are no real safeguard, so long as that organization keeps its reports confidential. Without the spur of publicity, detaining authorities will ignore its findings. The ICRC argues that confidentiality is a consequence of its necessary commitment to neutrality, but this does not follow. All that neutrality requires (as the ICJ noted in its *Nicaragua* decision) is that humanitarian assistance must be provided 'without discrimination of any kind'.[47] This is why the Red Cross is right to insist that its officials must ensure that their public statements 'do not contain political opinions or judgments which may cast doubt on the political neutrality of the Red Cross'. But its fetish for confidentiality – coyly described as 'a policy of discretion' – does not follow from its duty to stay impartial. The ICRC requires its employees to sign a 'commitment of discretion' that they 'will not divulge what they observe in the country where they work, particularly when visiting places of detention',[48] and the Hague Tribunal has given them an absolute immunity from being required to testify in war crimes courts.[49] This court ruling (by a majority) is controversial: the overarching principle surely is that there can be no confidence in iniquity, and Red Cross workers (like war correspondents and human rights monitors) should be required to testify if their evidence is crucial to the conviction or acquittal of a defendant on charges of crimes against humanity. The Red Cross should publicly call upon belligerents to waive confidentiality in its prison reports, as a necessary transparency measure to offer some real guarantee that its inspection regime will safeguard prisoners. Alternatively, it could adopt a 'freedom of information' approach under which its reports would be made public a year or two after they had been communicated to detaining authorities. Sunlight is the best disinfectant, and unless and until the public can access Red Cross reports and recommendations, prisoners-of-war will remain at the mercy of jailers who, if merciless, may never be called to account.

THE TRIAL OF SADDAM HUSSEIN

'Ladies and gentlemen, we got him,' gloated Paul Bremer at his press conference on 13 December 2003. He might have added, 'But we are not sure what to do with him.' The president of Iraq – for so he still was – had been hauled out of a hole in the ground near the Tigris River, and was soon displayed chained and caged, weary-eyed and bedraggled, like some primitive chieftain paraded in a Roman triumph. Then he was 'disappeared', probably to the safety of the American military base in Qatar, while the coalition worked out how and where to put him on trial. This decision was not straightforward. In principle, it is desirable to prosecute crimes against humanity at the scene of the alleged crime, where witnesses are readily available and justice can be seen by victims to be done. The trial can become a catharsis for a society on the mend, a symbolic rejection of violence and a sign of the re-establishment of the rule of law. This claim of the Iraqi people to exact retribution sounded fine in theory. It was made vociferously and insistently, especially by the Iraqi Governing Council, a group of pro-Western Iraqi exiles and local representatives of the various ethnic communities. It was endorsed by President Bush: 'They were the people who were brutalized by this man.'

But justice could neither be done nor be seen to be done in Baghdad, in the midst of a civil war in which the defendants' 'people' were killing the 'people' of the judges and prosecutors. Iraq's claim should have given way to the moral and legal right of the international community to try international crimes – certainly the genocide charges of gassing the Kurds and mass murdering the marsh Arabs. On Paul Bremer's desk was a report into the Iraqi justice system by the UN High Commission for Human Rights, describing the system as 'chronically dysfunctional' in all aspects.[50] Legal education and judicial appointments had been corrupted and politicized and few judges had any experience of trials lasting more than a day, or of considering charges with international law complications or 'political' overtones. Shia leaders, meanwhile, were screaming for Saddam's blood and revenge killings were ubiquitous: there was no way that the head of state could get a fair or even secure trial other than outside the country, in front of an international court, or at least before a 'hybrid tribunal' in which international judges would preside.

History demonstrates that it is no easy matter to bring a tyrant to justice in his own country. When he first appeared in the dock before the examining magistrate, Saddam used words reminiscent of Charles I when he faced down Cromwell's judges: 'I would know by what power I am called hither . . . I am your king, your lawful king . . . therefore I would know by what authority, lawful I mean, I am seated here' (see p. 7).[51] Saddam made the same point: 'Who are you? I want to know who you are. What does this court want? I preserve my constitutional rights as the President of Iraq. I do not recognize the power that authorized you . . . I do not want to make you feel uneasy, but you know this is all theatre by Bush.' It was a good question in both cases, asked by heads of state constitutionally clothed with immunity. Charles was executed and became a 'blessed martyr': when his family returned to power, they disembowelled his judges. That was not a happy precedent, but 400 years later there was an alternative – and much better – way to deal with political and military leaders accused of crimes against humanity who could not be fairly or safely tried by those they had persecuted, namely by putting them before an international criminal court, under the aegis of the United Nations.

An international tribunal in The Hague would have put the trial beyond America's sphere of influence. But the trial of Saddam was becoming the main justification for the invasion, and it had to be seen to be fair – especially to keep the British, with their stubborn attraction to international law, a willing coalition partner. A particular problem, however, was that an international court could not impose the death penalty, demanded by all factions in the country and by the Bush administration. Hanging Saddam could only be ordered by an Iraqi court – although there was no judge left in the country whose life or family had not been affected by his rule.

Eventually, the CPA reached an uneasy compromise, predicated on hope that the security situation would improve by the time the prosecution was ready to commence. It established the Iraqi Special Tribunal (IST), composed of the best local judges it could find who had the courage to volunteer. The US donated $75 million to fund the court, in a building within the high security 'Green Zone' which had previously displayed Saddam's gifts from fawning diplomats. The statute of the tribunal was drafted by US and UK lawyers, using UN war crimes precedents: the Sierra Leone 'hybrid model' was much in mind, so Article 4(d) specifically provided for the successor government 'to appoint non-Iraqi judges who have experience in the crimes encompassed in this statute' to sit with the judges from Iraq, in trial chambers of five. (The Appeals Chamber would have nine judges.) Moreover, Article 6(b) required the IST president to appoint, with assistance from the UN, non-Iraqi nationals to sit as observers in all cases and to assist judges 'with respect to international law and the experience of similar tribunals and to monitor the protection by the tribunal of general due process of law standards'. These important provisions reflected the hope that with distinguished judges from UN tribunals either as members of the court or as special observers, decisions by the makeshift IST could be seen to satisfy international standards.

The statute further provided for all the traditional indicia of a fair trial, although defendants would not be entitled to represent themselves (a result of the havoc Milošević-in-person was causing in The Hague). Article 33 specifically excluded former Ba'athists from involvement in the tribunal in any capacity – a rule that created a problem for recruiting experienced local lawyers and was later to encourage McCarthyite smears against some tribunal members. A prosecution team was quickly assembled, full of American legal and forensic talent – it was directed by Greg Kehoe, an ICTY veteran – and it began the task of investigating and collecting documentary evidence. There was no shortage of lawyers from around the world offering their services to defend Saddam (although several high-profile counsel dropped out when they discovered that he had less money to pay them than the media had made out). By the time the trial started, he had ten Iraqi and twenty-five international lawyers on his team, including former US Attorney-General Ramsey Clark. At this early stage, the IST was a model that could easily 'go international': with Security Council approval, it could have been moved to The Hague with international judges in the majority. That would have put its legitimacy beyond doubt: it had begun life as a creature of the US

Bremer administration, and occupiers are specifically prohibited by the Geneva Conventions from setting up special tribunals.

In the meantime, the lack of legal knowledge and experience of tribunal members was addressed by training courses in London, conducted mainly by US lawyers who made careful efforts to avoid 'judicial brainwashing'. The Iraqi judges learned their international law but were anxious to know how they could be true to their judicial oaths (taken under the 1968 Iraqi constitution) and still try Saddam Hussein, the president who had absolute immunity under Article 40 of that constitution from prosecution for any crime committed while in office. One answer was that they could not, if they remained a national court bound by the national constitution. If they were transformed into an international court, however, they could apply international law to strike down constitutional amnesties, even for heads of state (see chapter 7). These proceedings were not confidential (*The New York Times* was in attendance), but British fears of prejudicing the judges caused the training programme to be handed over to the International Bar Association, a body which at that time was more adept at providing lawyers with opportunities for professional networking and golf. At one of its secret training sessions, Saddam was put on mock trial, and was quickly convicted.[52] If this was meant as a rehearsal, it did not prepare anyone for the soap opera to come.

The interim Allawi government announced it was in favour of Saddam's execution, and then the government elected in 2005 made some changes to the statute. The tribunal became the 'Iraqi Higher Criminal Court', its new name making clear that it was embedded in the national judicial system. There were some new judicial appointments, allegedly for political reasons.[53] The provision for international judges suddenly disappeared – other than for unlikely cases to which a foreign state happened to be party. Instead there was a sinister new provision: 'No authority, including the President of the Republic, may grant a pardon or mitigate the punishment issued by the court.' Article 6(4) of the Human Rights Covenant (which the US, the UK and Iraq have ratified) insists that anyone sentenced to death must have the right to seek commutation or pardon after conviction, so this was a breach of international law. But the merciless Iraqi politicians wanted Saddam executed, and this new provision seemed designed to prevent President Talabani – a Kurd who had in the past expressed opposition to the death penalty when it was imposed on Kurds – from ever considering clemency.

The first case selected for trial was, curiously, the least serious. Saddam was accused, with seven officials, of responsibility for a reprisal killing in 1982 of 143 men in the Shia village of Dujail, after a failed attempt on his life. Although eyewitness descriptions of torture and summary execution were moving, they could not disguise the fact that many of the villagers were guilty of conspiracy to murder their president, and executions had followed a formal investigation by a co-accused, Judge al-Bandar, head of Iraq's 'Revolutionary Court'. The Dujail executions did not amount to an international crime, and the suspicion must be that the case was chosen either (or both) to play to Shia emotions or to obtain a speedy conviction, after which Saddam could be hanged. In that event, his execution would deprive the world of any trial and hence any authoritative judgment on his responsibility for genocide against the Kurds and the marsh Arabs.

None the less, the Dujail case became 'the trial of the twenty-first century' when it opened in October 2005. Saddam, neatly shaved and attired in grey pinstripe, was seen on television throughout the world, sitting in a large metal playpen and making pained or crude interruptions ('Go to hell!') to the unfailingly calm and polite Kurdish judge, Rizgar Mohammed Amin. As these proceedings went on, however, they became increasingly chaotic. Two defence lawyers were assassinated in the first few weeks; Saddam was assaulted by a court official and a guard's child was kidnapped. Security arrangements meant that defence lawyers had difficulty taking full instructions from their clients on visits to the prison, where their meetings were monitored by prison guards. One judge was killed earlier in the year and later Iraqi police stumbled upon a plot to kill the investigating judge, but three policemen were killed by a gunman as they attempted to arrest the suspect. As a simple matter of security, the trial was unfair to its lawyers and judges and court staff, as well as to defendants – it should not have taken place where and when it did.

The credibility of the trial in its early days hinged on its presiding judge, the only member of the tribunal prepared to show his face, a mask of patience and fairness – he even allowed the inevitable Ramsey Clark to address the court on Saddam's behalf. His attempt to produce a fair trial soon came under fire from Shi'ite politicians, and behind the scenes he was put under such improper pressure that in January 2006 he resigned. His deputy faced accusations from the de-Ba'athification authorities, so another Kurdish judge was brought in to preside. Judge Abdel Rahman was from Halabja: his friends and relatives had been gassed in the Anfal campaign and he had been reportedly jailed *in absentia* for anti-Saddam activity. Saddam and his lawyers claimed that Judge Rahman was biased and withdrew from the courtroom in protest. The defendant was ordered back and forced to hear the testimony of his alleged victims, although his lawyer refused to return and Saddam responded by going on hunger strike. As this rowdy atmosphere pervaded the court (so unlike those 'mock trials' held by the IBA in the calm of England's Lake District), witnesses for the prosecution were intimidated and witnesses for the defence seemed increasingly unlikely to answer their summonses. The trial was not, in its early months, a satisfactory proceeding – and important evidence and legal arguments, about Saddam's immunity and his responsibility for genocide, seemed far off.

The proceedings were televised and watched extensively in Iraq and in sound bites throughout the world. There was initial satisfaction at seeing the mighty, fallen – but also a disquietening sense that this event was not judicial but rather politically pre-ordained. The shouting matches in court between prosecution and defence lawyers and the interventions by defendants referred to and reflected the political divide in the country. Judge Rahman spent more time acting as television censor than as presiding jurist, ever alert to press the button that would blank television reception whenever a defendant made a remark which might inflame the insurgency. Behind the scenes a nine-judge appeals chamber was being assembled and Shia politicians openly boasted that once it turned down Saddam's first appeal, the new amendment to the court statute would require him to be rushed to the gallows without consideration of clemency. Against this background, the trial proceedings were a continuation of the war by other means and the heated political exchanges, appropriate to a public meeting rather than a court, were not out of place in this particular arena. Try as the judges undoubtedly did, they could not persuade informed observers that what they were doing was justice according to law. That was not their fault: it was yet another disaster attributable to a purblind American occupation which had stoked rather than smothered the fires of vengeance and factional hatred.

In sum, the trial of Saddam Hussein was simply too important to be left to and in Iraq. The national court was not equipped to try him or to render a fair verdict on all the evidence that could have been made available. An international criminal court, sitting with both local and international judges, could have achieved this. Given the deteriorating security situation in Baghdad, the argument for moving the trial to The Hague, or to Jordan or Kuwait, before a special court set up by agreement between the Security Council and the Iraqi government, was compelling. In rejecting it, the US ignored the Genocide Convention (which Iraq, the US and the UK had all ratified), which requires trial and punishment if not by a 'competent national court' then by an international penal tribunal.

The main reason why this was resisted is that no UN court can impose the death penalty. Indeed, as a party to the European Convention on Human Rights, Britain should not have permitted Saddam and the other prisoners to be handed over to the new Iraqi civilian government without first obtaining assurances that the death penalty would not be imposed. But the Iraqis were adamant, as one American lawyer involved in training their judges explained: 'Iraqis are fiercely proud of their legal tradition, as the country that created the first criminal code (the Code of Hammurabi) some 2,700 years ago. Since then, Iraq has always had a death penalty, and Iraqis consider its continued existence an important matter of their cultural heritage.'[54] It is precisely this primitive 'cultural heritage' that needs to be rethought in a country that continues to be plagued by blood vengeance.

Supporters of the death penalty for Saddam & Co. did have one point, however. If convicted, the Ba'athist leaders could hardly be imprisoned for life inside a country where they still had armed factional support. Britain learned one lesson from the martyrdom of

Charles I: instead of executing Napoleon, it sent him to exile in the South Atlantic. The UK opposes the death penalty, and doubtless it would make the Falkland Islands available, as a place where defendants, if convicted, would serve out a life sentence communing only with penguins, and would never be heard from again.

The trial of Saddam Hussein must be accounted a missed opportunity to bring to the bar of international justice one of the worst tyrants of modern times – a man whose own idea of justice, within the military-security regime he constructed, was to have his enemies killed in secret, or in some cases shot by firing squad on television. It might have shown the Arab world that there is an alternative to the tradition of vengeance: building upon the Genocide Convention (and avoiding the mistakes of the Milošević proceedings), it might have created an important precedent for international condemnation and punishment of heads of state who mass murder their own people, after a process which authoritatively establishes the facts and fairly examines all available defences. Instead, Saddam was not tried for an international crime and there are doubts about his role in the Dujail events. None the less he was deviously denied any right to seek commutation of his death sentence and was rushed to the gallows, his last moments obscenely and unlawfully captured on cell phone pictures taken by prison guards and instantly uploaded for the enjoyment of the Iraqi majority. Crimes against humanity should be condemned by humanity – by the international community, through global justice institutions, and not by courts and legislators consumed, however understandably, by feelings for that wild justice, revenge.[55]

14

The Guernica Paradox: Bombing
for Humanity

'It is too late in the day . . . to tell us that nations may not forcibly interfere with one another for the sole purpose of stopping mischief and benefiting humanity.'

John Stuart Mill, 'Vindication of French Revolution of February 1848'

'If tyranny becomes so unbearable as to cause the nation to rise, any foreign power is entitled to help an oppressed people that has requested its assistance.'

Hugo Grotius

As international lawyers scurried to the television studios of European capitals in the early evening of 24 March 1999 to explain the Pinochet judgment handed down that afternoon, they found themselves instead improvising answers to a more urgent question: is NATO's bombing of Serbia (which had begun that day) lawful? The following day George Robertson, the UK Defence Secretary and later head of NATO, gave to Parliament the considered British answer: 'We are in no doubt that NATO is acting within international law. Our legal justification rests upon the accepted principle that force may be used in extreme circumstances to avert a humanitarian disaster.'[1]

The right of humanitarian intervention an *accepted* principle?

As recently as 1986, the UK Foreign Office had concluded: 'The overwhelming majority of contemporary legal opinion comes down against the existence of a right of humanitarian intervention.'[2] It noted that no such right was contained in the UN Charter and it questioned whether state practice afforded any 'genuine' examples, but its real reason was based 'on prudential grounds, that the scope for abusing such a right argues strongly against its creation'. However, this is a diplomat's argument: the very purpose of legal definition is to narrow the scope for abuse, and international law would be an obscenity if it *required* the world to turn its back rather than act to save the lives of thousands of men, women and children, merely because the massacres were located in an unco-operative sovereign state. Yet it was this position, as bystander to genocide, that was cold-bloodedly adopted by Russia (and by many international law academics) arguing that if an attack on Serbia was not undertaken by the Security Council then it could not be undertaken at all. And it would not have been undertaken by the Security Council in the spring of 1999, even if 1.7 million Kosovars were in the process of being exterminated, because Russia would cast its veto (both for sentimental attachment to Serbia and fear of creating a precedent for Chechnya), followed by China, dogmatic about reading Article 2(4) of the UN Charter literally. Later in 1999, China was responsible for hundreds of deaths in East Timor, over the ten days following the UN referendum, when it refused to allow a 'coalition of the willing' to enter the country to protect civilians until the Indonesian president agreed. In 2012, after thousands had been killed by the Assad dictatorship in Syria (see p. 605), Russia (its closest ally and main arms supplier), together with China, vetoed a mildly critical Security Council resolution. What had become of the UN's much-vaunted doctrine, adopted by the General Assembly in 2005, that it had a 'responsibility to protect' people whose states had fallen so far down in their duty to look after their innocent civilians that they were busy killing them?

The 'responsibility to protect', charmlessly abbreviated to R2P, was an ingenious way around the humanitarian roadblock of Article 2(4) – the Westphalian rule in the UN Charter that states must refrain from threatening or using force against each other. R2P holds that each state has a responsibility to protect the lives of its citizens, and only when it cannot or does not protect them – e.g. when it is killing them, or cannot end a civil war in which they are being killed – does the responsibility devolve on the Security Council, and upon no other body or group of nations. R2P was devised by a high-level committee, led by former Australian foreign minister Gareth Evans, in the wake of confusion over the unauthorized intervention in Kosovo, and much watered down before acceptance by the General Assembly in 2005. R2P was mentioned in Security Council Resolutions 1970 (to refer the situation in Libya to the ICC) and 1973, to empower NATO to enforce a no-fly zone and use 'all necessary means' to protect civilians. That R2P had its limits, however, was very soon apparent, as Russia and China were not prepared for the Security Council to condemn or take forceful action against Syria. It is not always China or Russia that plays the dog in the manger: the worst example of a superpower stand-off was when the US and UK prevented the Security Council from intervening to save hundreds of thousands from being macheted to death in Rwanda, by pretending that what was happening was not genocide.

There were some post-war precedents for life-saving humanitarian interventions prior to Kosovo: India's invasion of East Pakistan to stop the genocide in what, thanks to that intervention, became Bangladesh; Tanzania's invasion of Uganda to remove the mad and bad Idi Amin; the US action in Grenada to restore peace and wrest power from the murderers of Maurice Bishop. All such interventions saved lives, although the UN purported to disapprove of them at the time. Whilst R2P is all very well if it encourages the Security Council to take unanimous action under Chapter VII to stop crimes against humanity, the irresponsible use by the 'big five' permanent members of their veto means that some last-resort right of humanitarian intervention is still required to save innocent lives.

In 1999, the problem crystallized in Kosovo, where Milošević and his nationalist Serb government were committing atrocities against the predominantly Muslim population of this province, and were about to extirpate hundreds of thousands of them from their homes and farms.

So, on the cusp of the millennium, the Western alliance had to wrestle with what might be termed the Guernica paradox: when can it be right to unleash terror on terrorists, to bomb for human rights, to kill to stop crimes against humanity? They decided in relation to Kosovo that it was right to use force in extreme circumstances to avoid a humanitarian disaster, but this simple proposition begged many questions. When are circumstances 'extreme'? Who decides the amount of force necessary – or proportionate – to deal with the disaster? These are the questions which had to be asked after an intervention that took the form of bombing from 15,000 feet, a height calculated to cause civilian casualties while protecting allied pilots. As with modern war of any kind, the result of NATO's bombing was tragedy and terror, the greatest anguish being that some of it was inflicted on the very people that the West had intervened to save in the name of that 'indignant pity' first identified by Theodore Roosevelt as the wellspring for humanitarian intervention. *Guernica* came once again to life, its screaming victims this time hit by accident rather than design.

These arguments bypassed the threshold question of whether NATO's action was lawful at all. There is a specific right, under Article 51 of the UN Charter, for states to go to war in self-defence (as Britain did in 1983 to recapture the Falkland Islands from their Argentinian invaders), but no NATO member was at risk from what remained of the state of Yugoslavia (Serbia, Kosovo and Montenegro). Alternatively, under Chapter VII the Security Council might determine that war on a sovereign state was necessary to restore international peace and security – the basis for the Gulf War on Iraq in 1991. But although the Security Council had passed a number of resolutions about Kosovo in the year before the bombing, none authorized the use of force. It was not asked for a mandate, for the very good reason that Russia and China made clear they would veto any such move. Since international law has the habit of pulling itself up by its own boot-straps (actions by states which have no precedent in 'state practice' serve in their turn as evidence of a new 'state practice', thereby helping to create a new rule of customary international law which will justify similar state actions in the future), the legitimacy of NATO's attack on Serbia must be settled.

A similar question had to be considered in 2011, over NATO's bombing of Libya, empowered (up to a point) by Resolution 1973. Did 'mission creep' and the ambiguities of the English language turn what was meant to be approval for an air patrol into a licence for regime change? The question-begging formula cobbled together by diplomats in Resolution 1973 stated that NATO must protect civilians by all necessary measures, and made no mention of removing Gaddafi. But if he was not removed, then civilians would be massacred by Gaddafi. Having gone so far as to create a no-fly zone and to encourage the rebel forces by bombing their enemies, was it not morally imperative for NATO to go further, even beyond its mandate, to ensure that rebel forces won the war, because if they lost it, Gaddafi's revenge would have involved the massacre of tens of thousands of civilians in rebel towns?

The only answer that satisfies common sense and common morality, and is consistent with legal positivism, is to acknowledge that there is a strictly limited right of humanitarian intervention, and to go on to define those strict limits. The lesson to be learnt from those two great débâcles of our time – unlawful intervention in Iraq and unlawful non-intervention in Rwanda – is that international law does provide a right to intervene to prevent a humanitarian catastrophe, available to states as a very last resort when the Security Council ignores a catastrophe or its projected action is blocked by a superpower veto. There are ample precedents in state practice, and the right in any event builds on international law defences of necessity and of distress (which excuses actions taken to prevent serious and imminent peril to life). The responsibility to protect is fine as far as it goes, but too often it comes up against a brick wall, namely a threat of veto by one of the five permanent Security Council members. It is in that situation, exemplified by Kosovo, that any responsibility to protect innocent civilians must allow intervention without Security Council authorization, if certain limiting conditions are fulfilled, or (as in the case of Libya) must permit a regional force like NATO to exceed its Security Council mandate in order to prevent crimes against humanity.

THE RIGHT OF HUMANITARIAN INTERVENTION

There is hostility to 'liberal humanitarian interventionism' which lingers from the US invasion of Iraq. The notion that George Bush was either a liberal or a humanitarian is misplaced, and there was no human emergency in Iraq at the time he invaded – only afterwards, and as a consequence of that invasion. As chapter 13 explains, the US government and their UK supporters were very clear at the time that they were going to war on the grounds of self-defence against Saddam's illegal build-up of what turned out to be non-existent weapons of mass destruction. The White House specifically disavowed any claim to be acting on humanitarian principles and the formal advice of the British Attorney-General was that no such right (if it even existed) could justify the invasion. It cannot be too clearly stated that the invasion of Iraq was not an exercise in humanitarian, let alone liberal, interventionism. The promotion of human rights has been a retrospective and false excuse proffered (especially by Tony Blair) after the weapons of mass destruction turned out to be a chimera. There was no crime against humanity or extensive loss of life to stop in 2003 – the time for that intervention was 1988, with the gassing of the Kurds at Halabja, but it had long passed.

Some international lawyers doubt the existence of any such right: as one textbook bluntly puts it, 'international law does not recognise a right of humanitarian intervention, except under the authority of the UN'.[3] This is a mistake, because custom – a primary source of international law – certainly provides examples over several centuries. Customary international law is moving towards the position that there is an *erga omnes* duty to punish perpetrators of crimes against humanity, which implies a right to intervene so far as to have them arrested and put on trial or at least to stop their ongoing crimes. A powerful attack on legal scholarship that denies the right has been delivered by historians at Princeton and Cambridge, who observe that 'legal scholars, though considering history, actually do so superficially'.[4] In fact, writings on the definition of the right go back to the 'just war' theories of St Augustine. Later (in the thirteenth century) St

Thomas Aquinas argued for the right to take up arms against tyrants. Grotius added that any intervention must come at the request of the potential victims. Other philosophers insisted that there must be no mixed motives – no interest in obtaining territory or mineral wealth, for example. These preconditions were capable of crystallization into preconditions for the exercise of a right of humanitarian intervention.

In 1655, just seven years after the Treaty of Westphalia, Cromwell threatened intervention to stop 'violation of the honest maxims of humane policy' by the Duke of Savoy, the ruler of Piedmont, who had ordered all Protestants to convert to Catholicism on pain of death and had massacred 300 of them, burning their homes '*pour encourager les autres*'. Milton penned a famous sonnet, 'On the Late Massacre in Piedmont', lamenting that fellow Protestants 'whose bones/ lie scattered on the Alpine mountains cold' who had been 'slain by the bloody Piedmontese that rolled/ mother with infant down the rocks'. Oliver Cromwell wept for pity, and then planned a humanitarian intervention using the British fleet, master of the Mediterranean, to blockade Nice (then Piedmont's sea-port). The duke gave in, and signed a treaty (with England as guarantor) promising tolerance of Protestantism.[5] Interestingly, Cromwell had collected a large sum to pay for post-war reconstruction and to repair damage 'caused by the war, as pillaging, burning and the like' – his prescience in this respect shaming Donald Rumsfeld, 350 years later, who gave no thought to regenerate Iraq after 'stuff happens'.

When early international lawyers like Grotius and Vattel searched for definitions of a 'just' war, they routinely included the rescue of oppressed peoples: 'If tyranny becomes so unbearable as to cause the Nation to rise, any foreign power is entitled to help an oppressed people that has requested its assistance.'[6] This was, after all, a logical development of Locke's theory of government by consent: if tyrants can be overthrown when they abuse their power and destroy the people they are obliged to protect, then it follows that other governments may lawfully render 'humanitarian' assistance to those battling for their lives. Indeed, if the tyrant is a colonial power committing widespread atrocities and is opposed by a majority of the native people, this 'right of humanitarian assistance' is really a right in aid of self-determination. The difficulty arises in law when the victims are not in the majority in a state – when they are peoples of a province, or a race, or both. Just how bogus may be a claim made on their behalf was demonstrated by Hitler's claim of a right to invade Czechoslovakia in order to protect German minorities from alleged Czech brutality, and then to invade Poland to save German minorities there from the allegedly inhumane Poles.

Hitler gave the so-called 'right of humanitarian intervention' a bad name, but there were better precedents. The nineteenth century saw many high-minded debates over its application, at least in Britain, beginning with the great example of ending the slave trade – a policy which caused the country great economic loss and damaged its relations with Spain, France and the US, with several thousand naval and military lives lost in various anti-slavery operations. These downsides for the national interest made the policy genuinely selfless: it involved incursions on sovereignty by seizing and confiscating the ships of other countries, with incursions on foreign land to liberate slaves awaiting transportation. Then came the Philhellenes – described as 'the first modern human rights group'[6] – as their poets (Byron and Shelley), philosophers (Bentham) and liberal politicians (the Whigs) condemned the Ottoman massacres and demanded that Lord Castlereagh and his Tory government take military action against their great ally (the Ottoman Empire was a pro-British bulwark against Russian expansion).[7] Many massacres later, the interventionists won: in 1827 a British fleet, joined by French and Russian warships, destroyed the Turkish and Egyptian fleets at the battle of Navarino – the decisive victory that led to the creation of modern Greece. Navarino was a disaster for the foreign policy pursued by Conservative governments, but it was invoked as a famous victory by Liberal leader Gladstone in his Midlothian campaign demanding intervention to stop massacres in Bulgaria. 'Damaging to our honour and fatal to our interests. Navarino over again,' his Conservative opponent Disraeli wrote to Queen Victoria.[8] But Gladstone's oratory prevailed: the moral indignation of the Liberals again triumphed over Tory *realpolitik*. It was not unmixed with an imperial sense of superiority and a degree of Christian smugness (although the Church of England – 'the

Tory party at prayer' – opposed all these interventions), but Gladstone's direct appeal was to human decency and the parable of the good Samaritan.

The liberal tradition of intervention to stop massacres was, therefore, well established by 1898, when the US acted to free Cuba from Spanish domination. President McKinley drew heavily on liberal rhetoric: 'We took up arms only in obedience to the dictates of humanity and in the fulfillment of high public and moral obligations. We had no design of aggrandisement and no ambition of conquest.'[9] He probably believed this, as did most Americans (his successor, Theodore Roosevelt, actually spoke of a 'duty' to intervene in order to stop 'systematic and long-extended cruelty and oppression'). But curtailing Spanish brutality in Panama and Cuba by extirpating the Spanish brought strategic benefits; as a result, the US in 1906 insisted on keeping Puerto Rico and (ironically) Guantanamo Bay.

In 1984 a US intervention in the Caribbean that could have been justified as a response to a humanitarian emergency was undertaken when the governing party of Grenada fell apart, and one side started murdering the other, including Prime Minister Maurice Bishop, his pregnant partner and dozens of his supporters who had come out in the street to chant 'We want our leader'. President Reagan, however, was neither liberal nor humanitarian: he justified the intervention with the bogus claim that America had to send in the Marines to protect some pampered students at a private medical school, who were in fact safe and far from the shooting. His real reason was fear that the murderous faction were Stalinists (Bishop, a socialist, had been bad enough) and there was hope of restoring a previous pro-American prime minister, who believed in flying saucers. Reagan was admonished for breaching Grenada's sovereignty by his close friend Mrs Thatcher, who had just come triumphant through the Falklands War and considered a squabble between black politicians beneath her notice. The UK, which should have acted to stop the violence, at least collaborated with the US in putting the killers on trial, thus ensuring that the death penalty was not imposed. A dozen or so were convicted and spent many years in the island's prison obtaining law degrees and then doctorates from London University: whenever the government tried to release them (they were providing an expert legal service to prisoners) the public objected. They had not forgotten the massacre, and they had not found Maurice Bishop's body. They remained grateful, on the whole, for American intervention – the right act for the wrong reason.

Prior to Kosovo, there were three examples of interventions against state sovereignty without Security Council authorization which did in fact avert or curtail humanitarian disasters, an objective which motivated the intervening states but which they did not specifically advance to justify their actions. India's invasion of East Pakistan in 1971 stopped the campaign of mass murder and rape by the Pakistani army and led to self-determination by Bangladesh. There was some strategic advantage to India, but it certainly had the consequence of stopping genocide. Nonetheless it was greeted with a chorus of Cold War diplomatic disapproval, because this was achieved by a Soviet ally. That was the reason for the universal Western condemnation of Vietnam's invasion of Cambodia which put an end to Pol Pot's regime after it had killed 1.7 million Cambodians. There is no more revealing example of the stupidity of the doctrinaire anti-Soviet policy in this period than the Carter/Reagan embrace of the Khmer Rouge (partly to curry favour with its sponsor, China) notwithstanding evidence of their perverted assumption of a 'responsibility to destroy' a substantial section of Cambodia's population. Vietnam justified its invasion on the tenuous ground of self-defence (there had been some border clashes) and it had the strategic advantage of installing Hun Sen's friendly government, but in retrospect its action saved hundreds of thousands of innocent Cambodian lives, and put an end to the crimes against humanity now being prosecuted, so many years later, at the ECCC.

There was less international outrage in 1979 when Tanzania invaded Uganda to overthrow the crazed Idi Amin, who had already killed 100,000 of his people. Diplomats muted their criticism because Tanzania's President, Julius Nyerere, was not a Soviet ally. Despite the compelling human rights justification, Tanzania too claimed, quite incredibly, that it had acted in self-defence. It was as if the right of humanitarian intervention, articulated so clearly in the nineteenth century, could no longer be used in diplomatic discourse, because Article 2(4) of the Charter was a full-blooded reassertion of Westphalian sovereignty.

The end of the Cold War saw the revival of humanitarian intervention, firstly and uncontroversially in relation to the US-led action against Saddam Hussein in the first Gulf War. That, however, was to remedy his blatant breach of Article 2(4) – he had unlawfully invaded Kuwait. UN support for humanitarian relief operations against warring tribes was the basis for the UN's intervention in Somalia in 1992 – here again, the Security Council was unanimous, with China casting its vote, for the first time, in favour of a humanitarian intervention. Its collapse (the US withdrew after 'Black Hawk Down') influenced the 'big five' powers to turn a blind eye to the genocide in Kosovo a few years later.

After the First World War, when the rights of minorities were overseen by the League of Nations, the question of secession was squarely addressed in two reports of jurists called upon by the League to determine the future of Finland's Aaland Islands. They reported in 1920 that the League would be entitled to consider the claim of a minority group to secede in the event of 'a manifest and continued abuse of sovereign power, to the detriment of a section of the population of a State'.[10] It was this 'Aaland Islands Question' which loomed over Kosovo in 1999: a historically defined province of Serbia, comprising 90 per cent Albanian Muslims who were being driven out of their homes and out of the country by Milošević's continued abuse of Serbia's sovereign power. If the Kosovars had in these circumstances a right to secede, would their cries for assistance entitle NATO to respond? This would depend, first and foremost, on whether any right of humanitarian intervention (or right to assist secession) could survive outside the binding international law regime established by the United Nations Charter, which prevails over any other international agreement (see Article 103 of the Charter) and to which indeed Article 7 of the North Atlantic Treaty genuflects by providing that membership of NATO does not affect 'the primary responsibility of the Security Council for the maintenance of international peace and security'.

The heart of the UN Charter is Article 2. Paragraph 4 provides:

(4) All members shall refrain in their international relations from the threat or use of force against the territorial integrity or political independence of any state, or in any other manner inconsistent with the purposes of the United Nations.

Article 2(7) allows the UN itself to 'intervene in matters which are essentially within the domestic jurisdiction of any State . . .', but only through application of Chapter VII enforcement measures by the Security Council, which must first 'determine the existence of any threat to the peace, breach of the peace, or act of aggression' (Article 39). It may then, if measures short of armed force are insufficient, 'take such action by air, sea or land forces as may be necessary to maintain or restore international peace or security' (Article 42).

Critics of NATO's action argued that these sections of the Charter cover the field and by implication extinguish any pre-existing customary law right of humanitarian intervention, whether by a single state or a regional group, without Security Council approval. They placed additional reliance on the second sentence of Article 53 – 'no enforcement action shall be taken under regional arrangements or by regional agencies without the authorization of the Security Council' – although this in fact refers (as the opening sentence of Article 53 makes clear) only to situations where the UN has *already* utilized regional agencies. To fall within the 'just war' permitted by Chapter VII of the Charter, Security Council condemnation of the enemy for crimes against humanity is not enough: there must be a resolution to use force, passed by at least nine of the fifteen members without any of the five permanent members (US, China, Russia, France and Britain) casting a veto.

This was the case made on behalf of Yugoslavia when it took NATO countries to the International Court of Justice in May 1999 in a forlorn effort to injunct the bombing campaign.[11] Where it breaks down is in its failure to demonstrate that the Charter outlaws the use of force other than pursuant to Chapter VII. This cannot be the Charter's effect because Article 51 provides that it shall not 'impair the inherent right of individual and collective self-defence' of a state subject to armed attack, irrespective of whether or not the Security

Council decides to intervene. This is one 'inherent' right which has not been abrogated by the UN Charter, and the same may be said of the customary international law right of humanitarian intervention. The only legal precedent that Yugoslavia's lawyers relied upon to dispute its existence was a comment by the ICJ in the 1986 *Nicaragua Case*, that the US Congress was entitled to criticize the Sandinista human rights record but not to seek to improve it by mining Nicaraguan harbours, destroying oil refineries and sending the Contras as surrogate soldiers.[12] The right of humanitarian intervention arises in an emergency, to stop the continuing commission of crimes against humanity: it has never been suggested that a state's poor human rights record alone could justify armed intervention. The ICJ in *Nicaragua* was demolishing a hypothetical 'right of ideological intervention' urged to justify destabilization of a particular political system: it was not deciding whether a regional group of states was entitled to use force to stop another state in the region mass murdering a section of its people. Indeed, the ICJ goes on to emphasize that 'the UN Charter . . . by no means covers the whole area of the regulation of the use of force in international relations' and explains that 'customary international law continues to exist alongside treaty law [i.e. the Charter]'.[13] So NATO's critics were wrong to this extent: the UN Charter does not 'cover the field' and exclude the use of force pursuant to any rule of customary law which has crystallized independently of it.

Whether the right of humanitarian intervention did exist in customary international law was an issue ducked by the International Court of Justice, two months into the NATO bombing, when it delivered its ruling rejecting Yugoslavia's request for 'provisional measures'. It declared itself 'profoundly concerned with the use of force in Yugoslavia' (as well it might be, since it has a responsibility under the UN Charter to help maintain peace and security) and 'in the present circumstances [the bombing] raises very serious issues of international law'.[14] Fatuously, it then went on to demand that all parties act in conformity with their obligations under international law – obligations which it had declined to elucidate (other than to describe them as 'very serious').

Yugoslavia was knocked out on a technicality. It had always refused to consent to the Court's jurisdiction until, a month into the bombing, it opportunistically decided to avail itself of this international tribunal: most defendant states refuse to consent to jurisdiction in these circumstances, so the predictable result was a refusal to adjudicate, since (as Judge Higgins commented) 'the jurisdiction of the court – even if one might regret this state of affairs as we approach the twenty-first century – is based on consent'. The Court did not lack jurisdiction, however, under the Genocide Convention, to which both the UK and Yugoslavia were fully fledged parties, and the latter (with breathtaking hypocrisy, given its own persecution of the Kosovars) accused NATO of genocidal intent towards the Serbs. The Court delivered a legal ruling that 'the threat or use of force against a State cannot in itself constitute an act of genocide within the meaning of Article II of the Genocide Convention', so it is not genocide to mount a lethal attack on a state which is oppressing a section of its own people. Further than this, the ICJ refused to be drawn.

It was Václav Havel who best expressed the purpose of NATO's intervention, namely to punish a nation state for committing crimes against humanity. In a speech to the Canadian parliament six weeks into the bombing, he updated the definition of the 'just war':

This war places human rights above the rights of the State . . . although it has no direct mandate from the UN, it did not happen as an act of aggression or out of disrespect for international law. It happened, on the contrary, out of respect for a law that ranks higher than the law which protects the sovereignty of states. The alliance has acted out of respect for human rights as both conscience and international legal documents dictate.

Havel was referring to what might be termed the evolving principle of humanitarian necessity, whereby force of a proportionate kind may be used to prevent a humanitarian catastrophe. This is the 'Good Samaritan' paradigm, writ large: the obligation to stop mass murder of innocents must override the rule about not intervening in the affairs of other states. This exception to sovereignty can be developed juristically from defences familiar in most national legal systems: *necessity* (which excuses unlawful actions taken to prevent serious and imminent peril) and *distress* (which permits illegality to protect life during an emergency). The International Law Commission, dominated by state-serving lawyers, allows these defences only to states which use force to protect themselves or their national interests, rather than to save people in other states from being massacred – a backward view, blinkered by sovereignty. It is better morally to build on the ICJ decision in the *Corfu Channel Case* in 1949, which condemned Albania for neglecting to warn foreign shipping that its waters were mined. This rogue state had overlooked 'elementary considerations of humanity, even more exacting in peace than war'.[15]

These elementary considerations are built into the Charter, which begins with a reaffirmation of faith in fundamental human rights and sets out as a purpose the promotion of respect for human rights and fundamental freedoms. So when Article 2(4) says that

All members shall refrain in their international relations from the threat or use of force against the territorial integrity or political independence of any state, or in any *other manner inconsistent with the purposes of the UN* . . .

it really means to prohibit any armed attacks which are inconsistent with Charter purposes, and does not necessarily exclude those which are directed to uphold those purposes (unless they are actually *contrary to* or *condemned by* a specific Security Council resolution). This interpretation might permit the use of force where it is directed not to the conquest of territory or the overthrow of a political system, but to the rescue of innocent persons at risk of extermination, or the entry into a country in order to capture someone wanted for crimes against humanity. It is interesting to note that in its first draft, Article 2(4) of the UN Charter simply read: 'All members of the Organisation will refrain from the threat of force.' Australia proposed the amendment that inserted 'against the territorial integrity or political independence of any member state' – a limiting amendment which was intended to permit interventions that do not envisage foreign domination or dismemberment. Invasion to capture war criminals, for example, would be a permitted intervention. The Article bans incursions which are inconsistent with UN purposes, but the responsibility to protect innocents from lethal harm is central to UN purposes. This interpretation would justify Israel's incursion into Ugandan sovereignty, committed in order to rescue the hostages at Entebbe airport: the military action was taken to protect nationals, after evidence showed that Uganda's president, Idi Amin, was collaborating with the hijackers. It would also justify the US incursion into Pakistan to capture (if possible) Osama bin Laden, wanted for crimes against humanity, in circumstances where it was a reasonable inference that he was under the protection of a Pakistan government agency. The wider principle would retrospectively legitimize the Tanzanian invasion of Uganda which put an end to Idi Amin's reign of terror (an incursion condemned by the UN at the time but greeted with universal relief). Other instances might include the US invasion of Grenada when murderers took over the government, and India's intervention in 1971 both to stop genocide in, and permit the right to self-determination of, Bangladesh. Mixed motives make some of these interventions questionable, especially when the intervenor keeps territory or installs a more congenial government or political system. But if only, say, Kenya, Uganda and South Africa had invaded Rwanda in April 1994 to stop the genocide after Security Council action had been vetoed by Britain and the US (as it undoubtedly would have been), who would now complain about its illegality?

An important precedent for humanitarian intervention with Security Council acquiescence but not approval was the 'Safe Havens' operation in northern Iraq after the Gulf War. Displaced Kurds hostile to Saddam were massing there, vulnerable to his violent reprisals. The Security Council passed Resolution 688, calling for humanitarian relief efforts, but the US, Britain and France went further and invaded Iraq to establish protected enclaves. Eventually Iraq agreed to their presence and the position was regularized, but the initial intervention could only be squared with Articles 2(4) and 2(7) on the assumption that these paragraphs of the Charter did not exclude the use of multinational forces in a humanitarian emergency, so long at least as this promoted a Security Council-approved purpose and the invading states harboured no territorial ambitions. These are reasonable limitations on a 'right' which would otherwise have too much scope for abuse. It would hardly be exorbitant for international law to allow humanitarian intervention to stop or punish state perpetration of crimes against humanity, where (a) the violating state has been condemned by the Security Council and action against it will further a clear Security Council purpose; (b) the intervenors represent a regional alliance, or at least a coalition of UN members with no territorial ambitions or other prospects of national profit; and (c) the armed force is a proportionate response which has a reasonable prospect of stopping or deterring the perpetrators.[16]

The moral imperative must be to stop crimes against humanity whenever they occur, not merely when the five permanent members of the Security Council have unanimously resolved to act. A UN structured (understandably, in 1945) for collective defence against aggressor states like Nazi Germany and imperial Japan finds itself constitutionally debarred from stopping internecine violence by states which oppress their own people if those states include or are in close alliance with one of the five members entrusted with a superpower veto. Indeed, so obsessed is China with sovereignty at all costs that it has threatened to exercise its veto to prevent UN action in any state which does not welcome UN forces, notwithstanding that state's responsibility for continuing genocidal attacks. (This was China's position when Indonesian militias were killing East Timorese after the referendum in September 1999.) Although not many vetoes have been cast formally since the Cold War ended in 1990 (compared with 240 previously), the Security Council is poleaxed by the very threat of a veto, on matters great and small.[17] Some threats are puerile: China blackballed valuable peacekeeping operations in Macedonia and Guatemala for no better reason than that these countries had dealings with Taiwan. Others are irrational: Russia has stood firm in its protection of North Korea (despite its breaches of the Nuclear Non-Proliferation Treaty) and throughout 1999 it was joined by France in protecting Saddam Hussein against any further UN insistence on inspecting his assumed progress towards nuclear and ballistic weapons (had these inspections gone ahead and proved he had no weapons of mass destruction, the US could not have invaded Iraq in 2003). On 10 December, the last Human Rights Day of the twentieth century, the Security Council was still deadlocked in debate over Iraq, while CNN was showing a drunk Boris Yeltsin grabbing the Chinese premier for support and hurling a slurred threat at the US ('Remember, we have as many nuclear weapons as you do') for criticizing the Russian army's merciless actions in Chechnya. It was hard to believe that the world had much improved since Khrushchev banged his shoe on the UN table, but all this evidence of superpower irresponsibility underlined the necessity for an international law principle permitting intervention in a humanitarian emergency, if need be without the unanimous support of permanent members of the Security Council. The search began for a legal basis for requiring the 'big five' members of the Council to act so as to save civilian lives, or at least to permit other states to intervene without awaiting their unanimous support.

WE BOMBED IN KOSOVO

'These wretched and unhappy little countries in the Balkan peninsula can, and do, have quarrels that cause world wars,' explained a once-popular guidebook for American tourists. 'Loathsome and almost obscene snarls in Balkan politics, hardly intelligible to a Western reader, are still vital to the peace of Europe, and perhaps the world.'[18] President Clinton had to play geography teacher to his people, explaining where Kosovo was before proclaiming, 'We could not stand aside and let history forget the Kosovo Albanians.' We could – and would if the philosophy of Henry Kissinger and John Bolton had prevailed, since US national interests were not remotely involved ('We have no dog in this fight,' as James Baker crudely put it). What made it all the more remarkable that the US would go to war against Slobodan Milošević was that his crimes against humanity they had tolerated for years, and his role as powerbroker in the Balkans they had assiduously courted.

It was Milošević, an old communist boss in the process of reinventing himself as an aggressive Serb nationalist, who first lit the racist fuse in 1989 with his rhetoric against the 1.7 million Albanians in Kosovo. They constituted 90 per cent of the population of the province and had enjoyed under Tito a considerable degree of autonomy. This Milošević ended, in the name of Kosovo's historical importance to Serb nationalism: he introduced direct rule from Belgrade and oversaw pro-Serb discrimination in public offices. For the next eight years the Kosovars lived in a sullen silence within their own 'alternative state', led in passive resistance by Ibrahim Rugova.[19] In 1990 Milošević had announced the 'time for struggle', which he simultaneously positioned himself to lead, and called upon the Muslims ranged against his Bosnian Serb surrogates to 'surrender or die'. There was evidence that he personally approved the infamous killing of 200 patients and staff at Vukovar hospital at the outset of hostilities with Croatia in late 1991, and he bore heavy responsibility for some of the outrages unleashed against Muslims in Bosnia thereafter. But at Dayton, when he was relied upon to deliver agreement from the Bosnian Serbs, no Western diplomat wanted to complicate matters by raising the question of Serbia's southern province, whose ethnic Albanians wanted either independence or absorption into a 'greater Albania'. So, after Dayton, the Kosovo teenagers who had in previous years thrown the odd stone at Serb soldiers acquired guns and took to assassinations, calling themselves the Kosovo Liberation Army (KLA). Sporadic attacks by these terrorists-cum-freedom fighters provoked (as they intended) reprisals and further repression by Serb security forces, which in turn (as the KLA also intended) caused Albanian victims to support the KLA *en masse*.

The first massacre by Serb troops – in Kosovo's Drenica valley – came in March 1998, and caused a refugee exodus. Throughout the year Western diplomats struggled, without success, to find a solution to the increasing violence. Milošević refused to accept NATO peacekeepers in Kosovo, and the KLA, the new champions of Kosovar aspirations, refused to accept anything short of independence. In October 1998 an excessively brutal Serb military offensive against the KLA drove 400,000 Albanians from their homes: many returned, however, after a ceasefire agreement was brokered by Richard Holbrook which introduced to the province unarmed monitors from the Organization for Security and Co-operation in Europe (OSCE). But by the year's end Yugoslavia had breached this agreement by refusing to reduce its troops and police, and Serb atrocities, 'reprisals' though some of them were, were meted out with a savagery that deeply shocked the OSCE monitors, going far beyond legitimate counter-terrorism. 'Police action' directed by the Yugoslav army killed defenceless old men, women and children. Forty-five bodies were left for television camera crews to pick through in the village of Racak in January 1999 and it was this atrocity more than anything else which convinced the US administration that NATO must meet force with force.[20] Its European allies agreed, after watching Milošević defiantly refuse the ICTY prosecutor, Louise Arbour, permission to enter Kosovo in order to gather forensic evidence from these crimes against humanity, as seen on television sets around the world. In the early months of 1999 about 1,800 civilians were killed in Kosovo by the Serbs, in fighting and in deliberate massacres; after eight years of Serb atrocities in the Balkans these latest slaughters, replete with lies and defiance from Milošević, were the last straw for the Western alliance. The Security Council had adopted a number of resolutions under Chapter VII in relation to Kosovo – number 1160 (March 1998) imposed an arms embargo and called on the Serbs to reconsider the 'political status' of Kosovo, while further resolutions in September and October had demanded an end to ethnic repression and threatened 'further measures' if Milošević refused a political settlement.

In the end, what tipped NATO into an enforcement action which the Security Council itself would not take was that the killings and deportations were part of a carefully premeditated plan to 'ethnically cleanse' the province of its 1.7 million Albanians by persecuting them so severely that most would flee, thereby creating a refugee crisis for neighbouring states. On 23 March NATO reported to the UN (and its figures have never been doubted) that 100,000 Kosovars had been forced from their homes in the previous three months, and that the number was increasing – evidence that the plan for mass deportation was underway. Although killings were not central to it (the goal was 'depopulation, not extermination'), this purpose would none the less amount to a 'crime against humanity' as defined by Article 7(1)(d) of the Rome Statute. It was a widespread and systematic attack directed as a matter of government policy against an ethnic group, and it took the form both of *persecution* on racial and cultural grounds and of *forcible transfer of population* (defined in Article 7 as 'forced displacement of the persons concerned by expulsion or other coercive acts from the area in which they are lawfully present').

At the peace conference at Rambouillet in March, both sides were presented with an ultimatum: a political settlement giving Kosovo autonomy and self-government within the Federal Republic of Yugoslavia, with human rights protected by a continuing NATO presence. This was reluctantly accepted by the KLA (it meant abandoning independence for this dubiously workable 'autonomy') but rejected by Milošević. It is not clear why: his apologists in the West have claimed that he justifiably resisted Appendix B, which gave NATO troops rights to unimpeded transit through Serbia and was therefore an unacceptable infringement on his sovereignty, although it was not much more sinister than a routine 'status of forces' agreement, giving peacekeepers direct access to Kosovo through a hostile country where they would need some immunity. But Milošević and his negotiators never once raised Appendix B, or mentioned it as a stumbling block.[21] There is evidence that the real reason Milošević refused the Rambouillet Agreement was in order to enable the ethnic cleansing of Kosovo to continue: NATO's very failure to arrest Karadžić and Mladić had convinced him that it would not take an action that would imperil its own force. In Priština, a week before the bombing, Serbs suddenly put signs on their houses announcing their nationality, so Milošević's men in ski masks would pass them by.

NATO had no game plan for this war, other than a naive belief that the bombs would quickly work, as they had at Dayton, to bring Serbia to its senses. Instead, war at first united the Serbs around Milošević, who quadrupled his troops in Kosovo and let them loose on a murderous rampage, in the course of which they massacred about 10,000 Kosovars and raped and tortured many more, unrestrained by the presence of OSCE monitors, who were pulled out (for fear they would be held hostage) just before the bombing commenced. Towns and villages were destroyed, and over a million inhabitants were put to flight. The refugee crisis destabilized Montenegro and Macedonia and created an endless stream of human misery to testify to the barbarity of Serb soldiery. Serb apologists like Lord Carrington perversely claimed that 'the bombing caused the ethnic cleansing',[22] but it did no such thing. In the first few days, many bombing missions targeted empty buildings, but the very first attack on 24 March became an excuse for the Serbs to unleash murderous violence on the Kosovars, speeding up the premeditated ethnic cleansing operation so as to uproot the Albanian population virtually in its entirety. This crime was 'caused' by politically directed racial hatred, not by bombing; the barbaric behaviour of the Serb forces in the first week of the NATO campaign is an indication of what was always in store for the Kosovars, and retrospectively underlined the need that existed for the international community to come to their rescue.

Where Western political leaders can certainly be faulted, both militarily and morally, was in their foolish promise at the outset that ground troops would not be committed to the battle. This was designed to take care of the 'Mogadishu factor' for the Americans and some nervousness from Serbia's friends in NATO (notably Greece), but it persuaded Milošević that an air war could only serve to sustain him in power. The decision to bomb from 15,000 feet minimized allied casualties – incredibly, not a single NATO life was lost in the seventy-eight-day campaign – but this put at certain risk innocent civilian lives, Serb and Albanian, 500 of which were lost in what was euphemistically described as 'collateral damage'. NATO refused to strike in less than perfect weather conditions, afraid that low-level bombing might endanger its pilots. The 1999 war has been dubbed 'the first post-heroic war', conducted by one side in a safety perfect except for the certainty of civilian casualties, a 'virtual war' for airmen and citizens of NATO democracies alike, as they witnessed the spectacle on television, or through cameras mounted on gunsights.[23]

One great humanitarian purpose was achieved, however, namely the restoration of the Kosovars to their homeland. This took over two months because in the first weeks NATO indecisively targeted empty buildings; only later did it mount a massive attack on economic infrastructure, like power grids and bridges, to 'turn the lights out in Belgrade' and undermine middle-class support for the war. But this late shift to infrastructure bombing brought allegations of war crimes against NATO, a concern voiced by Mary Robinson and others who were no friends to Serbia. The strategy came perilously close to breaching the rule expressed in Article 8 of the ICC Charter, which follows the Geneva Convention by making it a war crime to direct attacks against non-military objects, or in ways likely to cause incidental civilian damage disproportionate to military advantage. NATO's 'espresso machine war' (cynically so called because it shook enemy morale when electricity failures denied the Belgrade middle classes their morning coffee) involved bombing civilian bridges, a TV station and even a water purification plant. It is questionable whether these last three examples can be justified under the rubric of 'military necessity', although NATO scrupulously took legal advice about its targets from legal teams serving the US, British and French forces, which sometimes came to different conclusions. For example, the bombing of the Serbian TV station (which killed sixteen technicians) was opposed by the French, but the Americans insisted it was a military target because it supported the war effort. (The US argument is clearly wrong: the station was not inciting war crimes or genocide, like Rwanda's radio Libre des Mille Collines.) The Americans were, however, right to stop using cluster bombs, as soon as they realized these caused an unnecessary number of civilian casualties: the British kept dropping them throughout the war, and they took about 160 of the 500 civilian lives lost in the campaign. These and other targeting decisions were taken by NATO honestly, if mistakenly: isolated misjudgements cannot amount to war crimes, but they show that it is time to tighten that over-elastic test, 'legitimate military objective'. On the other hand, is it not legitimate to undermine the morale and disrupt the comfort of 'innocent' civilians who are guilty of supporting – indeed, electing – a government which criminally persecutes minorities?

This unprecedented attention to obeying the laws of war was a result of the existence of the ICTY, which had jurisdiction over all 'serious violations' committed in the territory of the former Yugoslavia, including any which might be committed by NATO. (Subsequently the prosecutor did examine the legality of NATO bombing, and concluded that no war crimes had been committed.) In order to avoid the humiliation of a Western general being placed in the Hague dock, lawyers sat at NATO command computer screens and assessed the legality of every proposed target and air strike: the texts of the Geneva Conventions were available on-screen.[24] One consequence was that NATO refused to launch a 'cyberwar' (by bombing banks or 'offensively hacking' into their computers) to close down Serbia's financial systems.[25] This decision was overcautious: cutting off water to a population is disproportionate because civilians can die of thirst or dysentery; when those civilians are as insouciant about crimes against humanity as were most Serbs, throwing their finances into disarray would have served them right and helped, psychologically, to secure the military objective of surrender.

But is it right to punish a people for the wickedness of their leaders or their soldiers? (This question had real point in Iraq, where sanctions caused suffering and death to a populace which lacked the power to remove Saddam Hussein.) When the Hague Tribunal was set up, many argued that it would demonstrate how war crimes were committed only by a handful of evil individuals, thus relieving their countrymen of the stigma of 'collective responsibility' for crimes against humanity. This idealistic notion has been called into question – by historians who revealed just how many Germans were 'Hitler's willing executioners', and by 'Hutu power' in Rwanda. Most of Serbia's eight million citizens were guilty of indifference towards atrocities in Kosovo. The only answer that can be given – and it has relevance to economic sanctions as well as bombing – is that 'punishing the people' can be justified if those people have real power to remove the rulers for whose decisions they are to be punished. That could not have been said of the Kurds and Shi'ites in Iraq, but was sadly true of Serbia, a country where, despite a courageous opposition, the majority of the public supported Milošević and his commanders throughout the Kosovo events albeit without full knowledge (although they could have found out) about the brutality with which they implemented their popular plan for ethnic cleansing.

The indictment of Slobodan Milošević was a legal act of some historic significance, based as it was on evidence which had been assessed as probative by David Hunt, an Australian judge of great criminal trial experience. The allegation put about by the Russian and Greek governments – that this indictment was 'political' – was false: it was not a partisan political decision but a deliberative judgment by an institution independent of national interests. It had an immediate impact on the conduct of the war, since it precluded the kind of diplomatic compromise (with the inevitable amnesty for Milošević) that some NATO members – Italy in particular – were privately urging. It also provided legitimacy for further incursions on Serbian sovereignty, since there was now good reason to believe that crimes against humanity had been committed by its head of state, the 'good reason' being the determination of a body established by the Security Council exercising Chapter VII power. It provided, too, some impartial support for NATO allegations of crimes against humanity which the Serb government publicity machine was ridiculing as propaganda: journalists could report, to a world audience, that these charges were based on convincing evidence. The indictment of Milošević marked the moment when the international criminal court system exercised, through its independent judgment, an influence on the way international affairs – in this case, a war – was conducted.[26] Its influence must not be overstated, but the indictment ended talk of a 'deal' involving amnesty and strengthened Tony Blair's hand in seeking approval, if necessary, for a ground war. It is significant that although most diplomats from NATO countries cursed the indictment when it was first delivered, its consequences were, with hindsight, beneficial.

A few weeks later, the indicted criminal surrendered his country, although not himself. By a 'peace agreement' signed on 9 June the Serbs agreed to leave Kosovo, 'bag and baggage', within the week: it was to become a completely autonomous province run by the Security Council and policed by NATO. Astonishingly, the great majority of refugees chose to return, even from the beaches of Australia, to their burned-out homes – a few were actually killed by land mines in their rush to re-enter their villages. NATO could take heart from the fact that so many human beings had regained their lost political rights along with the liberty to live in their homes, free from the nationalist rampages of Serb security forces. The KLA instantly showed its gratitude for this restoration of their human rights by murdering hundreds of Kosovo Serbs – a few of them collaborators, but most just guilty of being in the wrong place at the wrong time.

Human rights initiatives cannot be judged by the lack of humanity shown by their beneficiaries. What probably made these reprisal killings inevitable was that the surrender agreement made no provision for justice. Although Milošević and six of his senior commanders had already been indicted, NATO lost sight of its one proclaimed war aim – to punish the perpetrators of ethnic cleansing. Security Council Resolution 1244 of 10 June, concluding the war, asked only 'full co-operation of all concerned, including the international security presence, with the International Tribunal for the Former Yugoslavia'. This was the same feckless formula of Dayton, which failed to produce the arrest of Karadžić or Mladić. The moral purpose of the war was betrayed by NATO diplomats who failed to insist, as a condition for stopping it, on the surrender of those its object was to punish.

And so, once again, the world watched genocidal killers exit the bloodstained stage, this time in wraparound sunglasses and black bandanas. Lorry loads of Serb soldiers gestured obscenely at bereaved families and shouted defiant confessions about the number of Kosovars they had killed, as they went home to guard their indicted political leaders and high army commanders. The lack of any provision for justice was NATO's real defeat in the war. No doubt it felt pressure, as did the UN, from the pragmatic imperative of getting over a million refugees back into some kind of housing in the months before winter, but it succumbed without a thought for the consequences of leaving Milošević's crimes unrequited. Firstly, the KLA took the law into its own hands, wreaking vengeance on the remaining Serbs so unrelentingly that Kosovo was at one point in danger of becoming an 'ethnically cleansed' province – cleansed of its Serb minority, that is, and of its gypsies (Roma people were blamed by the KLA for siding with the Serbs). NATO handed the liberated province over to the UN, which treated it as a protectorate and placed it under the command of former human rights warrior Bernard Kouchner, with the help of 40,000 UNMIK troops from thirty-five countries. Despite this show of force, the reprisal killings only stopped after Milošević fell from power in the October 2000 elections. Then Kosovo could begin its quest for independence from the hated state which once made its people the victims of a crime against humanity.

The first to quake at humanitarian intervention was, ironically enough, the race whose history has made it necessary. Israel refused to support NATO's action against Serbia, because its right-wing government worried about Arab demands for a Kosovo-style 'autonomy' for Galilee. Shimon Peres was ashamed: 'For the first time after the Nazi Holocaust, when the world does not stand by, we do not know what to say?' But in NATO, too, Kosovo was an awkward precedent – certainly for Spain, which has used state terror against Basque separatists, and for Turkey, engaged in a war with its Kurds (which they had tactically suspended to save the life of Ocalan, their captured leader). It was precisely the fear of opening cans of ethnic worms which caused NATO's rhetoric to emphasize the humanitarian emergency and to avoid mention of Kosovo's right to self-determination, which was at the heart of the whole matter. By failing to adopt this goal as a war aim and a principle of peace, NATO and the UN faced a constitutionally confusing future in the province. The KLA (like Falintil in East Timor) was fighting for control of a discrete patch of earth where the great majority were suffering under a brutal, militarized state, and international law was on their side. It should have been declared to be on their side – in the Dayton Accords (and in the judgments of the *East Timor Case*). But the West long ago developed a knee-jerk hostility to the right of self-determination, because it was asserted first by colonial rebels and later by communist-backed liberation groups. But the lesson of Kosovo and East Timor is that in an age of human rights enforcement it should no longer be necessary for peoples to fight and die for their international law rights: the world must develop an enforcement system which will do this for them. Until international law clearly confronts the problem of secession, and lays down some ground rules for its exercise – including the existence of cast-iron guarantees for dissenters and minorities in the new seceded state – liberation struggles will be endless, and some great power claims, Russia's over Chechnya and most dangerously China's over Taiwan, will continue to trouble the peace of the world.

JUST WAR

There is nothing to stop a state murdering and extirpating its own people: for them, if the Security Council fails to reach superpower agreement, salvation can only come through other states exercising the right of humanitarian intervention. Thanks to Kosovo, that right has re-entered international law, but must be qualified in ways which restrict its potential for abuse. The preconditions for a lawful humanitarian mission without a Security Council mandate may be stated as follows:

(1)   A target state where there is convincing evidence of continuing commission of crimes against humanity either by the government or, if the country is a failed state (i.e. ungovernable), by armies, militias or organized terrorist groups.

(2)   Security Council resolutions which have identified the situation as a threat to world peace and imposed sanctions or other non-violent inducements which have been ignored. Peaceful solutions must have failed.

(3)   An intervention with the primary and dominant object of stopping crimes against humanity or punishing their perpetrators. Where victims are an ethnic majority within a definable territory, the overall object may be to assist their right to self-determination from a state which has by its barbaric behaviour forfeited any entitlement to rule them.

(4)   A collective armed response, preferably through a regional organization or a 'coalition of the willing', supported by the majority of the permanent members of the Security Council. (The mission must end if, notwithstanding that support, it is subsequently condemned by a Security Council resolution.)

(5)   There should be support, or at least acquiescence, from a regional bloc or representative group (if any) with which the

target state is most closely affiliated (e.g. in the case of Libya in 2011, the League of Arab states).

(6) The mission states must not stand to profit, e.g. by acquisition of territory or resources or through settlement of old scores.

(7) The methods of warfare must comply with the Rome Statute and the Geneva Conventions, and be proportionate to the legitimate objectives.

(8) The intervention must be assessed, at its outset and in subsequent stages, to have a reasonable prospect of securing those objectives.

(9) The interveners must be prepared to pick up the pieces, not hit and run. That means commitment from the outset to resource whatever reconstruction or reconstitution is necessary for a return to normality, preferably under the aegis of the UN.

(10) The interveners must not only be confident of winning on the battlefield, they must be equally sure of winning a subsequent battle in the courtroom if accused of aggression. The enemy leaders they accuse of committing crimes against humanity (precondition (1) above) must (if possible) be taken alive and then fairly tried on those charges before an international tribunal.

These are the ten principles by which the lawfulness of NATO's intervention over Kosovo must be judged. They were met in the following ways:

(1) Serb policy in Kosovo, namely the use of terror to drive the ethnic majority from their homes and from the country, amounted to the crime of persecution. This does not bear moral equivalence to the Holocaust, NATO rhetoric notwithstanding: Hitler exterminated, Milošević extirpated. But Serb action was none the less an ongoing crime against humanity, in pursuance of a preconceived plan to terrorize and deport Albanians.

(2) A number of Security Council resolutions to this effect were passed in the twelve months before the bombing. Resolution 1199 (September 1998) was pursuant to Chapter VII, and branded Serb behaviour in Kosovo as a threat to the peace. That

behaviour did not stop, and the last-ditch solution, Rambouillet, was rejected by Milošević.

(3) NATO's immediate objective was to force Serbia to accept the Rambouillet Agreement, which would end the persecution of Kosovars and turn the province into an 'autonomous' NATO protectorate within a wider Yugoslavia. The bombing escalated in response to the Serb army's barbarity at the outset of the war and hence to the need to win it so as to enable the return of all the Kosovar refugees.

(4) NATO was the appropriate regional organization to exercise military power, and it did so throughout the war without Security Council opposition. Indeed, when Russia moved a resolution on 26 March 1999 to condemn the NATO attack on Serbian sovereignty a few days after it commenced, it lost by 12 votes to 3.

(5) The European Union strongly supported the intervention.

(6) NATO allies had little to gain from the intervention: northern Kosovo has some mineral wealth, but there were no oilfields or other resources which could begin to offset the massive cost of bombing and then of reconstruction.

(7) The high-altitude bombing was of questionable morality, but it did not contravene the laws of war. The use of cluster bombs soon proved disproportionate, and some infrastructure targets (notably the TV station, water supply and several civilian bridges) were not 'legitimate military objectives', but no 'grave breaches' of the Geneva Conventions were committed.

(8) NATO miscalculated in its belief that bombing of strategic targets would bring about quick Serbian acceptance of Rambouillet. Continuing and escalating the bombing war was reasonably thought necessary in order to bring about some sort of a surrender, which it did after seventy-eight days. A ground war (even a threat of ground war) would have brought an earlier and much more satisfactory surrender, although at the expense of some NATO casualties.

(9) NATO followed through appropriately by handing control of Kosovo to the UN, and by providing many of the protectorate's

administrators and peacekeepers. The European Union, comprising most NATO countries, provided €4.65 billion to transform the Balkans.[27] The UN secured peaceful elections in Kosovo, and faced up to its obligation to prepare that territory for independence, which was declared in 2008.

(10) The allies called initially for war crimes trials, but failed to make surrender of all Hague Tribunal indictees a condition of the ceasefire agreement. They did, however, maintain economic and political pressure, which has led to the handover of Milošević and other significant indictees (including several KLA leaders), and eventually the capture of Mladić, Karadžić and Gotovina.

On balance, then, Kosovo was a just and lawful war, and the victims of Serbia's crimes against humanity are better off as a result of it. NATO failed to condition Yugoslavia's surrender on the handover of indicted war criminals, but this was not a terminal set-back, since Milošević was subsequently handed over. The immediate motive for surrendering him was Serbian self-interest in obtaining international aid to reconstruct bombed bridges and power grids, but there was a more hopeful reason why it was publicly acceptable. The Serb media, liberated from censorship imposed by the Milošević regime, began to expose some of its atrocities – most gruesomely, how the bodies of Albanians killed by Serb forces had been dug up from mass graves in Kosovo, taken across the border and reburied beneath a police station outside Belgrade, and in another case transported in a freezer lorry which had been tipped into the Danube in eastern Serbia.[28] These extraordinary steps to hide the evidence of war crimes had of course been taken under Milošević's command in an effort to impede the Hague Tribunal's investigations. They proved that international justice was having an impact, generating a fear of conviction through the skill of the prosecution's forensic scientists in identifying decomposed bodies from dentistry records and the happenstance of old X-rays. They were evidence, moreover, of something more important than Milošević's guilt, namely the fear induced in political and military leaders by the existence of an international criminal court – a fear which may in time deter them from committing such crimes in the knowledge that the accumulating evidence can never be hidden for ever.

So a commitment to retributive and deterrent punishment of those who bear greatest responsibility for the crimes against humanity which created the emergency in the first place must be the tenth and final precondition for humanitarian intervention. Although such a doctrine is essential, in morality and in law, if innocent lives are to be saved, it still has many opponents. NATO's critics, certainly, were men acquainted with strange bedfellows: Dr Kissinger ('The whole business was misconceived') joined Noam Chomsky ('If you can't do no harm, then do nothing' – a recipe for turning a blind eye to genocide) and Fidel Castro ('Shameful . . . international legality is being violated'). They are supported in their objections by some international law academics, upset that humanitarian intervention has no Latin pedigree and no sufficient *opinio juris*[29] – although in fact the 12-3 vote in the Security Council on 26 March 1999 against the Russian resolution accusing NATO of breaching the UN Charter produced plenty of *opinio*. This came not only from NATO member states, but from non-permanent members like Slovenia, Malaysia, Bahrain and Argentina, all chiding the resolution's three proponents – Russia, China and Namibia – whose refusal to authorize armed enforcement to stop ethnic cleansing had prevented the Security Council from exercising its responsibility for maintaining peace and security.[30] Some academics have argued that military action which is morally justified but none the less unlawful (because it has not been authorized by the Security Council) should be dubbed 'exceptional illegality' – a suggestion that is exceptionally silly, because a state's admission of the unlawfulness of its humane action will either (or both) drain popular support from a justifiable intervention or drain popular support from an unjustifiable international law.[31] That the right has evolved in the way described above, strictly limited by preconditions, was apparent when the US and its allies were casting around for legal reasons to invade Iraq: it was never suggested at that time that their regime-change operation could be defended as 'humanitarian'.

THE RESPONSIBILITY TO PROTECT

THE R2P PRINCIPLE

After the Kosovo intervention had once again exposed the inability of the Security Council to intervene if pole-axed by an unco-operative superpower, the UN went back to the drawing board. The problem, inevitably, was its member states' attachment to sovereignty, and it was only by deconstructing this concept that some of its officials – notably Kofi Annan and Francis Deng – thought they could square the vicious circle. 'Sovereignty carries with it certain responsibilities for which governments must be held accountable . . . ultimately to the international community' their argument went.[32] To flesh out this insight, the Canadian government in 2000 sponsored an International Commission on Intervention and State Sovereignty (ICISS), co-chaired by former Australian Foreign Minister Gareth Evans and Mohammed Sahnoun, an Algerian diplomat. It duly came up with *'The Responsibility to Protect' – Principles for Military Intervention.* This postulated an R2P duty on the Security Council whenever there was, or was likely to be

large scale loss of life which is the product either of deliberate state action, or state neglect, or inability to act, or a failed state; or large scale ethnic cleansing, whether carried out by killing, forced expulsion or acts of terror or rape.

This set a high threshold for contemplating a military intervention, which then was subject to four 'precautionary principles'. 1) There should be no mixed motives: the object must be to halt or avert human suffering. 2) Every peaceful way forward should have been tried and exhausted. 3) Proportionality must govern the scale of the intervention – there should be use only of the minimum force necessary to achieve the humanitarian objective. 4) There must be a reasonable prospect of success.

These R2P principles were to be applied by the Security Council, but there was a need 'to make the Security Council work better than it has', by the five permanent members agreeing not to apply their veto power to prevent military interventions 'for which there is other-wise majority support' (a tilt at Russia for its veto over Kosovo). Importantly – and unacceptably for some states – the ICISS Report allowed 'last resort' humanitarian intervention, outside the Security Council's Chapter VII jurisdiction, either by vote of the General Assembly, or by a regional organization such as NATO, provided it subsequently sought Security Council authorization. It warned that should the Security Council fail to discharge its responsibility to pro-tect, 'in conscience-shocking situations crying out for action, concerned states may not rule out other means to meet the gravity and urgency of that situation' – they would break international law, in other words, but be applauded for doing so.

The R2P formula tried to be all things to all men (and women): the 'precautionary principles' were too few and the position of states which unilaterally intervened 'in conscience-shocking situations cry-ing out for action' was bizarre, whilst the threshold test made no mention of stopping or punishing crimes against humanity. But it was a welcome beginning for an intervention blueprint, or it would have been if the 9/11 attacks had not occurred a few weeks after it was published, diverting attention from it, and had the US (joined by the UK and Spain) not ignored it entirely when deciding to invade Iraq to remove Saddam Hussein at a time when there was no 'large-scale loss of life' and the precautionary principles screamed for caution. But many wrongly perceived the invasion as an example of R2P, and most states feared that instead of squaring the circle, the ICISS Report had formed it into a pentagon – or at least an excuse for Pentagon-led regime change. When the UN adopted something called 'responsibil-ity to protect' at the world summit in 2005, it was a very watered down version of the original proposal. It decreed only that:

Each individual state has the responsibility to protect its population from genocide, war crimes, ethnic cleansing and crimes against humanity . . . we are prepared to take collective action, in a timely and decisive manner, through the Security Council, in accordance with the Charter, including Chapter VII, on a case by case basis and in co-operation with relevant regional organisations as appropriate, should peaceful means be inadequate and national authorities are manifestly failing to protect their populations from genocide, war crimes, ethnic cleansing and crimes against humanity.

Was this, as some immediately dubbed it, 'R2P lite', or was it R2P at all? The ICISS definition had been cut off at the knees, largely because of the false perceptions that the Iraq invasion had been an application of it (a perception enhanced when one ICISS member, Michael Ignatieff, cheered on the invaders as if they were crusaders for human rights). Although the basis for intervention had been more precisely defined in terms of combating war crimes and crimes against humanity, the 'precautionary principles' had been removed and everything had been left to the Security Council to decide, without guidelines or preconditions, on 'a case by case basis'. There was no presumption, as in the ICISS formulation, that the Security Council would act at all, no leeway for NATO to bomb first and ask for approval afterwards, and certainly no suggestion that any state might heed the cry for action in 'conscience-shocking situations'. The danger, of course, in this new, watered-down but UN-approved version, is that it places all responsibility on the shoulders of an unreformed Security Council, without any obligation on 'big five' members to withhold a veto if intervention has majority support, and virtually implies that humanitarian intervention without Security Council Chapter VII authorization is unlawful. That means no more Kosovos, as well as no more Iraqs (although there always will be more Iraqs if great powers are determined on aggression, and there will not be more Kosovo interventions if they can be inhibited from acting when one or other of the 'big five' refuses authorization). This is the danger of 'R2P lite': without guidelines to determine at what point intervention is justified there will be no intervention, even when the circumstances cry out for it. At best the World Summit approval of R2P, subsequently endorsed by the Security Council, should stand as an international law commitment by member states to protect their own citizens from crimes against humanity, and a declaration that they will assist other states to comply with their commitment – even (or especially) if that assistance takes the form, in the last resort, of military action endorsed by the Security Council. But R2P must not be allowed to be a substitute for the broader right of humanitarian intervention, when the ten preconditions are met and the Security Council is powerless because of a permanent member veto.

It is at this point that the advocates of R2P stumble into incoherence. If, under the UN version of R2P, NATO or a 'coalition of the willing' or an individual state, performs a genuine humanitarian rescue without a Security Council mandate (think Kosovo, or safe havens in Iraq, or invasions to remove Idi Amins or Pol Pots) have they committed a crime against humanity or, post 2017, the crime of aggression? Gareth Evans, the intellectual author and indefatigable champion of R2P, even in its watered-down version (which he described at the time it was produced at the World Summit as 'a huge wasted opportunity') suggests that such an intervention would be 'unlawful' but nonetheless 'legitimate'.[33] So Good Samaritan states are guilty of an international crime, but have a moving plea in mitigation. This is a fudge, and international law cannot be allowed to develop irrationally. For example, in 2011 came the Gaddafi dilemma: Resolution 1973 empowered civilian protection but not regime change (i.e. removal of Gaddafi by force). But as Obama, Cameron and Sarkozy announced, a month into NATO's bombing campaign, 'it is impossible to imagine a future for Libya with Gaddafi in power. It is unthinkable that someone who has tried to massacre his own people can play a part in their future governance.'[34] On this basis, NATO turned an essentially defensive mandate into a permission to bomb Gaddafi and his government into oblivion (whichever way his convoys were going – advancing or retreating – they were attacked). Was this a lawful extension of their mission, exercising the right of humanitarian intervention to save lives, or was it unlawful but 'legitimate' in a praiseworthy sense, because it did save lives, or was it unlawful and illegitimate? The diplomats had cobbled together a question-begging formula which directed NATO to protect civilians 'by all necessary measures' but not to remove Gaddafi – who, if not removed, would massacre them. The only sensible way forward is to avoid the fudge of a distinction between legality and legitimacy, and acknowledge that there is a strictly defined right of humanitarian intervention – and to go on to define it, by way of the ten preconditions set out at p. 755.

LIBYA AND SYRIA – 2 R2P OR NOT?

Where the 'responsibility to protect' principle has had some resonance is to encourage the Security Council and regional bodies to take preventive or at least intermediate measures at an early stage, where mass atrocities are threatened. The best example is Resolution 1970, which referred the situation in Libya to the ICC, just ten days after the commencement of attacks on protesters in Benghazi. That did not, of course, stop Colonel Gaddafi, but in Kenya in 2008 the post-election violence (which had cost 1,000 lives and displaced 300,000) was cooled by the speedy African Union action to send in a panel of 'Eminent African Personalities' led by Kofi Annan, which resulted in due course in a reference to the ICC and the indictment of the leaders of the inter-ethnic conflict. Less successful has been intervention in the continuing conflict in Darfur, where the 'responsibility to protect' spurred the Security Council to mandate the African Union to send in 7,000 ill-equipped and reluctant Nigerian soldiers (paid for by the European Union) to observe the ethnic cleansing. The ICC indictments have not to date been effective: their investigators cannot access some conflict areas and have no power to arrest the government officials (including Prime Minister al-Bashir) who are charged with genocide. There has from time to time been talk of sending in NATO, but China (a supporter of the Sudanese government and the main importer of its oil) and Russia (the main supplier of its weapons) have demurred. These two superpowers were, of course, responsible for the Security Council's paralysis over Syria, when the Assad regime began committing crimes against humanity in 2011 by killing protesters, and continued to do so in 2012. In both cases, the argument for military intervention came up against the 'do more good than harm' test (Kosovo precondition 8). An invasion of either Sudan or Syria would have been difficult, humanitarian missions would have had to leave, more civilians would have been killed and there was no clear or effective alternative government. This problem will always counsel against the use of force, but the failure of R2P in both cases was that a divided Security Council did not take non-military measures under Article 41 of the Charter: by July 2012 it had not even referred the situation in Syria to the ICC.

SRI LANKA – GETTING AWAY
WITH MASS MURDER

Another unhappy example of how a member state was allowed to get away with mass murder notwithstanding acceptance of the 'responsibility to protect' principle is provided by the case of Sri Lanka. In 2009 its government and army took the opportunity to launch a massive bombardment of the 400,000-strong Tamil community in the north of the island, bombing and shelling from air, sea and land, killing about 40,000 in order to rid the country for ever of the Tamil Tigers – an armed guerrilla movement that sought independence for its people. These attacks took place when the long civil war turned in the government's favour – an excuse for killing thousands of Tamils and the forcible displacement of over 350,000, in an offensive in which army officers were responsible for torture and rape as well as summary executions. One factor that undoubtedly helped the government's refusal to account for its military's atrocities is that the civilian victims were sympathetic to a desperate and vicious secession movement. The Tigers had embarked on a terrorist campaign some years before, and as the army closed in they actually killed some of their own people who had disobeyed their orders and were trying to escape from the target area. The opportunity to finish off the separatist movement was too good – or too bad – for the government of President Mahinda Rajapaksa to pass up. It banned all foreign journalists (a tactic later used by Syria) and all NGOs except the Red Cross, secure in the knowledge that the latter would not breach confidentiality and tell of any horrors its workers might witness. Although the military took several months to subdue the Tamil strongholds, the Security Council failed to apply the R2P principle – inaction that might be excused by the lack of concrete information, as well as the fact that this was the end-stage of a lengthy civil war. In due course, however, the truth emerged, captured in fleeting and grainy images on hand-held or cell phone cameras. They showed summary executions, naked female bodies on the beach, violated and drowned, lines of captives beaten over the head with rifle butts, shot where they crouched in handcuffs, and so on.

'Our troops carried a gun in one hand and a copy of all the Human

Rights Charters in the other,' boasted the cynical, lying Rajapaksa. UN Secretary-General Ban Ki-moon insisted that perpetrators be investigated and prosecuted – Rajapaksa pretended to agree, but did nothing, so the UN set up a panel of experts, headed by a former Indonesian attorney-general, to provide a report on accountability in Sri Lanka. Of course Rajapaksa did not allow its members to enter the country, but they interviewed many survivors and formed an accurate picture of the war crimes committed by both sides. The conduct of the war by the Sri Lankan army 'represented a grave assault on the entire regime of international law designed to protect individual dignity during both war and peace'. It accused the government army and navy of indiscriminate shelling of civilian areas and camps, abducting members of the local media, starving civilians in the conflict zone of food and medical supplies, as well as torturing captured Tamil soldiers and raping civilian women. It had justifiably harsh words, too, for the Tigers and their tactic of holding hostage their own civilians, and murdering them if they disobeyed orders.[35] After a report as condemnatory as this, the Security Council had an R2P duty to follow up, preferably by way of a reference of the situation in Sri Lanka to the ICC Prosecutor – necessary since Sri Lanka was not a party to the Rome Statute. But this was never a serious possibility, because China stymied any action shortly after the report was released, publicly threatening a veto: the Sri Lankan government, it stated, must be allowed to handle the matters raised in the report without the international community 'complicating the issue'.

R2P seemed dead in the water, like so many Tamil victims. With superpower support, the Sri Lankan government was not even apologetic – it had destroyed an organization that some states loathed because it was terrorist, but more states (especially in Africa) rejected because it was secessionist. But NGOs took up the case and there were powerful demands for further investigations – the HRC experts had not been allowed to enter the country, and any independent panel of experts which was permitted to investigate might gather conclusive evidence. So Rajapaksa, under this pressure, established in May 2011 'The Lessons Learnt and Reconciliation Commission' – a sham truth commission packed with former government officials, which was not interested in establishing the truth but rather in supporting the government's propaganda. It had no power to protect witnesses who dared to criticize the army, and human rights groups refused to cooperate with it. The report, published in December 2011, concentrated upon condemning the Tigers, and on whitewashing the military which it claimed had given 'the highest priority' to protecting civilians. As this was an obvious lie, the report tried to gild it by attributing blame for the murder and rapes of Tamils to rogue elements rather than military commanders. The Commission was condemned by all the main human rights organizations, as well as by its own words. If governments try to avoid international obloquy by setting up enquiries, these must involve international figures with a reputation for independence, like the commissioners recruited by Bahrain, who were given access to government offices and permitted to interview victims (in confidence) and military officers. There will be continuing demands for proper accountability, and in 2012 the US persuaded the HRC, by a narrow majority, to demand some answers from the Sri Lankans. But R2P as a principle requiring international action notably failed the Tamils. To add insult to their injuries, the Commonwealth Heads of Government meeting (CHOGM) rebuffed all attempts to raise the matter, and actually endorsed Sri Lanka by selecting its capital, Colombo, as the site for its 2013 meeting.

THE GADDAFI PRECEDENT

For an astonishing forty-two years, Colonel Muammar Gaddafi, who seized power in a military coup in Libya in 1968, strutted the world stage, his increasingly crazed ramblings at the UN becoming such an excruciating embarrassment to other world leaders that even China and Russia were prepared, in 2011, to unleash a Chapter VII force that eventually brought about his brutal end. Resolution 1970 of February 2011, which referred the situation in Libya to the ICC Prosecutor (who subsequently indicted him for crimes against humanity, together with Saif, his son and heir, and his brother-in-law, the intelligence chief Al-Senussi) was an important precedent. It marked the first time that a unanimous Security Council had approved the use of the ICC – the US, Russia and China had abstained in 2005 over the referral of Darfur which led to the Bashir indictment. International criminal law had finally come of age: Resolution 1970 conferred international jurisdiction over crimes committed by a sovereign government which had determined to kill its own civilians. A few weeks later the Security Council went a step further, in Resolution 1973, which mandated NATO to create a 'no-fly zone' over Libya and to use 'all necessary measures' to protect its civilians. As Gaddafi's brutal forces engaged the rag-tag rebel army, the measures that became necessary were more forceful than many of the Resolution's initial supporters had wished: they had not envisaged 'regime change' but rather the use of force to bring about a truce, or at least an agreed resignation by Gaddafi. But one lesson from other post-war conflicts is that international criminals cannot be trusted: Gaddafi repeatedly declared bogus ceasefires and refused to engage with diplomats or ICC prosecutors: his sovereign right to rule obsessed him, until a NATO jet struck a convoy in which he was travelling. A group of rebels found him cowering in a roadside tunnel: they beat him, threw him across the bonnet of their jeep and rammed an iron pipe through his sphincter. 'What you are doing is not permitted' were his last words before they shot him in the head.

THE CRIMES OF THE COLONEL

The crimes of Colonel Gaddafi are far too many to list.[36] Early in his reign he ordered that dissidents abroad should be hunted down and killed like 'stray dogs' – his assassins were supported from his embassies ('peoples' bureaus', he insisted upon calling them). He gave refuge and financial support to most terrorist movements, such as Baader-Meinhof and Abu Nidal, who trained in camps outside Tripoli. His oil wealth also funded genuine liberation movements like the ANC, which is why Nelson Mandela remained his firm friend (twice visiting, at Gaddafi's request, the Lockerbie bomber, Al-Megrahi, in his prison in Scotland). One of his more malicious enterprises was to have his intelligence services supply the IRA with funds and with the Semtex used in hundreds of bombings to take the lives of innocent civilians in Northern Ireland

and mainland Britain. His responsibility for thousands of civilian deaths throughout the world cannot be doubted: he was listed as an 'unindicted co-conspirator' in the charges brought against Charles Taylor in the Special Court for Sierra Leone, because he had sponsored Taylor and Foday Sankoh, the brutal rebel leader whose 'Operation No Living Thing' had lived down to its name in Freetown. There was no way that Libya's intelligence services (run by Al-Senussi) could have committed an atrocity on the scale of the Lockerbie bombing without Gaddafi's knowledge and approval, and a few months later they brought down a French passenger jet over Chad. (Gaddafi was charged with this crime in France, until an appeal court ruled that as head of the Libyan state he had 'sovereign immunity'.) Blood money was paid to the victims' relatives in appeasement – $2.7 billion for Lockerbie, $1 million per family for the UTA bombing – although it failed to appease.

Libya sought nuclear weapons through the AQ Khan network, but in 2003, increasingly concerned that he would be the target of terrorism – his moronic 'green book' was anathema to al-Qaida as well as to most of his own people – Gaddafi decided to come in from the cold. Tony Blair, with the approval of President Bush (who could not be seen to sup with the devil) went to Libya to do 'the deal in the desert'. Gaddafi agreed to give up nuclear ambitions and provide information about his dealings with Khan and the IRA, in return for Western co-operation in suppressing those who were out to destroy his dynasty. The British, shamefully, did co-operate, prosecuting members of the Islamic Fighting Group who were dedicated to his overthrow and rendering others of his enemies back to Libya for torture and imprisonment. There were oil deals for British Petroleum in exchange, but Gaddafi's most wanted prize was the return of his proxy, the Lockerbie bomber Al-Megrahi. He was released in 2009, thanks to conniving British politicians who wanted Libya's oil and naïve Scottish politicians who thought they were being compassionate when they were just being stupid. The man who had put the bomb aboard the fatal flight in which 250 innocent people were blown out of the air was allowed to make a triumphant return to Tripoli, welcomed by Saif and said by the Scots to have only three months to live. But he was always available to attend rallies for

Gaddafi, and lived long enough – for almost three years – to see him overthrown.

Until 2011, Gaddafi got away with murder because important states were desperate to share in his oil wealth. He had bought off the relatives of the victims of his airline terrorism with blood money and insincere apologies. In February 2009 he was elected chairman of the African Union, which he turned into a major opponent of the ICC, guaranteeing Omar al-Bashir (wanted for genocide in Darfur) a safe conduct through the continent. What neither Gaddafi himself, nor the states which courted or at least suffered him, realized was the depth of the hatred that he had built up inside Libya over many years as a result of brutal repression, non-Islamic 'green book' religion, and discrimination against the tribes in Libya's oil-rich east. He could never be forgiven for one great atrocity – the slaughter of 1,270 prisoners (mostly political dissidents) at Tripoli's Abu Salim prison, back in 1996. His response to a mild protest seeking better food and medical treatment had been to have the prisoners released into a courtyard and machine-gunned by soldiers positioned in the towers. Barbarity on this scale could never be forgiven. Fifteen years later, on 15 February 2011, some human rights lawyers in Benghazi took up the case on behalf of relatives, and were arrested. Lawyers and judges gathered outside the courthouse to demand their release, and two days later a popular protest erupted in the city, stirred by the success of the rebellions in neighbouring Tunisia and in Egypt, where President Mubarak had resigned a few days previously. In Benghazi a gimcrack rebel leadership formed – the Transitional National Council (TNC) – which included some early defectors from the Libyan army and government. Gaddafi's reaction was to have his soldiers shoot to kill protesters, and to make blood-curdling threats to come and liquidate the 'rats' of Benghazi: his army would 'purify all decisions from these cockroaches'.

RESOLUTION 1970

Just eleven days later, on 26 February, after urging from France and Britain to acknowledge its 'responsibility to protect' and (crucially, and at the same time) a decision by the League of Arab States to suspend Libya until its government stopped the violence, the Security Council unanimously invoked Chapter VII powers and passed Resolution 1970.[37] It imposed an arms embargo, a travel ban on the sixteen most powerful officials of the state and a freeze on the assets of Gaddafi and his sons. Most importantly, the Resolution read:

Considering that the widespread and systematic attacks currently taking place in the Libyan Arab Jamahiriya against the civilian population may amount to a crime against humanity . . .

Recalling the Libyan authorities' responsibility to protect its population . . .

Reaffirming its strong commitment to the sovereignty, independence, territorial integrity and national unity of Libya . . .

Acting under Chapter VII of the Charter of the UN and taking measures under its Article 41

Decides to refer the situation in Libya since 15 February 2011 to the Prosecutor of the ICC.

Decides that the Libyan authorities should co-operate fully with and provide any necessary assistance to the court and the Prosecutor pursuant to this Resolution and, whilst recognizing that states not party to the Rome Statute have no obligation under the Statute, urges all States and concerned regional and other international organisations to co-operate fully with the Court and the Prosecutor.

This Resolution was groundbreaking, firstly because it was unanimous. China and the US, which had abstained from voting for the Darfur Resolution of 2005, all voted in favour, as did the non-permanent members of the Council. Libya of course was not a party to the ICC, but that did not matter: the Court's jurisdiction was conferred by virtue of the Chapter VII power to determine that there is a threat to, or breach of, the peace, or an act of aggression, and to act under Article 41 or 42 to 'maintain or restore international peace and security'. A reference to the ICC Prosecutor is a 'measure not involving the use of armed force', so it falls under Article 41.

Resolution 1970 involved a determination that a government

which puts down an internal revolt by killing peaceful protesters, a) could be committing a crime against humanity and b) its actions could threaten international peace and security. In other words, ten days of army killing in one region of Libya was sufficiently 'systematic' to amount to a crime against humanity. More controversially, the Resolution treated an internal revolt as likely to impact upon *international* peace and security if it was countered by lethal force. The reasons for this determination were not spelled out, other than by mention of the plight of thousands of refugees who had by this time crossed into Tunis, and the assumption that a crime against humanity affects the world. This precedent means that in future even a revolt within a region of a state, if it lasts a few weeks, causes a potential refugee problem and is put down with disproportionate and lethal force could result in a Chapter VII determination by the Security Council to make an ICC reference.

There is an interesting disjunct in a Resolution which purports fully to preserve Libyan sovereignty, yet which has the consequence of making its leaders amenable to an ICC Treaty that they have not ratified and which requires them to co-operate with a court they do not recognize. This is a consequence of Article 2(7) of the Charter, which allows enforcement measures ordered under Chapter VII to override the bar on UN intervention in matters that are 'essentially within the jurisdiction of any state'. The preamble to Resolution 1970 refers to 'gross and systematic violations of human rights': to the extent that these may amount to an international crime, there will henceforth be a legal basis for UN intervention. It is interesting to note the preambular recall of Libya's 'responsibility to protect its population' – a reference to the responsibility of every state under the Responsibiity to Protect (R2P) doctrine. Some have argued that Resolution 1970 is an *application* of R2P, although this is misleading: Libya's position was that, on or before 26 February, it was responsibly protecting its population by putting down an insurrection, which would have been an entirely legitimate use of its sovereign powers. It was the fact that it was putting down a peaceful protest by killing the protesters that engaged the Security Council's duty to refer this *prima facie* evidence of a crime against humanity to the ICC Prosecutor.

Resolution 1970 is significant for confirming international jurisdiction over crimes committed in civil wars and internecine struggles by rulers who kill their own people. For that reason it marks an important stage in the delivery upon the promise of Nuremberg, that political and military leaders will face justice on earth and not in heaven. As the first unanimous vote of confidence in the ICC, it signalled an end to the years of unreasoning hostility epitomized by Jesse Helm's 'bomb the Hague Bill' empowering the president to do just that if any US soldier were captured by the Court. It brought within the Court's jurisdiction, if not within its grasp, a man whose international power and oil wealth had given him impunity for forty-two years, even from other international courts. (There had been sufficient evidence to charge him, along with Charles Taylor and Foday Sankoh, in a conspiracy to foment civil war in Sierra Leone, but the Sierra Leone Court Prosecutor, David Crane, said he feared a diplomatic storm would engulf the Court if he embarrassed such a powerful head of state by indicting him.)

Of course Gaddafi refused to comply with Resolution 1970, and specifically rejected its demand that he allow humanitarian aid convoys into besieged towns such as Misrata. Other towns in the east of the country rose against the government, and its troops reacted mercilessly: hundreds of civilians were killed in the next three weeks. Moreover, it became clear that Gaddafi was recruiting mercenaries from Chad and Niger to fight for him. The battle for Benghazi began with bloodthirsty televised threats by Saif to kill its people 'to the last bullet', if they did not surrender.

RESOLUTION 1973

It was the Gulf Co-operation Council (a pro-Western body) that first called on the UN, in early March, for a 'no-fly zone' and 'all necessary measures' to protect civilians. Then (on 10 March) came a decisive intervention by the League of Arab States, urging the Security Council to go further, by establishing 'safe areas' in the country (whilst, of course, 'respecting its sovereignty', which was a *non sequitur*) and to co-operate with the TNC because Gaddafi's 'grave crimes' had deprived him of legitimacy. This was a remarkable *volte-face* by a body hitherto opposed to any intervention anywhere: it was a measure of the personal embarrassment that Gaddafi had caused Arab leaders by his insults and *braggadocio* (he had proclaimed himself the 'African King of Kings' and the 'Imam of the Muslims') that they were prepared to cut him loose.[38]

The Security Council moved quickly. On 17 March it passed Resolution 1973, which authorized member states (operating through NATO) 'to take all necessary measures . . . to protect civilians and civilian populated areas under threat of attack . . . while excluding a foreign occupation force of any form on any part of Libyan territory'.[39] The Resolution set up a 'no-fly zone' over the country, froze the assets of diplomats who had been recruiting mercenaries, and extended the asset freeze to cover all funds emanating from Libya or used by or for the benefit of the Libyan authorities. There was no exception for funds for legal representation at the ICC, or to enable Libya to challenge, in the courts of the UK and France, the 'mission creep' whereby NATO was progressively dismantling its defences. This was regrettable, since the Libyan government did instruct British law firms, but they could not access Libyan funds to pay their bills (and there was an understandable reluctance to act free of charge for the Colonel).

Resolution 1973 was a rushed measure passed in the excitement of the early days of the Arab Spring – if Ben Ali and Mubarak could be overthrown, it seemed logical to support a rebellion against a crazed and unpredictable leader who had killed more civilians than they had. Even so, the Resolution was not unanimous: Russia and China abstained, as did Brazil, Germany and India. It was within the Security Council's powers under Article 42 to determine that Article 41 measures were inadequate and that operations using force were necessary to restore peace and security. There is no doubt that Libya had failed to co-operate with the ICC Prosecutor, but he had not, by the time Resolution 1973 was passed, issued any indictments. There had been more evidence of torture and killings by Gaddafi forces, and the use of mercenaries and an increasing refugee exodus provided the necessary threats to international security. Condemnation of Gaddafi by the League of Arab States was of special importance: NATO countries were nervous that any use of force might be perceived as an Iraqi-style Western intervention. Resolution 1973 would not have been tabled had there been any real opposition from Arab or African regional groups.

But what did the Resolution mean? Its first demand was for a ceasefire and an end to attacks on civilians. Gaddafi believed he was entitled to reject it on the basis that he constituted the sovereign authority in the country (and Resolution 1973 had *reaffirmed* a strong commitment to sovereignty). That meant that NATO was mandated to take 'all necessary measures', short of boots on the ground ('a foreign occupation force' was specifically ruled out). The 'no-fly zone' was almost immediately established, and NATO went on to destroy ammunition dumps and then to attack convoys of government troops, whether or not they were progressing towards towns full of civilians. It was by now intervening in a civil war, and on the side of the rebels. It soon moved beyond the measures related to the 'no-fly zone' (airfields, military command posts, anti-aircraft batteries) and carried out raids intended to attack the security apparatus of the Libyan state.

On 15 April the NATO leaders – Obama, Cameron and Sarkozy – issued a joint statement congratulating themselves (not unreasonably) for preventing a bloodbath in Benghazi. They conceded that they had no mandate to remove Gaddafi by force, but went on: 'it is impossible to imagine a future for Libya with Gaddafi in power . . . it is unthinkable that someone who has tried to massacre his own people can play a part in their future governance . . . Colonel Gaddafi must go, and go for good.' These were fighting words, indeed a call to overthrow Gaddafi, since he had made very clear that he would die in the last ditch. It was, on one hand, impossible to reconcile with Resolution 1973's purported commitment to Libyan sovereignty, but, on the other, it was a cool-headed appraisal of what measures would be necessary – nothing short of the removal of Gaddafi – to protect civilians. The logic of these NATO leaders was simple:

Gaddafi promises to die in Libya, but not by his own hand.
So long as he lives, the bloodshed will continue.

Resolution 1973 calls for 'all necessary measures' to protect civilians. It follows that the measure most necessary is to kill Gaddafi.

In other words, Resolution 1973 had become a justification for tyrannicide, in circumstances where there was no other way to stop mass murder by the tyrant. Gaddafi was a man of infinite treachery whose word could not be trusted: there could be no 'negotiated cease-fire' with an enemy who declared ceasefires every week without any intention of honouring them and whose orders were to show no mercy towards civilians. But even if war law gave NATO the right to kill the enemy commander, the fact that something is lawful does not mean it is wise. His death as a result of direct targeting or bombing would certainly have discomfited many of NATO's allies. Instead, the fighting ebbed and flowed in the months that followed. In June Gaddafi, his son Saif and brother-in-law (the intelligence chief Al-Senussi) were indicted by the ICC Prosecutor for crimes against humanity, i.e. mass murder and persecution. This, some commenta-tors objected, ended any prospect of a negotiated peace, but there had never been a prospect of a negotiated peace with Gaddafi. As the war continued, the balance tipped against him: NATO bombing depleted his defences and frightened away his mercenaries; many of his minis-ters and officers, worried that they might become the next ICC indictees, defected to rebels who, armed and secretly trained by NATO proxies, steadily improved their discipline and fighting ability. Tripoli fell to the TNC in August, and Gaddafi's wife and some of his family took refuge in Niger.

TRIPOLI OR THE HAGUE?

At this point, justice became a possibility, but a very problematic one. NATO leaders mistakenly insisted that Gaddafi's fate should be a matter for the Libyan people, whose own gimcrack leadership, the TNC, put a $1 million bounty on his head and offered a pardon to his killer. Later, the TNC insisted that it wanted to organize his trial, but there was no extant judicial system in which this could take place. It was obvious that the rebels wanted to execute Gaddafi by any means possible, and it would not be possible were he dispatched to the ICC. But liberation had come to the Libyans by courtesy of international law and they had a reciprocal duty to abide by it. Resolution 1970 directed Libya to co-operate with the ICC, whose Prosecutor had brought down the indictments. Without NATO's actions under Resolution 1973, and its air, sea and logistical support to the rebels, the regime could not have been overthrown. The TNC had an international legal duty to hand over captured indictees to the ICC, and it should have been left in no doubt that this was what the Security Council expected. At this time, the chant 'Al-Assad to The Hague' was being heard in Syria. 'Gaddafi to The Hague' should have been the UN's condition for continuing its support for what was, in reality, a civil war for regime change.

The Security Council, however, fell silent on the subject and the NATO leadership seemed content that Gaddafi, like Saddam, should be killed by his own people. His end was brutal: his convoy was hit by a NATO airstrike and he was shot by a rebel group who were never subsequently disciplined for the war crime of killing a captured enemy. His son Saif was later caught and became the subject of a tug-of-war, both between his captors and the TNC and then between the TNC, which insisted on its right to put him on trial in Libya, and the EU (and most human rights organizations) which argued that he could not be tried fairly in Libya and which wanted him tried in The Hague. A sensible compromise would have been a 'hybrid' court with ICC judges and prosecutors in the majority, sitting if security permitted in Libya – but any such arrangement with the ICC would have meant dispensing with the death penalty, which the TNC refused initially to countenance.

The dispute drew attention to a flaw in the 'complementarity' principle enshrined in the Rome Treaty, namely the risk that trials in domestic courts, which 'complementarity' encouraged, might turn out to be gravely unfair to fallen political and military leaders also wanted by the ICC for crimes against humanity. This issue – which arises after every successful revolution, when there is a popular desire for revenge – was swept under the carpet when the Treaty was negotiated. It was simply assumed to be a good thing for states to punish their own dictators, and only when they sought to protect them by sham trials and investigations intended to go nowhere need the ICC become involved. So Article 17 of the Rome Treaty wrests jurisdiction from states which are not genuinely willing to punish perpetrators, and which begin bogus proceedings 'for the purpose of shielding the person concerned from criminal responsibility'. Nothing was said about the much more common problem of new governments which want to execute old leaders as quickly as possible, with trials that are a sham because guilt is preordained. The Romanian tribunal convened to kill the Ceauşescus after a two-hour 'hearing' provides the worst example (the judge committed suicide from shame a few weeks afterwards), but the politically manipulated court that hastened Saddam Hussein to the gallows is another. However much it may be an irony that the ICC can actually protect fallen tyrants from the death they once decreed for thousands of their subjects, international justice must pursue its commitment to fair trial. Once indicted, a defendant should be prosecuted by his own country only if his trial can be fair and his fate, at worst, imprisonment for life.

The Rome Statute can achieve this only through judicial case-law. Article 17(3) entitles the court to consider whether a state is unable to carry out its proceedings 'due to a total or substantial collapse or unavailability of its national judicial system'. It is necessary to interpret 'proceedings' as proceedings which are fair, and to consider whether they can be conducted independently and impartially. Although the death penalty is not mentioned as a factor in the Statute, the ICC should certainly take into account any unfairness likely at the sentencing stage and later when 'mercy' (i.e. commutation of a death sentence) is considered. In order to ensure Saddam's hanging, the Iraqi parliament abolished his right to such commutation from the president, because President Talabani was a known opponent of the death penalty (at least for his fellow Kurds). Actions of this kind should be considered by the ICC, in determining whether 'complementarity' – i.e. deference to domestic proceedings – would mean a rush to the gallows.

Saif Gaddafi was captured shortly after his father was butchered. He faced ICC indictment for killing peaceful demonstrators and mobilizing mercenaries. Libya, although not a party to the ICC, had been referred to it by the Security Council under its Chapter VII powers, in terms that required 'the Libyan authorities shall co-operate fully with and provide any assistance to the court and the Prosecutor'. In other words, Libya was under an international duty to surrender Saif to The Hague. Foolishly however, the ICC Prosecutor rushed to Tripoli and announced that the ICC would lend assistance to local authorities if they wanted to put him on trial. This was a serious error, because the decision about whether any indictee in these circumstances should be tried in The Hague had to be made by the court, and not prematurely by an announcement from its prosecutor. As should have been obvious at the time (and became very obvious afterwards) the Libyan justice system was dysfunctional and unlikely for some time to cope with a fair trial for any Gaddafi. In these circumstances, and notwithstanding the TNC's claim of sovereignty (it had not at that stage been elected), the Security Council should have insisted that Saif be transported to the ICC's prison – where he could be safe – pending a determination on where and under which law to try him. (Article 62 of the Rome Statute says that the place of trial shall be at the seat of the court 'unless otherwise decided'.) Instead, the precipitate behaviour of the ICC prosecutor caused an ICC defence team to visit Saif in Zintan (where he was being held by a local militia) pursuant to a promise of safety by the TNC, which it could not guarantee and should not have made. Australian barrister Melinda Taylor was there detained by a local militia – unfamiliar with the duties of counsel to assist their clients – and spent a month in prison whilst TNC officials published defamatory allegations against her.[40] The Security Council – and, it must be said, the president of the ICC – failed to condemn the Libyans (who should one day be prosecuted for contempt of the ICC) and chose to negotiate in secret for the release of their lawyers. This incident illustrates the risk of the 'complementarity principle' being turned into an excuse for abandoning indictees to the untender mercy of local lynch law, and underlines the need for the Security Council to show much firmer support for the Court's lawyers and investigators in their frequently dangerous work.

THE AFTERMATH – LAURENT GBAGBO

NATO's performance in Libya has been hailed as a 'model' intervention and a validation of the R2P principle.[41] It certainly saved the lives of tens of thousands of more-or-less innocent citizens (the people of Benghazi were mainly rebel sympathizers) and it did so without loss of a single NATO life, at a cost of several billion dollars – cheap compared to any other modern intervention. Although there were abstentions from Resolution 1973, NATO received armed assistance from the UAE, Turkey, Jordan and especially Qatar, and was supported throughout by the Arab League. Importantly, although the US took the lead in the initial bombing, provided much of the intelligence and paid half the bill, France and the UK undertook most of the work, so the engagement was not perceived as an American operation. There was, however, a failure to understand, and certainly to explain, the legal consequences of Resolution 1973 – Anders 'Fogh of War' Rasmussen, the NATO chief, seemed particularly confused. There were few signs that the great object lesson of the Iraq intervention – i.e. that intervening powers must plan for the aftermath – had been learnt, a failure that became plain in 2012 as Libya descended into bitter internecine conflicts, brutal treatment of prisoners-of-war and borderline chaos.

NATO is only a military alliance and has no qualifications for planning post-war reconstruction, although that does not absolve the Security Council from responsibility. Gaddafi's Libya, for all its authoritarianism, had an infrastructure which delivered on basic needs, and it was largely destroyed. Out went his lickspittle judges, his pliant politicians, his forcibly loyal administrators and his tribal security arrangements, as well as his policemen and his professors. And they could not quickly be replaced. NATO's faith in the TNC, never more than an organization of convenience, was astonishingly naïve: it was treated as a 'government in waiting' even when it could not protect its own military leader from being killed by his own troops. Even after Iraq, there was the ingenuous belief that 'democracy conquers all', as if post-revolution, fighters would surrender their arms and abide by the law – even though there was no law and no constitution available to replace the Colonel's diffusion of power through his family and his tribe. Humanitarian intervention, whether it comes through the Security Council or some 'coalition of the willing', must have as a precondition some plan for its aftermath. It was the difficulty of envisaging an aftermath (other than replacing Assad) that made intervention in Syria in 2011 something that no state was prepared to recommend, and no regional grouping would countenance beyond a notably unsuccessful 'observer mission' in 2012, which observed killings by government troops and snipers but had no power to stop them.

In the case of the Ivory Coast, however, intervention was limited and relatively easy. There was an African consensus in favour and the 'regime change' was only to bring in a regime that had won a democratic election. This election had taken place in November 2010 and, according to all impartial observers, had resulted in a clear win for the leader of the Muslim North, Alassane Ouattara, over the incumbent prime minister Laurent Gbagbo, who refused to accept the result. The African Union and ECOWAS (Economic Community of West African States) insisted that Gbagbo should go, but their diplomacy – and their emissaries including at one point South African President Thabo Mbeki – failed to move him or his Christian cronies, their resistance supported from afar by American evangelicals like Pat Robertson and Glenn Beck. With a legitimate claim to the presidency and a substantial army at his back, Ouattara swept down from the north and quickly occupied most of the country, with Gbagbo's forces concentrated in Abijan, along with a UN peacekeeping force in loose co-operation with French troops. It was at this point – as a massacre was looming – that ECOWAS requested the Security Council to intervene by using 'all necessary measures' to protect civilians and transfer power to Ouattara.[42] On 30 March 2011 the Security Council unanimously passed Resolution 1975, which recognized Ouattara as the legitimate president and gave UN forces (the peacekeepers and the French) a Chapter VII mandate to do exactly that, 'to prevent the use of heavy weapons against the civilian population'.

As a result of Resolution 1975, the outcome of the battle for Abijan was never in doubt. Ouattara's forces were accused of massacres as they swept to victory with the help of French air cover which destroyed Gbagbo's heavy weapons and bombarded his residence, whilst his loyal troops attacked UN headquarters and shelled civilians. Nonetheless, the death toll was much lower than it would otherwise have been without the UN intervention, and the R2P conditions were satisfied because there was a legitimate and experienced regime taking power in a country which war had not devastated. Even so, there were cavils from all the usual suspects – Russia, China, Brazil and India – which urged a restrictive interpretation of the Resolution and complained about the use of peacekeepers to support one side of a conflict.[43] But when that side is the right side – legitimate, democratic and entitled to hold power – neutrality could only work in favour of the spoiler. This lesson, although pointed out by the Brahimi report, has not been fully learnt: what is the point of peacekeepers when there is no peace to keep? The critics complained that the UN was using force only against Gbagbo, but not against the Ouattara troops, which had also massacred civilians. This is a point that does need to be addressed, but at the stage of ICC prosecution rather than in the middle of a war. It was right for the Security Council to support the forces of the legitimate government in Sierra Leone, even though its allies (the Kamajors, led by Chief Hinga Norman) had committed war crimes in the cause of their defence of democracy. Norman was indicted, and Ouattara or any of his commanders who gave orders to kill indiscriminately should be indicted as well – a task for the ICC prosecutor. Chief Hinga Norman had fought valiantly to protect democracy in Sierra Leone and had been made minister for home affairs: he was arrested whilst attending a cabinet meeting and taken to the Special Court prison, where the guards saluted him.

In this sense, the pejorative description 'victors' justice' – the insult flung at the Nuremberg trial – is invalid in respect of an international criminal law which holds all parties to account for crimes against humanity. In 1946 Russia got away with its barbaric massacre of the Polish elite in Katyn Forest, and Britain escaped examination of its bombing of Dresden, but impunity can no longer be allowed to those who commit war crimes in a just war. There can be no convenient compassion of the kind shown by Nixon to Lt Calley, freed after conviction for the brutal killings of the villagers of My Lai, and no immunities of the kind accorded to the commanders who turned a blind eye to the 'sadists on the night shift' at Abu Ghraib, or to the British Army officers who remained silent about the beating to death of Baha Mousa.[44] The US is shamed and diminished by the fact that none of its officials who authorized the torture and inhumane treatment of detainees during the 'war on terror' has faced charges. All war is hell, and any form of 'humanitarian intervention' must strictly comply with pre-condition 7 (see p. 756) which requires it to be conducted proportionately and in accordance with the Geneva Conventions. Chief Hinga Norman was a brave man who did more than anyone else to save Sierra Leone for democracy: he died before the Court could pass judgment, a martyr to the principle that 'victors' justice' now means justice on victors as well as losers.

Epilogue

'There is nothing culture-bound in the great evils of human experience, re-affirmed in every age and in every written history and in every tragedy and fiction: murder, and the destruction of life, imprisonment, enslavement, starvation, poverty, physical pain and torture, homelessness, friend-lessness.'

Stuart Hampshire
Innocence and Experience (1989)[1]

It is against such elemental evils that the Universal Declaration of Human Rights was erected, in 1948, as a talismanic barricade – a pile of decent principles to impede the onward march of tyrants and tanks and torturers. The Declaration and its progeny, the good conventions, can only serve this purpose to the extent that their rules are capable of being enforced – the true sign of progress towards the great but still distant promise of Article 28: 'Everyone is entitled to a social and international order in which the rights and freedoms set forth in this Declaration can be fully realized.' The bottom line of that promise means that UN members must deal with states where genocide or widespread torture or mass murder takes place, and must prosecute the perpetrators of these crimes against humanity – because they deserve it (retribution), to discourage others from acting likewise (deterrence), as well as to establish, through the reasoned judgment of an impartial court, an accurate historical record to confound nation-alist myth-makers and atrocity-deniers. The very possibility that someone, somewhere, will be arrested, tried and sentenced for a 'grave breach' of a human rights rule means that international criminal law has taken on the positivist character of 'law' and is no longer merely a set of pious platitudes. It means that the Nuremberg legacy, that political and military leaders will be punished irrespective of any state immunity, will be realized. It means an end to impunity, the freedom that tyrants should never have to live happily ever after their tyranny.

The length of this book attests to the many other ways and means of enforcing human rights rules. Officials complicit in murder or torture deserve long jail sentences, but they can also be sued in civil actions. The states they serve may cling to outdated sovereign immunities, but the banks or corporations or warlords in whose interests they act may be mulcted in damages, or forced to pay compensation to victims for economic loss or for pain and suffering, however long afterwards (over half a century, in the case of the Swiss banks and German corporations which took advantage of the Holocaust). There are regional human rights courts to call some governments to account for denying to their citizens the right to speak and associate freely, or for abrogating *habeas corpus* and due process. Economic sanctions can be imposed by the UN or by other political groupings, against states which abuse their citizens or breach international standards: such governments may be denied aid or disqualified for debt relief or find their leaders' overseas accounts subjected to freezing orders, and their overseas travel severely restricted. States that decline to disgorge indicted war criminals will be barred from joining the European Union. Reporting mechanisms in human rights conventions can lead to bad publicity for violators, in response to which trade and tourism may diminish. For all the wishy-washiness of OECD guidelines and the Global Compact, they do impose disclosure duties on multinational corporations vulnerable to adverse publicity – as those caught up in the Iraqi 'oil for food' scandal discovered.

The most important fact about the global justice movement is that it has not been going for very long. Amnesty International began in the 1960s by organizing its members to write begging letters to tyrants, pleading with them to spare the lives of political prisoners. It was not until the arrest of Pinochet in 1998 that it went on to the offensive, demanding the release of all such prisoners and the prosecution of their persecutors. Its achievement, alongside that of

Human Rights Watch and other NGOs,[2] has in the fourteen years since been remarkable, and although powerful states continue to place themselves above international human rights law when it suits their national interest, that law is having some restraining influence. China imprisons democracy activists and Falun Gongers, although it could not massacre them again in Tiananmen Square. Russia covers up army death-squad killings in Chechnya, and protects the murderous Assad regime in Syria but it is not about to reopen the gulag or fill mental hospitals with dissidents. The Obama administration fails to close Guantanamo Bay and unleashes drones for summary executions, but the days when the CIA propped up Pinochet and every other vicious right-wing dictatorship (on the principle that 'he may be a son of a bitch, but he's our son of a bitch') are coming to an end. The positive results of the rise of human rights are slowly being seen: there are many more democratic countries in the world and only a few dozen seriously repressive dictatorships. Refugee numbers are largely accounted for by war in the Congo and the four million displaced Palestinians.[3] These are statistics against despair, although some democracies are brutally authoritarian and the number of persons left homeless by civil war (in effect, 'refugees' in their own countries) has increased alarmingly. Although the struggle for global justice is beginning to bear fruit, it will be a long time ripening: the cautiously optimistic message of this book is that the momentum has begun.

The first obstacle was the objection made in the 1990s by Asian leaders like Mahathir, Lee Kuan Yew and Suharto that human rights are 'culturally relative' and hence not universally applicable. They claimed that 'Asian values' (such as stability) were undermined by free speech, while the Universal Declaration embodied Western individualism at odds with their communitarian societies. But human rights principles afford individuals such elemental protections against the state that they are sought by intelligent beings everywhere. The Holocaust could be said to be 'culturally relative' in the sense that it developed from a tradition of German anti-Semitism, but by treating Jews as less than human (just as Serbs were later to reduce Bosnian Muslims and then Albanians to pseudo-human status), the Nazis committed crimes which cannot be excused by setting them within any national history or tradition. This is the case with all culturally ordained killing and torture inflicted for whatever reason: the footbinding of young girls in China; widow-burning (*sati*) in India; apostate-hunting in Iran; or the stoning to death of adulterers in Saudi Arabia.

'Cultural relativism' was most notoriously asserted to defend the practice of female circumcision (more accurately, female genital mutilation) inflicted upon many millions of girls aged between four and twelve, in dozens of countries in sub-Saharan Africa and the Middle East, usually as a tribal tradition believed to maintain honour, control sexual desire and enhance marriageability. The World Health Organization describes it:

Infibulation involves the amputation of the clitoris, the whole of the labia minora, and at least the interior two-thirds and often the whole of the medial part of the labia majora. The two sides of the vulva are then stitched together with silk, catgut or thorns, and a tiny sliver of weed or reed is inserted to preserve an opening for urine and menstrual blood. The girls' legs are usually bound together from ankle to knee until the wound has healed, which may take anything up to forty days.[4]

This is inflicted upon small girls with the consent of their mothers: should a culturally sensitive world send surgeons and anaesthetic, or rather condemn it as torture and inhumane treatment contrary to Article 5 of the Universal Declaration? Michael Ignatieff argued that genital mutilation should be 'made less dangerous' rather than prohibited: 'Western activists have no right to overturn traditional cultural practices, provided that such practice continues to receive the assent of its members.'[5] But his assumption that young girls are in any position to assent to a ritual intended by a patriarchal society to control and commoditize them as women is unreal and unacceptable (and the mothers' consent to the mutilation of their daughters is neither free nor informed). No claim of culture can be permitted to defend the torture of children, a crime against humanity when permitted on any scale. 'Culture' offers no escape clause for barbarism. Nor does the disingenuous appeal to 'regional standards and values' – the catch-cry, for example, of Caribbean politicians who really want their local judges to order executions of prisoners, unrestrained by the human rights rules imposed by their external human rights court, the London-based Privy Council.[6]

Objection to universality from some Arab, Asian and African governments is not shared by their people. When given the choice, they usually turn out to prefer the so-called Western values – as Suharto in Indonesia, Banda in Malawi, Marcos in the Philippines, Ershad in Bangladesh, Ben-Ali in Tunisia, Mubarak in Egypt, Saleh in Yemen and Gaddafi in Libya all discovered to their cost. When rulers condemn human rights as a threat to national order and stability, they really mean a threat to their own power. And if they have such a harmonious society, why must they insist on preserving from colonial times draconian security and sedition laws, secret police and censorship, or why do they need (in China, Burma, Singapore and Zimbabwe) to outlaw human rights NGOs?[7] The irony is that these 'traditional cultures' never approved such brutal actions as the Indonesian army's repression in East Timor, Mugabe's racist extirpation of white farmers, Nigeria's execution of environmental protesters, the excesses of the Taliban's 'Ministry for the Prevention of Vice and the Promotion of Virtue', or the vicious targeting and torture of those supporting opposition movement in Egypt and Syria, or the SLORC generals in Burma keeping the democratic leader, Aung San Suu Kyi, under long-time arrest (until 2011) separated from her dying husband. These militant rulers were just using the argument to pull themselves up by the straps of their own jackboots. This was the point made by South Korean president Kim Dae Jung, a former human rights activist, who derided Lee Kuan Yew's 'Asian-values' argument as unsupportable and self-serving because the real problem was not Western liberalism but 'authoritarian rulers and their apologists'.[8] Africa, too, has a few younger statesmen like Dr Navin Ramgoolam, prime minister of Mauritius, who has embraced universality and demanded removal of the authoritarian clauses in the African Charter.

The debate over 'universality' has changed with the Arab Spring: gone is the notion that representative government is somehow a revolutionary 'Western' addiction. However, the right of individuals or minorities to avoid persecution or discrimination at the hands of dominant parties, religions or cultures has become more important than ever, certainly in those states where 'secular' rulers have been replaced by governments representing intolerant majorities. A foretaste of the dangers to international peace has been provided in recent years by worldwide protests in Muslim countries against cartoons of the Prophet published in the West.

Expression cannot be free without the right to shock and offend and certainly not without the right to satirize and ridicule religions of all kinds. Any freedom may be limited on public order grounds – there is no right to cry 'fire' in a crowded theatre – but Muslim states which impose censorship on their own combustible faithful have no right to insist that non-Muslim states must impose it as well. Islamic practices which breach human rights – such as executing apostates or devaluing the evidence of women or allowing them to be beaten by husbands – are not laid down by the Koran. They derive from hard-line clerical opinions which have existed alongside, and in some societies have prevailed over, the more moderate views of other Islamic jurists. These views remain available for enlightened interpretations of Sharia law in respect of women and family issues, by judges prepared to follow the philosophical purpose of Sharia, namely to protect and promote human welfare.[9] Although Muslim states have produced the Cairo Declaration of Human Rights in Islam (1990) there exists no authoritative court or committee to provide interpretation or guidance, or to restrain primitives like Afghanistan's chief justice, who interprets Sharia to require the mutilation of thieves, the stoning of adulterers, and death for homosexuals and Christian converts. (He has debarred women from judicial office because he thinks menstruation renders them unfit to sit.) It will take a new generation of Muslim scholars to stake out the common ground shared by Sharia and human rights law. In the meantime, every encouragement must be given to modernizing movements in the Arab world. The most progressive is Al Jazeera, a beacon of media freedom which has infuriated authoritarian Arab governments even more than it infuriated George W. Bush, who considered it a potential bombing target.

The Westphalian doctrine of state sovereignty remains embodied in Article 2(7) of the UN Charter, which prohibits intervention in matters 'essentially within the domestic jurisdiction of any state'. The Charter was designed in 1945 as a mechanism for collective defence against sovereign nations like Nazi Germany, and not as means of dealing with today's more common danger of failed states or state-sponsored terrorism. Enforcement measures which depend upon the Security Council depend in reality upon unanimous approval by five permanent powers with their own diplomatic games to play (and in the case of Russia and China, their own minorities to oppress).

The 'Responsibility to Protect' principle is all very well when the Security Council, in its collective wisdom, accepts responsibility. But when it fiddles, men, women and children are burned to death. The superpower veto, threatened sometimes cynically or irresponsibly, deprives the Council of that moral authority that is necessary for a 'law' that prohibits intervention without Security Council approval. UNanimity cannot be the *only* test for legality, since the big-power veto is so often wielded for reasons that have nothing to do with justice or morality. 'R2P lite', which makes intervention pivot upon a Security Council resolution, cannot be conclusive – a right to humanitarian intervention, as with Kosovo and (arguably) in the later stages of NATO's Libyan campaign, must be a resort, if a last one after all else has failed, and only if the 'Kosovo pre-conditions' set out at pp. 755–6 are observed.

There has been loud objection to the ICC's concentration on Africa, but the simple fact is that more people are being killed in Central African wars than in the rest of the world. Sudan's vicious policy in Darfur produced a refugee crisis that destabilized Chad, and its sponsorship of the maniacal 'Lord's Resistance Army' continued to spread death and child slavery in parts of Uganda. In the Democratic Republic of Congo, after the massively corrupt Mobutu, a series of wars and tribal conflicts involving six neighbouring countries, fomented by animosity between the genocidal Interhamwe refugees from Rwanda (revived by international aid) and vengeful Rwanda government troops, has produced a staggering death toll in excess of four million: the biggest bloodbath since the Second World War. It was not until 2010 that the UN High Commissioner for Human Rights began some form of accountability by a report exposing Rwanda's role in perpetrating conflict in the DRC: Rwanda delayed the report's publication by threatening to pull out of peacekeeping efforts if it was criticized.[10]

There have been a few ICC indictments of paramilitary leaders, captured providentially or arrested in Europe, but this prospect cannot be expected to deter warlords unless there is some likelihood of their arrest: the ICC has been unable to catch Joseph Kony or his commanders in the Uganda bush; it has difficulty getting its lawyers and investigators into Darfur. The only way for the UN to deliver on its 'responsibility to protect' is by a process dubbed (by critics) 'humanitarian re-colonization' by which (as in Kosovo) satraps will be dispatched to head international administrations which help to rebuild institutions of government and to train local people for civic administration. There may be no alternative – the people of Sudan and the Congo would rather be colonized than cauterized (i.e. better fed than dead), but the very possibility infuriates leaders of other African states who uphold the right to be ruled by the likes of Mobutu, Mugabe, Kabila senior and al-Bashir.

The lesson of Iraq is that proportionality is everything. Ground war is horrific: however 'smart' the bombs or 'surgical' the air strikes; engagement with an armed enemy on its home ground will produce a toll of death and destruction that should not be contemplated unless it is reasonably reckoned to be less, in the long run, than allowing the tyranny to run its course. The proportionality test palpably failed to justify the invasion of Iraq – as the 2002 edition of this book foreshadowed.[11] The test was passed by NATO's aerial attack on Serbia to stop ethnic cleansing in Kosovo: as Václav Havel pointed out, this was the first war waged for ethical principle: 'no decent person can stand by and watch the systematic state-directed murder of other people'. It was passed by NATO's air offensive in Libya in 2011 – there was no way that civilians could be protected other than by the defeat of

Gaddafi. But never again must interventions without Security Council approval be based on the dangerous doctrine of 'preemptive self-defence'. Self-defence in international law requires any threat to be objectively established and imminent, while humanitarian intervention requires evidence of a human rights emergency, and in both cases the proportionality test must be satisfied.

The renunciation of 'preemptive self-defence' as any sort of international law doctrine is essential, both because it may otherwise be availed of by any state: the US and Israel already use it to justify 'targeted assassinations' and may soon use it to attack Iranian nuclear installations. The increasing number of states which have or can readily develop nuclear weapons will provide the next crisis: any attack on those states would satisfy Bismarck's definition of preventive war, 'committing suicide for fear of death'. The way forward in respect of Iran's nuclear truculence cannot be the Osirik-like first strike currently contemplated by hotheads in Washington and Israel, but rather a re-negotiation of the 1968 Non-Proliferation Treaty (NPT), to put in place an intrusive and strictly enforced inspection regime to which current non-parties like India, Pakistan and Israel would be forced to comply on pain of sanctions under Chapter VII of the Charter. This is just one area where US re-engagement with international law would have long-term benefits for world peace: after all, it may not always have hegemonic power to drop bombs on any nuclear installation in a Muslim nation or to shield Israel from the consequences if it does so. The ease with which the criminal – yet still unprosecuted – Pakistani scientist A.Q. Khan set up his procurement network to sell technology to Libya and North Korea underlines the overriding importance of an NPT binding upon every state, enforceable by the Security Council invoking its powers, if need be, to use force.

Diplomats still baulk at the consequences of the Nuremberg legacy because international law reduces their scope for compromise and appeasement. Their fondness for amnesties is ineradicable, despite the international law rule that they are invalid when purportedly bestowed on those who bear greatest responsibility for crimes against humanity. The US, under Obama, has at least sloughed off the hostility to the ICC of the early Bush years, and there has been revived interest in 'Wilsonian liberal democracy' – the dream that failed in 1919 when America refused to join the League of Nations.[12] But pragmatists remain unconvinced. Henry Kissinger warns of a 'dictatorship of the virtuous' which 'risks substituting the tyranny of judges for that of governments'.[13] But if governments are tyrannical, then the prospect that judges may bring them to heel must surely be welcome. Jurists, after all, cannot inflict torture, or line civilians up against a wall to be shot. When this unelected power-broker deplores any prospect of 'the ultimate dilemmas of international politics being assigned to unelected jurists', he is engaging in turf warfare: his real complaint is of a power shift away from diplomats who resolve such 'dilemmas' by rewarding aggressors with territories or amnesties or permission to keep their Swiss bank accounts, rather than by putting them on trial. He raises the bogey of an ICC prosecutor having a 'discretion without accountability' to prosecute people like himself, but he would be prepared for the US to join an ICC whose prosecutor is subject to direction by the Security Council, where the US can wield its veto. Ironically, this might be the best way forward: it would mean selective justice (in the sense that Americans would not be selected), but there is little prospect of that in any event because of the complementarity principle – American soldiers accused of crimes against humanity are generally prosecuted, although not always properly punished (Lieutenant Calley, for example, was effectively pardoned by Nixon for the murders of My Lai). Trials of non-American war criminals are better than no trials of war criminals at all. The Obama administration has been supportive of the ICC – to such an extent that the US has virtually become an associate member, a status that might be offered in future in return for some funding.

But can the ICC and other fledgling international courts overcome their crippling failure to work expeditiously and effectively – and especially, cost effectively? Critics point to the fact that Nuremberg processed twenty-three Nazi leaders within a year, while individual cases in modern war crimes courts take five years or more. The Milošević trial, for all its symbolic importance, did a disservice to the global justice movement by spotlighting the plodding pace and massive cost of such exercises. It is therefore necessary both to understand the problems that unique case threw up (see pp. 14–18) and to address very seriously the issues of cost and delay that have a potential to undermine the ICC. Part of the problem is the calibre of some international judges, selected by the unmeritocratic process of state nomination and then General Assembly vote (always on bloc allegiance and never on the candidate's ability). The trial of Charles Taylor took three years, but then the judges were incapable of handing down a verdict until thirteen months had elapsed – a disgraceful delay. The ICC needs an oversight body, like the UN's Internal Justice Council, which can both protect judicial independence and improve judicial performance. Other problems, as a recent study has shown, can be resolved only by amendments to the Rome Statute. It is absurd that three judges have to sit to decide all procedural issues; large amounts of time and money could be saved if there was no requirement to translate every word into French in cases with no Francophone connection; it is unfair and time-consuming to allow victims' lawyers to intervene at the trial rather than the sentencing stage; the courts should impose strict time limits on oral advocacy and insist both that prosecutors should limit indictments to worst cases and that defendants should not be permitted to waste time by tactics such as changing lawyers.[14]

The difficulties encountered by war crimes tribunals have led some to suggest that truth and reconciliation commissions provide an alternative. TRCs have sometimes been devices to bury rather than understand the past, and the Sri Lankan Commission in 2011 was a cynical exercise in trying to shore up government propaganda. But such commissions, if independent or international experts are allowed to sit on them, can be a genuine forum for truth-telling and a means of mapping a post-conflict future. But they do not usually produce confessions from political and military leaders or powerful state officials.[15] Those who bear the greatest responsibility seem to bear least sense of guilt: they usually defend their actions as having been required by the national interest. The TRC process, involving public confrontation with victims, allows a degree of individual reconciliation when policemen and soldiers apologize, but not the sense of closure for grieving relatives which comes after a trial and sentence of major culprits. The message that most helps people come to terms with human loss – that their suffering has not been in vain because the perpetrator is locked away and other perpetrators may be deterred – is not available, and Bishop Tutu has for this reason come to regret South Africa's failure to prosecute those who refused to testify to his commission. Truth commissions may reveal truth, in the sense of finding out where bodies are buried and who ordered the disappearance and why, but that sort of truth, without a follow-up prosecution, is unlikely to produce much satisfaction. Naming and shaming is no path to reconciliation when those who are named remain unashamed.

Trials provide evidence not only for conviction or acquittal, but for historians. They can provide the best evidence: documents of proven authenticity and testimony which has been vigorously cross-examined and then judicially analysed. Nuremberg still confounds Holocaust-deniers, but the under-reported Tokyo Tribunal has been largely ignored in Japan. It matters that state-directed crimes against humanity are accurately recalled in state-approved history books. This became an international issue when China, unusually but rightly, condemned Japan for the manner in which its schoolbooks whitewashed the rape of Nanking and its wartime atrocities in Manchuria. Selective amnesia about international crimes is not confined to Japanese historians: the Chinese themselves overlook the millions wiped out in Mao's 'cultural revolution'; Turkish textbooks deny the Armenian genocide (it is a criminal offence to admit it); and Spanish schoolbooks avoid all mention of Franco's recently discovered mass graves. This has attracted too little attention: the extent to which states own up to their international crimes should be investigated by NGOs and made an issue by the UN Human Rights Council.[16] One test is to look for memorials to victims and compare them with monuments to perpetrators. (The ashes of Vyshinsky and Stalin remain in pride of place in the Kremlin; the most vicious Japanese war criminals rest in shrines honoured by the prime minister.) Another aspect of education that deserves human rights attention is the extent to which the seeds of ethnic hatred are implanted in state schools (for example, Palestinian authority textbooks are predictably anti-Semitic; Israeli school history predictably Zionist) and in religious schools sanctioned by the state. Tolerance must not only be taught by example, it must be taught.

The case for forcible regime change without Security Council approval will rarely be made out: the case for UN peacekeeping operations is made out so often that the organization cannot cope. Its only unqualified success has been Cyprus ('We have been here for over forty years and will have to stay another forty, but at least there have been no massacres'). The cowardly betrayals by the Dutch at Srebrenica and the Belgians in Rwanda are infamous but more often – as in Central Africa today – the UN simply lacks professional troops and effective management. It has a $5 billion peacekeeping budget and 80,000 troops in the field,[17] but 77 per cent of these 'blue berets' are contributed by developing countries and often come without adequate equipment, modern weaponry or proper discipline, and sometimes with a taste for petty corruption or sexual exploitation. In 2012 its 17,000 troops from various countries were dotted throughout the Congo, as a country the size of Europe, vainly attempting to staunch the fighting that has claimed over four million lives since 1998. In South Sudan, the UN's newest state, which came into being in 2011, over 2000 UN blue berets have been forced to witness inter-tribal mass murder and rape without taking sides – neutral both in the build-up to the atrocity and afterwards. Hence the headlines that began in 2012: 'UN troops left us to be killed'.[18] The only silver lining in South Sudanese violence, which is most aggressively perpetrated by the man Africa refuses to arrest (the indicted Bashir), is that after twenty-five Chinese workers were kidnapped in 2012, the Chinese government agreed to deploy a platoon of soldiers to the UN mission. China has never before agreed to send troops on any UN humanitarian mission, so this may signal a change in policy from the obsessive anti-interventionism of the past.[19] Eventually, the UN must acquire its own rapid reaction force if it is to stop genocide in places like Rwanda and Darfur, where speedy deployment of a unified and trained force would have saved so many lives.

The organization's fundamental peacekeeping failure was spelled out by the Brahimi Report. Its 'reluctance to distinguish victim from aggressor' and its adherence to traditions of neutrality, respect for national sovereignty, and use of force only in self-defence had resulted in the UN's 'complicity with evil'.[20] Future mandates must permit aggressive military action by bigger and better forces, directed against 'spoilers' – parties which ignore human rights and break peace agreements – and against their accomplices: arms suppliers, drug and gem traders and parasitical crime syndicates. Human rights must also be enforced in occupied territories, as part of 'post-conflict peace building'. The UN must 'establish custom services, set and collect business and personal taxes, attract foreign investment, adjudicate property disputes and liabilities for war damage, reconstruct and operate all public utilities, create a banking system, run schools and pay teachers and collect the garbage'. It must impose on the territories it occupies 'a common UN justice package', including a model penal code reflecting basic standards of criminal law and procedure, to punish burglars and muggers while UN police round up the war criminals for delivery to the International Criminal Court. The importance of this work can be appreciated from the consequences of the US failure to do it in Iraq.

But whilst doing it, the UN remains irredeemably politicized, riddled with nepotism, and with insufficient safeguards against corruption. Its internal culture is driven by lobbying and regional bloc power-play, in which rich states can buy appointments for their candidates by offering aid in return for votes. The most important positions are in the gift of the Secretary-General or else go (like the Secretary-Generalship itself) on the principle of 'Buggins's turn', to a politician or diplomat (rarely to an independent expert) from a particular regional bloc. Thus failures like Ruud Lubbers (High Commissioner for Refugees) and José Bustani (Director-General of the Organization for the Prohibition of Chemical Weapons) were appointed to crucial jobs that should have been advertised and allotted according to merit and expertise, not nationality or friendship with the Secretary-General. The Brahimi Report politely identified this fatal stumbling block, the enemy within the organization itself: 'Put simply, the UN is far from being a meritocracy . . . the hiring, promotion and delegation of responsibility rely heavily on seniority and personal and political connections.'

The UN has had one recent success in the field of administrative justice. This had always been denied to its own staff, who cannot sue the organization in national courts where they are stationed, because it has immunity. They had to fall back on a sclerotic administrative law system dating from the League of Nations, which had no independent judges to hear allegations of unfair dismissal, sexual harassment, corrupt management and the like. Finally, at the insistence of the UN staff unions, a proper justice system was established in 2009. The judges are recommended by an independent justice council, which advertises (in *The Economist* and *Le Monde*) for applicants with ten to fifteen years of judicial experience, reduces the number of candidates to the most meritorious thirty to forty, then invites them to The Hague to sit a written examination paper before undergoing a searching interview. This is the only way to select judges on merit, and should be adopted for ICC and all other international judicial appointments.

Meanwhile the human rights movement still struggles against its traditional enemies – armies, churches and states – but with international law as an increasingly useful weapon. Most crimes against humanity are committed by professional soldiers, blessed by religious leaders and tacitly approved by governments. The new role of peacekeeping has muted the military brass but not changed its tune: generals avoid real courts in favour of the court martials and special military commissions that prove Clemenceau's point that 'military justice is to justice what military music is to music'. Religion is often a factor in war crimes, from the ju-ju priests of tribal conflicts in Africa to the Islamist preachers who recruit suicide bombers for al-Qaida and Hamas. The Serb orthodox church has absolved Milošević and hidden Karadžić, while the Vatican has shielded priests and nuns who took part in the Rwanda genocide. It tried to stop supplies of 'morning after' pills reaching refugee women raped by Serb battalions in Kosovo and it facilitates the spread of HIV/AIDS through its dogmatic opposition to condom-distribution programmes. Its widespread and systematic protection of paedophile priests, who have molested over 100,000 children, arguably qualifies as a crime against humanity. As for governments, *realpolitik* still rules when superpower interests are at stake: balancing the interests of their arms manufacturers against the rights of potential victims in far-off countries is like weighing hard cash against hot air. The five permanent Security Council members (and Israel) are the main suppliers of military equipment to the Third World and (the UK excepted) the least interested in limiting 'conventional' weapons.

There has been a marked reluctance by 'suprapowers' – thriving democracies of the global south such as India, South Africa and Brazil – to take up the human rights cause. These governments are usually found in the ranks of the non-interventionists, opposed to the mildest criticisms of other nations. In the case of South Africa, which owes its abandonment of apartheid to international pressure, this practice sits uneasily with its own history, whilst India received international support to emerge from colonialism. But diplomats form alliances of which their people would often be ashamed if they knew of them: how many Africans, for example, know that their diplomats in 2010 pledged the African Group, a powerful bloc vote in the UN, to oppose resolutions critical of a country without that country's consent – a shameful retreat (coming from a continent where people have suffered grave human rights abuses) from their duty to stand up for the oppressed. These hypocrites – for so they are – voted in favour of a resolution to congratulate Sri Lanka on its victory over the Tamil Tigers, without any mention of the indiscriminate killing of thousands in the course of achieving it.[21] The US and UK, of course, turn a blind eye to all the injustices heaped on women by Saudi Arabia, whose wealth buys silence (it was even given a place on the board of the newly created UN agency for women, because it contributed to its funding).

There has been a marked failure of UN country representatives to speak critically of the governments where they are stationed, even when UN employees are summarily arrested, as they were during Sri Lanka's war on the Tamils. There, the UN took neutrality to an extreme: whilst the government hired a Washington PR agency to 'spin' the war its way, the UN withheld evidence of civilian casualties which would have confounded the propaganda. In Zimbabwe, the UN representative was never in attendance at the trials of human rights defenders, and was never heard speaking out against abuses. In Asia, the continent where silence over human rights has been the norm, there has been one heartening development: the establishment in 2009 of the ASEAN Intergovernmental Commission on Human Rights. Its terms of reference are extremely narrow – it must respect sovereignty and the right of every member state 'to lead its national existence' free from 'external interference', and it is required to pursue 'a constructive and non-confrontational approach' – presumably by pulling punches and avoiding criticism of Asian governments. But some of the individuals chosen as commissioners have respectable track records, and the Commission is at least a start for a much-needed human rights initiative in the region.

That the US remains leader of the free world should realistically be welcomed, given the alternative candidates. It has the most advanced democratic institutions, and under Obama and Hillary Clinton its humanitarian instincts and support for international justice cannot be doubted. Regrettably US 'targeted killings' by drone strikes have executed hundreds of terrorist suspects, and many unsuspected bystanders. The consequence has been to expand the pool of sympathizers with the victims, and to dissipate the moral authority necessary for the US to promote human rights and justice. The failure to close Guantanamo continuously damages the cause of freedom. George W. Bush, who cheerfully admitted in his autobiography to ordering torture (water boarding), cannot travel to some European countries for fear of arrest. The mote in its own eye is its prison system: the nation has approximately 3,200 on its death rows, where conditions in some state penitentiaries are described by UN inspectors as barbaric and where the poor have very limited access to justice. It seems to have forgotten the wise words of Eleanor Roosevelt:

Where, after all, do universal rights begin? In small places, close to home – so close and so small they cannot be seen on any maps of the world . . . unless these rights have meaning there, they have little meaning anywhere. Without concerted citizen action to uphold them close to home, we shall look in vain for progress in the larger world.

The global justice movement is a human rights offensive. In the past, NGOs pleaded with tyrants to be less tyrannical and published reports which exposed state-sponsored torture and murder about which nothing could be done. Today, tyrants can be threatened, credibly, with international justice. In only eight years, General Pinochet metamorphosed from strutting untouchable to a desperate mass-murder suspect and was forced to cancel the party for his ninetieth birthday because he was under house arrest for a multi-million-dollar tax fraud as well.[22] The whirligig of time brought the daughter of one of Pinochet's torture victims to the presidency of Chile, whilst another whirligig has brought the President of Liberia to the dock of a UN court and now to prison for the rest of his life. Colonel Gaddafi was brought down by a NATO airstrike as he was dodging an International Criminal Court indictment whilst Karadžić and Mladić are making their desperate excuses for Srebrenica from the dock at their trials.

These events astonish because they were inconceivable just a decade and a half ago, when futurists could see no future for human rights in the twenty-first century, other than as support for supplicants before sovereign power. Nor could they have foretold how its discourse would become less pious and politically correct. We are beginning to call a savage a savage, whether he or she is black or white. We are becoming less respectful of old men with beards, be they mullahs or rabbis or patriarchs, who ordain cruelty in the name of religion. There is less mealy-mouthedness about intolerable behaviour and fewer attempts to suggest that hideous traditional practices are 'culturally relative' or that authoritarian governments are reflecting 'communitarian values'. The American Secretary of State can call Russia and China 'despicable' for their threats in the Security Council to veto any action against Syria, as the world watches while Assad's regime guns down its own people. There must be some optimism about the future, more so than expressed in 2006 in the third editon of this book, when the Epilogue lamented:

'But any optimism about the future must be tempered by continuing failures to uphold and enforce human rights standards. The worst man left in the world, Colonel Gaddafi, rides high: his massive oil wealth enabled him to pay $2.7 million blood money to relatives of the victims of the Lockerbie bombing which he undoubtedly approved and probably ordered. As the person most responsible for modern terrorism, Gaddafi is a reminder that the powerful have impunity so long as they stay in power – a comforting thought for Mugabe and Kim Jong Il and some forty other dictators, emperors and absolute monarchs.'

Ironical, six years later, as the world's store of tyrants begins to empty. Each edition of this book ends by sounding a little more positive about the struggle for global justice. It was first written as a controversial call for delivery on the Nuremberg legacy, for trials that would warn brutal political and military leaders that they could no longer look confidently forward to a genial retirement with amnesty and Swiss bank account, but might instead spend their twilight years in the company of their lawyers in The Hague. It is pleasing to record that international criminal justice is now here to stay, but even more satisfying to note how its momentum has inspired the governments of reformed states to settle debts with human rights villains in their own recent history. Latin America has led the way, with Videla and Artiz imprisoned for life, Alberto Fujimori convicted in Peru of crimes against humanity, Rios Montt facing genocide charges in Guatemala and ex-Uruguayan dictator Juan Maria Bordaberry convicted of murder. Post-Pinochet, Chile is mopping up: two officers who tortured and killed Michelle Bachelet's father, an airforce general who remained loyal to Allende, now face trial. Local war crimes courts in the Balkans – especially the Bosnian War Crimes Chamber – are processing suspected war criminals with a fairness that cannot yet be accorded to the effort by Bangladesh, which may yet come good. The UK is finally confronting its old colonial demons, most notably in civil cases brought over Mau-Mau torture in Kenya and civilian massacres in Malaysia. (There is backsliding, of course, notably by Spain, whose Supreme Court dismissal of Judge Garzón veiled the fact that his real crime, in their eyes, was to have opened Franco's mass graves.) But as

Ben Ali's officials are jailed for shooting protesters and Mubarak is convicted for the same reason, these are hopeful signals of impunity's end. There remain, at time of writing, many struggles unresolved, notably against Big Power complicity and cruelty – e.g. Russia and China refusing to sanction Assad – and deliberate breaches of human rights laws (the most flagrant being President Obama's summary drone executions). If there is one focus for the human rights movement of the future, it must be to work out a legal way to prevent abusive nations from acquiring a nuclear weapons capacity. But the momentum that has carried the global justice movement so far so fast since the millennium offers hope that it will meet these challenges in the future.

Notes

PREFACE

1. Hitler's speech is reproduced in UK Foreign Office, *Documents on British Foreign Policy, 1919–1939*, 3rd series, 9 vols. (HMSO, 1949–55), vol. 7, p. 258.
2. See, for example, David Chandler, *From Kosovo to Kabul* (Pluto, 2002).
3. John R. Bolton (later US ambassador to the UN), 'Abolish UN Sovereignty?', *Washington Times* (22 August 2000).

1. THE HUMAN RIGHTS STORY

1. Tom Bingham, *Lives of the Law* (Oxford University Press, 2011), p. 5.
2. Philip Bobbitt, *The Shield of Achilles* (Penguin, 2002), pp. 502–3.
3. *R. v. Hampden* (1637), 3 State Trials 825.
4. See generally Geoffrey Robertson, *The Tyrannicide Brief* (Chatto, 2005).
5. Andrew Marvell, *An Horatian Ode Upon Cromwell's Return from Ireland* (1650).
6. Simon Schama, *Citizens: A Chronicle of the French Revolution* (Penguin, 1989), p. 659.
7. John Locke, *Second Treatise of Government: Of the Beginning of Political Societies* (1690).
8. Cesare Beccaria, *Of Crimes and Punishments* (1764).
9. Quoted in J. A. Joyce, *The New Politics of Human Rights* (Macmillan, 1978), p. 7.

10. Letter of 12 January 1789, *The Papers of Thomas Jefferson*, ed. J. Boyd, (Princeton University Press, 1958), ch. 14, p. 436.

11. Thomas Paine, *The Age of Reason* (1794). See Michael Foot and Isaac Kramnick (eds.), *The Thomas Paine Reader* (Penguin, 1987) and John Keane, *Tom Paine – A Political Life* (Bloomsbury, 1995).

12. See Schama, *n*. 6 above, pp. 521, 781.

13. Ibid., p. 851.

14. *Marbury* v. *Madison* (1803), 5 US (1 Cranch) 137, p. 163.

15. Jeremy Bentham, *Supply without Burthen; or Escheat Vice Taxation* (1795), Objection V.

16. See Jeremy Waldron (ed.), *Nonsense upon Stilts – Bentham, Burke and Marx on the Rights of Man* (Methuen, 1987).

17. V. I. Lenin, *Report to the First Congress of the Third International* (1919).

18. See L. Oppenheim (ed.), *International Law: A Treatise* (Longmans, Green and Co, 1912), section 292.

19. Theodore Roosevelt, 'On Human Rights in Foreign Policy, State of the Union Message 1904', republished in Walter Laqueur and Barry Rubin (eds.), *The Human Rights Reader* (Penguin, 1978).

20. See Bingham, *Lives of the Law, n.* 1 above, p. 39.

21. C. K. Hall, 'The First Proposal for an International Criminal Court', *International Review of the Red Cross*, no. 322 (ICRC, 1998).

22. The evidence that this does amount to genocide, as defined in the Geneva Convention, is set out in Geoffrey Robertson, *Was There an Armenian Genocide?*, University of St Thomas, *Journal of Law and Public Policy*, vol. IV, no. 2 (Spring 2010).

23. Michael Oren, 'The Mass Murder They Still Deny', *New York Review of Books* (10 May 2007).

24. Michael J. Kelly, 'Genocide, the Power of a Label', *Case Western Review Journal of International Law* (2008), vol. 40, pp. 151–2.

25. See Robertson, '*Was There an Armenian Genocide?*', para. 38; Peter Balakian, *The Burning Tigris* (Heinemann, 2003), pp. 212–16.

26. See Jan Burgers, 'The Road to San Francisco', *HRQ* 14 (4) (1992), pp. 447, 455–9.

27. See Walter Laqueur, *Stalin, the Glasnost Revelations* (Macmillan, 1990), pp. 123–7.

28. Under *Glasnost*, a Politburo commission was established to investigate

archival material relating to the show trials: its report in 1989 established that the confessions had been obtained by torture and that the defendants had been seduced to give their public performances at first by promises of clemency and later by promises to protect family members. See Laqueur, *n.* 27 above, pp. 297 ff.

29. George Katkov, *The Trial of Bukharin* (Batsford, 1969).

30. See Burgers, *n.* 26 above, pp. 459–64. One rare exception was a declaration adopted by the Institut du Droit International in New York in 1929.

31. Dan Plesch, *America, Hitler and the UN: How the Allies Won World War II and Forged a Peace* (I. B. Tauris, 2011), p. 104.

32. See Geoffrey Robertson, *The Statute of Liberty* (Vintage, 2009), pp. 31–2.

33. Ibid., p. 33.

34. Harry S. Truman, *Memoirs*, vol. 1, *Years of Decision* (Doubleday, 1955), p. 292.

35. See John P. Humphrey, *Human Rights and the United Nations: A Great Adventure* (Transnation, 1984), pp. 29–32.

36. See generally Johannes Morsink, *The Universal Declaration of Human Rights* (University of Pennsylvania Press, 1999), pp. 14–20.

37. See Johannes Morsink, 'World War Two and the Universal Declaration', *HRQ* 15(2) (1993), p. 357.

38. Morsink, *n.* 36 above, p. 268.

39. Ibid., p. 274.

40. Drafting session, UN Commission on Human Rights, 1st session, 5th meeting (1947), 11 UN Doc. E/CN.4/AC.1/SR.5.

41. Cited in Stephen Marks, 'The Roots of the Universal Declaration of Human Rights in the French Revolution', *HRQ* 20 (1998), pp. 483–4.

42. Morsink, *n.* 36 above, pp. 222–6.

43. Upendra Baxi, 'Mambrino's Helmet? Human Rights for a Changing World' (Har-Anand, New Delhi, 1994).

44. Immanuel Kant, *Foundations of the Metaphysics of Morals*, tr. L. W. Beck (Prentice Hall, 1990), pp. 49–50.

2. THE POST-WAR WORLD

1. The evidence has been summarized by Jeremy Isaacs and Taylor Downing in *Cold War* (Bantam, 1998), pp. 186–95, 231–2.

2. ECOSOC Resolution 1235 (XLII) of 6 June 1967.

3. Declaration on Principles of International Law Concerning Friendly Relations and Co-operation among States in Accordance with the Charter of the United Nations, Resolution 2625 (XXV) (24 October 1970).

4. See William Shawcross, *Sideshow – Kissinger, Nixon and the Destruction of Cambodia* (André Deutsch, 1979).

5. Andrei Sakharov, *Memoirs* (Hutchinson, 1990), ch. 35.

6. See Philip Alston, 'The Commission on Human Rights' in Philip Alston (ed.), *The United Nations and Human Rights: A Critical Appraisal* (Oxford University Press, 1992), pp. 126ff.

7. See Geoffrey Robertson, *The Independence of the Judiciary, Some Recent Problems*, IBA, November 2011.

8. 'Walkout at Iran Leader's speech', BBC News (20 April 2009).

9. E.g. 'Libya to head human rights body', *The Australian* (21 January 2003), p. 9; 'Libya elected to head UN rights body', *The Times* (21 January 2003), p. 16.

10. 'The United Nations', *Economist* (10 September 2005), p. 30.

11. UN General Assembly, Resolution 60/251, 16th session (3 April 2006).

12. Amnesty International, *Detention and Torture of Political Suspects* (23 July 2006).

13. Sanja Kelly and Judy Breslin (eds.), *Women's Rights in the Middle East and North Africa* (Freedom House, New York, 2010).

14. Human Rights Council, *Report on Rapporteur Mission to Philippines* (16 April 2008), A/HRC/8/3/Add.2.

15. Human Rights Watch, *Nigeria: Post-election Violence Killed 800* (16 May 2011).

16. Gareth Sweeney and Yuri Saito, 'An NGO Assessment of the New Mechanisms of the UN Human Rights Council' (2009) 9(2), *Human Rights Law Review* (2003).

17. Robert Evans, 'UN Chief tells Rights Body to Drop Rhetoric, and Blocs', Reuters (12 December 2008).

18. Secretary-General's remarks to Human Rights Council, Geneva (12 December 2008).

19. E. B. Solomont, '*Shalev*: Goldstone Overshadowing Real Issues', *Jerusalem Post* (15 October 2009).

20. Aluf Benn, 'Despite its Flaws, the Goldstone Report Has Changed Israel's Behaviour in Gaza', *Guardian* (3 April 2011).

21. Richard Goldstone, *Washington Post* (2 April 2011).

22. Statement by Christine Chinkin, Hina Jiliani and Desmond Travers, *Guardian* (14 April 2011).

23. Committee Against Torture, *Annual Report of the Sub-committee on the Prevention of Torture* (3 February 2011), CAT/C/46/2.

24. See *Johnson* v. *Jamaica* (1997), 4 1HRR21, Comm. no. 588/1994, 22 March 1996.

25. *John Ballantyne & others* v. *Canada* (31 March 1993), Comm. nos. 359 and 385/1989 *HRLJ* (1993), p. 171.

26. *Nicholas Toonen* v. *Australia* (31 March 1994), Comm. no. 488/1992.

27. Philip Alston and James Crawford (eds.), *The Future of UN Human Rights Treaty Monitoring* (Cambridge University Press, 2000), p. 5.

28. Concluding Observations of HRC: Libyan Arab Jamahiriya, 6/11/98 CCPR/C/79 Add. 101. Compare US State Department Country Report on Human Rights Practices, 'Libya': 4 March 2002.

29. See Geoffrey Robertson, *The Case of the Pope – Vatican Accountability for Human Rights Abuses* (Penguin, 2010).

30. Ibid., pp. 112–20.

31. Torkel Opsahl, 'The Human Rights Committee' in Alston (ed.), *n.* 6 above, p. 374.

32. See the decision in *Otto Preminger Institute* v. *Austria* (20 September 1994), 19 EHRR 34, followed by *Wingrove* v. *UK* (25 November 1996), 24 EHRR 1.

33. *Norris* v. *Ireland* (1989), 13 EHRR 186; *Dudgeon* v. *UK* (1982), 4 EHRR 149.

34. *Ex parte Pinochet (No. 2)* (1999), 1 All ER 577.

35. Adrian Saunders, 'Strengths and Weaknesses of a Regional Appellate Court', paper delivered at Gray's Inn, 10 February 2005, p. 15. See also Derek O'Brien, 'The Caribbean Court of Justice and its Appellate Jurisdiction: A Difficult Birth', *Public Law* (Summer 2006), p. 344.

36. Tom Farer, 'The Rise of the Inter-American Human Rights Regime', *HRQ* 19 (3) (1997), pp. 511–12.

37. *Compulsory Membership in an Association Prescribed by Law for the Practice of Journalism*, Advisory Opinion no. OC-5/85 of 13 November 1985, series A: Judgment and Opinions no. 5.

38. Rachel Murray, 'Report on the 1996 Sessions of the African Commission on Human and Peoples' Rights', *HRLJ* 18 (1997), p. 16; 'Report on the 1999 Sessions of the ACHPR', *HRLJ* 22 (2001), p. 172.

39. African Commission on Human and Peoples' Rights, Banjul, Comm. no. 25/89, opinion delivered 4 April 1996.

40. Jamil Mujuzi, *The Africa Court's First Decision* (2010), 20(2), *Human Rights Law Review*, p. 372.

41. Jonathan Power, *Like Water on Stone: The Story of Amnesty International* (Penguin Books, 2001), ch. 4.

42. See *The Massacre of Political Prisoners in Iran 1988*, Report of an Inquiry conducted by Geoffrey Robertson (Abdorraham Boroumand Foundation, 2011).

43. See Philip Gourevitch, 'The Genocide Fax', *New Yorker* (11 May 1998), p. 42; *When Good Men Do Nothing*, BBC *Panorama* programme broadcast on 8 December 1998.

44. L. R. Melvern, *A People Betrayed – The Role of the West in Rwanda's Genocide* (Zed Books, 2000), p. 231.

45. 'Investigations Condemn UN Chief', *Guardian* (17 December 1999), and see Romeo Dallaire, *Shake Hands with the Devil* (Arrow, 2004), chs. 12–13.

46. Gérard Prunier, *The Rwanda Crisis 1959–94: History of a Genocide* (Hurst, 1995), p. 261.

47. See Philip Gourevitch, *We Wish to Inform You that Tomorrow We Will be Killed with Our Families* (Picador, 1998), pp. 154–8, 271–81.

48. Richard Goldstone, *For Humanity* (Yale University Press, 2000), p. 110.

49. *A Cry from the Grave* (Antelope Films; producer: Leslie Woodhead), screened BBC2 (27 November 1999).

50. The fairest instant history is provided by Jan Willem Honig and Norbert Both, *Srebrenica – Record of a War Crime* (Penguin, 1996).

51. David Rohde, *A Safe Area* (Pocket Books, 1997), p. 336.

52. Yasushi Akashi, 'The Limits of UN Diplomacy', *Survival*, vol. 37, no. 4, p. 96.

53. Michael Ignatieff, *The Warrior's Honour* (Chatto & Windus, 1998), p. 73.

3. THE RIGHTS OF HUMANKIND

1. *The Paquete Habana* (1900), 175 US 677.

2. See Geoffrey Robertson, *The Case of the Pope – Vatican Accountability for Human Rights Abuses* (Penguin, 2010), pp. 79–95.

3. *Barcelona Traction Case* (1970), ICJ Reports 3 at p. 32.

4. Ian Brownlie, *Principles of International Law* (6th edn) (Oxford University Press, 2003), p. 490.

5. See Igor Lukashuk, 'The Law of the International Community' in *International Law on the Eve of the 21st Century* (UN, 1997), p. 51 at 62–3.

6. *Salomon* v. *Customs & Excise* (1967), 2 QB 116 at 143, *per* Lord Diplock.

7. *Prosecutor* v. *Norman* (*Child Soldiers Case*), SCSL-04-14-AR72, 31 May 2004. The author dissented, on the basis that the necessary consensus to impose individual liability on those who conscript children did not emerge until the Rome Statute (1998), which was subsequent to the defendant's alleged conduct.

8. AFRC Appeal Judgment, 22 February 2008. See Leila Nadya Sadat (ed.), *Forging a Convention for Crimes Against Humanity* (Cambridge University Press, 2011).

9. *Kajelijeli*, Trial Judgment, case no. ICTR-98-44A, para. 936.

10. *Akeyesu*, Trial Judgment, case no. ICTR-96-4-T, para. 697.

11. *Peck* v. *UK* (2003), 36 EHRR 41, at para. 109.

12. See Geoffrey Robertson, *The Case of the Pope – Vatican Accountability for Human Rights Abuses* (Penguin, 2010).

13. *East African Asians Case*, 3 EHRR 76 (1973).

14. *Tyrer* v. *UK* (25 April 1978), 2 EHRR 1, *Costello-Roberts* v. *UK* (25 March 1993), 19 EHRR 112.

15. *T and V* v. *UK*, 30 EHRR 121 (16 December 1999).

16. *Prosecutor* v. *Anton Furundžija*, Hague Tribunal (10 December 1988), case no. IT-95-17, para. 153.

17. *Ex parte Pinochet* (*No. 3*) (1999), 2 All ER 97, pp. 108–9.

18. *Ireland* v. *UK* (1976), 2 EHRR 25.

19. *Denmark* v. *Greece* (1986), *Yearbook of the European Convention II*, p. 690.

20. See Amnesty International, URGENT ACTION 320/ii; MDE 14/043/2011 (2 November 2011).

21. 'Interpol Criticised over Effort to Have Separatist Arrested in the UK', *Guardian* (25 November 2011), p. 24.

22. *Kent* v. *Dulles* (1958), 357 US 116.

23. See Samuel Walker, *In Defence of American Liberties: A History of the ACLU* (Oxford University Press, 1990), pp. 232ff., and note the Supreme Court confirmation in *RAV* v. *City of St Paul, Minnesota*, 505, US 377 (1992).

24. Ian Buruma, 'China in Cyberspace', *New York Review of Books* (4 November 1999).

25. *Observer and Guardian* v. *UK* (1991), 14 EHRR 153.

26. *Tolstoy* v. *UK* (13 July 1995), 20 EHRR 442.

27. *Goodwin* v. *UK* (1996), 22 EHRR 123.

28. *Lautsi & Ors.* v. *Italy* (2011), ECHR Application No. 30814/06 (18 March 2011).

29. Case of *Leyla Sahin* v. *Turkey*, App. no. 44774/98, judgment of 10 November 2005, para. 111.

30. *Church of New Faith* v. *Commissioner for Payroll Tax* (1983), 57 ALJR 785 (High Court of Australia).

31. *X* v. *United Kingdom* (1981), 4 EHRR 188.

32. See ECHR, *Mayzit* v. *Russia*, 6/7/05, 20 January 2005, case no. 63378/00, Appeals Chamber, SLSC, *AFRC Case*, December 2005 (Justice Robertson).

33. *Woolmington* v. *DPP* (1935), AC 462.

34. See the Privy Council decision, *A-G of Hong Kong* v. *Lee Kwong-Kut* (1993), AC 951, and the ECHR in *Salabiaku* v. *France* (1988), 13 EHRR 379; also, the South African Constitutional Court in *State* v. *Mbatha* (1996), 2 LRC 208; the Canadian Supreme Court in *R.* v. *Oakes*, 26 DLR (4th) 200 and the English Courts in *R.* v. *DPP ex parte Kebilene* (2000), 2 AC 326.

35. *Hauschildt* v. *Denmark* (24 May 1989), 12 EHRR 266.

36. *Ex parte Pinochet (No. 2)* (1999), 1 All ER 577.

37. See Gabriel García Márquez, 'The Future of Colombia', *Granta Magazine* (1990).

38. See 'Ali Daghir and the Forty Nuclear Triggers' in Geoffrey Robertson, *The Justice Game* (Chatto & Windus, 1998), p. 285.

39. *Sherman* v. *US* (1958), 356 US 369 at p. 382.

40. See *Sorrells* v. *US* (1932), 287 US 435.

41. *Jacobsen* v. *US* (1992), 112 S St 1535.

42. *Bunning* v. *Cross* (1978), 141 CLR 54 at pp. 74–5; *R.* v. *Hsing* (1991), 57 ACrimR 88.

43. *Police* v. *Lavelle* (1979), 1 NZLR 45; *R.* v. *Smurthwaite* (1993), 98 Cr App R 437; and see Geoffrey Robertson, 'Entrapment Evidence: Manna from Heaven, or Fruit of the Poisoned Tree?', *Criminal Law Review* (November 1994), p. 805.

44. *Amato* v. *The Queen* (1982), 69 CCC 2d 31; see also *Mack* v. *The Queen* (1988), 44 CCC 3d 513 at p. 541.

45. *Bannikova* v. *Russia* (2010), ECHR 18757/06 (4 November 2010), para. 34.

46. *Ramanauskas* v. *Lithuania* (2008), ECHR 74420/01 (5 February 2008), para. 55.

47. See *n.* 45 above, para. 47.

48. See *n.* 46 above, at para. 70.

49. *Teixeira de Castro* v. *Portugal* (1998), 28 EHRR 101, at para. 38.

50. *Khudobin* v. *Russia* (2006), ECHR 898, para. 135.

51. See *n.* 45 above, para. 57.

52. *Klassa* v. *Federal Republic of Germany* (1978), 2 EHRR 214 and see *Kruslin* v. *France* (1990), 12 EHRR 547, where statutory provisions were held to be insufficient.

53. *Conka* v. *Belgium* (2002), ECHR 51564/99 (5 February 2002), para. 135.

54. *Gusinsky* v. *Russia* (2004), ECHR 70276/01 (19 May 2004).

55. Ibid.

56. Resolution 40/146, December 1985, welcoming the principles adopted by the 1985 UN Congress on the Prevention of Crime and Treatment of Offenders.

57. See the Code.

58. IBA Human Rights Institute Report, *Judicial Independence Undermined: A Report on Uganda* (September 2007).

59. See Tony Halpin, 'Human Rights Activist Gets Four Years for Tax Evasion', *The Times* (24 November 2011).

60. IBAHRI, 'The Gambia: Freedom of Expression on Trial' (February 2010).

61. 'Ukraine Condemned as Former PM is Jailed in Political Verdict', *Guardian* (12 October 2011).

62. Andrew Osborn, 'Judges Forced out after Accusing Kremlin of Hijacking Judiciary', *Daily Telegraph* (2 December 2009).

63. And of important tribunal decisions. It is extraordinary that one of the most important decisions on judicial independence and the need for fairness in dealing with allegations against a judge – namely the Mustill Tribunal Report of its enquiry into the conduct of Trinidad Chief Justice Sharma – has gone entirely unreported. See *In the Matter of an Enquiry under s137 of the Constitution of Trinidad and Tobago*, Rt Hon. Lord Mustill, Sir Vincent Floissac and Mr D. Morrison, QC 14 December 2007 (copies may be obtained from Kirsty Brimelow QC, at Doughty Street Chambers).

64. *Prosecutor* v. *Fofana and Kondewa*. Decision on Preliminary Motion based on lack of Jurisdiction (Judicial Independence), case no. SCSL-04-14-PT-035-11.

65. See 'Show Trials', in Geoffrey Robertson, *The Justice Game* (Vintage, 1998), p. 226.

66. *Oló* v. *Equatorial Guinea*, Comm. no. 468/1991, UN Doc. CCPR/C/49/D/468/1991 (1993).

67. *Busyo, Wongodi, Matubuka* v. *Democratic Republic of the Congo*, Comm. no. 933/2000, UN Doc. CCPR/C/76/D/933/2000, views of 31 July 2003.

68. See Afua Hirsch, 'System for Appointing Judges is "Undermining International Court"', *Guardian* (8 September 2010).

69. See Caroline Binham, 'Election Shines Light on War Crimes Court', *Financial Times* (14 September 2011).

70. Ibid.

71. Ruth Mackenzie and ors., *Selecting International Judges: Principle, Process and Politics* (Oxford University Press, 2010).

72. *Bridges* v. *California*, 314 US 252 (1941).

73. *R* v. *Kopyto*, 1987, 47 DLR (4th) 213.

74. *AG* v. *Hertzberg* (2008), SGHC 218.

75. *Lithgow and others* v. *UK* (1986), 8 EHRR 329, para. 121.

76. *Chorzów Factory Case* (1928), PCIJ series A, no. 17.

77. See *James* v. *UK* (1986), 8 EHRR 123, para. 60.

78. *Lithgow and others* v. *UK*, as *n.* 75 above, para. 121.

79. *Chorzów Factory Case*, as *n.* 76 above. See also *American International Group Inc.* v. *Iran* (1983): 'fair market value at the date of nationalization'; and *Amco* v. *Indonesia* (1985): 'the full compensation of prejudice, by awarding to the injured party the *damnum emergens* [loss suffered] and the *lucrum cessans* [expected profits]'.

80. Resolution 1803 (XVII) (14 December 1962).

81. Resolution 3201 (S–VI) (1 May 1974).

82. See, for example, *James* v. *UK*, as *n.* 77 above at para. 54.

83. *World Duty Free Company Ltd* v. *Republic of Kenya*, ICSID case no. ARB/00/7, Award 4 October 2006, para. 157.

4. TWENTY-FIRST CENTURY BLUES

1. Stephen Trombley, *The Execution Protocol* (Century, 1993), pp. 12, 36.

2. Raymond Bonner, 'Absence of Executions: A Special Report', *New York Times* (22 September 2000).

3. James Liebman, Jeffrey Fagan and Valorie West, *A Broken System: Error Rates in Capital Cases, 1973–95* (2000) Columbia Law School, Public Law Research Paper No. 15.

4. See *Newsweek* (12 June 2000).

5. *The State* v. *Makwanyane & Mchunur* (1995), (3) SA 391, 16 *HRLJ* 154 (1995), p. 195, para. 272.

6. *Mbushuu* v. *The Republic* (30 January 1995) [1995] TLR 97, Tanzanian Court of Appeal.

7. See ICCPR, Article 6(2) and (6).

8. The Second Optional Protocol to the ICCPR, signifying 'an international commitment to abolish the death penalty', has been signed by only forty-six states, although thirty-nine European nations have forsworn executions other than 'in time of war or imminent threat of war' by acceding to the Sixth Protocol of the ECHR see *Ocalan* v. *Turkey* (Application No. 46221/99) for the European Court's position.

9. See William A. Schabas, *The Abolition of the Death Penalty in International Law* (Grotius, 1993), pp. 99–103.

10. *The State* v. *Makwanyane & Mchunur, n.* 5 above, p. 194, para. 269.

11. Schabas, *n.* 9 above, p. 310, excerpt from general comment on Article 6 by Human Rights Committee.

12. *Woodson* v. *The State of North Carolina* (1976), 428 US 280.

13. *Patrick Reyes* v. *The Queen* (2002), UKPC 11.

14. For example, Article 4(4) of the American Convention on Human Rights provides: 'In no case shall capital punishment be inflicted for political offences or related common crimes.'

15. HRC Doc. A/44/40, notwithstanding a contrary decision by the Privy Council: *Robinson* v. *The Queen* (1985), 2 All ER 594. The dissenting judgment of Lords Scarman and Edmund-Davies, p. 604, reflects the international law rule: 'there can, save in very special circumstances such as a national emergency, be no greater public interest than that one who is accused of an offence conviction of which carries with it a sentence of death has a proper

opportunity of defending himself . . . it is a serious error of law to hold that a man accused of a capital offence can be denied the option of defence by a legal representative of his own choosing'.

16. *Mbenge* v. *Zaire*, HRC Doc. A/38/40.

17. This follows from Article 6(2), echoing the general rule against retrospective law embodied in Article 15 of the Covenant (see p. 101).

18. See Articles 99 and 100 of Geneva Convention III (1949) and Article 68 of Geneva Convention IV (1949).

19. *Safeguards Guaranteeing Protection of the Rights of Those Facing the Death Penalty*, ECOSOC res. 1984/50 (25 May 1984), endorsed by General Assembly, res. 39/118 (14 December 1984). See Articles 4, 6 (which goes too far by requiring mandatory appeals against conviction in death sentence cases even when defendants do not contest their guilt) and 8.

20. *Neville Lewis* v. *AG of Jamaica* (2001), 2 AC 50.

21. See Geoffrey Robertson, *The Justice Game* (Chatto & Windus, 1998), ch. 4. An example of a senior domestic court refusing to buckle under government pressure for an immediate execution, and insisting that execution be stayed until every possible point could be carefully and calmly considered, is provided by the High Court of Australia in *Tait* v. R. (1962), 108 CLR 620.

22. *Breard* v. *Greece* (*Angel Breard Case*), US Supreme Court, 523 US 371, 14 April 1998. The Execution of Angel Breard: Apologies are Not Enough. Amnesty International Index, AMR 51/27/98.

23. *Germany* v. *USA* (*LaGrand Case*), ICJ decision, 27 June 2001.

24. Roger Hood, *The Death Penalty* (Oxford, 1995), pp. 91–2.

25. Covenant, Article 6(5); American Convention, Article 4(5); ECOSOC safeguards, Article 3; Convention on the Rights of the Child, Article 37.

26. Justice Anthony Kennedy, in *Roper* v. *Simmons*, case no. 03–633, 1 March 2005.

27. Res. 3/87, case no. 9647, *Roach & Pinkerton* v. *US, Annual Report of the Inter-American Commission on Human Rights 1986–7*, HRLJ 8 (1987), p. 345.

28. *Ford* v. *Wainwright* (1986), 477 US 399. The common law always permitted a reprieve of a death sentence to test an allegation that the prisoner was insane; see the approval of the judgment of Justice Smith by the Supreme Court of Victoria in *Tait* v. *R., n.* 21 above.

29. *Tyrer* v. *UK* (1978), 2 EHRR 1, para. 80; Anthony F. Granucci, 'Nor Cruel

and Unusual Punishments Inflicted: The Original Meaning', *Californian Law Review* 57(4) (1969), p. 839.

30. *Pratt and Morgan* v. *A-G of Jamaica* (1994), 2 AC 1.

31. *Soering* v. *UK* (1989), 11 EHRR 439.

32. *Knight* v. *Florida* (1999), 120 S. Ct 459. Justice Stevens has also found *Pratt and Morgan* at least arguable: *Lackey* v. *Texas* (1995), 514 US 1045.

33. *Trop* v. *Dulles* (1958), 356 US 86 at p. 101.

34. *Thompson* v. *Oklahoma* (1988), 487 US 815.

35. *Minority Schools in Albania* (1935), PCIJ Ser. A/B, no. 64, at p. 17.

36. Francesco Caportorti, *Study on the Rights of Persons Belonging to Ethnic, Religious and Linguistic Minorities*, UN Doc. E/CN$_4$ Sub 2/284.

37. *Sandra Lovelace* v. *Canada* (1981), Comm. no. R. 6/24, UN Doc. A/3/40, p. 166.

38. *The Belgian Linguistics Case No. 2* (1968), 1 EHRR 252, p. 832. This was decided by reference to family and educational rights provisions of the European Covenant, but the same reasoning would apply under Article 27.

39. See *TK* v. *France* (1987), Comm. no. 220/1987 (note dissent of Professor Rosalyn Higgins), UN Doc. A/45/40; and see Nigel Rodley, 'Conceptual Problems in the Protection of Minorities: International Legal Developments', *HRQ* 17 (1995), p. 48. *Guesdon* v. *France No. 2* (1990), Report of HRC, UN Doc. CCPR/C/39/D/219/1986.

40. *Her Majesty's Attorney General* v. *Trustees of the British Museum* (2005), EWCH 1089.

41. *Autocephalous Greek-Orthodox Church of Cyprus* v. *Goldberg and Feldman Fine Arts Inc.* (1990), 917 F.2d 278, and see *Iran* v. *Barakat Galleries* (2007), EWHC 705.

42. *Temple of Preah Vihear Cambodia* v. *Thailand* (1962), ICJ 6.

43. *Attorney-General of New Zealand* v. *Ortiz* (1983), 2 All ER 93; 78 ILR 608, at 631.

44. This is not to say that an action would succeed in either court. The Greek case might now be rejected because of delay or (in the ICJ) because the British declaration under the Court's optional clause is limited to 'situations subsequent to 1st January 1974'. If the retention of the Elgin Marbles is a continuing wrong, then this would not rule the case out of court.

45. *Lubicon Lake Band* v. *Canada* (1984), HRC Comm. no. 167, UN Doc. Supp. no. 40 A/45/40.

46. A definition suggested by the UN Working Group on Indigenous Populations. See Corntassel and Primeau, 'Indigenous "Sovereignty" and International Law: Revised Strategies for Pursuing "Self Determination"', *HRQ* 17 (1995), p. 343.

47. See Robert T. Coulter, 'The UN Declaration on the Rights of Indigenous Peoples: A Historic Change in International Law' (2009), 45 *Idaho Law Review*, p. 539.

48. *Mabo* v. *Queensland* (1992), 175 CLR 1.

49. *Republic of Fiji* v. *Prasad*, Fiji Court of Appeal, 1 March 2001. See George Williams, 2 *Melbourne Journal of International Law* (2001), p. 144.

50. R. Higgins, comment on 'Post-modern Tribalism and the Right to Secession' in Brolmand, Lefeber & Zieck (eds.), *Peoples and Minorities in International Law* (Martinus Nijhoff, 1993), p. 33.

51. *AD* v. *Canada* (1980), HRC Comm. no. 78/1980, UN Doc. A/39/40, p. 200.

52. See Jen Robinson, *Justice for West Papua*, Sydney University Lecture (13 March 2009).

53. Hugh Lunn, 'How the West Was Lost', *The Weekend Australian* (21–22 August 1999).

54. See John Saltford, *UN Involvement with the Act of Self-Determination in West Irian (Indonesian West New Guinea)* (2000) 69 71, at 184.

55. See the *Western Sahara Case* (1975), ICJ Reports 12, para. 57.

56. See D. J. Harris, *Cases and Materials on International Law* (Sweet & Maxwell, 1998), pp. 122–31.

57. Diane F. Orentlicher, 'Separation Anxiety: International Responses to Ethno-Separatist Claims', *Yale Journal of International Law* 23 (1998), p. 43.

58. The story is fully told in David Vine, *Island of Shame. The Secret History of the US Military Base on Diego Garcia* (Princeton University Press, 2009), and in *Chagos Islanders* v. *Attorney General* (2003), EWHC 2222 (9 October 2003, Mr Justice Ousley).

59. See http://www.cablegatesearch.net/Reference ID 09LONDON1156.

60. *Frontier Dispute Case (Burkina Faso* v. *Republic of Mali)* (1986), ICJ Reports (1986), p. 566.

61. See the analysis by Antonio Cassesse in *UN Law/Fundamental Rights: Two Topics in International Law* (Sijthoff and Noordhoff, 1979), pp. 154–5.

62. See James Crawford (ed.), *The Rights of Peoples* (Oxford, 1988), p. 56.

63. *Re Secession of Quebec* (1998), 2 SCR 217.

64. *South-west African Cases*, ICJ Rep. (1962), p. 319; ICJ Rep. (1966), p. 6.

This is a rare example of states (Ethiopia and Liberia) invoking the jurisdiction on behalf of other non-state 'peoples'.

65. Richard Falk in Crawford, *n.* 62 above, p. 19.

66. W. H. Auden, 'September 1, 1939', *Another Time* (1940).

67. *Legal Consequences of the Construction of a Wall in the Occupied Palestinian Territory* (9 July 2004), ICJ, separate opinion of Justice Rosalyn Higgins, para. 18.

68. *Rouquette et al.*, 5 March 1999, Conseil d'État (2000), 13 *Interights Bulletin* 53.

69. *Grootboom* v. *Oosteberg*, Municipality (2000), BCLR 277.

70. 'A Global War against Bribery', *Economist* (14 January 1999).

71. See Simon Jenkins, *The Times* (24 March 2000), and David Rieff, 'Did Live Aid Do More Harm than Good?' *Guardian* (24 June 2005).

72. Mohammed Bedjaoui, 'The Right to Development', cited by Henry Steiner and Philip Alston (eds.), *International Human Rights in Context* (Oxford University Press, 1996), p. 118, para. 34.

73. See Virginia A. Leary, 'The Paradox of Workers' Rights as Human Rights' in L. Compa and S. Diamond (eds.), *Human Rights, Labour Rights and International Trade* (University of Pennsylvania Press, 1996), p. 22, and Philip Alston, *Labour Rights as Human Rights* (Oxford University Press, 2005), p. 14.

74. Alston, *n.* 72 above, p. 23.

75. *Young, James and Webster* v. *UK* (1981), 4 EHRR 38.

76. See Patrick Macklem, 'The Right to Bargain Collectively in International Law' in Alston, *n.* 72 above, p. 61.

77. See *JB* v. *Canada* (1982) Comm. no. 118/1982, UN Doc. CCPR/C/28/D/118/1992.

78. See *Swedish Engine Drivers Union* v. *Sweden* (1981), 1 EHRR 617.

79. *Wilson* v. *UK* (2002), 35 EHRR 523, at para. 46.

80. *Khulumani* v. *Barclays National Bank Ltd*, 504 F. 3d 254, 260 (2nd Cir., 2007); and Lee Kristen Hutchens, 'International Law in the American Courts – *Khulumani v Barclay National Bank*: The Decision Heard "Round the Corporate World"' (2008) 9 (5) *German Law Journal*, 639.

81. *Kiobel* v. *Royal Dutch Petroleum* (2nd Cir., 17 September 2010), p. 49.

82. Rein Müllerson, *Human Rights Diplomacy* (Routledge, 1997), p. 52.

83. Examples are found in the European Commission and Court cases upheld

against the Greek Colonels, and in the Inter-American Court rulings that widespread electoral fraud is of international concern: *Mexico Elections Decision* (case nos. 9768 and 9780) (1990). See James Crawford, *Democracy in International Law* (Cambridge University Press, 1994).

84. *The Republic of Fiji v. Chandrika Prasad*, Fiji Court of Appeal, 1 March 2001.

85. See Leo Lewis, 'Rebel Artist attacks Beijing after Police Interrogate Wife', *The Times* (30 November 2011), p. 38.

5. WAR LAW

1. Bert Rölling, *The Law of War and National Jurisdiction Since* 1945 (Hague Academy, Recueil des Couis, 1960), p. 445.

2. See Edward Luttwak, 'A Post-Heroic Military Policy', *Foreign Affairs* (July/ August 1996), p. 33. But surveys show the 'Mogadishu factor' has been much less potent since 9/11.

3. *Henry V*, Act 4, Scene 7, and see Theodor Meron, 'Shakespeare's *Henry V* and the Law of War' in *War Crimes Law Comes of Age* (Oxford University Press, 1998).

4. See Geoffrey Robertson, *The Tyrannicide Brief* (Chatto & Windus, 2005).

5. Comment by Geoffrey Best, *War and Law Since 1945* (Clarendon Press, 1994), p. 41.

6. Preamble to Hague Convention II (1899), repeated in 1949 Geneva Conventions (I: Article 63; II: Article 62; III: Article 142; IV: Article 158) and in 1977 Geneva Protocols.

7. *The Llandovery Castle* (1921), Annual Digest of Public International Law Cases, 1923–4, case no. 235.

8. See Best, *n.* 5 above, pp. 171–9.

9. See Geneva Convention I: Article 50; II: Article 51; III: Article 130 (including 'compelling a prisoner-of-war to serve in the forces of the hostile power, or wilfully depriving a prisoner-of-war of the rights of fair and regular trial'); and IV: Article 147 (including 'unlawful deportation or transfer or unlawful confinement of a protected person, compelling a protected person to serve in the forces of a hostile power . . . taking of hostages').

10. See Phillip Webster, Tim Reid and Roland Watson, 'Red Cross Warned of Abuse Again and Again', *The Times* (11 May 2004), p. 1.

11. Protocol Additional to the Geneva Conventions of 12 August 1949 and Relating to the Protection of Victims of Non-International Armed Conflicts (Protocol II) (1977), Article I (material field of application).

12. Geneva Protocol I relating to the Protection of Victims of International Armed Conflicts, Article 90(5)(c).

13. Ingrid Detter, *The Law of War* (Cambridge University Press, 2000), p. 252.

14. Request for Advisory Opinion on Nuclear Weapons by the World Health Organization (8 July 1996), summarized in *HRLJ* 17 (1996), p. 392.

15. See James Chace, 'After Hiroshima: Sharing the Atom Bomb', *Foreign Affairs* (January/February 1996), p. 129.

16. Michael Mandelbaum, 'Lessons of the Next Nuclear War', *Foreign Affairs* (March/April 1995), p. 22.

17. Jonathan Medalia, 'Comprehensive Nuclear Test-Ban Treaty: Background and Current Developments', Congressional Research Service (3 August 2011).

18. Ibid.

19. *The Corfu Channel Case* (1949), ICJ 4.

20. *Nuclear Tests Case (Australia v. France)* (1974), ICJ 253, para. 53.

21. *Legality of the Use by a State of Nuclear Weapons in Armed Conflict*, ICJ advisory opinion (8 July 1996), para. 22. Reported in *HRLJ* 17 (1996), p. 253ff.

22. Ibid., dissent of Judge Korona, p. 6.

23. *Legality of the Use by a State of Nuclear Weapons in Armed Conflict*, ICJ advisory opinion (8 July 1996), para. 15 (argument of US).

24. Ibid., para. 35.

25. Ibid., para. 95.

26. *Military and Paramilitary Activities in and against Nicaragua*, ICJ Reports (1986), p. 94, para. 176.

27. See *n.* 23 above, para. 97.

28. Amnesty International, *Shattered Lives: The Case for Tough International Arms Control* (2003).

29. See Arms Trafficking, Mercenaries, and Drug Cartels, Hearing Before the Permanent Sub-Committee on Investigations of the US Senate (27 and 28 February 1991).

30. Louis Blom-Cooper QC, *Guns for Antigua: Report of the Commission of*

Inquiry into the Circumstances Surrounding the Shipment of Arms from Israel to Antigua and Transshipment to Colombia (Duckworth, 1990).

31. John F. Burns, 'Britain Joins a Draft Treaty in Cluster Munitions', *New York Times* (29 May 2008).

32. Common Article 2.

33. See James G. Stewart, 'Corporate War Crimes – Prosecuting the Pillage of Natural Resources', Open Society Justice Initiative, (2011).

34. IG Farben case, *US* v. *Krauch et al*, 8 Trials of War Criminals 1081, p. 1133.

35. Wilfred Burchett and Derek Roebuck, *The Whores of War* (Penguin, 1977).

36. UN General Assembly Resolution 44/81, Rep. A/44/717, *The Use of Mercenaries as a Means to Violate Human Rights and to Impede the Exercise of the Right of People to Self-determination* (8 December 1989).

37. Blom-Cooper, *n.* 30 above.

38. Arms Trafficking, Mercenaries and Drug Cartels, *n.* 29 above.

39. Thus, in American law there is no basis for incriminating acts of enlistment in foreign forces outside the jurisdiction: Neutrality Act: Title 18 s.959(a); *Wiborg* v. *US* (1896), 163 US 632. The UK Foreign Enlistment Act (1870) does apply to British nationals who render services to armies at war with friendly states, but its provisions have become a dead letter: Report of the Committee of Privy Counsellors Appointed to Inquire into the Recruitment of Mercenaries (1976), Cmnd. 6569.

40. See *Robertson & Nicol on Media Law* (5th edn, Penguin), pp. 675–8.

41. *Prosecutor* v. *Brdanin and Talic*, case no. IT-99-36-AR73.9, Decision on Interlocutory Appeal (11 December 2002), paras. 36 and 46.

42. *Goodwin* v. *UK* (App. no. 17488/90) (1996), ECHR 16, para. 39.

43. See *Prosecutor* v. *Brima and others*, case no. SCSL-2004-16-AR73, Appeals Chamber judgment (26 May 2006), separate and concurring opinion of Justice Geoffrey Robertson QC, para. 28.

44. *Prosecutor* v. *Norman* (*Child Soldiers Case*), SCSL-04-14-AR72, 31 May 2004.

45. Graça Machel, *The Impact of War on Children* (UNICEF, 2001), p. 8.

46. Report of ICC Preparatory Committee (14 April 1998).

47. In Act 4, Scene 7 the French attack on the boys in the baggage train was described as 'expressly against the law of arms' according to Captain Fluellen. See Meron, *n.* 3 above, p. 52.

6. AN END TO IMPUNITY?

1. *United States* v. *Ohlendorf* (Case 9) (1946–7), IV Trials of War Criminals before the Nuremberg Military Tribunals, p. 498.

2. *Barcelona Traction Case* (*Spain* v. *Belgium*), ICJ Rep. (1970), para. 33.

3. *The Antelope* (1825) 23 US (10 Wheat) 66.

4. Gary Bass, *Stay the Hand of Vengeance: The Politics of War Crimes Tribunals* (Princeton University Press, 2000), ch. 3.

5. See Peter Balakian, *The Burning Tigris* (Heinemann, 2003).

6. Proceedings of the International Conference on the Repression of Terrorism, League of Nations (1937).

7. Ian Cobain, 'Execution by Electric Chair for Hitler', *Guardian* (2 January 2006).

8. Foreign Office Paper (18 July 1942).

9. Richard Overy, *Interrogations* (Allen Lane, 2001), p. 6.

10. UK Aide-mémoire (May 1945), Sir Hartley Shawcross, *Life Sentence – The Memoirs of Lord Shawcross* (Constable, 1995), pp. 90–91.

11. Conference minutes, quoted by Sir Hartley Shawcross, *Tribute to Justice Jackson* (New York Bar, 1969).

12. Ann and John Tusa, *The Nuremberg Trial* (Macmillan, 1983), p. 66.

13. Ibid., Report (1 June 1945), Jackson to Truman.

14. Quoted by Michael Biddiss, 'Victor's Justice?', *History Today*, vol. 45(5) (May 1995), p. 40.

15. Overy, *n.* 9 above, p. 54.

16. Robert E. Conot, *Justice at Nuremberg* (Weidenfeld & Nicolson, 1983), p. 68.

17. Ibid., p. 325. And see Michael Walzer, *Just and Unjust Wars* (Basic Books, 1991), p. 148ff., for a discussion of the Laconia Order (U-boats must not attempt to rescue all survivors) and its US and British equivalents.

18. Conot, *n.* 16 above, p. 160.

19. Ibid., p. 329.

20. 'The Nuremberg Judgment', *American Journal of International Law* 41 (January 1947), p. 172.

21. *Re Krupp and others* (1948), 15 ILR 620.

22. *Re Ohlendorf and others* (1948), 15 ILR 656.

23. Tusa, *n.* 12 above, pp. 421 and 423.

24. See Albert Pierrepoint, *Executioner: Pierrepoint* (Harrap, 1974), p. 148.

25. Shawcross, *n*. 10 above, p. 133.

26. John W. Dower, *Embracing Defeat: Japan in the Wake of World War 2* (W. W. Norton, 1999), p. 453. Dower's is the best, and most recent, analysis of the long-term damage done by Hirohito's immunity. He concludes (p. 562): 'Even Japanese peace activists who endorse the ideals of the Nuremberg and Tokyo Charters, and who have laboured to document and publicize Japanese atrocities, cannot defend the way the war crimes trials were carried out; nor can they defend the American decision to exonerate the Emperor of war responsibility and then, in the chill of the Cold War, release and soon afterwards openly embrace accused right-wing war criminals like the later Prime Minister Kishi Nobusuke.'

27. Ibid., p. 437.

28. See Yves Beigbeder, *Judging War Criminals* (Macmillan, 1999), p. 72.

29. Ibid., p. 69.

30. Simon Wiesenthal, *'Justice Not Vengeance'* (Weidenfeld & Nicolson, 1990), pp. 91, 208–9.

31. Ibid., ch. 30.

32. Resolution 95(1) of the UN General Assembly (11 December 1946).

33. The debate over the need for linkage is summarized by Stephen Ratner and Jason Abrams, *Accountability for Human Rights Atrocities in International Law* (Oxford University Press, 1997), pp. 45–57; and see the decision of Justice Toohey in the High Court of Australia, *Polyukovich* v. *Commonwealth* (1991), 172 CLR, pp. 501, 664–77.

34. See Samantha Power, *A Problem from Hell* (Penguin, 2002), p. 19.

35. See Geoffrey Robertson 'Was there an Armenian Genocide?' University of St Thomas, *Journal of Law and Public Policy*, vol. IV, no. 2 (Spring 2010), pp. 84–5.

36. *Reservations to the Convention on Genocide Case* (1951), ICJ Rep. 15, p. 23.

37. *Barbie* (1988), 78 ILR 125, pp. 137–40.

38. See William A. Schabas, *Genocide in International Law* (Cambridge, 2nd edn, 2009), p. 149.

39. See Geoffrey Robertson, *The Massacre of Political Prisoners in Iran, 1988* (Boroumand Foundation, 2011), pp. 107–8.

40. See the commentary to Article 19 (Prohibition of Genocide) of the ILC

Draft Code of Crimes against the Peace and Security of Mankind (report of the ILC on the work of its 43rd session, 1991). The definition of genocide in Article 6 of the Rome Statute of the International Criminal Court is identical to that in the 1949 Genocide Convention.

41. *Prosecutor* v. *Akeyesu* (1998), 37 ILM, p. 1399.

42. *Kevin Buzzacott* v. *Hill and Downer*, Federal Court of Australia (1 September 1999), 96 FLR 153.

43. *Buck* v. *Bell* (1927), 274 US 200 US Supreme Court. The Australian policy was directed by an English eugenicist, A. O. Neville, who gloried in the title of 'Chief Protector of Aborigines' in Western Australia. The policy was formally adopted by Australian states in 1937, but abandoned after the Second World War. The film *Rabbit-Proof Fence* (2002) illustrates it accurately.

44. *A-G of Israel* v. *Eichmann* (1962), 36 ILR1, pp. 18 and 277; *Extradition of Demjanjuk* (1985), 776 F2d 571.

45. *Ex parte Pinochet (No. 3)* (1999), 2 ER 97, pp. 108–9 (Lord Browne-Wilkinson). The quotation is from *Extradition of Demjanjuk, n.* 44 above.

46. *Al-Adsani* v. *UK* (2002), 34 EHRR 11.

47. *Filártiga* v. *Peña-Irala* (1980), 577 F. Supp. 860.

48. *The Greek Case* (1969,) 12 *Yearbook of European Convention Law*, p. 505.

49. See *Bati* v. *Turkey*, no. 33097/96, ECHR (3 June 2004), paras. 114 and 117.

50. *Ireland* v. *UK*, European Court of Human Rights, Series A no. 25, paras. 96–7.

51. *Selmouni* v. *France* (1999), 29 EHRR 403.

52. *Prosecutor* v. *Bredanin* (1 September 2004), Appeal Judgment, paras. 243–52.

53. See the Privy Council decision in *Re Piracy Jure Gentium* (1934), AC 586.

54. Letter dated 24 January 2011 from the Secretary-General to the President of the Security Council – Report of the Special Adviser to the Secretary-General on legal issues related to piracy off the coast of Somalia, UN Doc. S/2011/30.

55. Richard Dowden, 'By Robbing the Rich, Somali Pirates Have Helped the Poor', *The Times* (4 February 2012).

56. See Martin N. Murphy, *Somalia: The New Barbary? Piracy and Islam in the Horn of Africa* (Columbia University Press, 2011).

57. See *n*. 54 above.

58. Jeffrey Gettleman, 'The Pirates are Winning!' *New York Review of Books*, (14 October, 2010).

59. Robert Wright, 'Borders to Control', *Financial Times* (2 March 2011).

60. See *n*. 54 above.

61. Ian Drury, '"Failure to Prosecute Pirates Beggars Belief" Say MPs', *Daily Mail* (5 January 2012).

62. *Lotus Case (France v. Turkey)* (1927), PCIJ Ser. A, no. 10.

63. *A-G of Israel* v. *Eichmann* (1962), 36 ILR, pp. 28, 26 (District Court), p. 277 (Supreme Court).

64. *Barbie* (1988), 89 ILR, pp. 125, 130.

65. *Democratic Republic of the Congo v. Belgium*: ICJ ruling on Belgian arrest warrant of 11 April 2000 (14 February 2002).

66. Yoram Sheftel, *The Demjanjuk Affair – The Rise and Fall of a Show Trial* (Gollancz, 1994), p. 216. This account of the case is by Demjanjuk's much-vilified Israeli defence lawyer.

7. SLOUCHING TOWARDS NEMESIS

1. Ernesto Sábato, Prologue to *Nunca Más, Report of the National Commission on the Disappearance of People* (Faber, 1986).

2. See Toine Van Dongen, 'Vanishing Point – The Problem of Disappearances', 90(1) *Bulletin of Human Rights* (1997), p. 23.

3. *Nunca Más, n.* 1 above, pp. 29–31.

4. Jacobo Timerman, *Prisoner without a Name, Cell without a Number* (Knopf, 1981), p. 148.

5. See Christopher Joyce and Eric Stover, *Witnesses from the Grave* (Bloomsbury, 1991), ch. 12.

6. See Diane F. Orentlicher, 'Settling Accounts: The Duty to Prosecute Human Rights Violations of a Prior Regime', 100(8) *Yale Law Journal* 2588 (1991), p. 227.

7. *Einsatzgruppen Case (US* v. *Ohlendorf and others)*, IV Trials of War Criminals (1950), p. 498.

8. *Bautista* v. *Colombia* (October 1995), HRC 55 Comm. no. 563/1993, paras. 8.6 and 10; HRLJ 19, p. 24.

9. 'UN Divided over "Disappearances", Al Jazeera (6 February 2007).

10. UN Doc. A/6716 (1967).

11. Collected in Naomi Roht-Arriaza, *Impunity and Human Rights in International Law and Practice* (Oxford University Press, 1995), ch. 3.

12. *Janes Case (US v. Mexico)*, 4 *Reports of International Arbitral Awards* (1926), p. 82.

13. *West Case (US v. Mexico)*, 4 *Reports of International Arbitral Awards* (1927), p. 270.

14. *Velasquez Rodriguez Case* (29 July 1988), *HRLJ* 9, p. 212; and see Julianne Kokott, 'No Impunity for Human Rights Violations in the Americas', *HRLJ* 14, p. 153.

15. See, for example, *Bleier v. Uruguay* (1982), Comm. no. 127/30 UN Doc. A/37/40; *Baboeram v. Suriname* (1985), Comm. no. 196/19833148-159/1993, UN Doc. A/40/40.

16. See Naomi Roht-Arriaza, 'State Responsibility to Investigate and Prosecute Grave Human Rights Violations in International Law', *California Law Review* 78(2) (1990), p. 451; at p. 481 commenting on *Donnelly v. UK* (1976), YB ECHR 84.

17. IAC 66, OAS/Ser L/V/III 29 Doc. 4, and see Padilla, 'Reparations in *Aloeboetoe v. Suriname', HRQ* 17(3) (1995), p. 541.

18. Ian Brownlie, *Principles of Public International Law* (6th edn) (Oxford University Press, 2003), p. 303.

19. *Trajano v. Marcos*, 878 F2d 1439 (9th Circuit); *Re Estate of Ferdinand Marcos Litigation* (1992), 978 F2d 493, 498 (9th Circuit).

20. *Filártiga v. Peña-Irala* (1980), 630 F2d 876 (2nd Circuit).

21. *Kadić v. Karadžić* (1995), 70 F3d 232 (2nd Circuit), is the decision permitting the action to proceed.

22. *Phillip v. Director of Public Prosecutions* (1992), 1 AC 545, PC.

23. *US v. Klein* (1871), 80 US (13 Wall) 128.

24. *The Federalist* no. 74 (1788) (Bourne edition, 1947), p. 79.

25. *Murphy v. Ford* (1975), 390 F. Supp. 1372.

26. *A-G of Trinidad v. Lennox Phillip, (No. 2)* (1995), 1 AC 396.

27. *Mustapha v. Mohammed* (1987), LRC Const & Admin 16, applied in *A-G of Trinidad v. Lennox Phillip, n.* 26 above.

28. *Prosecutor v. Kondewa*, SCSL-04-14-AR72, decision on amnesty provided by the Lomé Accord, 25 May 2004, separate opinion of author.

29. *Comprehensive Peace Agreement Between the Government of Liberia and the Liberians United for Reconciliation and Democracy [LURD] and the Movement for Democracy in Liberia [MODEL] and Political Parties, Accra* (August 2003), Article 34.

30. Protocol additional to the Geneva Conventions of 12 August 1949 and relating to the protection of victims of non-international armed conflicts (Protocol II), 8 June 1977, in force 7 December 1978.

31. See Inter-Am. Comm. HR Case 10.480 (El Salvador), report no. 1/99, para. 116 (1999), stating: 'The preparatory work for Article 6(5) indicates that the purpose of this precept is to encourage amnesty . . . as a type of liberation at the end of hostilities for those who were detained or punished merely for having participated in the hostilities. It does not seek to be an amnesty for those who have violated international humanitarian law.'

32. *Azanian Peoples Organisation [AZAPO] and others* v. *President of the Republic of South Africa*, 1996 (4) SA 672 (CC), 691.

33. HRC, General Comment no. 20 (on Article 7), 44th session (1992).

34. Inter-American Commission on Human Rights, Uruguay Report, *HRLJ* 13, p. 340, paras. 21–7; ibid., Argentina Report, pp. 336–9.

35. Inter-American Commission on Human Rights, El Salvador Report (24 September 1992): 'State Responsibility for Los Hojas Massacre', *HRLJ* 14 (1993), p. 167.

36. *Barrios Altos Case (Chumbipuma Aguirre et al.* v. *Peru)*, 75 Inter-Am. Ct HR (Ser. C) (Judgment) (2001), para. 41.

37. *Prosecutor* v. *Furundžija*, case no. IT-95–17/1, judgment 10 December 1998, para. 155.

38. Jack Straw, interview for BBC, 21 January 2003. See Hansard (19 March 2003), col. 936, for the prime minister's comments.

39. *Nicaragua* v. *US* (1996), ICJ Reports, para. 186.

40. Vienna Declaration and Programme of Action, 25 June 1993, World Conference on Human Rights, A/CONF.157/23 (12 July 1993), para. 60.

41. *Chile in Transition* (Americas Watch, 1989), p. 73.

42. Carlos S. Nino, 'The Duty to Punish Past Abuses of Human Rights Put into Context: The Case of Argentina', *Yale Law Journal* 100 (1991), p. 2624.

43. Belinda Aquino, 'The Human Rights Debacle in the Philippines' in Roht-Arriaza, *n.* 11 above, p. 231.

44. Richard Carver, 'Zimbabwe: Drawing a Line through the Past' in Roht-Arriaza, *n.* 11 above, p. 252.

45. *Prosecutor* v. *Sam Hinga Norman*, SCSL-2003–08-PT, decision of president on TRC appeal against denial of public hearing, 28 November 2003.

46. 'Bolivia: A Historic Ruling against Impunity', *ICJ Review* 51 (1993).

47. The El Mozote massacre was first reported by Ray Bonner in the *New York Times*. It was committed by a battalion trained in the US, but Assistant Secretary of State Thomas Enders told a Senate committee it had never taken place. See Mark Danner, *The Massacre at El Mozote* (Vintage, 1994).

48. See M. Ensalaco, 'Truth Commissions for Chile and El Salvador: A Report and Assessment', *HRQ* 16 (1994), p. 664.

49. Sábato, *n.* 1 above, pp. 160–61.

50. Quoted by Aryeh Neier in *War Crimes* (Random House, 1997), p. 37.

51. Jonathan Tepperman, 'Truth and Consequences', *Foreign Affairs* (March/April 2002), p. 128.

52. *Azanian People's Organization* v. *The President of the Republic of South Africa* (1996), 4 South Africa Law Reports 637, Ismail Mahomed CJ, para. 32.

53. Desmond Tutu, *No Future without Progress* (Rider, 1999), pp. 24–30. But compare Martin Meredith, *Coming to Terms – South Africa's Search for Truth* (Perseus, 1999), which gives a much more critical and pessimistic account of the Commission.

54. Richard J. Goldstone, *For Humanity – Reflections of a War Crimes Investigator* (Yale University Press, 2000), p. 72.

55. *Weekly Mail* (24 February 1995), pp. 7–8, cited by Parker, 'The Politics of Indemnities, Truth Telling and Reconciliation in South Africa', *HRLJ* 17, p. 1.

56. Amnesty Committee, Truth and Reconciliation Commission, Decision in the application of Dirk Coetzee (0063/96): see Henry Steiner and Philip Alston, *International Human Rights in Context* (2nd edn) (Oxford University Press, 2000), p. 1242.

57. Aryn-Baker, 'Bahrain's Stillborn Revolution', *Time* magazine (23 January 2012).

58. See Anna Funder, *Stasiland: Stories from Behind the Berlin Wall* (Granta, 2003), p. 17.

59. Jane Perlez, 'Hungarian Arrests Set Off Debate: Should '56 Oppressors be Punished?', *The New York Times* (3 April 1994), p. 10. Nick Thorpe, 'Four in Court for Hungarian Uprising Massacre', *Guardian* (12 October 1999), p. 17.

60. Susanne Walther, 'The Berlin Wall Shootings', in Roht-Arriaza, *n.* 11 above, p. 99. And see Tony Paterson, 'No Escape from Jail Term for East German Leader', *Guardian* (9 November 1999), p. 14.

61. *Sowaniuk* v. *UK*, App. no. 63716/00, admissibility decision, 29 May 2001.

62. *Kelly & ors* v. *UK*, Strasbourg, App. no. 30054/96, 4 May 2001.

63. Chris Bird, 'Chief of "Balkan Auschwitz" Gets 20 Years in Jail', *Guardian* (5 October 1999).

64. See Robert O. Paxton, 'The Trial of Maurice Papon', *New York Review of Books* (16 December 1999), p. 32.

65. IAC *Annual Report* (26 September 1986), p. 193, and see Kokott, 'No Impunity for Human Rights Violations in the Americas', *HRLJ* 14 (1993), p. 153.

66. John Aglionby, 'UK Embassy Lied Over Fate of Timor Journalists', *Guardian* (1 December 2005).

8. THE CASE OF GENERAL PINOCHET

1. DINA head Manuel Contreras, seeking parole from his prison sentences for directing the Letelier bombing, has testified that Pinochet gave him verbal orders for this and other assassinations. This chimes with the American prosecutor's case against the DINA operatives who effected the bombing. Lawrence Barcella Jr, 'The Case We Made 22 Years Ago', *Washington Post* (6 December 1998); Richard J. Wilson, 'Prosecuting Pinochet: International Crimes in Spanish Domestic Law', *HRQ* 21 (1999).

2. See Inter-American Commission on Human Rights, Report 36/96 (15 October 1996) and Report 29/98 (2 March 1998).

3. Judge Juan Guzmán, of the Santiago Appeals Court, seized with all cases against Pinochet, stated, 'I am prevented from issuing any kind of arrest warrant' (*El Mercurio*, 5 August 1998). After Pinochet's arrest in London three months later, the Chilean government petitioned the pro-Pinochet Supreme Court to appoint one of its own justices to take the cases over from Judge Guzmán so that the military tribunals could not assert jurisdiction. The court refused, by 13 votes to 3, to permit even this distant possibility of Pinochet standing trial in Chile. However, in July 1999, shamed by international criticism, Chile's Supreme Court at least allowed that disappearances still

unresolved could be characterized as the ongoing crime of 'kidnapping' which continues after, and therefore beyond and outside, the amnesty. Some twenty army torturers and one junta member (Humberto Gordon) were arrested in consequence.

4. Wilson, *n*. 1 above, p. 927.

5. See Hugh O'Shaughnessy, *Pinochet: The Politics of Torture* (Latin American Bureau, 1999).

6. *R. v. Evans, ex parte Augusto Pinochet Ugarte* (28 October 1998), Divisional Court (Chief Justice Bingham, Justice Collins (quoted) and Justice Richards).

7. *Ex parte Pinochet (No. 2)* (1999), 1 All ER 577.

8. Article 1, Montevideo Convention on the Rights and Duties of States (1933).

9. The Papal States were conquered in 1870 by Italy, which by the Treaty of Locarno recognized their traditional claim to sovereignty. There is no reason why any other state should recognize the Vatican, however, any more than the bantustans were recognized as states independent of South Africa.

10. See Geoffrey Robertson, *The Case of the Pope* (Penguin, 2010).

11. See Malcolm Shaw, *International Law* (4th edn) (Cambridge University Press, 1998), p. 143.

12. See *The South-west Africa Case*, ICJ Reports (1971), p. 16.

13. Edwin Borchard, 'Government Responsibility in Tort', *Yale Law Journal* 34 (1924), pp. 4–5.

14. See J. L. Brierly, *The Law of Nations: An Introduction to the International Law of Peace* (6th edn) (Oxford University Press, 1963), pp. 9–11, discussing J. Bodin, *De Republica* (1576).

15. As one of them, Vattel, memorably put it: '[A] Head of State who commits murder and other grave crimes in the course of war is chargeable with all the evils, all the horrors, of the war; all the effusions of blood, the desolation of families, the rapine, the violence, the revenge, the burnings, are his work and his crimes. He is guilty towards the enemy, of attacking, oppressing, massacring them without cause, guilty towards his people, of drawing them into acts of injustice, exposing their lives without necessity, without reason, towards that part of his subjects whom the war ruins, or who are great sufferers by it, of losing their lives, their fortune, or their health. Lastly he is guilty towards all mankind, of disturbing their quiet, and setting a pernicious example'

(quoted in Quincy Wright, 'The Legal Liability of the Kaiser', *American Political Science Review* 13 (1919), p. 120).

16. *Parlement Belge* (1880), 5 PD 197.

17. See respectively *Porto Alexandre* (1920), 1 ILR 146; *Krajina v. Tass Agency* (1949), 2 All ER 274.

18. *Trendtex Trading Corporation Ltd v. Central Bank of Nigeria* (1977), 2 WLR 356.

19. See criticisms of the 1952 'suggestion of immunity' procedure in *Isbrandtsen Tankers Inc. v. President of India* (1971), 446 F2d 1198 (2nd Circuit).

20. See Ian Brownlie, *Principles of Public International Law* (6th edn) (Oxford University Press, 2003), p. 326, and *Littrell v. USA (No. 2)* (1995), 1 WLR 82.

21. *Io Congreso del Partido* (1983), 2AC 244.

22. *The Schooner Exchange v. McFaddon* (1812), 7 Cranch 116.

23. *Saudi Arabia v. Nelson* (1993), 113 S Ct 1471.

24. *Siderman de Blake v. Republic of Argentina* (9th Circuit, 1992), 965 F2d 699.

25. *Al-Adsani v. Government of Kuwait* (1996), 107 ILR 536. The ECHR was narrowly divided (9–8) in declining to require the UK to end state immunity for torture in civil actions. See *Al-Adsani v. UK* (2002) 34 EHRR 11.

26. *Letelier v. Republic of Chile* (DDC, 1980), 448 F. Supp. 665.

27. For this reason, a more satisfactory extrajudicial settlement was achieved by negotiation between France and New Zealand over the sinking by French secret agents of the Greenpeace vessel *Rainbow Warrior*, moored in Auckland before a proposed voyage to protest at nuclear tests in the south Pacific. The agreement between the countries provided, *inter alia*, for France to pay $7 million to New Zealand: it had suffered no material damage, other than the insult of having the duties it was owed in international law treated with contempt by the French. The Letelier family was eventually compensated by the post-Pinochet government, after a special commission set up under a 1914 treaty for the resolution of disputes between Chile and the US; see 31 ILM 1 (1992).

28. M. Cherif Bassiouni, *Crimes Against Humanity in International Criminal Law* (2nd edn) (Kluwer Law International 1999), pp. 499–508. And see Brownlie, *n.* 20 above, pp. 313–14.

29. UN Doc. A/CONF 157/23, para. 60.

30. 'US Diplomatic and Consular Staff in Tehran', ICJ Reports (1980), p. 3, para. 91.

31. *Kilroy v. Windsor*, reported in *International Law Review* (1981), p. 605.

32. *Lafontant v. Aristide* (EDNY, 1994), 844 F. Supp. 128.

33. *In re Estate of Ferdinand E. Marcos*, US Court of Appeals 9th Circuit (21 October 1992), 978 F.2d 493.

34. *Estate of Ferdinand Marcos* (1994), 25 F.3d 1467 (9th Circuit).

35. *The Times* (26 February 1999).

36. See Ralph G. Steinhardt, 'Fulfilling the Promise of Filártiga: Litigating Human Rights Claims against the Estate of Ferdinand Marcos', 20 *Yale Journal of International Law* 65 (1995).

37. *Ex parte Pinochet (No. 1)* (1998), 4 All ER 897 at 939–40 *per* Lord Nicholls.

38. UN General Assembly Resolution 95(I) (11 December 1946).

39. Of the six judges in the majority, Lord Hutton clearly agreed with *Pinochet (No. 1)* that it was not a function of a head of state to commit serious international crimes, and this seems to have been the conclusion of Lord Phillips, at least in the case of torture. Lord Millet (who took the broad-brush approach that there could be no immunity to charges of crimes against humanity) thought that immunity might attach to purely ceremonial state functions, but not to crimes committed in the capacity of commander-in-chief or head of government. Lords Hope and Saville argued from exactly the opposite premise: that torture was an official act, and the Torture Convention applied to a crime it defined as only capable of commission by officials, therefore the Convention itself had necessarily abolished the immunity. Lord Browne-Wilkinson agreed with this argument on a hypothetical basis, but also seemed to think that a crime would fall outside the function of a head of state if it had a *jus cogens* quality and universal jurisdiction had been clearly established. He found that in the case of torture, universal jurisdiction was established by the Convention itself, in its requirement that parties either 'extradite or prosecute' suspected torturers found within their borders. See R. v. *Bow Street Magistrates ex parte Pinochet Ugarte (No. 3) (1999)*, 2 All ER, pp. 97–192.

40. Sir Arthur Watts, 'The Legal Position in International Law of Heads of States, Heads of Government and Foreign Ministers', *Recueil des Cours* 247 (1994), p. 82.

41. Quoting Sheldon Glueck (1946), *Harvard Law Journal* 59 (1946), p. 396.

42. *Ex parte Pinochet (No. 3), n.* 39 above at p. 177.

43. Citing *Prosecutor v. Furundžija,* ICTY case no. 17–95–17/I-T, para. 153.

44. 'Top Cardinal Made Plea for Pinochet', *Sunday Times* (11 February 1999), p. 24.

45. Castro's recent abuses of power fall short of crimes against humanity as strictly defined, although his imprisonment of HIV/AIDS sufferers smacks of persecution. The Cuban gulag was a reality for too many, too long; see Armando Valladares, *Against All Hope* (Alfred A. Knopf, 1987).

46. Lord Justice Simon Browne, *R. v. Home Secretary, ex parte Belgium* (15 February 2000), p. 28.

47. See *Case Concerning the Arrest Warrant of 11 April 2000 (DRC v. Belgium)*, 2002 ICJ 121 (14 February 2002). Decisions of the International Court of Justice are binding only between the parties; none the less they are entitled to great respect in so far as they elucidate rules of international law.

48. Ibid., para. 61.

49. US v. *Noriega*, 746 F. Supp. 1506, 1521–22 (SD Fla. 1990).

50. See *n*. 48 above, para. 61.

51. The ICJ decision was delivered on 14 February 2002. Understandably, it makes no mention of the Special Court for Sierra Leone, which was established by an agreement concluded only a few weeks before, and which had not been implemented at that stage. The Appeals Chamber of the SCSL has subsequently held that it falls within paragraph 61. See *Prosecutor* v. *Charles Taylor*, case no. SCSL-03-01-I-059, decision on immunity from jurisdiction, 21 May 2004; available at: www.sc-sl.org./LinkClink.aspx?fileticket=7oeBn4Ru/Eg=&tabid=191 (outlining the status of the Court).

52. The United Nations Conference on International Organization was attended by fifty countries and the UN Charter was signed on 25 June 1945. The United Nations came into existence on 24 October 1945.

53. *DRC* v. *Belgium*, above *n*. 48, para. 3.

54. Ibid., para. 5.

55. Ibid., para. 46.

56. Ibid., para. 51.

57. Ibid., para. 75. And see Geoffrey Robertson QC, 'Ending Impunity: How International Criminal Law Can Put Tyrants on Trial', *Cornell International Law Journal*, vol. 38, no. 3 (Autumn 2005), p. 649.

58. See *Statute for the Special Court of Sierra Leone*, Article 6(2) (16 January 2000), UN Doc. S/2002/246; available at: www.sc-sl.org/LinkClick.aspx?fileticket=4CInd1MJeEw%3d&tabid=176.

59. This common-sense solution was referred to by Lord Hope in *Ex parte Pinochet (No. 3)*, although he found no authority in its support. See *n. 39* above at p. 146.

9. THE BALKAN TRIALS

1. Deferral hearing, Bosnian Serb Leadership Investigation (15 May 1995).
2. *In re Yamashita* (1946), 327 US 1. The irony of citing this precedent is that the 'command responsibility' theory was misapplied to the facts at the trial of Yamashita (who was wrongly convicted), and rejected as a basis for criminal liability at the 1971 trial of Captain Ernest Medina over the My Lai massacre: see Ann Marie Prévost, 'Race and War Crimes: The 1945 War Crimes Trial of General Tomoyuki Yamashita', *HRQ* 14 (1992), p. 303. The question of when a commander is criminally responsible if his troops run amok requires a more careful analysis than is provided by either case.
3. 'War Crimes Court Urges Sanctions against Serbs: Goldstone Attacks NATO Inaction', *Guardian* (7 June 1996).
4. Anthony Parsons, *From Cold War to Hot Peace* (Penguin, 1995), p. 230.
5. An anonymous example of this argument is 'Human Rights in Peace Negotiations', *HRQ* 18 (1996), p. 249.
6. Charles Lane and Thom Shanker, 'Bosnia: What the CIA Didn't Tell Us', *New York Review of Books* (9 May 1996), p. 11.
7. Gary Bass, *Stay the Hand of Vengeance* (Princeton University Press, 2000), pp. 211–13.
8. Report of the Secretary-General Pursuant to Paragraph 2 of Security Council Resolution 808 (3 May 1993), S/25704.
9. 'Effects of Awards of Compensation Made by the United Nations Administrative Tribunal' (1954), ICJ Rep. 47.
10. *Tadić Case (Prosecutor v. Duško Tadić)* (1995), ICTY, The Hague, *HRLJ* 16, p. 426 (Trial Chamber), p. 437 (Appeals Chamber).
11. Ibid., Appeals Chamber, p. 451, para. 70.
12. *Nicaragua v. US* (1986), ICJ Rep. 4.
13. *Tadić Case, n.* 10 above, p. 458, paras. 96–7.
14. Ibid., p. 469, para. 141.
15. *The Kanyabashi Case* (18 June 1997), *HRLJ* 18 (1997), p. 343.

16. See Lyal S. Sunga, 'The First Indictments of the International Criminal Tribunal for Rwanda', *HRLJ* 18 (1997), p. 329.

17. 'When God was Absent', *Economist* (16 February 2002).

18. See Gary Bass, above *n.* 7, pp. 217–18; Richard Goldstone, *For Humanity: Reflections of a War Crimes Investigator* (Yale University Press, 2000), pp. 20–23.

19. William W. Horne, 'The Real Trial of the Century', *The American Lawyer* (1996), p. 61.

20. 'Failure to Arrest War Crimes Suspects Mars Talks', *The Times* (14 June 1996).

21. *Kupreskić Case*, AC ICTY case no. IT-95-16-A, 23 October 2001, para. 41.

22. Statute of the ICTY, Article 21(4)(d). See Judge Vorah's opinion in the *Tadić Case* (27 November 1996), importing the European Convention 'equality of arms' principle.

23. ICTY, Rule 89(c).

24. Ibid., Rule 93.

25. Opinion of Judge Sidhwa in *Rajić Decision* (13 September 1996), IT-95-12-R61.

26. The best example of an international court explaining the danger of convicting upon eyewitness evidence is the Privy Council in *Reid and Dennis* v. *R.* (1990), AC 363.

27. Lane and Shanker, *n.* 6 above, p. 10.

28. Catherine Niarchos, 'Women, War and Rape: Challenges Facing the International Tribunal for the Former Yugoslavia', *HRQ* 17 (1995), p. 649.

29. The *Celebići Case: Prosecutor* v. *Zejnil Delalić and others*, IT-96-21-T (16 November 1998), para. 476.

30. *Tadić Case, n.* 10 above, Decision on the Prosecutor's Motion (10 August 1995), Protective Measures for Victims and Witnesses.

31. ICTY, *Rule* 75A.

32. For example, *Kostovski* v. *The Netherlands* (1989), Series A no. 166; *Ludi* v. *Switzerland* (1992), 15 EHRR 173.

33. *Blaskić Case* (5 November 1996), IT-95-14-T.

34. *The Prosecutor* v. *Mile Mskić and others* (3 April 1996), Review of Indictment under Rule 61, Trial Chamber 1 (*Vukovar Hospital Decision*).

35. *Tadić* judgment (7 May 1997), para. 653. See also the Appeals Chamber

judgment, *Tadić Case* (15 July 1999), and its sentencing judgment (26 January 2000).

36. International Law Commission Report (1991), p. 266 (Draft Code, Article 94).

37. *Mauthausen Case* (1946–7), Vol. XI Law Reports, 15.

38. *Gustav Becker and others* (1946–7), Vol. VII Law Reports, 67.

39. *Zyklon-B Case (Trial of Bruno Tesch and others)* (British Military Court, Hamburg, 1946), 1 War Crimes Reports, pp. 93, 103.

40. *The Justice Case (The Trial of Josef Altstoetter and others)*, Vol. VI Law Reports, 88.

41. *International Tribunal First Annual Report* (28 July 1994); and see note by Secretary-General to the UN General Assembly (29 August 1994), A/49/342, para. 15..

42. Tom Walker, 'Defiant Karadzic in Suicide Pledge', *Sunday Times* (14 October 2001).

43. See Chris Stephen, *Judgement Day* (Atlantic Books, 2004), p. 128.

44. Samantha Power, 'Rwanda: The Two Faces of Justice', *New York Review of Books* (16 January 2003).

45. Stephen, *Judgement Day, n.* 45 above, p. 183.

46. *Prosecutor* v. *Milošević,* decision on the assignment of the defence counsel, ICTY Appeals Chamber, 1 November 2004.

47. David Rennie, 'Vatican Accused of Shielding War Criminal', *Daily Telegraph* (20 September 2005).

48. See Ed Vulliamy, 'Face to Face with Radovan Karadžić', *Observer* (4 December 2011).

49. Ian Traynor, 'Bosnian Serbs Convicted of Srebrenica Genocide', *Guardian* (11 June 2010), p. 17.

50. Ibid.

51. See Lara J. Nettelfield, *Courting Democracy in Bosnia and Herzegovina: The Hague Tribunal's Impact on a Post-war State* (Cambridge University Press, 2010).

52. Richard H. Steinberg (ed.), *Assessing the Legacy of the ICTY* (Martinus Nijhoff, 2011), p. 261.

53. Ibid., p. 283.

10. THE INTERNATIONAL CRIMINAL COURT

1. Quotations in this paragraph are from Amnesty International, *The International Criminal Court – Making the Right Choices*, part 1 (January 1997), pp. 76–7. The section on 'defences' continues until p. 88.

2. 'A New World Court', *Economist* (13 June 1998).

3. Jorgen Wouters, 'America v. Its Allies', *ABC World News* (17 July 1998).

4. A point well made by Ruth Wedgwood, 'Fiddling in Rome – America and the International Court', in *Foreign Affairs* 77 (November/December 1998), p. 20.

5. *Yugoslavia* v. *UK*, ICJ (2 June 1999), para. 40.

6. This definition combines the nub of paragraph 1 of Article 7 with sub-paragraph 2(a), which clumsily adds to the essential elements of the crime.

7. William A. Schabas, *An Introduction to the International Court* (Cambridge University Press, 2001), p. 32.

8. M. Cherif Bassiouni, *Crimes Against Humanity in International Criminal Law* (2nd edn, Kluwer Law International, 1999), pp. 273–5.

9. *USA et al.* v. *Göring et al.*, International Military Tribunal judgment, 30 September – 1 October 1946 (1947), 41 *American Journal of International Law* 172, at p. 186.

10. This argument is forcefully made by Simon Young, 'Surrendering the accused to the International Criminal Court', *BYIL* (2000), p. 317.

11. Decision on application by the Redress Trust, Lawyers Committee for Human Rights and the International Commission of Jurists for leave to file *amicus* briefs and to present oral submissions, Special Court for Sierra Leone, SCSL-2003–07 (Appeals Chamber), 1 November 2003.

12. Rome Statute of the International Criminal Court, Article 53(3)(b). Even more oddly, the prosecutor may be required to proceed by a chamber comprising only one judge: see Article 57(2).

13. For the background to the Sierra Leone principal defender's office, see paras. 81–9 in the author's concurring judgment in *Prosecutor* v. *AFRC* (decision on counsel withdrawal, SCSL-04-16-AR73, 8 December 2005).

14. See the report of the Office of Internal Oversight Services on the investigation into possible fee-splitting arrangements between defence counsel and indigent detainees at the ICTR and ICTY (1 February 2001), especially paras.

9–15; follow-up investigation into possible fee-splitting arrangements (26 February 2002), A/56/836.

15. See William A. Schabas, above *n.* 7, p. 184.

16. The right to counsel of choice for an indigent accused means the right to choose from a list of counsel prepared to act for the payment on offer from the registry. See the Rwanda Tribunal decision in the *Ntakirutimana Case* (1997), *HRLJ* 18 (1997), p. 340.

17. See *Prosecutor* v. *Semanza*, case no. ICTR-97-20-I, decision on prosecutor's motion for judicial notice, 3 November 2000; also the SCSL Appeals Chamber decision on judicial notice, *Prosecutor* v. *Fofana*, SCSL-04-14-AR73, 16 May 2005.

18. *Prosecutor* v. *Delalić* (case no. IT-98-21-T), 19 January 1998 (Trial Chamber), para. 32.

19. *Prosecutor* v. *Simić et al.* (case no. IT-95-9-PT). Decision under Rule 73 concerning witness testimony, 27 July 1999, decides that Red Cross privilege is a matter of customary international law. However, the privilege should be that of the witness, and capable of waiver as a matter of conscience or, in extreme cases, of being overridden for the public good. See author's concurrence in *Prosecutor* v. *AFRC* (26 May 2006), decision on testamentary privilege.

20. *Edwards* v. *UK* (1992), 15 EHRR 417.

21. Rome Statute, Article 80: 'Nothing in this Part of the Statute affects the application by State Parties of penalties prescribed by their national laws.'

22. *Prosecutor* v. *Norman*, SCSL-04-14-AR72, decision on preliminary motion on lack of jurisdiction (judicial independence), 13 March 2004, para. 3.

23. See Philippe Sands, *Lawless World: America and the Making and Breaking of Global Rules* (Penguin, 2005), ch. 3.

24. Human Rights Watch, *Entrenching Impunity – Government Responsibility for International Crimes in Darfur* (December 2005).

25. See Human Rights Watch, 'Uprooted and Forgotten: Impunity and Human Rights Abuses in Northern Uganda' (19 September 2005).

26. See Steven D. Roper, 'State Co-operation and International Criminal Court Bargaining Influence in the Arrest and Surrender of Suspects', *Leiden Journal of International Law*, vol. 21(2) (2008), 457.

27. Joe Bavier, 'Congo War-driven Crisis Kills 45,000 a Month: Study', Reuters (22 January 2008).

28. Phil Clark, 'Grappling in the Great Lakes', in Bowen, Charlesworth and Farrell (eds.) *Great Expectations: The Role of International Law in Restructuring Societies after Conflict*' (Cambridge University Press, 2009).

29. Simon Tisdall, '"Conflict in Darfur is My Responsibility", says Bashir', *Guardian* (21 April 2011), p. 1.

30. Report of the Secretary-General, International Commission of Enquiry on Darfur (January 2005); 'EU Mission Sees Abuses, but not Genocide, in Darfur', Reuters (9 August 2004).

31. Rome Statute, Article 61(2); Rules of Procedure and Evidence, Rules 121–6.

32. *Prosecutor* v. *Haroun*, 'Decision informing the UN Security Council about the lack of co-operation by the Republic of Sudan', 25 May 2010.

33. David Hoile, 'The International Criminal Court: Europe's Guantánamo Bay?', Africa Research Centre (2010).

11. JUSTICE IN DEMAND

1. Tom Finn, 'Five shot Dead in Yemen as Protesters Vent Fury at Presidential Immunity Deal', *Guardian* (25 November 2011).

2. Human Rights Watch, *Justice in Motion: The Trial Phase of the Special Court for Sierra Leone* (October 2005), vol. 17, no. 14a.

3. *Prosecutor* v. *Allieu Kondewa*, decision on preliminary motion on lack of jurisdiction: whether establishment of Special Court violates constitution of Sierra Leone, SCSL-2004-14-AR72(E) (Appeals Chamber), 25 May 2004.

4. See Samantha Power, *A Problem from Hell. America and the Age of Genocide* (Harper, 2003), p. 154.

5. David Scheffer, *All the Missing Souls – A Personal History of the War Crimes Tribunals* (Princeton, 2012).

6. 'Extraordinary Chambers for Khmer Rouge Trials', presentation by Nav Soursday to ICC, The Hague, 24 November 2005.

7. Charles Henry Durrant, 'A Perspective on the Extraordinary Chambers in the Courts of Cambodia', *The Barrister* (2010).

8. Jessica Winch, 'Cambodia: What Next for the Extraordinary Chambers?', *Crimes of War* (29 October 2010).

9. The 1973 Act is described by Suzannah Linton, 'Accountability for the

Crimes of the 1971 Bangladesh War of Liberation', *Criminal Law Forum*, vol. 21(2), March 2010, and by Cadman and Bafadel, 'Courting Controversy', *Criminal Bar Quarterly* (Autumn 2011), p. 10.

10. Antonio Cassesse, *Self-determination of Peoples* (Cambridge University Press, 1995), p. 226.

11. See the *Western Sahara Case* (1975), ICJ Rep. 12.

12. Statement by Senator Gareth Evans, Australian Minister for Resources (20 March 1986).

13. *East Timor Case (Portugal v. Australia)* (1995), ICJ Rep. 90.

14. Lynne O'Donnell, 'Jakarta's Final Solution', *The Australian* (17 September 1999).

15. Elisabeth Becker and Philip Shenon, 'With Other Goals in Indonesia, US Moves Gently on East Timor', *New York Times* (9 September 1999).

16. Michael Binyon, 'The World Wrings Its Hands but is Reluctant to Intervene', *The Times* (7 September 1999).

17. See John Aglionby, 'Indonesia's President Says He will Punish Ex-army Chief', *Guardian* (1 February 2000).

18. Don Greenlees, 'Day of Reckoning for East Timor', *Weekend Australian* (March 16–17 2002).

19. See David Cohen, *Intended to Fail: The Trials before the Ad Hoc Human Rights Court in Jakarta*, International Centre for Transitional Justice (2003).

20. *Ending the Cycle of Impunity*, Tapol (Indonesian Human Rights Campaign) Report (24 January 2000).

21. Noel Malcolm, *Kosovo: A Short History* (Macmillan, 1998), p. 25.

22. *Intended to Fail, n.* 19 above.

23. Ahdaf Souleif, *Cairo – My City, Our Revolution* (Bloomsbury, 2012), pp. 21–7.

24. Katerina Dalacoura, 'The 2011 Uprisings in the Arab Middle East', *International Affairs*, vol. 88, No. 1 (January 2012), p. 63.

25. Nate Wright, 'Former President Caged but Defiant as Millions Tune in for Historic Trial', *The Times* (4 August 2011).

26. Lara Pitel and James Hider, 'Arab Spring Topples Fourth Leader as Saleh Resigns', *The Times* (24 November 2011).

27. Yasmine El Rashidi, 'Egypt on the Edge', *New York Review of Books* (12 January 2012).

28. Nicholas Blanford, 'UN Indicts Hezbollah Henchmen over the Murder of Lebanese Prime Minister', *The Times* (1 July 2011).

29. Human Rights Council, Report of the Independent International Commission of Inquiry on the Syrian Arab Republic, 23 November 2011, UN Doc. A/HRC/S-17/2/Add. 1.

12. TERRORISM: 9/11 AND BEYOND

1. Ahmed Rashid, *Taliban* (Yale University Press, 2000), pp. 73–4.

2. Ibid., chap. 13.

3. Peter Bergen, *Holy War, Inc.: Inside the Secret World of Osama bin Laden* (Weidenfeld & Nicolson, 2001), p. 64.

4. Yonah Alexander and Michael S. Swetnam, *Osama bin Laden's al-Qaida: Profile of a Terrorist Network* (Transnational, 2001).

5. Quoted in para. 19 of HMG publication 'Responsibility for the Terrorist Atrocities in the US, 11 September 2001', tabled in the House of Commons, 4 October 2001.

6. *The Times* (5 October 2001).

7. Ian Brownlie, *Principles of International Law* (6th edn) (Oxford University Press, 2003), p. 90.

8. *Corfu Channel Case* (1949), ICJ Rep. 4.

9. *Case Concerning United States Diplomatic and Consular Staff in Tehran* (1980), ICJ Rep. 3.

10. *Case Concerning Military and Paramilitary Activities in and Against Nicaragua* (Merits) (1986), ICJ Rep. 14.

11. Ruling of UN Secretary-General, 6 July 1986, ILR 74, 241.

12. 22 ILM (1983), 1190–8.

13. Brownlie, *n*. 7 above, p. 436, citing *Ireland* v. *UK* (1978), 18 January, para. 158–9; and *Velasquez Rodriguez Case*, Inter-American Court (1988), ILR 95, 232.

14. See *n*. 10 above, para. 194–5.

15. General Assembly Resolution 2625 (XXV) (1970) (Declaration on Principles of International Law Concerning Friendly Relations among States).

16. *The Caroline Case* (1841), 29 BFSP 1137–8; (1842) BFSP 195–6.

17. International Military Tribunal, Nuremberg, 30 September 1946, 41 AJIL 205 (1947).

18. Yoram Dinstein, *War, Aggression and Self-Defence* (3rd edn) (Cambridge University Press, 2000), p. 218.

19. Christopher Greenwood, 'International Law and the United States: Air Operation against Libya', *West Virginia Law Review*, vol. 89 (1986–7), p. 933.

20. Dinstein, *n.* 18 above, pp. 208–9.

21. See Ruth Wedgewood, 'Responding to Terrorism: The Strikes Against Bin Laden' (1999), 24 *Yale Journal of International Law* 559.

22. Julian Borger and Richard Norton-Taylor, 'Pentagon split over war plan', *Guardian* (15 October 2001).

23. Letter, Mr John Negroponte (US ambassador to UN) to Security Council, 7 October 2001.

24. *The Times* (18 October 2001).

25. Judgment at Nuremberg, 41 AJIL 207 (1947).

26. *Nicaragua Case*, ICJ Reports 1986, p. 14, para. 195.

27. 'Some Lawmakers Prefer bin Laden Dead', *New York Times* (16 November 2001).

28. *Johnson v. Eisentrager* (1950), 339 US 763. The Germans had been convicted by a US military commission and were serving prison sentences in Germany: the fact that they were convicted prisoners was a better basis for denying *habeas corpus* than the fact that Germany was not US sovereign territory. General Yamashita was allowed to take his *habeas corpus* petition to the US Supreme Court from the Philippines, which at the time was under US sovereignty.

29. *Rasul v. Bush* (2004), 542 US 466, US Supreme Court, 28 June 2004, majority judgment of Justice Stephens. See Ronald Dworkin, 'What the Court Really Said', *New York Review of Books* (12 August 2004), p. 24.

30. Sean Aughey, 'Obama and Human Rights', *The World Today*, vol. 67 (January 2011), pp. 29–30.

31. See Clive Stafford Smith, *Bad Men: Guantanamo Bay and the Secret Prisons* (Weidenfeld & Nicolson, 2007).

32. Walter Pincus, 'Saddam Hussein's Death is a Goal, says Ex-CIA Chief', *Washington Post* (15 February 1998).

33. *McCann v. UK* (2008), ECHR 385.

34. UNHRC, Report of the Special Rapporteur on Extrajudicial, Summary or Arbitrary Executions, 'Study on Targeted Killings' (28 May 2010), A/HRC/14/24/Add. 6.

35. Ibid.

36. Harold Koh, Address to the American Society of International Law (25 March 2010).

37. See *n.* 34 above, p.26.

38. See *Nicaragua* v. *United States*, Merits (1986), ICJ Rep 14, paras. 154–5.

39. Scott Wilson, 'Gaza's Buzz of Death', *Guardian Weekly*, 30 December 2011.

40. Chris Woods, 'Over 160 Children Reported among Drone Deaths', The Bureau of Investigative Journalism (11 August 2011); Adam Eutous, 'How the White House Learned to Love the Drone', Reuters (18 May 2010).

41. Ibid.

42. Jane Mayer, 'The Predator War', *The New Yorker* (26 October 2009).

43. See *Al-Aulaqi* v. *Obama* (US District Court for Columbia 2010), 727 F.Supp 2d. 1, and Charlie Sauage, 'Secret US Memo Made Legal Case to Kill Citizen', *New York Times* (8 October 2011).

44. See Professor Cassese's submission to the Israeli Supreme Court, discussed in Nils Melzer, *Targeted Killings in International Law* (Oxford University Press, 2008), pp. 61–2.

45. William Shawcross, *Justice and the Enemy* (Public Affairs, 2011) pp. 157–8.

46. Jemima Khan, 'Nintendo Warfare', *New Statesman* (23 November 2011), p. 27.

47. See 'Behind the Hunt for bin Laden' (2 May 2011); 'Bin Laden Raid Revives Debate on Value of Torture', *New York Times* (3 May 2011).

48. Mark Hosenball, 'US Commandos Knew bin Laden Likely Would Die', Reuters, (22 May 2011).

49. 'Senior Administration Officials Defend Military Tribunal For Terrorist Suspects', *New York Times* (15 November 2001).

50. Editorial, 'A Travesty of Justice', *New York Times* (16 November 2001).

51. *New York Times* (24 November 2001).

52. One reason why the ECHR decided that UK courts martial did not satisfy the requirements of fair trial – see *Morris* v. *UK* (2002), 34 EHRR 1253, 26 February 2002.

53. Evan J. Wallach, 'The Procedural and Evidentiary Rules of the Post World

War II War Crimes Trials', 37 *Columbia Journal of Transnational Law*, p. 851.

54. *Application of Yamashita* (1946), 327 US 1, at pp. 48–9 (Justice Rutledge).

55. The details that follow are taken from Jess Bravin's coverage of the first week of hearings of the special military commission which sat at Guantanamo Bay. See 'As War Talks Open, Tribunal's Legality is Challenged', *Wall Street Journal* (25 August 2004) and following articles on 26, 27 and 30 August.

56. ABA, *Report of the Taskforce on the Treatment of Enemy Combatants* (August 2002), p. 2; Lord Goldsmith, Associated Press report (24 June 2004), *British Official Rips US Guantanamo Plan*; and Clare Dyer, 'Law Lord Castigates US Justice', *Guardian* (26 November 2003).

57. Allan Gerson and Jerry Adler, *The Price of Terror* (HarperCollins, 2001). Some of the families think that the Libyans were assisting what was really an Iranian operation planned by Ahmed Jibril, to revenge the accidental shoot-down of an Iranian airbus full of Mecca-bound pilgrims by USS *Vincennes*. Al-Megrahi's latest self-serving defence is set out in John Ashton, *Megrahi – You Are My Jury* (Birlinn, 2012). But if the bomb was loaded in Malta, the circumstantial case against him remains, without a credible answer.

58. Jeremy Rabkin, 'Terrorists Must Face US Justice', *The Australian*, (23 November 2001), p. 11.

59. The 9/11 Commission report, *Final Report of the National Commission on Terrorist Attacks upon the United States*, authorized edition (W. W. Norton, 2004), p. 376.

60. *Youngstown Sheet and Tube Co v. Sawyer* (1951), 343 US 579, at 704 (Justice Douglas).

61. *A-G of Ontario v. Canada Temperance Federation* (1946), AC 193, at 206 (Privy Council).

13. TOPPLING TYRANTS: THE CASE OF SADDAM HUSSEIN

1. Tony Blair, speech to Parliament, 5 March 2004. See Thomas Cushman (ed.), *A Matter of Principle – Humanitarian Arguments for War in Iraq* (University of California Press, 2005), p. 345.

2. Press conference, US Government Archives, 24 February 2001.

3. Speech to Senate Foreign Relations Committee, 17 July 2001.

4. George Packer, *The Assassin's Gate – America in Iraq* (Faber, 2005), p. 45.

5. Ibid.

6. 'Powell's Evidence Against Saddam – Does it Add Up?', *Guardian* (6 February 2003). Even this war-cynical paper thought these allegations 'striking and significant'.

7. See, for instance, Thomas Powers, 'Secret Intelligence and the War on Terror', *New York Review of Books* (16 December 2004), p. 50. There has been no explanation as to why the CIA discounted evidence that the Iraqi nuclear programme had been dead for a decade and that the nation no longer held WMD: see James Risen, *State of War: The Secret History of the CIA and the Bush Administration* (Free Press, 2006).

8. Cited, amongst many other places, in Packer, *n.* 4 above, p. 61.

9. See Geoffrey Robertson, *The Justice Game* (Vintage, 1999), ch. 15.

10. Ibid., p. 343.

11. Jeremy Greenstock 'What Must be Done Now', *Economist* (6 May 2004).

12. See Packer, *n.* 4 above, p. 98.

13. Richard Norton-Taylor, 'Bush-Blair Deal before Iraq Revealed', *Guardian Weekly* (3 February 2006), p. 1.

14. William Shawcross, 'Justice Demands the Invasion of Iraq', *The Australian* (20 March 2003).

15. See, for instance, 'Confronting Iraq', editorial in the *Economist* (12 September 2002), based on findings by the Institute of Strategic Studies.

16. See Kenneth Adelman, 'Desert Storm II will be a Walk in the Park', *The Times* (29 August 2002).

17. Anthony Lewis, 'Bush and Iraq', *New York Review of Books* (7 November 2002).

18. Interview in the *Financial Times* (17 September 2002).

19. See Brian Urquhart, 'The Prospect of War', *New York Review of Books* (19 December 2002), reviewing Kenneth M. Pollack, *The Threatening Storm: The Case for Invading Iraq* (Random House, 2002).

20. See Philippe Sands, *Lawless World: America and the Making and Breaking of Global Rules* (Penguin, 2005) and appendix.

21. Elizabeth Wilmhurst, *Principles of the International Law on the Use of Force by States in Self-Defence* (Chatham House, 2005), p. 7, draws upon the ICJ advisory opinion in *Nicaragua v. USA* (Merits, 1986, ICJ Rep. 14).

22. Ibid., p. 9.

23. See Michael Howard, 'The Bush Doctrine: It's a Brutal World, So Act Brutally', *Sunday Times* (23 March 2003).

24. Advice to prime minister, 7 March 2003 by UK Attorney-General.

25. 'The World Must Hold Saddam to Account', *Guardian* (13 September 2002), p. 4, reporting George Bush's speech to the UN General Assembly.

26. Michael Glennon, 'Why the Security Council Failed', *Foreign Affairs*, vol. 82, no. 3, p. 16.

27. Speech to UN General Assembly, 20 September 1999.

28. *US* v. *List et al.*, 11 *Trials of War Criminals* 757 (1948).

29. Lord Goldsmith, *Legal Authorisation for An Interim Administration*, 26 March 2003, published in the *New Statesman* (26 May 2003).

30. See Karin J. Greenburg and Joshua L. Dratel, *The Torture Papers – The Road to Abu Ghraib* (Cambridge University Press, 2005), p. 126, citing Ashcroft's memorandum to the President (1 February 2002).

31. Ibid., p. 129, citing memorandum from William H. Taft IV, Legal Adviser, State Department, to counsel to the President (2 February 2002).

32. Ibid., p. 136, citing memorandum 'Status of Taliban Forces under Third Geneva Convention', (7 February 2002).

33. Ibid., p. 172, citing memorandum 'Standards of Conduct for Interrogation' (1 August 2002).

34. Ibid., pp. 227–8, citing Department of Defense Joint Task Force 170, memorandum 'Counter Resistance Strategies' (11 October 2002).

35. The history is traced in Lord Bingham's opinion in *A* v. *Home Secretary* (2005), UKHL 71, paras. [10] to [17].

36. *Rochin* v. *California*, 342 US 165 (1952).

37. *Soering* v. *UK* (1989), 11 EHRR 439.

38. *Selmouni* v. *France* (1999), 29 EHRR 403, paras. [99] to [101].

39. See *Still At Risk*, Human Rights Watch report (April 2005).

40. See Anthony Lewis, 'Making Torture Legal', *New York Review of Books* (15 July 2004), p. 4.

41. Greenburg and Dratel, *n.* 30 above, p. 975.

42. Sheik Mohammed Bashir, Friday prayers, Baghdad, 11 June 2004, quoted by Mark Danner in 'Abu Ghraib: The Hidden Story', *New York Review of Books* (7 October 2004), p. 44.

43. Greenburg and Dratel, *n.* 30 above, p. 908.

44. ICRC report, ibid., p. 383.

45. Mark Danner, 'The Logic of Torture', *New York Review of Books* (24 June 2004), p. 70.

46. 'Ministers Last to Know of Report', *Guardian* (11 May 2004).

47. *Nicaragua* v. *US*, ICJ Reports (1986), p. 14.

48. Article 10, *Collective Labour Convention between ICRC and its Staff Association*.

49. *Prosecution* v. *Simić*, case no. IT-95-9, decision concerning the testimony of a witness, 27 July 1999.

50. See Akbar Khan, 'Judging the Judges', *Independent* (9 August 2004).

51. Geoffrey Robertson, *The Tyrannicide Brief* (Chatto & Windus, 2005), pp. 155–6.

52. 'Saddam Judges Were Secretly Trained in Britain', *The Times* (18 October 2005).

53. See Sonya Sceats, 'The Trial of Saddam Hussein', Chatham House briefing paper (October 2005).

54. Michael Scharf, 'Should Saddam Hussein be exposed to the death penalty? Yes', Grotian Moment Blog, 23.11.2005, www.law.case.edu/saddamtrial/.

55. See Michael A. Newton, 'Justice Abandoned', *International Herald Tribune* (25 November 2004).

14. THE GUERNICA PARADOX: BOMBING FOR HUMANITY

1. Hansard (25 March 1999), col. 617.

2. Foreign Policy Document no. 148 (1986), *British Yearbook of International Law* 56, section 2, para. 22. It did concede that 'the best case that can be made in support of humanitarian intervention is that it cannot be said to be unambiguously illegal'.

3. Gillian Triggs, *International Law: Contemporary Principles and Practices* (2nd edn, Butterworths, 2011), p. 639.

4. Brendan Simms and D. J. B. Trim, *Humanitarian Intervention – A History* (Cambridge University Press, 2011), p. 12.

5. Ibid., pp. 53–4.

6. Vattel, cited by Michael J. Bazyler, 'Re-examining the Doctrine of

Humanitarian Intervention', *Stanford International Law Journal* 23 (1987), p. 547. See Louis Henkin *et al.*, *Human Rights* (Foundation Press, 1999), p. 708.

7. Gary Bass, *Freedoms Battle – The Origins of Humanitarian Intervention* (Vintage, 2009), p. 48.

8. Ibid., p. 311.

9. *N.* 4 above, p. 309.

10. *Report of the International Committee of Jurists Giving an Advisory Opinion upon the Legal Aspects of the Aaland Islands Question*, cited in Henkin *et al.*, *n.* 6 above, p. 462. And see Antonio Cassesse, *Self-Determination of Peoples* (Cambridge University Press, 1995), pp. 27–33.

11. See Mark Littman, *Kosovo: Law and Diplomacy* (Centre for Policy Studies, 1999), appendix I: Submissions of Counsel for Yugoslavia to the International Court of Justice.

12. *Nicaragua* v. *USA*, judgment of 27 June 1986, paras. 266–8.

13. Ibid., para. 176.

14. *Yugoslavia* v. *UK*, judgment delivered at The Hague on 2 June 1999, para. 16.

15. *Corfu Channel Case* (1949), ICJ Rep. 22.

16. These are the circumstances in which the 'responsibility to protect' must arise. See p. 760 *et seq*, and *A More Secure World: Our Shared Responsibility* (UN, 2004); *The Responsibility to Protect: Report of the International Commission on Intervention and State Sovereignty* (Ottawa, 2001).

17. Richard Butler, 'Bewitched, Bothered and Bewildered: Repairing the Security Council', *Foreign Affairs* (September/October 1999), p. 9.

18. American journalist John Gunther, *Inside Europe* (1940), quoted in Misha Glenny, *The Balkans* (Granta, 1999), p. xxxiii.

19. See William W. Hagen, 'The Balkans' Lethal Nationalism', *Foreign Affairs* (July/August 1999), p. 52.

20. Barton Gellman, 'The Path to Crisis: How the US and Its Allies Went to War', *Washington Post* (18 April 1999).

21. Timothy Garton-Ash, 'Kosovo – Was It Worth It?', *New York Review of Books* (21 September 2000), p. 56.

22. Quoted in Littman, *n.* 11 above, p. 16.

23. Edward Luttwak, 'Letting Wars Burn', *Foreign Affairs* (July/August 1999), p. 41; Michael Ignatieff, 'Future War', *The World Today*, vol. 56, no. 2 (February 2000), and *Virtual War – Kosovo and Beyond* (Chatto & Windus, 2000).

24. Ignatieff, *n.* 23 above, pp. 197–8.

25. Julian Borger, 'Pentagon Kept the Lid on Cyberwar in Kosovo', *Guardian* (9 November 1999), p. 15.

26. See Marc Weller, 'The Kosovo Indictment of the International Criminal Tribunal for Yugoslavia', *International Journal of Human Rights*, vol. 3 (Winter 2000), p. 207.

27. See letter from European Commissioner Chris Patten to *The Times* (30 November 2001).

28. Noel Malcolm, 'Milošević Was Doomed by Press Freedom', *Sunday Telegraph* (1 July 2001), p. 18.

29. Ian Brownlie, *Principles of Public International Law* (6th edn, Oxford University Press, 2003), p. 712; Michael Byers, *War Law: International Law and Armed Conflict* (Atlantic Books, 2005), part III.

30. Nicholas J. Wheeler, *Saving Strangers: Humanitarian Intervention in International Society* (Oxford University Press, 2002), pp. 276–81.

31. See Michael Byers and Simon Chesterton in Holzgrefe and Keohane (eds.), *Humanitarian Intervention* (Cambridge University Press, 2003), ch. 5.

32. See Alex J. Bellamy, *Responsibility to Protect* (Policy Press, 2009), p. 23.

33. Gareth Evans, *The Responsibility to Protect – Ending Mass Atrocity Crimes Once and For All* (Brookings, 2008), pp. 146–7.

34. Joint Declaration, 15 April 2011.

35. *Report of the Secretary-General's Panel of Experts on Accountability in Sri Lanka*, UNHRC, 31 March 2011.

36. See Geoffrey Robertson, 'Gaddafi Getting Away with Murder', *Guardian* (21 September 2009); 'This Evil Despot Must Be Brought to Justice', *Independent* (23 February 2011); 'The Case for Prosecuting Libya's Muammar Gaddafi', *Daily Beast* (1 March 2011); 'When Tyrannicide is the Only Option', *Independent* (1 April 2011).

37. S/RES/1970 (2011), 26 February 2011.

38. See Alex J. Bellamy and Paul D. Williams, 'The New Politics of Protection? Cote d'Ivoire, Libya and the Responsibility to Protect', *International Affairs*, 87:4 (2011), 842.

39. S/RES/1973 (2011), 17 March 2011.

40. 'Libya Accuses ICC Lawyer of Smuggling "Spy Devices"', *Guardian* (26 June 2012).

41. Ivo H. Daalder and James G. Stavridis, 'NATO's Victory in Libya', *Foreign Affairs* (March/April 2012), p. 2.

42. See Thomas J. Bassett and Scott Straus, 'Defending Democracy in Cote d'Ivoire', *Foreign Affairs* (July/August 2011), p. 135.

43. N. 38 above, pp. 835–6.

44. See A.T. Williams, *A Very British Killing – The Death of Baha Mousa* (Jonathan Cape, 2012).

EPILOGUE

1. Stuart Hampshire, *Innocence and Experience* (Harvard University Press, 1989), cited by Michael Perry, 'Are human rights universal?', *HRQ* 19 (1997), p. 483.

2. There are some 800 NGOs that claim to support human rights, but not all do so with wisdom and a few are cuckoos in the nest: see 'Yanukovich's Friends: A Human Rights Group that Defends Dictators', *Economist* (2 December 2004), p. 30.

3. *The State of the World's Refugees: Human Displacement in the New Millennium*, Office of UNHCR (Oxford University Press, 2006). See *Guardian* (19 April 2006), p. 14.

4. 'A Traditional Practice that Threatens Health – Female Circumcision', *World Health Organization Chronicle* 51 (1986), reproduced in Henry Steiner and Philip Alston (eds.), *International Human Rights in Context* (Oxford University Press, 1996), p. 242.

5. Michael Ignatieff, 'The Attack on Human Rights', *Foreign Affairs* (November/December, 2001), pp. 112–13.

6. See Derek O'Brien, 'The Caribbean Court of Justice and its Appellate Jurisdiction: A Difficult Birth', *Public Law* (Summer 2006), p. 354.

7. Yash Ghai, 'Human Rights and Governance: The Asia Debate', *Australian Yearbook of International Law* 15 (1994), p. 5.

8. Kim Dae Jung, 'Is Culture Destiny? The Myth of Asia's Anti-Democratic Values', 73 *Foreign Affairs* 189 (1994).

9. See Mashood A. Baderin, *International Human Rights and Islamic Law* (Oxford University Press, 2003), pp. 219–30; Isobel Coleman, 'Women, Islam and the New Iraq', *Foreign Affairs* (January/February 2006), p. 24.

10. 'Leaked UN Report Accuses Rwanda', Guardian (27 August 2010), p. 8.

11. See *Crimes against Humanity* (2nd edn) (Penguin Books, 2002), pp. 511–12: 'There must be a tripwire, by way of a new Security Council ultimatum about inspections, which Saddam must defy before the US can plausibly wage a "just war" on Iraq . . .'

12. See Francis Fukuyama, *After the Neocons: America at the Crossroads* (Profile Books, 2006), pp. 40–42.

13. Henry Kissinger, 'The Pitfalls of Universal Jurisdiction', *Foreign Affairs* (July/August 2001).

14. See 'Expediting Proceedings at the International Criminal Court', War Crimes Research Office, ICC (June 2011).

15. See *Prosecutor* v. *Norman*, case no. SCSL-2003–08, decision on appeal by the Truth and Reconciliation Commission for Sierra Leone, 28 November 2003, para. 22.

16. In 2006, after a poll showing that 42 per cent of Russians believed Stalin had been a force for good, the European parliament debated the need for truth in history: see Charles Bremmer, 'History calls communists to account', *The Times* (26 January 2006), p. 43.

17. Kofi Annan, *Investing in the United Nations: Report* (7 March 2006), para. 5.

18. See Tristan McConnell, *The Times* (14 January 2012).

19. Leo Lewis, 'Combat Troops Join UN Mission to Guard Workers', *The Times* (21 February 2012).

20. *Report of the Panel on UN Peace Operations* (August 2000), UN Doc. A/55/305-S/2000/809.

21. See Ken Roth, Introduction to Human Rights Watch World Report 2011, pp. 4–6.

22. 'Pinochet Cancels Birthday Party', *Guardian* (26 November 2005), p. 22.

Appendix A:
Human Rights in History

1139	Second Lateran Council forbids the use of the crossbow in wars between Christians
1215	Magna Carta
1648	Peace of Westphalia: protection of religious minorities in Germany Trial of Charles I
1679	Habeas Corpus Act
1688	'Glorious Revolution' and English Bill of Rights
1690	*Second Treatise of Government* by John Locke
1764	*Of Crimes and Punishments* by Cesare Beccaria
1776	*Common Sense* by Thomas Paine American Declaration of Independence
1789	French Revolution: 'The Declaration of the Rights of Man and the Citizen' (France)
1792	*The Rights of Man* by Thomas Paine Alien Tort Claims Act (US)
1803	*Marbury v. Madison*: US Supreme Court asserts power to make laws conform to constitutional guarantees
1807	Abolition of slavery in England
1843	*Anarchical Fallacies* by Jeremy Bentham
1844	*On the Jewish Question* by Karl Marx
1863	The Red Cross founded by Henri Dunant *Lieber Code*: a war law manual for armies in the field
1865	America abolishes slavery
1868	St Petersburg Conference on limiting armaments
1885	Berlin Conference on Africa: ensuing treaty between European states forbids trading in slaves
1898	US declares war on Spain because of its oppression in Cuba
1899	First Hague Conference on arms limitation
1900	US Supreme Court decision in *The Paquete Habana*

1904	Theodore Roosevelt proclaims the right of humanitarian intervention
1907	Second Hague Conference on arms limitation
1915	Armenian genocide
1919	Versailles Peace Conference
	Charter of the League of Nations
1923	Hague agreement to confine aerial bombing to military targets
1925	Geneva Protocol against Use of Poison Gas
1926	Anti-Slavery Convention
1928	Kellogg-Briand Pact
	Chorzów Factory Case (Permanent Court of International Justice)
1933	Hitler in power: first League of Nations petition against the Nazis for discriminating against Jews lodged by Franz Bernheim
1935	*Minority Schools in Albania* decision (Permanent Court of International Justice)
1936	London agreement on rules of submarine warfare
1936–8	The Moscow show trials
1937	Draft Convention for the Prosecution and Punishment of Terrorism
1939	Declaration of Second World War
	H. G. Wells writes to *The Times* urging human rights as a war aim
1940	*H. G. Wells on The Rights of Man* (Penguin Special)
	Darkness at Noon by Arthur Koestler
1941	Franklin D. Roosevelt makes 'Four Freedoms' speech
1942	1 January: Allies declare protection of human rights as a war aim
1944	Dumbarton Oaks: Allied powers determine to establish UN
1945	April: British army enters Belsen and Buchenwald concentration camps
	26 June: Charter of UN signed at San Francisco
	July: Potsdam Conference: Allies confirm they will hold trials of major war criminals
	6 August: Atom bomb dropped on Hiroshima
	8 August: Nuremberg Charter proclaimed
	Animal Farm by George Orwell
1946	30 September: Judgment delivered at Nuremberg
	US v. *Yamashita* (US Supreme Court)
	11 December: UN General Assembly Resolution 96(i) recognizes the Nuremberg Charter and Judgment as stating customary international law
1948	10 December: Universal Declaration of Human Rights adopted by UN General Assembly, Paris
	11 December: Genocide Convention

1949	*Corfu Channel Case* (International Court of Justice)
	Geneva Conventions I-IV, on treatment of prisoners-of-war and civilians during war
	Soviet Union tests atom bomb: arms race begins
1950	European Convention on Human Rights
1950–53	Korean War
1951	Refugee Convention
	International Court of Justice Opinion on Genocide Convention
1953	Death of Stalin
	Electrocution of Julius and Ethel Rosenberg
1956	February: Khrushchev condemns Stalin and show trials at 20th Party Congress
	November: Soviet Union invades Hungary
1960	Massacre at Sharpeville, South Africa
1961	Berlin Wall goes up
	Amnesty International founded
	Trial of Adolf Eichmann
	Bay of Pigs invasion
1962	Cuban Missile Crisis
1964	US bombing of Vietnam begins
1966	Twin Covenants: Covenant on Civil and Political Rights and Optional Protocol on Economic, Cultural and Social Rights
1967	First UN sanctions against South Africa
	Seven Day War: Israel settles Gaza Strip
1968	Tehran Proclamation on Universality of Human Rights
	USSR invades Czechoslovakia
	Convention on the Non-Applicability of Statutory Limitations to War Crimes and Crimes against Humanity
1969	Convention on the Elimination of All Forms of Racial Discrimination (CERD)
	Inter-American Convention on Human Rights
	Vienna Convention on the Law of Treaties
1970	Convention on Return of Cultural Property
	Friendly Relations Resolution, UN General Assembly
1971	Convention on the Suppression and Punishment of the Crime of Apartheid
1973	UN General Assembly adopts principles for co-operation in punishment of crimes against humanity
	Sakharov's open letter to US Congress calling for trade sanctions on the Soviet Union

Pinochet coup in Chile

1974   *Nuclear Test Case* (*Australia* v. *France*) (International Court of Justice)

1975   UN declaration against torture

Helsinki Accords

1976   Military junta seizes power in Argentina

Ireland v. *UK*, European Court of Human Rights condemns inhumane treatment of detainees in Northern Ireland

1977   Charter 77 launched in Prague

UN imposes mandatory trade sanctions on South Africa and Rhodesia under Chapter VII of the Charter

Carter administration adopts human rights as foreign policy objective

Geneva Convention Protocols I and II

Human Rights Committee (HRC) established pursuant to Optional Protocol of the Civil Covenant

1978   Pinochet grants amnesty to death squads and torturers and to himself

1979   Convention against the Taking of Hostages

1980   *Filártiga* v. *Peña-Irala*

1 June: CNN begins broadcasting

1981   Convention on the Elimination of All Forms of Discrimination against Women

African Charter on Human and Peoples' Rights

1983   US invasion of Grenada

1984   Convention Against Torture

1985   *Nunca Más: Report of the National Commission on the Disappearance of People* by Ernesto Sábato, followed by trial of Argentinian junta

1986   *Burkina Faso* v. *Mali*: the International Court of Justice ignores the right of self-determination

UN General Assembly declares the existence of 'a right to development'

Nicaragua v. *US* (International Court of Justice)

1986–8   Proceedings in Israel against Ivan Demjanjuk

1988   Saddam Hussein uses poison gas on Kurds at Halabja: 8,000 killed

Velasquez Rodriguez Case (Inter-American Court)

Iran mass-murders its political prisoners

1989   Convention on the Rights of the Child

Massacre in Tiananmen Square

Collapse of communism in eastern Europe: demolition of Berlin Wall

1990 Iraq invades Kuwait

1991 Civil war begins in Yugoslavia

   'Operation Desert Storm' liberates Kuwait

1992 US ratifies Civil Covenant

   Torture Victims Protection Act (US)

1993 *Pratt & Morgan* v. *Jamaica* (Privy Council) limits death penalty

   International Criminal Tribunal for the Former Yugoslavia
    established by Security Council Resolutions 808 & 881

   June: UN Human Rights Conference in Vienna

   October: 18 American peacekeepers killed in Mogadishu

1994 April-June: 800,000 massacred in Rwandan genocide

   Security Council establishes Rwanda Tribunal in Arusha

1995 Nuclear Non-Proliferation Treaty

   Lennox Phillip v. *DPP of Trinidad* (Privy Council) settles limits of
    amnesties in domestic law

   15 May: Indictment by Hague Tribunal of Bosnian Serb
    leadership (Karadžić and Mladić)

   July: Fall of Srebrenica: 7,000 massacred

   Beijing Conference on Women's Rights

   Dayton Peace Accords

1996 Opinion on Legality of the Threat or Use of Nuclear Weapons
   (International Court of Justice)

   Tadić Case: Hague Tribunal Appeals Chamber ruling on
    jurisdiction

1997 Duško Tadić convicted and sentenced

   Ottawa Convention on banning anti-personnel land mines

1998 Report of South African Truth and Reconciliation Commission

   Death in Kampuchea of Pol Pot, but his chief lieutenants,
    Khieu Samphan and Nuon Chea, are welcomed back by
    Hun Sen

   17 July: 120 nations vote to approve the Rome Statute for the
    International Criminal Court

   16 October: General Pinochet arrested in London

   December: *Ex parte Pinochet (No. 1)*: House of Lords rules
    against immunity from charges of crimes against humanity for
    ex-heads of state

1999 OECD Convention against Third World bribery

   24 March: *Ex parte Pinochet (No. 3)*: Law Lords rule no
    immunity for ex-heads of state under Torture Convention

   NATO bombs Serbia to stop ethnic cleansing in Kosovo

15 April: Lockerbie suspects surrender. Flown to Camp Zeist

9 June: Milošević accepts ceasefire agreement

7 July: Lomé Agreement: : illegal amnesties in Sierra Leone

7 August: al-Qaida truck bombs explode at US embassies in Kenya and Tanzania: 234 killed

4 September: Result of East Timor ballot: 78.5 per cent vote for independence

12 September: President Habibie permits UN troops to occupy East Timor

8 October: Pinochet ordered to be extradited to Spain to face torture charges

Switzerland returns Maurice Papon to France

November: Appeal court jails Egon Krenz for commanding Berlin Wall shootings

2000   31 January: UN HRC report and Indonesian HRC report both condemn Indonesian army officers for crimes against humanity in East Timor and call for prosecutions

3 March: General Pinochet returns to Chile

September: UN Millennium Summit

31 December: President Clinton signs Rome Treaty

2001   31 January: Lockerbie verdict convicts Al-Megrahi

1 March: Fiji Appeals Court rules undemocratic government unlawful

24–28 June: Slobodan Milošević handed over for trial in The Hague

August: General Krstić convicted of Srebrenica genocide: sentenced to forty-six years imprisonment

11 September: al-Qaida attack on Twin Towers and Pentagon: 2,973 killed

October: US begins bombing in support of war on Taliban government in Afghanistan

17 November: Democratic and peaceful elections in Kosovo

2002   16 January: Special court, with international judge majority, established to try war crimes in Sierra Leone

12 February: Trial of Slobodan Milošević begins in The Hague

14 March: Lockerbie conviction upheld by Scottish Appeal Court

11 April: 60 ratifications of Rome Treaty

6 May: President Bush 'unsigns' Rome Treaty

1 July: ICC jurisdiction commences

2 August: American Service-members' Protection Act (ASPA)

12 September: President Bush addresses UN and announces US doctrine of pre-emptive self-defence

8 November: Security Council unanimously adopts Resolution 1441, which establishes UNMOVIC

2003 19 January: US offers Saddam Hussein amnesty if he leaves Iraq

28 January: Hans Blix (UNMOVIC) and Mohamed ElBaradei (IAEA) report to Security Council. They are critical of Iraq but ask for more time to complete their inspections

5 February: US Secretary of State Colin Powell presents 'irrefutable and undeniable' CIA evidence that Iraq is hiding WMD

14 February: Dr Blix makes second report to Security Council: no WMD yet, but prohibited weapons remain 'unaccounted for'

7 March: UK proposes 17 March deadline for Iraq to disarm or face war

8 March: Sierra Leone Special Court judge approves indictment of Charles Taylor

10 March: President Chirac promises that France will vote 'Non' to a second resolution. Kofi Annan warns that US will breach UN Charter if it declares war without Security Council approval

17 March: US and UK offer Saddam Hussein and sons amnesty if they leave Iraq within forty-eight hours

19 March: 'Operation Shock and Awe'

April: US establishes Coalition Provisional Authority under Paul Bremer

13 December: Saddam Hussein captured

2004 February: Secret ICRC report on abuse at Abu Ghraib prison

April: Red Cross report leaked to *Wall Street Journal*; publication of Abu Ghraib pictures

June: US Supreme Court decides *Rasul* v. *Bush* and *Hamdi* v. *Rumsfeld*

August: Special military commission hearings begin at Guantanamo Bay

2005 April: Darfur situation referred by Security Council to ICC

October: Trial of Saddam Hussein begins

December: Truth commission report on East Timor

2006 January: Election of Hamas government in Palestine

Iran reported by IAEA to Security Council over nuclear plans

February: UN abolishes Human Rights Commission

First ICC indictee, Congo warlord Thomas Lubanga, in custody

11 March: Milošević dies mid-trial from heart attack

5 April: Charles Taylor appears in SCSL dock

May: UN elects Human Rights Council

Cambodia and UN appoint judges to Khmer Rouge Tribunal

2007   3 May: Convention on Rights of Persons with Disabilities

13 September: UN General Assembly: Declaration of Rights of Indigenous Peoples

2008   July: Bosnian Serb leader Radovan Karadžić captured

27 July: 'Operation Cast Lead': Israeli attack on Gaza commences

2009   26 January: First trial at the ICC – of Thomas Lubanga – begins.

February–April: Sri Lankan army and navy bombard Tamils

October: ASEAN Intergovernmental Commission on Human Rights established

2010   10 June: First convictions for genocide at Srebrenica: Ljubiša Beara and Vujadin Popović jailed for life

July: First conviction, and thirty-five-year sentence, in Cambodian Court for Duch, prison commandant who tortured and executed 15,000

1 August: Convention on Cluster Munitions comes into force

15 December: ICC Prosecutor indicts six highly placed Kenyan politicians

17 December: 'Jasmine Revolution' begins in Tunisia with self-immolation of Mohamed Bouazizi

23 December: Convention on Disappearances enters into force

2011   14 January: Ben-Ali flees Tunisia

27 January: Tahrir Square protest begins

11 February: Mubarak resigns

17 February: Demonstrations begin in Benghazi

26 February: UN Security Council Resolution 1970 unanimously refers situation in Libya to ICC Prosecutor

17 March: Resolution 1973 authorizes NATO to use 'all necessary measures' to protect civilians in Libya

By Resolution 1975, Security Council authorizes 'all necessary measures' to protect Ivory Coast civilians

April: Croat General Ante Gotovina jailed for twenty-four years for war crimes

1 May: Osama bin Laden killed

26 May: Ratko Mladić captured and sent to The Hague

20 July: The last wanted ICTY indictee, Goran Hadzić, captured by Serb war crimes investigators

30 September: US citizen Anwar al-Awlaki killed by US drone in Yemen

28 October: Alfredo Astiz and other former Argentinian officers sentenced to life imprisonment for torturing and 'disappearing' dissidents

21 November: Trial of Nuon Chea, Khieu Samphan and Ieng Sary begins in Cambodian Court

5 December: Laurent Gbagbo, former President of the Ivory Coast, transported to The Hague to face charges of crimes against humanity

2012   16 January: ICC approves indictments on four senior Kenyan politicians

Guatemala court orders house arrest and trial on charges of genocide (the massacre of 1,600 indigenous people in 1982/3 of former dictator, General Rios Montt

5 March: 'Invisible Children', video about ICC indictee Kony goes viral on internet: 90 million viewers in five days

14 March: ICC records its first conviction – of Thomas Lubanga, for recruitment of child soldiers

26 April: Special Court for Sierra Leone convicts Charles Taylor of aiding and abetting war crimes

6 May: Pre-trial hearing begins at Guantanamo Bay in KSM case

16 May: Mladić trial, for genocide at Srebrenica and murder at Sarajevo, opens

30 May: Charles Taylor sentenced to fifty years in prison

July: UN hosts delegates from 150 countries for month-long session to finalize treaty to ban sales of conventional weapons to human rights abusers

6 July: Argentinian court jails former dictator Jorge Videla for fifty years, for ordering kidnap and killing of mothers and then stealing of their babies for adoption by military families

7 July: Mali asks ICC Prosecutor to investigate massacres and destruction of cultural heritage by Islamist rebel troops

19 July: Military court in Tunisia sentences Ben Ali's interior minister and security officials to lengthy prison terms for killing Arab Spring protesters

19 July: International Court of Justice in *Belgium* v. *Senegal* rules that Senegal is in breach of the Convention against Torture for its failure to put Hissène Habré on trial: it must do so forthwith, or extradite him for trial in Belgium.

Appendix B:
Universal Declaration of Human Rights

PREAMBLE

Whereas recognition of the inherent dignity and of the equal and inalienable rights of all members of the human family is the foundation of freedom, justice and peace in the world,

Whereas disregard and contempt for human rights have resulted in barbarous acts which have outraged the conscience of mankind, and the advent of a world in which human beings shall enjoy freedom of speech and belief and freedom from fear and want has been proclaimed as the highest aspiration of the common people,

Whereas it is essential, if man is not to be compelled to have recourse, as a last resort, to rebellion against tyranny and oppression, that human rights should be protected by the rule of law,

Whereas it is essential to promote the development of friendly relations between nations,

Whereas the peoples of the United Nations have in the Charter reaffirmed their faith in fundamental human rights, in the dignity and worth of the human person and in the equal rights of men and women and have determined to promote social progress and better standards of life in larger freedom,

Whereas Member States have pledged themselves to achieve, in co-operation with the United Nations, the promotion of universal respect for and observance of human rights and fundamental freedoms,

Whereas a common understanding of these rights and freedoms is of the greatest importance for the full realization of this pledge,

Now, therefore The General Assembly proclaims This Universal Declaration of Human Rights as a common standard of achievement for all peoples and all nations, to the end that every individual and every organ of society, keeping this Declaration constantly in mind, shall strive by teaching and education to promote respect for these rights and freedoms and by progressive measures, national and international, to secure their universal and effective recognition and observance, both among the peoples of Member States themselves and among the peoples of territories under their jurisdiction.

ARTICLE 1

All human beings are born free and equal in dignity and rights. They are endowed with reason and conscience and should act towards one another in a spirit of brotherhood.

ARTICLE 2

Everyone is entitled to all the rights and freedoms set forth in this Declaration, without distinction of any kind, such as race, colour, sex, language, religion, political or other opinion, national or social origin, property, birth or other status. Furthermore, no distinction shall be made on the basis of the political, jurisdictional or international status of the country or territory to which a person belongs, whether it be independent, trust, non-self-governing or under any other limitation of sovereignty.

ARTICLE 3

Everyone has the right to life, liberty and security of person.

ARTICLE 4

No one shall be held in slavery or servitude; slavery and the slave trade shall be prohibited in all their forms.

ARTICLE 5

No one shall be subjected to torture or to cruel, inhuman or degrading treatment or punishment.

ARTICLE 6

Everyone has the right to recognition everywhere as a person before the law.

ARTICLE 7

All are equal before the law and are entitled without any discrimination to equal protection of the law. All are entitled to equal protection against any discrimination in violation of this Declaration and against any incitement to such discrimination.

ARTICLE 8

Everyone has the right to an effective remedy by the competent national tribunals for acts violating the fundamental rights granted him by the constitution or by law.

ARTICLE 9

No one shall be subjected to arbitrary arrest, detention or exile.

ARTICLE 10

Everyone is entitled in full equality to a fair and public hearing by an independent and impartial tribunal, in the determination of his rights and obligations and of any criminal charge against him.

ARTICLE 11

(1) Everyone charged with a penal offence has the right to be presumed innocent until proved guilty according to law in a public trial at which he has had all the guarantees necessary for his defence.

(2) No one shall be held guilty of any penal offence on account of any act or omission which did not constitute a penal offence, under national or international law, at the time when it was committed. Nor shall a heavier penalty be imposed than the one that was applicable at the time the penal offence was committed.

ARTICLE 12

No one shall be subjected to arbitrary interference with his privacy, family, home or correspondence, nor to attacks upon his honour and reputation. Everyone has the right to the protection of the law against such interference or attacks.

ARTICLE 13

(1) Everyone has the right to freedom of movement and residence within the borders of each state.

(2) Everyone has the right to leave any country, including his own, and to return to his country.

ARTICLE 14

(1) Everyone has the right to seek and to enjoy in other countries asylum from persecution.

(2) This right may not be invoked in the case of prosecutions genuinely arising from non-political crimes or from acts contrary to the purposes and principles of the United Nations.

ARTICLE 15

(1) Everyone has the right to a nationality.

(2) No one shall be arbitrarily deprived of his nationality nor denied the right to change his nationality.

ARTICLE 16

(1) Men and women of full age, without any limitation due to race, nationality or religion, have the right to marry and to found a family. They are entitled to equal rights as to marriage, during marriage and at its dissolution.

(2) Marriage shall be entered into only with the free and full consent of the intending spouses.

(3) The family is the natural and fundamental group unit of society and is entitled to protection by society and the State.

ARTICLE 17

(1) Everyone has the right to own property alone as well as in association with others.

(2) No one shall be arbitrarily deprived of his property.

ARTICLE 18

Everyone has the right to freedom of thought, conscience and religion; this right includes freedom to change his religion or belief, and freedom, either alone or in community with others and in public or private, to manifest his religion or belief in teaching, practice, worship and observance.

ARTICLE 19

Everyone has the right to freedom of opinion and expression; this right includes freedom to hold opinions without interference and to seek, receive and impart information and ideas through any media and regardless of frontiers.

ARTICLE 20

(1) Everyone has the right to freedom of peaceful assembly and association.

(2) No one may be compelled to belong to an association.

ARTICLE 21

(1) Everyone has the right to take part in the government of his country, directly or through freely chosen representatives.

(2) Everyone has the right of equal access to public service in his country.

(3) The will of the people shall be the basis of the authority of government; this will shall be expressed in periodic and genuine elections which shall be by universal and equal suffrage and shall be held by secret vote or by equivalent free voting procedures.

ARTICLE 22

Everyone, as a member of society, has the right to social security and is entitled to realization, through national effort and international co-operation and in accordance with the organization and resources of each State, of the economic, social and cultural rights indispensable for his dignity and the free development of his personality.

ARTICLE 23

(1) Everyone has the right to work, to free choice of employment, to just and favourable conditions of work and to protection against unemployment.

(2) Everyone, without any discrimination, has the right to equal pay for equal work.

(3) Everyone who works has the right to just and favourable remuneration ensuring for himself and his family an existence worthy of human dignity, and supplemented, if necessary, by other means of social protection.

(4) Everyone has the right to form and to join trade unions for the protection of his interests.

ARTICLE 24

Everyone has the right to rest and leisure, including reasonable limitation of working hours and periodic holidays with pay.

ARTICLE 25

(1) Everyone has the right to a standard of living adequate for the health and well-being of himself and of his family, including food, clothing, housing and medical care and necessary social services, and the right to security in the event of unemployment, sickness, disability, widowhood, old age or other lack of livelihood in circumstances beyond his control.

(2) Motherhood and childhood are entitled to special care and assistance. All children, whether born in or out of wedlock, shall enjoy the same social protection.

ARTICLE 26

(1) Everyone has the right to education. Education shall be free, at least in the elementary and fundamental stages. Elementary education shall be compulsory. Technical and professional education shall be made generally available and higher education shall be equally accessible to all on the basis of merit.

(2) Education shall be directed to the full development of the human personality and to the strengthening of respect for human rights and fundamental

freedoms. It shall promote understanding, tolerance and friendship among all nations, racial or religious groups, and shall further the activities of the United Nations for the maintenance of peace.

(3) Parents have a prior right to choose the kind of education that shall be given to their children.

ARTICLE 27

(1) Everyone has the right freely to participate in the cultural life of the community, to enjoy the arts and to share in scientific advancement and its benefits.

(2) Everyone has the right to the protection of the moral and material interests resulting from any scientific, literary or artistic production of which he is the author.

ARTICLE 28

Everyone is entitled to a social and international order in which the rights and freedoms set forth in this Declaration can be fully realized.

ARTICLE 29

(1) Everyone has duties to the community in which alone the free and full development of his personality is possible.

(2) In the exercise of his rights and freedoms, everyone shall be subject only to such limitations as are determined by law solely for the purpose of securing the recognition and respect for the rights and freedoms of others and of meeting the just requirements of morality, public order and the general welfare in a democratic society.

(3) These rights and freedoms may in no case be exercised contrary to the purposes and principles of the United Nations.

ARTICLE 30

Nothing in this Declaration may be interpreted as implying for any State, group or person any right to engage in any activity or to perform any act aimed at the destruction of any of the rights and freedoms set forth herein.

Appendix C: Ratifications of Human Rights Conventions (As of 19 July 2012)

Instrument	Number of State Parties
Forced Labour Convention (1930)	175
Statute of the International Court of Justice (1946)	193*
Acceptance of the Compulsory Jurisdiction under the Optional Clause to the ICJ Statute	67
Convention on the Prevention and Punishment of the Crime of Genocide (1948)	142*
Geneva Conventions (1949)	194*
Convention for the Suppression of the Traffic in Persons and of the Exploitation or the Prostitution of Others (1950)	82
Convention Relating to the Status of Refugees (1951)	145
Convention Relating to the Status of Stateless Persons (1954)	74
Supplementary Convention on the Abolition of Slavery, the Slave Trade, and Institutions and Practices Similar to Slavery (1956)	123*
Abolition of Forced Labour Convention (1957)	172*
Vienna Convention on Diplomatic Relations (1961)	187*
International Covenant on Economic, Social and Cultural Rights (1966)	160
International Covenant on Civil and Political Rights (1966)	167*
Optional Protocol to the International Covenant on Civil and Political Rights: Rights of Individual Petition (1966)	114

* Ratified by the United States

Appendix D: Excerpts from the Rome Statute of the International Criminal Court

Adopted by the United Nations Diplomatic Conference of Plenipotentiaries on the Establishment of an International Criminal Court on 17 July 1998.

PREAMBLE

Conscious that all peoples are united by common bonds, their cultures pieced together in a shared heritage, and concerned that this delicate mosaic may be shattered at any time,

Mindful that during this century millions of children, women and men have been victims of unimaginable atrocities that deeply shock the conscience of humanity,

Recognizing that such grave crimes threaten the peace, security and well-being of the world,

Affirming that the most serious crimes of concern to the international community as a whole must not go unpunished and that their effective prosecution must be ensured by taking measures at the national level and by enhancing international co-operation,

Determined to put an end to impunity for the perpetrators of these crimes and thus to contribute to the prevention of such crimes,

Recalling that it is the duty of every State to exercise its criminal jurisdiction over those responsible for international crimes,

Reaffirming the Purposes and Principles of the Charter of the United Nations, and in particular that all States shall refrain from the threat or use of force against the territorial integrity or political independence of any State, or in any other manner inconsistent with the Purposes of the United Nations,

Emphasizing in this connection that nothing in this Statute shall be taken as authorizing any State Party to intervene in an armed conflict in the internal affairs of any State,

Determined to these ends and for the sake of present and future generations, to establish an independent permanent International Criminal Court in relationship with the United Nations system, with jurisdiction over the most serious crimes of concern to the international community as a whole,

Emphasizing that the International Criminal Court established under this Statute shall be complementary to national criminal jurisdictions,

Resolved to guarantee lasting respect for the enforcement of international justice,

Have agreed as follows ...

PART 2. JURISDICTION, ADMISSIBILITY AND APPLICABLE LAW

Article 5

Crimes within the jurisdiction of the Court

1. The jurisdiction of the Court shall be limited to the most serious crimes of concern to the international community as a whole. The Court has jurisdiction in accordance with this Statute with respect to the following crimes:

(a) The crime of genocide;
(b) Crimes against humanity;

(c) War crimes;

(d) The crime of aggression.

2. The Court shall exercise jurisdiction over the crime of aggression once a provision is adopted in accordance with articles 121 and 123 defining the crime and setting out the conditions under which the Court shall exercise jurisdiction with respect to this crime. Such a provision shall be consistent with the relevant provisions of the Charter of the United Nations.

Article 6

Genocide

For the purpose of this Statute, 'genocide' means any of the following acts committed with intent to destroy, in whole or in part, a national, ethnical, racial or religious group, as such:

(a) Killing members of the group;

(b) Causing serious bodily or mental harm to members of the group;

(c) Deliberately inflicting on the group conditions of life calculated to bring about its physical destruction in whole or in part;

(d) Imposing measures intended to prevent births within the group;

(e) Forcibly transferring children of the group to another group.

Article 7

Crimes against humanity

1. For the purpose of this Statute, 'crime against humanity' means any of the following acts when committed as part of a widespread or systematic attack directed against any civilian population, with knowledge of the attack:

(a) Murder;

(b) Extermination;

(c) Enslavement;

(d) Deportation or forcible transfer of population;

(e) Imprisonment or other severe deprivation of physical liberty in violation of fundamental rules of international law;

(f) Torture;

(g) Rape, sexual slavery, enforced prostitution, forced pregnancy, enforced sterilization, or any other form of sexual violence of comparable gravity;

(h) Persecution against any identifiable group or collectivity on political, racial, national, ethnic, cultural, religious, gender as defined in paragraph 3, or other grounds that are universally recognized as impermissible under international law, in connection with any act referred to in this paragraph or any crime within the jurisdiction of the Court;

(i) Enforced disappearance of persons;

(j) The crime of apartheid;

(k) Other inhumane acts of a similar character intentionally causing great suffering, or serious injury to body or to mental or physical health.

2. For the purpose of paragraph 1:

(a) 'Attack directed against any civilian population' means a course of conduct involving the multiple commission of acts referred to in paragraph 1 against any civilian population, pursuant to or in furtherance of a State or organizational policy to commit such attack;

(b) 'Extermination' includes the intentional infliction of conditions of life, inter alia the deprivation of access to food and medicine, calculated to bring about the destruction of part of a population;

(c) 'Enslavement' means the exercise of any or all of the powers attaching to the right of ownership over a person and includes the exercise of such power in the course of trafficking in persons, in particular women and children;

(d) 'Deportation or forcible transfer of population' means forced displacement of the persons concerned by expulsion or other coercive acts from the area in which they are lawfully present, without grounds permitted under international law;

(e) 'Torture' means the intentional infliction of severe pain or suffering, whether physical or mental, upon a person in the custody or under the control of the accused; except that torture shall not include pain or suffering arising only from, inherent in or incidental to, lawful sanctions;

(f) 'Forced pregnancy' means the unlawful confinement of a woman forcibly made pregnant, with the intent of affecting the ethnic composition of any population or carrying out other grave violations of international law. This definition shall not in any way be interpreted as affecting national laws relating to pregnancy;

(g) 'Persecution' means the intentional and severe deprivation of fundamental rights contrary to international law by reason of the identity of the group or collectivity;

(h) 'The crime of apartheid' means inhumane acts of a character similar to those referred to in paragraph 1, committed in the context of an institutionalized regime of systematic oppression and domination by one racial group over any other racial group or groups and committed with the intention of maintaining that regime;

(i) 'Enforced disappearance of persons' means the arrest, detention or abduction of persons by, or with the authorization, support or acquiescence of, a State or a political organization, followed by a refusal to acknowledge that deprivation of freedom or to give information on the fate or whereabouts of those persons, with the intention of removing them from the protection of the law for a prolonged period of time.

3. For the purpose of this Statute, it is understood that the term 'gender' refers to the two sexes, male and female, within the context of society. The term 'gender' does not indicate any meaning different from the above.

Article 8

War crimes

1. The Court shall have jurisdiction in respect of war crimes in particular when committed as a part of a plan or policy or as part of a large-scale commission of such crimes.

2. For the purpose of this Statute, 'war crimes' means:

(a) Grave breaches of the Geneva Conventions of 12 August 1949, namely, any of the following acts against persons or property protected under the provisions of the relevant Geneva Convention:

    (i) Wilful killing;

    (ii) Torture or inhuman treatment, including biological experiments;

    (iii) Wilfully causing great suffering, or serious injury to body or health;

    (iv) Extensive destruction and appropriation of property, not justified by military necessity and carried out unlawfully and wantonly;

    (v) Compelling a prisoner-of-war or other protected person to serve in the forces of a hostile Power;

    (vi) Wilfully depriving a prisoner-of-war or other protected person of the rights of fair and regular trial;

    (vii) Unlawful deportation or transfer or unlawful confinement;

    (viii) Taking of hostages.

(b) Other serious violations of the laws and customs applicable in international armed conflict, within the established framework of international law, namely, any of the following acts:

(i) Intentionally directing attacks against the civilian population as such or against individual civilians not taking direct part in hostilities;

(ii) Intentionally directing attacks against civilian objects, that is, objects which are not military objectives;

(iii) Intentionally directing attacks against personnel, installations, material, units or vehicles involved in a humanitarian assistance or peacekeeping mission in accordance with the Charter of the United Nations, as long as they are entitled to the protection given to civilians or civilian objects under the international law of armed conflict;

(iv) Intentionally launching an attack in the knowledge that such attack will cause incidental loss of life or injury to civilians or damage to civilian objects or widespread, long-term and severe damage to the natural environment which would be clearly excessive in relation to the concrete and direct overall military advantage anticipated;

(v) Attacking or bombarding, by whatever means, towns, villages, dwellings or buildings which are undefended and which are not military objectives;

(vi) Killing or wounding a combatant who, having laid down his arms or having no longer means of defence, has surrendered at discretion;

(vii) Making improper use of a flag of truce, of the flag or of the military insignia and uniform of the enemy or of the United Nations, as well as of the distinctive emblems of the Geneva Conventions, resulting in death or serious personal injury;

(viii) The transfer, directly or indirectly, by the Occupying Power of parts of its own civilian population into the territory it occupies, or the deportation or transfer of all or parts of the population of the occupied territory within or outside this territory;

(ix) Intentionally directing attacks against buildings dedicated to religion, education, art, science or charitable purposes, historic monuments, hospitals and places where the sick and wounded are collected, provided they are not military objectives;

(x) Subjecting persons who are in the power of an adverse party to physical mutilation or to medical or scientific experiments of any kind which are neither justified by the medical, dental or hospital treatment of the person concerned nor carried out in his or her interest, and which cause death to or seriously endanger the health of such person or persons;

(xi) Killing or wounding treacherously individuals belonging to the hostile nation or army;

(xii) Declaring that no quarter will be given;

(xiii) Destroying or seizing the enemy's property unless such destruction or seizure be imperatively demanded by the necessities of war;

(xiv) Declaring abolished, suspended or inadmissible in a court of law the rights and actions of the nationals of the hostile party;

(xv) Compelling the nationals of the hostile party to take part in the operations of war directed against their own country, even if they were in the belligerent's service before the commencement of the war;

(xvi) Pillaging a town or place, even when taken by assault;

(xvii) Employing poison or poisoned weapons;

(xviii) Employing asphyxiating, poisonous or other gases, and all analogous liquids, materials or devices;

(xix) Employing bullets which expand or flatten easily in the human body, such as bullets with a hard envelope which does not entirely cover the core or is pierced with incisions;

(xx) Employing weapons, projectiles and material and methods of warfare which are of a nature to cause superfluous injury or unnecessary suffering or which are inherently indiscriminate in violation of the international law of armed conflict, provided that such weapons, projectiles and material and methods of warfare are the subject of a comprehensive prohibition and are included in an annex to this Statute, by an amendment in accordance with the relevant provisions set forth in articles 121 and 123;

(xxi) Committing outrages upon personal dignity, in particular humiliating and degrading treatment;

(xxii) Committing rape, sexual slavery, enforced prostitution, forced pregnancy, as defined in article 7, paragraph 2(f), enforced sterilization, or any other form of sexual violence also constituting a grave breach of the Geneva Conventions;

(xxiii) Utilizing the presence of a civilian or other protected person to render certain points, areas or military forces immune from military operations;

(xxiv) Intentionally directing attacks against buildings, material, medical units and transport, and personnel using the distinctive emblems of the Geneva Conventions in conformity with international law;

(xxv) Intentionally using starvation of civilians as a method of warfare by depriving them of objects indispensable to their survival, including wilfully impeding relief supplies as provided for under the Geneva Conventions;

(xxvi) Conscripting or enlisting children under the age of fifteen years into the national armed forces or using them to participate actively in hostilities.

(c) In the case of an armed conflict not of an international character, serious violations of article 3 common to the four Geneva Conventions of 12 August 1949, namely, any of the following acts committed against persons taking no active part in the hostilities, including members of armed forces who have laid down their arms and those placed hors de combat by sickness, wounds, detention or any other cause:

(i) Violence to life and person, in particular murder of all kinds, mutilation, cruel treatment and torture;

(ii) Committing outrages upon personal dignity, in particular humiliating and degrading treatment;

(iii) Taking of hostages;

(iv) The passing of sentences and the carrying out of executions without previous judgment pronounced by a regularly constituted court, affording all judicial guarantees which are generally recognized as indispensable.

(d) Paragraph 2(c) applies to armed conflicts not of an international character and thus does not apply to situations of internal disturbances and tensions, such as riots, isolated and sporadic acts of violence or other acts of a similar nature.

(e) Other serious violations of the laws and customs applicable in armed conflicts not of an international character, within the established framework of international law, namely, any of the following acts:

(i) Intentionally directing attacks against the civilian population as such or against individual civilians not taking direct part in hostilities;

(ii) Intentionally directing attacks against buildings, material, medical units and transport, and personnel using the distinctive emblems of the Geneva Conventions in conformity with international law;

(iii) Intentionally directing attacks against personnel, installations, material, units or vehicles involved in a humanitarian assistance or peace-keeping mission in accordance with the Charter of the United Nations, as long as they are entitled to the protection given to civilians or civilian objects under the law of armed conflict;

(iv) Intentionally directing attacks against buildings dedicated to religion, education, art, science or charitable purposes, historic monuments, hospitals and places where the sick and wounded are collected, provided they are not military objectives;

(v) Pillaging a town or place, even when taken by assault;

(vi) Committing rape, sexual slavery, enforced prostitution, forced pregnancy, as defined in article 7, paragraph 2(f), enforced sterilization, and any other form of sexual violence also constituting a serious violation of article 3 common to the four Geneva Conventions;

(vii) Conscripting or enlisting children under the age of fifteen years into armed forces or groups or using them to participate actively in hostilities;

(viii) Ordering the displacement of the civilian population for reasons related to the conflict, unless the security of the civilians involved or imperative military reasons so demand;

(ix) Killing or wounding treacherously a combatant adversary;

(x) Declaring that no quarter will be given;

(xi) Subjecting persons who are in the power of another party to the conflict to physical mutilation or to medical or scientific experiments of any kind which are neither justified by the medical, dental or hospital treatment of the person concerned nor carried out in his or her interest, and which cause death to or seriously endanger the health of such person or persons;

(xii) Destroying or seizing the property of an adversary unless such destruction or seizure be imperatively demanded by the necessities of the conflict;

(f) Paragraph 2(e) applies to armed conflicts not of an international character and thus does not apply to situations of internal disturbances and tensions, such as riots, isolated and sporadic acts of violence or other acts of a similar nature. It applies to armed conflicts that take place in the territory of a State when there is protracted armed conflict between governmental authorities and organized armed groups or between such groups.

3. Nothing in paragraph 2(c) and (d) shall affect the responsibility of a

Government to maintain or re-establish law and order in the State or to defend the unity and territorial integrity of the State, by all legitimate means.

Article 12

Preconditions to the exercise of jurisdiction

1. A State which becomes a Party to this Statute thereby accepts the jurisdiction of the Court with respect to the crimes referred to in article 5.

2. In the case of article 13, paragraph (a) or (c), the Court may exercise its jurisdiction if one or more of the following States are Parties to this Statute or have accepted the jurisdiction of the Court in accordance with paragraph 3:

(a) The State on the territory of which the conduct in question occurred or, if the crime was committed on board a vessel or aircraft, the State of registration of that vessel or aircraft;

(b) The State of which the person accused of the crime is a national.

3. If the acceptance of a State which is not a Party to this Statute is required under paragraph 2, that State may, by declaration lodged with the Registrar, accept the exercise of jurisdiction by the Court with respect to the crime in question. The accepting State shall cooperate with the Court without any delay or exception in accordance with Part 9.

Article 13

Exercise of jurisdiction

The Court may exercise its jurisdiction with respect to a crime referred to in article 5 in accordance with the provisions of this Statute if:

(a) A situation in which one or more of such crimes appears to have been committed is referred to the Prosecutor by a State Party in accordance with article 14;

(b) A situation in which one or more of such crimes appears to have been committed is referred to the Prosecutor by the Security Council acting under Chapter VII of the Charter of the United Nations; or

(c) The Prosecutor has initiated an investigation in respect of such a crime in accordance with article 15.

Article 14

Referral of a situation by a State Party

1. A State Party may refer to the Prosecutor a situation in which one or more crimes within the jurisdiction of the Court appear to have been committed requesting the Prosecutor to investigate the situation for the purpose of determining whether one or more specific persons should be charged with the commission of such crimes.

Article 15

Prosecutor

1. The Prosecutor may initiate investigations *proprio motu* on the basis of information on crimes within the jurisdiction of the Court.

2. The Prosecutor shall analyse the seriousness of the information received. For this purpose, he or she may seek additional information from States, organs of the United Nations, intergovernmental or non-governmental organizations, or other reliable sources that he or she deems appropriate, and may receive written or oral testimony at the seat of the Court.

3. If the Prosecutor concludes that there is a reasonable basis to proceed with an investigation, he or she shall submit to the Pre-trial Chamber a request for authorization of an investigation, together with any supporting material collected. Victims may make representations to the Pre-trial Chamber, in accordance with the Rules of Procedure and Evidence.

4. If the Pre-trial Chamber, upon examination of the request and the supporting material, considers that there is a reasonable basis to proceed with an investigation, and that the case appears to fall within the jurisdiction of the Court, it shall authorize the commencement of the investigation, without prejudice to subsequent determinations by the Court with regard to the jurisdiction and admissibility of a case.

Article 16

Deferral of Investigation or Prosecution

No investigation or prosecution may be commenced or proceeded with under this Statute for a period of 12 months after the Security Council, in a resolution adopted under Chapter VII of the Charter of the United Nations, has requested the Court to that effect; that request may be renewed by the Council under the same conditions.

Article 27

Irrelevance of Official Capacity

1. This Statute shall apply equally to all persons without any distinction based on official capacity. In particular, official capacity as a Head of State or Government, a member of a Government or parliament, an elected representative or a government official shall in no case exempt a person from criminal responsibility under this Statute, nor shall it, in and of itself, constitute a ground for reduction of sentence.

2. Immunities or special procedural rules which may attach to the official capacity of a person, whether under national or international law, shall not bar the Court from exercising its jurisdiction over such a person.

Article 28

Responsibility of Commanders and other Superiors

In addition to other grounds of criminal responsibility under this Statute for crimes within the jurisdiction of the Court:

1. A military commander or person effectively acting as a military commander shall be criminally responsible for crimes within the jurisdiction of the Court committed by forces under his or her effective command and control, or effective authority and control as the case may be, as a result of his or her failure to exercise control properly over such forces, where:

(a) That military commander or person either knew or, owing to the circumstances at the time, should have known that the forces were committing or about to commit such crimes; and

(b) That military commander or person failed to take all necessary and reasonable measures within his or her power to prevent or repress their commission or to submit the matter to the competent authorities for investigation and prosecution.

2. With respect to superior and subordinate relationships not described in paragraph 1, a superior shall be criminally responsible for crimes within the jurisdiction of the Court committed by subordinates under his or her effective authority and control, as a result of his or her failure to exercise control properly over such subordinates, where:

(a) The superior either knew, or consciously disregarded information which clearly indicated, that the subordinates were committing or about to commit such crimes;

(b) The crimes concerned activities that were within the effective responsibility and control of the superior; and

(c) The superior failed to take all necessary and reasonable measures within his or her power to prevent or repress their commission or to submit the matter to the competent authorities for investigation and prosecution.

Article 29

Non-Applicability of Statute of Limitations

The crimes within the jurisdiction of the Court shall not be subject to any statute of limitation.

Article 33

Superior Orders and Prescription of Law

1. The fact that a crime within the jurisdiction of the Court has been committed by a person pursuant to an order of a Government or of a superior, whether military or civilian, shall not relieve that person of criminal responsibility unless:

(a) The person was under a legal obligation to obey orders of the Government or the superior in question;

(b) The person did not know that the order was unlawful; and

(c) The order was not manifestly unlawful.

2. For the purposes of this article, orders to commit genocide or crimes against humanity are manifestly unlawful.

Appendix E: Excerpts from the Charter of the United Nations

WE THE PEOPLES OF THE UNITED NATIONS DETERMINED to save succeeding generations from the scourge of war, which twice in our lifetime has brought untold sorrow to mankind, and to reaffirm faith in fundamental human rights, in the dignity and worth of the human person, in the equal rights of men and women and of nations large and small, and to establish conditions under which justice and respect for the obligations arising from treaties and other sources of international law can be maintained, and to promote social progress and better standards of life in larger freedom,

AND FOR THESE ENDS to practise tolerance and live together in peace with one another as good neighbours, and to unite our strength to maintain international peace and security, and to ensure, by the acceptance of principles and the institution of methods, that armed force shall not be used, save in the common interest, and to employ international machinery for the promotion of the economic and social advancement of all peoples,

HAVE RESOLVED TO COMBINE OUR EFFORTS TO ACCOMPLISH THESE AIMS. Accordingly, our respective Governments, through representatives assembled in the city of San Francisco, who have exhibited their full powers found to be in good and due form, have agreed to the present Charter of the United Nations and do hereby establish an international organization to be known as the United Nations.

CHAPTER I. PURPOSES AND PRINCIPLES

Article 1

The Purposes of the United Nations are:

(1) To maintain international peace and security, and to that end: to take effective collective measures for the prevention and removal of threats to the peace, and for the suppression of acts of aggression or other breaches of the peace, and to bring about by peaceful means, and in conformity with the principles of justice and international law, adjustment or settlement of international disputes or situations which might lead to a breach of the peace;

(2) To develop friendly relations among nations based on respect for the principles of equal rights and self-determination of peoples, and to take other appropriate measures to strengthen universal peace;

(3) To achieve international co-operation in solving international problems of an economic, social, cultural, or humanitarian character, and in promoting and encouraging respect for human rights and for fundamental freedoms for all without distinction as to race, sex, language, or religion; and

(4) To be a centre for harmonizing the actions of nations in the attainment of these common ends.

Article 2

The Organization and its Members, in pursuit of the Purposes stated in Article 1, shall act in accordance with the following Principles.

(1) The Organization is based on the principle of the sovereign equality of all its Members.

(2) All Members, in order to ensure to all of them the rights and benefits resulting from membership, shall fulfil in good faith the obligations assumed by them in accordance with the present Charter.

(3) All Members shall settle their international disputes by peaceful means in such a manner that international peace and security, and justice, are not endangered.

(4) All Members shall refrain in their international relations from the threat or use of force against the territorial integrity or political independence of any

state, or in any other manner inconsistent with the Purposes of the United Nations.

(5) All Members shall give the United Nations every assistance in any action it takes in accordance with the present Charter, and shall refrain from giving assistance to any state against which the United Nations is taking preventive or enforcement action.

(6) The Organization shall ensure that states which are not Members of the United Nations act in accordance with these Principles so far as may be necessary for the maintenance of peace and security.

(7) Nothing contained in the present Charter shall authorize the United Nations to intervene in matters which are essentially within the domestic jurisdiction of any state or shall require the Members to submit such matters to settlement under the present Charter; but this principle shall not prejudice the application of enforcement measures under Chapter VII.

CHAPTER VII. ACTION WITH RESPECT TO THREATS TO THE PEACE, BREACHES OF THE PEACE, AND ACTS OF AGGRESSION

Article 39

The Security Council shall determine the existence of any threat to the peace, breach of the peace, or act of aggression and shall make recommendations, or decide what measures shall be taken in accordance with Articles 41 and 42, to maintain or restore international peace and security.

Article 40

In order to prevent an aggravation of the situation, the Security Council may, before making the recommendations or deciding upon the measures provided for in Article 39, call upon the parties concerned to comply with such provisional measures as it deems necessary or desirable. Such provisional measures shall be without prejudice to the rights, claims, or position of the parties concerned. The Security Council shall duly take account of failure to comply with such provisional measures.

Article 41

The Security Council may decide what measures not involving the use of armed force are to be employed to give effect to its decisions, and it may call upon the Members of the United Nations to apply such measures. These may include complete or partial interruption of economic relations and of rail, sea, air, postal, telegraphic, radio, and other means of communication, and the severance of diplomatic relations.

Article 42

Should the Security Council consider that measures provided for in Article 41 would be inadequate or have proved to be inadequate, it may take such action by air, sea, or land forces as may be necessary to maintain or restore international peace or security. Such action may include demonstrations, blockade, and other operations by air, sea, or land forces of Members of the United Nations.

Article 51

Nothing in the present Charter shall impair the inherent right of individual or collective self-defence if an armed attack occurs against a Member of the United Nations, until the Security Council has taken measures necessary to maintain international peace and security. Measures taken by Members in the exercise of this right of self-defence shall be immediately reported to the Security Council and shall not in any way affect the authority and responsibility of the Security Council under the present Charter to take at any time such action as it deems necessary in order to maintain or restore international peace and security.

Article 55

With a view to the creation of conditions of stability and well-being which are necessary for peaceful and friendly relations among nations based on respect for the principle of equal rights and self-determination of peoples, the United Nations shall promote:
(a) Higher standards of living, full employment, and conditions of economic and social progress and development;

(b) Solutions of international economic, social, health, and related problems; and international cultural and educational cooperation; and

(c) Universal respect for, and observance of, human rights and fundamental freedoms for all without distinction as to race, sex, language, or religion.

Article 56

All Members pledge themselves to take joint and separate action in cooperation with the Organization for the achievement of the purposes set forth in Article 55.

Article 68

The Economic and Social Council shall set up commissions in economic and social fields and for the promotion of human rights, and such other commissions as may be required for the performance of its functions.

Index

Notes are marked with *n*.

ALLEN LANE
an imprint of
PENGUIN BOOKS

Recently Published

David Thomson, *The Big Screen: The Story of the Movies and What They Did to Us*

Halik Kochanski, *The Eagle Unbowed: Poland and the Poles in the Second World War*

Kofi Annan with Nader Mousavizadeh, *Interventions: A Life in War and Peace*

Mark Mazower, *Governing the World: The History of an Idea*

Anne Applebaum, *Iron Curtain: The Crushing of Eastern Europe 1944-56*

Steven Johnson, *Future Perfect: The Case for Progress in a Networked Age*

Christopher Clark, *The Sleepwalkers: How Europe Went to War in 1914*

Neil MacGregor, *Shakespeare's Restless World*

Nate Silver, *The Signal and the Noise: The Art and Science of Prediction*

Chinua Achebe, *There Was a Country: A Personal History of Biafra*

John Darwin, *Unfinished Empire: The Global Expansion of Britain*

Jerry Brotton, *A History of the World in Twelve Maps*

Patrick Hennessey, *KANDAK: Fighting with Afghans*

Katherine Angel, *Unmastered: A Book on Desire, Most Difficult to Tell*

David Priestland, *Merchant, Soldier, Sage: A New History of Power*

Stephen Alford, *The Watchers: A Secret History of the Reign of Elizabeth I*

Tom Feiling, *Short Walks from Bogotá: Journeys in the New Colombia*

Pankaj Mishra, *From the Ruins of Empire: The Revolt Against the West and the Remaking of Asia*

Geza Vermes, *Christian Beginnings: From Nazareth to Nicaea, AD 30-325*

Steve Coll, *Private Empire: ExxonMobil and American Power*

Joseph Stiglitz, *The Price of Inequality*

Dambisa Moyo, *Winner Take All: China's Race for Resources and What it Means for Us*

Robert Skidelsky and Edward Skidelsky, *How Much is Enough? The Love of Money, and the Case for the Good Life*

Frances Ashcroft, *The Spark of Life: Electricity in the Human Body*

Sebastian Seung, *Connectome: How the Brain's Wiring Makes Us Who We Are*

Callum Roberts, *Ocean of Life*

Orlando Figes, *Just Send Me Word: A True Story of Love and Survival in the Gulag*

Leonard Mlodinow, *Subliminal: The Revolution of the New Unconscious and What it Teaches Us about Ourselves*

John Romer, *A History of Ancient Egypt: From the First Farmers to the Great Pyramid*

Ruchir Sharma, *Breakout Nations: In Pursuit of the Next Economic Miracle*

Michael J. Sandel, *What Money Can't Buy: The Moral Limits of Markets*

Dominic Sandbrook, *Seasons in the Sun: The Battle for Britain, 1974-1979*

Tariq Ramadan, *The Arab Awakening: Islam and the New Middle East*

Jonathan Haidt, *The Righteous Mind: Why Good People are Divided by Politics and Religion*

Ahmed Rashid, *Pakistan on the Brink: The Future of Pakistan, Afghanistan and the West*

Tim Weiner, *Enemies: A History of the FBI*

Mark Pagel, *Wired for Culture: The Natural History of Human Cooperation*

George Dyson, *Turing's Cathedral: The Origins of the Digital Universe*

Cullen Murphy, *God's Jury: The Inquisition and the Making of the Modern World*

Richard Sennett, *Together: The Rituals, Pleasures and Politics of Co-operation*

Faramerz Dabhoiwala, *The Origins of Sex: A History of the First Sexual Revolution*

Roy F. Baumeister and John Tierney, *Willpower: Rediscovering Our Greatest Strength*

Jesse J. Prinz, *Beyond Human Nature: How Culture and Experience Shape Our Lives*

Robert Holland, *Blue-Water Empire: The British in the Mediterranean since 1800*

Jodi Kantor, *The Obamas: A Mission, A Marriage*

Philip Coggan, *Paper Promises: Money, Debt and the New World Order*

Charles Nicholl, *Traces Remain: Essays and Explorations*

Daniel Kahneman, *Thinking, Fast and Slow*

Hunter S. Thompson, *Fear and Loathing at Rolling Stone: The Essential Writing of Hunter S. Thompson*

Duncan Campbell-Smith, *Masters of the Post: The Authorized History of the Royal Mail*

Colin McEvedy, *Cities of the Classical World: An Atlas and Gazetteer of 120 Centres of Ancient Civilization*

Heike B. Görtemaker, *Eva Braun: Life with Hitler*

Brian Cox and Jeff Forshaw, *The Quantum Universe: Everything that Can Happen Does Happen*

Nathan D. Wolfe, *The Viral Storm: The Dawn of a New Pandemic Age*

Norman Davies, *Vanished Kingdoms: The History of Half-Forgotten Europe*

Michael Lewis, *Boomerang: The Meltdown Tour*

Steven Pinker, *The Better Angels of Our Nature: The Decline of Violence in History and Its Causes*

Robert Trivers, *Deceit and Self-Deception: Fooling Yourself the Better to Fool Others*

Thomas Penn, *Winter King: The Dawn of Tudor England*

Daniel Yergin, *The Quest: Energy, Security and the Remaking of the Modern World*

Michael Moore, *Here Comes Trouble: Stories from My Life*

Ali Soufan, *The Black Banners: Inside the Hunt for Al Qaeda*

Jason Burke, *The 9/11 Wars*

Timothy D. Wilson, *Redirect: The Surprising New Science of Psychological Change*

Ian Kershaw, *The End: Hitler's Germany, 1944-45*

T M Devine, *To the Ends of the Earth: Scotland's Global Diaspora, 1750-2010*

Catherine Hakim, *Honey Money: The Power of Erotic Capital*

Douglas Edwards, *I'm Feeling Lucky: The Confessions of Google Employee Number 59*

John Bradshaw, *In Defence of Dogs*

Chris Stringer, *The Origin of Our Species*

Lila Azam Zanganeh, *The Enchanter: Nabokov and Happiness*

David Stevenson, *With Our Backs to the Wall: Victory and Defeat in 1918*

Evelyn Juers, *House of Exile: War, Love and Literature, from Berlin to Los Angeles*

Henry Kissinger, *On China*

Michio Kaku, *Physics of the Future: How Science Will Shape Human Destiny and Our Daily Lives by the Year 2100*

David Abulafia, *The Great Sea: A Human History of the Mediterranean*

John Gribbin, *The Reason Why: The Miracle of Life on Earth*

Anatol Lieven, *Pakistan: A Hard Country*

William Cohen, *Money and Power: How Goldman Sachs Came to Rule the World*

Joshua Foer, *Moonwalking with Einstein: The Art and Science of Remembering Everything*

Simon Baron-Cohen, *Zero Degrees of Empathy: A New Theory of Human Cruelty*

Manning Marable, *Malcolm X: A Life of Reinvention*

David Deutsch, *The Beginning of Infinity: Explanations that Transform the World*

David Edgerton, *Britain's War Machine: Weapons, Resources and Experts in the Second World War*

John Kasarda and Greg Lindsay, *Aerotropolis: The Way We'll Live Next*

David Gilmour, *The Pursuit of Italy: A History of a Land, Its Regions and Their Peoples*

Niall Ferguson, *Civilization: The West and the Rest*

Tim Flannery, *Here on Earth: A New Beginning*

Robert Bickers, *The Scramble for China: Foreign Devils in the Qing Empire, 1832-1914*

Mark Malloch-Brown, *The Unfinished Global Revolution: The Limits of Nations and the Pursuit of a New Politics*

King Abdullah of Jordan, *Our Last Best Chance: The Pursuit of Peace in a Time of Peril*

Eliza Griswold, *The Tenth Parallel: Dispatches from the Faultline between Christianity and Islam*